P. Austin Nuttall

Dictionary of Scientic Terms

Salzwasser

P. Austin Nuttall

Dictionary of Scientic Terms

1. Auflage | ISBN: 978-3-84605-112-2

Erscheinungsort: Frankfurt, Deutschland

Erscheinungsjahr: 2020

Salzwasser Verlag GmbH

Reprint of the original, first published in 1869.

DICTIONARY OF
SCIENTIFIC TERMS

By P. AUSTIN NUTTALL, LL.D.

EDITOR OF "THE CLASSICAL AND ARCHÆOLOGICAL DICTIONARY," "STANDARD
PRONOUNCING DICTIONARY," AND NUMEROUS EDUCATIONAL WORKS

STRAHAN & CO., PUBLISHERS
56 LUDGATE HILL, LONDON
1860

[BY SPECIAL PERMISSION]

TO THE

RIGHT HON. ROBERT LOWE

CHANCELLOR OF HER MAJESTY'S EXCHEQUER

AND THE ELOQUENT REPRESENTATIVE OF UNIVERSITY COLLEGE, LONDON

THIS LITTLE WORK

IS RESPECTFULLY DEDICATED

BY HIS HUMBLE AND DEVOTED SERVANT

THE EDITOR

PREFACE.

THE educational systems of the United Kingdom are on the eve of a great social revolution. The refinements of classic lore, and the time-consuming studies of the learned languages, are rapidly yielding to the practical utilities of science and art. The Government of the country has at length directed its attention to the promotion of those branches of knowledge which are so essential to the well-being and prosperity of a great manufacturing and commercial nation, but which, in our general system of education, have been sadly neglected. Dr. Playfair and many competent observers have, indeed, attributed the decline in the superiority of certain branches of English manufacture, as compared with those of other nations, to a want of scientific and technical education in our schools and public institutions. Fortunately, the warning thus given has produced its results. The department of Science and Art, which owes its origin to the great Exhibition of 1851, is now connected with the Privy Council on Education. In the speech from the throne, on the opening of Parliament in 1852-3, the intention of the Government to form some comprehensive scheme for the promotion of Science and Art was fully declared; and in March, 1853, the Lords of the Treasury acceded to the proposal of the Privy Council to unite in one department "the kindred and analogous institutions of the Government School of Mines and Science, the Museum of Practical Geology, the Geological Survey, the Museum of Irish Industry, and the Royal Dublin Society, all of which are supported by Parliamentary grants."

In February, 1856, the whole department of Science and Art, by an order in Council, was transferred to the Committee of Privy Council for Education; and in 1857 the sum of £73,855 was voted for this department. In 1858 the question of grants in aid of education was referred to a royal commission. After three years' investigation that commission made a Report, which had the effect of producing a crisis in the system of education. After the fullest consideration, the Committee of Privy Council framed the scheme known as the Revised Code, which was designed to raise the character and efficiency of education, and now regulates the distribution of the large sums yearly expended among the aid-receiving schools. On Mr. Lowe, as Vice-President of the Committee of Council for Education, and the present Chancellor of the Exchequer, chiefly devolved the labour and responsibility of framing the new Code, and carrying it through Parliament.

A select committee, consisting of nineteen members of the House of Commons, was some time ago appointed to inquire into the provision for giving instruction in theoretical and applied sciences ; and in July of last year they published their Report. The witnesses examined by them included teachers of science, schoolmasters, engineers, architects, gun-makers, and several skilful manufacturers. In this Report the committee, after suggesting the importance of a reorganization of secondary instruction, so as to provide for a larger amount of scientific knowledge, arrive at the following conclusion :—" That certain endowed schools should be selected in favourable situations for the purpose of being reconstituted as science schools, having in view the special requirements of the district. That superior colleges and schools for special scientific instruction would require extraneous aid for their support, in addition to fees." The committee expressed an opinion " that some slight addition to the emoluments of science teachers would probably tend most materially to promote the establishment and permanence of elementary science classes, and that the provisions of the Public Libraries and Museums Act should be altered so as to enable public bodies to levy a slightly-increased rate for scientific purposes, and that the education of higher science teachers should be encouraged by the granting of degrees in science at Oxford and Cambridge, as at other universities, and by the opening of a greater number of fellowships to distinction in natural science as well as in literature."

When we consider (writes a learned contemporary) that " many of our grammar schools are now quite out of date, it will be a great boon to empower some authority to reconstruct them according to more approved models, and more especially to convert some of them, at least, into schools of science. It is gratifying, therefore, to find that the committee of the House of Commons have come to precisely the same conclusions respecting these endowed schools. Having recommended that elementary instruction in physical geography, and in the phenomena of nature, should be given in elementary schools, and that all whose necessities do not oblige them to leave school before the age of fourteen should receive instruction in the elements of science as part of their general education, the committee of the House of Commons resolved that the reorganization of secondary instruction, and the introduction of a larger amount of scientific teaching into secondary schools, are urgently required, and ought to receive the immediate consideration of Parliament and of the country."

The desire to promote scientific education is not confined to the metropolis alone, but is daily extending itself to the provinces, and especially to the manufacturing districts of the country. In Yorkshire a series of public meetings of schoolmasters was lately held, for the purpose of enforcing the claims of science for an introduction into schools, and to urge schoolmasters to qualify themselves in accordance with the requirements of the department of Science and Art to give instruction therein. At Leeds thirty-five schoolmasters at once joined the scientific class, and at Sheffield nearly an equal number. In addition to the members of the general council of the Yorkshire board and of the Yorkshire union, the principal resident manufacturers, clergy, and ministers have taken part in the proceedings. Altogether, there are now in Yorkshire at least one hundred schoolmasters preparing themselves, either privately or in connection with the special classes, to undergo the ensuing examinations of the department of Science and Art, and to become qualified science teachers. In addition to the special classes for schoolmasters, upwards of twenty new science schools have, through the agency of the Yorkshire Union of Mechanics' Institutes, been established.

Scientific education, aided by suitable elementary works, is thus day by day becoming an object of primary importance, and of indispensable necessity. In our private and public schools, when the scholar has learnt to read, to write, and to calculate, he has only obtained the tools of instruction. "To acquire a knowledge of the works of God and of man, of the miracles of nature and of art" (says that distinguished physicologist, Sir David Brewster), "is the first step in the civilization of the people. Without such information, the highest as well as the humblest of our race is unfit for a place in the social scale. He may have learned to read his Bible, and may have read it; he may have committed to memory every sentence of the Decalogue; and he may have packed into the storehouse of his brain all the wisdom of Solomon, and all the divine precepts of one greater than Solomon, while he is ignorant of everything above him, around him, and within him."—The smattering of science in the school will acquire solidity in the university, and will reappear in the workshop with valuable applications. It was the chemical teaching of Dr. Black that made James Watt the greatest inventor of his age; and it was the rush of electricity through a mile of wire that gave the electric telegraph to the world. But it is to the middle, and even to the upper classes, and through them to the nation (says Sir David Brewster), that scientific teaching will offer its richest benefits. The functionaries who administer our affairs are in number legion. Without science, without that elevation of character which positive knowledge confers, we can readily understand how the greatest interests of the State are mismanaged, how interests equally great are neglected, and how the public wealth is recklessly squandered. Incompetent subordinates assume the importance and discharge the duties of their chiefs; and while the deep problems of practical science receive a wrong solution, the feelings and interests of inventors and discoverers are utterly disregarded.

The language of practical science, which it is the object of the compiler of the present Work to elucidate and render familiar to the general student, is comparatively of modern introduction. Though Dr. Johnson reared a monument of imperishable fame in his Dictionary of the English language, he did not venture into the wide field which science, in its many aspects, presented to his view; but he drew from the varied sources of general literature the meaning of all those words of which the English language was composed, and which, for every purpose of general communication, might be considered as complete. When, however, the political and polemical disputes which for ages had agitated the country began to subside, inquiring minds had leisure to turn their attention to the more peaceful occupations of science and art. The discoveries of Galileo had led the way to a deeper inquiry into the laws and movements of the physical universe; and when Newton entered upon the stage of life, there was an expanded field opened for the exercise of his powerful genius. His profound researches into nature diffused the general spirit of inquiry, and revealed new discoveries in the regions of science, until Linnæus in the vegetable kingdom, and Buffon in animated life, laid such facts before the public as required a new nomenclature to render them intelligible to the community; and, as the facts which had to be stated were quite beyond the range of knowledge, and consequently without the means of comprehension, possessed by the Anglo-Saxon projectors, there were no roots in the language out of which to evolve a series of terms fitted to state the circumstances which those authors had to communicate, and the Greek and Latin languages were searched, and searched successfully, to supply the deficiency. The result was, that a set of compound words were formed, well calculated to express precise ideas of the several objects of scientific consideration, and singularly indicative of their several natures. Thus Astronomy, Geography, Botany, and Physiology obtained their distinctive terms; and when, through the celebrated philosophers, Scheele, Priestley, Dalton, Davy, Babington, Watt, Saussure, Lyell, De la Beche, and a host of others, the patent and occult properties and actions of natural bodies had to be designated, the same course was pursued; and compound terms from both the ancient languages, but especially from the Greek, have been incorporated, and now form an integral portion of the English language.

In the Supplement to Craig's valuable Dictionary of the English language, compiled by the Editor of the present work, and recently published by Messrs. Routledge, the writer observes that as new ideas, new arts, and new discoveries are constantly springing into existence with the ever-onward progress of civilization, the philological labours of the lexicographer can never cease to be in demand. "Through the inventions of art and the cultivation of science, a language becomes amplified and copious. The discoveries and improvements in machinery and manufactures are constantly adding new terms, which, formed in the first instance from the rude nomenclature of the working artisan, and considered as purely technical, at length become the ordinary language of society. With the words of such a mintage, definition is often difficult, and etymology sometimes impossible."—In terms derived from the classical languages, however, there is less difficulty, because they are generally self-explanatory. Thus, when a new idea or a new discovery connected with science or the arts presents itself to the mind, the Greek or Latin language is the great technological mine into which the lexicographer or the scholar may safely dive. Hence we have PHONOGRAPHY (sound-describing), PHOTOGRAPHY (light-describing), TELEGRAM (describing afar), and numerous terms of Greek origin recently introduced into the nomenclature of science. In the "Report of the Privy Council on Public Health and Diseases of Cattle," numerous terms have been thus adopted to indicate certain diseases, which are fully explained in the pages of the present work; as ANTHRAX (a carbuncular or inflammatory fever in cattle); STOMATHRAX (an inflammatory disease of the stomach) ; STRONGYLUS (a parasitical action of the respiratory organs of pigs and calves), &c.

With the view of promoting the objects under consideration, the present Dictionary has been compiled, so as to render the language of science intelligible, not only to the professional student, but to the general reader, who may be desirous of ascertaining the derivation, meaning, and general application of the numerous words which, with the progress of scientific knowledge, are coming into daily use. In this undertaking the Editor has been materially aided by the labours of Webster, Worcester, Goodrich, Craig, Ogilvie, Brand, Paxton, Hoblyn, Faraday, Cuvier, Lyell, and other distinguished authorities.

In a work where brevity has been the great object of the writer, occasional omissions or oversights may possibly be discovered, but which, the Editor hopes, when the difficulties attending such a varied compilation are taken into consideration, will receive every indulgence from a generous public.

INTRODUCTION TO THE CLASSIFICATION AND STUDY OF THE SCIENCES.

" Didicisse fideliter artes
Emollit mores, nec sinit esse feros."

THE physical and mechanical sciences embrace an ample range in the vast field of human knowledge, and every effort that tends to promote their cultivation among the great masses of the community is deserving óf commendation and support.

SCIENCE (Lat. *scientia*), as connected with literature, means any branch of knowledge in which the properties of mind or matter are to be made the subject of reasoning, with a view to discover and apply first principles. Science, in truth, is the knowledge of things reducible to practice, and in popular language is meant simply to apply to physical, mathematical, or natural phenomena, not with reference to principles, but to results. Thus a man of science may be an astronomer, geologist, electrician, zoologist, botanist, ornithologist, engineer, mechanician, chemist, medical practitioner, or other profession connected with the arts and sciences. The art of building is taught by the science of architecture; the art of curing diseases, by the science of medicine, &c. The terms *art* and *science* are, however, often used indiscriminately for the same thing, both being intimately connected. Art may be defined to be an ingenious disposal and arrangement of natural objects and materials, so as to supply the various necessities of mankind, or minister to their wants and enjoyments. Thus we have the art of Pyrotechny, of Weaving, of Masonry, &c., of which science is the directing genius.

In the study of the sciences, the necessity of classification, and of simplifying the nomenclature of science, is too manifest to admit of dispute. Indeed, a clear understanding of the classification and terms of any science is a necessary preliminary to its practical study. This is the master-key by which the mystic portals of physical and artistic knowledge can be opened. Without this, science appears involved in a labyrinthian maze; but when the first difficulty is surmounted, to which the present work may prove a useful auxiliary, the path becomes smooth and easy, and every obstacle appears to vanish.

PHYSICS, or Natural Philosophy, may be looked upon as the most interesting of all the sciences. Chemistry, which, since the establishment of the new nomenclature, has led to many important discoveries, has been of the most extensive utility to the arts. The age in which we live, says the intelligent author of "The Traveller's Remembrancer," is eminently utilitarian, and science is now only regarded in proportion as it presents useful results. The power of steam, the phenomena of galvanism, electricity, and magnetism, the polarization of light, and its chemical action, are now familiar instances of the truth of this observation. The application of steam power, the hydraulic press, the precipitation of metals by galvanic action, the lighting of cities by means of gas, the miner's safety lamp, the disinfection of foul air by chlorine, &c., are so many triumphs of modern science, and attest the utility of physical and chemical studies.

In physical science, NATURAL HISTORY embraces an extensive range, and is usually classed under three important divisions—ZOOLOGY, BOTANY, and MINERALOGY. As explained in the body of this Dictionary, Natural History has for its object the study of the various forms of bodies existing upon or under the surface of the earth : it examines the structure of such things as contain any trace of organization necessary for the exercise of the vital functions, investigates the organization of functions of living beings, and classifies those beings as such according to their analogies.

ZOOLOGY embraces an account of all animal creation, the principal classes being the MAMMALIA, AVES, REPTILIA, PISCES, INVERTEBRATA, and INSECTA.

The *first* and most important class is subdivided by naturalists into nine orders :—1. The BIMANA, or two-handed animals, as MAN ;—2. QUADRUMANA, or four-handed animals, as Apes and Monkeys ;—3. CARNIVORA, or beasts of prey, as Lions, Tigers, &c. ;—4. MARSUPIALIA, or pouch animals, as Opossums, &c. ;—5. RODENTIA, or gnawing animals, as Rats, Mice, &c. ;—6. EDENTATA, or animals wanting some of the teeth of other animals ;—7. PACHYDERMATA, or thick-hided animals, as Elephants, &c. ;—8. RUMINANTIA, or ruminating animals, as Oxen, Sheep, &c. ;—9. CETACEA, or the Whale tribe,—all of which are explained in the body of the Dictionary under their respective heads.

Naturalists class animal life by commencing from the highly-organized animals (such as those which walk, fly, and have nerves) to such as have very little structure, and in many cases cannot be classed with certainty as animals or vegetables ; thus classing, first, Man and Mammals, as above enumerated ; secondly, Birds ; thirdly, Reptiles ; fourthly, Fishes ; fifthly, Articulates, such as Insects and Crabs ; sixthly, Molluscs (Shell-fish); seventhly, Radiata (Star-fishes); eighthly, Corallites, or Corals ; and lastly, Protozoans, which are principally jelly-like organisms, with little structure.—In vegetable life there is an analogous descent from the noble forest tree to the gelatinous lichen, or, lower still, to the green slime sometimes seen upon walls. Mr. Samuelson, a naturalist, took a glass of water, and in a few days found its interior lined with slime, which proved to be a mass of thousands of monads, all trembling with life. In a few days more they became free, and were moving about in all directions.

The *second* class of animals (AVES, or BIRDS) are distinguished, as regards the blood and the structure of the heart, by the same characters as the first class ; but they are also covered with feathers, and furnished for the most part with wings. Moreover, they are oviparous. The knowledge of the forms, habits, manners, &c., of birds is called ORNITHOLOGY, which Linnæus, in his " Systema Naturæ," divides into six orders (see *Ornithology* in the Dictionary); but other naturalists have expanded their number, and have classed them as under :—1. INSESSORES, or Perching Birds ;—2. RAPTORES, or Rapacious Birds ;—3. RASORES, or Birds which scratch the ground to obtain their food ;—4. NATATORES, or Swimming Birds ; and 5. GRALLATORES, or Wading Birds. But the universal applicability of this or any other system has not been as yet established. The number of birds now known amounts to about 5,000.

The *third* class (REPTILIA) are vertebrated animals with cold red blood, respiring by lungs, with bodies naked, or covered with scales. Cuvier divides this class into four orders, founded on their organization :—1st order, CHELONIA, consisting of seven genera, including Land Tortoises, Fresh-water Tortoises, and Sea-water Tortoises, or Turtles ;—2nd order, SAURIA, consisting of twenty-eight genera, exemplified in the Crocodile, Alligator, Lizard, &c. ;—3rd order, OPHIDIA, consisting of thirty genera, divided by Cuvier into three families. The Snake, Boa, Viper, Rattlesnake, &c., are examples of this order. Many of these genera are poisonous ;—4th order, BATRACHIA, consisting of seven genera, as typified in the Toad, Frog, &c., fossil remains of which have been abundantly found of a gigantic size.

The *fourth* class (PISCES, or FISHES) are vertebrated animals, with cold red blood, respiring by branchiæ, or gills, and moving in the water by the aid of fins. A knowledge of their form and habits is scientifically called ICHTHYOLOGY.—Cuvier divides this class into two sub-classes—the cartilaginous and the osseous—which he distributes into *nine* orders, three being in the former sub-class, and six in the latter.

Invertebrate animals are divided into MOLLUSCA, ARTICULATA, and RADIATA. The Mollusca is so called from the body being soft and molluscous. It is divided into four classes, the *Mollusca, Conchifera, Tunicata,* and *Cirripeda.* The first class is subdivided into five orders, founded on the organs of locomotion. The second, third, and fourth classes, the *Conchifera,* the *Tunicata,* and the *Cirripeda,* are each divided into two orders. The shell of the fourth class is always multivalve, or composed of a number of separate pieces.

The next great divisions of invertebrated animals are the *Articulata* and the *Radiata,* which are each divided into five classes. The fifth class of invertebrates are the *Annelides,* or Worms ; the sixth class, the *Crustacea,* which respire by branchiæ, or branchial laminæ ; the seventh class, the *Arachnides,* or Spiders ; the eighth class, the *Myriapoda ;* and the ninth class, the *Insecta,* or Insects—a knowledge of their forms, habits, &c., being termed ENTOMOLOGY.

Entomology has been subdivided into eleven orders, viz., *Thyanoura,* apterous or wingless insects ;—*Parasita,* so called from living on other animals ;—*Siphoniptera,* which have mouths with a sucker of two pieces ;—*Coleoptera,* or insects with four wings, the upper ones in the form of cases, as the Beetle, the Lady-bird, &c. ;—*Orthoptera,* with elytra coriaceous, as the Earwig, Cockroach, &c. ;—*Hemiptera,* with two wings covered, and an elytra, as in the Grasshopper ;—*Neuroptera,* with four naked, reticulated, transparent wings, as the Dragon-fly ;—*Hymenoptera,* with four naked, veined wings of unequal size, with a sting at the anus, as the Bee, Wasp, Gall-fly, &c. ;—*Lepidoptera,* with four membranaceous wings, covered with farina, as the Moth and the Butterfly ;—*Strepsiptera,* with two naked, membranous wings longitudinally folded ;—*Diptera,* with six feet, and two membranous, extended wings, as the Gnat, Horse-fly, &c.—Insects generally exist in four states ; first as an egg, next as a worm, or larva, then a chrysalis ; in which state it remains dormant for a certain term, when in due time it becomes a moth, a beetle, or other insect with wings, in which state it propagates its species and dies. Some insects envelop themselves in a fine web previously to entering into their chrysalis state, of which the silkworm is a beautiful exemplification.

To enumerate the species, or even genera, of the animal kingdom, and define them in a portable Dictionary like the present one, would be an impossibility. Hence the Editor has chiefly confined himself to Classes, Orders, Families, Tribes, &c., of animated nature, briefly adverting to the genus or species of any class or order when of more than usual importance. The following table, however, presents an approximate estimate, according to Swainson, of the number of species of animals existing on the surface of the earth :—

Vertebrated Animals :—

Quadrupeds	1,200
Birds	6,800
Reptiles and Amphibia	1,500
Fishes	8,000

Annulose Animals :—

Insects, apterous and winged	550,000
Worms, and other classes	2,500

Molluscs, or *Soft Animals :—*

Radiata, star-fishes &c.	1,000
Polypes, corals, &c.	1,500
Naked molluscs	600
Testacea, or shell-fish	4,500
Total......	577,600

Next to Zoology is the science of Vegetation, called BOTANY, which consists of a knowledge of plants, their several kinds, uses, and virtues. The principal writers on this interesting science are Linnæus and Jussieu. The Linnæan System of classification is founded on the fact that there is in vegetables, as well as in animals, a real distinction of sexes, and that each plant may be analyzed by its several organs of fructification, which consist of the *calyx,* or flower-cup; the *corolla,* or blossom; the *stamen;* the *pistillum;* the *pericarpium,* or seed-vessel; and the *semen,* or seed. Thus the vegetable kingdom was divided by this great naturalist into twenty-four classes, of which twenty-three belong to the flowering and one to the flowerless plants. These, again, are subdivided into *orders,* the orders into *genera,* these again into *species,* and many of these into *varieties.* The names of the classes and orders are of Greek derivation, and allude to the functions of the respective organs. The first eleven classes are distinguished entirely by the number of stamens, which are called Monandria, Diandria, Triandria, &c., as far as Dodecandria, from the Greek words one, two, three, &c., combined with *male* (*andria*), because the stamens of flowers are compared to males, and the pistils to females. Hence the orders are denominated Monogynia, Digynia, &c., to Polygynia, according as the flower has one or more pistils; so called from the Greek *monos* one, and *gyne* a female. Thus in the third class (*Triandria*) are found most of the natural order of Grasses.

The Natural System of plants, as devised by Jussieu, differs materially from the Linnean system; for it takes into consideration the entire organization and form of the plant, with its peculiar habits; and the most striking genus of a tribe of plants gives name to the order; as, for instance, the Rose forms the type of the natural order *Rosaceæ,* and the Violet that of the order *Violaceæ;* these orders being each described under their respective heads in this Dictionary. In the same manner Jussieu divided the entire vegetable kingdom into classes, orders, and genera. These classes have no appropriate names, but are distinguished by numbers, with a short definition of the essential character of each. The orders are chiefly named, as just stated, after some principal genus belonging to each. Thus the order Campanulaceæ derives its name from *Campanula* (the Canterbury Bell), which is a diminutive of the Latin *campana* a bell; the genus having been so called from the resemblance of its corolla to a bell.

A third system in the classification of the vegetable kingdom is the one devised by our distinguished countryman, Professor Lindley, which is based upon the most accurate and extensive information, and which, in the botanical teaching of our schools, appears in some measure to be supplanting the recognised systems of Linnæus and Jussieu. Dr. Lindley reduces the whole of the vegetable creation to two great divisions, the "Asexual, or Flowerless Plants," and the "Sexual, or Flowering Plants;" and these he subdivides into seven distinct classes; two of them under the Asexual plants, as the Thallogens and the Acrogens, and the other five under the Sexual, as the Rhizogens, the Endogens, the Dictyogens, the Gymnogens, and the Exogens—this last class being composed of innumerable races.

Such are the principal systems of botanical classification (says the Editor of the supplementary volume to the "National Cyclopædia") which have been presented to the world; and although there have appeared, at different times, about thirty systems, "it is still probable," says Dr. Smith, "that the best one, at the present moment, is so imperfect that it must be amended yearly."

We now enter upon the third grand division in physical science, called MINERALOGY, in which we learn the form, nature, and uses of inorganic matter; so denominated from many of the bodies being obtained from *mines*. This science, till lately, was without order or connection; but Werner has thrown much light upon this branch of natural history. According to him, minerals were divided into four classes,—earthy minerals, saline minerals, inflammables, and metals. Professor Mohs arranges minerals under three divisions or CLASSES. The characters of the *first* class, if solid, are sapid, with no bituminous odour; specific gravity, under 3·8. This class is divided into four orders, of which *gas* forms the first, and consists of two genera, *hydrogen* and *atmospheric air*. The second order is *Water*, the third, *Acids*, and the fourth, *Salt*. The genera of the fourth order are ten in number, of which common salt, saltpetre, muriate of ammonia, zinc, copper, and sulphate of iron are samples.

Bodies constituting the *second* class of minerals are insipid, their specific gravity being above 1·8. They consist of thirteen orders. The first is *Haloide*, or salt-like; the second is *Baryte;* the third, *Kerate*, or horny; the fourth, *Malachite;* the fifth, *Mica*, or *Talc;* the sixth, *Spar*. The seventh order is the *Gem*, consisting of thirteen genera, of which the diamond, the emerald, the topaz, the garnet, and the corundum are examples. The eighth order is *Ore*, of which tin, iron, zinc, and copper are examples; the ninth order, *Metal*, of which antimony, arsenic, and gold are specimens. The tenth order is *Pyrites;* the eleventh, *Glance;* and the twelfth, *Blende*. The thirteenth is *Sulphur*.

Bodies constituting the *third* class of minerals, if solid, are insipid; if fluid, they have a bituminous odour, their specific gravity being under 1·8. This third class consists of two orders; the first one being *Resin*, and the second *Mineral Coal*, which contains many species and varieties.

Of GEMS and PRECIOUS STONES, which are briefly explained in the body of the Dictionary, the following are the principal :—

Agate.	Corundum.	Hyacinth, or Jacinth.	Sapphire.
Amethyst.	Crystal Quartz, or	Jasper.	Topaz.
Beryl.	Rock Crystal.	Onyx.	Zircon.
Calcedony.	Diamond	Opal.	
Chrysolite.	Emerald.	Pearl.	
Cornelian.	Garnet.	Ruby.	

STONE is a general term, in Mineralogy, for natural, inorganic bodies, that are hard, brittle, and nearly insoluble in water. Of these the most valuable are :—

Alabaster.	Freestone.	Marble.	Pumice-stone.
Emery.	Granite.	Mill-stones.	Serpentine.
Flint.	Hone, or Polish-	Plaster of Paris.	Slate.
Fluor Spar, or Fluate of Lime.	ing Slate.	Porphyry.	
	Jade.	Pudding-stone.	

METALS are an important branch of Mineralogy. In remote antiquity only seven were known, viz., gold, silver, mercury, copper, iron, tin, and lead. But modern discoveries have added considerably to the number, the most important of which are antimony, arsenic, cobalt, platinum, zinc, bismuth, manganese, iridium, tungsten, chromium, potassium, sodium, and lithium (the bases of the mineral and vegetable alkalies), and barium, strontium, magnesium, and calcium, the bases of the alkaline earths, &c. (See article METAL.) The number of bodies now classed as metals are forty-two. A few of the principal metals are here given in alphabetical order :—

Antimony.	Copper.	Manganese.	Silver.
Arsenic.	Gold.	Mercury.	Steel.
Bismuth.	Iridium.	Nickel.	Tin.
Black-lead.	Iron.	Ochre.	Tungsten.
Brass.	Lead.	Pewter.	Zinc.
Cobalt.	Magnet.	Platinum.	

With Mineralogy, the important science of GEOLOGY, which teaches us the external structure of the globe we inhabit, is closely allied. "Geology," as Hugh Miller once observed, "is a glance in the direction of the eternity that has gone by," in the same manner as astronomy is a prolongation of our view through the infinite abyss of space, and as chemistry and botany extend our vision indefinitely through the material universe. Werner, who may be considered as one of the most intelligent writers on geology, supposes that the globe was once covered with a sort of chaotic compost, holding, either in solution or suspension, the component parts of the various rocks and strata which now present themselves at its exterior crust. The substances of which this crust is composed have been arranged by geologists under five classes. The first class comprehends the PRIMITIVE ROCKS, which were so named because it was assumed they were first formed through the agency of fire, and contain neither animal nor vegetable remains, nor even rounded pebbles : such are granite, serpentine, and porphyry. The strata lying immediately above the primitive rocks, where shells and fragments occasionally occur, are denominated TRANSITION ROCKS, which consist of Graywacke and Transition limestone. The class above these is called FLOETZ, or Secondary Rocks, which abound in organic remains. The agencies of the wind, the ocean, and the weather produced those inequalities which exist on the earth's surface, and the water retreated into low lands and valleys, where depositions of sand, gravel, clay, &c., took place, and produced the *Alluvial Rocks;* the last class consisting of rocks produced by volcanic agency.—It is presumed that these processes of Nature, operating through countless ages, are sufficient to account for the present condition and general appearance of the crust of the globe. It is manifest that all rocks, even the primitive ones, were once in a state of solution or liquidity, so as to admit of the innumerable forms and crystallizations in which they are now found.

As a corollary to the magnificent operations of physical science (says a modern writer) is the belief that life, which is spirit, would also be found co-extensive with those great powers of Nature which we find moulding our own globe, with all its various phenomena of heat and light, its clouds and meteors, its seas and continents, and its endless varieties of organic existence. Spectral analysis has reinforced this mighty thesis, by positively showing that elements similar to those of our own world also enter into the composition of the orbs beyond us. The falling meteor which takes its fire by contact with the air-envelope of earth, impinging upon it from its own region of ether, is found to contain minerals common to this planet. Fact, analogy, the economics of Nature, her endless realms of marvel, and the deep instinct of the uplifted heart and eye—all combine to make it more and more likely that life is infinite in series. The more that our knowledge of the material world extends, and that we see the precise nature of the laws of life, the more do we perceive how essentially provincial were the old ideas of the relations which men bore to each other. Now that the study of physical science has generated the habit of dealing with facts as facts, and has filled the very air with a horror of anything like assumptions, we can hardly understand why past generations could have been satisfied with the narrow, dogmatic rules which we have inherited only to set aside.

The rigorous demonstrations of MATHEMATICS admit of nothing that is vague; and therefore they have naturally led men to apply its principles to all those nobler sciences which admit of them; as Astronomy, Geography, Navigation, Physics, and Mechanics, which owe the great progress they have made to mathematical formulæ. Thus Geometry, so essential to the arts of design, by lending its forms and its language to the phenomena of crystallization, has elevated Mineralogy to the rank of an exact science.

In MECHANICAL SCIENCE the ingenuity of man is making wonderful advances. Engineering, Electricity, and Railways are effecting a vast social revolution throughout the entire globe, by which the great family of man may be eventually united in the peaceful bonds of friendship and commercial intercourse. Engineers, with their regiments of industrious workmen, have proved themselves, in numerous instances, the victors over the material forces of Nature; the makers of roads and railways, builders of bridges and viaducts, tunnellers of impassable mountains, delvers of mines, openers-up of strange lands, cutters of isthmus necks, diggers of canals, eager promoters of sanitary science, suppliers of water, drainers, builders, developers, improvers—whose vocation has turned so much of our once wholly wild and rugged earth into the agreeable and convenient world which we know and enjoy. The most important works which antiquity accomplished are not so remarkable as the works which are now performed through the agency of modern science, almost without notice. The Pyramids, the Appian Way, the Mausoleum, the Colossus of Rhodes, and the great Wall of China were certainly most wonderful undertakings; but the triumphs of engineering science, as recounted by the President of the Society of Engineers at one of their late meetings, are even more wonderful than the boasted "wonders of the world." There is the Pacific Railroad in America, now approaching to completion; the mountain railway which scales the Cenisian Alp; the Isthmus of Suez canal, now crowned as a practicable and successful enterprise, and justly called "one of the grandest works of modern time." The network of railway lines completed throughout India; the bridges thrown or throwing over the Mersey at Runcorn, over the Rhine at Kuilemberg, and over Niagara Falls—in the last instance with a span of twelve hundred and sixty feet; together with such feats of modern engineering as the iron cradles which have been built in England for dockyard use at Bermuda, the Thames Embankment works, the London Main Drainage improvements, and the Millwall Docks—all these are really more wonderful in their way, and ten times more useful, than the prodigious efforts of ancient kings and conquerors.

DICTIONARY

OF

SCIENTIFIC TERMS.

Aardwolf (Dutch, *earth-wolf*), in zoology, the name of a carnivorous digitigrade quadruped, which appears to form an intermediate link between the civet and the hyæna.

Ab'aca, in botany, a species of flax or hemp which grows in the Philippine Islands.

Abacis'cus (Lat. from Gr. *abax* a slab), in the arts, a term applied to the square compartment of a tessellated pavement, which incloses the entire design; sometimes called *Abacus*.

Ab'ajour(Fr. *a skylight*), in architecture, a sloping aperture for air or light in a vault or prison apartment.

Ab'atis (Fr. *a breastwork* or *rampart*). in military science, a number of felled trees, having the smaller branches cut off, and placed side by side with their points outwards, to prevent assailants from mounting the breastwork.

Ab'attoir (Fr. *a beating down*), the name of a slaughter-house for cattle.

Abattu'ta (Ital. *by beating*), in music, an expression signifying that after a break the time of any piece is to be beaten as before.

Abat-voix (Fr. *throwing down the voice*), in acoustics, a sort of sounding-board or canopy placed over a pulpit or rostrum for the purpose of concentrating the voice of the speaker.

Abax (Gr. *a slab*), in entomology, a genus of coleopterous insects.

Abdo'men (Lat. *a hiding-place*), in vertebrated animals, that cavity which contains the organs of digestion; the lower venter or belly.—In entomology, the hinder part of the body, which appears united to the fore part by a filament, as in the wasp.

Abdom'inals (Lat. *having venters* or *bellies*), in ichthyology, a term applied to that class of fishes which has the ventral fins placed behind

the pectorals, as in the herring or pike.

Abduc'tor (Lat. *that which draws back*), in anatomy, a muscle which serves to draw back the parts to which it is attached.

Abe'lia (so named from Dr. C. Abel, of the Chinese embassy), a genus of pretty flowering greenhouse plants; order Caprifoliaceæ.

Abelmos'chus, a genus of plants, of which the Abelmosk, or Syrian mallow, is the type.

Ab'erdevine (Fr.), a well-known songbird, the *Carduelis spinus* of Cuvier.

Abhal (Arab.), the fruit of a species of cypress, used pathologically as an emmenagogue.

A'bia, a genus of hymenopterous insects which inhabit the furze and alder.

A'bies (Lat. *a fir-tree*), a genus of coniferous trees, embracing a variety of species, as the pine, larch, spruce, &c. ; order Pinaceæ.—The *Abies Albertiana* is a beautiful specimen, lately brought from California, and so called in memory of the late Prince Albert.

Abiet'eæ (Lat. *abies*), in botany, a suborder of the Pinaceæ or Conifers.— *Abietic acid* is a kind of resin obtained from the *Pinus abies* of Linnæus.

Ab'ietine (Lat. *abies*), a kind of resin obtained from Strasburg turpentine.

Abilgaar'dia (so called from Professor Abilgaard, of Copenhagen), a genus of plants ; order Cyperaceæ.

Abla'nia, a genus of arboreous plants, natives of Guiana ; order Tiliaceæ.

Ab'lepsy (Gr. *ablepsia* blindness), in pathology, defect of sight; blindness.

Abo'ma, in zoology, the name of a large serpent which inhabits the fens of S. America.

Aboma'sum (Lat.), in physiology, the fourth stomach of ruminating animals.

Aborig'ines (Lat. *originals*), in ethnology, the primitive inhabitants of a country.

A'bramis (Lat.), a genus of fishes, the bream; family Cyprinidæ.

Abran'chians (Gr. *without gills*), a name applied to Cuvier's third order of the Annelides, comprising the earth and aquatic worms, the Lumbrici and Naiades.

Ab'razite (Gr. *without bubbles*), the name of a mineral which does not effervesce when liquefied before the blowpipe.

Abreuv'oir (Fr.), in masonry, the joint between two stones, or the interstice to be filled up with cement.

Abro'ma (Gr. *not fit for food*), in botany, a genus of evergreens; order Byttneriaceæ.

Abrot'anum (Gr. *immortality*), in botany, a species of Artemisia, the southernwood.

Abrus (Gr. *delicate*), a genus of leguminous plants, commonly called wild liquorice, from their roots having the property of common liquorice.

Absois'sa (Lat. *a cutting off*), in mathematics, that part of the diameter of a conic section which lies between the vertex and a semi-ordinate.

Absoon'sio (Lat. *concealment*), in anatomy, the cavity of a bone which receives and conceals the head of another bone.

Absin'thate (Lat. *not pleasant*), in chemistry, a salt formed by the combination of absinthic acid with a base.

Absin'thine (Gr. *disagreeable to the taste*), the bitter principle of wormwood.

Absin'thites (Lat.), a term applied to wines impregnated with wormwood.

Absin'thium (Lat.), a species of Artemisia, wormwood, so-called from its vermifuge properties.

Absor'bents (Lat. *absorbent properties*), in physiology, a term applied to the vessels which absorb and convey fluids to the thoracic duct, generally known as the lacteals and lymphatics.

Abster'gents (Lat. *cleansers*), in pathology, lotions and other applications for cleansing sores, ulcers, &c.

Abstrin'gent (Lat. *unbinding*), in pathology, a term applied to any medicine used for removing concretions or obstructions in general.

Absus (Lat.), in botany, the four-eared cassia, the *Cassius absus* of Linnæus.

Abu'ta (the vernacular name in Guiana), in botany, a genus of climbing plants; order Sanguisorbaceæ.

Abu'tilon, in botany, an annual plant, the *Sida abutilon* of Linnæus, growing in the East and West Indies; order Malvaceæ.

Aca'cia (Gr. *the Egyptian thorn*), a genus of leguminous plants, consisting of numerous species, some of which yield gum-arabic and catechu, others tannin; sub-order Papilionaceæ.

Acæ'na (Gr. *a thorn*), a genus of herbaceous plants of the Tetrandria-Monogynia class; nat. order Sanguisorbaceæ.

Acæ'nitus, a genus of insects, of the tribe of Ichneumonides.

Acal'epha (Gr. *a nettle*), in zoology, a class of marine, gelatinous, and radiate animals, which includes the sea-nettle, the jelly-fish, medusa, &c.—In botany, a genus of prickly plants; nat. order Euphorbiaceæ.

Acal'ysine (Lat. *wanting a calyx*), in botany, a term applied to flowers destitute of a flower-cup.

Acam'aca (Sp. *unwearied*), the name of a bird, of the genus Todus, the Brazilian fly-catcher.

Acamar'chus (Gr. *indefatigable architect*), a genus of corals; fam. Cellularia.

Ac'amus, a chambered fossil shell of a conical shape.

Acantha'ceæ (*the prickle-tribe*), a natural order of exogenous monopetalous plants, composed of shrubs or herbs, and chiefly tropical.

Acan'thæ (Gr. *prickles, thorns,* or *spines*, from which a great variety of scientific terms are formed), in botany, the prickles of thorny plants; and in zoology, the spinous processes of animals.

Acanthari'næ, a sub-family of Coryphænidæ fishes.

Acan'thicus (Gr. *prickly* or *thorny*), a genus of fishes furnished with sharp spines on the scale coating of their bodies; fam. Siluridæ.

Acan'thion, a genus of animals allied to the porcupine; order Rodentia.

Acan'thium, in botany, the coffee thistle.

Acanthi'za, a genus of birds, of the family Silviadæ, or Warblers.

Acan'thobole (Gr. *spine-striking*), an instrument in surgery for extracting splinters of bone, or any foreign substance, from a wound.

Acanthoceph'ala (Gr. *spine-headed*), worms which attach themselves to the intestines by the instrumentality of curved spines; fam. Entozoa.

Acanthoce'rus (Gr. *spine-horned*), a genus of coleopterous insects; fam. Scarabæidæ.

Acanthoci'nus (Gr. *spine-moving*), a genus of coleopterous insects; fam. Longicornes.

Acanthoder'ma (Gr. *spine-skinned*), a genus of fossilized fishes.

Acan'thodes (Gr. *spine-toothed*), a genus of fossil fishes, of the order Ganoidia.

Acanthome'ra (Gr. *prickle-thighed*), a name applied to certain genera of coleopterous and dipterous insects.

Acanthono'tus (Gr. *spine-backed*), a genus of fishes furnished with dorsal and anal spines.

Acan'thophis (Gr. *a prickly serpent*), a genus of serpents furnished with plates beneath the tail.

Acan'thopod (Gr. *prickle-legged*), a tribe of clavicorn and coleopterous insects; also a genus of fishes, with the ventral fins represented by two sharp spines; fam. Squamipennes.

Acanthop'tera (Gr. *prickle-winged*), a genus of coleopterous insects; fam. Cerambycidæ.

Acanthopteryg'ii (Gr. *prickle-finned*), an order of fishes distinguished from others by their hard, bony, and prickly back-fins, as in the perch.

Acanthos'celes (Gr. *prickle-legged*), a genus of coleopterous insects, fam. Carabidæ.

Acanthosper'mum (Gr. *a spine*, and *seed*), a genus of plants, of the order Compositæ.

Acanthos'tachys (Gr. *spine*, and *stachys* a spike), a genus of stove-plants, of the order Bromeliaceæ

Acanthu'rus (Gr. *spine-tailed*), a genus of lancet-fish, of the order Acanthopterygii.

Acan'thus (Gr. *a thorn*), in botany, the plant bear's-breech, or brank ursine; nat. order Acanthaceæ.—In architecture, a kind of ornamental foliage which resembles the leaves of the acanthus, and is introduced into the capitals of the Corinthian and Composite orders.

Aca'nus (Gr. *a spiny shrub*), a genus of fossil fishes.

Acar'dia (Gr. *without a hinge*), a genus of fossil bivalve shells of the oyster kind.

Acar'do (Gr. *ut supra*), a genus of flat bivalve shells.

Ac'ari (Gr. *mites*), small spider-like animals, of the order Aptera.

Acar'ida, or **Acar'ides** (Gr. *mites*), a division of the Arachnides, including the mite (*acarus*), the tick (*ricinus*), &c.

Acar'na (Gr. *a thistle*), a genus of plants of the thistle tribe.

Acar'nar (Arab.), the name of a brilliant star of the first magnitude, in the constellation Eridanus.

Acar'py (Gr. *wanting fruit*), in botany, unfruitfulness.

Acas'ta (Gr. *sharpness*), in conchology, a genus of Cirripeds, with subconic compressed shells.

Acathar'sia (Gr. *uncleanness*), in medicine, impurity of the blood; and in surgery, the sordes proceeding from a wound.

Acau'lous (Gr. *wanting the stalk*), in botany, those plants which are without the stem or *caulis*, and have their flowers resting on the ground.

Accen'tor (Lat. *a tuner*), a genus of birds belonging to the Parinæ, or Titmice; fam. Silviadæ.—In music, one who takes the lead of a band or chorus.

Accentu'ra (Ital.), a term in music to express the manner in which particular passages are to be executed.

Accipen'ser (Lat. *the sturgeon*), a genus of malacopterygious fishes, from which the isinglass of the shops is made; fam. Sturionidæ. It is sometimes found eighteen feet long.

Accip'iter (Lat. *a hawk*), a genus of rapacious birds; sub-family Accipitrinæ.

Accordatu'ra (Ital. *accordance*), in music, a particular mode of tuning a stringed instrument.

Accor'dion (from *accord*), a small musical wind instrument, with keys, the tones of which are produced by the play of wind upon metallic reeds.

Accrescimen'to (Ital. *increase*), in music, the increase of a note by one half of its original duration, which is indicated by a dot.

Accrete (Lat. *grown together*), in botany, a term applied to the increase of additional substance, or two parts of a plant grown together.

Aceph'ala (Gr. *headless*), a term applied to the inhabitants of bivalve and other shells, of the order Mollusca.—In entomology, an order of insects.

Aceph'alism (Gr.), the state of a fœtus without a head.

Aceph'alobrach (Gr.), a fœtus without head and arms.

Acephalochi'rus (Gr.), a fœtus without head and hands.

Aceph'alocyst (Gr. *a headless bladder*), a genus of Entozoa, or intestinal animal, which has the appearance of a simple bladder, without any visible organs.

Acer (Lat. *sharp*), a genus of plants, the maple.

Acera'ceæ (Lat. *acer* sharp), a natural order of monopetalous exogens, allied to the lindens, of which the maple is the type; their sap yields a saccharine substance, of which sugar can be manufactured.

A'cerans (Gr. *without horns*), in entomology, a family of insects without antennæ or wings.

A'ceras (Gr. *without spurs*), a genus of plants, of the order Orchidaceæ.

Ac'erate (Lat. *sharp*), in chemistry, a salt, of which lime is the basis.

Acera'tum (Gr. *hornless*), in botany, a species of plant, of the order Elæocarpaceæ.

Aceri'na, a genus of fishes; order Acanthopterygii.

Aces'tis (Gr. a *healer*), a factitious sort of borax, made of Cyprian verdigris, &c.

Acetab'ulum (Lat. *a vinegar cruet*), in anatomy, the cavity which receives, as in a socket, the head of the thigh-bone.—In botany, a species of Tubularia, navel-wort.

Ace'tary (Lat. *sourness*), a term applied to the pulpy substance contained in the base of certain fruits, as the pear.

Ace'tas, Ace'tate (Lat. *acidity*), in chemistry and pharmacy, salt or acetate formed by the union of acetic acid with a metallic or alkaline base; an acetate, of which there are various compounds, as acetate of ammonia, of copper, of morphia, of barytes, of soda, of iron, of lead, &c.

Acetom'eter (Lat. and Gr. *a vinegar measurer*), an instrument for ascertaining the strength of acids.

Acetom'etry (Gr. *measurement of acids*), the process of ascertaining the strength of acids.

Acetosel'la (Lat.), in botany, a species of oxalis, of the order Oxalidæ; the wood sorrel.

Ace'tum (Lat.), the chemical name for vinegar.

Ace'tyl (Lat. *acetum* vinegar), in chemistry, a term applied to the supposed base of vinegar and other acids.

Achæ'nium (Gr. *not gaping*), in botany, the name of a small one-seeded fruit, which does not open when ripe.

Achæ'us (Gr.), a genus of crustaceans; fam. Brachyura.

Acha'nia (Gr. *closed*, in allusion to the corolla not opening), a genus of plants; order Malvaceæ.

Achati'na (Gr. *agate*), a genus of land-snails, with oblong ventricose shells; fam. Helicidæ.

Achatinel'la (Gr.), a sub-genus of agate-shells; fam. Helicidæ.

Acher'ner (Arab.), a star of the first magnitude, of the constellation Eridanus.

Acheron'tia (Gr. from *Acheron*, the fabled hell of antiquity), in entomology, a genus of Lepidoptera; fam. Crepuscularia.

A'chias, a genus of dipterous insects; fam. Muscidæ.

Achil'la (Gr. from *Achilles*, who applied one of its species, the milfoil, in curing Telephus), a genus of composite plants.

Achil'les Tendon, in anatomy, the name of the strong tendon inserted in the leg, so called from the mythological story of Achilles being held by the heel when dipped in the river Styx.

Acnime'nes, a beautiful flowering plant; order Gesneraceæ.

Ach'irite, in mineralogy, a silicate of copper, or green malachite, so called from Achir Malmed, who first introduced it into Europe.

Achi'rus (Gr. *without fins*), a genus of flat-fishes; fam. Pleuronectidæ.

Achlamyd'ea (Gr. *without a tunic*), in botany, a term applied to those plants which have neither corolla nor calyx.

Ach'mite, the name of a dark red-brown mineral, the bisilicate of iron and of soda.

Achnan'thes (Gr. *froth-flower*), a genus of sea-weeds, so called from the fine down with which they are covered.

Achnodon'ton (Gr. *chaff-toothed*), in botany, a genus of plants; order Graminaceæ.

Achor (Gr.), in pathology, a kind of pustule which contains a yellowish matter, generally occurring on the heads of children.

Ach'ras (Gr. *the wild pear*), a genus of plants, of the order Sapotaceæ.

Achroma'tic (Gr. *without colour*), a term applied to optical instruments which are free from colour, or the confusing effects of chromatic aberration.

Achro'matism (Gr. *ut supra*), freedom from colour, as applied to optical instruments.

Achy'la, in botany, a species of sea-weed, of the order Confervaceæ.

Achyran'thus (Gr. *chaff-flower*), a genus of evergreen shrubs, so called from their chaff-like envelopes; order Amarantaceæ.

Achyro'nia (Gr. *chaff*), a genus of leguminous plants, natives of Australia; sub-order Papilionaceæ.

Achyroph'orus (Gr. *chaff-bearing*), a genus of herbaceous plants, with chaff-bearing receptacles; sub-order Tubulifloræ.

Acian'thus (Gr. *a sharp-pointed flower*), a genus of tuberose plants, of the order Calyceraceæ.

Acicar'pha (Gr. *pointed straw*), a genus of plants, of the order Calyceraceæ.

Acidim'eter (Gr. *acid-measurer*), an instrument for ascertaining the strength of acids.

Acido'ton (Gr. *sharp-pointed*), a genus of stinging nettles, of the order Euphorbiaceæ.

Acid'ulum (Lat.), in chemistry, a salt in which the acid is in excess, as tartaric or oxalic acid.

Acina'ciform (Gr. and Lat. *scimitar-shaped*), in botany, a term applied to leaves which are sharp and convex on one side and straight on the other.

Acine'sia (Gr. *incapability of moving*), in pathology, loss of motion.

Acine'ta (Gr. *immovable*), a genus of plants, of the order Orchidaceæ.

A'cini (Lat. *grape stones*), in botany, a term applied to the small grains of which the fruit of the mulberry or blackberry is composed: "Varii generis reperiuntur acini."—*Col.*

Acin'opus (Gr. *grape-footed*), in zoology, a genus of coleopterous insects.

Acio'a (the Guiana name), a genus of arboraceous plants, a native of Guiana, of the order Chrysobalanaceæ.

Acio'tis (Gr. *ear-pointed*, in reference to the form of the petals), a genus of plants, natives of the West Indies; order Melastomaceæ.

Acipen'ser (see *Accipenser*).

Acis, in botany, the name of a bulbous-rooted plant, of the order Amaryllidaceæ, so called from the mythological Acis.

Acisanthe'ra (Gr. *anther-pointed*), a genus of plants, of the order Lythraceæ.

Acmade'nia (Gr. *gland-pointed*, from its glandulous anthers), a genus of plants, of the order Rutaceæ.

Acme (Gr. *height* or *summit*), in pathology, the crisis of a disease.—In the arts, the summit of perfection.

Acmel'la (Lat. from Gr. *akme* a point), a genus of plants, of the composite order, the Virginian hemp; sub-order Tubulifloræ.

Acme'na, in botany, an ornamental species of plants, of the order Myrtaceæ, so called from Acmena, a nymph of Venus.

Acne (Gr.), in pathology, a hard and inflamed tubercle, which occurs in different parts of the body.

Acnes'tis (Gr. *that cannot be rubbed*), in quadrupeds, that part of the spine between the shoulder-blades which the animal cannot reach.

Acni'da (Gr. *nettle-like*, in appearance but without its sting), in botany, a genus of annuals, of the order Chenopodiaceæ; the Virginian hemp.

Acocanthe'ra (Gr. *sharp-pointed anther*), a genus of plants, of the order Solanaceæ, natives of the Cape of Good Hope.

Acol'ogy (Gr. *discourse on curing diseases*), in pathology, the doctrine of therapeutic agencies.

Acon'dylose (Gr. *without a knuckle*), in botany, a term applied to stalks without joints.

Acon'itine, an alkaline poison extracted from the plant *Aconitum* (which see).

Aconi'tum (Lat. from *Acone*, a place in the Crimea, famous for its poisonous plants), a species of plants, generally poisonous, of the order Ranunculaceæ; wolf's-bane: "Miscent aconita novercæ."—*Ovid.*

Acon'tias (Gr.), a genus of small swift-darting serpents, sometimes called the Jaculum or dart-snake.

Acop'ic (Gr. *not wearisome*), that alleviates or prevents weariness.

Acop'ica (Gr. *ut supra*), in pharmacy, a medicine that alleviates wearisomeness.

Aco'pium (Lat.), in pathology, a warm fomentation.

Acor (Lat.), in pathology, acidity of the stomach.

Aco'ria (Gr. *insatiability*), voracious appetite.

Ac'orus (Gr. *wanting the pupil of the eye*), a genus of plants, of the order Araceæ; the sweet flag.

Acos'mia (Gr. *wanting beauty*), a genus of leguminous plants, of the sub-order Cæsalpineæ, natives of Brazil.

Acot'yla (Gr. *wanting a cavity*), in zoology, a species of Acalephæ, which has neither lateral cavities nor a central mouth.

Acotyledo'neæ, or **Acotyle'dons** (Gr. *without seed-lobes*), in botany, an important division of the vegetable kingdom, comprehending those plants which are without seed-lobes; the Cryptogamia of Linnæus; the highest tribe are the ferns, and the lowest the fungi and algæ, which have no leaves.

Acotyle'donous (Gr. *ut supra*), in botany, an epithet applied to plants which have no seed-lobes.

Acou'meter (Gr. *sound-measurer*), an instrument for measuring the extent of hearing.

Acou'rus (Gr. *unshaven*), in ichthyology, a genus of malacopterygious fishes; fam. Cobitidæ.

Acous'tics (Gr. *akouo* to hear), the science of sounds, and of hearing.

Acra'lia (Gr. *akre* extremity), in anatomy, a term applied to any extreme parts of the body, as the hands or toes.

Acran'thus (Gr. *irritated*), in herpetology, a genus of round-tailed lizards, with long tongues, of the order Lacertidæ.

Ac'rasy, Acra'tia (Gr. *wanting strength*), in pathology, irregularity or undue prevalence of one particular quality in the human constitution more than another; constitutional weakness of the body.

Acremo'nium (Gr. *akremon* a branch), in botany, a term applied to a curious little fungus growing on dead sticks; order Fungi.

Acrid'ians (Lat. *acris* sharp), a family of orthopterous insects, of the tribe Locustanæ, of which the Acridium is the type.

Acrid'ium (Gr. *akris* a locust), a genus of insects, of the locust family.

Acridoph'agi (Gr. *locust-eaters*), a tribe who feed on locusts.

Acriop'sis (Gr. *akris*, and *opsis* the eye), a pretty flowering shrub, of the order Orchidaceæ.

Ac'risy (Gr. *wanting judgment*), that on which no judgment can be passed, more especially as applied to a disease, the crisis of which is uncertain.

Acri'ta (Gr. *doubtful*), in zoology, a term applied to that division of the animal kingdom which comprehends the Polypes, Infusoria, Intestina, &c.

Acrocar'pe (Gr. *having seed at the extremities*), in botany, a sub-order of the Mosses.

Acroceph'alus (Gr. *top-headed*), a genus of plants, the flowers of which are on the uppermost branches; order Lamiaceæ.

Acrocer'idæ (Gr. *extreme-horned*), in entomology, a family of dipterous or double-winged insects, of which the Acrocera is the type.

Acroco'mia (Gr. *top-tufted*), a genus of arboriferous plants, of the order Palmaceæ.

Ac'rodont (Gr. *akros*, and *odontes* teeth), in zoology, a term applied to those fossil Saurians which have the teeth anchylosed to the top of the alveolar process.

Ac'rodus (Gr. *extreme teeth*), in geology, a genus of fossil sharks.

Ac'rogens (Gr. *extreme productions*), in botany, a term applied to those cellular plants, which increase chiefly in length, and not in thickness.

Acrogloch'in (Gr. *spear-pointed*), a species of herbaceous plants, of the order Chenopodiaceæ.

Ac'rolith (Gr. *stone extremities*), in sculpture and architecture, a statue of wood, with extremities of stone or marble.

Acroma'nia (Gr. *extreme madness*), in pathology, the height of insanity.

Acro'mion (Gr. *akros*, and *omos* a shoulder), in anatomy, the humeral extremity of the shoulder-blade.

Acron'ical (Gr. *at the summit*), in astronomy, a term applied to the rising and setting of a star about the same time as the sun.

Acronych'ia (Gr. *akros*, and *onyx* a claw), the name of a pretty shrub, with white clustering flowers and fragrant odour; order Rutaceæ.

Acrop'athy (Gr. *disease at the extremities*), in pathology, diseased action and pain at the extremities of the body.

Acrope'ra (Gr. *akros*, and *pera* a small sack), a genus of plants with purple and yellow-spotted flowers; order Orchidaceæ.

Acrophyl'lum (Gr. *akros*, and *phyllum* a leaf), a flowering plant, of the order Cunoniaceæ.

Acropo'dium (Gr. *summit-footed*), in botany, a genus of leguminous shrubs, of the sub-order Papilionaceæ; so called from the legumes being stalked within the calyx.—In zoology, a term applied to the upper part of the foot.

Ac'ropy (Gr.), defective articulation.

Acrosper'mum (Gr. *akros*, and *sperma* seed), a genus of fungus growing on dead herbs and putrid mushrooms.

Ac'rospire (Gr. *high-spired*), in botany, the sprout or plumule, which appears at the end of flowers during germination.

Acrote'ria (Gr.), in architecture, the small bases serving to support statues.

Acrote'riasm (Gr. *extremity*), in surgery, amputation of the extremities.

Acrothym'ion (Gr. *akros*, and *thymon* a wart), in pathology, a rugated, bleeding wart, of a conical shape.

Ac'rotism (Gr.), in pathology, defect of pulsation.

Actæ'a (Gr. *akte* the elder tree), the botanical name of a genus of herbaceous plants, the bane-berry; order Ranunculaceæ.

Actin'ia (Gr. *aktin* a sun-ray), a radiated marine animal, or animal-flower, of the class Acalephæ.

Actinia'ria (Gr. *aktin*), an order of Polypi, which have a radiated appearance like the Actinia.

Actin'ic (Gr. *sending out rays*), relating to actinism.

Ac'tinism (Gr. *aktin*, as " the actinic force of the solar ray"), in natural philosophy, a term applied to the radiation of light or heat.

Actinoc'amax (Gr. *aktin*, and *kamax* a peg), in fossilization, the name of an extinct class of Cephalopods, found in the chalk formation.

Actinocar'pus (Gr. *aktin*, and *karpos* fruit), in botany a genus of composite plants; sub-order Tubulifloræ.

Actinoc'rinite (Gr. *aktin*, and *krinon* a lily), in geology, the name of a fossil crinoidian, found in the limestone formation.

Actin'olite (Gr. *aktin*, and *lithos* a stone), in geology, a variety of green-coloured hornblende, chiefly consisting of silica, magnesia, lime, and alumina. It is one of the principal constituents of *Actinolite schist*, a species of laminated or slaty rock.

Actinom'eris (Gr. *a divided ray*), an ornamental genus of plants; order Compositæ.—*Nuttall.*

Actinom'eter (Gr. *a ray measurer*), an

instrument for measuring the intensity of the sun's rays.

Actinos'toma (Gr. *aktin*, and *stoma* a mouth), in zoology, an order of Helianthoides, whose mouths are encircled with radiated tentacula.

Actinozoa'ria (Gr. *atkin*, and *zoon* an animal), in zoology, a term applied to radiated animals ; the Radiata.

Acu'leates (Lat. *aculeus* a prickle), in entomology, a tribe of hymenopterous insects, the females and neutrals of which are provided with stings.

Acu'lei (Lat. *ut supra*), in botany, a term applied to those spines or prickles which spring from the bark of the tree, and not from the wood.

Acus (Lat. *a needle*), in zoology, a term applied to the sand-eel or ammodyte, and also to the needle-fish.

Ada'gio (Ital.), in music, a term denoting slow time.

Ad'amant (Lat. *not to be subdued*), a stone formerly supposed to be of impenetrable hardness ; a name applied to the diamond, and also to the loadstone. The crystals of the mineral corundum are called *Adamantine spar*, from their excessive hardness.

Ada'mia, a genus of plants, natives of the Nepaulese territory ; so called from John Adam, a promoter of natural history, and some time governor of India ; nat. order Hydrangeaceæ.

Adanso'nia, or **Baobab tree**, a tree of gigantic growth, the largest production in the vegetable kingdom ; so called from Michael Adanson, a celebrated French botanist. It grows to a vast age, and its trunk has been found to measure thirty feet in diameter. Some specimens on the coast of Africa are said to be 5,000 years old.—*Hooker*.

Ad'apis, in geology, a genus of fossil mammalia found in the Eocene formation of Paris.

Addax, a species of antelope.

Adduc'tor (Lat. *that which draws to*), in anatomy, a muscle whose action is to draw one part to another ; its antagonistic muscle is called the *Abductor*.

Adelobot'rys (Gr. *obscure raceme*), a genus of plants growing in Guiana ; order Melastomaceæ.

Adelobran'chiata (Gr. *concealed gills*), a name given to those molluscs whose respiratory organs are externally concealed, and also to a family of the Gasteropods.

Adeloder'ma (Gr. *adelos* hidden, and *derma* skin), in malachology, a name given to a sub-order of Gasteropods, whose respiratory organs are concealed by the skin.

Adelopneu'mona (Gr. *concealed lungs*), a name applied to an order of Gasteropods, whose respiratory organs are invisible.

Adel'opode (Gr. *concealed feet*), in zoology, an animal whose feet are not visible.

Adel'phia (Gr. *brotherhood*), a name applied to plants, in the Linnæan system of botany, whose stamens are aggregated into a bundle ; whence the term *Adelphic*, as applied to such plants.

Adenal'gia (Gr. *aden* a gland, and *alge* pain), in pathology, pain seated in a gland, attended by a painful swelling.

Adenan'dria (Gr. *a male gland*), a genus of evergreen herbaceous plants ; order Rutaceæ.

Adenanthe'ra (Gr. *aden*, and *anthera* an anther), a genus of handsome trees, of the order Leguminosæ. *A. pavonia* is one of the largest trees in the East Indies, the timber of which is much esteemed.

Adeni'tis (Gr.), in pathology, inflammation of the glands.

Adenocalym'na (Gr. *concealed gland*), a genus of plants, of the order Bignoniaceæ.

Adenocar'pus (Gr. *aden* and *carpos* fruit), a genus of leguminous ornamental shrubs ; sub-order Papilionaceæ.

Adenog'raphy (Gr. *aden*, and *graphe* description), in physiology, a description of the glands.

Adenoi'dal (Gr. *aden*, and *oidos* similar to), glandiform, like a gland.

Adenol'ogy (Gr. *aden*, and *logos* a treatise on), a discourse on the nature and use of the glands.

Adenomesenteri'tis (Gr. *aden*, and *mesenterion* mesentery). in pathology, inflammation of the mesenteric glands.

Adenopharyngi'tis (Gr. *aden*, and *pharynx*), in pathology, inflammation of the glands of the tonsil and pharynx.

Adenoph'ora (Gr. *aden*, and *phoreo* to bear), a genus of perennial herbs, natives of Siberia ; order Campanulaceæ.

Adenophthal'mia (Gr. *aden*, and *ophthalmos* the eye), inflammation of the Meibomian glands, which are situated at the edge of the eyelids.

Adenophyl'leæ (Gr. *aden*, and *phyllon* a leaf), the name of a group of plants, of the order Oxalidaceæ, which have small glandulous tubercles on the leaves.

Adeno'sis (Gr. *aden* a gland), a family of glandular diseases.

Adenot'omy (Gr. *aden*, and *tome* a cutting), in anatomy and surgery, the cutting of a gland.

Adeph'agans (Gr. *gluttons*), a family of voracious coleopterous insects.

Adeps (Lat.), in anatomy, the fat of the abdomen.

Adesma'ceæ (Gr. *long-footed*), a family of boring Mollusca, including the Pholidæ, Teredineæ, &c.

Ades'mia (Gr. *without bands*), a genus of S. American herbaceous plants; sub-order Papilionaceæ.

Adian'tum (Gr. *dryness*, alluding to the want of moisture in the leaves), a genus of ferns, maiden's-hair.

Adiaphneus'tia (Gr.), impeded or defective perspiration.

Adiaphore'sis (Gr. *indifference*), in pharmacy, suppressed cutaneous perspiration.

Adi'na (Gr. *crowded*), a genus of glabrous shrubs, with flowers disposed in heads (whence the name); natives of China; order Cinchonaceæ.

Ad'ipocere (Lat. *adeps*, and *cera* fat wax), a fatty spermaceti substance produced in dead animal bodies by burial in moist places, or by long immersion in spirit or water.

Ad'ipose (Lat. *adeps* fat), belonging to or consisting of waxy fat; an epithet much used in pathology and anatomy; thus, *Adipose cells* are those vesicles which contain the fat; *Adipose membrane*, the tissue which encloses the fat in animal bodies; *Adipose tumour*, a large fatty swelling; *Adipose vein*, a vein arising from the descending trunk of the cava, which spreads itself on the coat of fat that covers the kidneys.

Adip'sia (Gr. *free from thirst*), absence of thirst.

Adip'son, a medium that tends to allay extreme thirst.

Adit (Lat.), the horizontal or inclined entrance to a mine.

Ad'jutant (Lat. *an assistant*), in natural history, the *Ardea gigantea*, or gigantic crane, one of the most voracious carnivorous animals in existence; it swallows bones with impunity.

Adjuto'rium (Lat. *a helper*), in anatomy, a term applied to the humerus, for its usefulness in raising the arm.

Adminic'ulum (Lat. *support*), in natural history, a term applied to the abdominal semi-circular row of teeth, which enables certain subterranean insects to force their way to the surface.

Adna (Lat. *adnatus* growing to), in malacology, a term applied to those cup-shaped shells found attached to stones on the sea-coast; a genus of Balani or Barnacles.

Adnas'cent (Lat.), in botany, growing to or on.

Adna'ta, Tu'nica (Lat. *an adhering tunic*), in anatomy, one of the coats of the eye, situated between the conjunctiva and sclerotica; called also *Albuginea*.

Ad'nate (Lat. *growing together*), in botany, a term applied to a leaf when it is found adhering to the stem by its surface; also to an anther, when adherent to the filament in its entire length.

Adoscula'tion (Lat. *a kissing*), in botany, a term applied to the impregnation of plants through the agency of the pollen, which falls on the stigma.

Adox'a (Gr. *inglorious*), a genus of plants, the moschatel; order Saxifrageæ.

Adula'ria (from Mount Adula, in Switzerland), in mineralogy, a semi-transparent variety of felspar; moonstone.

Adyna'mia, or **Adynamy** (Gr. *wanting strength*), in pathology, a prostration of physical energy; a diminution of the vital powers; debility.—*Adynamic*, without power, applied to invalids.

Æchmea (Gr. *a point*), a genus of plants; order Bromeliaceæ.

Æcid'ium (Gr. *like a wheel*), in botany, a genus of minute fungi, growing in the leaves and bark of trees, like small membraneous bags.

Æ'dilite (Gr. *a modest-looking stone*), in mineralogy, a silicate of alumina, of a light grey striated appearance, found in Sweden.

Ædoiot'omy (Gr.), dissection of the organs of generation.

Ægagrap'ilus (Gr. *aix* a goat, and *pilos* a ball of hair), a concretionary hairy ball, found in the stomachs of ruminating animals.

Ægerid'eæ (Gr. *aix*, and *eidos* resemblance), a family of lepidopterous insects; the hornets.

Æ'gialites (Gr. *a beach*), a name given to a family of wading birds.

Æ'gilops (Gr. *goat-eyed*), in botany, a genus of the Graminaceæ, called hard-grass.

Ægiph'ila (Gr. *aix*, and *philos* dear), a genus of West Indian plants, goat's-friend; order Verbenaceæ.

Ægochlo'a (Gr. *aix*, and *chloa* grass), a genus of plants; order Polemoniaceæ.

Ægoph'ony (Gr. *goat-like voice*), in pathology, a tremulous sound of the voice resulting from a diseased state of the chest, similar to the bleating of a goat.

Æo'lian (Lat. *Æolus*, the god of the winds), pertaining to the winds.—*Æolian harp*, a stringed instrument, which yields agreeable sounds when acted on by a current of air.

Æol'ipile (*Æolus*, and Gr. *pila* a ball), an instrument used in showing how water may be converted into steam.

A'erate (Gr. and Lat. *aer* air), to impregnate a liquid with carbonic acid.

Aera'ted (Lat.), charged with air, applied to water charged with carbonic acid gas.

Aera'tion (Lat.), act of charging with air or gas.

Aerhy'drous (Gr. *aer*, and *hydor* water), in mineralogy, applied to those minerals which contain water in their cavities.

Ae'rial (Lat.), in natural philosophy, an epithet of very general use, as applied to objects connected with the air; as *Aerial perspective*, that branch of perspective which treats of the relative diminution of the colours of bodies in proportion to their distance.—In painting, the secondary objects, as seen through the medium of the atmosphere, are so termed.

Aer'ides (Lat. *aer* the air), a genus of plants, the air-plant; order Orchidaceæ.

Aerif'erous (Lat. *containing air*), in botany, an epithet applied to the vesicles of certain fuci, which enable them to swim on the surface of the water.—In zoology, applied to the bronchial vessels.

Aerifica'tion (Lat. *aer*, and *fio* to become), in natural philosophy, the act of becoming air, or of being changed from a solid or liquid to an aeriform state.

A'eriform (Lat.), resembling air.

A'erify (Lat.), to infuse air into, or fill with air.

Aerodynam'ics (Gr. *air-power*), in natural philosophy, the science which treats on the force and properties of air, when in motion.

Aerog'nosy (Gr. *knowledge of air*), in natural history, the science which treats of the properties of air, and of the part it performs in the economy of nature.

Aerog'raphy (Gr.), a description of the atmosphere or air which circumvolves the earth.

A'erolites, or **A'eroliths** (Gr. *aer* and *lithos*, air-stones), in meteorology, luminous stones, or mineral masses, which fall from the atmosphere; or, as some philosophers affirm, from the more distant regions of the solar system. Of their physical or meteorological origin, however, nothing certain is known; but the subject is sufficiently interesting to deserve inquiry. These wonderful phenomena are mentioned in the earliest periods of antiquity, yet their physical origin has never been satisfactorily explained. In China there exist catalogues of remarkable meteors of every description, which have appeared there during a period of 2,400 years. From A.D. 960 to 1270, no fewer than 1,479 meteors are registered by the Chinese observers. Pliny relates that a shower of stones (for such he calls them) fell in Lucania. In 1762, many of these meteoric stones fell near Verona, in Italy, some of them weighing 200 and 300 pounds in weight. In Siberia, a mass of native iron was discovered by Professor Pallas, which weighed 1,600 pounds; and one was discovered, in Peru, of the enormous weight of fifteen tons.

That these meteoric phenomena are of cosmical origin has been demonstrated by Olmsted, at Newhaven, in Connecticut, who proved that during the celebrated display of aeroliths, in November, 1833, they all emerged from precisely the same quarter of the heavens, near the star γ, in the constellation Leo; and that they did not deviate from this particular point, though the star changed its apparent height and azimuth during the observation; thus demonstrating that these bodies are independent of the diurnal or rotatory motion of the earth.—The verified instances of the fall of aerolites in modern times are innumerable. In 1789 a fire-ball broke over the Landes, near Bordeaux, and discharged stones that fell on a shed and killed several cattle. In 1798, at Benares, there was a shower of stones, many of them weighing two pounds. In 1790 a meteor burst over Agen, a French village; the stones that fell were at first soft, but they gradually hardened. An aerolite that fell at Manerkirch, in Bavaria, in 1768, was triangular, and weighed thirty-eight pounds; it buried itself two feet. — "These bodies," says an able writer in the *Quarterly Review*, "afford us glimpses into the history of matter foreign to the world in which we ourselves live. They represent another domain of nature; yet connected with our own by the signal fact, also derived from them, that the matter is the same in kind as that which surrounds us here. One-third of the whole number of· elementary substances enter into their composition; iron largely predominating over the rest, and associated· occasionally with minerals, resembling closely the hornblende, augite, and olivine of our rocks."

Aerol'ogy (Gr. *aer*, and *logos* treatise on), the science of air; a treatise on air in general, and its various properties; whence *Aerologist*, one versed in aerology.

Aerom'etry (Gr. *aer*, and *metron* air-measurer), in natural philosophy, that portion of physics which relates to the expansion and density of the air, and the means of measuring it; whence *Aerometer*, an instrument for measuring the density and lightness of the atmosphere.

A'eronaut (Gr. *aer*, and Lat. *nauta* a sailor), one who floats through the air in a balloon; whence *Aeronautics*, the art of sailing in the air; and *Aeronautism*, the art and science of ballooning.

Aeropho'bia (Gr. *dread of air*), a symptom of hydrophobia.

A'erophyte (Gr. *air-plant*), in botany, a plant which derives its nutriment exclusively from the air and the moisture which it contains.

Aeros'copy (Gr. *air-inspector*, or *perception by the air*), the science which shows by observation the state of the atmosphere, and its variations; the faculty of perception by the medium of the air, peculiar to the antennæ of some insects.

Aerostat'ics (Gr. *the statics of air*), the science which treats of the weight or pressure of the air, and other elastic fluids; whence *Aerostatic*, relating to aerostation.

Aerosta'tion (Lat. *air-weighing*), the science of weighing air; the art of raising heavy bodies through the air; aerial navigation.

Æru'go (Lat.), a subacetate of copper; verdigris.

Æschynan'thus (Gr. *a modest flower*), a genus of twining parasitic plants, of the order Gesneraceæ.

Æs'chynite (Gr. *sensitiveness*), in mineralogy, a yellow-brown ore from the Ural Mountains.

Æschyno'mene (Gr. *modest*), a genus of leguminous plants; order Papilionaceæ.

Æs'culus (Gr. *esca* nourishment), a genus of arborescent plants, the horse-chesnut; order Sapindaceæ.

Æthione'ma (Gr. *a scorched filament*), a genus of plants, of the order Cruciferæ.

Æthu'sa (Gr. *warmth*), a genus of umbelliferous plants, one of which, the fool's parsley, is poisonous.

Ætiol'ogy (Gr. *treatise on causes*), in pathology, the doctrine of the causes of disease.

Æti'tes (Gr.), in mineralogy, a variety of ironstone, eagle-stone, which makes a noise when shaken.

Ætoba'tis (Gr. *aetos* an eagle, and *batis* a bramble), in ichthyology, a genus of skate, the eagle-ray, with long thorny tails.

Affettuo'so (Ital. *tender*), in music, a term denoting that the strain is to be played in a slow and gentle manner.

Affinage (Fr.), in metallurgy, the process of refining metals, or obtaining them in a state of purity.

Afze'lia, a genus of leguminous plants, of the order Papilionaceæ.

Ag'alaxy (Gr. *without milk*), in pathology, want of milk in the mother after parturition.

Agal'lochum, in botany. the name of aloes wood, of which there are three varieties: the calamba, the common lignum aloes, and the calambaz, the last of which is used by cabinet-makers.

Agal'myla (Gr. *a forest ornament*), a genus of flowering plants.

Ag'ama (Gr. *wonder*), in herpetology, a genus belonging to the Iguana family, resembling the common lizards; fam. Agamidæ.

Ag'amæ (Gr. *without sex*), in botany, a term applied to the cryptogamous or acotyledonous division of the vegetable kingdom; whence *Agamous*, as applied to cryptogamic plants, which have the organs of reproduction, but are flowerless.

Ag'ami (Sp.), in ornithology, a species of crane, inhabiting the woods of Central America; the trumpeter crane.

Aganis'ia (Gr. *soft*, or *pleasing*), a genus of plants, of the order Orchidaceæ.

Aganos'ma (Gr. *a mild scent*), a genus of plants, of the order Apocynaceæ.

Agapan'thus (Gr. *a love-blossom*), a genus of bulbous-rooted plants, the African lily; order Liliaceæ.

Agape'tes (Gr. *beloved*), a genus of showy evergreen shrubs, natives of the East Indies; order Vaccineaceæ.

Ag'aphite, in mineralogy, a variety of turquoise.

Agar'icus, a very extensive genus of the mushroom family, of the natural order Fungi, so called from *Agaria*, a town in Sarmatia; whence *Agaric*, of the nature of the mushroom. This word gives the following combinations used in natural history: *Agaricicolus*, living among mushrooms; *Agariciformis*, having the form of a mushroom; *Agaricinus*, like a mushroom. —*Agaric mineral* is a calcareous earth or carbonate of lime, resembling a fungus in colour and texture.

Agas'tachys (Gr. *admirable spikes*), a genus of plants, of the order Proteaceæ.

Agastra'ria (Gr. *without intestines*), a name applied to those organic animal bodies which, like the sponges, have no intestinal canal; *Agastria* is the type.

Agas'tric (Gr.), in natural history, applied to animals without a stomach or intestines.

Ag'asyllis (Gr.), a genus of plants, of the order Umbellaceæ.

Ag'ate (Lat.), an ornamental stone (the Scotch pebble), used in the coarser kind of jewellery; it is a variety of chalcedony, and is chiefly composed of quartz, variegated with colouring matter, and seems to be of igneous origin; whence *Agatine*, of the nature of agate.

Ag'athæa (Gr. *beautiful flower*), a genus of pretty-flowering plants, of the order Tubulifloræ.

Ag'athis (Gr. *a cluster*), a genus of coniferous trees; the Dammar pine, a native of New Zealand.

Agathophyl'lum (Gr. *a fine leaf*), the Madagascar nutmeg tree; order Lauraceæ.

Agathos'ma (Gr. *a good smell*), a genus of evergreen shrubs; order Rutaceæ.

Agathyr'sus (Gr. *a pretty pannicle*), a genus of composite plants, allied to the sow-thistle; sub-order Tubulifloræ.

Ag'ati (Sans.), a genus of leguminous trees of the East Indies; sub-order Papilionaceæ.

Agave (Gr. *admirable*), a genus of plants which belong to the pine-apple, the American aloe; fam. Bromeliaceæ.

Agelai'næ (Gr. *gregarious*), a sub-family of gregarious birds, natives of S. America, of which the maize bird (*Agelaius*) is the type.

Agenne'sia (Gr. *impotency*), male sterility.

Agera'sia (Gr.), immature old age.

Agera'tum (Gr. *not subject to old age*), a genus of ornamental plants, of the order Compositæ.

Ageus'tia (Gr.), loss of taste.

Agglu'tinant (Lat. *uniting parts together*), in pathology, a medicine which has the property of uniting different parts.

Aggrega'ta (Lat. *called together*), in zoology, a family of naked Acephala, whose bodies become united in one mass in the later stages of existence.

Agil'ia (Lat. *agile*), in zoology, a family of Rodents, comprehending the dormouse, squirrel, &c.

Agita'to (Ital.), in music, a rapid and broken style of performance, calculated to awaken surprise.

Aglai'a (Gr. *beauty*, or *splendour*), in botany, a genus of plants, of the order Aurantiaceæ.—In ornithology, a genus of very beautiful Brazilian finches, of the sub-family Tanagrinæ.—In astronomy, the name of one of the recently-discovered planets, first observed by Luther, the German astronomer, in 1857.

Aglamor'pha (Gr. *beautiful form*), an elegant stove-plant, a genus of fern.

Aglaone'ma (Gr. *a splendid filament*), a genus of plants, of the order Araceæ.

Aglaophe'nia (Gr. *aglaos*, and *phene* the osprey), a class of elegant plant-like corals, resembling the waving plumes of the osprey.

Aglau'ra (Gr. *bright tailed*), in zoology, a genus of dorsi-branchiate annelides, distinguished by their bright colouring.

Aglone'ma (Gr. *a beautiful grove*), a showy flowering plant, of the order Araceæ.

Ag'nail (Sax. *pain of the nail*), in pathology, disease of the nails; whitlow.

Agna'tha (Gr. *without jaws*), in entomology, a family of neuropterous insects, whose mouths are so small as to be scarcely observable.

Agnos'tes (Gr. *unknown*), in palæontology, a genus of fossil trilobites, existing in the Silurian formation.

Agnothe'rium (Gr. *agnus* a lamb, and *therion* a wild beast), in palæontology, a fossil quadruped, found in the Miocene formation of France.

Agom'phians (Gr. *toothless*), in entomology, a name applied to the rotiferous infusoria, which have no teeth.

Agon'ic (Gr. *without angles*), in natural philosophy, an epithet applied to two lines on the surface of the globe, in which there is no declination of the magnetic needle from the meridian.

Agon'idæ (Gr. *contention*), in ichthyology, a family of acanthopterygious fishes, with prolonged jaws, and covered with mail plates; the mailed bullheads, of which *Agonus* is the type.

Agou'ti (Ind.), in zoology, a genus of the Rodentia, which do not burrow like the rabbit, but lodge under rocks or trees.

Agrimo'nia (Gr.), a genus of plants, of the order Rosaceæ; agrimony; the only British species is the *A. eupatoria*, a well-known herb, used medicinally as a tonic.

Agrion'idæ (Gr. *agrios* rustic), a family of neuropterous insects, the dragon-flies, of which *Agrion* is one of the genera.

Agri'opus (Gr. *agrios*, and *pous* foot), a genus of hog-fishes.

Agrob'ates (Gr. *agrios*, and *batis* a thorn-bush), in ornithology, a genus of Warblers, of the sub-order Philomelinæ.

Agrod'roma (Gr. *a field-runner*), in ornithology, a genus of the lark tribe.

Agron'omy (Gr. *field-law*), the rules or science of agriculture.

Agroph'ilus (Gr. *field-loving*), a genus of ground finches, of the family Fringillidæ.

Agropy'rum (Gr. *field-wheat*), a genus of plants, of the order Graminaceæ.

Agrostem'ma (Gr. *a field-stem*), a genus of plants, the wild lychnis, of the order Caryophyllaceæ.

Agros'tis (Gr. *agros* rustic), the name of the bent grass ; order Graminaceæ.

Agrostog'raphy (Gr. *agros*, and *graphe* description), a description of the grasses, of which Bishop Stillingfleet enumerates about 300 species.

Agrostol'ogy (Gr.), a treatise on the various grasses of the field.

Agryp'nia (Gr.) in pathology, indisposition to sleep; sleeplessness.

Agrypnoo'oma (Gr. *sound sleeping*), a continued tendency to sleep.

A'gynous (Gr. *without female sex*), in botany, applied to flowers that are without the organs of female fructification ; the term being synonymous with male flowers.

A'gyrate (Gr. *without a circle*), in botany, a term applied to those ferns which are without the elastic ring, or annulus.

Agyr'ium (Gr. *clustered*), a genus of speckled gregarious fungi, growing on wood ; order Fungi.

Ai'guille (Fr.), an instrument used by engineers and miners for piercing a rock for the lodgment of powder.—In physical geography, *Aiguilles* are the sharp needle like points of lofty mountains.

Aikin'ia, a genus of flowering plants, of the order Gesneriaceæ, so called in honour of Arthur Aikin.

Ailan'tus (Sans. *a heavenly tree*), a genus of trees of towering growth, natives of the East Indies and China ; order Terebinthaceæ.

Ailu'rus (Gr. *a cat*), a small carnivorous animal, allied to the raccoon, about the size of a large cat, with a red brilliant fur.

Aimoph'ila (Gr. *loving the thicket*), a genus of American ground finches, of the family Fringillidæ.

Air (Gr.), an invisible, transparent fluid, which we constantly breathe, and which is essential to the support of animal and vegetable existence. It envelops the entire globe, and constitutes the atmosphere that surrounds it. Air is 816 times lighter than its bulk of water ; 1,000 cubic inches at the ordinary temperature and pressure weighing 305 grains. It consists of about 80 parts, in bulk, of nitrogen, and 20 parts of oxygen, and about one-thousandth part of carbonic acid. Air, when inhaled into the lungs, unites with the carbon of the blood, and forms carbonic acid, a process which produces the heat necessary to sustain the proper temperature of the animal system.—In zoology, *Air-cells* are membraneous receptacles communicating with the lungs, and in birds extending through the different parts of the body, by which their specific gravity is diminished, and they are rendered fitter for sustentation in the air.—In botany, air-cells are cavities in the leaves and stems of certain algæ, which render them buoyant in water.—*Air-plants* are orchideous plants which live for many months suspended in the air.—*Air-vessels* are spiral vessels or ducts in plants containing air, and supposed to answer the same purpose in the vegetable system as lungs do in the animal.

Air is a useful prefix to numerous words connected with science and art, of which a brief enumeration may be here given.—*Air-balloon* is a balloon inflated with gas, in distinction from a fire-balloon, which ascends through the rarefaction of the air contained in it by the application of heat.—*Air-bladder*, the air-bag, sound, or swim, in fishes, which they have the power of compressing and dilating at pleasure, as they require to sink or ascend.—*Air-fountain*, a contrivance for producing a jet of water by the elastic force of air compressed in a close vessel, and made to act on the surface of the water to be raised.—*Air-gun*, a pneumatic instrument, so constructed as to propel bullets with immense force by means of condensed air.—*Air-lamp*, a pneumatic machine, formed by the combination of inflammable air and electricity, which, by turning a stopcock, produces a flame that may be restrained or continued at pleasure.—*Air-pump*, a machine for extracting the air, and producing a vacuum.—*Air-trunk*, a contrivance to prevent the stagnation of putrid effluvia in jails or apartments. It is an open tube passing from the ceiling to the open air, by which the heated or foul air escapes.

Ai'ra (Gr.), a genus of plants, hair-grass, of the order Graminaceæ.—*Airopsis* is a plant of the same genus and order.

Air-poise, a term applied to any instrument used for weighing the air.

Aizo'on (Gr. *ever alive*), a genus of plants, of the order Tetragoniaceæ.

Aja'va, the seed of a plant brought from Malabar, used medicinally as a carminative.

Ajow'an, a species of umbelliferous plants, used in the East Indies for diseases of cows and horses.

Aju'ga (Gr. *not yoked*), a genus of herbaceous plants, the bugle. of the order Labiatæ.

Ak'era (Gr. *wanting horns*), in zoology, a family of Mollusca, without horns or feelers.

Ala (Lat. *a wing*), in botany, a term applied to the hollow of a leaf or pedicle, which is made with the stalk. The plural *Alæ* is used for those parts of leaves called lobes or leaflets; and also applied to the side petals of papilionaceous flowers, placed between those other petals distinguished as the vexillum and carina, and which constitute the top and bottom of the flower.—In anatomy, the term has various applications, especially to the cartilages of the nostrils, and the cartilaginous parts of the ear; *Alæ nasi* are the lateral or movable parts of the nose; *Alæ vespertilionum* (bat's wings) are the broad ligaments situated between the uterus and the fallopian tubes. The term is generally applied to the wings of birds and insects.—*Alar*, belonging to a wing.—*Alate*, having wings.

Al'alite (from *Ala* in Piedmont, and Gr. *lithos* a stone), in mineralogy, a variety of augite, or diopside, which occurs in prismatic crystals of a shiny lustre.

Alangia'ceæ, or **Alan'giæ** (Malabar, *alangium*), in botany, an order of handsome tropical trees, allied to the Myrtaceæ or Myrtles; its fruit is a drupe.

Ala'ria (Lat. *winged*), a genus of Algæ, so-called from their wing-shaped appearance.

Al'aris (Lat. *wing-like*), in anatomy, an epithet applied to the pterygoid processes of the sphenoid bone, and to the inner vein of the bend of the arm.

Alas'modon (Gr. *without a portion of teeth*), in conchology, a species of shells, of the genus Unio, which have cardinal but no lateral teeth.—*Alasmodina* comprehends a class of shells of which the *Alasmodon* is the type.

Alater'nus (Lat. *treble-winged*), a Linnæan genus of plants, the buckthorn, of the order Rhamnaceæ.

Alba'rium (Lat. *whiteness*), a fine white lime or stucco, produced from burnt marble.

Alba'ta (Lat. *white*), in metallurgy, a composition of tin, zinc, nickel, and copper, usually called German silver.

Al'batross, a genus of large aquatic birds, the Diomedia, some of which, from wing to wing, measure fourteen or fifteen feet.

Albert Coal, a beautiful carbonaceous product from New Brunswick, of the nature of coal and asphaltum.

Albi (Lat.), in natural history, botany, and zoology, a prefix of frequent occurrence, denoting whiteness, of which the following is a brief enumeration:—*Albicaulis*, white-stemmed, or white-tailed; *albicollis*, having a white neck; *albicornis*, having white horns, or white or pale-coloured antennæ; *albicostatus*, or *albicostus*, white-sided; *albidactylus*, white-fingered, applied to a butterfly with digited white wings; *albiflorus*, having white flowers; *albilabris*, white-lipped; *albimanus*, white-handed, or having white tarsi; *albinervus*, having white nervures or veins in the leaves; *albipennis*, white-winged; *albipes*, white-footed; *albirostris*, white-billed or beaked; *albitarsis*, having white tarsi, &c.

Al'bicore, in natural history, a fish which pursues the flying-fish.

Albin (Lat. *white*), a white mineral (a variety of apophyllite), which consists of an aggregation of crystals.

Al'binism (Lat. *whiteness*), a state in which the skin is white, the eye of a pink colour, and the hair flaxen. This peculiarity exhibits itself in rabbits, mice, &c., as well as in man.

Albi'no (Lat. *white*), a term applied to the white descendants of a black parentage, in whom albinism, as previously explained, is manifested. This phenomenon is frequently witnessed in the inter-tropical regions of Africa, America, Ceylon, &c. In Africa the Albinos are called *dongos;* in Java, *chracrelas;* and in Ceylon, *bedhas.*

Albir'eo (Arab.), in astronomy, a star of the third magnitude, in the constellation Cynas.

Al'bite (Lat. *white*), in mineralogy, a four-angled variety of felspar, generally of a white colour.

Albo'ra, in ichthyology, a species of fish of the genus Erethynus, found in the Mediterranean Sea.—In pathology, a kind of itch, or rather leprosy, attended by fetid evacuations from the mouth and nostrils.

Albor'ga, a kind of sandal-wood made of mat weed.

Albu'ca (Lat. *whiteness*), a genus of

bulbous-rooted flowering plants, of the order Liliaceæ.

Albu'go Lat.), in pathology, a disease of the eye (leucoma), which consists of a white speck on the cornea that attends inflammation.—*Albugeneous*, in anatomy, is an epithet applied to membranes distinguished by their white colour, as the *albugeneous* membrane of the eye. *Albugeneous fibre*, says Palmer, is white, firm, hard, elastic, and insensible, and constitutes, by its union in fasciculi, or small bundles, and its various dispositions, different membraneous expansions, as the periosteum, duramater, sclerotica, the proper coverings of the kidneys, spleen, testicles, the sheaths of tendons, capsules, and ligaments of joints, the tendons themselves, and faciæ.

Al'bulo (Lat. *silvery whiteness*), a genus of fishes, of the family Salmonidæ.

Albu'men (Lat.), a thick glairy substance found in the white of an egg, and identical with the serum of the blood. In physiology, it forms one of the nutritive compounds of food, consisting of nearly the same ingredients as fibrine and caseine, which are identical with blood and muscular fibre. Its principal ingredients are carbon, hydrogen, nitrogen, and oxygen.—In botany, albumen is that fleshy or horny consistence which is secreted in certain seeds.—*Albuminous*, belonging to, or containing albumen.

Albur'num (Lat. *whiteness*), the white and soft part of the wood of trees, which lies between the inner bark of the hard wood, properly called sapwood.

Al'cadæ (Arab.), in ornithology a family of web-footed birds, of which the *Alca*, or auk, is the type, including the penguins, the puffins, gillimots, &c.; their wings are not adapted for flight, but perform the office of fins.

Al'cahist (Arab.), in alchemy, an old term for a universal solvent.

Alcan'na (Arab.), a name given to the dye which is extracted from the Egyptian privet.

Aloe'do (Lat.), a genus of beautifully feathered birds (the kingfishers), which live on the banks of rivers, and feed on small fishes; fam. Halcyonidæ.

Al'chemy (Arab.), a chemical art by which its professors (the *Alchemists*) pretended to transmute all metals into gold, and prepare a panacea against disease and death, called *Elixir vitæ*.

Al'cohol (Arab.), in chemistry, highly rectified spirit; a term applied to the intoxicating principle of spirituous liquors, wine, beer, &c., which is obtained by repeated distillation. From this term there are various formatives; as *Alcoholic*, of the nature of alcohol;—*Alcoholize*, to convert spirituous liquors into alcohol by rectification;—*Alcoholization*, process of rectifying spirits;—*Alcoholmeter*, an instrument for ascertaining the quantity of spirit in any vinous liquid;—*Alcoholate*, a species of salt, in which alcohol replaces, or appears to replace, the water of crystallization.

Al'coran (Arab.), the Mohammedan bible, or sacred book, containing the articles and precepts of the Mussulman faith, as written and promulgated by Mohammed.

Al'cyone (Arab.), a bright star in the constellation Pleiades.

Alcyo'neæ, a group of polypiferous Acrita, more nearly allied to animal life than the sponges; the *Alcyonium*, a genus of sponges, is the type.—*Alcyonella* is a fresh-water specimen; *Alcyomidium* is a gelatinous variety, inhabiting deep water, and attached to stones, &c.—*Alcyonite* is a petrified Alcyonium.

Aldebar'an (Arab.), a bright reddish looking star of the first magnitude, in the constellation Taurus; the Bull's Eye.

Al'dehyde (Arab.), in chemistry, a limpid volatile liquid, of a suffocating odour, the product of the oxidation of alcohol and ether.—*Aldehyde-ammonia* is a crystalline compound of the two bodies;—*Aldehydic acid* is a solution of oxide of silver in aldehyde; the solution being decomposed by means of hydrosulphuric acid.

Alder, a genus of forest trees, the Alnus of botanists, the leaves of which resemble the hazel.—*Alder buckthorn* is the shrub *Rhamnus frangula*.

Alecto'ria, in botany, a genus of Lichens, which occur in long tufts.

Alector'idæ (Gr. *like a cock*), a family of American gallinaceous birds (the Alectors), without spurs; order Cracidæ.

Alectorol'ophus (Gr. *a cockscomb*), in botany, a species of the Linnæan genus Rhinanthus; the plant cockscomb, or yellow rattle.

Alem'bic (Gr.), a vessel used in chemical operations.

Alem'broth, in chemistry, a compound of the bichloride of mercury and sal-ammoniac, from which is prepared the white precipitate of mercury; the salt of wisdom of the old alchemists, or the philosopher's salt.

Al'epis (Gr. *without scales*), in ichthyology, a genus of scaleless fishes, with small heads and broad bodies. — *Alepidote*, a term applied to any fish not covered with scales.

Alepisan'tus (Gr. *a scaleless Saurian*), in ichthyology, a genus of thin-bodied malacopterygious fishes, of the family Scomberidæ.

Alepoceph'alus (Gr. *scaleless heads*), a genus of abdominal fishes, with large scales on the body, but none on the head.

Alethop'teris, a genus of fossil plants, of which various species have been found in the Palæozoic and Mesozoic formations.

Ale'tris (Gr. *the miller's wife*), a genus of N. American plants, of the order Liliaceæ; so called from the powdery dust with which the plant is covered.

Aleuris'ma (Gr. *flour*), a genus of Fungi, of the tribe Ascomycetes.

Aleuri'tis (Gr. *flour*), a genus of plants, of the order Euphorbiaceæ, which have the appearance of being covered with flour.—*A. triloba* supplies the candle-nuts of the South-Sea Islanders, which serve for food as well as for torches.

Aleurom'eter (Gr. *flour-measurer*), an instrument for determining the quantity of gluten in flour.

Alexan'dra, in astronomy, the name of one of the recently discovered planets, first observed by Goldschmidt, in 1857.

Alexandri'na, a genus of leguminous plants, of the sub-order Papilionaceæ.

Alexephar'mic (Gr. *poison repellent*), that which has the quality of repelling poison.—*Alexepharmics*, or *Alexeterics*, are antidotes to poisons.

Alexipyret'ic (Gr. *fever dispellent*,) in pathology, a medicine that operates as a remedy against fever.

Aley'rodes (Gr. *flour*), a genus of white-looking hemipterous or half-winged insects; fam. Aphidæ.

Algæ (Lat. *sea-weeds*), in botany, an order of cryptogamous plants, which comprise sea-weeds, lavers, and the floating scum - like substances of ditches and rivers. They constitute the second grand division of the vegetable kingdom, the *Cellulares*. They grow extensively at the bottom of the sea, or in fresh water. After stormy weather, vast quantities may be found on the rocks, or on the beach of the sea. They are wholly composed of cellular tissue, ascending from the simplest form to a very compound state, the lowest being filiform and leafless, and the highest leafy, with a fructification included in an indehiscent pericarpium. The colour of the lowest grade is green; that of the highest is purple or red. In the philosophical arrangement of Dr. Lindley, in his "Vegetable Kingdom," the *Algæ* are thus classed according to their respective orders :— 1. *Diatomaceæ*, which are crystalline fragmentary bodies, brittle, and multiplied by spontaneous separation ;—2. *Confervaceæ*, filamentary, or membraneous bodies, multiplied by zoopores, generated in the interior at the expense of their green matter ;—3. *Fucaceæ*, cellular or tubular unsymmetrical plants, multiplied by simple spores formed externally ; — 4. *Ceraminæ*, cellular or tubular unsymmetrical plants, multiplied by tetraspores ;—5. *Characeæ*, symmetrically branched plants, multiplied by spiral nucules filled with starch.

Alg'aroth-powder, in chemistry, the oxychloride of antimony, used in the preparation of tartar-emetic.

Al'gebra (Arab. *al-jebr-e-al mokabalah*, restoration and reduction, or the reduction of a whole to a part), the science of computing abstract quantities by means of signs or symbols, instead of arithmetical figures; a species of calculation which takes the quantity sought, whether it be a number or a line, or any other quantity, as if it were granted, and, by means of one or more quantities given, proceeds by consequence, till the quantity at first only supposed to be known, or at least some power thereof, is found to be equal to some quantity or quantities which are known, and consequently its own value or quantity, or number, is determined.—*Algebraic equation* is an equation of which the terms contain only algebraic quantities.—*Algebraic geometry* is a name given to the application of algebra to geometrical problems.—*Algebraic curve* is a figure whose intercepted diameters bear always the same proportion to their respective ordinates.

Al'geneb (Arab.), in astronomy, a star in the constellation Perseus, in which constellation the star *Algal*, called Medusa's Head, also appears.

Al'gia (Gr. *pain*), in pathology, a term used at the end of a word, to denote pain in the part spoken of.

Algide (Lat. *to be cold*), in pathology, a term applied to febrile diseases which are accompanied with great coldness.

Al'gorah (Arab.), a star of the third magnitude, in the constellation Corvus.

Algoro'ba Bean (Arab.), the bean of *Ceratonia siliqua*; the Carob tree, or St. John's bread.

Al'goroth (Arab.), in chemistry, the submuriate of antimony, obtained as a white powder by mingling the chloride of mercury with water.

Alha'gi (Arab.), a genus of plants, the manna tree, believed by Arab writers to be a supernatural production. In hot weather the manna exudes from the leaves and branches. It is found in Mesopotamia, and other places in Asia and Africa.

Alhen'na, or **Alken'na** (Arab.), in botany, the plant *Lawsonia alba*, with the pulverized leaves of which the Egyptian women dye their nails yellow.

Alhir'to (Arab.), in astronomy, a star of the third magnitude, in the constellation Capricornus.

Alicula'ria (Lat. *drink*), in botany, a genus of scale mosses, of the order Jungermanniaceæ.

Al'iform (Lat.), wing-shaped.

Al'ioth (Arab.), in astronomy, a star of the third magnitude, in the constellation Ursa Major.

Al'iped (Lat. *wing-footed*), in zoology, an animal whose toes are connected by a membrane, which, like those of the bats, serve for wings.

Alis'ma, a genus of plants, the water-plantain, a type of the nat. order Alismaceæ, which contains three genera, *Alisma, Damasoma,* and *Sagittaria*; their flowers being in racemes, umbels, or pannicles.

Al'itrunk (Lat. *ala* a wing, and *trunk*), in entomology, the hinder segment of the body of an insect, with which the legs are connected.

Al'kali (Egyp. *kali*, a marine plant, the glass-wort), a term originally applied to certain plants of a soapy quality, but often used to designate their calcined produce, and in modern chemistry applied to bodies possessing similar chemical properties. It is the property of the alkalies to change vegetable blues to green, yellows to brown, and red to violet. The alkalies are arranged under three classes :—1. Those which have a metallic base combined with oxygen, soda, and lithia;—2. Ammonia, containing no oxygen;—3. Those containing oxygen, hydrogen, and carbon. The *Alkaline earths* are lime, baryta, and strontia.—*Alkalescent, Alkaline,* &c., are epithets applied to any substance of an alkaline nature.—*Alkaloid* (Gr. *like alkali*) is a term applied to certain compounds obtained from organic bodies, which possess the alkaline principle, in order to distinguish them from the mineral alkalies, from which they differ in their general properties, but agree in their being composed of the same elements.—*Alkahest* is the pretended universal solvent of the alchemists; the word being first used by Paracelsus, and adopted by his followers, to signify a universal dissolvent or liquor, which, if found out, was to have the power of resolving all compounds into their elementary constituents.

Alkalim'eter (*alkali*, and Gr. *metron* a measure), a graduated measure used by chemists for ascertaining the amount of alkali in any substance; the operation being called *Alkalimetry*.

Al'kanet, a purple dye, obtained from the root of the dyers' bugloss.

Alkar'sine, in chemistry, a compound of hydrogen, carbon, arsenic, and oxygen.—*Brande*.

Al'kool (Arab.), a preparation of antimony, used by the ladies of the East in staining the eye-lids and eye-lashes.

Al'lagite, in mineralogy, a massive opaque mineral, with a conchoidal fracture; it consists of manganese, silica, carbonic acid, and lime.

Allaman'da (so called in honour of Dr. Allamand, of Leyden), a genus of plants, with yellow flowers, a native of Guiana; order Apocynaceæ. In medicine, an infusion of the leaves makes a valuable cathartic.

Al'lanite, an opaque mineral, found in West Greenland, so named from Thos. Allan, of Edinburgh; its component parts consist of oxide of cerium, oxide of iron, silica, lime, and alumina; sp. gr. 3·1.

Allantoi'dia (Gr. *like a sausage*), a genus of ferns, of the order Polypodiaceæ.

Allan'tois (Gr. *ut supra*), in comparative anatomy, a thin transparent membrane, situate between the amnion and the chorion, or external and internal membrane, which contains the fœtus; the vesicle or sac which projects at the lower end of the alimentary canal in the embryo animal, organized by the hypogastric arteries and umbilical vein.—*Allantoid*, having the appearance of allantois. —*Allantoic acid* is an acid found in the allantois and amnion of the fœtal calf, formerly called *Amniotic acid*.

Allantox'icon (Gr. *sausage poison*), a poison exhibited in putrid sausages made of liver and blood.

Alle'gro (Ital.), in music, a quick and sprightly movement.—*Allegretto* is the diminutive of allegro, and not so quick.—*Allegressimo* is the superlative of allegro, and signifies very brisk and lively.

Al'lemande (Fr.), a slow piece of music.

Allia'ria (Lat. *garlic*), a genus of plants, with a strong smell, like garlic; hedge garlic, or Jack-in-the-hedge; order Cruciferæ.

Alliga'tor (Port.), a large Saurian of the Crocodile family, which inhabits the American rivers.

Alliga'tor Apple, a species of the custard-apple, which grows wild in the marshy grounds of Jamaica; the tree which produces it is the *Annona palustris*, which yields a kind of cork-wood.

Al'lium (Lat. *garlic*), in botany, a genus of bulbous-rooted plants, which yield a strong aromatic smell, as the onion, garlic, leek, shallot, and numerous other pot-herbs of an edible character; order Asplodeleæ.

Al'lochroite (Gr. *varied colour*), in mineralogy, a species of dodecahedral garnet found in Norway, consisting of silica, alumina, lime, oxide of iron, oxide of manganese, and carbonate of lime.—*Allochrous* is an epithet applied to a mineral which has various colours.

Allogo'nus (Gr. *a reciprocal angle*), in mineralogy, a kernel-shaped crystal, with the form of a dodecahedron.

Allop'athy (Gr. *other disease*), in pathology, the art of curing disease by inducing symptoms different or otherwise from those of the primary disease; the ordinary medical practice as opposed to Homœopathy.—*Allopathic* pertains to allopathy, or the ordinary method of medical practice.

Al'lophane (Gr. *varied appearance*), a mineral of various colours, found in Derbyshire and Thuringia; massive, and extremely brittle; consisting of alumina, silica, water, carbonate of copper, and sulphate of iron; sp. gr. 1·85.

Allos'orus (Gr. *varied heap*), in botany, a genus of ferns, of the order Polypodiaceæ.

Allosper'mum (Gr. *other seed*), a genus of composite plants, of the sub-order Tubulifloræ.

Allot'ropy (Gr. *another mode*), in chemistry, the capacity to undergo a change of physical properties without change of medical composition.—*Faraday*.

Allox'an (Gr. *other acidity*), the action of nitric with uric acid.—*Brande*.

Allu'vium (Lat. *a washing down*), in geology, the increase of earth on a shore or on the bank of a stream by the deposit of earthy matter carried thither by water.—*Alluvial* is a term generally applied to those superficial stratified deposits of sand and gravel, in many places abounding with the remains of existing animals and plants. Such deposits occur, in many parts, hundreds of feet above the level of the present ocean, or that of any existing water by which they could have been formed. In many places the alluvial formations are of considerable thickness, and, in some instances, partially consolidated into rock. When the Boulder formation is present, the alluvial beds overlie it; the term is therefore properly restricted to such stratified deposits as have occurred since the convulsive period, when the erratic boulders were spread over many portions of the earth's surface. See *Diluvium*.

Almacan'tar (Arab.), a small circle of the sphere parallel to the horizon, which passes through the centre of the sun.—*Almacantar staff*, an instrument used to take observations of the sun when it rises or sets.

Al'magist (Arab. and Gr. *megistos* greatest), a collection of problems in astronomy and geography drawn up by Ptolemy of Egypt.

Alma'gra (Sp.), in mineralogy, a fine deep-red ochre, which is very heavy and friable; it is used as a medicine and as a paint.

Al'ma-Ma'ter (Lat. *a fostering mother*), a term applied to a university, or to a college or seminary of education.

Alman'dine (Fr. from Arab.), in mineralogy, an inferior kind of ruby; a precious garnet.

Al'monds (Fr.), in anatomy, two round glands on the sides of the basis of the tongue; the tonsils.

Almug Tree (Heb.), a tree mentioned in Scripture, supposed to be the Shittim wood.

Alnus (Sax.), a genus of trees allied to the birch; the alder; order Betulaceæ.

Aloe, pl. **Aloes** (Gr.), a tree or species of wood used in the East for perfumes. The medicinal gum, or inspissated bitter juice of this plant, is highly purgative. There are various species: as *A. caballina*, or horse aloes; *A. spicata*, or Cape aloes; and *A. vulgaris*, or Barbadoes aloes.—*Aloes wood* is a resinous fragrant substance derived from the *A. agallochum* and the *Aquillaria ovata*.—*Aloetic acid* is a precipitate obtained by heating nitric acid on aloes.

Alonso'a, a genus of flowering S. American plants, of the order Solaneæ.

Alope'cia (Gr. *alopex* a fox), in pathology, the falling off of the hair; baldness.

Alopecu'rus (Gr. *alopex*, and *oura* a tail), the grass foxtail, of the order Graminaceæ.

Alo'sa, a migratory fish, the shad, of the Clupeæ or Herring family.

Alpa'cha, in zoology, a species of Peruvian sheep, the llama, of the order Ruminantia, and tribe Camelidæ; its fur or wool is fine and soft, and of late years has become of great importance as an article of commerce.

Alpes'tris (from *the Alps*), in botany, an epithet applied to those plants which grow on elevated mountains.

Alphon'sin, in surgery, an instrument for extracting balls, called after Alphonso Ferrier, the inventor.

Alphon'sin Tables, a series of astronomical tables, compiled in 1252, by Aphonso XII., King of Castile and Leon.

Alpine (Lat. *Alpinus*), in natural history, an epithet applied to the Alps or any mountainous country, or to the productions thereof.

Al'quifou, in mineralogy, a kind of lead ore, found in Cornwall, commonly called potter's ore, because used by them to give a green varnish to their wares.

Alsine (Gr. *a shady grove*), a genus of herbaceous plants (chickweed), of the order Caryophyllaceæ.

Alsodei'a (Gr. *leafy*), a genus of Madagascar plants, of the order Violaceæ or Violets, and of the tribe Alsodineæ.

Alt-az'imuth (Gr. and Arab.), in astronomy, a term applied to an instrument for observing both the altitude and azimuth of a celestial body.

Alter'ative (Lat. *to alter*), in pathology, a medicine which gradually re-establishes the healthiness of the natural functions of the body.

Alter'nant (Lat. *alter* another), in mineralogy, an epithet applied to a rock which is composed of alternating laminæ or layers.

Alternanthe'ra (Gr. *alternate anthers*), a genus of plants whose stamens are alternately fertile and barren; order Amaranthaceæ.

Alter'nate Genera'tion, in zoology, a form of reproduction in which the young do not resemble the parent of the animal, but the grand-parent.

Althæ'a (Gr. *to heal*), a genus of plants, including the hollyhock (*A. rosea*), and the marshmallow (*A. officinalis*); order Malvaceæ.

Al'theine, in chemistry, the name of a salifiable base found in *Althæa officinalis*.

Al'tica (Gr. *nimble*), in entomology, a genus of minute coleopterous insects, which jump to a great height, and with amazing quickness.

Altim'etry (Lat. and Gr. *measuring of heights*), the science or art of measuring altitudes, generally by means of the quadrant, whether accessible or otherwise.

Al'tingia (so called from *Alting*, the German botanist), a magnificent class of trees, which attain a great height and magnitude, especially the species *Altingia excelsa*; order Coniferæ.

Altiros'tres (Lat. *high-beaked*), in ornithology, a name given to those scansorial or climbing birds, which have their beaks elevated but not large.

Alto (Ital. *high*), in music, the higher part of the gamut; the counter-tenor, or highest natural pitch of the adult male voice, usually from F, the fourth line in the base, to C, the third space on the treble.—*Altissimo* is the superlative of *alto*; the musical scale in altissimo commencing with F, the octave above the fifth line in the treble.—*Alto-clef* is one of the names of the C clef, when placed in the third line.

Altom'eter (Lat. and Gr. *a measurement of heights*), an instrument for measuring heights and distances; a name for the theodolite.

Al'to-relie'vo (Ital. *high relief*), in sculpture and architecture, that species of ornamentation which projects from the surface to which it is attached nearly as much as if the figures were isolated from the body of the work.

Alto-rip'iendo (Ital. from Lat. *altus* high), in music, the tenor of the great chorus.

Alu'del (Lat. *without lute*), in chemistry, a kind of subliming pot, without a bottom. In operating, the aludels are fixed into one another, as many as there is occasion for, without luting. At the bottom of the furnace there is a pot which holds the matter to be sublimed, and at the top there is a head to retain the flowers that rise up.—*Quincy*.

Al'ula (Lat. and Fr. *a wing*), in ornithology, the bastard wing or group of feathers attached to the joint of the carpus.—In entomology, a small scaly convexo-concave appendage fixed to the base of the wing of some dipterous insects.

Al'um (Lat. *alumen*), in mineralogy, an earthy chalk, a sulphate of alumina, or of potash. It occurs as an efflorescence in sulphureous shales, lavas, &c., or as stalactites in delicate capillary crystals. It consists of sulphuric acid, alumina, potash, and water.—In medicine, *A. exsiccatum*, dried alum; *A. rupeum*, rock alum; and *A. Romanum*, Roman alum.

Alu'mina (Lat. *alumen*), in chemistry, the oxide of *Aluminum*, which forms the basis of all clays, and to which the plastic property of clay is owing. —*Aluminum*, in a state of purity, resembles platina in appearance; but when burnished it has the lustre of polished tin.

Al'umite, in mineralogy, a hard variety of alum stone, sometimes used for mill-stones.

Alum-meal, a name for the granular alum which occurs in the manufacture of salt.

Alum'nus (Lat.), one educated at a college or public institution, of which he is called the Alumnus.

Alum-slate, or **Schist**, in mineralogy, a variety of clay-slate or shale, which, when exposed to the action of the atmosphere, effloresces into soft delicate fibres of the ferro-sulphate of iron. Alum-slate occurs near Whitby, in Yorkshire, and at Hurlet and Campsie, near Glasgow, at which large manufactories have been long in existence.—*Alum-stone* is a crystallized mineral, which occurs at La Tolfa, in Italy; it consists of sulphuric acid, alumina, potash, and iron.

Alu'ta (Lat.), in mineralogy, a sort of leather stone, which is soft and pliable, and not laminated.

Alva-Mari'na (Lat. *a sea-weed*), in commerce, the scientific name for certain dried sea-weeds, which in the arts are used for stuffing cushions, beds, bolsters, &c.

Alve'oli (Lat.), in anatomy, the sockets of the teeth; the alveolar processes. In botany, the small honey-comb-like cavities, which are symmetrically arranged on certain plants.—*Alveolar*, belonging to the sockets in which the teeth are fixed.

Al'veolites (Lat. *honey-combed*, and Gr. *a stone*), in geology, a genus of fossil zoophytes, composed of small hemispherical cells.

Alvus (Lat.), the abdomen or lower intestines.—In pathology, *Alvine concretions* are those formed in the large intestines by accumulation of fæces.

Amal'gam, or **Amal'gama** (Gr. *a welding together*), the mixture of metals by amalgamation, particularly by the agency of mercury. Native amalgams in Sweden, Hungary, and other places, in a semi-fluid, massive, or crystallized state, are composed of mercury 64, and silver 36.

Amal'thus, a fossil Cephalapod; a genus of the Ammonite family.

Aman'dola, in mineralogy, a variety of green marble.

Amani'ta (Gr. *a fungus*), a genus of mushrooms, said to be poisonous.—*Amanitine* is a name of the venomous principle contained in poisonous fungi.

Amarantha'ceæ (Gr. *ever-blooming*), a nat. order of apetalous plants, of which the *Amaranth* is the type:

"Immortal amaranth! a flower which once
In Paradise, fast by the tree of life,
Began to bloom."—*Milton*.

The principal species cultivated in this country are, the globe amaranth, the cockscomb, love-lies-bleeding, and the prince's feather.—*Amaranthine* is a general epithet applied to an unfading flower.

Amaryllida'ceæ, or **Amaryllid'eæ** (Lat.), a nat. order of indigenous, bulbous-rooted plants, of which the *Amaryllis* is the type. This order contains the narcissus, the daffodil, the belladonna, and the blood-flowers.

Amasthen'ic (Gr.), in optics, an epithet applied to a lens photographically perfect, or which unites all the chemical rays into one focus.

Amauro'sis (Gr. *obscure*), in pathology, a disease of the eye, attended with weakness or loss of vision, the retina and optic nerves being paralytically affected; sometimes called *Gutta serena*.

Amazon Stone, a species of stone found on the river Amazon, and also in New Zealand and other South-Sea Islands; it is manufactured into hatchets and other warlike implements; also a green variety of felspar, found on the Ural Mountains.

Amber (Arab.), in mining, a fossil, yellow-coloured resin, easily cut with a knife, and supposed to be of vegetable origin. Its component parts are carbon, hydrogen, oxygen, and ashes. It is highly electric, and is called in Greek *electron*, whence the term *electricity*. Insects are frequently found enclosed within amber. In the arts it is extensively used, especially as mouth-pieces of tobacco pipes.

Am'bergris (Arab. and Fr. *gris* grey), a substance used as a perfume, found in the intestines of the spermaceti whale, and considered to be a morbid product analogous to biliary calculi.

Ambig'enal (Lat. *double-kneed*), in geometry, a term applied to one of the triple hyperbolas of the second order, having one of its infinite legs falling within an angle formed by the asymptotes, and the other without.

Am'bitus (Lat.), in conchology, a term applied to the outline or circumference of the valves.—In botany, the encompassing border of a leaf.

Amblyg'onite (Gr. *oblique-angled*), a crystallized mineral, of a greenish-white colour, consisting of alumina, lithia, and phosphoric acid ; sp. gr. 3.

Amblyop'ia (Gr. *dull-eyed*), imperfect sight, incipient amaurosis.

Ambly'opus (Gr. *ut supra*), a genus of eel-like fishes, with very minute eyes ; family Gobideæ.

Amblyp'terus (Gr. *obtuse-finned*), in palæontology, a genus of fossil fishes, with obtuse rounded fins.

Amblyrhyn'chus (Gr. *obtuse-snouted*), in herpetology, a genus of spiny-backed lizards ; fam. Iguanidæ.

Ambon (Gr.), in anatomy, the margin or tip of a socket, in which the edge of a bone is lodged.

Amboy'na-wood, in the arts, the name of a beautifully mottled wood, the produce of the *Pterospermum Indicum*.

Ambre'ic Acid, in chemistry, an acid formed by the combination of ambrein with nitric acid.—*Ambreate* is a salt formed from the combination.

Am'brein, in chemistry, the fatty matter of ambergris, changed by nitric acid into ambreic acid.

Ambrosia'ceæ (Gr. *immortal*), an order of annual composite plants, of which *Ambrosia* is the type.

Ambulac'ra (Lat. *an alley*), in zoology, the narrow longitudinal portions of the echinus or sea-urchin shell.

Ambulato'res (Lat. *walkers*), in ornithology, a term applied to an order of walking birds, which are nearly feathered to the toes.

Amel, the material used in the art of enamelling.

Amenorrhœ'a (Gr. *wanting the monthly course*), in pathology, irregularity or defectiveness of the menstrual discharge.

Amen'tia (Lat.), in pathology, want of intellect ; madness ; idiotcy.

Amen'tum (Lat. *a thong*), in botany, a term applied to the male inflorescence of the birch, willow, or hazel ; a form of inflorescence resembling a pike.

Ametabo'lia (Gr. *without change*), in entomology, a class of insects which do not undergo the metamorphosis of other insects.

Am'ethyst (Gr. *not intoxicating*), in mineralogy, a precious stone, of two varieties, one an adamantine spar or corundum, the other a beautiful violet-coloured transparent quartz ; it consists of silica, alumina, manganese, and oxide of iron.

Amhers'tia, in botany, a genus of fine flowering plants, so named in honour of the Countess Amherst ; order Leguminosæ.

Amian'thus (Gr. *undefiled*), a variety of the mineral asbestos, which occurs in long flexible fibres, and when woven in cloth is capable of resisting the action of fire ; it is composed of silica, magnesia, lime, and alumina. —*Amianthoide* (Gr. *like the amianthus*), a mineral of an olive-green colour and silky lustre, which occurs in long capillary filaments ; its component parts are silica, oxide of iron, lime, manganese, and magnesia.

Am'miolite, in mineralogy, an antimoniate of quicksilver, imported as a kind of red powder from Chili.

Am'mite (Gr. *sand*), in mineralogy, a variety of sandstone, oolite, or roestone.

Ammocœ'tes (Gr. *sand-bed*), a genus of round-mouthed fishes, which bury themselves in sand, and have worm-like habits ; they have the lowest grade of vertebral organism.

Am'mochryse (Gr. *gold-sand*), in mineralogy, a soft yellow-looking stone, found in Germany.

Ammody'tes (Gr. *sand-ducker*), a genus of apodal fishes, the sand-eels.

Ammo'nia (so called from the temple of Ammon, in Libya, which was visited by the camels from whose dung the muriate of ammonia was first produced), in chemistry, an important volatile alkali, obtained from the decomposition of animal matter, or artificially by subjecting bones, horns, hoofs, &c., to heat, in iron cylinders ; or from portions of vegetable matter which contain nitrogen. Ammonia chemically consists of 3 atoms of hydrogen, 1 of nitrogen ; or hydrogen 17·64 and nitrogen 82·36. When moderately heated ammonia expands, but by a strong heat it is decomposed, and when decomposed it is found to consist of three volumes of hydrogen and one of nitrogen, condensed into one volume, or if estimated by the weight, according to the atomic system of chemistry, we shall find :

3 atoms of hydrogen $=$ 3... 17·64
1 atom of nitrogen $=$ 14... 82·36

Equivalent to ...... 17...100

The salts of ammonia are decomposed by the fixed alkalies and alkaline earths, with the evolution of ammonia. When a salt of magnesia, and a soluble phosphate, are added to them, precipitation takes place, and crystals are the result, which are compounds of the phosphate of ammonia and the phosphate of magnesia. The proper application of ammonia to peat land is very important.

Ammonia has a variety of compounds, of which the following are among the most important :—*Acetate of ammonia*, a salt produced by the union of acetic acid with ammonia as its base, and consisting of 1 atom of acetic acid = 51; 1 atom of ammonia = 17; 7 atoms of water = 63; atomic weight, 131.—*Bicarbonate of ammonia*, 2 atoms of carbonic acid = 54; 1 atom of ammonia = 17; 2 atoms of water = 18; atomic weight, 86.—*Carbonate of ammonia*, 1 atom of carbonic acid = 22; 1 atom of ammonia = 17; atomic weight, 39.—*Muriate of ammonia*, 1 atom of muriatic acid = 37; 1 atom of ammonia = 17; atomic weight, 54.—*Nitrate of ammonia*, 1 atom of nitric acid = 54; 1 atom of ammonia = 17; 1 atom of water = 9; atomic weight, 80.—*Oxalic of ammonia*, 1 atom of oxalic acid = 36; 1 atom of ammonia = 17; 2 atoms of water = 18; atomic weight, 71.—*Sesquicarbonate of ammonia*, 3 atoms of carbonic acid = 66; 2 atoms of ammonia = 34; 2 atoms of water = 18; atomic weight, 118.—*Sulphate of ammonia*, 1 atom of sulphuric acid = 40; 1 atom of ammonia = 17; 2 atoms of water = 18; atomic weight, 75.

Ammoni'acum, a gum resin, obtained from the *Dorema ammoniacum*, from which it naturally exudes. Its varieties are *lapis ammoniacus*, in lumps, and *guttæ ammoniacæ*, in drops.

Am'monites (so called from the ram's horn on the head of the Libyan deity Ammon), in palæontology, an extinct order of molluscous animals, curved like a coiled snake, which are found in great abundance and variety in the secondary strata of the earth's crust.

Am'nion (Gr. *amnos*, a lamb), in anatomy, an internal membrane of the womb, which envelops the fœtus.—In botany, the thin semi-transparent membrane in which the embryo of a plant is enveloped.—*Amniotic acid*, an acid obtained from the *liquor amnii* of the cow.

Amo'mum (Gr. *harmless*, so named from its being a counter-poison), a genus of aromatic herbaceous plants, anciently used in embalming and in the preservation of bodies. Several species produce cardamoms or grains of paradise; order Scitamineæ.

Amor'phous (Gr.), without regular shape.

Amorphozo'a (Gr.), animals without any definite shape, applied to sponges and their congeners.

Am'pelite (Gr. *the vine*), in mineralogy, a species of black earth, so named from having been used for killing insects on vines. It is a generic name given to slates, and is also applied to cannel coal, and to some kind of schist.

Amphi, a Greek prefix, of frequent use in scientific words, signifying *around, about*, or *both*.

Amphiarthro'sis (Gr. *amphi*, and *arthron* a joint), in anatomy, the form of a joint which has the properties of two others, named *diarthrosis* and *synarthrosis*, and allows a slight action.

Amphib'ium (Gr. *amphi*, and *bios* life), that which lives in two elements, as in air and water.

Am'phicome (Gr. *amphi*, and *kome* hair), a kind of figured stone, anciently used in divination.

Amphid (Gr.), an epithet applied to compounds consisting of acids and bases, as distinguished from *haloid* compounds.

Amphihexahe'dral (Gr. *amphi*, and *hexahedral* six-sided), a term applied to crystals whose faces, counted in two different directions, give two hexahedral outlines.

Am'phipoda (Gr. *amphi*, and *podes* feet), in zoology, an order of Crustacea, with feet for both swimming and walking.

Amphipros'tyle (Gr. *amphi*, and *stylos* a column), in architecture, an edifice having a portico or equal number of columns at each end, and thus presenting two fronts, but without columns at the sides or flanks.

Amphi'scians (Gr. *amphi*, and *skia* a shadow), the inhabitants of the tropics whose shadows in one part of the year extend to the north and in the other to the south.

Am'phitrite (Gr.), in astronomy, the name of one of the recently-discovered planets, first observed in 1854. Its mean distance from the sun is 243,530,000 of miles, and the time of its periodical revolution is four years and thirty days.

Amphod'elite, a reddish crystallized mineral from Finland.—*Dana*.

Amplex'us (Lat. *embrace*), a term applied to corals of a cylindrical shape, which are divided by transverse septa into numerous chambers that embrace each other with reflected margins.

Ampul'la (Lat.), in the arts, a globular-shaped bottle, with a narrow neck, chiefly used as household ornaments.—In botany, applied to a leaf in which the petiole is dilated and hollowed out in the shape of a hollow vessel, open at the upper end.

Ampulla'ria (Lat.), in malacology, a genus of spiral univalve Molluscs, which are found in the ponds and rivers of S. America, Africa, and India.

Am'ula (Lat.), in architecture and sculpture, an ornamented vase, usually made of marble or bronze, and found in temples and public edifices.

Amygda'leæ (Gr. *almonds*), a nat. order of polypetalous exogens, of which *Amygdalus*, the almond tree, is the type. It is distinguished by its producing the kind of fruit called a drupe, as in the peach, nectarine, plum, cherry, almond, apricot, prune, damson, all of which belong to this order. Another of its characteristics is, that the leaves of this species yield prussic acid; the stamens are numerous, and rise from the orifice of a tubular calyx.—*Amygdala amara* are the kernels of a variety of *Amygdalus communis*, or bitter almond.—*Amygdala dulcis* is a variety of the *Amygdalus*, the sweet almond, chiefly composed of fixed oil.—*Amygdalæ oleum* is the oil extracted from the kernels of both varieties of almonds.

Amyg'daline (Gr. *amygdalus*), in chemistry, a crystalline principle contained in the bitter almond.—*Amygdalinic acid* is an acid obtained from amygdaline.

Amyg'daloid (Gr. *like an almond*), in geology, a variety of trap rock, resembling almonds, generally vesicular, with embedded round or almond-shaped minerals, such as agate, calcareous spar, calcedony, jasper, or zeolites.—*Amygdalite* is the name of the almond-stone.

Am'ylate (Lat. *starch*), in chemistry, a compound of starch with a base.—*Amylic acid* is a volatile acid obtained from starch.—*Amyline* is the fecula or crystallized starch of wheat.

Am'ylum (Lat. *starch*), in pharmacy, a preparation of starch obtained by diffusing flour through a large quantity of water, by which the saccharine and mucilaginous matters are dissolved—the fibrous parts floating on the surface, while the fecula is allowed to subside. It consists of oxygen, carbon, and hydrogen.

Amyrid'eæ (Gr. *myrrha*, myrrh, the type of the order), a nat. order of ornamental trees; the leaves, bark, and fruit of which abound in odoriferous resins and gums.

Ana (Gr. *again*), in pharmacy, a term used by physicians, importing the like quantity, as honey and wine, *ana*, ℥ ii; that is, honey and wine, each two ounces.

A'nabas (Gr. *to ascend*), a genus of fishes belonging to the Perch family, remarkable for the power they possess of quitting their native element, and making their way on land.

Anabe'næ (Gr. *to ascend*), a family of Saurians, which, like the chameleon, are in the habit of climbing trees.

An'ableps (Gr. *to look up*), a genus of fishes, of the tribe Cyprinidæ, which inhabit the rivers of Guiana.

Anabro'sis (Gr. *corrosion*), in pathology, a wasting away of any portion of the body.

Anacamp'tics (Gr. *to bend back*), in optics, the science of reflected light; Catoptrics.—An *anacamptic* sound, a sound that produces an echo; an *anacamptic* hill, a hill that sends back an echo.

Anacan'thus (Gr. *ana*, and *akanthus* a spine), a genus of fishes, the skate, which have neither fins nor spine on the tail.

Anacardia'ceæ (Gr. *ana*, and *kardia* the heart), in botany, a natural order of polypetalous exogens, which contains among its genera the cashew (which produces a black caustic oil), the sumach, the mango, and the pistachia.

Anacar'dium (Gr. *ana*, and *kardia* the heart), a genus of plants to which belongs the cashew-nut, and so called from its being heart-shaped.

Anacathar'tics (Gr. *ana*, and *katharos* pure), in pharmacy, any medicine that operates upwards; a cough attended with expectoration.

Anach'ronism (Gr. *ana*, and *chronos* time), any error in chronology, or the computation of time, by which historic events are misplaced.

Anaclas'tic (Gr. *to bend back* or *refract*), in optics, breaking the rectilinear course of light.—*Anaclastic glasses* are sonorous glasses or phials, which emit a vehement noise by means of the human breath.

Anaclas'tics (Gr. *ana*, and *klao* to break), that branch of optics which treats of the reflection of light; Dioptrics.

Anacli'sis (Gr. *ana*, and *klino* to lie down), in pathology, the attitude of a sick person in bed, which affords important indications in various cases.

Anacon'da, in herpetology, a species of boa or large serpent of Ceylon, and other parts of Asia.

Anacyc'lus (Gr. *without a circlet of flowers*), a genus of composite plants, the ring-flower.

Anæ'mia (Gr. *ana*, and *haima* blood), in pathology, a deficiency of blood.

Anæsthe'sia (Gr. *without feeling*), in pathology, deprivation of the sense of touch or feeling.

Anæsthet'ic (Gr. *a* priv. and *aisthesis* feeling), tending to deprive of sensation.

Anagal'lis (Gr. *dispelling grief*), a genus of plants with wheel-shaped corollas and a capsule opening in two halves, the one fitting into the other;—the pimpernel, or poor man's weather-glass, which opens in the morning, and closes in the afternoon; in wet weather the petals remain closed.

An'aglyph (Gr. *ana*, and *glypho* to engrave), anything in relief; an ornamental piece of sculpture, engraving, chasing, or embossing.

An'agogy (Gr.), in pathology, the rejection of blood from the lungs.

Anal'cime (Gr. *weakness*), in mineralogy, a variety of zeolite, occurring usually in trap rocks; when rubbed, it becomes *weakly* electric, whence the name; it consists of silica, alumina, soda, and water; sp. gr. 3.

Anal'cipus (Gr. *weak-footed*), a genus of birds, of the family Dicrurinæ, or Drongo Shrikes.

Analep'sis (Gr. *a recovering*), in pathology, restoration from sickness to health.—*Analeptic* is a medicine which tends to restore the body to health and vigour.

An'alogue (Gr. *resemblance*), in palæontology, applied to an animal or plant in the fossil state, which bears a strong resemblance to some recent genus or species.

Anal'ysis (Gr. *unloosing*), in physics, the separation of a compound body into its several parts.—In botany, it is synonymous with dissection in zoology.—In geometry, it is the method of establishing the truth of a proposition by certain analytical processes.

Anamorpho'sis, or **Anamor'phosis** (Gr. *change of figure*), the distorted representation of an object.—In botany, the degenerated appearance of a plant through excess of development.

Anamp'sis, a genus of acanthopterygious fishes, with fusiform bodies. —*Cuvier*.

Ananchi'tes (Gr. *a gem*), in palæontology, a genus of helmet-shaped fossil Echinidæ.

Anapai'ma, a tree of majestic size, which abounds in the rocky districts of British Guiana; and in commerce is appreciated for its fine, close-grained wood.

Anaplero'sis (Gr. *to fill up*), in surgery, restoration of parts destroyed, as in the healing of a wound.

Anar'richas (Gr.), the Linnæan name of a genus of acanthopterygious fishes, allied to the Blennies.—The *A. lupus* is the sea-cat or wolf-fish of the British seas, which attains the length of six or seven feet, and is extremely voracious.

An'as (Lat. *a duck*), a genus of web-footed birds, of the family Anatidæ (which see).

Anasar'ca (Gr. *ana*, and *sarx* flesh), in pathology, a dropsical disease.—*Anasarcous*, relating to the dropsy.

Anastal'tic (Gr. *ana*, and *staltikos* contracting), in medicine, styptic; astringent.

Anas'tasis (Gr. *a raising up*), in pathology, recovery from sickness; the transference of humours to other parts of the body.

Anastat'ic (Gr. *reproducing*), in the arts, a term applied to a new scientific process, by which designs produced either by the ordinary mode of printing from types, copper, or steel plates, wood, stone, &c., or by manual operations of writing or drawing in prepared ink or chalk, may be readily transferred to the metal plate, and an indefinite number of copies produced at a really trifling cost.—*National Cycl. Suppl.*

Anastat'icon (Gr. *resurrection*), a cruciferous plant, known as the rose of Jericho, which, however dry it may be, has the property of recovering its original form, when immersed in water; order Cruciferæ.

Anas'toma (Gr. *ana*, and *stoma* a mouth), a genus of terrestrial Testacea, belonging to the land Volutes.

Anastomat'ic (Gr.), in pathology, a medicine intended to remove obstructions, by opening the mouths of vessels, and promoting circulation.

Anastomo'sis (Gr.), in physiology, the joining together the organs of circulation, as of the veins and arteries; the opening of the mouths of vessels of organized bodies to discharge their fluids into other vessels.—In botany, the union of the veins of leaves.—In entomology, the union of the nervures of the wings of insects.—*Anastomosing* is applied in anatomy, when blood-vessels open the one into the other; and in botany, when two parts, growing in different directions, unite and grow together.

Anas'tomus (Gr.), a genus of fishes with compressed heads and vertical mouths.

Anas'trous (Gr. *without stars*), in astronomy, a name applied to the twelve portions of the ecliptic, formerly possessed by the signs, but which, owing to the precession of the equinoxes, have since been deserted.

An'atase (Gr. *extension*), in mineralogy, the octahedral oxide of titanium; octahedrite. (See *Titanium*.)

Anat'idæ (Lat. *duck family*), a family of birds of the order *Natatores* or Swimmers, including the *Anserinæ*, or geese and swans; the *Anatinæ*, or river ducks; the *Fuligulinæ*, or sea-ducks; the *Phœnicoptinæ*, or flamingoes, and the *Merganidæ*, or Mergansers, all of which have the bill very broad and the feet webbed.

Anat'ifer (Lat.), a genus of Cirripeds (Barnacles), furnished with multivalve shells, by which they are enabled to adhere to rocks, or ships' bottoms.

Anat'omy (Gr. *cutting up*), the art of dissecting animal bodies; the science which treats of the internal structure of the human body.—*Comparative Anatomy* is the science which teaches the differences in the structure and organization of the animal kingdom.—*Vegetable Anatomy* teaches the structure of plants.

An'bury, a kind of gall produced by insects on the roots of cabbages, turnips, hollyhocks, &c.

Anceps, (Lat.), in botany, two-edged.

An'chovy (Sp. *anchova*), a small sea-fish, of the Clupeæ or Herring tribe, closely resembling the common sprat, and extensively used in the manufacture of sauce.—*Anchovy pear* is the succulent fruit of the *Persea gratissima*, which in commerce is highly esteemed as an edible butyraceous production of the tropics.

Anchu'sa (Gr. *paint*), a genus of plants, the Bugloss, so called from one of the species, *A. tinctoria*, being used for staining the skin; order Boragineæ.

Anchylo'sis (Gr. *to bend*), in pathology, a stiffness of the joints, arising from inflammation of the membrane lining the joints.—*Anchylotic*, pertaining to anchylosis.

Ancillarin'eæ, in conchology, a subfamily of Volutes, of which the *Ancillaria*, a genus of spiral univalve testacea, is the type.

Ancip'ital (Lat. *anceps* double), in botany, double-edged, compressed so as to form two opposite angles or edges.

Ancis'trum (Gr. *a hook*), a genus of herbaceous plants, of the order Sanguisorbeæ.

An'cones, in architecture, the name of certain ornaments which depend from the corona of Ionic doorways; a sort of shoulder pieces, or brackets, which bear up the mouldings under which they are placed; ornaments cut in the key-stone of arches, serving to support busts, &c.

An'cony, in metallurgy, a bloom wrought into the figure of a flat iron bar.

Ancyloblephar'on (Gr. *construction of the eyelid*), in pathology, a disease of the eye, by which the eyelids are closed, and vision obstructed.

Ancyl'odon (Gr. *bent tooth*), a genus of acanthopterygious fishes; of the family Chætodon, and sub-family Sciæna.

Andal'usite, a mineral of a flesh-red colour and vitreous lustre; thus named from Andalusia, in Spain, where it was first found.

Andan'te (Ital.), in music, distinct and exact.—*Andantino*, in a gentle manner, and slower than andante.—*Andante largo* denotes that the movement must be slow, distinct, and accurate.

An'darac, red orpiment.

Andrea'a, a genus of mosses, of a brown or black colour.

Andre'na, in entomology, a genus of bees, which have three-clefted tongues.

Andrody'namis (Gr. *male power*), in botany, a name applied to those plants which have a full development of petals and stamens.

Androg'ynous (Gr. *male and female*), in botany, an epithet applied to plants which grow male and female flowers on the same root; as also to flowers containing stamens and pistils within the same envelope.—In zoology, applied to animals which naturally, as in the snail, combine, in their own structure, the organs necessary for the reproduction of the species.

An'droid (Gr. *like a man*), an automaton resembling a human being.

Androm'eda (Gr.), in astronomy, one of the constellations in the northern hemisphere.--In entomology, a species of butterfly. In botany, a genus of plants, of the order Ericeæ.

Andropet'alous (Gr. *a male petal*), in botany, a term applied to double flowers, which are produced by the stamens being converted into petals.

Androph'agi (Gr. *man-eater*), cannibals.

Androt'omy (Gr. *dissecting of men*), dissection of human bodies of the male sex.

Anely'tra (Gr. *without a sheath*), in entomology, those insects which have two or four membraneous wings, naked or hairy.

Anemog'raphy (Gr.), description of the winds.

Anemol'ogy (Gr. *treatise on wind*), the science which treats on the cause, nature, and velocity of the wind.

Anemom'eter (Gr. *wind measurer*), an instrument for determining the velocity and force of the wind.—*Anemometrograph* is an instrument for indicating on paper the force of the wind.

Anem'one (Gr. *the wind*), a beautiful flowering plant, the *Pulsatilla*, or wind flower, of the order Ranunculaceæ.—*Anemonin* is an inflammable cystallizable substance of the nature of camphor, obtained from the anemone.

Anem'oscope (Gr. *view of the wind*), an instrument for indicating the direction which the wind blows.

Anen'tera (Gr. *without intestines*), in entomology, a class of polygastric infusoria, which have several stomachs but no intestinal duct.

An'eroid (Gr.), applied to a peculiar kind of barometer, which consists of a small box, from which air is exhausted.

An'eurism (Gr. *dilatation*), in pathology, the diseased state of an artery, or other vessel, in which it is widened at any part, so as to form a bag or pouch. There are different kinds of aneurism : *A. cordis*, as the dilatation of the heart ; *A. verum*, the uniform dilatation of all the coats of an artery ; *A. spurium*, the dilatation of an artery in one direction, through disease of its coats ; *A. varicosum*, a disease arising from a lancet passing through a vein, and wounding the subjacent artery.

Anfrac'tuous (Lat. *winding*), in botany, applied to the lobes of an anther, which are folded back on themselves, and doubled and bent, as in the cucumber.

Angel'ica (Lat.), a garden herb used in medicine and confectionery ; an umbelliferous plant ; so called from its agreeable smell and medicinal qualities. *A. archangelica* is a well-known garden herb, sometimes candied with sugar, or eaten as celery.

Angeli'na, the name of one of the recently-discovered planets, first observed by Tempel, in 1861.

Angel-shot, chain-shot, being two halves of a cannon-ball fastened to the ends of a chain.

Angel-water, a perfume consisting of rose, orange-flower, and myrtle-water, scented with musk and ambergris.

Angi'na Pec'toris (Lat.), a tightening or contraction of the thorax.

Angiocar'pous (Gr. *fruit vessel*), in botany, an epithet applied to seed vessels which are enclosed within a covering that does not form a part of the fruit itself, as the filbert, acorn, &c.

Angiog'raphy (Gr. *angeion*, a vessel), in physiology, a description of the human body, as the veins, nerves, lymphatics, &c.

Angiol'ogy (Gr.), a treatise on the blood-vessels of the body.

Angiosper'mous (Gr. *angeion*, and *sperma* seed), in botany, applied to plants the seeds of which are enveloped in a pericarp.

Angiospo'rous (Gr.), in botany, applied to fungi which have their spore enclosed in cells.

Angios'tomous (Gr.), in conchology, applied to shells which have a straight opening nearly the length of the shell.

Angiot'omy (Gr.), the science or art of dissecting the vessels of the body. —*Angiotomist* is one who is skilled in angiotomy.

An'gle (Lat. *a corner*), the inclination of two lines to each other, which meet together at a point called the vertex.—In geometry, *a right angle* is an angle formed by one straight line falling perpendicularly upon another straight line, and containing 90 degrees, or one-fourth of the circle. —*Acute angle*, an angle containing less than 90 degrees.—*Rectilinear angle*, an angle contained between two straight lines.—*Curvilinear angle*, an angle formed by two curved lines.—*Obtuse angle*, an angle greater than a right angle, or containing more than 90 degrees.— *Oblique angles* are either acute or obtuse, in opposition to right angles. —*Spherical angles* are formed by the meeting of two arches of great circles, which mutually cut each other at the surface of the sphere.—In optics, the *angle of polarization*, or *angle of incidence*, is the angle which a ray of light, refracted, makes with a perpendicular to the surface on which it falls ;—*Angle of reflection* is always equal to the angle of incidence ;— *Angle of refraction* is the angle which a ray of light makes with the surface of the refracting medium ;— *Visual angle* is the angle which is formed by two straight lines passing from the eye to the extreme points of any object.—In zoology, the *facial angle* is the angle made by the intersection of two lines, the one drawn from the farthest projection of the frontal bone over the anterior margin of the upper jaw ; the other from the external opening of the ear along the floor of the nasal cavity.—In mechanics, the *angle of draught* is the angle made by the line of direction with a line upon the plane, over which the body is drawn, and perpendicular to that line of direction.—In Military Architecture and Fortification, the term *Angle* is of very extensive application : —*Angles* are formed by the several lines used in fortifying a place, or making it defensible, and are either real or imaginary;—*Real angles* are those which appear in the erection;—*Imaginary angles* are those which are only subservient to the processes of delineation or construction;—*Angle at the centre* is an angle formed by two radii drawn from the centre to two adjacent lines;—*Angle of the polygon* is formed by two of the sides of a polygon;—*Angle of the triangle* is half the angle of the polygon;—*Angle of the bastion* or *flanked-angle*, that formed by two faces of the bastion;—*Diminished angle*, the meeting of the outer side of the polygon with the face of the bastion;—*Angle of the curtain*, or *angle of the flank*, is made between the curtain and the flank;—*Angle of the shoulder*, or *angle of the épaule*, is made by the flank and face of the bastion;—*Angle of tenaille* is formed by two rasant lines of defence, or faces of two bastions produced;—*Angle of the counter-scarp* is made by the two sides of the counter-scarp meeting before the line of the curtain;—*Angle forming the face* is that made by one flank and one face;—*Angle of the moat* is that made before the curtain where it is intersected;—*Re-entering* or *re-entrant angle*, that which has its vertex turned inwards.—*Salient angle*, that turned outwards towards the field.—*Craig, Mil. Dict.*

Angle Capital, in architecture and sculpture, an Ionic capital, placed on the flank columns of a portico, which has one of its volutes placed horizontally at an angle of 130° with the plane of the frieze.

An'glesite, in mineralogy, native sulphate of lead; so named from the Island of Anglesea, where it occurs in white or yellowish prismatic crystals, with a glassy lustre.

Ango'la, a light kind of cloth, manufactured from the Angora goat's wool, and used for paletots, cloaks, &c.—*Angola weed* is the name of a lichen, the *Ramolina furfuracea*.

Ango'ra Wool, the long white hair of the Angora goat (*Capra Angorensis*), which is highly appreciated for its silkiness of appearance, and its beautiful adaptation to the manufacture of shawls, lace, braiding, &c.

Angostu'ra Bark, an aromatic bitter bark, obtained in South America from the *Galipea cusparia* or *officinalis*.

Angaa'va, the name of a red Indian gum, which has some resemblance to dragon's-blood.

Angu, a species of bread produced from the Cassava plant, which is extensively used as food by the in-

habitants of South America and the West Indies.

Anguil'la (Lat. *an eel*), type of the family Anguilliformes or Eels; a name given by Cuvier to the only family of his Malacopterygii Apodes, fishes with elongated forms, and thick and soft skins.

Angui'na (Lat. *anguis* a snake), a family of Ophidian reptiles, of which *Anguis* is the genus, now subdivided into Ophiosaurus, Pseudopus, Acontias, and Anguis proper.—*Anguiviperæ* (Lat. *viper-snakes*) is the name of a family of venomous serpents, with snake-formed bodies.

An'gular Capi'tal, in sculpture and architecture, a term applied to the modern Ionic capital, the volute being placed at an angle of 135° on all the faces. (See *Angle Capital*.)

Angulif'erous (Lat. *being angulated*), in conchology, an epithet applied to a shell which has the last whorl angulated, or to one which is triangular in shape, as the *Murex anguliferus*.

Anguliros'tres (Lat. *angled beaks*), a tribe of passerine birds, whose beaks are angulated.

An'gulo-den'tate (Lat. *angulus*, and *dens* a tooth), in botany, a term applied to leaves angularly toothed.

Anhy'drite (Gr. *without water*), in mineralogy, a variety of the sulphate of lime, so called from its having none of the water of crystallization; its fracture is conchoidal and splintery; sp. gr. 2·85.

Anictan'gium (Gr. *an open vase*), a genus of mosses in which the theca is unenclosed.

An'imal (Lat. *anima*, the breath of life), in zoology, a living being, with an organized material body, endowed with the powers of sensation, digestion, and voluntary action. In natural history, the animal kingdom forms one of the three grand divisions of material objects; the vegetable and mineral kingdoms forming the other two.—According to Cuvier, the primary divisions of the animal kingdom are, the *Vertebrata*, the *Articulata*, the *Mollusca*, and the *Radiata*.—The *Vertebrata* comprehend those animals with a bony skeleton, consisting of a cranium, spinal column, and four limbs; the classes of which are the *Mammalia*, *Aves*, *Reptilia*, and *Pisces*, described under their respective heads.—The *Articulata* are animals without a skeleton, divided into a number of ring-like segments, having their integuments sometimes hard, and sometimes soft, and the muscles always attached to the envelope; with or without limbs; respiring through tracheæ or air-vessels, sometimes through branchiæ; the nervous system composed of two long cords, swelling at intervals into knots or ganglions. Other different classes of the Articulata are, the *Annelides, Crustaceæ, Arachnides,* and *Insects.*—The *Mollusca* are animals without a skeleton, the muscles being attached to the skin; the body almost always covered with a mantle, which is either membraneous, fleshy, or secreting a shell; the nervous system composed of scattered masses, or ganglions, connected by filaments; with distinct organs of digestion, circulation, and respiration. The various classes of the Mollusca are the *Cephalopoda, Pteropoda, Gasteropoda, Acephala, Brachiopoda, Cirrhopoda.*—The *Radiata* are animals which have the organs of sensation and motion arranged round a common axis, in two or more rays, or in two or more lines, extending from one extremity to the other; no circulation in vessels. The classes are the *Echinodermata, Entozoa, Acalepha, Polypi,* and *Infusoria.*

Animal'cula (Lat.), very minute animals, which can scarcely be seen without the aid of a microscope. The *Infusoria* are examples, to which the reader is referred.

An'imal Heat, in physiology, the natural heat or temperature which animals possess in themselves. This heat is chiefly owing to the production of carbonic acid, by the union of oxygen with the carbon of the blood in the processes of respiration and circulation. The animal temperature in man, and other mammiferous animals, when in health, is from 94° to 100° Fahrenheit.

An'imality (Lat. *animal*), the vital activity of animal organization.

Animal Magnet'ism, an agent of a peculiar and mysterious nature, supposed to have a powerful influence on the system, when acted upon by contact or voluntary emotion, on the part of the operator.

An'imal Sub'stances, in physiology, a term applied to substances produced by the operation of the animal functions, consisting of carbon, hydrogen, oxygen, and nitrogen. When in a state of decomposition or putrefaction they produce ammonia (which see).

An'ime, a substance derived from the *Hymenæa courbaril,* of a resinous nature, and used in perfumery and the making of plaisters.

An'imism (Lat. *anima* the soul), in psychology, the doctrine that the living phenomena of organized bodies are produced by some actuating or vital power distinct from those bodies. In a more limited sense, the doctrine that all the phenomena of the human system are produced by the agency of the *soul,* the *anima mundi.* Animism is opposed to *materialism.*—*Animist* is one who maintains the doctrine of animism.

Anin'ga, a root growing in the West Indies, used in refining sugar.

An'ion (Gr. *ana* and *ion,* growing upwards), in electricity, an electro-negative element; that is, an element which is evolved at the surface where the electrical current enters an electrolyte.—*Faraday.*

Anisan'thus (Gr. *anisos* unequal, and *anthos* a flower), in botany, a genus of ornamental bulbous-rooted plants, of the order Irideæ.

An'ise (Gr. and Arab.), in botany, a genus of annual plants, originally brought from Egypt, but now extensively cultivated in Europe. The seeds possess an agreeable aromatic odour; in medicine, they are carminative, and useful in dyspepsia.

An'iso, a Greek prefix, signifying *unequal,* of frequent use in botany and natural history: as *anisocheles,* unequally serrated; *anisodon,* unequally toothed; *anisomerus,* consisting of unequal parts; *anisomericus,* having the parts unequally disposed; *anisopetalus,* having unequal petals; *anisophyllus,* unequally leaved; &c.

Anisodac'tyli (Gr. *unequal digits*), in ornithology, an order of birds with unequal toes, the various genera of which consist of small birds, with beautiful plumage.

Anisodyn'amous (Gr. *having unequal power*), in botany, an epithet applied to endogenous plants, which, having only one cotyledon, or seed-lobe, grow at first with more force on one side of their axis than on the other.

Anisopeta'lum (Gr. *unequal petals*), a genus of plants with bulbous roots and little erect spikes of brownish flowers; order Orchidaceæ.

Anisostem'onous, in botany, applied to a flower whose stamens correspond neither with the calyx nor corolla in number or power.

Anisostomid'eæ (Gr. *unequal cutting*), in entomology, a family of insects, of the order Coleoptera.

Anisos'tomous, in botany, denotes that the divisions of a calyx or corolla are unequal.

Anneal'ing (Sax. *burning*), the heating and tempering of glass, &c., for the purpose of rendering it less brittle.

Annel'ida, Annel'idans, An'nelida, Annella'ta, Annulo'sans (Gr. *ring-like*), in zoology, names given to a division of the Articulata, or articulate animals, comprising the common earth-worm and the various allied animals.

Annot'to, a red colouring matter, obtained from the seeds of the *Bixa*, and used in the colouring of cheese, butter, &c.

An'nuent (Lat. *bending*), in anatomy, a term applied to the muscles that assist in bending the head forward, as in nodding or bowing.

An'nular Crystal (Lat. *annulus* a ring), a hexagonal prism with six, or an octohedral prism with eight, marginal faces, disposed in a ring about each base.

Annula'ria, in geology, a genus of fossil plants, with leaves arranged in ring-like whorls.

An'nular Lig'ament, in anatomy, the circular band that unites the iris and the sclerotic membrane to the choroid coat of the eye.

Annula'ta (Lat. *ringed*), in zoology, the first class of Cuvier's third division of the animal kingdom, the Articulata; they are nearly all aquatic, with the exception of the Lumbrici, or earth-worms.

An'nulet (Lat. *a little ring*), in architecture, a small square moulding, accompanying another; a term of frequent use in heraldry, as a mark of family distinction.

An'nulus (Lat. *a ring*), in anatomy, a ring-like opening, asthe *annulus abdominalis,* or the abdominal ring, the opening through which the spermatic cord in man, and the circular ligament of the uterus in woman, passes, formed by the separation of the external oblique muscle of the abdomen. It is through this opening that the intestines protrude in inguinal rupture. — In botany, the *annulus* is the membrane which encircles the stem of the fungus.—In natural history, *annulus* has a variety of useful combinations: as, *annulicaudus,* ring-tailed; *annulicornis,* having ringed-horns or antennæ; *annulifereus,* bearing rings; *annulipes,* ring-footed.—In anatomy, *annulus foraminis* is the muscular margin of the *foramen ovale,* or opening situated in the partition separating the right and left auricles in the fœtus; *annulus ovalis* is the ring that surrounds the *fossa ovalis,* or oval depression, presented by the septum of the right auricle.

Ano'a, a ruminating animal.

An'odyne (Gr. *without pain*), a medicine which assuages pain, by the application of paregorics, narcotics, or soporifics.—*Anodynous,* allaying pain.

An'olis, a genus of saurian reptiles, belonging to the Iguana family.

Anomali'na (Gr. *irregular*), a genus of fossil shells found in the tertiary strata of the earth's formation.

Ano'mia (Gr. *without rule*), a genus of *Acephalus testacea,* of the family Ostraceæ or Oysters.—The *Anomile* is a fossil species of Anomia.

Anomodon'tia (Gr. *irregularity of teeth*), in palæontology, an extinct order of reptiles, with teeth wanting, and other irregularities of form.

Anomop'teris (Gr. *an irregular fern*), a fossil fern found in the New Red sandstone formation.

Anomorhom'boid (Gr. *irregular rhomboid*), the name of a crystalline spar, of no regular form, but always fracturing into irregular rhomboids.

Anomou'ra (Gr. *irregularly tailed*), a section of ten-footed Crustaceans, with tails of intermediate lengths, as the hermit-crab.

Ano'na (Lat.), in botany, the name of the custard-apple.

Anona'ceæ (Malay), a nat. order of exogenous evergreen plants, of which the *Anona,* or custard-apple, is the type.

Anoplothe'rium (Gr. *unarmed wild beast*), in geology, an extinct herbivorous animal, shaped like a pig, and found in the tertiary strata near Paris.

Anoplu'res (Gr. *without weapon or tail*), in entomology, an order of parasitic insects without wings or sting.

Anop'sy (Gr. *wanting sight*), a visual defect, in which the eye and orbit are wanting.

Anorex'y (Gr.), want of appetite.

Anor'thite (Gr. *not right*), a siliceous mineral, a variety of felspar, without right angles in its crystals; composed of silica, alumina, lime, magnesia, and oxide of iron.

Anos'mia (Gr.), loss of smelling.

Anos'toma (Gr. *an upward mouth*), in malacology, a genus of univalve testacea.

Ano'tis (Gr. *without an ear*), a pretty little plant, which flowers from June to September; order Rubiaceæ.— *De Candolle.*

Anou'ra, the name of a family of batrachian reptiles, which lose the tail on arriving at full age.

Ansel'lia, a genus of plants, with large showy flowers, discovered at Fernando Po by Mr. Ansell, whose name it bears; order Orchidaceæ.

An'seres (Lat. *geese*), in ornithology, the third order in the Linnæan system, including all the web-footed water-fowls, of which *Anser*, a goose, is the type; fam. Anatidæ.

Antac'ids, in medicine, alkaline or carbonic substances, to remove acidity.

An'tæ (Lat.), in architecture, pilasters, or door-posts, supporting the lintels attached to a wall; the pier-formed ends of the side walls of temples, when prolonged beyond the face of the walls.

Antal'kaline (Gr. *anti* against, and Arab. *alkali*), in pathology and chemistry, a medicine to neutralize the presence of alkalies.

Antarc'tic (Gr. *opposite the Bear*), relating to the south pole, or to the region within the antarctic circle.

An'tares, a star of the first magnitude, in the constellation Scorpio.

Ante, a Latin prefix, signifying *before*.

Antœ'cians (Gr. *dwelling opposite*), in geography, those inhabitants of the earth under the same meridian and at the same distance from the equator, but on opposite sides, one party north, the other south. They have the same hours of day and night, but different seasons; it being winter with one when it is summer with the other.

Antedilu'vian (Lat.), a term relating to things existing before the Deluge.

Ant-eggs, in entomology, little white balls, found in the hillocks of ants, usually supposd to be their eggs, but which in fact are the young brood in their embryo state.

An'tefixæ (Lat.), in architecture, ornamental blocks placed at intervals on the cornice along the sides of a roof; likewise heads of animals placed as water-spouts below the eaves of temples, cathedrals, and churches.

An'telope, in zoology, a genus of ruminating animals.

An'te-mural, in architecture, an outer or boundary wall.

Anten'næ (Lat.), in entomology and ichthyology, hornlike processes on the heads of certain insects and crustaceans, which serve as tentacles or feelers.

Antephia'tic (Gr.), efficacious against the nightmare.

Antes (Lat.), in architecture, square pillars on each side of the doors of temples, or at the front of a building.

Antes'tature (Lat. *standing before*), in military science, a small entrenchment, consisting of sacks of earth, or palisados, thrown up hastily as a defence.

Anthe'lion (Gr. *anti*, and *helios* the sun), a mock sun.

Anthe'lix (Gr. *anti*, and *helix* a spiral), in anatomy, a part of the external ear, within the helix.

Anthelmin'tics (Gr. *against worms*), in pathology, medicines to destroy worms.

An'themis (Gr. *flowery*), a genus of composite herbs, the camomile, of great importance in pathology, from their use in intermittent fevers, dyspepsia, &c.; sub-order Anthemideæ.

Anther (Gr. *a flower*), part of a flower containing the pollen or fertilizing dust, by which the seed-vessel is fructified.

An'thias, a genus of fishes, of the family Percidæ.

Anthic'ides, a family of coleopterous insects, of which *Anthicus* is the type.

Antho'bians (Gr.), animals that live on flowers.

Anthobran'chia (Gr. *flower-gills*), in ichthyology, a family of Mollusca, which have their branchiæ in the form of panicles.

Anthocar'pus (Gr. *flower-fruit*), in botany, a term applied to fruits formed of masses of inflorescence in a state of cohesion, as the pine-apple and fir-cone.

Anthoceph'alous (Gr. *flower-headed*), having a head formed like a flower.

Anthoce'ros (Gr. *a horn-like flower*), a plant, of the order Cryptogamiæ hepaticæ.

Anthochæ'ra (Gr.), a large-sized tenuirostral bird, of the family Meliphagidæ or Honey-suckers.

Anthocy'anine (Gr. *blue flower*), the blue colouring matter of plants.

Antho'dium (Gr. *full of flowers*), the inflorescence of a compound flower.

An'thodon (Gr. *tooth-flower*), a genus of shrubs, of S. America; order Hippocrataceæ.

An'tholites (Gr. *flower-stones*), in geology, a fossil plant found in the coal formation.

Anthol'ogy (Gr. *discourse on flowers*), a work which treats on choice flowers; a collection of flowers, or elegant extracts.

Anthol'ysis (Gr. *anthos*, and *lysis* a breaking up), a change of flowers from their usual state to some other condition.

Anthomī'za (Gr. *a flower fly*), a genus of birds, of the family Meliphagidæ or Honey-suckers.

Anthoph'ila (Gr. *flower-loving*), in entomology, a name applied to those insects which live by sucking flowers; the Bee family. They form the fourth family of the Hymenoptera according to Cuvier's arrangement.

Anthophyl'lite (Gr. *leaf-stone*), the prismatic Schiller spar; a massive mineral of a yellowish grey colour, consisting of silica, alumina, oxide of iron, magnesia, lime, and oxide of manganese; sp. gr. 3.

Anthophyl'lum (Gr. *a flower leaf*), in zoology, the name of a lamelliferous coral, of a conical shape, found in the Palæozoic formation.

Anthosper'mum (Gr. *a flower seed*), a heath-like shrub (the amber tree), from the Cape of Good Hope.

Anthos'toma (Gr. *a flower-like mouth*), a family of Entozoaria.

Anthoxan'thine (Gr. *yellow flower*), a genus of plants (spring-grass), with sweetly-scented leaves and yellow flowers; order Gramineæ.

Anthozo'a (Gr. *animal flowers*), in natural history, a class of Polypes, which resemble flowers, as the Actinia and allied species.

Anthracid'eæ, a tribe of dipterous insects, of which *Anthrax* is the type.

An'thracite (Gr. *anthrax* charcoal), a variety of coal, consisting chiefly of carbon; it has the shining appearance of black-lead. There are several varieties of coal which go by this name, particularly in Ireland, Wales, and North America.

Anthracom'eter (Gr. *anthrax*, and *metron* a measure), an instrument for determining the quantity of carbonic acid which exists in any gaseous admixture.

Anthrac'onite (Gr.), a dark-coloured calcareous spar, with a compact fracture and glimmering lustre.

Anthracothe'rium (Gr. *anthrax*, and *therion* a wild beast), an extinct genus of mammiferous animals, many species of which have been discovered in the lignite of the gypseous strata of Paris and Tuscany; some of the appearance of the hog or hippopotamus.

Anthrax (Gr.), a hard inflammatory tumour, a carbuncle.—In zoology, a genus of dipterous insects, type of tribe Anthracideæ.

Anthropog'eny (Gr. *generation of man*), the study of human generation.

Anthropoglot'tis (Gr. *tongue of man*), in zoology, an appellation given to animals which have tongues resembling that of man.

Anthropog'raphy (Gr.), a description of the varieties of the human race.

Anthrop'olite (Gr.), any stone which contains the remains of man, like those found in the island of Guadaloupe.

Anthropol'ogy (Gr.), the science which treats of the physical and intellectual properties of man.

Anthropop'athy (Gr. *feeling of man*), human passions or affections.

Anthropoph'agy (Gr. *anthropos*, and *phago* to eat), eating of human flesh; cannibalism.—*Anthropophagi*, man-eaters, cannibals.

Anthropos'copy (Gr. *inspection of man*), the art of discovering a man's character by the lineaments of his body.

Anthropos'ophy (Gr. *anthropos*, and *sophia* wisdom), the knowledge of the nature of man or of human nature.

Anthroposomatol'ogy (Gr. *anthropos*, and *soma* the body), a discourse on the structure of the human body.

Anthus (Lat.), in ornithology, a genus of insectivorous birds, allied to the Wagtails; sub-fam. Motacillinæ.

Anthyl'lis (Gr. *a downy flower*), a leguminous plant, the kidney vetch; order Leguminosæ.

Anthyster'ic (Gr. *anti*, and *hystera* the womb), in pathology, applied to medicine used against hysteria.

Anti, a Greek prefix to numerous scientific words, signifying *against*, or *opposed to*.

Anti'ades (Gr.), the tonsils or almonds of the ear.—*Antiaditis*, inflammation of the tonsils.—*Antiadonicus*, swelling of the tonsils.

Anti'aris (Jav. *antiar*), the name of the far-famed upas poison tree of Java, the juice of which is of a most deadly nature. It attains a large growth, and its exhalations produce very unpleasant effects to those who remain long in its vicinity; order Urticaceæ.—*Antiarine* is the active principle of the upas poison.

Antiarthri'tic (Gr.), curing gout.

Antiasthma'tic (Gr.), preventing or curing asthma.

Antiattri'tion, a compound of plumbago and some oily substance, applied to machinery to prevent friction.

Antibrach'ium (Lat. *the upper part of the arm*), in anatomy, the forearm articulating with the upper arm and the hand.

Anticacheo'tics (Gr.), in pathology, remedies for a disordered state of the body.

Anticard'ium (Gr. *anti*, and *kardia* the heart), the pit of the stomach; the hollow part below the breast.

Antich'ronism (Gr. *anti*, and *chronos* time), deviation from the right order of time; anachronism.

Antic'ipant (Lat. *conceiving beforehand*), in pathology, a term applied to an attack of a periodic disease earlier than its wonted return, or to the paroxysm of a fever, &c., recurring at a shorter interval than the preceding.

Anticli′nal (Gr. *anti*, and Lat. *inclino* to incline), in geology, a term denoting an axis or imaginary line, where strata dip in opposite directions. The line of a ridge or bend in strata is denominated the *Anticlinal line*.

An′ticor (Gr. *anti*, and *cor* the heart), an inflammatory swelling in the chest of a horse, near the heart.

Antidota′rium (Lat. *a laboratory*), a dispensatory.

Antidysenter′ia (Gr. *anti*, and *dysenteria* flux), in pathology, applied to medicines used in the cure of dysentery.

Antidysu′ria (Gr. *anti*, and *dysuros* difficult urination), applies to medicine used in the cure of dysentery.

Antienneahe′dral (Gr.), in crystallography, having nine faces on two opposite parts of the crystal.

Antifeb′rile (Gr. *good against fever*), in pathology, applied to medicines in cases of fever.

Antigalac′tic (Gr. *anti*, and *gala* milk), a medicine which tends to diminish the secretion of milk.

Antihe′lix (Gr. *anti*, and *helix* gyration), the semi-circular prominence of the ear, situated before and within the helix.

Anti-ic′teric (Gr. *anti*, and *ikteros* jaundice), a medicine for curing the jaundice.

Antilith′ic (Gr. *anti*, and *lithos* a stone), in pathology, a remedy for stone in the bladder, or for gravel.

Antim′eter (Gr. *anti*, and *metron* a measure), in optics an instrument for the precise measurement of angles.

Antimo′nious Acid (Gr.), an acid consisting of two equivalents of antimony and four of oxygen.—*Antimonite* is a compound of antimonious acid and a base; the grey ore or sulphate of antimony, extensively used for commercial purposes.

An′timony, in mineralogy, a brittle metal, of a white silvery colour, with a brilliant lustre. After being fused, it crystallizes into an octahedron. Antimony occurs in the mineral state as a sulphuret, associated with quartz, sulphate of barytes, carbonate of lime, &c. According to Dr. Ure, the ore consists of 72·86 parts of the metal, and 27·14 of sulphur; sp. gr. 4·13. Antimony combines with all metals, even gold, and is one of the principal in type-metal, Britannia metal, &c. Of the chemical combinations of antimony, the following may be enumerated:—*Bromide of antimony*, consisting of bromide 64·3, antimony 35·7.—

Crude antimony, 2 atoms of sulphur = 16; 2 atoms of antimony = 128; atomic weight 64.—*Deutoxide of antimony*, 2 atoms of oxygen = 16; 1 atom of antimony = 64; atomic weight 80. — *Iodide of antimony* consists of iodine 74·7, antimony 25·3. —*Perchloride of antimony*, 5 atoms of chlorine = 180; 2 atoms of antimony = 128; atomic weight 308.— *Peroxide, or Glass of antimony*, 5 atoms of oxygen = 40; 2 atoms of antimony = 64; atomic weight 168.—*Sesquichloride of antimony*, 3 atoms of chlorine = 108; 2 atoms of antimony = 128; atomic weight 236. — *Sesquioxide of antimony*, consisting of 3 atoms of oxygen = 24; 2 atoms of antimony = 128; atomic weight 152.

The preparations of antimony, used in medicine, are numerous, among which the following may be mentioned, viz., the *Sulphuret of antimony*, *Precipitate of antimony*, *Tartarized antimony*, *Wine of Tartarized antimony*, and *Powder of antimony*. The only salt of antimony, which has been found of any importance, is tartarized antimony, commonly known as *tartar emetic*.

An′timony Yellow, a preparation of antimony, of a durable colour, used in enamel and porcelain painting.

Anti′pathes (Gr.), a genus of corals allied to the Gorgonia.

Anti-peristal′tic (Gr. *anti*, and *peristallo* to contract around), in pathology, a term applied to a reversed action of the bowels; opposed to the vermicular motion.

Anti-phlogis′tian (Gr. *anti*, and *phlogistos* burnt), an opponent of the theory of combustion; also, any medicine that tends to counteract preternatural heat.

Antip′odes (Gr. *anti*, and *podes* feet), in geography or cosmology, those people who stand on opposite sides of the globe; as the inhabitants of New Zealand.

Antique Bronze, in the arts, an alloy of copper and tin, used for statuary, casts, &c.

Antiq′uities (Lat. *antiquus* ancient), the remains of science and art, which have been transmitted to us by the ancients, comprehending their monuments, coins, inscriptions, edifices, literature, offices, habiliments, weapons, manners, ceremonies, laws, religion, &c.

Antirrhi′num (Gr. *anti*, and *rhin* a snout), a genus of pretty flowering plants, of the order of Scrophulariaceæ.

Antis (Lat.), in architecture, a term applied to a portico, when pillars are placed in a line in front.

Antis'cii, or **Antis'cians** (Gr. *anti*, and *skia* a shadow), in geography, the people who inhabit different sides of the equator, and whose shadows at mid-day extend in different directions.

Antiscorbu'tics (Gr. *anti*, and *scorbutus* scurvy), medicines for the cure of scurvy.

Antisep'tic (Gr. *anti*, and *sepo* to putrefy), in pathology, a remedy against putrefaction. — The principal antiseptic medicines are alcohol, anthemis, assafœtida, camphor, cinchona, and cusparia.

Antis'pasis (Gr. *anti*, and *spao* to draw), in pathology, a revulsion of the humours to other parts.—*Antispastics* are medicines which cause a revulsion.

Antispasmod'ics (Gr.), medicines to relieve cramp or spasms of the muscles.

Antisyph'ilitic (Gr.), antivenereal; efficacious against syphilis.

Antithe'nar (Gr. *anti*, and *thenar* the sole of the foot or palm of the hand), in anatomy, the name of two muscles, the abductors of the thumb and of the great toe.

Antitrag'icus (Gr.), a muscle of the outer ear.

An'tlia (Gr. *a baling out*), in entomology, the spiral apparatus by which butterflies and other insects pump up the juices of plants.

Antœ'ci (Gr. *anti*, and *oikeo* to inhabit), in geography, those people who inhabit the same meridian, but on the opposite side of the equator.

Antri'tis (Lat. *a cave*), in pathology, inflammation in any cavity of the body.

Antrum (Lat. *a cave*), in anatomy, a term applied to certain cavities of the body.

Antwerp Blue, a colour rather lighter in tint than Prussian blue.

Antwerp Brown, a colour made by painters from asphaltum ground in drying oil.

Anus (Lat.), in anatomy, the lower orifice of the visceral duct or rectum; the fundament.

Aor'ta (Gr. *aeiro* to take up or carry), in anatomy, the great vessel which arises from the left ventricle of the heart, and conveys the blood through the arteries to every part of the body. It is the main trunk of the arterial system, which rises behind the pulmonary artery.—*Aortitis*, inflammation of the aorta.

Apag'ma (Gr. *a breaking from*), in pathology, the fracture of a bone, or a forcing out from its proper place.

Apa'telite (Gr. *a deceiving stone*), in mineralogy, a hydrous sulphate of peroxide of iron.

Ap'atite (Gr. *apatao* to deceive), a variety of phosphate of lime, crystallized in six-sided prisms. It consists of lime and phosphoric, fluoric, and muriatic acids; sp. gr. 3·25.

Apep'sy (Gr.), want of digestion. (See *Dyspepsy*.)

Apet'alæ (Gr. *without flower-leaves*), in botany, the third grand division of the Dicotyledons, comprehending those plants whose flowers are without petals.—*Apetalous* is an epithet applied to this class of plants.

Aphanip'tera (Gr. *obscurely winged*), in entomology, an order of insects, of which the common house-flea is the type.

Aphan'isite (Gr. *not bright*), a copper ore, of a dark bluish green, consisting of arsenic acid and oxide of copper.

Aphanis'tic, in mineralogy, not distinct.

Aph'anite (Gr. *obscure*), in mineralogy, a variety of the hornblende.

Aphe'lion (Gr. *apo*, and *helios* the sun), in astronomy, that point of the orbit of a planet or comet which is farthest from the sun.

Aphel'ian, a bright star in the constellation Gemini.

Aph'ides, Aphid'ii (Gr. *aphis* the plant-louse, or vine-fretter), a family of hymenopterous insects, furnished with two elytra and two wings, and antennæ with ten or eleven joints; generally known by the name of wood-lice.—The *Aphidiphagi* are a family of coleopterous insects which live on the Aphides.

Aphidiv'orous (Gr. *aphis*, and Lat. *voro* to devour), in entomology, feeding on the aphis, as the lady-bird.

Aphlogis'tic (Gr. *without flame*), uninflammable; without flame or fire; applied to the safety lamp invented by Sir H. Davy.

Apho'nia, or **Aph'ony** (Gr. *without voice*), the loss of speech or voice.

Aph'rite (Gr. *foam*), in mineralogy, a species of carbonate of lime (earth-foam), of a frothy silvery appearance.

Aph'rizite (Gr. *ut supra*), a variety of black tourmaline.

Aphrod'itæ (Gr. *like Venus*), a fam. of dorsibranchiate Annelides, adorned with shining silken hairs or bristles, of which the Aphrodite is the genus or type.

Aph'rodite (Gr.), a silicate of magnesia.

Aphtha (Gr. *inflammation*), in pathology, a disease (the thrush), in which small white ulcers appear upon the gums, tongue, lips, and palate.—*Aphthous*, partaking of the nature of aphtha; ulcerated in the mouth or throat.

Aphthæ (Gr. *to fasten upon*), small white ulcers inside the mouth.

Aphyl'læ (Gr. *without leaves*), in botany, a class of the second grand division of plants, the Cellulares, comprehending those which have no leaves, as the Algæ, Fungi, and Lichens. — *Aphyllous*, having no leaves.

Apia'riæ (Lat. *apis* a bee), bees which live either solitary or in communities, containing the genera Xylocopa, Bombus, and Apis.

Apic'ra (Gr.), a genus of Cape plants, which resemble the aloe, but want its bitterness; order Hemerocallideæ.

Ap'idæ (Lat. *apis* a bee), a section of bees, which constitute the Anthophila of some naturalists.

Apiocri'nite (Gr. *apion* a pear, and *krinon* a lily), in geology, a genus of fossil Crinoidians, shaped like a pear at the top.

A'pion (Gr.), a genus of coleopterous insects; fam. Curculionidæ.

Apis (Lat. *a bee*), a genus of hymenopterous insects; fam. Anthophila.

Apis'tes (Gr. *treacherous*), in ichthyology, a genus of acanthopterygious fishes, remarkable for a strong sub-orbital spine, with which they can inflict severe wounds when handled; fam. Scoropænidæ.

A'pium, a genus of umbelliferous plants; celery, much used as a salad.

Aplanat'ic (Gr. *without deviation*), in optics, applied to glasses contrived to correct the abberration of the rays of light.

Aploce'ros (Gr. *a simple horn*), a genus of ovine antelopes, consisting of three species; order Rodentia.

Aplodon'tia (Gr. *simple tooth*), a genus of Rodents, allied to the sand-rats.

Aplo'me (Gr.), a dodecahedral or twelve-sided variety of the garnet.

Aplys'ia (Gr. *a* priv., and *plyzo* to wash), in botany, an inferior kind of sponges. —In zoology, a genus of marine slugs, type of the sub-family Aplysianeæ, of the tribe Tectibranchia or Sea-slugs.

Apnœ'a (Gr.), loss of breath; suffocation.

Apo, a Greek preposition signifying *from*, often used as a prefix to scientific terms.

Apocar'pous (Gr. *apo*, and *karpos* fruit), in botany, a term applied to flowers and fruits in which the carpels are separate.

Apocom'etry (Gr.), the art of measuring distant objects.

Apocyn'eæ (Gr.), in botany, an extensive order of exogenous plants, consisting chiefly of tropical shrubs and trees, which possess powerful medicinal qualities; *Apocynum*, or dog's bane, being the type.

Ap'oda (Gr. *without feet*), in zoology, a term applying to different orders and classes of animals:—1st, the class Echinodermata;—2nd, a section of Lizards;—3rd, a family of Serpents;—4th, a family of Batrachians; — 5th, Linnæus' first order of Fishes;—6th, a sub-order of the Malacopterygii. All these are characterized by the want of feet, or of ventral fins.

Apodes (Gr. *ut supra*), in ichthyology, an order of fishes, consisting of those which have anguilliform bodies, are without ventral fins, and have the branchial aperture spiracled.

Ap'ogee (Gr. *from the earth*), in astronomy, the point of the orbit of a planet which is at the greatest distance from the earth.

Ap'ogon (Gr. *without a beard*), a genus of small red-coloured acanthopterygious fishes; family Percidæ or Perches.

Apolep'sy (Gr.), an obstruction of the blood.

Apol'ysis (Gr. *releasing*), in pathology, debility of limbs, or looseness of bandages.

Apomecom'etry (Gr. *mekos* distance, and *metron* measure), measuring from a distance.

Aponeuro'sis (Gr. *apo*, and *neuron* a nerve), in anatomy, a fibrous or tendonous expansion of a nerve, tendon, or chord, which, when it occurs in the thigh, is termed the *fascia lata*.

Apoph'ygy (Gr. *escape*), in architecture, that part of the column where it begins to spring out of its base; sometimes called the spring of the column.

Apophyl'lite (Gr. *apo*, and *phyllon* a leaf), a mineral, which occurs in square prisms, the solid angles of which are replaced by triangular planes, which, by a deeper replacement, assume the form of rhombic planes. It exfoliates before the blowpipe, hence the name apophyllite. The name *ichthyophthalmite*, or fish-eye stone, is given to it from its pearly-like lustre. A specimen from Iceland consisted of potash, silica, lime, and water.

Apoph'ysis (Gr. *apo*, and *phyo* to produce), in anatomy, a term signifying a process, protuberance, or projection of a bone or other part. In botany, a fleshy tubercle, situated under the basis of the pericarp of certain mosses.

Ap'oplexy. (Gr. *apo*, and *plesso* to strike), in pathology, a disorder which suddenly strikes the brain, and takes away all consciousness and power of voluntary motion, during which the patient lies in a somnolent state, though the action of the heart and lungs still continues.

Aporobranchi'ata, or **Aporobran'chians** (Gr. *wanting gills*), in natural history, an order of Arachnides, or Spiders, which have no stigmata or respiratory organs upon the surface of the body.

Apos'tasis (Gr. *a throwing off*), the termination or crisis of a disease by secretion; the throwing off of exfoliated or fractured bones; an abscess. —*Apostematous*, pertaining to an abscess.

Apoth'ecary's Weight, in pharmacy, the weight by which drugs are dispensed. —Like the common troy weight, it contains only twelve ounces to the pound, and differs from it only in its minor subdivisions.—The *Apothecaries' Company* is one of the City Companies of London, who are the vendors of genuine medicines, and have also the power of examining and licensing dispensers of medicine in town and country.

Apot'ome, or **Apot'omy** (Gr. *a cutting from*), in mathematics, the remainders of, or difference between, two incommensurable quantities.

Apotrep'sis (Gr. *apo*, and *trepo* to return), in pathology, the solution of a suppurating tumour.—*Hooper*.

Appara'tus (Lat. *a preparation*), an instrument for the performance of any operation or function.—In surgery, the term is applied to certain methods of performing operations.—*Pneumatic apparatus* consists of certain contrivances for collecting the gases from chemical processes, and experimentalizing thereon.

Appendic'ulate (Lat. *furnished with appendages*), in botany, an epithet applied to stalks or leaves which have one or more additional organs attached.—In anatomy, *Appendiculæ epiploicæ* are small appendages of the rectum and colon, which are filled with adipose matter, and produced by the peritoneal tunic.

Appog'giata (Ital. *a prop* or *support*), in music, a gently blended utterance of the tone.

Appoggiatu'ra (Ital.), in music, a small note, by way of embellishment, before one of longer duration.

Approach'es, in military science and fortification, the trenches excavated during a siege, by which the assail-

ants can advance to the foot walls, under a covered way, being exposed to the fire of fenders.

Apron (Gael. *apran*), a term quent use in the mechanical practical science.—In nava tecture, it is a piece of curve fixed above the foremost en keel, behind the lower par stern.—In gunnery, it is a lead to cover the touch-ho piece of ordnance.—In naval it is a platform or flooring raised at the entrance of a little higher than the bottom which the dock gates are s carpentry, it is a horizontal timber, in wooden flighted used for the support of the pieces or rough strings and in the half spaces or landi carriage building, a piece of or other material used in carriage as a defence from rain.—*Apron-lining* is the the apron-piece.

Ap'sides, sing. **Apsis** (Gr. *to* in astronomy, the two extri opposite points of the orl planet; that point nearest to being called the *perihelion*, farthest off, the *aphelion*. orbit of the moon the most point is denominated the *apo* the opposite one the *perigee*. chitecture the apsis is the roof of any building, or the c a throne; the inner part of churches, in which the al placed; also in which the saints were preserved with care.

Ap'tera (Gr. *without wings*), mology, a class of insects w without wings, as the flea, lo —*Apterology* is a discourse class Aptera.

Apteryg'ians (Gr. *without fins* of Mollusca, which compreher not adapted for swimming.

Apus (Lat. *a small fish*), a nar rally applied to those leaf-fo tomostraca that inhabit pools and stagnant waters.

Apyrex'ia (Gr.), in pathology, tromission of fever or of the

Apy'rous (Gr.), capable of resi action of fire; formerly ap those minerals which endure heat without change, as asbe

Aqua (Lat. *water*), a term m in medical and chemical tions, and Anglicised in vari pounds, as *aquafortis* (La *water*), nitric acid; *aqua m* a medical water; *aqua reg*

muriatic acid; *aqua aëris fixi*, carbonic acid; *aqua alkalinamuriatica*, a bleaching liquid, prepared from muriate of soda and powdered manganese; *aqua Benedicti Rolandi*, a solution of crocus of antimony in wine; *aqua fernelii*, a mixture of corrosive sublimate and lime water; *aqua florum aurantium*, orange-flower water; *aqua græca*, a weak solution of the nitrate of silver; *aqua grysea*, an aqueous solution of nitrate of mercury; *aqua rosæ*, rose water; *aqua sappharina*, or *aqua cærula*, blue eye-water, made by mixing sal ammoniac with lime-water; *aqua vegeto-minerale* (Goulard water), made of lead and vinegar.—The artificial waters are:—*aqua distillata*, distilled-water; *aqua tosti panis*, toast-water; *aqua calcis*, lime-water; *aqua picis*, or *picis liquidæ*, tar-water; *aqua menthæ piperita*, peppermint-water; *aqua menthæ viridis*, spearmint-water; *aqua pimentæ*, allspice-water.

Aquæduc'tus (Lat.), in anatomy, a term applied to various channels or canals in the animal system, and more especially to the human body, as the *Aquæductus Fallopii*, which winds through the petrous portion of the temporal bone;—*Aquæductus vestibuli*, a canal which commences in the vestibule of the internal ear, and terminates between the layers of the dura-mater;—*Aquæductus cochleæ*, a foramen of the temporal bone, for the entrance and exit of the blood-vessels connected with the ear;—*Aquæductus Sylvii*, the passage or canal which extends from the under and back parts of the brain into the fourth ventricle.

Aqua-Mari'na (Lat. *sea-water*), in mineralogy, a stone of a bluish-green, of the colour of sea-water; the beryl.

Aqua'rium (Lat. *aqua* water), an artificial pond or cistern for cultivating aquatic plants or small marine animals, usually made of glass or other materials, so that the objects contained therein are fully exposed to the view of the spectators; a Vivarium. There are two kinds of aquaria (says the editor of the "National Cycl. Supp."), viz., *Marine Aquaria*, which contain sea-water, and are intended for the preservation of marine animals; and *Fresh-water Aquaria*, intended for lacustrine and fluviatile animals. The fresh-water aquarium is the easiest to manage; for the marine aquarium must be filled with sea-water, either real or artificial, which is often difficult to supply.

Aqua'rius (Lat. *water-carrier*), in as-

tronomy, the eleventh sign of the zodiac.

Aquat'iles (Lat. *aqua* water), in natural history, a term applied to animals or plants which inhabit the water, as aquatic birds, reptiles, insects, plants, &c.

Aquatil'lia (Lat.), a name given by different naturalists to sections, tribes, or families of birds, crustacea, mollusca, and hemipterous insects, all of which live in water.

Aqua-tinta (Lat. *aqua*, and Ital. *tinta*), in the arts, a mode of etching which produces the appearance of Indian-ink drawings.

Aqua-toffa'nia (Lat. and Ital.), a poisonous fluid, prepared by a woman named Toffana, of Naples, who is said to have destroyed upwards of 600 persons with it.

Aqua-vitæ (Lat. *water of life*), a name applied to brandy or spirit of wine.

Aq'ueduct (Lat.), an artificial channel for water.

A'queous Humour of the eye, a transparent limpid fluid which fills the space between the cornea and the crystalline lens.

Aquifolia'ceæ (Lat. *water-leaves*), in botany, a nat. order of plants, belonging to the polycarpous division of polypetalous Exogens, of which the *Aquifolium*, or common holly, is the type.

Aq'uila (Lat. *an eagle*), in astronomy, the name of a constellation near Capricornus and Aquarius.

Aquilaria'ceæ, or **Aquilari'neæ** (Lat.), in botany, a nat. order of tubuliferous Exogens, of which the *Aquilaria*, or eagle-wood, is the type.

Aquile'gio (Lat.), a genus of herbaceous plants.

Aquili'næ (Lat.), in ornithology, a sub-family of the Falconidæ, or Falcons, including the Eagles, and various genera, all consisting of large birds.

Aq'uilon (Lat.), the north wind.

Ar'abesque (Fr.), a style of ornamental architecture attributed to the Arabians.

Arabid'eæ (Arab.), in botany, a tribe of plants of the order Cruciferæ, of which the *Arabis*, or wall-cress, is the type.

Ar'abine (Arab.), the mucilage of gum Senegal, gum Arabic, and of linseed.

Ar'abo-Tedes'co (Arab. and Germ.), in architecture, a peculiar style consisting of German Gothic, with Moorish or degraded Grecian.

Ar'achis (Gr. *without branches*), in botany, a genus of papilionaceous plants, the earth-nut; order, Leguminosæ.

Arach'nida, or **Arach'nides** (Gr. *like*

spiders), a class of invertebrate animals, including spiders, mites, and scorpions, and comprehending Cuvier's second-class of the Articulata.

Arachni'tis, in pathology, inflammation of the arachnoid membrane of the brain.

Arach'noid (Gr.), in zoology and botany, a term applied to objects which are like a spider's web.—In anatomy, a tunic of the vitreous humour of the eye.—The *Arachnoid membrane* is a cobweb-like membrane, situate between the pia and the dura-mater of the brain.

Arachnol'ogy (Gr.), the science of the Arachnida; that part of natural history which treats of spiders.

Aræos'tyle (Gr. *width between columns*), in architecture, an arrangement of columns with certain widths between them.

Aræosys'tile (Gr.), in architecture, an arrangement of columns with an interval of half a diameter between the coupled columns, and of three diameters and a half between the piers.

Aragoa'ceæ (from *Arago*, the French physiologist), in botany, a natural order of beautiful exogenous plants, of the class Corollifloræ, natives of New Granada.

Ar'agonite, in mineralogy, a columnar crystal, of snowy whiteness.

Ar'agu, in commerce, a scientific term applied to crude stick-lac, as extracted from the tree.

Aralea'ceæ, in botany, a natural order of Exogens, of which the *Aralia*, a shrub of N. America, is the type.

Aranei'dans (Lat. and Gr. *like spiders*), a family of Arachnides, comprehending the various genera of spiders.

Arauca'ria (so called from *Araucaros*, a tribe of Chili Indians), in botany, a genus of gigantic firs, which are found fossil in the coal formation.

Arbor (Lat. *a tree*), in mechanical science, the part of a machine which sustains the rest.

Arbor-Dia'næ (Lat. *tree of Diana*), in chemistry, the name given to a beautiful arborescent appearance, which takes place in a vessel containing a solution of nitrate of silver, when mercury has been thrown into it.— *Arbor Martis* (tree of Mars) is produced by dissolving iron filings in aquafortis, until the acid is saturated, and then pouring gradually into the liquid a solution of fixed alkali, when a strong effervescence takes place, and the iron, instead of falling to the bottom of the vessel will often rise to cover its sides, and present the appearance of vegetable florescence.

Arbores'cent Star-fish (Lat. *growing like a tree*), a genus of Asterias, the *Caput Medusæ*.

Arbor'iculture (Lat.), the art of cultivating trees and shrubs.

Arboriza'tion (Lat.), in mineralogy, the figuration of a tree or plant in minerals or fossils.

Arbor-Vitæ (Lat. *tree of life*), in botany, the *Thuya occidentalis.*— In anatomy, a term applied to the medullary ramifications of the brain.

Arbu'tus (Lat.), a genus of plants, with fruit similar to the strawberry; order Ericaceæ.

Arc (Lat. *a bow*), in geometry, the segment of a circle; an arch.— In astronomy, a *diurnal arc* is that part of a circle described by a celestial body between its rising and setting, as the *nocturnal arc* is that described between its setting and rising.—*Arc of progression* or *direction*, an arc of the zodiac which a planet appears to pass over when its motion is according to the signs.— *Equal arcs* are those which contain the same number of degrees, and whose radii are equal.

Arca (Lat. *an ark*), a genus of bivalved Mollusca, the shells of which are transverse, and nearly equal in their valves.

Ar'cadæ (Lat.), in malacology, a fam. of marine Mollusca, which includes the Arca, Nucula, Pentunculas, Byssoarcea, and Trigonia.

Arcbou'tant (Fr.), in architecture, a flying buttress.

Arch (Lat. *a bow*), in mathematics, the part of a circle or eclipse (see *Arc*).— In architecture any solid work formed into an arc of a curve, supported at the two extremities.—There are various terms of art connected with the arch of a building; thus, the pedestals upon which an arch rests, are called its *piers;* the portions of the pedestal from which the arch is said to spring are termed the *flanks;* the lower tier of the arch-stones is called the *intrados* or *soffit;* the upper, the *extrados* or *back;* the arch-stones are termed *voussoirs;* and the highest stone, the *keystone*, the top of which is termed the *crown.*—*Triumphal Arch* is a stately gate, adorned with sculptures, &c., and erected in honour of some distinguished individuals who had deserved a tribute of honour; as, for instance, the *Arc de Triomphe* at Paris.

Archæol'ogy (Gr. *archaios* ancient), the science which describes the objects of antiquity.

Archan'gel (Gr. *chief*), in botany, the name of the death nettle and other species of the genus Lanium.

Arc'hetype (Gr. *arche* beginning), in mechanical science, an original model or pattern.

Arc'hil, a sort of lichen; the name of a violet-red paste, used as a dye stuff.

Archime'dean Screw (so called from *Archimedes*, the Greek mechanician), a spiral machine for raising water, consisting of a tube rolled in a spiral form round a cylinder, a modification of which has been introduced for propelling steam-vessels.

Arc'hitect (Gr. *archos*, and *tekton* an artificer), a professor of the science and art of building; a person capable of designing and superintending the erection of any great building or edifice.—*Architecture* is the art or science of building. It is divided into *Civil Architecture*, which comprehends the erection of public edifices and domestic buildings;—*Military Architecture*, or *Fortification*, and *Naval Architecture*, which (besides the building of ships and smaller vessels) includes the erection of docks, ports, moles, &c., though generally classed under the science of civil engineering.—In the erection of public edifices, of an ornamental character, there are different orders of architecture, as the Tuscan, Doric, Ionic, Corinthian, and Composite, which are noticed under their respective heads.

Arc'hitrave (Gr. *archein* to govern, and Lat. *trabs* a beam), in architecture the chief beam, or that part of a column which is immediately upon the capital.

Arc'hivolt, in architecture the ornamented band of mouldings round the arch-stones of an arch, terminating horizontally on the imposts. In the Tuscan order, the architrave has only one face; in the Doric and Ionic it has two crowned; and in the Corinthian and Composite the mouldings are the same as those of the architrave.

Arc'hograph (Lat. *arcus* a bow, and Gr. *grapho* to describe), an instrument for drawing a circular arch without the use of a central point.

Arch-stone, in architecture, the key-stone that binds an arch.

Arctic (Gr. *northern bear*), belonging to the arctic regions.—*Arctic circle* is one of the lesser circles of the sphere, described as being 23½° from the north pole.

Arctic'tis (Gr. *a weasel-bear*), a genus of marsupial animals, consisting of two Indian species, *A. albifrons*, about the size of a large cat, and *A. ater*, the size of a large terrier dog; both having long prehensile tails.

Arc'tomys (Gr. *a bear-rat*), in zoology, a genus of Rodents, the marmot, or bear-rat, which passes the winter in a state of torpor.

Arc'tonyx (Gr. *bear-clawed*), a genus of omnivorous Pachyderms, the pig-bear.

Arctostaph'ylus (see *Arbutus*).

Arctu'rus (Gr. *the bear's tail*), a brilliant star of the first magnitude, in the constellation Boötes.

Ar'deadæ (Lat.), in ornithology, a family of large wading birds, including the herons and cranes; of which the *Ardea*, or heron, is the type.

Ardisie'æ (Gr. *spear-like* or *pointed*), in botany, a tribe of plants, of which *Ardisia* is the type; order Myrsiniaceæ or Myrrh plants.

A'rea (Lat.), in geometry, the superficial contents of any figure.

Are'ca (Malabar), the betel-nut tree.—*A. oleracea* is a remarkable genus of lofty palm trees, known as the cabbage tree.

Are'na (Lat. *sand*), the space of an amphitheatre or circus covered with sand, for the exhibition of combats or equitation.

Arena'ria (Lat. *arena*), in ornithology, a genus of wading birds, the sanderling.—In botany, a genus of plants, of the order Caryophylleæ.

Aren'dalite (from *Arendal*, in Norway, and *lithos* a stone), in mineralogy, the name of a fine crystal, a variety of epidote.—*Dana*.

Areng, a genus of palm trees, from which palm-wine and sago are produced.

Aren'icole (Lat. *sand inhabitants*), in zoology, a genus of Dorsibranchiata annulata or sand-worms, which are about a foot in length, and inhabit the sea-shore.

Are'ola (Lat.), the coloured circle round the nipple of woman; also, an inflamed ring round pustules arising from variola or vaccinia.

Are'olæ (Lat.), in entomology, the smaller spaces into which the wings of insects are divided by the nervures.—In botany, the areas or small spaces on the surface of certain plants, as in the fossil genera Sigillaria.

Areom'etry (Fr.), art of measuring the specific gravity of fluids.—*Areometer* is the instrument by which they are weighed.

Ar'gali, in zoology, a species of wild sheep, found in the elevated steppes of Siberia, and the mountain chains of Central Asia.

Ar'gand Lamp, in practical science, a lamp so named from the inventor, in which the burner is in the form of a hollow cylinder, with a series of perforations around the circumference for the egress of gas. A free supply of oxygen being thus admitted to the interior as well as to the exterior of the flame, a very brilliant light is obtained.

Argem'one (Gr. *argemon*, a disorder in the eye), a genus of Mexican plants, the prickly poppy.

Ar'gent (Lat. *silver*), in heraldry, the white colour used in armorial bearings.

Argen'tan (Lat. *silvery*), in metallurgy, an alloy of nickel with copper and zinc; German silver.

Argen'tate, a term applied to fulminating silver, as *argentate of ammonia*.

Argen'tite, in metallurgy, sulphuret of silver.

Argil (Gr. *whiteness*), in mineralogy, pure clay or alumina.—*Argillite* is the name of clay-slate. — *Argillaceous schist* is indurated laminated clay or slate.—*Argil* has various combinations in natural history: as, *Argillo-arenaceous*, consisting of clay and sand; *Argillo-calcareous*, a species of calcareous earth; *Argillo-calcite*, a species of calcareous earth, with a large proportion of clay; *Argillo-murite*, a variety of magnesite. *Argilliformis*, resembling clay; *Argillo-ferruginous*, containing clay and iron; *Argillo-gypseus*, containing clay and gypsum; *Argillo-silicius*, containing clay and silex.

Argo, a ship or constellation; a shell-fish.

Argol (old Fr.), crude tartar, or tartar of wine, obtained from the inside of wine vessels.

Argonau'ta (*argo*, and Lat. *nauta* a sailor), a genus of shell-fish, of which the principal species is the *Argo*; the nautilus.

Argus-shell, a species of beautifully variegated porcelain shell.

Argyre'ia (Gr. *silvery whiteness*), in botany, a tribe of exogenous plants, of the natural order Convolvulaceæ.

Argyr'tes (Gr. *argyros* silvery), a genus of coleopterous insects, belonging to the Mycetophagi or Mice-eaters.—*Argyros* is of frequent occurrence in natural history, as a prefix, denoting silvery whiteness: as *Argyranthemus*, having flowers of a silvery whiteness; *Argyrocephalus*, having a white silver-like head; *Argyrophthalmus*, having silver-like eyes; *Argyrophyllus*, having silver leaves; *Argyropygus*, having the lower part of the abdomen white; *Argyrostigma*, having the flowers spotted with silver-like spots.

Ariad'ne, the name of one of the re-cently-discovered planets, first observed by Pogson in 1857.

Ar'icine, in chemistry, an alkali found in the Arica bark, containing one atom more of oxygen than quinine.

A'ries (Lat. *a ram*), in astronomy, a constellation figured as a ram, which is the first sign of the zodiac, and is marked thus ♈.

Aril, or **Aril'lus** (Lat.), in botany, a peculiar wrapper of certain seeds, formed by a fleshy expansion of the umbilical cord.

Ario'so (Ital.), in instrumental music, a sustained vocal style.

Aris'ta (Lat.), in botany, the beard of corn, or other grasses.

Aristolo'chia (Gr. *best parturition*), in botany, a natural order of plants, with hermaphroditic flowers.—The genus Aristolochia includes different species, which for their medical virtues have obtained a prominent place in our pharmacopœias: as *A. clematis*, which is slightly diaphoretic; *A. anguicida*, snake-killing birthwort; and *A. serpentaria*, which in cases of protracted ague increases the efficacy of cinchona.

Arith'metic (Gr. *measurement* or *calculation*), the science of numbers, or the art of computation by figures.—*Integral arithmetic* is the science of whole numbers.—*Fractional arithmetic* is divided into Vulgar and Decimal Fractions.—*Arithmetical complement* is that which a number wants of the next highest decimal denomination.—*Arithmetical complement of logarithm* is the sum or number which a logarithm wants of 10,000,000. — *Arithmetical mean* is that number or fraction which lies between two others.—*Arithmetical progression* is a series of numbers which increase or decrease by equal steps. — *Arithmetical ratio* is the difference between any two terms in arithmetical progression.

Arithmom'eter (Gr.), a circular logarithmic scale for the mechanical performance of arithmetical calculations.

Armadil'lo (Sp.), in zoology, a quadruped covered with a bony shell, of the family Mammalia, which includes the three-banded and the six-banded armadillo, the giant armadillo, the Chlamyphorus, and the Touay.

Ar'mature, in physics, applied to two pieces of soft iron fastened to the poles of a magnet, and connected at their ends by a third piece, so as to increase its power.

Arme'nian Bole, in the arts, a soft earth, of a red colour, employed in painting and gilding.

Arme′nian Stone, a mineral, of a greenish blue colour; a variety of blue carbonate of copper, used in medicine as a purgative.

Arme′ria (Lat. *Sweet William*), a genus of plants of the order Plumbagineæ. —*A. vulgaris* is the common thrift, which forms pretty borders for our gardens.

Armil′la (Lat. *a bracelet*), in anatomy the *Armilla membrosa* is a circular ligament which binds the tendons of the wrist and hands.—*Armillary sphere* is a hollow artificial sphere geographically illustrative of imaginary lines surrounding the earth.—*Armillary trigonometry* is an astronomical instrument consisting of five semicircles, which being divided and graduated assist in solving many useful problems.

Aroi′deæ, in botany, a natural order of plants, the Arum family, with which it agrees in all its essential properties. (See *Arum*.)

Aro′ma (Gr. and Lat.), in botany, the fragrant or spicy odour of flowers, roots, and vegetable substances.—*Aromadendron* is a genus of plants, comprehending the elegant aroma tree of Japan; order Magnoliaceæ.—*Aromatic confection* is a medicine for diarrhœa, composed of chalk and aromatics. — *Aromatic vinegar* is acetic acid, flavoured with aromatics.

Aro′matite (Gr. *aroma*), a mineral resembling myrrh.

Arou′ra (Gr. *ploughing*), a Grecian measure of fifty feet; an Egyptian measure of 100 square feet.

Arpeg′gio (Ital.), in music, the distinct sound of the notes of an instrumental chord accompanying the voice; imitation of the harp, by striking the chords in rapid succession.

Ar′quebusade (Fr.), an aromatic spirituous lotion applied to bruises and sprains.

Ar′quifoux, in the arts, a kind of lead ore used by potters to give their ware a green varnish.

Ar′ragonite (from *Arragon* in Spain, where it was first discovered), in mineralogy, a species of carbonate of lime; sp. gr. 2·6 to 3·0. It occurs in Devonshire and Buckinghamshire, and also at Leadhills, in Scotland.

Arris (Ital.), in architecture, the edge of two surfaces meeting each other.—*Arris fillet* is a slight piece of timber used in raising slates against a wall or chimney, that obliquely cuts across a roof. Sometimes it is called *eaves-lathe*, *eaves-catch*, or *eaves-boards*.—*Arris gutter* is the wooden gutter fixed to the eaves of a building.

Ar′row-headed Char′acters, in ancient art, a term applied to certain marks found stamped on the bricks of Babylon, and cut upon the marble monuments at Persepolis. They have also been found at Nineveh and Susa, and also in Armenia.

Ar′row-root, a farinaceous substance, consisting of starch, albumen, volatile oil, chloride of calcium, and water. It is obtained from the root of the *Maranta arundinacea*, and the tubers of *Carcuma angustifolia*. Dissolved in milk or water it forms a light and digestible food for children and invalids.

Arsen′iate (Gr. *arsenikon*), in chemistry, a neutral salt, formed by the union of arsenic acid with a metallic oxide. The principal arseniates are barytes, potassa, soda, lime, oxide of silver, and protoxide of lead.

Ar′senic (Gr. *arsenikos*), in mineralogy, a soft brittle metal, which is a violent corrosive poison. Native arsenic contains from 2 to 3 per cent. of antimony, and 1 per cent. of iron and water; sp. gr. 5·75. It enters into most of the compositions for the specula of reflecting telescopes, and for other optical purposes. Its oxides are used in dyeing and several of the arts. Its sulphurets are valuable pigments. Its principal mineral compounds are :—*Arsenic acid*, composed of 2 equivalents or atoms of arsenic, and 5 of oxygen ; atomic weight 115·4. —*Oxide of arsenic*, composed of arsenic and oxygen, colour snow-white, sometimes reddish or greenish; cleavage, octahedral ; fracture, conchoidal ; taste, astringent. — *Sulphuret of arsenic*, or *orpiment*, a trisulphuret of arsenic, consisting of arsenic and sulphur; the colour is a lemon-sulphur, passing into gold-yellow. — *Sulphuret of arsenic*, *realgar*, or *hemi-prismatic*, a bisulphuret of arsenic, composed of arsenic and sulphur; it is of a brilliant red colour, and splendid vitreous lustre.

Arsen′ical Soap, in taxidermy, a preparation used in anointing the skins of animals previous to stuffing. It is composed of arsenic, camphor, white soap, salt of tartar, and powdered lime.

Arsen′ico-Sul′phurets, in chemistry, compounds obtained by dissolving arsenic in a solution of caustic alkali, soda, and ammonia.

Ar′senite, in chemistry, a salt formed by the union of arsenious acid with a base ; the oxide of arsenic, a very dangerous poison.

Arsen′iuret, in chemistry, a combination of arsenic with a metallic or other base. The arseniurets are numerous: as, arseniuret of nikel, or antimonial silver; arseniuret of bismuth; axotomous arsenical pyrites; prismatical arsenical pyrites; white arsenic, or arsenious acid, &c.

Artemis'ia, an extensive genus of plants, remarkable for the bitterness of some of its species; a term applied to southern-wood, or magwort, and wormwood.

Arteriot'omy (Gr.), the cutting of an artery: the operation of letting blood from the artery.

Art'ery, in anatomy, a vessel or tube which conveys the blood in a direction from the heart to all parts of the body. The blood of the arterial system, after having reached the extremities of its innumerable ramifications, passes through the capillaries into the veins, by which it is again transmitted to the heart.—*Arteritis* is an inflammation of the arteries.

Arte'sian Wells (so named from Artois, in France, where they were first brought into use), a perforation or deep boring made in the earth, through which the water springs, from various depths, to the surface.

Arthrem'bolum (Gr. *an inserted joint*), in surgery, an instrument for rectifying disjointed bones.

Arthri'tis (Gr. *arthron* a joint), in pathology, any inflammation of the joints, especially the gout.

Arthro'dia (Gr.), in anatomy, a joint in which the head of one bone is received into the socket of another; a ball and socket joint.—*Arthrodic*, pertaining to *arthrodia*.

Arthrody'nia (Gr.), pain in the joints.

Arthropuo'sis (Gr.), suppuration in the cavity of a joint.

Arthro'sis (Gr.), inflammation of the joints.

Ar'tichoke (Fr.), a genus of composite plants, of the thistle tribe, Cardiaceæ. The Jerusalem artichoke (*Helianthus tuberosus*) is a plant with a root resembling the potato.

Artic'ulata (Lat.), one of the principal divisions of the animal kingdom, applied to those animals which have a jointed structure but no internal skeleton, and comprehending insects, spiders, crustacea, worms, &c.

Articula'tion (Lat.), in anatomy, the adapting of one bone or joint in the skeleton of an animal to another. —In botany, the knots or joints inserted in certain plants, as the grasses, cane, &c.

Artil'lery (Fr.), a term denoting the science or art which relates to the materials, ingredients, and composition of whatever belongs to engines of war, as the composition of shot,

the arrangement of cannon in passes, or in the field, &c. Under this head are comprehended various implements of modern warfare, as cannon, mortars, howitzers, and other large pieces of ordnance, for discharging shot and shells.

Artiste (Fr.), in the arts, a term to denote one who is particularly dexterous in the art which he practises, of whatever nature it may be, as an opera-dancer, hair-dresser, cook, &c.

Artocar'peæ (Gr. *bread-fruit*), a nat. order of plants, of which the *Artocarpus*, or bread-fruit tree, is the type. It is a native of the South-Sea Islands, and forms an important article of food to the natives.—The *Artocarpus integrifolia* is a native of the Indian Archipelago, and yields a fruit of sixty or seventy pounds weight.

Arts (Lat. *artes*), those branches of knowledge which require ingenuity and manual skill, and are used to denote the whole circle of the arts and sciences, or of an academical education; hence the degrees of A.B. Bachelor of Arts, and A.M. Master of Arts. They are divided into the liberal and mechanical arts: the former comprehending poetry, painting, sculpture, architecture, &c.; the latter, engineering, carpentry, masonry, smith-work, &c. Poetry, painting, music, sculpture, engraving, &c., are called the *Fine Arts*.

Arum (Egyp.), a genus of plants belonging to the nat. order Aroideæ (which see).—The *A. maculatum*, wake-robin, or cuckoo-pint, is the only British species.

Arunde'lian Marbles, certain tables containing the chronology of ancient history, particularly of Athens, from the year 1582 to 353 B.C. They were purchased by Thomas Lord Arundel, whence the name.

Arun'do (Lat. *a reed*), a genus of plants belonging to the Gramineæ, the water-reed.—The *A. phragmites*, or marsh-reed, is the only British species.—In anatomy, the *Arundo brachii* is the radius of the arm.

Arvic'olæ (Lat.), a genus of rodent animals, of which the field-rat is the type.

Ary'tenoid (Gr. *like a pitcher*), in anatomy, applied to two small cartilages at the top of the larynx.

Asafœ'tida (Lat. *fœtid gum*), a gum resin of a very fœtid description, obtained from the Persian plant, *Ferrula asafœtida*.

As'aphus (Gr. *doubtful*), in palæontology, a genus of Trilobites, found in the Silurian formation.

in chemistry, a crystallizable
ice obtained from the root of
rum Europæum, composed of
is of carbon, 11 of hydrogen,
f oxygen.

ite (Gr. *asbestos*), in minera-
ie stralstein or actinolite. —
rous asbestinite is a variety
iolite.

(Gr. *indestructible*), a mine-
imbustible substance of fibrous
re; a term also applied to
amphibolic or hornblendic
ls, such as actinolite, tremolite,
i common asbestos, the crys-
e not so fine or flexible as
of amianthus. The other
is are, mountain - feather,
iin-cork, and mountain-wood.
te asbestos consists of silica,
iia, lime, alumina, and protox-
ron.

i (Gr. *askeris*), a genus of in-
. worms, two species of which
he human intestines, *A. lum-*
es, and *A. vermicularis.*

i (Lat.), a term of frequent ap-
in in astronomy.—*Right as-*
of the sun or a star, is that
of the equinoctial, reckoned
ries, which rises with the sun
ht sphere.—*Oblique ascension*
rch of the equator intercepted
n the first point of Aries and
int of the equator which rises
r with a star in an oblique
—*Ascensional difference* is
erence between the right and
ascension of the same point to
ace of the sphere.—The term
ing applies to such stars as
ng above the horizon in any
l of the equator; thus, *As-*
r latitude is the latitude of a
when proceeding towards the
iole; and *Ascending node* is
int of a planet's orbit wherein
s the ecliptic.

Gr. *without shadow*), in geo-
those inhabitants of the tor-
ie who have no shadow at

i (Gr. *like a leather bottle*), a
pplied to those acephalous
:a which are shaped like a

(Gr. *askos* a bottle), in botany,
iw appendage, resembling a
itcher or bottle, which occurs
tem or leaves of some plants.
ir. *askos*), in pathology, a kind
sy of the abdomen, so named
ie bottle-like appearance of
iase.

ieæ (*Asclepius*, the god of
ie), a nat. order of Exogens,
h the *Asclepius*, or swallow-

wort, is the type. It consists of
shrubs and herbs which abound in
tropical climates.

Ash-blue, in chemistry, a product of
lime-water and copper.

Ashlar, in architecture, a term applied to freestone, as it comes from
the quarry. In mechanics, however,
the word is more generally used for
stones hewn for the facing of walls:
when smooth, it is termed *plane-
ashlar;* when fluted, *tooled-ashlar;*
when irregularly · cut, *random-ash-
lar;* when wrought with a narrow
tool, it is said to be *pointed;* when
the tool is not very narrow, it is
called *chiselled* or *boasted-ashlar.*

Ash'lering, in carpentry, the fixing of
upright quarterings between the rafters and floors of garrets.

Aspar'agus (Gr.), a genus of shrubby
plants (sparrow-grass), with scale-
like leaves.—*A. officinalis* is a delicate culinary vegetable.

Aspergil'lum (Lat.), a mollusc inhabiting a tubular shell, and living in
sand.

Asphalte, or **Asphal'tum** (so called
from the asphalt lake, or Dead
Sea), a bituminous stone, used as a
cement, consisting of bitumen, charcoal, and hydrogen gas, extensively
used in paving and covering roofs.

Asphode'liæ, a natural order of endogenous plants; the first division of
which contains the oliaceous plants,
the onion, garlic, hyacinth, &c.; and
the second division, the asparagus,
gum-dragon tree, &c.

Asphu'relates (Gr. *a,* and *sphura* a
hammer), in mineralogy, a series of
semi-metallic fossils, including bismuth, antimony, cobalt, zinc, and
quicksilver.

Asphyx'ia, or **Asphy'xy** (Gr. *without
pulsation*), in pathology, the state of
the body in which the pulse is so
low as not to be felt; but now applied by the faculty to the symptoms
of suffocation produced by an accumulation of carbonic acid in the
blood; the vital phenomena being
suspended, but life not extinct.

Aspidia'ria (Gr. *aspis* a shield), in geology, a genus of fossil coal plants, of
the Lepidodendron family.

Aspidu'ra (Gr. *aspis,* and *oura* a tail),
a species of fossil Echinodermata,
with serpent-like tails, from the lias
of Yorkshire.

Aspredi'næ (Lat. *roughness*), in ichthyology, a sub-division of the Siluridæ or Leaf-fishes, of which the *As-
predo* is the type.

Ass (Lat. *asinus*), in zoology, the
Equus asinus of Linnæus; a sub-genus of the Horse family.

Assam Tea, in botany, a valuable kind of tea, raised and manufactured in the upper district of India.

As'say, or **Assay'ing** (Fr.), in the science of metallurgy, a process for determining the quantity of gold or silver in any ore or metallic admixture; or, in its extended signification, of ascertaining the quantity of any one metal contained in any mineral or metallic compound, as copper or tin.—*Analysis* determines the different ingredients; *Assay*, only the quantity of any particular ingredient.—*Assay Balance* is a very delicate balance, used in chemical analysis, and in assaying metals.

As'sident, in pathology, an epithet applied to symptoms that accompany disease.—*Assident signs* are those particular indications which attend disease.

Asta'cidæ, Asta'cinæ (Lat. *a shell-fish*), in ichthyology, the family of lobsters, comprehending those crustaceans which have long tails, of which the *Astacus*, lobster or crawfish, is the type.

Aster (Gr. *a star*), a genus of plants, with pretty radiated flowers, as the Christmas daisy and China-aster of our gardens.

Aste'rias (Gr.), a genus of radiated animals (the star-fish), belonging to the section Stelleridæ, subdivided into the scutellated or shield-like, and the radiated star-fishes.

As'teroides (Gr. *like stars*), in astronomy, a name applied to the four small planets, Ceres, Vesta, Juno, and Pallas, which revolve between Jupiter and Mars.

Asthen'ic (Gr. *want of strength*), in pathology, applied to diseases attended with great physical debility. —*Asthenia*, bodily debility.

Asthenol'ogy (Gr.), discourse on diseases that debilitate the system.

Asthenop'sia (Gr.), weakness of vision.

Asth'ma (Gr.), a disease attended with difficulty of breathing and frequent coughing.

Astræ'a (Gr. *aster*), a genus of polypifers or stony corals, belonging to the tribe *Polypi vagini*. These animals fix their calcareous habitations in the rocks, and present one living mass of brilliant covering.—In astronomy, the name of a planet discovered by Encke in 1845.

As'tragal, Astrag'alus (Gr. *astragalos*, an ankle bone), in anatomy, the bone of the foot which forms part of the ankle joint.—In architecture, a small semicircular moulding at the bottom and top of columns.—In botany, a genus of plants, the milk-

vetch some species of which yield the gum-dragon and gum-tragacanth of commerce.

Astra'pia (Gr. *lightning*), in ornithology, a genus of birds of the family Sturnidæ or Starlings, distinguished by brilliant plumage, and excessively long tails.

Astrocri'nites (Gr. *aster* a star, and *krinon* a lily), a genus of fossil Crinoideans, found in the carboniferous limestone formation.

Astroder'minæ (Gr. *aster*, and *derma* skin), a subdivision of the family Caraphænideæ; type of the genus Astroderma.

Astrog'raphy (Gr. *aster*, and *grapho* to describe), the science which describes the nature, position, and properties of the stars.

As'trolabe (Gr. *aster*, and *lambanein* to take), an astronomical instrument, composed of two or more circles, having a common centre.

Astrol'ogy (Gr. *aster* a star, and *logos* discourse), the pretended art of foretelling events by nativities and the position of the heavenly bodies; at one time looked upon as a science, but now generally exploded as false and unphilosophical.

Astron'omy (Gr. *aster*, and *nomos* a law), the science which ascertains by observation and mathematical deduction the nature of the bodies occupying the celestial spaces, and examines their various movements.

As'troscope (Gr. *aster*, and *skopeo* to view), an astronomical instrument for making observations of the stars, and ascertaining their position in the heavens.—*Astroscopy* is the art of examining the stars by the agency of telescopes.

Astrothemat'ic (Gr. *aster*, and *thema* position), the places of the stars in an astrological scheme of the heavens.

As'tro-theology (Gr. *aster*, and *Theos* God), theology founded on observation of the heavenly bodies, presenting proofs of the existence and omniscience of a Deity.

Asymp'tote (Gr. *not coincident*), in mathematics, a right line which continually approaches nearer and nearer to a curve, without ever meeting it.

Atalan'ta, in astronomy, the name of one of the recently-discovered planets, which was first observed by Goldschmidt in 1855.

Ate, in chemistry, a Latin termination applied to compounds of which the acid contains the greatest quantity of oxygen.

At'eline (Gr. *no end*), in mineralogy, imperfect, or amorphous.

Athenæ'um, the name of a club or

place of literary resort; a seminary or public library, with reading-room, &c.; so called from a celebrated edifice at Athens.

Athori'cera (Gr. *pointed horn*), in entomology, a division of the Diptera or two-winged insects; so called from the last joint of the antennæ being terminated by a bristle.

Athero'ma (Gr. *porridge of meal*), in pathology, a diseased state of blood-vessels, characterized by a pulpy deposit.

Athle'tæ (Gr. *athlos* labour), contenders for victory at the public games of Greece.

Atlan'tides (from *Atlas*), in architecture, the figures of men supporting an entablature, instead of columns, called also Caryatides.—In astronomy, the Pleiades.

Atlas, in anatomy, the uppermost part of the neck, so named from its supporting the cranium, as Atlas is represented sustaining the globe.

Atmol'ogy (Gr. *atmos* vapour, and *logos* a discourse), the doctrine which treats of heat and moisture.

Atmom'eter (Gr. *atmos*, and *metron* a measure), an instrument for measuring the amount of evaporation from a moist surface in a given time; an evaporometer.

At'mosphere (Gr. *atmos* vapour, and *sphaira* a globe), the sphere or mass of air surrounding the earth, from 40 to 50 miles high.

Atmospher'ic Pressure, the weight of the atmosphere on a surface; the mean being 14·7 lbs. to the square inch.

Atmospher'ic Tides, certain changes which take place in the atmosphere, caused by the attraction of the sun or moon, when in opposition or conjunction.

Atom (Gr. *not to be divided*), in nat. philosophy, a particle of matter which can no longer be diminished in size; the smallest particle of which we can conceive any natural substance composed.

Atom'ic The'ory, in chemistry, the doctrine which teaches that the atoms of elementary substances become combined in certain definite proportions; and that all bodies are composed of ultimate atoms, their weight differing in different bodies. The relation in weight among the molecules of bodies constitutes the basis of the atomic theory, which establishes the important fact that bodies do not combine at random, but in definite proportions by weight. Thus, admitting the principle that all atomic weights are multiples by whole numbers of the atomic weight

of hydrogen, it follows that all atomic weights whatever will be expressed in whole numbers; the number for hydrogen being 1. Professor Graham, in his "Elements of Chemistry," presents a tabular view of the different elementary bodies, with the symbols by which they are indicated. In this table the *Chemical Symbols* and *Equivalents* are modes of expressing by letters and figures the definite proportions in which the substances chemically combine with one another, as elucidated in the annexed table. Thus hydrogen is represented by H 1; Oxygen by O 8; and water by H O. Iodine being denoted by I, and Fluorine by F, the symbols H I and H F denote hydriodic and hydrofluoric acid respectively. It happens, however, that many of the elementary bodies have names beginning with the same letter. In such cases the single letter is usually appropriated to one of them, and the others are denoted by that letter joined with some other letter of their names. Thus carbon is denoted by C, calcium by Ca, cobalt by Co, and chlorine by Cl. The names of the elements in the different languages of Europe not always beginning with the same letter, it has been agreed to form them from the Latin names of the elements; thus copper (*cuprum*) is represented by Cu, iron (*ferrum*) by Fe, tin (*stannum*) by Sn, &c. The great advantage of these symbols is, that they enable us to represent chemical decompositions in the form of equations. Thus, for the action of zinc on hydrochloric acid, we have—

$$H\ Cl + Zn = Zn\ Cl + H,$$

which means that hydrochloric acid and zinc, when placed in contact, produce chloride of zinc and free hydrogen. The left-hand side of the equation represents the state of things before the action, and the right-hand side shows the change produced. The annexed table contains an alphabetical list of the elementary bodies at present known, together with their symbols and their equivalents; hydrogen being taken as unity. The Italic words in parentheses are the Latin names of certain elements, as previously explained :—

ELEMENTS.	SYMBOLS.	EQUIV.
Aluminium	Al.	13·70
Antimony (*Stibium*)	Sb.	64·60
Arsenic	As.	37·70
Barium	Ba.	68·70
Bismuth	Bi	71·00
Boron	B.	10·90

Bromine	Br.	78·40
Cadmium	Cd.	55·80
Calcium	Ca.	20·50
Carbon	C.	6·12
Cerium	Ce.	46·00
Chlorine	Cl.	35·42
Chromium	Cr.	28·00
Cobalt	Co.	29·50
Columbium (*Tantalum*)	Ta.	185·00
Copper (*Cuprum*)	Cu.	31·60
Fluorine	F.	18·68
Glucinium	G.	26·50
Gold (*Aurum*)	Au.	199·20
Hydrogen	H.	1·00
Iodine	I.	126·30
Iridium	Ir.	98·80
Iron (*Ferrum*)	Fe.	28·00
Lead (*Plumbum*)	Pb.	103·60
Lithium	L.	6·00
Magnesium	Mg.	12·70
Manganese	Mn.	27·70
Mercury (*Hydrargyrum*)	Hg.	202·00
Molybdenum	Mo.	47·70
Nickel	Ni.	29·50
Nitrogen	N.	14·15
Osmium	Os.	99·70
Oxygen	O.	8·00
Palladium	Pd.	53·30
Phosphorus	P.	15·70
Platinum	Pl.	98·80
Potassium (*Kalium*)	K.	39·15
Rhodium	R.	52·20
Selenium	Se.	39·60
Silicium	Si.	22·50
Silver (*Argentum*)	Ag.	108·00
Sodium (*Natrium*)	Na.	23·30
Strontium	Sr.	43·80
Sulphur	S.	16·10
Tellurium	Te.	64·20
Thorium	Th.	59·60
Tin (*Stannum*)	Sn.	57·90
Titanium	Ti.	24·30
Tungsten (*Wolfram*)	W.	99·70
Vanadium	V.	68·50
Uranium	U.	217·00
Yttrium	Y.	32·20
Zinc	Zn.	32·30
Zirconium	Zr.	33·70

Any of the symbols in the table express one atom; when two or more are expressed, it is 2B or B2, that is, two atoms of boron. Fe + O, or FeO, is one equivalent of iron united to one of oxygen; and 2Fe + 3O, or Fe2O3, the combinations of two atoms of iron and three of oxygen.

Aton′ic (Gr. *wanting tension*), in pathology, wanting energy.

Atrabila′rian (Lat. *black bile*), in pathology, a term applied to hypochondriasis, or melancholy, arising from superabundance of bile.

At′rophy (Gr. *not nourishing*), a wasting away.

Atro′pia, a poisonous vegetable alkali obtained from the *Atropa belladonna*, or deadly nightshade.

Attic (Gr. *attikos*), in architecture, a story erected over a principal order, to finish the upper part of the building; never with columns, but frequently with small pilasters or antæ. —*Attic base* is the base of a column, consisting of an upper or lower torus, a scotia and fillets between them.

Attol′lens (Lat. *raising up*), in anatomy, an epithet applied to those muscles of the ear, eye, &c., which serve to draw them up.—*Attollens oculi*, the muscles of the eye.

Attrac′tion (Lat.), in physiology, the natural tendency of bodies to unite or approach each other.—*Attraction of gravitation* is that power which tends to draw all bodies towards the centre of the earth, and the earth towards the sun; a law which was first clearly demonstrated by Newton. —*Chemical attraction*, or *affinity*, is the tendency of certain bodies to unite so intimately as to lose their individual character, and to form compound substances. —*Capillary attraction* is that power which causes fluids to rise above their level in very small hair-like tubes. —*Electrical attraction* is the tendency which two bodies, when in different electrical states, have of coalescing, until, by union or approach, they pass into the same electrical condition.—*Magnetic attraction* is that power which a magnet has of attracting any piece of iron near it.—*Cohesion* is that power of attraction which binds the particles of bodies together into a mass.

At′trahent (Lat.), in physicology, attracting to.

At′tributes (Lat.) In painting, sculpture, and the fine arts generally, *attributes* are used to characterise certain figures, as the caduceus of Mercury, the trident of Neptune, or the club of Hercules.

Au′gite (Gr. *splendour*), a mineral of a brown or dark-green colour, a constituent of volcanic rocks. It consists of silica, protoxide of iron and manganese, lime, magnesia, and alumina.

Augustite (Gr. *brightness*), a scientific term for the emerald.

Auk (Icelandic or Dan.), a genus of web-footed aquatic birds, with fin-shaped wings, type of the family Alcadæ.

Aura (Gr.), a vapour or exhalation, defined by the early chemists as a pure essence exuding from animals and plants, and perceptible only by its odour.—*Aura electrica* is a term used in electricity, and applied to the sensation experienced, as if a cold wind

wing on the part exposed to
ity when received from a sharp
In pathology, *aura epileptica*
ecular sensation felt imme-
before an attack of epilepsy.
e (Lat. *aurantium* an
, a nat. order of thalamiflo-
gens, consisting of trees and
of great utility and beauty.
vers are fragrant, and the fruit
The order comprehends the
lemon, shaddock, and lime,
ave been divided into four-
nera.
at. *gold*), in chemistry, a
ation of auric acid with a
salt formed by its combina-
h an alkali. From *aurate of*
ia a detonating compound is
ed, analogous to fulminating
ometimes called fulminating

Lat.), in entomology, the first
rphosis of the maggot of an
or that state in which it is
rmed from the caterpillar to
fect winged fly; a chrysalis.
Lat.), the external part of the
ich projects from the head;
two venous chambers or apes of the heart. In the heart
re four cavities, two auricles
ventricles, termed the right
e left; the auricles are very
on the inside, but smoother
outside, and terminate in a
, flat, indented edge.
(Lat.), in botany, a pretty
us of the Primrose family.—In
logy, a genus of testaceous
ater mollusca.
at.), in astronomy, a brilliant
lation of the northern hemi-
(the Waggoner), consisting of
x stars, some of them of the
gnitude.
hy (Lat. *gold writing*), the
vriting, in which diluted gold,
of the common ink, is used.
Lat. *aura* an ear), in botany
ology, having lobes like the

rides, in chemistry, crystal-
lts, the electro-negative in-
t of which is the terchlorate
. Most of them crystallize in

in geology, a name given to
al of the bovine genus, whose
re found in gravel and allu-

orea'lis (Gr. *northern light*),
ctric phenomenon frequently
a clear frosty nights in the
n skies.
usi'vum, in the arts, a combina-
tin and sulphur (Mosaicum),

used as a pigment for giving a golden
colour to statuettes, or small plaster
figures. It may be made by melting
twelve ounces of tin with three ounces
of mercury; this amalgam is triturated with seven ounces of sulphur,
and three ounces of muriate of ammonia.

Ausculta'tion (Lat. *a listening*), in pathology, the art of detecting the
seat and nature of disease by listening to the sounds produced in the
lungs by respiration, or the action
of the heart, chiefly ascertained
through the aid of the stethoscope.

Auso'nia, the name of one of the recently-discovered planets, first observed by De Gaspari in 1861.

Austral Signs. The last six signs of the
zodiac, situated to the south of the
equator.

Austra'les Pisces (Lat.), a constellation
in the southern hemisphere; the
Southern Fishes.

Autoch'thones (Gr. *born of the earth*),
the aboriginal inhabitants of a country, supposed to have sprung from
the soil on which they live; a title to
which the ancient Greeks of Attica
laid claim.

Autog'enous (Gr. *self-produced*), in anatomy, applied to those parts of a vertebra which are developed from independent centres of ossification.

Au'tograph (Gr. *one's own handwriting*), the actual signature of a person;
the original writing, in opposition
to *apograph*, or mere copy.—*Autographic press* is a portable printing
machine for taking copies from a
lithographic stone. — *Autographic
telegraph* is an electric telegraph
for transmitting messages in the
handwriting of the person sending
them.

Autom'alite (Gr. *extraneous stone*), in
mineralogy, a variety of corundum,
of a dark green colour, sp. gr. 4·1;
its crystals are octahedral or tetrahedral, with truncated angles.

Automat'ic (Gr. *self-moving*), in physiology, applied to muscular movements
produced independently of the will.

Autom'aton (Gr. *self-moving*), a machine so constructed as to appear to
be self-acting, and to move, for a
considerable time, as if endowed with
animal life.

Au'tophon (Gr. *self-sounding*), a kind
of barrel-organ, the tunes of which
are produced by means of perforated
sheets of millboard.

Autop'sy (Gr. *one's own sight*), direct
or personal observation; ocular demonstration.—In surgery, a term applied to an examination of the body
after death.

Au tunite, a yellowish-green mineral, found in granite.

Av'alanche (Fr.), an immense accumulation of snow and ice, which, on being detached from the mountain's height, descends with terrible ponderosity, and often with devastating and fatal results.

Ave'na (Lat. *oats*), in botany, a genus of the Gramineæ, or Grass family; the oat-grass.—*A. sativa*, the common oat.

Aves (Lat. *birds*), in zoology, the second class of the Vertebrata, comprehending the feathered animals which are oviparous.

Avicu'lidæ (Lat. *little birds*), in ichthyology, a family of bivalve Mollusca, belonging to the tribe Atrachia, of which the Avicula is the type. It has a shell with equal valves, and a rectilinear hinge, often extended into wings on each side (whence the name); the shells interiorly are of a pearly lustre; and one of the species is the well-known oyster, *A. margaritifera*, from which the most valuable pearls are obtained.

Av'oirdupois (Fr. *to have weight*), a pound weight, containing 16 ounces, 256 drachms, or 7,000 grains; 28 pounds making 1 qr., and 4 qrs. 1 cwt.

Awl Tree, in commerce, the name of the Indian mulberry (*Morinda citrifolia*), the roots of which are used for dyeing.

Awm, a Dutch measure, equal to 34·16 imperial gallons.

Awn, in botany, the hairy-pointed beard of corn or other grasses.

Axe'stone, a mineral found in New Zealand, and other islands of the Pacific, with which hatchets, &c., are made by the inhabitants.

Axil, or **Axil'la** (Lat. *the arm-pit*), in botany, the angle formed by the separation of a leaf from its stem.

Ax'illary (Lat.), in botany, a term applied to flower-stalks, when proceeding from the axilla, or angle made by a leaf and stem, or branch and stem.—In anatomy, applied to the arteries, veins, glands, lymphatics, and plexus connected therewith.

Ax'inite, a mineral of a brown, grey, black, or blue colour, with axe-shaped crystals, and consisting of silica, alumina, lime, oxide of iron, and oxide of manganese.

Axis (Lat.), a straight line, either real or imaginary, passing through the centre of a body on which it may be supposed to revolve; a pivot on which anything turns.—In the sciences and the mechanical arts, the term is of very general application.—In astronomy, axis is an imaginary line supposed to pass through the centre of the earth and the heavenly bodies, about which they perform their diurnal revolutions.—In geometry, it is the straight line in a plane figure, about which it revolves to produce or generate a solid.—In mechanics, *the axis of a balance* is the line about which it moves, or rather turns about; *the axis of oscillation* is a right line, parallel to the horizon, passing through the centre, about which a pendulum vibrates; *the wheel and axis* is one of the mechanical powers, consisting of a wheel concentric with the base of a cylinder, and movable together with it about its axis.—In architecture, *spiral axis* is the axis of a twisted column drawn spirally, in order to trace the circumvolutions without;—*the axis of the Ionic capital* is a line passing perpendicularly through the middle of the eye of the volute.—In optics, an *axis* is that particular ray of light, coming from any object, which falls perpendicularly on the eye.—In anatomy, the *axis* is the second vertebra of the neck; it has a process, or tooth, which goes into the first vertebra, and this by some is called the *axis.*—In botany, the *axis* is a taper column, placed in the centre of some flowers or catkins, round which the other parts are disposed; or it signifies the stem round which the leaves, or modified leaves, are produced.—*Axal* is an epithet relating to the axis; thus *axal section* is a section through any body, whatever shape it may be.

Ax'minster Carpet (so called from having been first manufactured at Axminster), in the arts, a term applied to carpets manufactured in imitation of Turkey carpets, and noted for their thick and soft pile; they are woven in one piece.

Ay'mestry Limestone, in geology, one of the calcareous beds of the Upper Silurian series, which has been produced by coral and shell accumulations amidst the masses of argillaceous sediments. It occurs near Ludlow, Malvern, and some localities in Wales.

Aza'lea (Gr. *dry*), in botany, a beautiful shrubby plant, with richly-coloured bell-shaped flowers; order Rhododendreæ.

Az'imuth (Arab.), in astronomy, the arc of the horizon intercepted between the meridian and the vertical circle passing through a star or other celestial body.—The *azimuth of the sun*, or *of a star*, is an arch between the meridian of the place and any given vertical line.—*Azimuth circles* are great circles of the heavens intersecting one another in the zenith and nadir, and consequently are at right angles to the horizon.—The *azimuth compass* is an instrument used at sea to find the sun's magnetical azimuth. —*Azimuth dial* is a dial whose stile or gnomon is at right angles to the plane of the horizon.

Azo'ic (Gr. *wanting life*), in natural philosophy, a term applied to objects entirely destitute of organic life.

Azote (Gr. *destructive of life*), in chemistry, a kind of gas which is fatal to animal life; a name for nitrogen gas. Though destructive to animal life, it is one of the constituents of the atmosphere, of blood, muscular fibre, and many minerals. The name, nitrogen, is given to it from its being the base of nitre. The following are some of its compounds:—*Azobenzide*, consisting of 12 equivalents of carbon, 5 of hydrogen, and 1 of nitrogen;—*Azobenzoide*, 42 of carbon, 16½ of hydrogen, and 2½ of nitrogen;—*Azobenzule*, 42 of carbon, 15 of hydrogen,

and 2 of nitrogen.—*Azotite*, is a salt formed of nitrous oxide, &c.

Az'otized, impregnated with azote, or mephitic air.

Azure, in heraldry, one of the tinctures employed in blazonry; the blue colour in the armorial bearings of any person below the rank of a baron.— In engraving, this colour is expressed by fine horizontal lines.

Az'urite, or **Azure Stone**, in mineralogy, a fine azure blue, the lazulite or lapis lazuli of the lapidaries; structure, finely granulated; sp. gr. 3·0; hardness, 5—6; its constituent parts are phosphoric acid, alumina, magnesia, lime, oxide of iron, silica, and water.

Az'ygos (Gr. *without a fellow*), in anatomy, a term applied to various muscles, bones, and veins, which occur singly, and not in pairs; as *azygos processus*, a process of the sphenoid bone: *azygos uvulæ*, a muscle of the uvula; and *azygos vena*, a vein of the thorax.

Az'ymous (Gr. *wanting leaven*), a term applied to unleavened or unfermented dough.

B.

Babyrous'sa, in zoology, a species of wild hog, the horned hog of Java, the Celebes, and other of the Sunda Isles.

Bac'cate (Lat. *a berry*), in botany, having seed contained in a fleshy fruit; fleshy-berried.

Baccaula'ris (Lat.), in botany, a species of fruit with a succulent coating, and several distinct carpels.

Bacc'haris (Lat. *Bacchus*, from its wine colour), a genus of composite plants (ploughman's spikenard) used medicinally for its tonic properties.

Bacilla'reæ (Lat.), in botany, a group of minute algæ, which appear, from their power of spontaneous motion, to form the link that connects the vegetable and animal kingdoms.

Bacilla'ria (Lat. *bacillum* a little staff), in entomology, an extensive family of infusorial animalcula, of the siliceous shields of which many rocks are composed; the family comprehends about thirty genera.

Backer, in architecture, a small slate laid on the back of a large one at certain intervals.

Back-staff, an instrument formerly used as a sextant or quadrant, for taking altitudes, in surveying, navigation, &c.

Backstays, in navigation, certain ropes extending from the topmast head to both sides of the ship, used to sup-

port the mast when strained by a weight of sail.

Backstep, in military science, the retrograde movement of a body of men without changing front.

Bactris (Gr. *baktron* a cane; so called from the small stems being used for walking-sticks), a genus of palms, with spiny stems and pinnated leaves.

Bac'ulæ (Lat. *baculus* a stick), in fortification, a gate or portcullis, supported by two great stakes.

Bac'ulites (Lat. *baculus*), a genus of straight-chambered shells, with pinnated partitions, pressed by a marginal syphon, like the ammonites.

Baculom'etry (Gr. *staff-measuring*), the art of measuring distances by staves.

Badger, in zoology, a carnivorous quadruped, about two feet and a half in length; the *Meles* of Cuvier.

Badig'eon (Fr.), in the arts, a fine kind of mortar, for repairing defects in statuary; a preparation for colouring houses.

Bae'tis (Gr. *a skin jacket*), in entomology, a genus of neuropterous insects; one of the four genera of British May-flies; fam. Ephemeridæ.

Bags. In military science, *bags* are frequently used in works to cover a besieging army, or in field fortification. — *Earth-bags* and *sand-bags* have each their respective uses;

earth-bags contain about a cubical foot of earth, and are used to raise a parapet in haste, or to repair one that is beaten down; *sand-bags* are filled with earth or sand, to repair breaches, and the embrasures of batteries, when damaged by the enemy's fire.

Bag-shot-sand, in geology, a term applied to one of the Middle Eocene formations, consisting of extensive beds of sand, in which shells and the bones of a sea-serpent above 20 feet long have been discovered. They occur at Highgate and Hampstead, and other localities in Surrey, &c. According to Dr. Mantell, the boulders and masses of sandstone, which are abundant in some of the chalk valleys, and on the flanks of the Downs, are called Sarsenstone, or Druid Sandstone, from being the principal material employed in the construction of Stonehenge and other Druidical monuments.

Baikalite (from Lake *Baikal*, in Siberia, and *lithos* a stone), in mineralogy, a variety of augite.

Bailey's Beads, in astronomy, an appearance as of a string of beads round the sun in an eclipse.

Bala Limestone, in geology, a fossiliferous series of slaty calcareous strata, occurring in the Silurian system.

Bala Ruby (Sp.), a rose-coloured variety of spinel, not nearly so valuable as the oriental ruby or sapphire.

Balæ'na (Lat. *a whale*), in ichthyology, a genus of Cetaceans, which comprehends the *Balæna mysticetus*, or common Greenland whale, and other species, which are inhabitants of the polar seas and the Atlantic Ocean. —*Balæna boops* is a species of whale which attains the length of about 54 feet.

Balance (Fr.), one of the powers in mechanics.—In astronomy, one of the twelve signs of the zodiac, commonly called *Libra* (♎).—The *hydrostatic balance* is a balance used for determining the specific gravity of bodies, whether fluid or solid, by weighing them in water.—*Assay balance* is a balance used in assaying metals.—*Balance-wheel* is one of the wheels of a watch or chronometer, which answers the purposes of a clock pendulum, and regulates its motion.—In commerce, *balance-sheet* is the financial statement of a merchant or trader's affairs.

Balanite (Gr. *acorn-shaped*), in botany, a genus of ornamental plants, of the order Olacaceae.—In zoology, the name of a barnacle which is fixed by its shell.

Bala'nius (Gr. *balanos,* an acorn), in entomology, a genus of small weevil possessed of a long snout, by means of which it bores a hole into the common hazel-nut or filbert, for the purpose of depositing its egg, which is soon hatched into a larva or maggot.

Bal'anoid (Gr. *like an acorn*), in ichthyology, a family of barnacles, with shells arranged conically, like acorns.

Bala'nus (Gr. *an acorn-shell*), in ichthyology, a genus of Cirripeds, the shells of which consist of a testaceous tube, attached to rocks and other substances.

Baldwin's Phosphorus, the ignited anhydrous phosphate of lime.

Balis'tides (Gr. *speckled*), in ichthyology, a family of cheliform fishes, with oval bodies, mailed with plates, or covered by a hard coriaceous skin.

Ball-and-Socket, in anatomy and mechanics, a peculiar kind of joint, of which one part is shaped like a ball, and the other is a hollow socket, in which the other moves.

Ball-valve, a simple contrivance, by which a ball is placed in a circular cup with a hole in its bottom, the ball being surrounded by four arms. Being placed in a tube, it is made to act as a piston in pumping water.

Ballast Engine, a steam engine for dredging up shingle in a river, or drawing gravel or earth on a railway.

Ballis'tics (Gr. *ballo* to throw), the science of projecting heavy missiles by an engine.—*Ballistic pendulum* is an instrument for measuring the force or velocity of cannon or musket balls.

Bal'lium (Lat.), in military architecture, the open space or court-yard within a fortified castle.

Balloon (Fr. *ballon* a little ball), a large inflated bag, of a spherical shape, inflated with hydrogen gas, which, being lighter than the atmospheric air, causes it to ascend, and pass through the air.—In chemistry, a round vessel with a short neck, or a glass receiver of a spherical form.—In fireworks, a ball of pasteboard filled with combustible matter, which, when ignited, shoots into the atmosphere, and then bursts, scattering around brilliant sparks of fire, resembling stars.—In architecture, a ball or globe placed on the top of a pillar.

Ball, in military science, a general term applied to every kind of spherical or conical shot fired from a musket, rifle, or cannon: leaden balls being chiefly used for small arms, and iron ones for the artillery: their sizes and weights being distinguished by their calibres.—*Miné-ball* is, comparatively, a new species of military fire-arm, in which the ball, instead of being round, is conical; the base being concave, and the conical or pointed end being drawn towards its object with much more force and velocity than the common ball. It received its name from Captain Minié, the inventor.—In military science, there are various kinds of balls: as *Light-balls*, which are made of combustible materials, and are of great use in discovering the working parties of the besiegers by the strong light they throw on distant objects.—*Fire-balls* are bags of canvas, filled with combustibles, thrown from mortars for the purpose of firing houses, magazines, &c.—*Smoke-balls* are intended to conceal the position of the troops, and annoy the enemy.—*Sky-balls* are those which ascend to a great height, and are useful in showing the situation of forts or lofty buildings, which are about to be attacked.—*Stink-balls* are composed of combustible and suffocating materials. and are intended to stifle an enemy, or drive him out of his stronghold. — *Ball-cartridge*, the charge for a fire-arm, packed in paper, with a ball at the end.—*National Cycl. Suppl.*; *Military Dict.*, &c.

Balm, the name of the labiate plant Melissa, the juice of which is of a highly aromatic and odoriferous character.— *Balm of Gilead* is the fragrant balm extracted from the plant *Balsamodendron Gileadense*.

Balneum (Lat. *a bath*), in chemical science, a vessel filled with sand or water, in which another vessel is placed, requiring a more gentle heat than the naked fire. — The varieties of Balnea are usually designated by Latin epithets: as, *B. frigidum*, the cold bath; *B. pluviale*, the shower bath; *B. tepidum*, the luke-warm bath; *B. calidum*, the hot bath, from 95° to 100° Fahr.; *B. vaporis*, the vapour bath, from 100° to 130° Fahr.; *B. capitiluvium*, the head-bath; *B. maniluvium*, the hand-bath; *B. pediluvium*, the foot-bath; *Demi-bain*, the hip-bath; *B. aquosum*, the water-bath; *B. arenæ*, the sand-bath.

Balsam (Lat. *balsamum*), an unctuous, aromatic, healing substance, flowing spontaneously, or by incision, from certain plants; the natural mixture of resin with a volatile oil.—The name is also given to certain drug preparations, as *balsam of sulphur*, an admixture of sulphur and olive oil.—The true *balsams* are the brown balsam of Peru; the pale balsam of Tolu; balsam of Capivi, &c.

Balsama'ceæ (Lat. *flowing balsam*), a nat. order of exogenous plants, consisting of lofty trees flowing with balsamic juices; it has only one genus, the Liquid-amber.

Balsam'ina (Lat.), a genus of handsome flowering plants, natives of the East Indies. — *Balsamina hortensis* is a well-known odoriferous garden flower, order Balsaminaceæ.

Balsamina'ceæ, or **Balsamin'eæ** (Lat.), a nat. order of exogenous plants, consisting of succulent annual herbs.

Bal'uster, in architecture, a small column or pilaster, belonging to a balustrade, or row of balusters, for defence or ornament.

Bana'na (Sp.), a tall herbaceous plant, of the West Indies; also the fruit of the plant, used as food. It is known as the *Musa paradisiaca*; order Musaceæ. The fruit, when fully ripe, is exposed to the sun, and preserved as figs are, forming in this state an agreeable and wholesome food.

Ban'berry, the herb Christopher, the berries of which are very noxious.

Ban'dages (Fr.), in architecture, the rings or chains of iron inserted in the corners of a stone wall, or round the circumference of a tower, at the springing of a dome, which act as a tie to keep the walls together.

Ban'dala (Sp.), in the arts, a kind of fibre made from the strong outer layers of the *Musa textilis*, chiefly used in the manufacture of cordage.

Ban'delet, in architecture, any little bend or flat mould that encompasses a column like a ring.

Ban'dicoot, a genus of marsupial mammalians of Australia.

Banewort (Sax. *bane destruction*), in botany, the *Atropa belladonna*, or deadly nightshade, a poisonous herbaceous plant, found growing in waste grounds and hedges.

Ban'gia, a kind of hempen cloth, made from the fibre of a gigantic stinging-nettle in India.

Banian, or **Banyan** (Sans.), in botany, the *Ficus Indica*, or Indian fig tree, which spreads to such an extent that a single tree sometimes affords shelter to a cavalry regiment.

Bank'sia (after Sir J. Banks), a genus of umbellated bushy plants, found in the forest land or rocks over the whole known continent of Australia; order Proteaceæ.

Ba'phia (Gr. *baphea* dye), a genus of plants, the wood of which is imported into this country from Africa, as a dye stuff, by the name of cam-wood; order Leguminosæ.

E

Baptis′ia (Gr. *bapto* to dye), a genus of herbaceous leguminous plants of N. America, the tincture of which is used as a dye-stuff.

Barba (Lat. *a beard*), a term of frequent application in different branches of natural history.—In botany, it applies to any collection of long loose hairs into a tuft or crest.—In zoology, it is the beard or long tuft of hair dependent from the chin or under jaw of a mammiferous animal.—In ichthyology, it is a small kind of spine projecting from the mouth, with the teeth pointing backwards.—In ornithology, it consists of feathers which hang from the skin covering the gullet or crop of certain birds.

Bar′bacan (Fr.), in mediæval architecture, a watch-tower or fort placed on the wall of a town; or a small round tower situated before the outward gate of a castle-yard or ballium.

Barba′does Tar, a sort of bituminous oil, used in medicine and surgery.

Barba′rea (herb of St. Barbara), a genus of cruciferous plants (winter cress), of which there are two British species, *B. vulgaris* and *B. præcox*.

Barbel (Lat. *barba* a beard), in ichthyology, a genus of malacopterygious fishes, allied to the carp, which inhabits the rivers of England and Southern Europe.

Barbels (Lat. *barba* a beard), in ornithology, a family of scansorial or climbing birds, with bearded tufts and long conical bills.

Barbette (Fr.), in fortification, an earthen terrace, raised without a parapet, of sufficient height to enable the gunners to fire with a free range.

Bar′botine (Fr.), a vegetable production of the East Indies, the constituents of which are wax, gum, and bitter extract.—*Crabbe*.

Baril′la (Sp.), a plant cultivated for its ashes, and the alkali procured from them; an impure carbonate of soda imported from Spain and other places, and chiefly used in the manufacture of glass and soap.

Bar′itone (Gr. *heavy-toned*), in music, a low pitch of voice, or a tone ranging between the bass and tenor.

Ba′rium (Gr. *barys* heavy), in mineralogy, the metallic base of the mineral barytes, of the colour and lustre of silver; discovered by Sir H. Davy in 1807. When heated, it burns with a deep red light. It has a variety of chemical compounds, the principal of which are:—*Bromide of barium*, 1 atom of barium + 1 of bromine = 78·4; atomic weight, 147·1.—*Chloride of bromium*, 1 atom of barium + 1 of chlorine = 35·42; atomic weight,

104·12.—*Fluoride of barium*, 1 atom of barium + 1 of fluorine = 18·68; atomic weight, 87·38.—*Iodide of barium*, 1 atom of barium + 1 of iodine = 126·3; atomic weight, 195·0.—*Peroxide of barium* 1 atom of barium + 2 of oxygen = 16; atomic weight, 84·7.—*Protoxide of barium*, 1 atom of barium = 68·7 + 1 of oxygen = 8; atomic weight, 76·7.—*Sulphuret of barium*, 1 atom of barium + 1 of sulphur = 16·1; atomic weight, 84·8.

Bark (Germ.), in vegetable physiology, the external coating of the trunk and branches of trees, sometimes applied to medical or chemical purposes. Thus *Peruvian bark* is a very valuable medicine, the produce of the Cinchona, from many parts of South America, but chiefly from Peru; the medicinal property is termed *quinine*. Independently of its chemical properties, bark is of some importance for its organic products, which science and art have applied to many of the purposes of life. The *liber*, or bark of the lime tree, of the bread-fruit tree, and of the paper mulberry, is torn into slips, and manufactured into useful mats. Hence several kinds of bark, being used for processes in the arts or for medicines, enter extensively into commerce. Among these may be noticed the oak bark, cork bark, mimosa or wattle bark, the quercitron bark, cinnamon, cassia, &c. The oak bark it extensively used in tanning, for which it is valuable on account of the large proportion it contains of that peculiar astringent called *tannin*.—*Barkery* is the place where the tanners keep the bark used in the process of tanning.—In horticulture, a *bark-bed* is a bed formed of the spent bark used by tanners, which is placed inside of a brick pit in a glazed house, constructed for forcing artificial warmth by the fermentation of the materials of which it consists.

Barley (Sax. *bere*), the Hordeum of botanists, extensively used in malting, from which ale and porter are produced.

Bar′nacle (Fr.), in conchology, a family of sedentary crustaceans, protected by hard shell-like valves; the common name for the *Pentalasmis anatifera* is the duck barnacle, a Cirriped, with a shell attached to a fleshy stalk, found adhering to ships or floating timbers.—In ornithology, *Barnacle* or *Bernacle goose* is a species of goose which is found in high northern latitudes, and visits Britain in the autumn.—In farriery an instrument used for holding horses by the nose when an operation is to be performed.

Bar'olite (Gr. *heavy stone*), a poisonous mineral in lead veins, the carbonate of barytes, containing 80 per cent. of barytes, and 20 per cent. of carbonic acid; sp. gr. 4·3.

Barom'eter (Gr. *weight measurer*), an instrument for measuring the weight or pressure of the atmosphere, and showing the changes of the weather. It is a glass tube filled with mercury, hermetically sealed at one end; the other open, and immerged in a basin of stagnant mercury; so that, as the weight of the atmosphere diminishes, the mercury in the tube descends; and as it increases the mercury ascends, the column of mercury suspended in the tube being always equal to the weight of the incumbent atmosphere.—*Barometrograph* is an instrument which of itself inscribes on paper the variations of atmospheric pressure.

Bar'ometz, a vegetable production, the Scythian lamb, which consists of the prostrate heavy stem of the fern *Aspidium barometz*, which has the appearance of a crouching animal.

Bar'oscope (Gr.), an instrument to show the weight of the atmosphere.

Barose'lenite (Gr. *baros* weight, and *selenite*), in chemistry, the sulphate of barytes, heavy spar, which occurs in various rocks, both igneous and stratified.

Barras, the resin which exudes from wounds made in the bark of fir trees.

Barry, in heraldry, a field divided by horizontal lines into four or more parts.

Bar'sowite (Russ.), a snow-white mineral, so named from Barswski, in the Ural Mountains, where it occurs. With borax, it fuses into a transparent glass. Its constituent parts are silex, alumina, and lime.—*Dana.*

Barwood, a red dye-wood produced in Africa.

Barypho'nia (Gr. *barys*, and *phone* voice), in pathology, difficulty of pronunciation.

Barystron'tianite (Gr. *barys*, and *strontian*), a mineral of a greyish-white colour, which occurs at Stromness, and in the Orkneys; hence called Stromnite.

Bary'ta, or **Bary'tes** (Gr. *barys* heavy), in mineralogy, a ponderous alkaline earth; an oxide of barium, so called from its great density. It is of various colours, but generally of reddish white; sp. gr. 4·41—4·67.

Bary'to-calcite (Gr. *barys*, and Lat. *calx* chalk), a crystallized mineral of a yellowish or greyish colour, consisting of baryta and carbonate of lime: sp. gr. 3·6.

Basalt, a greyish-black mineral, of igneous or volcanic origin, occurring in globular masses, composed of concentric layers. The Giant's Causeway and the island of Staffa, with its celebrated excavation called Fingal's Cave, are remarkable examples of its columnar structure.

Basal'tine, a mineral with a foliated texture; basaltic hornblende, of a dark green or yellowish green colour; it consists of silica, alumina, iron, lime, and magnesia.

Bas'anite (Gr. *touchstone*), in mineralogy, a variety of siliceous slate, called Lydian stone, from its being used as a test in determining the purity of gold by the colour of the streak.

Bascule (Fr.), in military science, the lever which serves to lift a drawbridge, the fore part being called the *flèche*, and the hind part the *beauche*.

Base (Gr. and Lat. *basis*; Fr. *bas*; Ital. *basso*), a term of frequent occurrence in science and art.—In chemistry, it is applied to all substances capable of saturating acids, and thus constituting neutral salts, as the metallic oxides, ammonia, and morphia.—In medicine, the constituent principle of a compound body or medicine.—In geometry, it is the lowest side of the perimeter of a figure.—In conic sections, it is a right line in the hyperbola and parabola, arising from the common intersection of the second plane and the base of a cone.—In architecture, it is the lowest part of a column and pedestal.—In fortification, the exterior side of the polygon. — In music, it is often called *bass*, the lowest part in a concert, either vocal or instrumental.—In military science, the *base of operations* is that line of frontier or country occupied by troops, from which military operations advance, and munitions are supplied, and on which a retreat may be made when needful.

Basement, in architecture, the lowest story of a building on which an order is placed, with a base or plinth, die and cornice.

Basic (Lat. *basis*), in chemistry, compounds having a large proportion of base.

Basil, in botany, a name of the genus Ocymum, one of the species of which is much used for seasoning in the culinary art.

Bas'ilar, or **Bas'ilary** (Lat. *basis*), in anatomy, belonging to the base of the skull.—*Arteria basilaris*, basilar or basilary artery, is that artery which results from the union of the two vertebral arteries, so termed because it lies upon the basilary process of the occipital base.—In botany, the term is applied to any part placed at or near the base of another.

Basil'ica (Gr. *royal*), in anatomy, the anterior part of the axillary vein, running the entire length of the arm. —In ancient architecture, the court or public hall in which princes and magistrates sat to administer justice.

Basilis'cus (Gr.), in herpetology, a genus of saurian reptiles, the basilisk, belonging to the Iguana family.—In astronomy, a star of the first magnitude, in the constellation Leo.—In anatomy, applied to parts supposed to be very important in their functions; and in pharmacy, to compositions highly esteemed for their superior virtues in curing cutaneous or other disorders, as the ointment *Basilicon*.

Basin (Fr.), in geology, a hollow tract of country, filled with a series of aqueous deposits, the strata of which have generally a dip in a central direction.—In geography, that portion of the country which is drained by a river and its tributaries.

Basi-occip'ital (Lat. *basis*, and *occiput* the back of the skull), in anatomy, a bone of the head of lower vertebrate animals.

Basis (Lat.), in architecture, the pedestal of a column.—In anatomy, *basis cordis* is the superior part of the heart, to distinguish it from its apex or small point; *basis cerebri*, the lower and posterior part of the brain.—In pharmacy and medicine, the principal ingredient in a composition.—In chemistry, a term applied to all the metals, alkalies, and other bodies which unite with acids or gases.

Bas-relief, or **Basso-relie'vo** (Ital.), in sculpture, low relief, or the figures which do not stand out prominently from the ground. When the figures are prominently raised, they are said to be in *alto-relievo*.

Bass, Basso (Fr. *basse*; Ital. *basso*), in music, the deepest part of harmony, and that which gives concord to the different parts of a concert. It is played on the largest pipes or strings of an instrument, as the organ, lute, &c.—*Basso*, in choral score, is generally placed against the stave of the instrumental bass in preference to that of the vocal bass.—(*Busby*.) *Thorough bass* is continued bass; the fundamental bass continued throughout a composition; also, the accom-

paniment of a continued bass, marked by figures placed over or under the notes of the instrumental bass-staff. —*Basso concertante* is the bass of the little chorus.—*Basso repieno* is the bass of the grand chorus; and *basso continuo*, that part of a composition which is set for an organ.—*Basso-di-camera* is an instrument for performing double bass.—*Bass-clef* is the character placed at the beginning of a stave, in which the bass or lower notes of a composition are placed, and serving to determine the pitch and names of those notes.—*Bassetto*, the diminutive of *basso*, sometimes applied to the tenor violin.

Bassoon (Fr.), a musical wind instrument, serving as the proper bass to the oboe and clarionet.

Bastion (Fr.), in fortification, a strong projecting mass of masonry at the angles of a fortified work.—A *bastion* has two faces, and an opening towards the centre, called the gorge. —A *flat bastion* is made in the middle of the curtain, when it is too long to be defended by the *bastions* in its extremes.—A *demi-bastion* has only one face, with one flank and a demigorge. — A *double bastion* is one erected on the plane of another.— *Mil. Cycl.*

Basyle (Gr. *basis*, and *yle* matter), in chemistry, a term applied to the metallic radical of a salt; thus the base of a sulphate of soda is *soda*, or oxide of sodium, and the *basyle* is sodium. —*Graham*.

Bat'ardeau (Fr.), in fortification, a wall across a wet ditch, with sluices in it. —In civil achitecture, a coffer-dam for building the piers of a bridge.

Bath, in chemistry, a vessel filled with either water or sand, which encloses another vessel containing a substance to be heated or dried.—*Bath-metal* is a metallic alloy, composed of zinc and brass.

Bath O'olite (*Bath*, and Gr. *egg-stone*), in geology, a stone belonging to the Oolitic formation, much used in building and architectural works.

Bath-stone, a kind of limestone, much used in building, quarries of which are found near Bath, in Somersetshire.

Bat'olite (Fr. *bâton* a staff, and *lithos* a stone), in geology, a genus of cylindrical bivalve shells, some of considerable length, which form masses of rock in the High Alps.

Bat'on (Fr.), in heraldry, the mark of illegitimate descent.

Batrac'hia, or **Batrac'hians** (Gr. *batrachos* a frog), in zoology, an order of reptiles comprising frogs, toads, and others, which have naked skins and external branchiæ, or gills, in the early state.—*Batrachite* is a fossil batrachian, which occurs in the tertiary lignite, or brown coal-beds of the valley of the Rhine.

Bat'tery, a term of frequent use in physical and practical science.—In electricity, a battery consists of a combination of glasses with cooled surfaces, so connected that they may be charged at once, and discharged by a common conductor.—A *galvanic battery* or *pile* is an apparatus employed for accumulating the electric fluid, by means of plates of zinc and copper arranged alternately, connected together, and placed in diluted nitric acid; invented by Volta. Various improvements have been effected in electric batteries by Wollaston, Daniel, Grove, Smee, Wheatstone, and others. The battery invented by Professor Daniel consists of a certain number of cylindrical vessels of copper, open at the top, about sixteen inches high, and three inches diameter, and containing a saturated solution of sulphate of copper, with a little vitriolic acid. — In military science, *batteries* are the implements of war with which a besieged place is battered. They are of various kinds. A *mortar battery* is sunk into the ground, and has embrasures; *battery d'enfilade* is one formed to sweep the whole length of a given straight line; *cross batteries* are two batteries so situated as to play on the same object at a given angle; a *battery en écharpe* plays in an oblique direction; *battery de revers* plays on the back of the enemy.—*Camerade battery* is one in which several guns are engaged in firing on the same object at the same time.—To *batter in breach* is to direct a heavy cannonade of many pieces on one part of the revêtement from the third parallel.

Bat'tlement (Fr. *bâtiment*), in military science, a breast-work or parapet raised round the top of a building, with embrasures or interstices to look through, and at the same time assail and annoy a besieging force.

Battu'ta (Ital.), in music, the motion of the foot or hand in beating time and guiding the performers.

Bay (Sp. *bahia*), in architecture, a term applied to a compartment between the ribs of a groined roof; also to the square between the buttresses of a wall, or between the mullions of a window.—In naval architecture, the *bay* is the part on each side between decks situated between the bitts.—In geography, a bay (Ital. *baia*) is a portion of the sea extending into the land less than a gulf, and larger than a creek, the shore of which is usually of a curved appearance.—*Bay-salt* is a salt produced by exposure of sea-water to evaporation from the action of the atmosphere or the rays of the sun.

Bdella (Gr. *bdello*), a genus of Annelides, furnished with eight eyes, inhabitants of the Nile; also a genus of Arachnides, found under stones.

Bdel'lium (Lat. from Gr. *bdellion*), a resinous juice or gum resin, exuding from an oriental tree, supposed to be the Balsamodendron (Balsam tree).

Bead, in architecture, a kind of circular moulding, frequently used on the fascia of an architrave, and also in the mouldings of doors, imposts, cornices, &c There are various distinctive names, as *quirk bead*, *cock bead*, &c., which are more of a technical than scientific character.

Beak (Fr. *bec*), in architecture, a small fillet left on the edge of a larmier, forming a canal behind, to prevent the water from running down the lower bed of the cornice.—In naval architecture, that part situated before the forecastle, on the outside of the ship, fastened to the stem, and supported by the main knee.—In farriery, a little shoe about an inch long at the toe, turned up and fastened in upon the forepart of the hoof.

Beam Compasses, in geometry and mathematics, an instrument with sliding sockets, and several shifting points, for the purpose of drawing circles with very long radii.

Beam Tree, a species of wild pear tree, the *Pyrus aria*, so called from the wood being much used in the manufacturing of machine cogs and axletrees.

Bear, in astronomy, a northern constellation; the Ursus Major and Minor, the names of the *Great* and *Little Bear*.

Bearing, in geography and navigation, the point of the compass that one place bears or stands off from another.—In architecture, the length or distance which the ends of a piece of timber are inserted into walls or piers.—*Bearing wall*, or *partition*, is a wall which is built upon the solid, and is made to support another wall or partition, either in the same or in a transverse direction.—In heraldry, coats of arms or figures of armories.

Beau-ide'al (Fr.), in the fine arts, the conception of perfect beauty, as represented in painting, sculpture, or architecture; the beautiful in nature.

Beca-fico (Sp.), in ornithology, a beautiful little bird, that sings like a nightingale, and feeds on figs; the *Sylvia hortensis* of naturalists.

Bed Mouldings, in architecture, those mouldings which are between the corona and frieze of all the orders.

Bee, in entomology, the common name of the genus Apis, a honey-producing hymenopterous insect, celebrated for the wonderful accuracy of its architecture, its instincts, and the valuable products of its industry.—*Bee-bread* is a term applied to the pollen of flowers, from which the bee supplies its young with food.

Beetle (Sax. *bitel*), a coleopterous insect with four wings, of which there are numerous species. (See *Coleoptera*.)

Begonia'ceæ, in botany, a nat. order of endogenous plants, the flowers of which are unisexual; the type and only genus of this order is the Begonia.

Behen (Arab.), an old name given to the *Cucubalus behen* of British botanists; *Centaurea behen*, which is aromatic and astringent; and to *Statice limonium*, used as an astringent.

Belem'nite (Gr. *belemnon* a dart), in geology, a fossil shell (Arrow-head, or Thunderstone) of the Cephalopod order, found in the chalk or limestone formation. It is of a conical form, and divided into chambers, perforated by a siphuncle or pipe, and inserted into a laminar, solid, fusiform sheath.

Bell, in architecture, the naked vase or *corbeille* round which the foliage and volutes of the Corinthian and composite capitals are arranged.—*Bell roof* is a roof, the vertical section of which is concave at bottom and convex at the top.

Belladon'na (Ital. *fair lady*), in botany, a poisonous perennial plant, the Deadly Nightshade; a species of Amaryllis.—*Belladonna lily*, a liliaceous plant, with beautiful delicate flowers.

Bel'latrix (Lat. *a female warrior*), in astronomy, a star of the first magnitude, in the constellation Orion.

Beller'ophon, in palæontology, a genus of fossil shells found in the carboniferous limestone formation.

Bell-metal, in metallurgy, a metallic composition, consisting of 8 parts of copper and 2 of tin.—In small ringing bells, zinc is sometimes a constituent.

Bello'na, in astronomy, one of the recently discovered planets, first observed by Luther in 1854. Its mean distance from the sun is 264,650,000 miles.

Bel'lua (Lat. *bellua*, a large beast), in zoology, an order of Mammiferæ now comprehended under the Pachydermata of Cuvier's system.

Belly. In music, the *belly* of the harpsichord or piano-forte (as described by Dr. Busby) is that smooth thin boarding over which the strings are distended, and which, by its vibration, materially contributes to the tone. In a double bass, violoncello, violin, and all instruments performed on with the *bow*, it is that part of the body which lies immediately under the strings.

Belo'ne (Gr. *a needle*), in ichthyology, a sub-genus of the Pike family, one of which is known as the Needle or Garfish.

Belop'tera (Gr. *a winged javelin*), in geology, a genus of fossil shells, found in the London clay, with wing-shaped appendages.

Belos'toma (Gr. *belos* a javelin, and *stoma* a mouth), a genus of hemipterous insects, of the family Hydrocorisæ.

Belt, in astronomy, a name applied to certain zones seen to pass across the surface and parallel to the equator of the planet Jupiter.

Bel'vedere (Ital. *a fine view*), in Italian architecture, an ornamental erection at the top of a mansion, constructed for the purpose of obtaining an extensive view of the surrounding country.

Belvisia'ceæ, a nat. order of plants, of which *Belvisia cærulea* is the type, a plant which is loaded with large blue flowers, and grows about seven feet high.

Bembicid'eæ (Gr. *bembex* a top), a family of coleopterous insects, of which the Bembex, belonging to the Fossores, or burrowing wasps, is the type.

Ben Marca'to (Ital.), in music, an expression denoting that a passage is to be executed in a clear and pointed manner.

Ben Oil, an oil expressed from the decorticated seeds of *Guilandina moringa*, used in the manufacture of scented oils.

Bengal Lights, in pyrotechny, a species of firework, used as signals by night or otherwise, producing a steady and very vivid blue-coloured fire. The ingredients are 28 oz. of sulphur, 12 oz. of saltpetre, and 2½ oz. of realgar.

Ben'zamide, in chemistry, a compound of benzoic acid and amide, 1 atom each; it forms colourless transparent crystals.

Benzhy'dramide, in chemistry, a compound consisting of 42 atoms of carbon, 18 of hydrogen, and 2 of nitrogen.

Benzile, in chemistry, a compound consisting of 14 atoms of carbon, 5 of hydrogen, and 2 of oxygen.—*Hydrocyanite of benzile* is a chemical product obtained from a hot solution of benzine and prussic acid, forming large colourless crystals, and consisting of benzile and prussic acid, 1 atom each.—*Benzilic acid* is a compound consisting of 28 atoms of carbon, 11 of hydrogen, 5 of oxygen, and 1 of water.

Ben'zimede, in chemistry, an ingredient of the raw oil of bitter almonds, forming very white and flocky inodorous pearly needles and laminæ. It consists of carbon, hydrogen, oxygen, and nitrogen.

Benz'oate, in chemistry, a combination of benzoic acid with the metallic oxides.

Benzo'ic Ether, in chemistry, a colourless oily liquid, with a feeble aromatic smell and pungent taste.

Benzoin, in chemistry, a concrete resinous juice of the East Indian tree, *Styrax benzoin.*—*Flowers of benzoin* are white needle-like prisms, with a soft silky lustre and pungent taste.—*Hydrocyanite of benzoin* is a chemical product from a mixture of oil of bitter almonds, prussic acid, caustic potash, and alcohol.—*Benzoic acid* unites with the earthy and alkaline bases, and with the metallic oxides.

Benzole, or **Benzine**, in chemistry, a colourless liquid of agreeable odour, which freezes at 32° in a crystalline mass resembling loaf-sugar.

Benzone, in chemistry, a colourless oily liquid, which consists of 13 atoms of carbon, 5 of hydrogen, and 1 of oxygen.

Benzule, in chemistry, a compound obtained from the volatile oil of the bitter almond. It has various compounds; as, *Bromide of benzule*, 1 atom of benzule, and 1 of bromine; atomic weight = 185·03;—*Cyanogen of benzule*, 1 atom of benzule, and 1 of cyanogen; atomic weight = 133·07;—*Hydruret of benzule*, 1 atom of benzule, and 1 of hydrogen; atomic weight = 142·10;—*Iodide of benzule*, 1 atom of benzule, and 1 of iodine; atomic weight = 232·98;—*Sulphuret of benzule*, 1 atom of benzule, and 1 of sulphur; atomic weight = 122·78.

Berbera'ceæ, or **Berberid'eæ** (Arab.), in botany, a nat. order of exogenous plants, of which the Barberry is the type. It is an elegant shrub, which bears yellow flowers and red acid berries.—*Berberin* is the bitter principle, obtained from barberry and its root, and is extensively used in dyeing yellow.

Ber'gamite, in mineralogy, a variety of scapolite, found in Norway.

Ber'gamot, the fragrant fruit of the bergamot orange tree, from the rind of which an essential oil is obtained.

Bergmehl (Swed. *mountain meal*), in geology, a whitish, mealy-looking earth, containing infusorial animalcules.

Berme (Fr.), in fortification, a space of ground between the foot of the rampart and the side of the moat, to prevent the earth from falling down.

Ber'oë, in ichthyology, a genus of very minute radiated animals, with globular gelatinous bodies, remarkable for emitting a phosphoric light.

Ber'thierite (so called from Prof. Berthier, of Paris), a mineral found in lamellar masses, of a dark grey steel colour, and consisting of antimony, sulphur, iron, and zinc.

Beryl (Lat. *beryllus*), in mineralogy, a gem or precious stone.—The *aquamarina* is a beryl, which is transparent, and consists of silica, alumina, glucina, oxide of iron, and oxide of columbium.

Beryx, a genus of fishes, of the subfamily Percidæ, or Perches.

Ber'zeline, in mineralogy, the seleniuret of copper; also, surname of a mineral found in Italy.

Beta-or'ceine, a colouring matter obtained from the beet-root, composed of carbon, hydrogen, and protoxide of nitrogen.

Betel, an evergreen shrub of the East Indies, the *Piper betel*, the leaf of which forms a hot and acrid masticatory, in almost universal use in India and the Malayan Archipelago. It is aromatic and stomachic.—*Betel nut*, or *Areca*, is used in dyeing cottons.

Bethy'lus, in entomology, a genus of hymenopterous insects.—In ornithology, a genus of passerine birds.

Beton (Fr.), in the arts, a kind of concrete or hydraulic cement, mixed with gravel, pebbles, &c., and used in submarine works as a foundation.

Beton'ica, a genus of labiate plants (Betony), consisting of perennial deciduous herbs.

Betula'ceæ, or **Betulin'eæ** (Celtic *bes-the*), a division of the nat. order Amentaceæ, of which the Betula (including the alder and birch) is the type.

Bet'uline, in botany, a colourless resinous camphor (the *Betula nigra*), extracted from the bark of the black birch.

Beu'danlite, a mineral found associated with brown iron ore in the district of Nassau, and consisting of oxides of lead and iron.

Bezo'ar (Pers. *pashahar*, an antidote to poison), a concretion formed in the intestines of land animals, some of which were formerly celebrated for their supposed medicinal virtues. Those found in the intestines of herbivorous quadrupeds consist of the phosphate of ammonia and magnesia.

Bi (Lat. *bis* twice), in the language of science, a prefix to numerous terms, signifying twofold.

Bib'liolite (Gr. *bookstone*), in mineralogy, a species of schistous stones which present the figures of leaves or simple dendrites.

Bicar'bonate (Lat.), in chemistry, a carbonate containing two equivalents of carbonic acid to one of base.

Biceps (Lat. *two-headed*), in anatomy, applied to certain muscles.

Bichlo'ride (Lat.), in chemistry, a compound consisting of two equivalents of chlorine with one of another element.

Bichro'mate of Potash (Gr. *bis*, and *chroma* colour), a crystallized salt, the source of chrome pigments, obtained from chromate of iron, and used in dyeing and calico-printing.

Bicip'ital (Lat. *two-headed*), having two heads.

Bicus'pid (Lat. *double-pointed*), having two fangs or points.

Bidens (Lat.), having two teeth or prongs.

Bid'ery-ware, in commerce and the arts, a metallurgic compound, consisting of 16 parts of copper, 4 of lead, and 2 of tin, with a portion of spelter. Articles inlaid with gold and silver, and highly polished, are manufactured from it.

Bifid (Lat.), cleft in two parts.

Bif'orines, in natural history, a term applied to certain oval perforated sacs, consisting of two coats, found in the pulpy part of the leaves of some plants. When the biforine is placed in water, it discharges its spiculæ with considerable violence.

Bifur'cated (Lat.), divided into two prongs or forks.

Bignonia'ceæ (so called from M. Bignon), in botany, a nat. order of corolliflorous Exogens, of which the Bignonia, or Trumpet-flower, is the type. It consists of trees and shrubs, mostly climbing, and of great variety, with showy trumpet-shaped flowers, many of them of great beauty.

Biju'gate (Lat.), in botany, having two pairs of leaflets.

Bila'biate (Lat.), having two lips.

Bilat'eral (Lat.), having two sides.

Bile (Lat. *bilis*), in physiology, an animal secretion of a greenish-yellow colour and bitter taste, secreted from the blood, collected in the gall-bladder, and discharged into the lower end of the duodenum.

Biloc'ular (Lat.), containing two cells.

Bima'na (Lat. *two-handed*), in zoology, a term applied to the first order of the animal kingdom, consisting of the genus and species *Homo*, Man. In physical structure man is strikingly distinguished from the *Quadrumana*, which most nearly approach him, by many peculiarities, the chief of which are—the possession of hands on the fore limbs, with opposable thumbs; the structure of the pelvis and feet, by which he is enabled to support an upright position; the form of the teeth, and the adaptation of the organs of speech for articulate sounds; as also the superior magnitude of his brain, and the number of its convolutions. The normal varieties of man are—the Caucasian, the Mongolian, and the Negro. The anomalous races are—the Malayan, Polynesian, Australian, Tasmanian, the American Indian, and the Hyperborean.

Bima'nous (Lat.), having two hands; in zoology, applied to man.

Bimar'ginate (Lat. *bis*, and *margin*), in conchology, an epithet applied to shells which have a double margin as far as the lip.

Bime'dial (Lat. *bis*, and *media* middle), in mathematics, belonging to a quantity arising from two other quantities.

Bi'nary (Lat. *binarius* twofold).—*Binary arithmetic* is a kind of notation proposed by Leibnitz, in which, instead of the ten figures used in common arithmetic, and the progression from ten to ten, two only, 1 and 0, are employed.—*Binary theory of salts*, in chemistry, is a theory which supposes that oxygen salts are constituted on the same plan as chloride of sodium.

Binate (Lat. *bis*, and *natus* born), in botany, produced in twos; growing in couples.

Bin'ocle (Lat. *bis*, and *oculus* the eye), a dioptric telescope fitted with two tubes joined together.

Binoc'ular (Lat.), having two eyes; applied to optical instruments that have two apertures, so that both eyes may be used at the same time.

Bino'mial (Lat. *double-named*), in algebra, applied to a term consisting of two quantities joined by the sign + *plus*, or − *minus*.—The *binomial theory* is a formula by which a binomial quantity can be raised to any power, or for extracting any root of it.

Binox'ide (Gr. *bis*, and *oxygen*), in

chemistry, a term applied to the second degree of oxidation of a metal or other substance.

Bi'otine, a Vesuvian mineral, of a yellowish colour and brilliant lustre.

Bipapilla'ria (Lat. *bis*, and *papilla* a nipple), a genus of marine Mollusca.

Biped (Lat. *bis*, and *pedes* feet), in zoology, an animal with two feet, as man and a bird.

Bipelta'ta (Lat. *bis*, and *pelta* a shield), in ichthyology, a family of Crustaceans, of the order Stomapoda, in which the shell is divided into two shields, the interior one being very large.

Bipen'nate (Lat. *bis*, and *penna* a wing), in zoology, having two wings.

Bipes (Lat. *two-footed*), in ichthyology, a genus of eel-shaped reptiles.

Bipin'nate (Lat.), in botany, double pinnate; applied to compound leaves, of which the leaflets are pinnate.

Biquad'rate (Lat. *bis*, and *quadratus* square), in mathematics, the fourth part of a number on the square multiplied by the square; as $4 \times 4 = 16 \times 16 = 256$, the biquadratic power of 4.—*Biquadratic root*, the fourth root of any quantity; the square root of any number or quantity, marked $\sqrt[4]{}$.

Birds (Sax.) in ornithology, the general name for oviparous vertebrated animals of the feathered tribe (see *Aves*). The mandible of birds is naked and protracted. They are destitute of teeth, scrotum, womb, bladder, epiglottis, and diaphragm. Cuvier divided the Aves into the following orders:—Accipitres, Passerinæ, Scansoriæ, Gallinaceæ, Grallatoriæ, and Palmipedes, which are described in their respective places.

Biros'trites (Lat. *bis*, and *rostrum* a beak), in palæontology, a fossil two-beaked bivalve shell.

Biscutel'la (Lat. *bis*, and *scutella* a saucer), a genus of plants, the Bastard Mustard, of the order Cruciferæ.

Bisect (Lat. *bis*, and *seco* to cut), to divide into two equal parts.

Biser'rate (Lat.), doubly serrated.

Bish'opswort (Sax. *bisceop-wyrt*), in botany, a species of the umbelliferous genus, Honeywort.

Bismuth (Germ. *wismuth*), in mineralogy, a brittle metal of a reddish-white colour, and of lamellated structure. Its principal chemical compounds are, the protoxide and peroxide of bismuth, the chloride, bromide, and sulphuret of bismuth.—*Butter of bismuth* is the chloride of bismuth. —*Bismuth ores* are native or octahedral bismuth, bismuth ochre, pris-

matic bismuth glance, and needle ore, a kind of acicular bismuth.

Bison (Lat.), in zoology, a sub-genus of the ox (*bos*) which has never yet been tamed. The American bisons have huge heads, a conical hump between the shoulders, and a shaggy mane. The European bison still inhabits the extensive forests of Lithuania and the Caucasus.

Biston, in entomology, a genus of moths, of the family Geometridæ, several species of which are found in this country.

Bistort (Lat. *bistorta*), in pharmacy, an astringent medicine, obtained from the root of the *Polygonum bistorta*, or Snakeweed.

Bisul'cate (Lat.), cleft in two, cloven-footed.

Bisul'phate, Bisul'phuret, in chemistry, a sulphate, or sulphuret, having two equivalents of sulphur to one of base.

Biter'nate (Lat. *bis* and *terni*, three and three), in botany, a term applied to compound leaves.

Bitter (Sax. Swed. and Germ.), having a hot acrid taste, like wormwood.—In the sciences, *bitter* forms a prefix to numerous words connected with botany, chemistry, medicine, &c.; as, *Bitter-almonds*, of the order Amygdaleæ;—*Bitter-gourd*, a variety of cucumber, which has a bitter taste, and in medicine acts as a drastic purgative;—*Bitter-oak*, the *Quercus cerris*, of which there are numerous varieties;—*Bitter-salt*, the sulphate of magnesia (Epsom salts);—*Bittersweet*, a species of the nightshade, *Solanum dulcamara*;—*Bitterwort*, the British plant, *Genetiana amarella*.—*Bitter-spar*, in mineralogy, is a variety of dolomite, composed of carbonate of lime, carbonate of magnesia, a little iron, and manganese. —There are also many minor compounds, as *Bitter-apple*, *Bitter-ash*, *Bitter-bean*, *Bitter-cucumber*, *Bitter-damson*, &c.

Bitter Principle, in chemistry, a term applied to results of the action of nitric acid upon organized matter, of an intensely bitter taste.

Bitu'men (Lat. from Gr. *pitis* the pitch tree), a tar-like combustible substance, or mineral pitch, generally known by the name of *asphaltum*. It is a compound of carbon and hydrogen, and constitutes the inflammable principle of coal.—In science and the arts, the name is applied to a number of inflammable substances found in a liquid or viscid state, and known as naphtha, petroleum, mineral tar, maltha or mineral pitch, asphalt, elastic bitumen, and amber.—*Bitu-*

minous shale is an argillaceous or slaty clay, much impregnated with bitumen, common in the coal formation.—*Bituminous springs* are springs impregnated with petroleum, naphtha, &c., some of which, as in the United States and the Birman Empire, annually yield thousands of hogsheads, known by the name of *crystal oil*, and largely consumed in Europe and other parts of the world.

Bivalve (Lat. *double doors*), in conchology, having a shell of two valves, closing with a hinge.

Bizzar'ro (Ital.), in music, a term implying that the style of the movement to which it is prefixed is fantastical and irregular.

Black Flux, in metallurgy, a flux used in melting various metallic substances. It is made by deflagrating tartar with half its weight of potash; the substance remaining being a compound of the carbonate of potash and charcoal.

Black-lead, in mineralogy, a substance found in various rocks, especially in Cumberland, and much used for pencils, and for giving a metallic lustre to grates, &c. (See *Plumbago*).

Black Salt, in chemistry, a product of the muriate of soda, fused with a species of Myrobalan.

Black Spruce (Lat. *Abies nigra*), a valuable tree of N. America, the wood of which furnishes the spruce deals of commerce.

Black-wood (Lat. the *Dalbergia latifolia*), a valuable furniture wood, chiefly obtained from Malabar, and also from New South Wales.

Bladder (Sax. *blædr*), in anatomy, a membranous bag, situated between the pubis and the rectum in the male, and pubis and vagina in the female. Its use is to receive and retain the urine previous to its expulsion from the body by the urethra.

Blain (Sax. *blegan*), in farriery, an ulcerous distemper incident to horses. It is a bladder which grows at the root of the tongue, against the windpipe, and swells so as to stop the breath.

Blanching (Fr. *whitening*), a term of frequent use in the arts.—In horticulture, it is the art of rendering the stalks or leaves of plants white by covering them with earth, so as to exclude the action of light.—In metallurgy, *blanching* is the operation of covering iron plates with a thin coat or crust of tin.—In numismatics, it is the operation performed on the planchets of pieces of silver, to give them the requisite lustre.—*Blanching of copper* is done in various ways,

so as to make it resemble silver. *Blanchimeter* is an instrument used for ascertaining the bleaching power of chloride of lime and potash.

Blaste'ma (Gr. *a bud*), in botany, the axis of growth of an embryo.—In anatomy, the granular and gelatinous basis of the ovum.

Blas'toderm (Gr. *vital skin*), the seat of development of all parts of the body of birds; the granular membrane situated beneath the membrana vitelli of the ovum.

Blatta'ree, or **Blat'tidæ** (Lat.), a tribe of orthopterous insects, with five jointed tarsi, and wings folded longitudinally, the type of which is the Blatta, or Black-beetle.

Blechnum (Gr.) a genus of ferns, of the tribe Polypodium.

Ble'dius, a genus of beetles found commonly burrowing in wet clay or sand on the sea-coast; fam. Stenidæ.

Blende (Ger. *dazzling*), a term applied to minerals having a peculiar lustre.

Blen'nidæ (Gr. *blenna* mucus), a family of acanthopterygious fishes (the Blennies), belonging to the Marlcheeks, the type of which is the Blennius, divided by Cuvier into several sub-genera, remarkable for the slimy mucus with which their bodies are covered.

Blind'age, in military science, a temporary bomb-proof or splinter-proof roofing, constructed to afford cover to magazines, earthworks, &c.

Blocking, in architecture, a term applied to a course of stones, or bricks, erected on the upper part of a cornice, to form a termination.

Blood (Sax. *blod*), in anatomy and physical science, the red fluid which circulates in the veins and arteries of animals. The blood of vertebrated animals is red and warm; and, when allowed to cool, it separates into two substances, which in their component parts are nearly identical. According to the analyses of physiologists, the human blood consists of water, 780·145; fibrine, 2·100; colouring matter, 133·000; albumen, 65·090; crystalline fat, 2·430; oily matter, 1·310; extractive matter, 1·790; albuminate of soda, 1·265; alkaline chlorides, carbonates, phosphates, and sulphates, 8·370; carbonates of lime and magnesia, phosphates of lime, magnesia, and iron, peroxide of iron, 2·100; loss, 2·00 = 1000.

Blood-root, in botany, a small N. American plant, the *Sanguinaria Canadensis*, so termed from its roots yielding a red juice. It is called by the Indians *puccoon*, and by farriers *turmeric*.

Blood-running Itch, in farriery, a disease in horses, proceeding from an inflammation of the blood, by over-heating, hard riding, or too severe labour.

Blood-stone, in mineralogy, a green siliceous stone, classed among the gems; a variety of heliotrope spotted with jasper, as if with blood.

Blowpipe, in chemistry and mineralogy, an implement by which a small jet of air is directed into a flame, and that flame employed on a mineral substance to vitrify or fuse it. It is thus used by artists for the purpose of enamelling, and of softening and soldering small pieces of metal; by glass-blowers, in making thermometers and other glass instruments; and by chemists and mineralogists, in the examination of substances. Of late, this instrument has been greatly improved by the introduction of the self-acting or oxyhydrogen blowpipe.

Blue (Sax. *bleo*), in painting and the fine arts, one of the seven primary colours, which, mixed with red, produces purple, or with yellow makes green. The various shades of blue used in painting are—Prussian blue, Ultra-marine, Blue ashes, and Blue verditer.—Indigo forms the chief ingredient in blue used as a dye-stuff. *Prussian blue*, the ferrocyanate of peroxide of iron, prepared from bullocks' blood, carbonate of potash, sulphate of iron, and alum.—*Saxon blue* is sulphate of indigo.—*Blue verditer* is an impure carbonate of copper.—*Blue* is also a prefix to numerous compounds; as *Blue ointment*, or mercurial ointment; *Blue pill*, or mercurial pill; *Blue-stone*, or *blue vitriol*, the sulphate of copper; *Blue eye-water*, the solution of ammoniated copper.

Bluebell, in horticulture, a well-known beautiful British plant, with bell-shaped flowers, the *Campanula rotundifolia*.

Bluebottle, in botany, the annual plant *Centaurea cyanus*, which is frequently seen growing in our corn-fields.—In entomology, the common name of a species of dipterous insects, the *Musca vomitoria*.

Boa (Lat.), in herpetology, a genus of large prehensile-tailed serpents, with jaws capable of great dilatation.— The great *boa-constrictor*, when full-grown, is about thirty-five feet long.

Body (Sax. *bodig*), a term of frequent use in practical science.—In geometry, it is applied to any solid figure; and in physics it is a solid, extended, palpable substance of itself merely passive.—Among painters, the *colour*

is said to bear the *body* when, having been finely ground, it embodies with the oil in working, and does not separate from it.

Bog Moss, in botany, a genus of aquatic plants, the *Sphagnum palustre*, of the tribe Gymnostomi. The bogs, which are chiefly formed from the continued growth of this plant, are often of great depth, some of them having increased to eight feet in depth since the period of the Roman occupation of this country.

Bog Ore, in mineralogy, a species of iron ore formed in bogs or other places from the ore contained in chalybeate springs, and, in some instances, from the shields of infusoria.

Bohea (Chinese), an inferior kind of black tea, of which there are two sorts from China; the inferior, called Canton bohea, which is a mixture of coarse tea and the refuse of Congou; the better kind comes from the district of Bohea, in Fokien.

Boil (Sax. *bile*), in pathology, a swelling of a very painful inflammatory nature, sometimes as large as a pigeon's egg. It has always a central core, which suppurates, and eventually discharges its contents.

Boiler, in mechanical science, the vessel in which steam is engendered for propelling a steam-engine.

Boiling-point, in physics, the degree of temperature at which liquids are in a state of ebullition by heat. The boiling-point varies greatly for different substances, but is constant for the same under the same circumstances. Thus, of water the boiling-point is 212°; of alcohol, 176°; of ether, 96°; and of mercury, 66°.

Bole (Gr. *bolos* a clod), in mineralogy, a friable clayey slate or earth, usually coloured with oxide of iron. The kind called Armenian bole is used as tooth-powder, and as colouring to the sauce called the essence of anchovies. It consists of silica, alumina, and iron.— *Boletic acid* is an acid contained in the juice of the boletus.

Bole'tus, a species of fungi, of the mushroom kind, on which are the Boletobius and Boletophagus, the names of two extensive genera of beetles, which live on the boletus.

Bolo'gnian Stone, in mineralogy, a variety of the sulphate of barytes, found near Bologna, which, when powdered and heated with charcoal, shines in the dark.

Bol'sover Stone, in mineralogy, a yellow limestone, occurring at Bolsover, in Derbyshire. It is the stone of which the new Houses of Parliament are built.

Bolus (Lat.), in physiology, the mass formed by the food after mastication and insalivation, and thus prepared for its passage into the pharynx, is named the *alimentary bolus.* — In pathology, a form of medicine in which the ingredients are made up into a soft mass, larger than pills, to be swallowed at once.

Bomb (Teut.), in artillery or gunnery, a hollow ball or shell of cast-iron, filled with gunpowder or other combustible matter, to be thrown out from a mortar by means of a fuzee.—*Bomb-ketch* is a small vessel strongly constructed for the use of mortars at sea.—*Bomb-vessel* is a ship-of-war appointed for the bombardment of a town or place situated on the sea-coast.—*Bomb-chest* is a chest filled with combustibles for explosion underground.

Bomba'ceæ (Lat. *bombax* the cotton tree), a nat. order of dicotyledonous or exogenous plants, consisting chiefly of large tropical trees, with strong cotton-like flowers. From the quantity of cotton they produce they have been called cotton trees.

Bom'biates, a genus of salts, the combination of bombic acid with other bases.

Bombic (Gr. *bombyx*, the silk-worm), pertaining to the silk-worm.—*Bombic acid* is an acid obtained from the silk-worm, when in its chrysalis state.

Bombus, a genus of hymenopterous insects, with hairy bodies (the Humble Bees); fam. Apidæ.

Bomby'cidæ (Gr. *bombyx*, the silk-worm), a family of lepidopterous insects, chiefly distinguished by their possessing only rudimentary maxillæ; the caterpillars generally weave cocoons, as in the case of *Bombyx mori*, the silk-worm.

Bombycil'la (Gr.), a genus of birds, the type of the sub-family Bombycillinæ; a group of the Fruit-eaters, the Wax-chatterers.

Bond (Sax.), in architecture, the method of connecting different bodies together. — In masonry, or brickwork, the artistic disposition of stones or bricks in a building.—*Bond-stones* are stones used in uncoursed rubble work, having their length placed in the middle of the wall.—*Bond-timbers* are timbers placed in the horizontal direction in the walls of buildings, in tiers at certain distances apart, and on which the battens, laths, &c., are secured.

Bone (Sax. *ban*), in physiology and anatomy, the firm hard substance which forms the skeleton and supports the fabric of the higher orders of living animals. Bone is composed of solid cartilage, phosphate and carbonate of lime, phosphate of magnesia, and animal matter.—The office of bone, in the animal economy, is chiefly mechanical, and the mechanical purposes to which it is subservient require that it should be of different sizes and forms. In the human skeleton there are commonly enumerated 260 different bones, which present every variety of size and figure. Some are long and round, as the bones of the upper and lower extremities; others broad and flat, as the bones of the skull; and others short and square, as the separate bones that compose the vertical column. The bones may be enumerated under three different classes, with the English and the Latin names :—

1st. Of the BONES OF THE HEAD, which, including the teeth, are 55 in number, viz. :—

The frontal	*Os frontis*	1
The occipital	*Os occipitis*	1
The parietals	*Ossa parietalia*	2
The temporals	*Ossa temporum*	2
The sphenoid	*Os sphenoides*	1
The ethmoid	*Os ethmoides*	1
The nasal	*Ossa nasi*	2
The cheek	*Ossa malarum*	2
The lachrymal	*Ossa lacrymalia*	2
The upper jaw	*Ossa maxillaria superiora*	2
The lower jaw	*Os maxillare inferius*	1
The palatine	*Ossa palatina*	2
The turbinated	*Ossa turbinata*	2
	Vomer	1
The tongue bone	*Os hyoides*	1
The teeth	*Dentes*	32

To these may be added the proper BONES OF THE EAR, contained in the temporal bones :—

Mallei	2
Incudes	2
Stapedes	2
Orbicularia	2

2nd. The BONES OF THE TRUNK, of which there are 56 in number, viz. :—

Spine bones	*Vertebræ*	24
The ribs	*Costæ*	24
Breast bone	*Sternum*	1
Hip bone	*Ossa innominata*	2
Rump bone	*Os sacrum*	1
Coccygeal bones	*Ossa coccygis*	4

3rd. The BONES OF THE EXTREMITIES, of which there are 132, viz. :—

Collar bones	*Claviculæ*	2
Blade bones	*Scapulæ*	2
Arm bones	*Ossa humeri*	2
Fore-arm bones	*Radii et ulnæ*	4

Wrist bones	. . *Ossa carpi* . . .	16
Hand bones	. . *Ossa metacarpi* .	8
Finger bones	. . *Phalanges* . . .	24
Thumb bones	. . *Ossa pollicis* . .	6
Sesamoid bones	. *Ossa sesamoidea* .	4
Thigh bones	. . *Ossa femoris* . .	2
Knee pans	. . . *Patella*	2
Shin bones	. . . *Tibia*	2
Small leg bones	. *Fibula*	2
Tarsal bones	. . *Ossa tarsi* . . .	14
Metatarsal bones	*Ossa metatarsi* .	10
Toe bones	. . . *Phalanges* . . .	28
Sesamoid bones	. *Ossa sesamoidea*	4

Bone-dust, Bone-earth, and Bone-phosphate, in agriculture, very useful manures, from their containing the phosphate of lime, which is one of the necessary ingredients of nutritive vegetation, particularly of the cereal crops.

Boni'to (Sp.), in ichthyology, a long marine fish, remarkable for its persecution of the flying-fish and flying-squid; fam. Scomberidæ.

Bo'ops, in ichthyology, a genus of acanthopterygious fishes, of the family Chætodon. It is also the specific name of the Jubarta (*Balæna boöps*), a whale about fifty feet long, which inhabits the Greenland seas.

Boo'tes (Gr. *bous* an ox), in astronomy, a constellation of the northern hemisphere, which contains 39 stars. On the celestial globes, Boötes is represented with a club in one hand and the two dogs, *Canes venatici*, held by a string in the other.

Boragin'eæ (Lat. *borago* action of the head), in botany, a nat. order of flowering monopetalous Endogens, of which the plant Boragos is the type.

Boras'sus (Gr.), in botany, the Fan Palm, a genus of the Palm-tree tribe with gigantic leaves, and fruit as large as a child's head. The Hindoos consider it the king of trees.

Borate, in chemistry, a salt consisting of boracic acid with a basis, as Borate of lime, Borate of magnesia, Borate of soda, &c. (See *Borax*.)

Borax (Gr.), in chemistry, a compound of boracic acid and soda, the principal use of which is as a flux in the operations of the blowpipe.—*Boracic acid* is a compound of boron and oxygen, which occurs as a natural product in the hot springs of Lipari, and other places, and is a constituent of various minerals.—*Boracite* is a native borate of magnesia.—*Boraxated tartar* is a compound of borax with crystals of bitartrate of potash.

Bor'eal (Gr. *boreas* the north wind), in natural philosophy, applied to a pole of a magnet which points to the north.

Boril'la, a rich copper ore, in dust.

Boring, in mineralogy, a method of piercing the earth, so as to ascertain the extent of any mineral bed or vein rich enough to be worth sinking a shaft.—The same operation is undertaken in boring for water.

Bornine, in mineralogy, a name given to telluric bismuth, a mineral of light steel-grey colour and metallic lustre, occurring in crystalline masses, and composed of tellurium, bismuth, sulphur, and silver; sp. gr. 7·2—8·0.

Bornite, a tellurite of bismuth.—*Dana.*

Boron, in mineralogy, one of the elementary substances; the base of boracic acid. It is of a dark olive colour, without taste or smell. It bears intense heat in close vessels without fusing. Its specific gravity is about twice that of water. If heated to 600°, it suddenly takes fire, oxygen gas disappears, and boracic acid is generated. — *Boro-fluorides* are compounds formed by the union of the fluorides of boron, or fluoboric acid gas, with either potassium, sodium, or borium.—*Boro-hydrofluoric acid* is a compound of the boracic and fluoric acids.

Bos (Lat. *an ox*), in zoology, a genus of Mammalia, of which the domestic ox, the buffalo, bison, &c., are species; order Ruminantia.

Boschus (Lat.), in ornithology, a genus of the Anatinæ, or Duck family.

Bostric'hidæ (Gr. *bostrychus* a lock of hair), a family of wood-boring coleopterous insects, of which the Bostrychus, which is very destructive to timber, is the type.

Boswel'lia, a genus of East Indian trees, the Olibanum, one of the species of which, *B. thurifera*, yields the gum resin olibanum, the frankincense of the ancients, and now used in Catholic churches; order Terebinthaceæ.

Bot'any (Gr. *botane* a plant), that branch of natural science which comprehends all that relates to the vegetable kingdom. In the classification of the botanical nomenclature there are two principal systems—the sexual or artificial one of Linnæus, and that of Jussieu, which is according to the natural order of plants. The Linnæan system is founded on the number, situation, and proportion of the essential organs of fructification, denominated stamens and pistils. The names of the classes and orders are of Greek derivation, and allude to the functions of the respective orders. Thus the vegetable kingdom is divided by that great naturalist into 24 classes, of which 23 belong to flowering, and 1 to flowerless plants. The first eleven classes are distinguished entirely by the number of stamens, which are called Monandria, Diandria, Triandria, &c., as far as Dodecandria, from the Greek words one, two, three, &c. combined with male (*andria*), because the stamens of flowers are compared to males, and the pistils to females. Hence the orders, as far as Polygynia, are denominated Monogynia, Digynia, Trigynia, &c., according as the flower has one or more pistils; so called from the Greek *mone* (one), and *gune* (a female). Thus the jasmine, having two stamens and one pistil, is placed in the second class of the first order of that class, or Diandria Monogynia.—The following is a summary of the 24 classes, which owe their distinctions chiefly to the stamens and pistils:—1. Monandria, one stamen.—2. Diandria, two stamens.—3. Triandria, three.—4. Tetrandria, four.—5. Pentandria, five.—6. Hexandria, six.—7. Heptandria, seven.—8. Octandria, eight.—9. Enneandria, nine.—10. Decandria, ten.—11. Dodecandria, twelve.—12. Icosandria, twenty or more stamens, inserted into the calyx.—13. Polyandria, all above twenty inserted into the receptacle.—14. Didynamia, four stamens, two long and two short.—15. Tetradynamia, six stamens, four long and two short.—16. Monadelphia, the stamens united into the bodies by the filaments.—17. Diadelphia, the stamens united into the bodies by the filaments.—18. Polyadelphia, the stamens united into three or more bodies by the filaments.—19. Syngenesia, anthers united into a tube.—20. Gynandria, stamens inserted either upon the style or germen.—21. Monœcia, stamens and pistils in separate flowers, but on the same plant.—22. Diœcia, stamens and pistils, like the former, in separate flowers, but on two separate plants.—23. Polygamia, stamens and pistils separate in some flowers, united in others, either on one, two, or three distinct plants. — 24. Cyptogamia, stamens and pistils either not well ascertained, or not to be numbered with certainty.

The *Natural System of Plants*, as devised by Jussieu and De Candolle, differs most materially from the Linnæan System; it takes into consideration the entire organization of the plant, with its properties and peculiar habits. The most striking genus of a tribe of plants gives name to the order; as, for instance, the Rose (Lat. *rosa*), forms the type of the natural order Rosaceæ; and the Violet, that of the order Violaceæ. In this manner Jussieu divided the whole vegetable kingdom into 15 classes, and the genera into 100 orders, but which number has been gradually increasing with the general progress of discovery. The difference between the artificial system of Linnæus and natural order of Jussieu has been admirably illustrated by our distinguished countryman, Professor Lindley, in his work on the "Vegetable Kingdom."

In the Natural System the vegetable world has been classified under two grand divisions — the VASCULARES and the CELLULARES; and these again divided into classes and sub-classes.

VASCULARES. Class I. *Dycotyledons* or *Exogens*.—The plants of this class have stems consisting of concentric layers, formed by external annual additions, and are composed of vascular and cellular tissue; the flowers are furnished with male and female organs of reproduction, called stamens and pistils.—Class II. *Monocotyledons* or *Endogens*. The stems of this class are formed by the addition of new fibres to the interior of the stem already formed; flowers sexual, the seed consisting of one cotyledon.

CELLULARES. Class I. *Semi-vasculares*. Plants having vessels as well as cellular tissue; the stems are increased by simple elongation; the leaves veined and forked; the sexual organs distinct and visible under the microscope only. — Class II. The *Agamæ* are plants which increase by elongation or irregular expansion of their parts, and are wholly composed of cellular tissue, showing, under the microscope, no sexual organs whatever. These consist of the Fungi, Mosses, Lichens, Hepaticas or Liverworts, and Algæ. The Dicotyledons are divided into four sub-classes—the Thalamifloræ, Calycifloræ, Corollifloræ, and Monochlamydeæ.

Botryoi'dal (Gr.), resembling a bunch of grapes.

Boulders, in geology, fragments of rock embedded in diluvial deposits; sometimes found lying on the surface of the ground, and bearing marks of abrasion and transport.—*Boulder formations* are deposits of clay, gravel, &c., containing boulders, or fragments of triturated rocks.

Boustrophe'don (Gr. *ox-ploughing*), an ancient form of writing from right to left, and from left to right, like ploughing.

Bovey Coal, a species of wood-coal, or lignite, found at Bovey, near Exeter.—Lignites are chiefly found in rocks of tertiary formation. Their constituents are carbon, oxygen, and earthy matter.

Bo'vidæ (Lat. *boves* oxen), in zoology, a tribe of Ruminants, of which the genus Bos is the type.

Bow-line, in practical navigation, a term applied to a rope fastened near the middle of the perpendicular edge of the principal square sails; its use is to make the sails stand sharp and close to the wind.

Bow-pen, in the arts, a metallic ruling pen, the part holding the ink being formed of two cheeks bowed out towards the middle.

Box (Sax.), in botany, the common name of the Euphorbian genus of plants, the Buxus, or Box tree.—*Box-thorn*, the English name of the genus of plants Lycium.—*Box-wood*, the fine-grained wood of the box tree, extensively used in wood engraving, and the manufacture of various articles.—*Boxing the compass* is repeating the various points of the compass in order.

Boyau (Fr.), in fortification, a trench made by a besieging army, to serve as a covered line of communication or approach during the siege.

Brachely'tra (Gr. *brachys* short, and *elytron* a sheath), in entomology, a section of coleopterous insects or beetles, the Staphylinus of Linnæus.

Brachi'nus (Gr. *noise-making*), in entomology, a genus of coleopterous insects or beetles, so called from the noise they make in discharging an acrid fluid.

Brach'ionus (Gr. *brachion* an arm), a genus of rotiferous Infusoria, of which there are several genera.

Brach'iopods (Gr. *brachion*, and *podes* feet), in malacology, a class of bi-valved Mollusca, which, instead of feet, are furnished with two fleshy arms provided with numerous filaments.

Brachyglot'tis (Gr. *short-tongued*), in botany, a genus of garden plants of the order Compositæ.—*Brachys*, signifying short, forms a prefix to various scientific words connected with botany, zoology, ichthyology, mineralogy, &c.; as *Brachyrynchus*, a greenhouse plant;—*Brachytype*, a variety of calcareous spar;—*Brachytypous*, in mineralogy, of a short form;—*Brachyurus*, short-tailed, applied to a tribe of Crustaceæ, comprehending the Crabs, Lobsters, &c.

Brach'ium (Lat. *the arm*), among the Mammalia, that part which articulates with the scapula, and extends to the elbow; the *os humeri* of anatomy.—In entomology, the brachia are the first pair of legs in hexapod insects.

Bra'dypods (Gr. *slow-footed*), in zoology, a family of edentate mammals, including the two-toed and three-toed sloths.—*Brande*.

Brain (Sax. *bragan*), in physiology, the soft, whitish mass enclosed in the cavity of the skull, in which the nerves and spinal marrow terminate. It is divided into three parts—the cranium, or proper brain, which occupies the whole of the superior part of the cavity; the cerebellum, occupying the lower and back part of the cavity; and the medulla oblonga, situated at its base, beneath the cerebrum and cerebellum.

Bramah Lock, in mechanical science, an ingeniously-contrived lock, invented by him whose name it bears.—The *Bramah press* is constructed on hydrostatic principles by the same inventor.

Bran'chiæ (Lat.), in ichthyology, the gills or respiratory organs of fishes and other aquatic animals.

Branchif'eræ (Lat. *branchiæ*), in malacology, a family of Mollusca, including various genera, as the Fissurella, the Emarginula, and the Parmophorus.

Branchi'opods (Lat. *branchiæ*, and *podes* feet), an order of crustaceous animals with gills and feet. They are chiefly microscopic, and always in motion.

Branchios'tegens (Lat. *branchiæ*, and Gr. *stegos* a cover), an order of fishes with gills free, and covered with a membrane.

Bras'sica (Lat.), a genus of cruciferous plants, comprising the cabbage, cauliflower, broccoli, turnip, &c.

Braunite, a mineral of a dark brown colour, occurring massive and crystallized, and consisting of protoxide of manganese, oxygen, baryta, and water.

Bravou'ra (Ital. *courage*), in music, an air consisting of difficult passages, in which many notes are executed in one syllable.

Braxy (Sax. *broc* disease), a disease or scouring in sheep; the most virulent form of anthrax, which kills upwards of fifty per cent. of the sheep that annually die of disease in Scotland.—*Report of the Privy Council on Diseases of Cattle*.

Brazil, Brazilet'to, a kind of wood used for dyeing and for cabinet-work, brought from Brazil.

Brazil-wood, the heavy red-coloured wood of *Cæsalpinia Braziliensis*, used as a dye-stuff.

Brazil'ian Pebbles, pure rock-crystal lenses for eye-glasses and spectacles.

Brazing, in metallurgy, the soldering together of metals by means of an alloy, of which brass forms the principal ingredient.

Bread-fruit, the fruit of the *Artocarpus incisa* of the South Sea Islands.

Bread-nut, the fruit of the *Brosimum alicastrum,* a native of the West Indies.

Bread-root, the tuberous-rooted plant, *Psoralea esculenta,* of N. America, which produces abundant crops of roots, used like the potato in this country.

Brec'cia (Ger. *brechen* to break), in mineralogy, a species of rock composed of angular fragments cemented together ; a kind of pudding-stone.

Breis'lakite, a fibrous mineral found in the lavas of Vesuvius, which occurs in delicate capillary crystals and semi-metallic lustre.

Breve (Fr. and Ital.), in music, a note equal to four minims.

Brevipen'nes (Lat. *short-winged*), a term applied by Cuvier to the first family of the order Grallæ, of which the ostrich or emu is the type, whose wings are too short for flight.—In natural history, the word *brevis* (short) forms a prefix to numerous terms of a scientific character ; as, *brevicaudatus,* short-tailed ; *brevicaulis,* short-stemmed ; *brevicollis,* short-necked; *brevicornis,* short-horned; *brevidens,* short-toothed ; *breviflorus,* short or small-flowered, having small petals ; *brevifolius,* short or small-leaved ; *breviped,* short-footed ; *brevipennate,* short-winged ; *brevirostris,* or *brevirostrated,* short-billed ; *breviscapus,* short-stalked ; *brevisetus,* short-bristled ; *brevistylus,* short-styled ; *breviventris,* having a short abdomen.

Brev'isite, a white zeolitic mineral.

Bristol Stone, or **Bristol Diamond,** in mineralogy, a kind of rock crystal, a transparent variety of quartz, consisting of pure silica, so named from being found in a rock near Bristol.

Brisure (Fr.), in fortifications, a line of four or five fathoms, which is allowed to the curtain and crillon, to make the hollow tower, or to cover the concealed flank.

Britan'nia Metal, in the arts, a sort of mixed metal of which the best tea-pots are manufactured. It is made by melting an equal weight of plate-brass and tin, and when melted, adding the same quantities of bismuth and regulus of antimony.

Bromal, in chemistry, an oily colourless fluid, obtained by the action of bromine on alcohol.

Bromate, in chemistry, a salt formed by the combination of bromic acid with any salifiable base.

Brombenzo'ic Acid, an acid prepared from dry benzoate of silver and bromine.

Bromelia'ceæ, a nat. order of endogenous plants, of which the *Bromelia ananas,* or Pine-apple, is the type.

Bromic Acid, in chemistry, an acid consisting of 5 equivalents of oxygen and 1 of bromine. It reddens, and then destroys the colour of litmus paper. Its equivalent is 118·4.

Bromine (Gr. *a stench*), in chemistry, a substance obtained from the crystallizable residue of sea-water, called *bittern.* It is one of the elementary bodies, and about three times heavier than water. It corrodes the skin, stains it of a yellow colour, and is a powerful and dangerous poison. Bromine unites with iodine, hydrogen, sulphur, phosphorus, and selenium, as well as with many of the metals, forming compounds called bromides, among which are the following :— *Hydrobromic acid,* 1 atom of bromine, and 1 of hydrogen ;—*Bromic acid,* 1 atom of bromine, and 5 of oxygen ;— *Protobromide of phosphorus,* 1 atom of bromine, and 1 of phosphorus ;— *Perbromide* of *phosphorus,* 5 atoms of bromine, and 2 of phosphorus.

Bromus (Gr. *the wild oat*), in botany, the Brome-grass, an extensive genus of the order Gramineæ, or Grass tribe.

Bron'chia, or **Bronchi** (Gr. *bronchos* the windpipe), in anatomy, the ramifications of the windpipe, or trachea, which pass into the lungs.— *Bronchitis* is an inflammation of the bronchia.—*Bronchocele,* an enlargement of the thyroid gland.—*Bronchotomy,* an incision made into the trachea.

Bronze (Ital. and Fr.), in metallurgy, a red-brown metal, compounded of copper and tin, harder and more fusible than copper, and highly malleable when it contains from 85 to 90 per cent. of copper. Bronze for cannon is composed of 90 copper, and 10 of tin. English bell-metal, according to Dr. Thompson, consists of copper 80, tin 10·1, zinc 5·6, lead 4·3 = 100. Reflectors for telescopes consist of 66 parts of copper, and 33 parts of tin. Bronze for medals is formed of 100 copper, and 7 to 11 of tin and zinc.—*Bronzing salt* is chloride of antimony, so called from its being used in browning gun barrels, &c.—*Bronze liquid* is made by melting 14 ounces of vinegar, 2 drachms of sal-ammoniac, and half a drachm of sorrel (binoxalate of potash).—A liquid to imitate antique bronze is made by dissolving 1 part of sal-ammoniac, 3 parts of cream of tartar, and 6 of common salt in 12 parts of hot water, mixing with the solution 8 parts of a strong solution of the nitrate of copper.

Bronzite (from *bronze*), a mineral of a yellowish-brown colour, with a semi-metallic lustre, consisting of silica, magnesia, and oxide of iron.

Broom (Sax. *brom*), in botany, the common English name of the genus Spartium. The *Spartium scoparius* is a beautiful yellow-flowering leguminous shrub, of the sub-tribe Genista.

Brown Bess, in military art, a musket with a brown barrel and smooth bore, distinguished from the rifle.

Bruchus (Gr. *a grinding with the teeth*), in anatomy, a genus of insects of the family Rhynchophora, the females of which deposit their eggs in the seeds of leguminous plants, which on coming to maturity are devoured by the larva, where it undergoes its metamorphosis.

Brunia'ceæ (so named from M. Brun), a nat. order of ericaceous shrubs, with small pretty flowers, extremely ornamental in gardens.

Brunonia'ceæ (so called from R. Brown, the distinguished botanist), a nat. order of monopetalous Exogens, of which the Brunonia, a genus of Australian plants, is the type.

Brunswick Green, in the arts, a colouring obtained from submuriate of copper, by exposing metallic copper to the action of muriate of ammonia.

Bruta (Lat. *brutish things*), in zoology, an order of Mammalia according to Linnæus, but now constituting the Edentata of Cuvier, as the elephant, walrus, &c.

Bryo'nia (Gr. *sprouting out*), a genus of climbing plants, the Bryony, or wild hop.

Bry'onin, a crystallizable substance obtained from white bryony.

Bryophyl'lum (Gr. *a sprouting leaf*), a yellow flowering shrub, whose leaves possess the remarkable property of budding on their margins, and forming new plants, a property not possessed by any other plant.

Bryozo'a, or **Bryozoa'ria** (Gr. *bryon* moss, and *zoon* an animal), the minute Mollusca that live united in masses in a moss-like manner.

Bubo (Gr. *the groin*), in pathology, a swelling of the lymphatic glands, arising from syphilitic virus.—In ornithology, the horned owl.

Buccina'tor (Lat.), the large muscle of the cheek, so called from its use in blowing wind instruments.

Buc'cinite (Lat. *a horn*), in geology, fossil remains of shells, called Buccinum.

Buccinoi'dia (Lat. and Gr. *like a trumpet*), in malacology, a form of pectino-branchiate Gasteropods, of which Buccinum, a genus of bivalved Mollusca, is the type.

Bu'ceros (Gr. *ox-horned*), in ornithology, a genus and family of birds (Buceridæ) remarkable for their enormous bills.

Buchol'zite, an amorphous mineral, spotted black and white, consisting of silica, alumina, potash, and oxide of iron.

Buchu Leaves, the produce of a species of Barosma, of the Cape Colony, of an aromatic smell, and highly esteemed for their diuretic properties.

Buckland'ia (in honour of Dr. Buckland), a fossil plant from the Stonefield oolite.

Buck'landite, in mineralogy, a rare variety of augite, which occurs in minute crystals in the lake of Laach, on the Rhine.

Buckwheat (Germ. *buchweizen*), the *Polygonum fagopyrum*.

Buf'falo (Ital. and Sp.), in zoology, the *Bos bubalus*, a species of ox domesticated in India and Italy.

Bufoi'dæ (Lat. *bufo*), a family of amphibious reptiles, of which Bufo, a toad, is the type.

Bu'fonite (Lat. *bufo*), fossil teeth of fishes occurring in the oolitic formation of the Pycnodont family.

Buhl, in the arts, mother-of-pearl, gold, or other rich material used for inlaying.

Bu'limus (Lat.) a genus of land Mollusca.

Bu'limy (Gr. *hunger*), voracious appetite.

Bulla (Lat.), a genus of Mollusca belonging to the Sea-slugs; nat. order Bulladæ.

Bullate, in conchology, applied to a shell which is cylindrical and oval.—In botany, having a blistered-like appearance.

Bulli'næ, a sub-family of Mollusca, the Bullas.

Bull's-eye, in astronomy, the bright star Aldebaran, in the constellation Taurus.

Buni'adæ (Gr. *a hill*), a fam. of plants, of which Bunias is the type; order Cruciferæ.

Bunter (Ger.), in geology, a term applied to the new red sandstone.

Buphthal'mia (Gr. *ox-eyed*), in pathology, dropsy of the eye, hydrophthalmia.

Bupres'tidæ (Gr. *bous* an ox, and *pretho* to cause to swell), a family of coleopterous insects, richly coloured with metallic shades of green and blue; the genus Buprestes is the type of the family.

Burette (Fr.), in chemistry and assaying, an instrument for dividing a portion of liquid into decimal parts.

Bur'gundy Pitch, the juice of the *Pinus abies*, chiefly used in pharmacy as a plaster on the chest for coughs, &c.

Burman'niæ, in botany, a nat. order of epigynous Exogens; herbaceous plants, with tufted radicles.

Burrh Stone, in mineralogy, pure silex, used as mill-stone.

Bursæ Muco'sæ, in anatomy, mucus bags, or small sacs, situated about the joints.

Bursa'ria (Lat. *a pouch*), in entomology, a genus of Infusoria.

Bursera'ceæ, a nat. order of calyciflorous Exogens, of which the Bursera is the type; they consist chiefly of trees and shrubs, which abound in balsamic resin.

Bus'tamite, a mineral occurring in prismatic crystals of a pale grey-greenish or reddish colour. It consists of silica, protoxide of manganese, lime, and protoxide of iron.

Buteoni'næ, a sub-family of the Falconidæ (the Buzzards), of slender form, with long wings; order Raptores.

But'yrates, a genus of salts, formed by the combination of butyric acid with salifiable bases.—*Butyric acid* is an acid existing in butter, urine, and the gastric juice, composed of 8 atoms of carbon, 3 of oxygen, and 6 of hydrogen.

Buxus (Gr.), in botany, a genus of plants, the box tree.—*Buxus sempervirens* is one of the most useful of evergreen shrubs. The dwarf variety is used almost universally as a border-edging in the gardens of Europe.

Byrr'hidæ, in entomology, a family of clavicorn coleopterous insects, of which Byrrhus is the type. It includes a number of genera, the larvæ of some of which are very destructive in our museums, by feeding on the skins of birds, preserved insects, &c.

Byssa'ceæ (Gr. and Lat. *byssus* fine flax), a tribe of cryptogamic plants, including, among others, the genus Rhizomorpha, a phosphorescent, fibrous, silky-looking plant, often of great beauty, found in mines and dark places, and frequently on decayed wood.

Bys'sifera, a family of acephalous Mollusca, including those bivalves which, like the mussel, &c., are attached to foreign substances by a byssus.

Bys'solite (Gr. *byssos*, and *lithos* a stone), a mineral of a fibrous, silklike texture, existing in the Alpine mountains.

Byssus (Gr. *fine flax*), a bunch of silklike fibres, by which many bivalves adhere to other substances without the shell itself being deprived of the power of locomotion; as the pinna, the pearl, and hammer oyster.

Byttnera'ceæ, a nat. order of plants, of which Byttneria is the type, consisting of trees and shrubs, chiefly tropical.

C.

Cabacal'li (Sp.), a wood of British Guiana, which is impregnated with a bitter principle that protects it against the ravages of worms.

Cabbage-palm, a genus of palm trees, the Areca. — *Cabbage-wood* is the wood of the cabbage-palm, sometimes used in the manufacture of cabinet-work.

Cabbling, in metallurgy, a process by which flat masses of iron are broken into pieces, and after being reheated are wrought into bar-iron.

Cabomba'ceæ, in botany, a nat. order of hypogynous Exogens, the Watershields, consisting of aquatic plants, allied to the Water-lilies.

Cach'alot, in ichthyology, a genus of Cetacea, the Sperm whale.

Cachex'y (Gr.), in pathology, a bad state of body, arising from scurvy, syphilis, or other disorder.

Cach'olong, in mineralogy, a milk-white calcedony.

Cacoo'hymy (Gr. *bad chyme*), in pathology, an unhealthy state of the fluids of the body.

Cac'odyl (Gr. *ill-smelling*), a preparation of volatile arsenic, which produces a liquor of very fetid odour.

Cacoon, a commercial name for the seeds of the *Entada gigalobium*, used for making scent-bottles, purses, &c.

Cacoph'ony (Gr. *kakos* bad, and *phone* sound), a harshness of sound in the tones of music, or pronunciation of words.—In medicine, a depraved or altered state of the voice.

Cacoplas'tic (Gr. *kakos*, and *plasso* to form), in physiology, having a defective organization.

Cacta'ceæ (Gr.), a nat. order of epigynous Exogens, of which the Cactus is the type.

Cactus (Gr. so named by Theophrastus), a genus of pretty flowering plants, the Melon-thistle or Indian Fig of America, which comprehends a vast number of genera and species; order Cactaceæ.

Cadaver'ic (Lat. *cadaver* a corpse), in anatomy, a term applied to the venom which exudes from a dead body, and which often proves fatal to those who happen to wound themselves by the instrument used in the dissection of a human body.

Caden'za (Ital.), a musical cadence; the modulation of the voice in singing.

Cad'mia, a mineral; the recrement of copper; an oxide of zinc, which collects on the sides of furnaces when zinc is sublimed.

Cad'mium (Lat. *brass ore*), a white metal found among the ores of zinc, having a strong resemblance to tin, but harder; sp. gr. 8·6. It has various compounds; as, *Oxide of cadmium*, consisting of 1 atom of cadmium = 55·8 + 1 of oxygen = 8, making its atomic weight = 63·8;—*Chloride of cadmium*, 1 atom of cadmium and 1 of chlorine = 35·42; atomic weight = 91·22;—*Iodide of cadmium*, 1 atom of cadmium and 1 of iodine = 126·3; atomic weight = 182·1;—*Sulphuret of cadmium*, 1 atom of cadmium and 1 of sulphur = 16·1; atomic weight = 71·9.

Cæcum (Lat. *cæcus* blind), in anatomy, a tube with a closed end, especially applied to a part of the intestinal canal.

Caen Stone, a fine white stone brought from Normandy, much used in Gothic structures.

Cænozo'ic (Gr. *new life*), in geology, a term applied to the tertiary strata, which include the most recent remains of animal life.

Cæsalpin'ieæ, a sub-order of leguminous plants, of which Cæsalpinia is the type.

Cæsa'rian Operation, a term in surgery, applied to the operation of cutting a child out of the womb when the life of the mother is in danger, so called from Julius Cæsar having been thus brought into existence.

Caffe'in, a bitter substance obtained from coffee and tea. It is composed of 8 atoms of carbon, 3 of hydrogen, 2 of nitrogen, and 2 of oxygen.

Cain'ca Acid, in chemistry, an acid obtained from the root of the cainca, a Brazilian plant, used in intermittent fevers.

Cairngorm, in mineralogy, a variety of topaz, or rock crystal, obtained from a mountain in Perthshire, Scotland.

Caisson, in military science, a chest in which bombs, gunpowder, &c., are placed, for the purpose of explosion. —In civil engineering, a wooden frame used in laying the foundation of bridges.

Caj'aputi, an East Indian tree, the *Melaleuca cajaputi*, from the leaves of which the volatile oil cajeput is obtained.

Cal'abash, a tree, the *Crescentia cujete*, inhabiting the tropical parts of America, and bearing a gourd-like fruit, filled with a sourish pulp, eaten by the negroes; the shells are used as bottles for holding liquids; order Crescentiaceæ.

Caladi'eæ, in botany, a family of plants belonging to the nat. order Araceæ, of which the Caladium is the type.

Cal'amine (Lat.), in mineralogy, a native carbonate of zinc; when reduced to a powder by roasting it is called *calamina preparata*.

Cal'amite, a species of mineral, hornblende. In geology, a species of fossil plants, occurring in the coal formation.

Cal'amus (Gr. *a reed*), in botany, a genus of East Indian palms, one species of which attains a height of 500 feet. A sort of sweet-scented calamus, used as a perfume, is mentioned in Scripture (Exod. xxx. 23).—The Sweet Flag (*Acorus calamus*) is a British species of the Aroideæ, growing in pools.—In anatomy, *Calamus scriptorius* is a groove with a pen-like termination, situated in the fourth ventricle.—In zoology, Calamus is a genus of fishes belonging to the Chætodon family; sub-family Sparianeæ.

Calan'dra, in entomology, a genus of coleopterous insects, one species of which, *C. granaria*, in the larva state, is very destructive in our granaries; another species, *C. oryræ*, attacks rice; fam. Rhynchophora.

Cal'carate (Lat.), similar to or having a spur.

Calca'reo-argilla'ceous (Lat. *calx* chalk, and Gr. *argil* whiteness), in mineralogy, consisting of lime and clay.

Calca'reo-sili'ceous (Lat. *calx*, and *silex* flint), consisting of lime and silex.

Calca'reo-sul'phurous, having lime and sulphur in combination.

Cal'cedon, with jewellers, a foul vein, like calcedony, occurring in some precious stones.

Calced'onite, a mineral of a bright green or bluish colour, found at Leadhills in Scotland.

Calced'ony (from *Chalcedon* in Asia), in mineralogy, a hard precious stone, composed of 84 parts of silica and 16 of alumina, frequently botryoidal or stalactitic, generally semi-transparent, and of various colours. Its varieties are agate, onyx, plasma, heliotrope, and cornelian.

Calceola'ria (Lat. *a slipper*), a genus of plants from S. America, the Slipperwort, extensively cultivated as garden flowers; order Scrophulariaceæ.

Calcifica'tion (Lat. *calx* chalk, and *facio* to make), in chemistry, a hardening by the deposition of salts of lime.—*Calcify* is to change into lime.

Calcina'tion (Lat. *calx*), in chemistry, the process of subjecting a body to an intense degree of heat, to drive off its volatile parts. The fixed residues of such bodies as have undergone combustion are termed calces, or more generally oxides.

Calci'ner, in mineralogy, the name of a furnace where minerals are pulverized by heat.

Cal'cium (Lat. *calx* lime or chalk), in chemistry, the metallic base of lime. It is a bright metal, white as silver, which burns when heated a little, and lime is re-formed. Sir H. Davy calculates that 20 parts of calcium combine with about 7·5 of oxygen. Its chemical compounds are as follow: —*Protoxide of calcium*, 1 atom of calcium and 1 of oxygen = 8; atomic weight = 28·5;—*Peroxide of calcium*, 1 atom of calcium and 2 of oxygen; atomic weight = 36·5;—*Chloride of calcium*, 1 atom of calcium and 1 of chlorine = 35·42; atomic weight = 55·49;—*Iodide of calcium*, 1 atom of calcium and 1 of iodine = 126·3; atomic weight = 146·8;—*Bromide of calcium*, 1 atom of calcium and 1 of bromine = 78·4; atomic weight = 98·9;—*Fluoride of calcium*, 1 atom of calcium and 1 of fluorine = 18·68; atomic weight = 39·18;—*Sulphuret of calcium*, 1 atom of calcium and 1 of sulphur = 16·1; atomic weight = 36·6;—*Bisulphuret of calcium*, 1 atom of calcium and 2 of sulphur = 32·2; atomic weight = 52·7;—*Quintosulphuret of calcium*, 1 atom of calcium and 5 of sulphur = 80·5; atomic weight = 101;—*Phosphuret of calcium*, 1 atom of calcium and 1 of phosphorus = 15·7; atomic weight 36·2.

Calc-spar, in mineralogy, crystallized carbonate of lime; calcareous spar.

Cal'culating Machine, an implement with toothed wheels for automaton calculation.

Cal'culus (Lat.), in pathology, a term applied to a hard or stony consistence which forms in the bladder. — In mathematics, the *differential calculus* is the finding an infinitely small quantity, which, being taken an in-finite number of times, shall be equal to a given quantity.

Cal'edonite, a mineral of a green colour, consisting of the sulphate and carbonate of lead.

Cal'endar (Lat. *calendæ* calends), in chronology, a division of time, or register of the year, in which the months, weeks, days, festivals and holidays, &c., are distinguished.—A *calendar month* is one of the months consisting of 30 or 31 days, with the exception of February.—The *Calends* (*calendæ*) of Roman chronology, were reckoned backwards; thus the 1st of May begins the calends of May; the 30th of April was the second of the calends of May; the 29th, the third, &c., to the 13th, where the ides commence, which are also numbered in a retrograde order to the 5th, where the nones begin; and these are numbered after the same manner to the 1st of the month, which is the calends of April; and in the study of Roman history it is necessary that this system of chronologizing events should be clearly understood.

Cal'enture (Sp. from Lat. *caleo* to be hot), in pathology, a violent fever, chiefly affecting sailors in hot climates.

Cal'iber, or **Cal'ibre** (Fr.), in the arts, the bore of a cylindrical tube, especially of a piece of ordnance.—*Calibre compasses*, improperly called *callipers*, are used by gunners in measuring the diameter of shot and bomb-shells, by engineers and smiths in taking the diameter of round bodies, and by phrenologists in measuring the degrees of development in the various organs of the head.

Cal'ico-printing (from *Calicut*, a city of Hindostan) is the art of printing figures on cotton fabrics, now performed by very ingenious machinery.

Cali'go (Lat. *darkness*), in pathology, a disease of the eye, of which there are different kinds; as, *Caligo lentis*, true cataract; *C. cornea*, opacity of the cornea; *C. pupilla*, blindness from obstruction in the pupils, &c.

Calip'pic Period (from Calippus, the philosopher of Cyzicus), in chronology, a period of 76 years continually recurring, after which it was calculated that the lunations of the moon would return in the same order.

Calip'teryx (Gr. *kalos* beautiful, and *pteryx* a wing), in entomology, a genus of neuropterous insects, distinguished by their brilliant colours, of the fam. Libellulinæ, or Dragon-flies.

Calisthen'ics (Gr. *kalos* beautiful, and *sthenos* strength), in gymnastics, exercise of the body and limbs to promote strength and graceful movements.

Calking, in painting, covering the back of a design with black-lead or red chalk, and tracing through it on a waxed plate, by passing over each stroke of the design with a pointed instrument, so as to leave the colour on the plate or wall.

Cal'liope (Gr. *a beautiful sight*), in astronomy, a planet or asteroid discovered by Hind in 1852. Its mean distance from the sun is 277,870,000 miles, and its periodical revolution 4 years 356 days.

Cal'lithrix (Gr. *kalos*, and *thrix* hair), in zoology, the *Cercopthecus sabæus*, or Green Monkey.

Callitricha'ceæ (Gr.), in botany, a nat. order of aquatic Exogens (the Starworts), of which the Callitriche, an aquatic plant, is the genus and type.

Callus (Lat.), in pathology, a hard deposit; an excess of bony matter, often formed in the uniting of broken bones.

Cal'omel (Gr. *kalos* fair, and *melas* black), in pharmacy, the chloride of mercury, prepared by rubbing mercury with corrosive sublimate; the mercury being in the proportion of 200 to 36 of chlorine.

Calor'ic (Lat.), in natural philosophy, the principle of heat; the cause of the phenomena or effects popularly recognised as heat; a fluid or condition diffused through all bodies.

Calorim'eter (Gr. *heat-measurer*), an apparatus for ascertaining the relative quantities of heat given out in bodies when cooling, from the quantity of ice it melts.

Calorimo'tor (Lat. *heat-mover*), a form of the voltaic apparatus for evolving caloric.

Calotte (Fr.), in architecture, a concavity in the form of a cup or niche, lathed and plastered, serving to diminish the height of a chapel, alcove, or cabinet, which otherwise would appear too high for the breadth.

Cal'otype (Gr. *beautiful type*), a process of photography, in which the picture is produced by the rapid action of light on paper prepared with iodide of silver and gallo-nitrate of silver; sometimes called Talbotype, from the inventor.

Caltrop (Sax.), a term applied to a prickly plant, known by the name of *Paliurus australis*, or Christ's Thorn.—In military science, an implement with four iron points disposed in a triangular form, so that when thrown on the ground one of the points stands upright. Their use is to arrest the advance of cavalry by laming the horses.

Calum'ba, in pharmacy, a root, the *Cocculus palmatus*, used as a tonic medicine.

Calu'ria, in botany, the *Erica vulgaris*, or common Ling, much used for fuel and for making brooms.

Calycantha'ceæ (Gr. *kalyx*, and *anthos* a flower), a nat. order of rosal Exogens, of which the Calycanthus is the type.

Calycera'ceæ (Lat.), a nat. order of herbaceous Exogens, allied to the Teazelworts.

Calyciflo'ræ (Lat. *calyx*, and *flores* flowers), in botany, a division of dichlamydeous Exogens, in which the stamens are placed on the calyx.

Calym'ene (Gr. *a veil*), in geology, a genus of Trilobites, or fossil Crustaceans, found in the silurian rocks.

Calyp'so, in astronomy, a planet or asteroid, discovered by Luther, the German astronomer, in 1858.

Calyptræ'idæ, in ichthyology, a family of Gasteropods.

Calyp'trate (Gr. *kalyptra* a covering), in botany, applied to the calyx of plants when it comes off like an extinguisher.

Calyx, *pl.* **Cal'yces** (Gr. and Lat.), in botany, a flower-cup; the row of leaf-like organs which immediately surround a flower.

Cam, in mechanical science, a contrivance for changing a circular motion into an alternate one.

Cam'aieu, a kind of painting wherein there is only one colour, a monochrome, chiefly employed in representing basso-relievo.

Camber (Fr.), in architecture, the concavity of the under-side of a beam; whence *camber-beam*, &c.—*Camber-window*, among builders, is a window arched above.—In shipbuilding, *cambered deck* is an arched deck declining towards the stem and stern.

Cam'bistry (Ital. *cambista*, from Low Lat. *cambio*), the science of commercial exchanges, of the relative value of foreign coins, and of weights and measures.

Cam'bium, in botany, the mucilaginous fluid that lies between the young wood and the bark of a tree, which appears in the spring, and disappears after the formation of the wood, which then adheres firmly to the bark, but reappears whenever the plant is again called into growth.

Camboge, a gum resin, the juice of *Stalagmitis cambogioides*.

Cam'brian (*Cambria*, the ancient name of Wales), in geology, a name given to a group of rocks of a slaty structure, older than the silurian system.

Camel (Lat. *camelus*), in zoology, a large ruminant animal, type of the family Camelidæ, of great utility in traversing the sandy deserts of the East; by its aid a stout Arabian can travel at the rate of three miles an hour.—*Camel's hair* is a valuable article of commerce, being often as fine as silk, and much longer than sheep's wool.—*Camel's hay* is the name given to some of the fragrant grasses of the Andropogon genus.

Camelopar'dæ, in zoology, a family of Ruminants, the Giraffes, with enormously long necks and long slender legs. The genus consists of two species the *Camelopardalis antiquorum*, or Northern Giraffe, and *Camelopardalis australis*, or South African Giraffe.—In astronomy, the *Camelopard* is a constellation of thirty-two stars, situated between Cepheus, Perseus, Ursa Major and Minor, and Draco.

Cam'eo (Ital. and Fr.), in the arts, a term applied to gems or precious stones, in which the object represented is worked in relievo, and not in intaglio.

Cameralis'tics (Germ.), the science of revenue or public finance.

Cam'era Lu'cida (Lat. *a light chamber*), an optical instrument for the purpose of making the image of any object appear on the wall in a light room, either by day or night.

Cam'era Obscu'ra (Lat. *a dark chamber*), an optical machine, used in a darkened chamber, so that the light coming only through a double convex glass, all objects exposed to daylight, and opposite to the glass, are represented as inverted upon any white substance placed in the focus of the glass.

Camou'flet (Fr.), in military science, a charge of powder sunk in the wall of earth between two parallel galleries.

Campanula'ceæ (Lat. *campanula* a little bell), in botany, a nat. order of plants, of which Campanula, or Bell-flower, is the type.—*Campanularia* is a genus of corals, in which the polypi assume a bell shape.

Camphor (Arab.), in pharmacy, a resinous concrete juice; an exudation from different kinds of Asiatic trees, especially the *Laurus camphora* of Japan. It is of an acrid taste and keenly penetrating smell, and used medicinally as a stimulant.—*Camphora flores compositi* are the compound flowers of sulphur; camphor sublimed with benzoin.

Cam'phorates, in chemistry, salts formed by the combination of any base with the camphoric acid.

Camwood, in botany, a species of red dye-wood, chiefly imported from Brazil, and from the neighbourhood of Sierra Leone, and principally used for knife-handles, and articles of a similar nature.

Can'ada Balsam, an oleo-resin obtained from the *Abies balsamifera*, which is extensively used for medicinal and manufacturing purposes, and also as a transparent varnish for water-colour drawings.

Canal (Lat. *canalis*, from *canna* a reed), in anatomy, a duct or vessel in an animal body through which any of the juices flow.—*C. arteriosus* is a canal or blood-vessel which unites the pulmonary artery and aorta in the foetus.—*C. venosus*, a canal which conveys the blood from the *vena porta* of the liver to the ascending *vena cava* in the foetus.—*C. petitianus*, a triangular cavity formed by the separation of the anterior lamina of the crystalline lens from the posterior.—In hydraulics, *Canal lift* is a hydro-pneumatic elevator for raising boats from one level to another.—*Canal lock* is a sluice or stop-gate for raising or depressing the water to a certain level, and thus enabling boats to pass through.

Cancel'li (Lat. *lattice-work*), in anatomy, the network which forms the least compact part of bones.

Cancer (Lat. *a crab*), in astronomy, one of the twelve signs and the fourth constellation in the zodiac. *Tropic of Cancer*, a lesser circle of the sphere parallel to the equator.—In zoology, a genus of decapod Crustaceans, the Crab.—In medicine, a roundish, unequal, hard, and livid tumour, generally seated in the glandulous part of the body.

Candite, in mineralogy, a variety of the spinel found at Candy in Ceylon.

Can'diteers, in fortification, frames to lay fagots or brushwood on, for covering the workmen.

Candle or **Cannel Coal**, in mineralogy, a coal-black bituminous substance, which resembles jet, and does not soil the fingers when handled. The difference between cannel coal and jet exists solely in the presence or absence of foreign earthy matters.

Cano'pus, in astronomy, a star of the first magnitude in the constellation Argo.

Cantan'te, in music, an expression sometimes used to distinguish the vocal part of a composition.

Canta'ta (Ital.), a song intermixed with recitatives.

Canthar'ides (Gr.), a family of coleopterous insects, of which Cantharis, or Spanish-fly, is the type.—In chemistry, *Cantharidine* is the active principle of 'cantharides, which possesses extremely vesicating properties.

Cantile'na (Ital.), in music, a term sometimes used for distinguishing the treble melody from the bass and other inferior parts.

Caout'chouc, gum-elastic or India-rubber, which exudes from a tree in S. America; a mineral substance found in Derbyshire.—*Caoutchou-cine* is an inflammable oily liquid obtained from caoutchouc.

Cap (Lat. *caput* a head), in musketry, *percussion cap* is a metal capsule for the nipple of a gun-lock, containing a detonating powder to explode the charge in the barrel.

Cap'illary (Lat. *hairy*), in anatomy, a term applied to the minute vessels by which the terminal arteries and veins communicate with each other.—In botany, it applies to the fine hair-shaped fibres of a plant.—In natural philosophy, *Capillary attraction* is that property of a fluid by which it rises above the level in tubes of small diameter, in consequence of the attraction of the matter of the tube being greater than the power of gravitation.

Cap'ital (Lat. *caput* the head), in architecture, the uppermost portion of a pilaster or column, placed over the shaft, and beneath the entablature.

Capit'ulum (Lat.), in anatomy, the protuberance or small head of a bone received into the concavity of another bone.—In botany, a species of inflorescence, formed of many flowers upon a common peduncle.

Cap'nomor (Gr. *kapnos* smoke, and *moira* part), an oily substance obtained from the tar of wood.

Capon'niere (Fr.) in fortification, a passage leading from one passage to another, and usually protected by a wall or parapet.

Capparida'ceæ (Gr. *kapparis* the caper tree), in botany, a nat. order of Exogens, consisting of herbaceous plants, shrubs, and trees, of which Capparis is the type.

Capric Acid (Lat. *caper* a goat), in chemistry, an acid obtained from the milk of the goat, consisting of 18 atoms of carbon, 14 of hydrogen, and 3 of oxygen.

Capric'cio (Ital.), in music, an irregular, loose species of composition.—*Capriccioso* denotes a free or fantastic style.

Cap'ricorn (Lat. *goat's horn*), in astronomy, one of the twelve signs of the zodiac, represented on globes in the form of a goat. The sun enters it about the 21st of December.—*Tropic of Capricorn* is a small circle

of the sphere parallel to the equinoctial.

Caprifolia'ceæ (Lat. *caprifolium* honeysuckle), in botany, a nat. order of exogenous plants, of which Caprifolium (Woodbine) is the type.

Caprimul'gidæ (Lat. *goat-suckers*), in ornithology, a fam. of birds, of which the Caprimulgus (Goat-sucker or Moth-eater) is the type.

Cap'roate, in chemistry, a salt formed by the union of caproic acid with a base.

Capro'ic Acid, in chemistry, a clear oily liquid obtained from the salt of baryta by adding sulphuric acid to its solution. It consists of 12 atoms of carbon, 9 of hydrogen, and 3 of oxygen.

Cap'sicine, an alkaline principle found in some species of capsicum.

Cap'sicum (Gr. *kapto* to bite), a genus of tropical plants, the seeds and fruits of which are powerful stimulants, from which the condiment called Cayenne pepper is produced; order Solanaceæ.

Capstan (Fr.), a machine employed in ships to weigh anchors, or to draw up great weights.

Capstone, in geology, a kind of fossil oolite.

Capsule (Lat.), in botany, the membranous or woody seed-vessel of a plant.—In anatomy, a membrane, as the capsule of the crystalline lens, the capsular ligaments, &c.—In chemistry, a small evaporating dish.

Capuloi'da (Lat. *capulus* a cup), in ichthyology, a family of Pectini-branchiate Gasteropods, of which the Capulus, with a patelliform shell, is the type.

Carab'idæ (Lat.) in entomology, a family of coleopterous insects, of which the Carabus is the type.

Car'acol, in architecture, a staircase with a spiral curve.

Caran'a Resin (Sp.), a resin obtained from the *Bursera gummifera*, and used medicinally.

Car'apace, a thick shell which covers the tortoise, and protects the body of chelonian reptiles. The term is also applied to the upper surface of the Crustaceans.

Carat (Ital. and Fr.), a weight of 4 grains, with which diamonds are weighed. A term also used to express the fineness of gold. It means the twenty-fourth part of any given weight of that metal, or its alloy. If such a weight be pure gold, it is said to be 24 carats fine; if three-fourths only be gold, it is said to be 18 carats fine. The diamond carat, however, is a definite weight.

Carbazo'tic Acid, in chemistry, a crystallizable acid, composed of carbon, azote, and oxygen. It is formed from the action of nitric acid on animal and vegetable substances. *Carbazotate* is a salt formed of carbazotic acid and a base.

Carbide, in chemistry, a compound of carbon with hydrogen.

Carbon (Lat. and Fr.), in mineralogy, the pure inflammable principle of charcoal. Charcoal is infusible, insoluble in water, is capable of combining both with hydrogen and sulphur, is a conductor of electricity, and has a powerful affinity for oxygen. Carbon is obtained nearly pure in charcoal; but it is in the diamond that this elementary substance is found in its purest form.—In geology, carbon forms beds of considerable thickness, being the principal constituent part of coal, combined with oxygen.

Car'bonate (Lat. *carbo*), in chemistry, a compound substance formed by the union of carbonic acid with a salifiable base. The carbonates principally used in medicine are those of ammonia, lime, iron, magnesia, lead, soda, and potash. When there is an excess of base, the compound is called a subcarbonate; and when two equivalents of carbonic acid unite with the base, it is termed a bicarbonate or supercarbonate.

Carbon'ic Acid, in chemistry, a compound of carbon and oxygen; a mephitic gas, which, when breathed undiluted, is fatal to human life. It is the *choke-damp* of the miners.

Carboniza'tion (Lat. *carbo* coal), in chemistry, the process of burning a substance until nothing but the carbon is left.

Carbo-sul'phurets, in chemistry, a description of salts formed by the union of carbon, sulphur, and potassium, sodium, barium, ammonium, &c.

Car'buncle (Lat.), in mineralogy, a precious stone, of a deep red colour.—In surgery, a hard, inflammatory tumour, nearly allied to a boil, but of a more aggravated nature; the *anthrax* of the Greeks.

Car'buret, in chemistry, a combination of carbon with any metal, alkali, or other substance.—*Carburetted hydrogen* is an inflammable gas, generated in stagnant pools from the decomposition of dead vegetable matter, and often found in coal-beds, where it sometimes explodes, and produces much destruction of life. The miners call it *fire-damp*.

Carcino'ma (Gr. *karkinos* a crab), in pathology, a form of cancer.

Car'dia (Gr. *the heart*), in anatomy, the œsophagal orifice of the stomach, so called from its proximity to the heart. —*Cardiac* is an epithet applied to the blood-vessels and nerves which are distributed on the heart; also to the nerves which, originating from the cervical ganglia, unite to form, between the arch of the aorta and the bifurcation of the bronchia, the cardiac plexus.—In pathology, the term is applied to a painful affection of the heart.—*Cardialgia*, a pain affecting the epigastric region; heartburn.

Cardia'ceæ (Gr. *kardia* the heart), a family of acephalous Testacea, of which the Cardium, or Cockle (a genus of univalve Mollusca), is the type; so called from the shell being heart-shaped, with costated ribs.

Cardiag'raphy, an anatomical description of the heart.

Car'dinal (Lat.), in astronomy, the *cardinal signs* are Aries, Libra, Cancer, and Capricorn.—In navigation, the *cardinal points* of the compass are north, south, east, and west. — In arithmetic, the *cardinal numbers* are 1, 2, 3, 4, &c.—In ethics, the *cardinal virtues* are prudence, temperance, justice, and fortitude.—In the Romish hierarchy, an ecclesiastical prince, next in dignity to the Pope.

Car'dioid (Gr.), in alegbra, a peculiar curve, so called from its resemblance to the heart.

Cardiol'ogy (Gr. *kardia* and *logos*), in physiology, a discourse on the heart.

Cardi'tis (Gr.), inflammation of the heart.

Car'dium (Gr.), a genus of univalve Mollusca, the Cockle; fam. Cardiaceæ.

Cardua'ceæ (Lat. *carduus* a thistle), in botany, the thistle, formerly a suborder of asteroid or composite plants, of which Carduus is the type.

Ca'ries (Lat.), in pathology, ulceration or rottenness of a bone.

Cari'na (Lat. *a keel*), in botany, a term applied to the petals in papilionaceous flowers.—*Carinate*, or *Carinated*, is a term applied to a calyx, leaf, or nectary, when shaped like the keel of a ship.

Carin'thine, in mineralogy, a variety of augite, of a dark green or black colour, so called from being found in Carinthia.

Cariop'sis, in botany, a one-celled indehiscent pericarp, adhering to the seed which it contains, as the grain of grasses.

Carmin'ative (Fr. from Lat. *carmen*), in pathology, a term applied to those medicines which tend to dispel flatulence, as ginger, cardamom, aniso and caraway seeds; several ot the essential oils, as those of peppermint, anise, caraway, juniper; and aromatic tinctures.

Carmine (Fr.), a beautiful red pigment made of cochineal.

Carna'ria, or **Carniv'ora** (Lat. *flesh-devouring*), in zoology, an order of mammalian animals which live on flesh, as the tiger, lion, &c., and have their teeth peculiarly fitted for the mastication of animal matter.

Carno'si (Lat. *fleshy*), in zoology, an order of Polypi, or flesh animals, which consist of the Actinia, Zoanthus, and Lucernalia.

Carot'id (Gr. *karoo* to cause to sleep), in anatomy, the name of an artery on each side the neck. The common carotids are two considerable arteries that ascend on the fore part of the cervical vertebræ to the head, to supply it with blood. The right common carotid is given off from the arteria innominata; the left arises from the aorta.

Carpel (Gr. *karpos* fruit), in botany, a term applied to the separate pistils of which a compound fruit is formed. Each modified leaf which forms the pistil is called a *carpellum*. On the form of the carpella, and on their number and arrangement around the centre, depends the form of the pistil.

Carphol'ogy (Gr. *karphos* chaff, and *lego* to pluck), in pathology, a term applied to a certain stage of disease, in which the patient evinces a desire to pluck at the bed-clothes.

Carphosil'lerite (Gr.), a straw-coloured reniform mineral.

Car'politha (Gr. *karpos* fruit, and *lithos* a stone), in geology, the general term for fossil fruits.

Carpol'ogy (Gr. *karpos* fruit, and *logos*), in botany, a treatise on the classification and nature of fruits.

Car'rageen, a sea-lichen, the *Chondrus crispus*, or Irish Moss, used for making jellies, &c.

Carra'ra Marble, the name of a fine white marble.

Cartilagi'nii (Lat. *cartilago* cartilage), in ichthyology, a class of fishes, the skeleton of which is composed of cartilage, as in the skate, flounder, and other flat fish.—*Cartilaginous* is an epithet applied to all fishes whose muscles are supported by cartilages instead of bones.—In botany, the term is applied to leaves, the borders of which are hard and horny.

Cartog'raphy (Lat. *carta* a leaf of paper, and Gr. *grapho* to write), the art of preparing charts or maps.

Cartoon (Ital. *cartone*), in painting, a

sketch made as a pattern for tapestry; a design drawn on strong paper, to be afterwards traced through, and transferred on the fresh plaster of a wall to be painted in fresco.

Cartouch (Ital. and Fr.), in military science, a wooden case for holding balls to be fired out of a howitzer.—In architecture, the name of a medallion of a cornice — In Egyptian architecture, it is applied to those parts of a hieroglyphic inscription enclosed in oval-drawn lines.

Car'uncle (Lat. *caro* flesh), in pathology, a small fleshy excrescence.

Caru'to, the name of a beautiful dye, of a bluish-black colour, obtained from the fruit of *Genipa Americana*.

Caryat'ides (Gr.), in architecture, the figures of women instead of columns to support the entablatures of an edifice. Their origin is attributed to the taking of Carya by the Greeks, when the women were led away captive.

Caryophylla'ceæ (Gr. *karyon* a nut, and *phyllon* a leaf), in botany, a nat. order of Exogens (the Cloveworts), consisting of shrubs or herbs, of which the Caryophyllus, or Clove tree, is the type.—*Caryophyllic acid* is an acid obtained from the oil of cloves, consisting of 20 atoms of carbon, 12 of hydrogen, and 4 of oxygen. —*Caryophylline* is a solid substance extracted from cloves by means of alcohol; composed of 20 atoms of carbon, 16 of hydrogen, and 2 of oxygen.

Caryop'sis (Gr. *karyon* a walnut, and *opsis* appearance), a peculiar form of dry fruit, containing seed which is adherent to the pericarp.

Cascaril'la (Sp.), in pharmacy, a term applied to *Croton cascarilla*, a valuable aromatic and tonic. It is the produce of the Bahama Islands, and imported into Europe in thin brittle rolls.

Ca'seate (Lat. *cheese*), in chemistry, a salt resulting from *caseic acid*, which is obtained from cheese.

Ca'seine, the principle of cheese, and one of the most important elements of animal nutrition, as found in milk, and in the seeds of leguminous plants. It consists of 48 atoms of carbon, 36 of hydrogen, 6 of nitrogen, and 14 of oxygen.

Casemate (Fr. and Ital.), in fortification, a vault in the flank of a bastion for the reception of artillery.

Case Shot, in military science, a general term for musket-balls, old iron, stones, &c., put into cases, and discharged from a piece of ordnance; canister shot.

Cassamu'nar, an aromatic root of the ginger kind, brought from the East Indies, and pathologically recommended in epileptic, hysterical, and paralytic affections.

Cas'sia (Gr.), a genus of plants, of which the *C. lanceolata* produces the well-known purgative, senna; order Leguminosæ.

Cassida'ria (Lat. *cassis* a helmet), in malacology, a genus of gasteropod Mollusca, with ventricose shell; fam. Muricidæ.

Cassida'riæ (Lat. *cassida* a helmet), a family of monilicorn coleopterous insects; the Tortoise beetles.

Cassid'ea (Lat.), a genus of Mollusca, the shells of which are closely allied to Cassis; sub-family Cassinæ.

Casside'us (Lat.), in botany, a term applied to the upper petal of a flower when helmet-shaped.

Cassiope'ia (Gr.), in astronomy, a constellation in the northern hemisphere, containing 55 stars, and passing vertically over a large portion of Europe.

Cassis (Lat. *a helmet*), the name of an Echinite (the Helmet-stone), a section of the class Catocysti; also the name of a ventricose univalve, found both recent and fossil.

Cas'sius (Lat.), in the arts, a beautiful purple obtained from the muriate of gold by means of tin, highly valued for the beauty of the colour it gives to glass or enamel.

Cas'sowary, a genus of fissirostral birds, belonging to the Ostrich family.

Cassytha'ceæ (Gr.), in botany, an order of tropical Exogens, allied to the Lauraceæ, or Laurels, termed Dodder Laurels by Lindley, from their having the appearance of dodders, and like them seeming to live parasitically on other plants. Cassytha, or Dodder Laurel, is the only genus.

Casta'lia, in malacology, a genus of marine Mollusca, closely allied to the Unios, or Fresh-water Mussels.

Casta'nea (from *Castanea*, in Thessaly), an important genus of plants, which produces the well-known chestnut; order Corylaceæ.—*Castano-spermum* (Chestnut-seed) is the name of the Moreton Bay Chestnut, a leguminous tree which grows from forty to fifty feet high.

Cast'niadæ, in entomology, a family of lepidopterous insects, the Sphinx Moths, of which the genus Castnia is the type; tribe Crepuscularia.

Castor (Gr.), a genus of Rodents, the Beavers, one species of which secretes the fetid substance called *castor,* used medicinally as an antispas-

modic and excitant of the brain and vascular system.—*Castoreum* is the name applied to two bags situated in the inguinal regions of the beaver. —In astronomy, *Castor and Pollux* are two allegorical figures in the sign Gemini, which give name to the two bright stars in that constellation.

Cas'torate, in chemistry, a salt produced from the combination of castoric acid with a salifiable base.

Cas'torin, or **Cas'torine,** in chemistry, a crystallizable substance extracted from castor by the action of alcohol.

Castor Oil, in medicine, a mild and safe purgative, extracted from the seeds of a West-Indian plant, the Ricinus, of the order Euphorbiaceæ.

Casuarina'ceæ, a nat. order of amentaceous trees, of which the Casuarina (so called from its branches appearing like the plumes of the cassowary) is the type and only genus.

Catacaus'tics (Gr. *a burning*), in optics, the caustic curves formed by the reflection of the rays of light.—In the higher geometry, *Caustic* curves are those formed by reflection, and the catacaustic of a circle is a cycloid, formed by the revolution of a circle along a circle.

Cat'aclysm (Gr. *a deluge*), in geology, a term applied to the great mundane deluge.

Catacous'tics (Gr. *kata,* and *akouo* to hear), the science which treats of reflected sounds or echoes, which do not strike the ear direct, but previously come in contact with other bodies.

Catadiop'tric (Gr. *kata,* and *dioptomai* to see), in optics, reflecting light.

Catafal'co, in architecture, a temporary ceremonial tomb.

Cat'agraph (Gr. *kata,* and *grapho* to write), in painting, the first draft of a picture.

Catalep'sy (Gr. *a seizing*), in pathology, a sudden suspension of the action of the senses and of volition.

Catal'ysis (Gr. *kata,* and *luo* to loosen), in chemistry, a term applied to certain chemical phenomena, in which changes in the composition of substances are effected by the presence of another body.

Cataphon'ics (Gr. *kata,* and *phone* sound), in acoustics, the doctrine of reflected sounds.

Catap'tosis (Gr. *kata,* and *pipto* to fall), in pathology, a falling down suddenly, as in apoplexy or epilepsy.

Cat'apult (Lat.), an ancient military engine for throwing stones, &c.

Cat'aract (Gr. *kata,* and *russo* to dash),

a water-fall.—In surgery, a disease of the eye, produced by the opacity of the crystalline lens.

Catarrh (Gr. *kata*, and *rheo* to flow), in pathology, a term applied to a severe cold in the head, usually attended with a discharge from the nose or mucous membrane; inflammation of lining membrane of the air passages, which presents itself under two forms, viz.: *common catarrh*, or, in ordinary language, a cold; and *epidemic catarrh*, or *influenza*, in which the attack is very sudden.

Catastal'tic (Gr. *kata*, and *stello* to send), in pathology, acting from above downwards; applied to nervous action.

Catas'trophist (Gr. *katastrophe*, finality), one who maintains that the great changes of our globe have been the result of catastrophes or violent physical convulsions.

Cate'nary (Lat. *catena* a chain), in geometry, the name of a curve line formed by a rope hanging freely from two points of suspension, whether the points be horizontal or not.

Cath'arine Wheel, in Gothic architecture, an ornamented window, or compartment of a window, of a circular form, with rosettes, or radiating divisions, of various colours.—In pyrotechny, a revolving wheel, which throws out radiating fire-sparks as it turns.

Cathar'sis (Gr. *a cleansing*), in medicine, purgation of the fæces or humours, either artificially or naturally.—*Cathartic* is applied to medicines which increase the evacuations.

Cathar'tine (Gr.), the purgative principle of senna.

Cathæret'ic (Gr.), in the materia medica, applied to a caustic substance used to eat down warts and other excrescences.

Cath'eter (Gr. *a probe*), in surgery, a long and hollow tube for drawing off the urine when the patient is unable to pass it naturally. Catheters are made of silver, or of elastic gum.

Cath'etus (Gr. *perpendicular*), in architecture, a perpendicular line passing through a cylindrical body, as a baluster or column.—In geometry, a line or radius, falling perpendicularly on another line or surface; thus the catheti of a right-angled triangle are the two sides that include the right angle.—*Cathetus of reflection*, or of the eye, a right line drawn from the eye perpendicular to the reflecting line.—*Cathetus of obliquation*, a right line drawn perpendicular to the speculum in the point of incidence or reflection.—*Cathetus of incidence*,

in catoptrics, a right line drawn from a point of the object perpendicular to the reflecting line.

Cathode (Gr. *kata* down, and *odos* a way), in electro-chemistry, the way or surface by which the electric current leaves substances through which it passes. It is equivalent to negative pole.

Catkin, in botany, a kind of inflorescence, resembling a spike.

Catocys'ti (Gr. *kata* below, and *kyste* the bladder), a division of the family of Echini, which have the opening for the vent in some part of the base of the shell.

Catop'sis (Gr. *kata*, and *opsis* vision), a morbid quickness of vision.

Catop'trics (Gr. *katoptron* a mirror), in optics, the science of reflected vision, which explains the laws and properties of reflection, chiefly founded upon this truth—that the angle of reflection is always equal to the angle of incidence; and from thence deducing the magnitude, shapes, and situations of the appearances of objects seen by the reflection of polished surfaces, and particularly plane, spherical, conical, and cylindrical ones.

Cat's-eye, a beautiful siliceous mineral from Ceylon, which reflects pearly light. It is a variety of rhombohedral quartz, having an opalescence resembling the light from the eye of the cat: whence its name. It is harder than quartz, and consists of silex, alumina, lime, and oxide of iron.

Cat-silver, in mineralogy, a variety of mica.

Caucalin'idæ, in botany, a tribe of the Umbellifera, of which the Caucalis, or Bur-parsley, is the genus and type.

Cauca'sian (from *Caucasus*), in ethnology, a term applied to most of the European and several Asiatic nations.

Cauda (Lat. *a tail*), in entomology, that part of the abdomen which terminates in a long-pointed tail.—In astronomy, the term is prefixed to the names of several constellations, to denote the several stars in their tails; as, *Cauda Capricorni*, *Cauda Leonis*, &c.—In anatomy, *Cauda equina* (horse-tail) is the final division of the spinal marrow, so called from the form of the disposition of the nerves which issue from it.—In anatomy, the term is of frequent use as an adjective; as, the *caudal* vertebræ of an animal, or the *caudal* fin of a fish.

Cau'licoles (Lat. *caulis* a stalk), in architecture, the slender stalks under the leaves of the abacus of the Corinthian capital.

Cau'licule (Lat. *a little stalk*), in botany, the little stem in the embryo which unites the cotyledons, or seed-lobes, with the radicle.

Caulis (Lat. *a stem*), in botany, a term applied to the leaves growing fiom the main axis of a plant.

Caulocar'pus (Gr. *kaulos* a stem, and *karpos* fruit), in botany, a term applied to trees that produce both flowers and fruit.

Caun'terlode, in mineralogy, a lode which inclines at a considerable angle to the other contiguous veins.

Causal'ity, in phrenology, the faculty of tracing the relation of cause and effect.

Cau'salty, in mineralogy, the lighter parts of the ore carried off during the process of washing.

Caustic (Gr. *burning*), in surgery, destroying animal substances by powerful chemical action.

Causti'city (Gr.), that quality in animal substances by which they burn or corrode animal bodies to which they are applied.

Cau'tery (Gr. *kaio* to burn), in surgery, the destroying of animal tissues by the application of heat.

Cav'alier (Fr.), in fortifications, a work or mound raised for placing cannon thereon; a sort of interior bastion, which serves to protect the ramparts from the fire of an enemy on the neighbouring heights, or to direct a plunging fire into the trenches of the besiegers.

Cavati'na (Ital.), in music, a species of short air, usually inserted in obligato recitatives.

Ca'veating, in the science of fencing, the shifting of the sword from one side of an adversary to another.

Cavet'to (Ital. from Lat. *cavus* hollow), in ornamental carpentry, a hollow moulding, chiefly introduced into cornices whose profile is the quadrant of a circle.

Cav'icorn, a tribe of Ruminants with horns hollowed out like a sheath.

Cav'ies, in zoology, a tribe of Rodents, assimilating to the hare, but wanting the tail, and covered with hair-like bristles. They include the genera Hydrochærus, Cobaya, Dasyprocta, and Cavia.

Cavin (Fr.), in military science, a natural hollow adapted for covering a body of troops, and facilitating their advance.

Cav'olinite, a Vesuvian mineral; a variety of nepheline.

Cayman, in zoology, the Campsa, or Alligator, a genus of crocodiles peculiar to America.

Ceb'idæ, in zoology, a family of American monkeys, of which the Cebus is the type, composed of the genera Mycetes, Cebus, Callithrix, Harpales, and Pithecia.

Ceblepyri'næ (Gr. *handsome-headed*), in ornithology, a family of Shrikes, of which the Ceblepyris, or Caterpillar-catcher, is the genus and type.

Cebrion'idæ, an order of coleopterous insects, of which the Cebrio is the genus.

Cedrela'ceæ (Lat. *the cedar tree*), in botany, a nat. order of Exogens, of which the Cedrela is the type, the wood of which is usually compact, scented, and beautifully veined; the mahogany tree belongs to this order.

Ced'riret, a compound substance discovered in tar, which crystallizes into a kind of network, composed of red crystals.

Ce'drium, the resinous extract of the cedar tree, very useful in preserving books from the depredations of insects.

Celastra'ceæ (Gr.), in botany, a nat. order of calyciflorous Exogens, of which the Celastrus is the type.

Ce'lature (Lat. *cælo* to engrave), the art of engraving or embossing; that which is engraved.

Cel'estine (Lat.), a mineral of a reddish or delicate sky-blue colour, composed of sulphuric acid and strontia; sp. gr. 3·6 to 4·0.

Cell (Lat. *cella* a little chamber), in physiology, a vesicle or minute bag.

Cel'lular (Lat. *cellula*, a little cell), in anatomy, an epithet applied to certain organs and parts, as the lungs, bones, sinuses of the dura mater, &c.; in zoology, to the combs of bees and wasps; in botany, to the empty spaces, generally of a hexagonal figure, formed in the vegetable structure.—*Cellular tissue* is that part of plants which is composed of little cells or cavities.—*Cellulares* is a name applied to the second grand division of the vegetable kingdom, consisting of plants composed of cellular tissues only.—*Cellularia* is a genus of corals in which the cells are so arranged as to form branching stems.—*Cellularii* is a family of corals, in which each polypus is adherent in a corneous or calcareous cell, with thin parietes.

Cel'lulose (Lat. *cellula*), in physiology, a compound forming the fundamental material of the structure of plants, consisting of carbon, hydrogen, and oxygen.

Celt, in archæology, an implement of stone or metal found in ancient tumuli of the Celtic period in different parts of Europe.

Cement (Lat. *cementum*), any glutinous substance employed in uniting bodies together; a composition of lime, sand, and water, used for uniting stones or bricks; mortar.—*Cementation* is a chemical process, which consists in surrounding a body in the solid state with some powder of another body which is more combustible, or which unites with it without the whole contents becoming fused. Thus iron is converted into steel by cementation, by being surrounded with charcoal powder, which during combustion yields its carbon to the iron.—*Cement-stone*, in geology, a kind of septaria, obtained in various localities, for making cements and concretes.

Census (Lat.), in ethnology, an official enumeration of the inhabitants of a country, taken in Great Britain, by order of the legislature, every ten years.

Cen'tering, in architecture, the temporary frame or wood-work on which an arch is supported during its construction.

Cen'tigrade (Lat. *centum* and *gradus* a hundred degrees), the thermometer of Celsius, consisting of 100 degrees, used particularly in France. It begins at the freezing-point of water, between which and the boiling-point the scale consists of 100 equal parts. The degrees on Fahrenheit's scale being each equal to five-ninths of a degree, to find the correspondence of the degrees of the former with those of the latter, we multiply the degrees above or below the freezing of water by 5, and divide by 9.

Cen'tigramme (Lat. *centum*, and Fr. *gramme*), a French weight, the hundredth part of a gramme.

Cen'tilitre (*centum*, and Fr. *litre*), a liquid measure; in France, the hundredth part of a litre.

Cen'timetre (*centum*, and Fr. *mètre*), the hundredth part of the French mètre, nearly equivalent to one-third of an inch.

Cen'tipede (*centum*, and Lat. *pedes* feet), the name commonly given to insects of the order Myriopoda; the number of feet seems to increase with the age of the insect, and in some species to the number of twenty-six pairs.

Centner, in metallurgy and assaying, a hundred divided decimally.

Central, an epithet of frequent use in the sciences, denoting centrality.— In anatomy, the *central artery* is given off by the ophthalmics, and insinuates itself into the optic nerve in its passage to the retina.—In botany, the *central placenta* is the column in the centre of fruits to which the seeds are attached.—In astronomy, a *central eclipse* is when the centres of the heavenly bodies which are affected exactly coincide, or are directly in a line with the spectator.—In dynamics, the central forces are the powers which cause a moving body to tend towards, or recede from, the centre of motion.

Centre (Lat. *centrum*), in military science, the body of troops occupying the place in the line between the wings of an army.—*Centre* is a term of frequent application in practical science and the arts.—*Centre of attraction* is that point in a body into which, if all its substance be collected, its action upon any remote object would be just the same as if that body retained its form.—*Centre of a bastion* is a point in the middle of the gorge of a bastion, whence the capital line commences, and is generally at the angle of the inner polygon.—*Centre of a dial* is that point where the axis of the world intersects the plane of the dial; and also that point wherein all the hour-lines meet. —*Centre of gravity* is that point, in mechanics, about which all the parts of a body balance each in any situation whatever.—*Centre of motion* is that point which remains mathematically at rest when the other parts of the body are in motion.— *Centre of oscillation* is that point of a pendulum in which, if the weight of the several parts was collected, each vibration would be performed in the same time as when those weights are separate.—*Centre of percussion*, in a moving body, is that point wherein the percutient force is greatest.

Centrif'ugal (Lat. *centrum*, and *fugio* to fly from), in dynamics, having a tendency to recede from the centre; thus *centrifrugal force* is that force by which the parts of a body moving round a centre have a tendency to recede from it. — *Centripetal force* (from *centrum*, and *peto* to seek), on the contrary, is that which attracts or draws to the centre; as, the force of gravitation. It is by these two opposing forces, *centrifugal* and *centripetal*, that all the planetary bodies are governed, and revolve in their respective orbits.

Centrolin'eal (Lat. *centrum* a centre, and *linea* a line), in geometry, applied to lines converging to a centre; an instrument for drawing lines converging towards a point, though the point be inaccessible.

Centrolo'bium (Gr. *kentron* a spur or thorn, and *lobos* a lobe), a genus of leguminous plants, of the tribe Dalbergieæ.—*Centro-* forms a prefix to numerous genera of plants, fishes, birds, and insects, which our confined limits will not allow us to enumerate; as, *Centropetalum*, a genus of plants of the order Orchidaceæ;—*Centronotus*, a genus of fishes with oblong fusiform bodies, of the family Zeidæ; —*Centropus*, a genus of birds belonging to the hook-billed Cuckoos; —*Centrotus*, a genus of insects (so called from the thorax being furnished with a horn on each side), of the order Hemiptera.

Cephalal'gio (Gr. *kephale*, and *algos* pain), a medicine for the headache.

Cephalas'pis, (Gr. *kephale* the head), a genus of fossil placoid fishes, found in the old red sandstone formation.

Cephalat'omy (Gr.), in anatomy, dissecting the head.—In midwifery, the removal of the brain of a child impacted in the pelvis.

Cephali'næ (Gr.), in ichthyology, the Sun-fishes, of which the Cephalus (so called from the head forming the larger portion of the fish) is the type and genus: order Plectognathes.

Cephali'tis (Gr.), inflammation of the brain.

Cephal'ophus (Gr. *head-crested*), in zoology, a genus of Ruminants (the Tufted Antelope), distinguished by a prominent tuft of hair on the forehead.

Cephal'opods (Gr. *kephale*, and *podes* feet), an order of Mollusca, in which the viscera are contained in a muscular sac, from the opening of which the head projects. The Nautilus and Spirula form the living types of hundreds of species which have become extinct. Their remains are found in the secondary strata, and also in the palæozoic formations.

Cephalota'ceæ (Gr.), a nat. order of plants with exstipulate leaves, of which the Cephalotus, or New Holland Pitcher-plant, is the type and genus.

Ceph'alus. (See *Cephalinæ*.)

Cerama'ceæ (Gr. *keramos* a little measure), a nat. order of cellular Sea-weeds (the Rose-tangles), of which the Ceramium is the type.

Cerambyc'idæ (Gr. *keras* a horn, and *ambyx* a cup), in entomology, a family of coleopterous insects, living chiefly on decayed woods, of which Cerambyx is the type and genus.

Ceram'ic (Gr. *kera* wax), denoting the plastic arts; a term frequently applied to ornamental pottery.

Cer'asin (Lat. *cerasus* a cherry tree), a term applied to those gums which exude from the cherry and other trees of a similar nature.

Cerate (Lat. *ceratum*), a pharmaceutical preparation, of which wax is the principal ingredient.

Cer'atites (Gr. *keras* a horn), in geology, a genus of fossil Cephalopods in the triassic strata.

Cer'ato- (Gr. *keras*), in anatomy, a prefix in compound words, signifying connection with the cornua of the hyoid bone.

Ceratophylla'ceæ (Gr. *keras* and *phyllon*, a horn-leaf), a nat. order of plants, consisting of floating herbs.

Ceratoph'yta (Gr. *a horn-plant*), a tribe of corals of the family Corticati.

Cercæ (Gr. *kerkos* a tail), in entomology, the feelers in some insects projecting from the hind part of the body.

Cercodia'ne, in botany, a tribe of plants of the order Halorageæ.

Cercopi'næ (Gr. *kerkos* a tail, and *pous* a foot), in entomology, a family of small grasshoppers (the Jumping Cicadas), of which the Cercopis, or Cuckoo-spit, is the type, the species of which are very numerous.

Cerco'sis (Gr. *kerkos* a tail), in pathology, an elongation of the clitoris.

Ce'real (Lat. *Ceres* goddess of corn), belonging to or producing edible grain, as wheat, barley, &c.

Cer'ebrum (Lat. *the brain*), applied to the pulpy mass which occupies the cranial cavity of vertebrated animals. —*Cerebellum*, or little brain, is the hinder part of the head, under the occiput.—*Cerebritis* is inflammation of the brain.—*Cerebral*, in anatomy, is an epithet applied to those membranes, blood-vessels, and nerves which emanate from or supply the brain.— *Cerebric acid* is an acid extracted by ether from the matter of the brain after exposure to the action of boiling alcohol.

Ce'reolite (Gr. *kera* wax, and *lithos* a stone), a mineral substance, which in appearance and softness resembles wax.

Ceres, in astronomy, the name of one of the asteroid planets, discovered in 1801 by Piazzi; its mean distance from the sun being 263,740,000 miles, and its periodical revolution 4 years 220 days.

Cerine (Lat. *cera* wax), in chemistry, a substance which forms from 70 to 80 per cent. of bees'-wax; it is soluble in boiling alcohol.

Cerite (Lat.), a siliceous oxide of cerium; sp. gr. 4·7.

Cerith'inæ, a sub-family of Mollusca, the Club-shells, of which the Cerithium, a genus of pectinibranchiate Gasteropods, is the type.

Ce'rium (Lat.), a greyish mineral found in cerite.

Cerog'raphy (Gr.), painting or writing in wax.

Ce'rolite (Gr.), a mineral of a laminar

or compact structure, consisting of silica, alumina, magnesia, and water; sp. gr. 2·0—2·2.

Cer'thiadæ, Cer'thianæ (Gr. *keras* a horn), a family of birds, the Creepers, of which Certhia is the type. They are distinguished by the tail ending in sharp and horny points, whence the name.—*Certhia familiaris*, the Nut-hatch, or common Creeper, is a British species.

Ceru'leum (Lat. *ceruleus* sky-blue), a silicate of copper; a blue Roman pigment.

Ceruse (Lat.), in the arts, a preparation of white-lead, extensively used by painters. It is prepared from the subacetate of protoxide of lead by a current of carbonic acid, on exposing metallic lead, in minute division, to air and moisture; and also by the action of the vapour of vinegar on thin sheets of lead, by which the metal is both oxidized and converted into a carbonate.

Ce'rusite (Lat. *cerusa* white-lead), a valuable ore of lead, of great commercial importance.

Cer'vical (Lat. *cervix* the neck), in anatomy, a term applied to the blood-vessels, ligaments, bones, glands, &c., in the region of the neck.

Cesa'rean, in surgery, a term applied to the operation of cutting a child out of the womb.

Cestoi'dea (Gr. *like a cestus*), in entomology, a family of intestinal worms which infest the abdomen of certain fishes and birds, the body being flat and ribbon-like.

Cestra'cions, a family of fossil fishes, of which the Shark is the type.

Cestrin'eæ (Gr. *kestron* betony), in botany, a tribe of plants of the order Solaneæ, of which Cestrum, the Bastard Jasmine, is the type.

Ceta'ceæ (Gr. *ketos* a whale), an order of vertebrated mammiferous animals, inhabiting the northern seas. They have the form of fishes, with the exception of the horizontal tail, which enables them to rise speedily to the surface to breathe. Their blood is warm; they are viviparous, and suckle their young. They are divided into the *C. herbivora* and the *C. ordinaria*, the first composed of the Manati or Lamantins, the Halicores or Dudongs, and Stellerus; the latter, of the Whales, Dolphins, Narwhals, and Porpoises.

Cetine, in chemistry, an oily, colourless liquid obtained by distilling ethal repeatedly with glacial phosphoric acid; it is soluble in alcohol and ether, but not in water. It consists of 32 atoms of carbon and 32 of hydrogen.

Cetiosau'rus (Gr. *ketos*, and *sauros* a lizard), in geology, a genus of fossil Saurians found in the oolite formation.

Cetol'ogy (Gr. *ketos*), the natural history of the whale kind.

Ceto'niadæ, in entomology, a family of coleopterous insects, the Floral Beetles, of which the Cetonia is the type; they live and move among trees, plants, and flowers, their natural food.

Cetus (Gr.), in astronomy, a large constellation of the southern hemisphere (the Whale), which occupies the greatest space of any in the firmament, and contains 97 conspicuous stars.

Cevadil'la, or **Cebadil'la**, a species of Veratrum, or Indian caustic barley. Sevadic acid is obtained from the seeds of this plant.

Ceylonite (from *Ceylon*, where it is found), an opaque, black-looking mineral, which occurs in crystals. It consists of alumina, silica, magnesia, and oxide of iron; sp. gr. 3·64.

Chab'asite (Fr.), in mineralogy, a variety of zeolite, of a pale red colour, and found crystallized in the form of an obtuse rhomboid.

Chætodon'idæ (Gr. *chaite* a bristle, and *odontes* teeth), a family of acanthopterygious fishes, of which the Chætodon is the type; they are of great variety and beauty, distinguished from the perches chiefly by the operculum or gill-cover being without prickles.

Chailletia'ceæ, in botany, a nat. order of plants, of which the Chailletia is the type.

Chain, a series of connected links used in land-surveying, divided into 100 parts or links. The English or Imperial chain is 66 feet, and 10 square chains are equal to 1 imperial acre.—*Chain Rule*, or Rule of Equations, is an arithmetical formula of German origin, which is of great practical utility, particularly in exchange calculations.—*Chain-pump* is an hydraulic machine for raising water, consisting of two collateral square barrels, and an endless chain of pistons of the same form fixed at proper distances. The pistons or pallets bring up a full bore of water in the pump.—*Chain-shot* are two cannon-balls fastened together with a short chain, designed to mangle and ruin a ship's sails and rigging.—*Chain-wales*, broad and thick planks projecting horizontally from a ship's outside, formed to extend the shrouds from each other. In shipbuilding, strong links or plates of iron, the lower ends of which are bolted through a ship's sides to the timbers. —*Chain-timber*, a piece of timber in breadth equal to the length and breadth of a brick, used for strengthening brick walls.—*Chain-work*, applied to articles of manufacture in which cordage or thread is linked together in the form of a chain.

Chair, in the arts, a socket of cast-iron used upon the railways to support and secure the rails.

Chala'za (Gr. a *tubercle*), in botany, a spot on a seed indicating the nucleus.—In physiology, *Chalaza* is the name given to two membranous cords attached near to the poles of the yolk of an egg.—*Chalazium*, in pathology, is a little tubercle on the eyelid, vulgarly called a *sty*.

Chal'cidites (Gr. *shining like brass*), a family of hymenopterous insects, the Gadflies, which are very small, and usually ornamented with brilliant metallic colours.

Chalcog'raphy (Gr. *chalkos* brass), the art of engraving on brass or copper.

Chalk, in geology, a white fossil, or earthy limestone, much used in the arts; an opaque carbonate of lime, with an earthy fracture. In the south and south-east of England it forms extensive rocks, and in geology is the newest of what is known as the secondary formation. The greatest thickness of this formation in England is from 600 to 1000 feet. The organic remains are very numerous, and are all marine.—*Red chalk* is a clay deeply coloured with the peroxide of iron, of which it generally contains from 15 to 18 per cent.— *Black chalk* is a carbonaceous variety of shale, called also drawing-slate. — *French chalk*, steatite, or soapstone, a soft magnesian mineral. —In pathology, *Chalk-stones* are concretions formed in the joints of persons who have suffered long from gout; chiefly composed of uric acid and soda.

Chal'kolite (Gr. *chalk-stone*), a green-coloured mineral, crystallized in quadrangular prisms, consisting of oxide of uranium, phosphoric acid, oxide of copper, and water; sp. gr. 3·33.

Chalyb'eate (Gr. *chalyps* steel), a term applied to medicines and mineral waters that are impregnated with iron.

Chama'cea, or **Cham'idæ**, a family of conchiferous Mollusca, of which Chama, a gigantic bivalve shell, is the type.

Chamber, in gunnery, the hollow part of a mortar or gun, in which the charge is lodged. In mining, the cavity where the powder is lodged. —*Chamber of a lock*, in canals, is the space between the gates in which the vessels rise and sink from one level to another, in order to pass the lock.— *Chambers of the eye* are the minute spaces between the cornea and anterior surface of the iris, occupied by the aqueous humour.—In conchology, *chambered shells* are those shells of Cephalopods which have their cells divided by septa, as in the nautilus, ammonites, spirula, &c.

Chame'leon (Gr. *a lion on the ground*), a lizard-like reptile, of the family of the Saurians, noted in all ages for changing its colour,—a property owing to the rete mucosum containing two kinds of colouring matter; fam. Cameleonidæ. — In mineralogy, *Chameleon mineral* is a compound of manganesic acid and potash; so named from the variety of tints it displays when dissolved in water.

Chameleon'idæ, a family of Lizards, of which the Chameleon is the type and genus; they are furnished with four scansorial feet; the toes syndactyle, two before and two behind; the tail prehensile; the tongue vermiform, and capable of great extension.

Chamois Leather, a very soft and pliable leather, chemically prepared from different kinds of skin, dressed with fish-oil, and washed in strong alkali.

Cham'oisite, in mineralogy, an oxide of iron, combined with silica and alumina; so called from Mont Chamoison, in the Valais, where it is dug as an iron ore.

Cham'omile, in botany, the *Anthemis nobilis*, the flower-heads of which are used in medicine as strengthening.

Champawk (from the island *Champaca*, of which it is a native), a tree with large copper-coloured or yellow flowers, which are sweet-scented during the day, but fetid at night.

Chan'delier (Fr.), in fortification, a movable parapet, which serves to support fascines to cover the workers.

Chank, or **Chank-shell**, in conchology, an Eastern name for the Couch-shell (*Voluta gravis*), which is fished up in the gulf of Manaar, on the northwest side of Ceylon. The demand for these shells, caused by the religious rites of the Hindoos, was formerly very great.

Chantant (Fr. *chanter* to sing), a term applied to instrumental music composed in a melodious and singing style.

Chaos (Gr.), in physics, a confused mass of things; a word used to express a supposed confusion of matter previous to its being formed into regular order, or before those laws had come into operation by which harmony and order were first established in the material universe.—*Chaology* is a treatise on chaos, or chaotic matter.

Char'acter (Lat.), in natural history, the peculiar discriminating properties or qualities of animals, plants, or minerals. — In mathematics, the *Characteristic of a logarithm* is its index or exponent;—*Characteristic triangle of a curve* is a rectilinear right-angled triangle, whose hypothenuse makes a part of the curve.

Charadri'adæ, in ornithology, a family of Wading birds, of which the Charadrius, or Plover, is the type and genus. There are four British species — the golden plover, the dotterel, the ring dotterel, and the Kentish plover.

Charcoal, in chemistry, an oxide of carbon, produced by wood being burnt in close vessels.

Charge, in electricity, an accumulation of the electric fluid at any given part of an apparatus, which induces it to fly off with violence from the charged body. — In the veterinary art, a preparation, of the consistence of a thick decoction, used as a remedy for sprains and inflammation.—In heraldry, the figures represented on the escutcheon, by which the bearers are distinguished from one another.

Charian'theæ (Gr. *a beautiful flower*), in botany, a nat. order of the Melastomaceæ, of which the Charianthis is the type and genus.

Chart (Lat. *charta*), a hydrographic or marine map, or a delineation of coasts, shoals, isles, rocks, &c., for the use of seamen. Such was Dr. Johnson's definition; but in science there are various terms employed for expressing the different uses to which charts are applied, and which are thus briefly enumerated by Craig and other lexicographers:—*Globular chart* is a projection, so called from the conformity it bears to the globe itself ;—*Hydrographical charts* are sheets of large paper, on which several parts of the land and sea are described, with their respective coasts, harbours, &c. ;—*Mercator's chart*, like the plain charts, has the meridians represented by parallel right lines, and the degrees of the parallels, or longitude, everywhere equal to those at the equator ;—*Plain charts* have the meridian as well as the parallels of latitude drawn parallel to each other, and the degrees of longitude and latitude everywhere equal to those at the equator ;—*Selenographic charts* are particular descriptions of the appearances, spots,

and maculæ of the moon ;—*Topographic charts* are drafts of some small parts only of the earth, or of some particular place.

Chasseurs (Fr.), in military matters, a select body of light infantry, who are required to be particularly expert in their military operations.—*Chasseurs à cheval*, a kind of light horse, particularly employed in the French army.

Chato'yant (Fr.), in mineralogy, a term applied to stones of an undulating lustre, like that of a cat's eye in the dark.

Chats, in mining, a term applied to the second stratum of a mass of ore in the process of washing.

Cheek, in mechanical science, those pieces of timber in any machine which are double and alike, and form corresponding sides. — In shipbuilding, the term is applied to two pieces of timber fitted on each side of the mast, serving to strengthen it at the top.—*Cheek of a mortise*, the two solid parts on the sides of the mortise.

Cheiran'thus (Gr. *cheir* the hand, and *anthos* a flower), a genus of sweetscented plants, the Wallflower, the species of which are very numerous ; order Cruciferæ.

Cheirol'ogy (Gr. *hand conversation*), a mode of conversing with the fingers, usually practised by the deaf and dumb.

Chei'ropods. (See *Chiropods*.)

Cheirop'tera (Gr. *hand-winged*), in zoology, a family of Mammalia, of which Cheiropter (the Bat or Vespertilio) is the type. The distinguishing characteristic of this family consists in a fold of the skin, which, commencing at the sides of the neck, extends between the fingers of the fore limbs, supports them in the air, and enables them to fly.

Cheirothe'rium (Gr. *a handed wild beast*), in geology and palæology, the name given to an animal whose footprints, resembling those of a hand, are found impressed on new red sandstone. It is considered by Prof. Owen to have been a large Batrachian reptile, for which he proposes the name Labyrinthodon, from the peculiar labyrinthian structure of its teeth.

Cheleryth'rine, in chemistry, a peculiar substance, obtained from the plants *Chelidonium majus* and *Glaucium luteum*, which powerfully excites sneezing.

Chelid'ridæ (Gr. *chelys* a tortoise, and *drao* to act), in herpetology, a family of Chelonians (the Crocodile Tortoises), of which Chelydra is the type.

Chelo'nians, or **Chelon'ides** (Gr. *chelone* a tortoise), in herpetology, an order of reptiles, including the tortoise, turtle, &c., distinguished by the body being enclosed within a double shell, out of which the head, tail, and four extremities extend. The order is divided into four families, each comprehending different genera; as, the *Chelidridæ*, or Crocodile Tortoises; *Testudinidæ*, or 'Land Tortoises; *Emydæ*, or River Tortoises; *Trionycidæ*, or Soft Tortoises; and *Chelonidæ*, or Sea Turtles.

Chelys (Gr. *a tortoise*), a genus of Chelonians (which see).

Chem'ical, relating to chemistry, or resulting from the operation of chemical agencies. (See *Chemical Symbols and Equivalents*, under *Atomic Theory*.)—*Chemicals* are the various substances used in chemistry.

Chem'istry (Arab. *kimia;* Coptic *chems* obscure; Gr. *cheuma* a pouring out; Celtic *kheym* fire), in natural philosophy, the study (says Dr. Black) of the effects of heat and mixture, with a view of discovering their general and subordinate laws; that branch of natural science, as defined by Dr. Brande, which investigates the nature and properties of the elements of matter, and their mutual actions and combinations. Chemistry determines the proportions in which they unite, and ascertains the modes of separating them when united. It also inquires into the laws and powers which preside over and affect the agencies by which material combination or decomposition takes place.—*Organic chemistry* is the chemistry of vegetable and animal compounds; and *Inorganic chemistry* is that which investigates inorganic compounds.—In the *Atomic Theory* of chemistry there are certain *Chemical Symbols* and *Equivalents* which have been adopted for the purpose of expressing by letters and figures the definite proportions in which substances chemically combine; and these are presented in a tabular form under the article *Atomic Theory*, to which the reader is referred.

Chemo'sis (Gr. *gaping*), in pathology, an affection from which the membrane that lines the posterior surface of the eyelids is continued over the fore part of the eyeball.

Chenopodia'ceæ (Gr. *goose-footed*), in botany, a nat. order of Exogens, consisting of herbaceous plants, of which the Chenopodium, or Goosefoot, is the type.

Chœropot'amus (Gr. *river hedgehog*), in geology, an extinct genus of the or-der Pachydermata, considered as a link between the Peccary and the Anoplotherium.

Chert, a siliceous mineral, fusible and less splintery than flint.

Chert Stone, a mineral quarried in Derbyshire and Cornwall, and applied to the forming of the stones of pottery mills.

Chev'aux-de-frise (Fr.), in military science, a piece of timber traversed with revolving spikes, used in making a retrenchment to stop cavalry.

Chevron (Fr. *gable end*), an architectural ornament characteristic of the Norman style of building.—In heraldry, an honourable ordinary, representing two oblique rafters, or the gable end of a house.

Chev'ronel, a diminutive of chevron.

Chia'ro-oscu'ro (Ital.), in painting, the art of advantageously combining light and shade in a picture; a drawing in black and white.

Chias'tolite (Gr.), a mineral occurring crystallized in rectangular prisms, which present a black cross in their transverse section, whence the name. In contains silica, alumina, magnesia, and oxide of iron.

Chicken-pox, in pathology, the disease Varicella, or Water-jags, an eruption of vesicles on the skin, which burst and concrete into scabs.

Chickweed, in botany, a name given to various genera and species of plants: —1. Common Chickweed, *Stellaria media;*—2. Sea Chickweed, *Arenaria peploides;*—3. Mouse-ear Chickweed, the genus *Cerastium;*—4. Chick Winter-green, *Trientalis Europæa.*

Chic'ory, a perennial plant, from the root of which a powder is produced, used as a substitute for coffee.

Chil'drenite, a crystallized mineral, which is a compound of iron, alumina, and phosphoric acid.

Chil'iad (Gr. *chilias* a thousand), a collection or sum containing a thousand; a term applied to tables of logarithms, which were first arranged in thousands.—*Chiliagon* is a plane figure of a thousand sides and angles. —*Chiliahedron* is a figure of a thousand equal sides.

Chil'ian Pine, a fine lofty tree of Chili, the *Araucaria imbricata.*

Chilog'natha (Gr. *cheilos* a lip, and *gnatha* a jaw), in entomology, an order of Myriapoda, distinguished by having the two mandibles and the tongue so united as to form a large lower lip. They are found beneath the bark of trees, and in humid places.

Chi'loma (Gr.), in zoology, the upper lip or muzzle of a quadruped, when tumid and continued uninterruptedly from the nostril, as in the camel.

Chilop'oda (Gr. *chilias* a thousand, and *podes* feet), in entomology, an order of myriapodous invertebrate animals, or Centipedes, the genera of which have elongated antennæ, and a depressed body, covered with coriaceous plates.

Chil'tonite, in mineralogy, a variety of prehnite.

Chimær'idæ, a family of the cartilaginous order of fishes, of which Chimæra is the genus and type.

Chimes, in campanology, a term applied to a set of bells scientifically tuned to the modern musical scale, and struck with hammers acted on by a pinned cylinder, which revolves by means of clockwork; the term is also applied to the music produced by the bells in a steeple.

Chimpan'zee, a species of Quadrumana, the *Simia troglodytes*, or African Orang, which makes the nearest approach to the likeness of man.

Chir'idæ, a family of acanthopterygious fishes, of which the Chirus is the genus; tribe Blennidæ.

Chirol'ogy (Gr. *hand conversation*), the art of communicating or interchanging thoughts with the deaf and dumb by means of certain signs made with the hands and fingers.

Chironec'tidæ (Gr. *cheir* the hand, and *nectos* swimming), a family of Frog-fishes, of which the Chironectes, a genus of cheliform fishes, is the type.

Chiron'omy (Gr. *cheir*, and *nomos* law), the science that treats of gesticulation, or pantomime, and oratorical action.

Chi'roplast (Gr. *cheir*, and *plasso* to form), in music, an instrument used when learning the pianoforte, for accustoming the hand to a particular position when playing.

Chirop'odist (Gr. *cheir*, and *podes* feet), one who treats of or cures diseases of the hands or feet, and extracts corns.

Chi'ropoda (Gr. *cheir* and *podes*), mammiferous animals with hands.

Chirur'gery (Gr. *cheir*, and *ergon* work), that department of physiological science in which the hand is employed for the cure of disease. *Surgery* is now the term commonly used.—*Chirurgical*, relating to surgery.

Chlæna'ceæ (Gr. *a cloak*, or involucrum), a nat. order of handsome flowering trees or shrubs, natives of Madagascar.

Chlorace'tic Acid, an acid formed by the action of chlorine; an acetic acid exposed to bright sunshine.

Chloral (Gr. *chloros* yellowish green), in chemistry, an oily fluid of a peculiarly penetrating agreeable smell, obtained by the action of chlorine or alcohol. It consists of 4 atoms of carbon, 3 of chlorine, 1 of hydrogen, and 2 of oxygen.

Chlo'ranile (Gr.), in chemistry, a pale yellow substance, obtained in pearly scales by the action of chlorine on a warm alcoholic solution of chlorisatine. It consists of 6 equivalents of carbon, 2 of oxygen, and 2 of chlorine. —*Chloranilic acid* is an acid obtained from the chloranilate of potash by the action of hydrochloric acid.

Chlorantha'ceæ (Gr. *chloros*, and *anthos* a flower), in botany, an order of herbaceous plants, with aromatic taste, of which the Chloranthus is the type. The plants are natives of Tropical India, the West Indies, South America, and the Society Islands.

Chlorate (Gr.), in chemistry, a salt produced by the combination of chloric acid with a salifiable base.

Chloric, pertaining to chlorine.—*Chloric acid*, an acid composed of chlorine and oxygen.—*Chloriodate*, a compound of the chloriodic acid with a salifiable base.

Chloride (Gr.), in chemistry, a compound of chlorine with a metal or other elementary substance.—*Chloride of lime* is a preparation extensively used in the process of bleaching, of which Dr. Ure gives the following analysis:—Chlorine, 39·5; lime, 39·9; water, 20·6.—*Chloride of potash*, a valuable compound, prepared by passing chlorine gas into a mixture of 1 lb. of caustic lime and 1 lb. of potash with 8 lbs. of water.

Chlorine (Gr.), in chemistry, an elementary gas obtained from common salt, and so called from its yellow colour. It has a disagreeable odour, and is the most suffocating of all the gases; it speedily destroys all animal and vegetable colours when water is present, which renders it extremely useful in the process of bleaching.—*Hypochlorous acid* consists of 2 atoms of chlorine and 1 of oxygen;—*Chlorous acid*, of 2 atoms of chlorine and 4 of oxygen;—*Chloric acid*, of 2 atoms of chlorine and 5 of oxygen;—*Perchloric acid*, of 2 atoms of chlorine and 7 of oxygen.—*Chloronitrous gas* is obtained when fused chloride of sodium, potassium, or calcium in powder is treated with strong nitric acid.—*Chloriodic acid* is a compound of chlorine and iodine, and more properly termed the *chloride of iodine*.

Chloris'atine (Gr.), a chemical compound obtained in transparent four-sided crystals, when a solution of isatine is saturated with chlorine.

Chlorite (Gr.), a mineral occurring in the granite and metamorphic rocks (prismatic talc). It is of various shades of green, white, and yellow, and consists of silica, magnesia, oxide of iron, alumina, and water.

Chloro- (Gr.), a prefix to numerous scientific words, indicating a yellowish-green colour; as, *Chloroacetate*, a compound of chloroacetic and acetic acids with a base;—*Chloroacetic acid*, an acid obtained by hydrated acetic acid (vinegar) being exposed to the combined action of chlorine gas and the rays of the sun, and other manipulations;—*Chlorobenzide* is a colourless oily liquid, obtained by the distillation of chloride of benzole with an alkali;—*Chlorocarbonic acid gas* is a gas made by exposing a mixture of equal measures of dry chlorine and carbonic oxide gases to sunshine, when a rapid combination ensues, and they contract to half their volume;—*Chloropal*, a mineral found associated with opal, which is earthy and conchoidal;—*Chlorophane*, the name of a fluor-spar, which, when exposed to heat, exhibits the phenomena of phosphorescence in green colours;—*Chlorophyl*, a term applied to the green colouring matter found in leaves, stalks, and juice of plants;—*Chlorosamide*, a compound obtained by causing chloride of salicicule to absorb dry ammoniacal gas, the result being a yellow mass, which, when dissolved in boiling ether, separates on cooling in iridescent crystals of a yellow colour.

Chlo'roform (Gr. *chloros* green, and Lat. *formica* an ant, on account of its resemblance to formic acid), a valuable anæsthetic agent, obtained by distilling a mixture of chloride of lime and alcohol, and first applied in 1847 as a substitute for sulphuric ether, to produce, through its inhalation, insensibility to pain in surgical operations.

Chlorom'eter (Gr. *chloros*, and *metron* a measure), in chemistry, an instrument for testing the discolouring or bleaching powers of chloride of lime.

Chlo'romys (Gr. *chloros*, and *mys* a rat), in zoology, a genus of Rodents (the Yellow Rat), which inhabits the warmer latitudes of America, and bears some resemblance to the hare or rabbit.

Chlo'rophyl (Gr. *chloros*, and *phyllon* a leaf), in botany, the green colouring matter of the leaves of plants.

Chloro'sis (Gr.), in pathology, the disease known as green sickness, incident to females, and indicated by a greenish colour of the skin.

Choke-damp, in mining, the carbonic acid gas which escapes in mines.

Chole'ic Acid (Gr. *chole* bile), in chemistry, an acid obtained from bile, the chemical formula of which is $C_{76} H_{66} N_2 O_{22}$.—*Choloidic acid* is obtained when choleic acid is boiled with hydrochloric acid.

Choles'terine (Gr.), the fat of bile, the principal ingredient of biliary concretions.

Chondrine (Gr. *chondros* gristle or cartilage), a substance somewhat resembling gelatine, produced by the action of hot water on cartilage. It is the substance which forms the tissue of cartilage, as it occurs in the trachea, nose, &c.

Chon'drites (Lat. *chondrus* a sea-weed), in geology, the name of fossil marine plants found in the chalk and other formations.

Chondroglos'sus (Gr. *chondros*, and *glossa* the tongue), in anatomy, an epithet applied to a fasciculus of muscular fibre, extending from the lesser cornu of the hyoid bone to the tongue.

Chondrog'raphy, or **Chondrology** (Gr. *chondros* cartilage), in anatomy, a description of, or discourse on, cartilages.

Chondropteryg'ians (Gr. *chondros*, and *pteryx* a fin), in ichthyology, one of the two great sections in which the class Pisces is divided. It embraces those fishes the bones and fin spines of which are formed of gristle, viz., the sturgeons, sharks, rays, &c.

Chon'ikrite, a yellowish-grey mineral, consisting of silica, alumina, magnesia, lime, protoxide of iron, and water; it is found in round masses in the Isle of Elba.

Chord (Lat.), in geometry, a right line drawn from one part of an arc of a circle to the other.—In music, the union of two or more sounds forming an entire harmony.

Chorda (Gr. *chorde* a cord or tendon), in anatomy, a term of frequent application; as, *Chorda tympani*, a filament of the videan nerve which enters the tympanum;—*C. tendinea*, the tendinous strings which connect the *carneæ columnæ* of the heart to the auricular valves;—*C. vocales*, the vocal ligaments, or thyro-artænoid articulation.

Cho'rea (Lat. *a dance with singing*), in pathology, a disease which affects with irregular movements the muscles of voluntary motion; commonly known as *St. Vitus's Dance*.

Cho'rion (Gr.), in anatomy, the delicate structure which constitutes the exterior membrane of the fœtus in the womb.—In botany, the external membrane of the seeds of plants.—*Choroid*, resembling the chorion ; a term applied to the inner tunic of the eye, and also to the web of the pia mater.

Chorog'raphy (Gr. *choros* a region), the description of a district, place, or region.

Chrematis'tics (Gr. *chremata* riches), in political economy, the science of national wealth, or of the means of acquiring it.

Chris'tianite, in mining, a variety of anorthite.

Christmas Rose, in botany, the Black Hellebore, the roots of which are poisonous, but the fibres are used in medicine as a drastic purge.

Chro'mascope (Gr. *chroma*, and *skopeo* to view), an instrument for exhibiting colours.

Chromate (Gr. *chroma* colour), in chemistry, a salt formed by the union of chromic acid with a base.—*Chromate of potash* is a neutral salt; and the insoluble salts of chromic acid, such as the chromates of baryta, and oxides of zinc, lead, mercury, and silver, are prepared by mixing the soluble salts of these bases with a solution of chromate of potassa. The yellow chromate of lead is used as a pigment, under the name of chrome yellow.

Chromat'ic (Gr. *colour*), in music, applied to musical sounds, or semitones.

Chromat'ics (Gr.), in optics, the science which treats of the colours of light and natural bodies.

Chromatog'raphy, or **Chromatol'ogy**, a treatise on colours.

Chro'matrope (Gr. *chroma*, and *trepo* to turn), in optics, an apparatus for exhibiting the appearance of a stream of colours by the revolution of a double set of coloured circular arcs.

Chro'matype (Gr.), a photographic process on chemically-prepared paper.

Chrome Ochre, oxide of chrome, a pulverous mineral of a green colour, consisting of chromium and oxygen.

Chrome Yellow, a rich pigment derived from the chromate of lead.

Chromic Acid, a chemical preparation used by bleachers and calico-printers for dyeing orange or red.

Chromite (Gr.), a mineral containing chromium.

Chro'mium (Gr. *chroma* colour), in mineralogy, a metal discovered by Vauquelin in 1797. It was found in a rare Siberian mineral, which contained lead, and was called, from its colour, *red-lead*, but which is now known as *chromate of lead*.—Chromium is brittle and infusible, it is of a white colour, with a shade of yellow, and a metallic lustre. Its chemical equivalent is 28. Its principal chemical compounds are—*Protosulphuret of chromium*, formula Cr + S, or Cr S;—*Sesquichloride of chromium*, the chemical formula of which is Cr + 3 Cl, or Cr Cl3 ;—*Sesquifluoride of chromium*, formula C + 3 F, or Cr2 F3 ;—*Sesquisulphuret of chromium*, formula 2 Cr + 3 S, or Cr3 S3.

Chromo-lithog'raphy (Gr. *chroma*, and *lithos* stone), the art of printing coloured and tinted lithographs.

Chromo-typog'raphy (Gr. *chroma*, and *typos* type), a new process of letterpress printing in colours.

Chronic (Gr. *chronos* time), in pathology, an epithet applied to such diseases as are of long duration, in opposition to those of more rapid progress, termed *acute*.

Chronol'ogy (Gr. *chronos* time), the science which treats of the various divisions of time, or presents a tabular view of historical events.

Chronom'eter (Gr. *a measurer of time*), a time-piece, or watch, so perfectly constructed as to note time with exact precision ; it is used for ascertaining and keeping the longitude of a ship's course at sea.

Chron'oscope (Gr. *chronos*, and *skopeo*, to view), a chronometer; a pendulum.

Chrys'alis (Gr. *chrysos* gold), in entomology, the second stage of a metabolian insect, during which it is transformed from the caterpillar state to a perfect winged insect, as the butterfly or moth.

Chrysam'mic Acid (Gr.), in chemistry, an acid obtained by the action of nitric acid on aloes, which forms a fine golden-yellow powder.

Chrysid'idæ, or **Chrys'ides** (Gr. *chrysos* gold), a family of hymenopterous insects, of which Chrysis, or the Golden Wasp, is the type. This order is distinguished from others by being furnished with a tubuliferous ovipositor. They are all parasitic, and coloured with the richest metallic hues.

Chryso- (Gr. *chrysos* gold), a prefix to numerous scientific words of Greek origin, denoting a golden or bright yellow colour.

Chrysobalana'ceæ (Gr. *chrysos*, and *balanos* an acorn), in botany, a natural order of plants, which Dr. Lindley classes in his Rosal alliance. It consists of shrubs or trees, of which the Chrysobalanos is the type.

Chrysober'yl (Gr. *chrysos* golden, and

beryllos beryl), in mineralogy, a hard precious stone employed in jewellery; prismatic corundums found crystallized in the alluvial deposits of rivers. It consists of alumina, lime, silica, and oxide of iron.

Chrysocol'la (Gr. *chrysos*, and *kolla* gluten), in mineralogy, a variety of malachite, or copper ore, consisting of oxide of copper, silica, carbonic acid, and water.

Chrysolep'tic Acid (Gr. *chrysos*, and *lepis* a scale), an acid obtained in bright yellow scales from the washings of chrysammic acid. Its compounds are *chrysolepate of potash*, in long shining needles; *chrysolepate of silver*, in brownish-red needles; *chrysolepate of soda*, in long green needles.

Chrys'olite (Gr. *golden stone*), a crystallized mineral or precious stone. It consists of magnesia, silica, and oxide of iron : sp. gr. 3·5.

Chrysomel'idæ (Gr. *golden-limbed*), in entomology, a family of coleopterous insects, of which the Chrysomela is the type.

Chrys'oprase (Gr. *golden spar*), a variety of calcedony, much prized by jewellers, consisting chiefly of silica, oxide of nickel, and minute portions of magnesia, alumina, lime, and oxide of iron.

Chrys'otype (Gr.), a photographic process in which a solution of gold is used.

Chyle (Gr. *chylos* juice), in physiology, a milky fluid formed in the stomach during the process of digestion, and conveyed by the absorbent vessels of the intestinal canal to the thoracic duct.—*Chylification* is the process by which the chyle is converted into chyme.—*Chylopoietic* is a term applied to the organs engaged in the formation of the chyle.

Chyme (Gr. *chymos* juice), in physiology, the pulpy substance into which food is converted after being subjected to the action of the stomach, from which, on the addition of the biliary and pancreatic fluids, the chyme is subsequently separated.—*Chymification* is the process by which food is converted into chyme.

Cica'didæ (Lat. *cicada*, the grasshopper), a family of leaping hemipterous insects, the Singing Grasshopper, remarkable for their musical chirp.

Cic'atrix (Lat.), in surgery, the scar left after the healing of a wound.—*Cicatrisation* is the process of healing a wound.

Cichora'ceæ, a tribe of composite plants, constituting the sub-order Ligulifloræ.

Cicindele'tæ, a tribe of coleopterous insects, of which Cicindela, an insect of predatory habits, is the genus.

Cico'nia (Lat.), a genus of wading birds (the Storks), the largest of the Heron family.

Cil'ia (Lat.), in anatomy, the hairs which grow from the margin of the eyelids.—In botany, long hairs on plants or leaves.—*Ciliary*, belonging to the eyelashes.

Ciliobra'chiate (Lat. *cilium*, and *brachium* an arm), in physiology, having the arms provided with cilia, more especially applied to a class of Polypods.

Cil'iogrades (Lat. *cilium* an eyelash, and *gradior* to step), a tribe of the Acalephans, or Sea-nettles, which swim by means of cilia.

Cim'bia, in architecture, a fillet or band round the shaft of a column.

Cimic'ides (Lat. *cimex* a bug), an extensive tribe of hemipterous insects, of which *Cimex lectuarius*, or common Bed-bug, is the type.

Cim'olite, in mineralogy, a light grey silicate of alumina, from the island of Cimolo.

Cincho'na, a celebrated tree in Peru, which produces Peruvian bark, and also its extract, quinine, both extensively used in medicine.—*Cinchonaceæ* is a nat. order of plants, the Rubiaceæ of Jussieu and other botanists, of which Cinchona is the type.—*Cinchonine* is a vegetable alkali found in cinchona.—*Cinchonate* is a salt formed of cinchonic acid and a base.

Cineri'tious (Lat.), resembling ashes; grey.

Cin'gulum (Lat. *a girdle*), in zoology, a term applied to the neck of a tooth, or that constriction which separates the crown from the fang.

Cin'nabar, in mineralogy, a beautiful red pigment, the sulphuret of mercury. Vermilion is pure cinnabar, being a compound of mercury and sulphur in nearly the same proportion, viz. : mercury, 84·50; sulphur, 14·75 : sp. gr. 6·7—8·2.

Cinnam'ic Acid is an acid formed in translucent prisms from oil of cinnamon.

Cin'namon Stone, a mineral of a red colour found in Ceylon and Brazil. It is composed of silica, alumina, lime, and oxide of iron.

Cinnyr'idæ, in ornithology, a family of birds, the Sun-birds, which are distinguished by their brilliant plumage : Cinnyris is the type and genus.

Cinquefoil (Fr.), in botany, a five-leaved clover; the common name of plants of the genus Potentilla.—In architecture, a five-leaved ornament, in circular and other divisions of the windows of ancient churches.

Cip'olin (Ital. *cipola* an onion), in mineralogy, a green Italian marble, with white zones. That from Rome contains carbonate of lime, quartz, schist, and a little iron.

Circle (Lat. *circulus*), in geometry, a plane figure bounded by a curved line called its circumference, having all its parts equally distant from a common centre.—In science and the arts, *circle* has various applications:—*Astronomical circles* are instruments to measure angles; as equatorial and mural circles.—*Circles of declination* are great circles intersecting each other in the poles of the world.—*Diurnal circles* are parallels to the equinoctial, supposed to be described by the stars, and other points of the heavens, in their apparent diurnal rotation about the earth.—*Horary circle* on the globe is a brazen circle fixed to the north pole, and furnished with an index, showing the difference of meridians, and serving for the solution of many problems.—In dialing, *horary circles* are the lines which show the hours on dials.—*Circles of latitude* are great circles perpendicular to the plane of the ecliptic, passing through the poles thereof, and through every star and planet.—*Circles of longitude* are several less circles parallel to the ecliptic, still diminishing in proportion as they recede from it.—*Polar circles* are immovable circles parallel to the equator, and at a distance from the poles equal to the greatest declination of the ecliptic.—(*Worcester, Craig, National Cyc.,* &c.) — The *Quadrature of the circle* is a problem of great celebrity in the history of mathematical science, which has never yet been satisfactorily solved. (See *Quadrature.*)

Cir'cular Polariza'tion, in natural philosophy, and especially in the undulacory theory of light, a supposed circular rotation of the particles of ether in certain media, when a pencil of plane polarized light is allowed to pass through these media.—In mathematics, *Circular parts* consist of the fine parts of a right-angled or a quadrantal spherical triangle; they are the legs, the complement of the hypothenuse, and the complements of the two oblique angles.—*Circular sailing*, in navigation, is the art of sailing on the arc of a great circle, by which distance is often saved.

Cir'culating Dec'imals, decimals in which two or more figures are constantly repeated in the same order.

Circula'tion, in physiology, a term applied to the circulation of the blood, or the function whereby the blood is conveyed from the left ventricle of the heart through the arteries and veins and right auricle to the right ventricle, and thence through the lungs to the left auricle.

Cir'culus (Lat.), in anatomy, any circular portion of the animal body; as, *circulus oculi*, the orb of the eye.

Circum (Lat.), in frequent use as a prefix to compound words, signifying *around* or *about*.

Circumduc'tion (Lat. *circum*, and *duco* to lead), in physiology, a motion in which a bone is made to describe a cone, the apex of which is at the joint.

Cir'cumflexus (Lat. *bent round*), in anatomy, applied to certain nerves and vessels which wind round joints or bones.

Circumgyra'tion (Lat. *circling about*), motion in a circle.

Circumpo'lar (Lat. *circum*, and *polos* the pole), in astronomy, an epithet applied to those stars which appear to revolve round the north pole, and never set in the southern latitudes.

Circumvolu'tion (Lat. *a turning round*), in architecture, the windings in the spiral part of the Ionic capital.

Cirrho'sis (Gr. *yellowish*), in pathology, a shrinking of the liver.

Cirri (Lat. *cirrus* a tendril or fringe), in ichthyology, the soft filaments attached to the jaws of certain fishes.—In botany, the fine thread-like tendrils or filaments by which certain climbing plants attach themselves to stones, walls, trees, &c.

Cir'ripeds (Lat. *cirrus* a curl, and *pedes* feet), a class of Mollusca, the animals of which are furnished with an enveloping mantle and testaceous juices.

Cirro-cu'mulus (Lat.), in meteorology, an orbicular mass of clouds arranged in extensive beds.—*Cirro-stratus*, a flat cloud of great horizontal extension.

Cir'ropods (Gr. *fringe-footed*), in zoology, a class of invertebrate animals with curled jointed feet.

Cir'rus (Lat.), a curl cloud, named from its resemblance to a distended lock of hair.

Cir'socele (Gr. *kirsos* a dilated vein), in pathology, a morbidity of the spermatic veins in the groin.—*Cirsomphalus*, a tumour formed by a varicose dilatation of the veins round the navel.—*Cirsophthalmia*, a varicose or swelled state of the vessels of the eye.

Cista'ceæ (Gr. *kistos* a capsule), in botany, a nat. order of plants (the Rock Roses), of which Cistus, an elegant flowering shrub, is the type.

Citigra'da (Lat. *swift runners*), in entomology, a tribe of Arachnidans, or spiders.

Citric (Lat. *citreum*), of or belonging to the lemon.—In chemistry, *Citric acid* is obtained in crystals from the juice of lemons, consisting of carbon, hydrogen, and oxygen.—*Citrate* is a salt formed by the union of citric acid with a salifiable base, as the citrate of potash.

Civet (Ger. *zebeth*), a semi-fluid matter used as a perfume. It has an odour like musk, and is obtained from several species of carnivorous animals of the genus Viverra, or Civet Cat. The substance is secreted in a pouch.

Clairvoy'ance (Fr. *clear-sightedness*), a state of somnolence in which persons profess to see that which under ordinary circumstances is not apparent to the sight.

Class (Lat. *classis*), in zoology and botany, a scientific arrangement, containing the subordinate divisions of order, genus, and species.

Classman, a term in the University of Oxford equivalent to that of Wrangler and Optime at Cambridge.

Clausthale (from *Clausthal* in the Hartz), in mineralogy, the selenuret of lead, a mineral of a lead-grey colour and metallic lustre, found in veins of hæmatite. It consists of lead, selenium, and cobalt.

Clavicor'nes (Lat. *clavus* a club, and *cornu* a horn), in entomology, a family of insects whose antennæ end in a club-shaped enlargement, as the burying beetle.

Cla'vier, in music, an assemblage of all the keys of an organ or pianoforte.

Clavipal'pi (Lat. *the feelers of insects*), in entomology, a family of coleopterous insects, living on boleti and fungi, of the section Tetrametra.

Clay (Sax.), in geology, the plastic material which forms some of the important beds of the earth's formations. The London clay is an extensive deposit of blue and yellow clay, including beds of sandstone and coarse limestone, of which Roman cement is made. It belongs to the eocene, or earliest of the tertiary deposits, and contains the remains of tortoises, crocodiles, fishes, and marine shells, nearly the whole of which are of extinct species.—*Clay-slate*, an indurated slate, found in metamorphic or fossiliferous rocks, usually composed of silica, alumina, and iron.—*Clay-stone* is an indurated clay of a purplish colour; a variety of prismatic felspar.

Clayes (Fr.), in fortification, wattles made with stakes interwoven with osiers to cover lodgments.

Clear-story, or **Clere-story**, in architec-

ture, an upper story, or row of windows, in a Gothic church, tower, or other erection, rising clear above the adjoining parts of the building.

Cleavage, in mineralogy, applied to minerals which have a regular structure, and are said to admit of cleavage. The surfaces exposed by splitting are termed the *faces* of the *cleavage*. When minerals are divisible in two or more directions, they are then said to have a double, treble, or four-fold cleavage.—In geology, the word is said to indicate a phenomenon in slate and other rocks, by which they split up into thin plates, or slates, at a considerable angle to the plane of deposition or stratification.

Clef (Fr.), in music, a mark or character for the key, placed at the beginning of the staff or stave. It is termed the base, the tenor, or the treble clef. The mean clef gives the name of C to any line on which it is placed. It is called the soprano clef when placed on the first line; the mezzo-soprano when on the second; the alto, or contra-tenore, or counter-tenor, when on the third; and the tenor when on the fourth.

Cleft, in farriery, a disease which attacks the heels of horses, superinduced by surfeits or hard labour.

Cleido (Gr. *a clavicle*), in anatomy, a prefix to certain terms connected with the clavicle; as, *cleido-costalis*, a ligament which passes from the cartilage of the first rib to the inferior surface of the clavicle; *cleido-scapular*, applied to the articulations of the clavicle with the scapula.

Clema'tideæ (Gr. *klematis* a vine branch), in botany, a tribe of plants of the nat. order Ranunculaceæ: Clematis, or Virgin's Bower, is one of the genera. It consists of pretty climbing shrubs.

Cleom'eæ (Gr. *to shut*), in botany, a tribe of plants of the nat. order Capparidaceæ, of which Cleome, a pretty flowering plant, is the type.

Clere-story. (See *Clear-story*.)

Cler'idæ, a family of coleopterous insects, embracing nine genera, of which Clerus is the type.

Climac'teric (Gr.), a critical period of a person's life.

Climatol'ogy (Gr. *klima* climate, and *logos* a treatise), a discourse on the different climates of the earth; an investigation of the causes which form a climate.

Clin'ic, or **Clin'ical** (Gr. *lying down*), in pathology, a term applied to patients on a sick bed, such as visits made and instructions delivered there.—*Clinical physician*, one who practises medicine.—*Clinical lecture*, a lecture or instruction given at the bed-side of a patient.

Clink-stone, in mineralogy and geology, a species of trap rock, composed of felspar, sometimes termed trap porphyry. This mineral owes the name of clinkstone, as well as that of phonolite, to the sharp sound it gives when struck with a hammer. In basalt or wacke, when the felspar greatly prevails, and the texture becomes nearly compact, it passes into clinkstone; again, when clinkstone has a more earthy structure, it passes into claystone.

Clinom'eter (Gr. *klino* to bend, and *metron* a measure), an instrument for measuring the dip of mineral strata, constructed somewhat on the principle of the level.

Clion'idæ, in malacology, a family of naked Mollusca, of which Clio is the type; order Pteropoda.

Clit'oris (Gr.), in anatomy, the small, prominent, elongated organ which occupies the central and superior part of the vulva in female mammifera.

Clo'acæ (Lat.), in pathology, the openings in cases of necrosis, or mortification of the bones, which lead to the dead bone; the common excretory outlet of birds and some other animals.

Clonic (Gr. *klonos* violent emotion), in pathology, applied to spasmodic convulsion, with ultimate relaxation.

Clouds (Sax. *gehlod*), in natural philosophy, a collection of vapours suspended in the air, or floating, sometimes low and sometimes at a considerable height, in the atmosphere. Clouds assume a great variety of appearances — nebulous, striated, mackled, &c.—and have been thus classified by meteorologists under different names:—1. The *Cirrus*, or Curl-cloud, resembling a lock of hair or a feather. It is the thinnest of all the forms which the clouds assume, and rises to a height of from three to five miles above the level of the sea. The *Comoid* cirrus, or the "Mare's tail," is the true form of the cirrus. —2. The *Cumulus*, or Stacken-cloud, which increases from above in dense convex or conical heaps.— 3. The *Stratus*, or Fall-cloud, is the name given to an extended continuous level sheet of cloud, composed of fogs and mists. —4. The *Cirro-cumulus*, or Sonder-cloud, consists of well-defined small roundish masses of cloud.—5. The *Cirro-stratus*, or Wane-cloud, is a slightly-inclined sheet, attenuated at its surface.— 6. *Cumulo-stratus*, or Twin-cloud, is a compound of the cumulus and the cirro-stratus.—7. *Cumulo-cirro-stratus, Nimbus*, or Rain-cloud, is a dense cloud, spreading out into a crown, and passing beneath into a shower of rain.—*Howard*.

Clove (Sp. *clava*), in botany, the aromatic produce of the genus Caryophyllus.

Clover, in botany, the popular name of different genera of herbaceous plants, of great value in pasturing, viz.:— *Trifolium pratense*, or Red Clover; *T. repens*, or White Clover; *T. procumbens*, Procumbent Trefoil, Yellow Clover.

Clupe'idæ (Lat. *clupea* a herring), in ichthyology, a family of abdominal malacopterygious fishes, of which the Clupea, comprehending the herring, sprat, whitebait, shad, and pilchard, is the type and genus.

Clusia'ceæ, in botany, an order of exogenous tropical plants, of which the Clusia, or Balsam, is the type and genus.

Clyther'idæ, in entomology, a family of monilicorn coleopterous insects, of which the Clythera is the type.

Clytus (Gr. *noisy*), in entomology, a very extensive tribe of coleopterous insects; fam. Cerambycidæ.

Coal (Germ. *kohl*), in mineralogy, an inflammable fossil substance, of vegetable origin, found embedded in strata of different thicknesses. It appears to have been produced, in primeval ages, by the long-continued decomposition of wood, by which 9 atoms of carbonic acid, 3 of carburetted hydrogen, and 3 of water have been separated. The coal of the tertiary strata of the earth's crust is generally lignite-wood or brown coal.—In geology, the *coal formation, coal-fields*, or *coal measures* are a series of deposits consisting of coal, limestone, ironstone, sandstone, and shales of various kinds, estimated in Scotland at an entire thickness of 1,200 yards, or more. The coal-fields of England are numerous, and the coal is of superior quality.—*Coal-gas*, carburetted hydrogen gas, produced by the distillation of coal, and now generally used in lighting streets, houses, &c.— *Coal-tar*, produced in the distillation of coal. *Coal-plants*, plants the remains of which are found in the strata of the coal formation, and from the wood of which coal itself has been produced.—*Craig's Surveys*.

Cob, in mining, the process of crushing ore with hammers to separate the worthless parts.

Cobalt (Germ. *kobold*), in mineralogy, a metal of a grey colour, occurring chiefly in combination with arsenic; sp. gr. 7·83. The oxide of cobalt, when in the state of a hydrate, or when largely diluted by fusion with glass or borax, produces the rich blue colour so valuable in the manufacture of porcelain and pottery ware.—*Cobaltine* is a mineral of a silver or yellowish colour, with a tinge of red, occurring in cubic crystals and their varieties.—*Cobalto-cyanide* is a compound in which 1 atom of sesquicyanide of cobalt is united with 3 atoms of another cyanide.

Cobbing, in mining, a name for old furnace-bottoms, pieces of brick, &c., thrown into a smelting furnace.

Cobit'idæ (Lat. *cobio* a gudgeon), in ichthyology, a family of viviparous malacopterygious fishes, of which Cobitinæ is a sub-family.

Coc'cides, (Lat. *coccus*), a family of hymenopterous insects, the Plant-bug, of which the *Coccus cacti*, or Cochineal insect, is the type; whence the beautiful scarlet colour used as a dyestuff is derived. (See *Cochineal.*)

Coccinel'la (dim. of Lat. *coccinus* scarlet), a genus of coleopterous insects, popularly known as lady-birds, or lady-cows, which are very useful in the destruction of aphides, or woodlice.

Coc'colite(Gr.*kokkos*, and *lithos* a stone), in mineralogy, a variety of augite of a bluish-green colour, consisting of silica, alumina, lime, magnesia, oxides of iron, and manganese.

Coccothraus'tinæ (Gr. *kokkos*, and *thraustos* broken), a sub-family of Fringillidæ, or Hard-bills, of which the bill is remarkably strong, and adapted for breaking the seeds on which they feed.

Coc'culus In'dicus, a fruit of the East Indies, which contains a poisonous principle, called picrotoxin.

Coccus (Gr. and Lat. *an insect*), the Cochineal insect (*Coccus cacti*), which constitutes the valuable red dye-stuff, cochineal.

Coccyx (Gr.), in anatomy, a bone at the extremity of the os sacrum.—*Coccygeius* is a muscle of the os coccygis.

Coccyz'inæ (Gr. *kokkyx* a cuckoo), in ornithology, a section of the Cuculidæ, or Horn-billed Cuckoos, of which the genus Coccyzus is the type. They are distinguished by the hooked character of the bill.

Co'chineal (Sp.), a substance consisting of dried insects, extensively used as a beautiful scarlet dye, produced from the *Coccus cacti*. The colouring principle is obtained by the insect from the scarlet juice of the plant on which it feeds: with alum it yields the beau-

tiful lake called carmine.—*Cochineal fig*, a species of Cactus, so named from a wild kind of cochineal insect feeding on it.

Coch'lea (Gr. *kochlos* a shell-fish with a spiral shell), in anatomy, a part of the internal ear, of a conical form, indicated by a spiral groove.

Coch'leare (Lat. a *spoon*), a term of frequent use in medical prescriptions; as, *C. amplum*, a table-spoonful; *C. mediocre*, a dessert-spoonful; *C. minimum*, a tea-spoonful.

Cocks'comb, in botany, the common name of plants of the genus Celosia; order Amaranthaceæ. — *Cockscomb pyrites* is a variety of white or prismatic iron pyrites; colour nearly tin white.

Cocoon, an oblong ball or covering of silk, fabricated by the silkworm, and other insects, for their larvæ during the period of metamorphosis.

Cod-liver Oil, in medicine, a valuable oil obtained from the liver of the cod.

Coehorn, in military science, a small kind of mortar, first introduced by the celebrated engineer whose name it bears.

Coelacan'thidæ (Gr. *a hollow spine*), in geology, a family of ganoid fishes, so called from their having been armed with hollow spines. The Coelacanthus is the type and genus.

Coelelmin'tha (Gr. *a hollow worm*), a term applied to the intestinal worms which have an alimentary tube.

Coe'liac (Gr. *koilia* the belly), in anatomy, an epithet relating to the abdomen, or the intestinal canal.— *Coeliac passion* is a painful species of diarrhœa.

Coffea'ceæ, in botany, a tribe of plants, consisting of trees and shrubs, of which the genus Coffea is the type. There are numerous species, one of which, the common coffee tree, rises from 5 to 15 feet in height, with oval-oblong glabrous leaves, and axillary aggregate flowers; order Cinchonaceæ. (See *Caffein.*)

Coffer (Sax. *cofre*; Fr. *coffre*), in mineralogy, a trough in which tin ore is broken to pieces.—In fortification, a hollow lodgment across a dry moat.—In architecture, a square depression or sinking in each interval between the modillions of the Corinthian cornice.—*Coffer-dam*, in engineering, is an enclosure formed of piles, to exclude the surrounding fluid, and afford a protection to the works, while laying the foundations of piers, &c., under water.

Coin (Fr. from Lat. *cuneus* a wedge), in architecture, an angle formed by two surfaces of stone or brick; also a block to support a pilaster or column on an inclined plane.—In gunnery, a sort of wedge for raising or depressing the piece.

Coining Press, a powerful lever-press for striking impressions on coins or medals.

Coins, or **Quoins,** in gunnery, the name of the bevelled wedges placed under the breech of a cannon for the purpose of elevating or depressing it. —In printing, bevelled wedges of wood used for fastening the types together.

Col'chicum (Lat.), in botany, a genus of bulbous-rooted herbs, the Meadow Saffron, all the species of which are ornamental border flowers; order Melanthaceæ.

Coleop'tera, or **Coleop'terous** (Gr. *koleos* a sheath, and *pteron* a wing), in entomology, a very extensive order of winged insects, with six legs and four wings, of which the Beetle is the type. The upper wings form a horny covering, or case, called *elytra,* which protect the wings of flight. The Coleoptera are usually classed under four great sections, viz. :— *Pentamera,* those which have five-jointed tarsi; — *Hetromera,* those which have four-jointed tarsi to the two anterior pairs of legs, and four to the posterior pair;—*Tetramera,* those having four-jointed tarsi to all the legs; — *Trimera,* those which have three-jointed tarsi to all the legs.

Coleop'tilum (Gr. *a feathery sheath*), in botany, a sort of sheath which envelops the plumule of the Liliaceæ and Alismaceæ during the germination of the seed.

Col'ica, or **Colic** (Gr. *kolon* a part of the large intestine), in pathology, a painful spasmodic affection of the intestines, especially of the colon, attended with fever or inflammation; colic. There are many varieties of this dangerous complaint mentioned in medical works; as, *Colica accidentalis,* colic superinduced by particular articles of diet; *C. stercorea,* from accumulation of the contents of the bowels; *C. meconialis,* from the retention of the meconium; *C. calculosa,* from intestinal calculi; *C. pictorum saturnina,* or painter's colic, produced by the effects of lead.

Collima'tion (Lat. *collimo* to aim at), in astronomy, the *line of collimation* is the line of sight in any gradescent instrument that passes through the point of intersection of the wires fixed in the focus of the object-glass and the centre of that glass. —The *Error of collimation* is the difference between the existing and the required position, when the line of sight is not perpendicular to the horizontal or vertical axis.

Colliquamen'tum (Lat. *collique* to dissolve), in physiology, the first rudiments of animal generation; an extremely transparent fluid in an egg, observable after two or three days' incubation, containing the first rudiments of the animal.

Collo'dion (Gr. *kolla* glue), a solution of gun-cotton in a mixture of alcohol and ether, used for taking portraits by the photographic process.

Collum (Lat. *the neck*), in botany, that part of a plant from which the stem and root proceed; the portion between the plumule and the radicle.— In glass-making, that part of a glass vessel which sticks to the iron instrument used in removing the substance from the melting-pot.—Among jewellers, the horizontal face or plane at the bottom of a brilliant.

Collu'vies (Lat. *filth*), in geology, the fluid mass into which the substance of the earth was supposed to be dissolved by the great Deluge.

Collyr'ium (Gr. *kolyo* to check, and *rhoos* a flowing), in pathology, a lotion to check inordinate discharges; an eye-salve, applied to affections of the eyes.

Col'ocynth (Gr. *a gourd*), in botany, a fruit about the size of an orange, the *Cucumis colocynthis,* or Bitter Cucumber; order Cucurbitaceæ.— *Colocynthine* is the purgative principle extracted from the pulp of the above fruit.

Col'olites (Gr. *kolon,* and *lithos* a stone), in geology, a term applied to the tortuous masses representing the fossil intestines of fishes.

Colom'ba Root, in pharmacy, a bitter stomachic, the root of the *Cocculus palmatus,* useful in dyspepsia or diarrhœa.

Colon (Gr.), in anatomy, that portion of the larger intestinal canal situated between the rectum and the cæcum.

Colonnade' (Ital. from Lat. *columna* a column), in architecture, a series of open columns disposed in a circular form. A colonnade in front of a building is called a *portico;* when surrounding a building, a *peristyle;* and when double or more, *polystyle.* The colonnade is also designated, according to the intercolumniation— *pycrostyle,* when the space between the columns is one diameter and a half; *systyles,* when two diameters; *diastyle,* when three; and *aræostyle,* when four. If the columns are four in number, the building is termed *tetrastyle;* if six in number, *hexa-*

style; when there are eight, *octastyle;* and when ten, *decastyle.*

Coloph'onite (Gr. *red-coloured resin*), in mineralogy, a brownish-red variety of garnet, found in Norway, consisting of silica, alumina, lime, oxide of iron, magnesia, oxide of manganese, and water.

Coloph'ony, a dark-coloured resin from Colophon, in Asia Minor.

Colos'trum (Lat.), the first milk of the mammalia after parturition.

Colour (Lat.), in natural philosophy, a property inherent in light, which, although apparently colourless, is capable of being separated into seven tints or hues, designated *primitive colours,* viz., red, orange, yellow, green, blue, indigo, and violet; although it is now determined that the primitive colours consist only of three —red, yellow, and blue, by the various combinations of which the other tints are produced.—*Prismatic colours* are the colours in which the rays of light are decomposed or refracted through a prism, known as Newton's seven primitive colours.—*Substantive colours,* in dyeing, are such colours as unite immediately with the material to be dyed without a mordant. *Adjective colours* are such as will not unite with the material to be dyed without a mordant.—In heraldry, the colours are thus distinguished :—Red, *gules;* blue, *azure;* black, *sable;* green, *vert;* purple, *purpule;* yellow, *or* (gold); white, *argent* (silver).

Coluber'idæ (Lat. *coluber* a snake), in herpetology, a numerous family of poisonous serpents (the True Snakes), which comprehends twenty-seven genera.

Colum'bates, salts formed by the combination of any base with columbic acid.

Colum'bidæ (Lat. *columba* a pigeon), an extensive and interesting family of birds, comprehending pigeons, doves, turtles, &c., of which Columba is the general type. The Ring-dove or Cushat, *C. palumbus;* the Wood-pigeon or Stock-dove, *C. Œnas;* and the wild Rock-pigeon, *C. Livia,* the stock from which the domestic pigeon is derived, are the best known species in this country.

Colum'bites, a mineral of a dark brown colour, occurring in small crystals, being a combination of tantalium with the oxides of manganese and iron.

Colum'bium, the name of a metal discovered in the above mineral.

Columel la (Lat. *a little column*), in anatomy, applied to the central part or axis of the cochlea of the ear.— In conchology, the central pillar round which a spiral shell is wound.

Columellia'ceæ, in botany, a nat. order of Exogens, of which the Columellia, an evergreen shrub, is the type and genus.

Column (Lat. *columna*), in architecture, a cylindrical pillar, used to support or adorn a building, the different parts of which are the base, the shaft, and the capital. Columns are distinguished by different orders of architecture, as the Tuscan, Doric, Ionic, Corinthian, and Composite. The Tuscan is of a massy, rude, and simple character; the Doric is next in strength and massiveness to the Tuscan; the Ionic is more slender than the Tuscan and Doric; the Corinthian is more delicate in its form and proportions, and enriched with ornaments; and the Composite is a combination of the Ionic and Corinthian. —In physics, the term is applied to a quantity of any fluid showing an altitude greater than the diameter of its base, as a "column of air."—In botany, the central point of the union of portions of seed-vessels.—In military science, a formation of troops, narrow in front, and deep from front to rear; thus distinguished from line, which is extended in front, and thin in depth.

Colum'næ Car'neæ (Lat. *fleshy columns*), in anatomy, small muscular bands covering the inner surface of the ventricle of the heart.

Colure (Gr. *kolouros*), in astronomy, an imaginary great circle of the celestial sphere, intersecting another similar circle at the celestial poles; one passing through the equinoctial points of Aries and Libra, and the other the solstitial points of Cancer and Capricorn. The first is termed the *equinoctial,* and the other the *solstitial* colure.

Colym'bidæ (Gr. *kolymbos* a diver), a family of diving-birds, of the order Anseres, including several sub-families, of which Colymbus is the genus.

Colza (Fr.), in botany, a species of cabbage, the *Brassica campestris,* from the seeds of which *colza oil* is expressed.

Coma (Gr. *hair*), in astronomy, the hairy appearance that surrounds a comet when the earth is between the comet and the sun.—*Coma Berenices* is a constellation of the northern hemisphere, which contains forty-three stars.—(Gr. *koma* profound sleep), in pathology, a morbid condition of the brain, attended with the loss of sensation and voluntary action.

Combina'tion (Lat. and Fr.), in mathematics, changes or variations in every possible manner among a certain number of objects or symbols taken in sets

—In chemistry, the union of two or more substances in such a manner as to form, by chemical affinity, a new compound. Bodies combine with each other only in relative proportions, termed equivalents (see *Atomic Theory*); thus, water is a compound of 1 atom of oxygen and 1 of hydrogen. The composition of bodies is fixed and invariable. Thus, sulphuric acid is always composed of 16 parts of sulphur and 24 of oxygen, and water of 1 of hydrogen and 8 of oxygen: an atom of sulphuric acid is therefore represented by $16 + 24 = 40$; and water by $1 + 8 = 9$.

Combreta′ceæ, in botany, a nat. order of exogenous plants, chiefly tropical, consisting of trees and shrubs, of which Combretum is the type.

Combus′tibles (Lat. *combustio* a burning up), in chemistry, certain substances which are capable of combining more or less rapidly with oxygen.

Combus′tion (Lat. *a burning up*), in chemistry, the process in which, by the aid of heat, a substance unites with oxygen, or sometimes with chlorine; thus, the carbon of wood or coal unites with the oxygen of the atmosphere in ordinary combustion, forming carbonic acid gas. All union of carbon, hydrogen, sulphur, phosphorus, &c., with oxygen, is combustion.

Comet (Gr. *kometes*), in astronomy, a luminous body revolving with amazing velocity round the sun in an elliptical orbit, and having usually a tail or train of light.

Compar′ative Anat′omy, the anatomy of all organized bodies, compared with a view of illustrating the general phenomena of organic structure. (See *Anatomy*.)

Compass. In navigation, the *mariner's compass* is an instrument so contrived as to allow free motion to a magnetic needle; thus indicating the magnetic meridian, by which the true course of a ship at sea is ascertained.

Com′passes, a mathematical instrument for dividing and drawing circles, and measuring distances between two points. The compasses in general use have two legs, movable on a joint; but there are various kinds of compasses for different scientific objects.—The *Triangular compasses* have two legs similar to common compasses, and a third leg fixed to the bulb by a projection, with a joint so as to be movable in every direction. —*Hair compasses* are constructed by a small adjusting screw to one of the legs, so as to take an extent even to

a hair's breadth.—*Spring compasses* are such as are expanded by a spring, and closed by a screw.—*Proportional compasses* have two pairs of points, movable on a shifting centre which slides in a groove, and thereby regulates the proportion that the opening at one end bears to that of the other.

Compensa′tion Balance, in horology, the balance of a chronometer or watch, so contrived that the two opposite actions counteract each other's effect, and assist in correcting the errors occasioned by the variation of the temperature.—*Compensation bars* are bars formed of two or more metals, so that the expansion of the one counteracts that of the other. They are chiefly used in producing perfect equality in the balance of pendulums, chronometers, &c.

Com′plement, a term of frequent use in different branches of science. — In trigonometry, the *complement of an angle* is what is wanted to make a right angle of 90°; — the *complement of a number* is what is required to make it 1, 10, or 100.—In astronomy, *complement* is the distance of a star from the zenith, or the arch comprehended between the place of the star above the horizon and the zenith.—In fortification, *complement of the curtain* is that part in the interior side which makes the demi-gorge.

Complex′us (Lat. *embrace*), in anatomy, the name of a muscle of the back of the neck, which regulates the movement of the head.

Compo, in building, a concrete or mortar used by bricklayers and plasterers.

Compose (Lat.), in musical science, to arrange musical notes so as to produce new pieces.—In the art of letter-press printing, to arrange loose types into words and sentences.

Compos′itæ (Lat. *compounded*), in botany, a nat. order of plants; the most extensive family of the vegetable kingdom, the flowers of which, like those of the daisy, are of a radiated or star-like form.

Com′posite (Lat.), in architecture, the last and richest of the five orders of architecture, being composed of the Ionic and Corinthian.—In botany, belonging to the nat. order Compositæ.

Com′position (Lat.), a term of frequent application in different departments of science and art.—In music, it is the arranging and disposing of musical notes into different parts, so as to produce general harmony.—In painting, composition is that combination of the different parts by which an agreeable impression is made on the mind of the spectator, each part being subordinate to the whole.—In mechanics, *composition of motion or forces* is an assemblage of several directions of motions resulting from various forces acting in different directions.

Compound (Lat. *compono*), an epithet applied to different branches of art and science, as denoting the union or mingling of two or more ingredients or substances.—In the science of simple arithmetic, the addition of compound quantities produces *Compound* addition, *Compound* subtraction, *Compound* multiplication, and *Compound* division; each of which consists of more than one denomination, as 2*l.* 6*s.* 4*d.*—In algebra, *Compound quantities* are such as are linked by the signs + and —; as, $a + b, c - d, xy + ab$.—In chemistry, *Compound radicle* is a term used to denote a certain class of compound bodies, possessing the property of uniting with the elements, and of forming combinations with them, analogous in their properties to the combinations of two simple bodies. —In music, *Compound time* implies that two or more measures are joined in one.

Compres'sion (Lat.), in pathology, a term applied to a compressed state of the brain or other organ.—In surgery, the term is used for the repression of hæmorrhage from diseased or wounded blood-vessels, as also in the treatment of aneurisms, wounds, or sores, by means of bandages.—In physics, it implies the action exercised upon a body by external force, which presses the constituent molecules into closer contact.—In botany, it applies to leaves when flattened laterally; in conchology, to shells when one valve is flatter than another.

Comp'tonite, a mineral which occurs in translucent white crystals among the lavas of Vesuvius; so called in honour of Lord Compton, Earl of Northampton.

Conca'vo-convex, concave on one side, and convex on the other.

Concen'trated (Lat.), in chemistry, an epithet applied to a fluid when, by evaporation or other means, it is deprived of the excess of the solvent body which it previously contained.— In pathology, the term is applied to the pulse when there is a contracted condition of the artery.

Conceptac'ulum (Lat.), in botany, a term applied to a one-valved pericarp, opened longitudinally on one side, and distinct from the seeds.

Concerti'na (Ital.), a musical instrument, whose notes are produced by the action of air on steel bars, similar in principle to the accordion.

Conch (Lat. *concha* a shell), a marine bivalve shell.—In anatomy, *concha auris* is that portion of the external ear which represents a large oval cavity.—*Concha naris* is the turbinated portion of the ethnoid bone.

Concha'ceæ (Lat. *concha*), a family of lamellibranchiate Mollusca, generally marine, which comprehends the genera Cardium, Iridina, Donax, Tellina, Mactra, Amphidesma, and Crassatella.

Con'chifers (Lat. *concha*), a class of Mollusca, the inhabitants of bivalve shells.

Conchoid (Gr. *like a shell*), in mathematics, a peculiar curve for solving the tri-sections of an angle and the duplication of the curve.—*Conchoidal*, like a shell.

Conchol'ogy (Gr. *koncha* a shell), a treatise on shells, being that department of malacology which treats of the form, relation, and classification of the shells of the testaceous Mollusca.

Conchom'eter (Gr.), an instrument for measuring shells.

Conchyliom'etry (Gr. *koncha* a shell, and *metron* measure), the art or science of taking the measurement of shells or their curvatures.

Concor'dia (Lat.) in astronomy, a planet or asteroid, discovered by Luther in 1860.

Concrete (Lat. *concrescere* to grow together), in engineering and architecture, a term applied to a mass of stone-chippings or ballast cemented together with lime and sand; used in making foundations.—In chemistry, a substance which differs from a fluid; thus camphor is termed a *concrete* oil.—*Concretion* is a mass formed by the aggregation of separate parts. In surgery, it consists of hard substances that sometimes grow in different parts of the body; those forming in the solids are termed concretions or ossifications, and those in cavities containing fluids, calculi.—*Concretionary deposits*, in geology, are the recent alluvial deposits, including calcareous and other deposits from springs.

Concus'sion (Lat. *a shaking together*), in pathology, a term applied to injuries of the brain, independently of fracture of the skull.

Condensa'tion (Lat.), in physics, the act of rendering a body more dense by mechanical pressure, or by chemical affinity.—In pathology, a term used to express a condition of the lungs in which, from the obliteration of the air-cells, that organ has acquired an unnatural hardness and solidity of structure; also an increase of the density of blood, or other animal fluid.

Conden'ser (Fr. from Lat. *condenso*), in electricity, an apparatus by which the electric fluid is accumulated.—*Volta's electrical condenser* is an instrument used for rendering apparent such portions of electricity as are too weak to be indicated by the electrometer only.—In pneumatics, the condenser is an instrument by which a given volume of common air or gas may be condensed into much less space; that part of a steam-engine attached to the cylinder in which the steam is compressed.—The *Condenser gauge* is a tube of glass, 32 inches long, open at both ends, the upper end being fixed to the condenser, and the lower end dipping into the mercury. Its use is to indicate the degree of exhaustion within the condenser.—The *Condenser pump* is an air pump attached to the condenser of the steam-engine.

Condi'tion (Lat.), in mathematics, an *equation of condition* is an equation which will not always be true, but requires certain conditions to be satisfied.

Con'droite (Gr. *chondros* grain), a yellow-brown mineral, which occurs in small grains; the hemiprismatic chrysolite, consisting of magnesia, silica, oxide of iron, alumina, and potash.

Conduc'tor (Lat.), in natural philosophy, a body that receives and conducts electricity or heat.

Con'durrite, an ore or oxide of copper, so called from the Condurra mine, in Cornwall, where it was found.

Condyle (Gr. *a knuckle*), a rounded projection at the end of a bone.

Con'dyloid (Gr. *like a joint*), in anatomy, a term applied to foramina of the occipital bone, through which the lingual nerves and the cervical veins pass.—The *Condyloid process* is the posterior protuberance of the lower jaw.

Condyl'opods (Gr. *joint-footed*), in zoology, a sub-division of the Articulata, comprising the Myriapods, Spiders, Insects, and Crustaceans.

Cone (Gr. *konos*), in geometry, a solid body with a circular base, ending in a point at the top.—In botany, a mass of hard scales or bracts covering naked scales; the fruit of fir trees.—*Cone of rays* is a term used in optics, when all the rays of light are on a given surface.

Conferva'ceæ (Lat. *confero* to join), in botany, a nat. order of water-plants, or Algæ, of which Conferva is the type and genus.

Con'fluent (Lat. *confluens* flowing together), in pathology, a term applied to those pustules on the skin which are so numerous as to form patches, the matter of which runs together.

Congen'ital (Lat. *born with*), in pathology, an epithet applied to disease or infirmity existing in an individual at the time of his birth.

Con'geries (Lat.), a mass of things heaped together.

Conges'tion (Lat.), in anatomy, an accumulation of blood or other fluid in the vessels.

Con'gius (Lat.), in pharmacy, eight pints, marked C.

Conglom'erate (Lat. *conglomero*), in geology, applied to rocks composed of rounded fragments worn · by the action of water, but cemented together.

Congreve Rocket, in the military art, a very destructive kind of rocket, filled with inflammable matter, invented by Sir W. Congreve.

Co'nia (Lat.), a poisonous alkali obtained from hemlock.

Conics (Gr. *konos* a cone), the doctrine of *Conic sections*, or that part of mathematics which treats of the properties, measurements, and subdivisions of the cone. The figures formed by the division of a cone are five in number, viz.: the Triangle, the Circle, the Ellipse or Oval, the Parabola, and the Hyperbola. Thus, if a perfect cone with a circular base be cut at right angles to the base by a plane passing through the apex, the section will be a triangle; if the cone be cut through both sides by a plane parallel to the base, the section will be a circle; if the cone be cut slanting quite through both sides, the section will be a parabola; and if the plane cut only one side of the cone, and be not parallel to the other, the section will be a hyperbola.

Conif'eræ (Lat. *cone-bearing plants*), a nat. order of plants, the Pinaceæ of Lindley, including the pine, cedar, juniper, savin, cypress, and arborvitæ. (See *Pinaceæ*.)

Con'ilite, a genus of fossil Cephalopods, allied to the Orthoceratites, the shell of which is conical, straight, or slightly curved.

Coni'næ, the cones, a sub-family of the Strombidæ, or Wing-shells.

Coniomyce'tes (Gr. *a cone mushroom*), a sub-order of sporiferous Fungi, in which the spores are single.

Coniros'tres (Lat. *cone-beaked*), a tribe of birds belonging to the order In-

sessores, or Perching birds, which comprises the Crows, Finches, Plantain-eaters, and Hornbills.

Conite (Lat. *conus*), a flesh-coloured mineral, consisting of carbonates of magnesia and lime, and oxide of iron.

Con'jugate Foci (Lat.), in optics, the union of two foci.

Conjunc'tion (Lat. *a joining*), in astronomy, the meeting of two or more heavenly bodies in the same degree of the zodiac, represented thus ☌. A planet is in conjunction with the sun when it appears in the same straight line with the earth.

Connara'ceæ (Gr.), in botany, a nat. order of exogenous plants, of which the Ceylon Sumach, a genus of shrubs with white flowers, is the type.

Connate (Lat.), in physics or botany, growing together.

Conoid (Gr. *like a cone*), in anatomy, a gland in the third ventricle of the brain.—In mathematics, a term applied to the surface generated by the revolution of a conic section about its axis.

Conosper'midæ (Gr. *konos*, and *sperma* seed), a tribe of exogenous plants, of the nat. order Proteaceæ, of which Conospermum is the type and genus.

Conostyl'eæ (Gr. *konos*, and *stylos* a style), a tribe of the nat. order Hæmodoraceæ, or Blood-roots, of which Conostyles, a native of New Holland, is the typical genus.

Constric'tor (Lat. *constringo* to bind tight), in anatomy, applied to muscles which close any orifice.—In herpetology, a term applied to the larger class of serpents, as the *Boa constrictor*, so called from its power of winding round and crushing its prey.

Construc'tion (Lat.), in architecture, the art of distributing the different forces and strains of the parts and materials of a building in so scientific a manner as to avoid failure and insure durability.— In geometry, the manner of describing a figure or problem.—In algebra, *construction of equations* is the method of reducing a known equation into lines and figures, in order to a geometrical demonstration.

Construc'tiveness (Lat.), in phrenology, a term applied to a development or organ at that part of the frontal bone above the spheno-temporal suture, next acquisitiveness. Its presumed tendency is to construct mechanical contrivances or works of art.

Contact (Lat. *contactus*), a term applied in geometry to the point where a curvilinear line touches a straight one, called *point of contact ;* the *angle of contact* is formed by the meeting of a curvilinear line and a straight one.—*Contact theory*, in electrical science, is the hypothesis by which two different conductors placed in contact with each other produce a decomposition, and mutual transference of their electric fluids.

Conta'gion (Lat.), in pathology, the communication of disease by touching the sick or his clothes.

Contents (Lat.), in geometry, the area or quantity included in a certain span or length.—*Superficial contents* is length multiplied by breadth. — *Solid contents* is the superficial contents multiplied by the thickness.

Con'tinent (Lat.), in geography, a wide extent of land embracing many countries, as the continent of Europe, of Asia, of Africa, or America.

Contornia'ti (Ital.), in numismatics, certain bronze medals supposed to have been struck in the time of Constantine the Great and his successors.

Contra, a Lat. preposition signifying *against*, frequently used in composition.

Contra-basso (Ital.), in music, the largest kind of bass violin for playing double bass.

Contra-in'dicant (Lat.), in pathology, a symptom forbidding the usual treatment of a disorder.

Contral'to (Ital.), in music, the part immediately below the treble.

Contra-rota'tion (Lat. *contra*, and *rota* a wheel), circular motion in a direction contrary to some other similar motion.

Contrate Wheel, in horology, a wheel moved by opposite cogs.

Contravalla'tion (Lat.), in fortification, a trench guarded by a parapet wall ; a counter-fortification to hinder the sallies of the besieged.

Contre-bas (Fr.), in music, a double bass.

Conus (Gr. *a cone*), in malacology, a genus of Gasteropods, the shell of which is a cone.—In botany, a mode of inflorescence which is a cone or spike, the carpels of which are in the form of scales.

Convec'tion (Lat. *carrying*), the power which fluids have of transmitting heat or electricity by currents.

Conver'gent, or **Converg'ing** (Lat.). In optics, *converging rays* are those rays of light which proceed from the various parts of an object to a common focus.—In mathematics, a *converging series* is that in which the magnitudes of the terms gradually diminish.

Conversa'tion Tubes, in acoustics, a term applied to pipes made of elastic gum or metal, which are calculated for conveying messages to any part of a building.

Convolu'tions (Lat. *rolling together*). In anatomy, *convolutions* are the foldings of the small intestines; and also the windings and turnings of the brain.

Convolvula'ceæ (Lat. *convolvo* to entwine), a nat. order of herbaceous plants, usually twining and milky, of which Convolvulus, with its sweet-scented flowers, is the type.

Co-or'dinates (Lat.), in geometry, the abscissa and its ordinates taken in conjunction. The co-ordinates either determine the position of a point in space, or in a plane, which is understood to contain all the figures under contribution.

Copai'ba, or **Capiv'i**, in pharmacy, a balsam of liquid resin used in medicine, especially as a diuretic. It is an exudation from the *Copaifera officinalis* of S. America.

Copal, a transparent resin obtained from the *Rhus copallinum* of Mexico, from which *Copal varnish* is prepared with oil of turpentine.—The *Copal tree* is a native of Malabar; the *Valeria Indica*. When wounded it discharges a clear, pellucid resin, which, after a time, becomes yellow and brittle like glass.

Coper'nican, in astronomy, a term applied to the system propounded by Copernicus, who taught that the earth revolves round the sun.

Copper (Dutch *koper*, from Lat. *cuprum*), a metal of a pale reddish colour, sonorous, and very malleable and ductile. In its native state it occurs in cubical and octahedral crystals, and sometimes in macules or in thin plates. Its equivalent is 32; symbol Cu; sp. gr. 8·5—8·9. The ores of copper are very numerous, the principal being sulphuret of copper and iron (copper pyrites) and sulphuret of copper (nitrous copper ore). The more important compounds of copper are here enumerated:—*Bisulphuret of copper*, occurring in black or bluish-green incrustations, and consisting of copper, 66; sulphur, 32;—*Black copper*, of a blackish-brown colour, friable and heavy; consisting of copper, 79·83; oxygen, 20·17;—*Blue copper*, of an azure colour, consisting of deut-oxide of copper, 70; carbonic acid, 24; water, 6: sp. gr. 3·5—3·77;—*Grey copper* is of an iron-black colour, containing about 40 per cent. of copper, and variable quantities of arsenic, iron, sulphur, silver, and sometimes antimony: sp. gr. 4·4—5·2;—*Green carbonate of copper*, of various shades of green, containing about 70 per cent. of copper, 20 of carbonic acid, and 8 or 9 of water;—

Hydrous phosphate of copper, the colour emerald green, consisting of phosphoric acid, 21·687; oxide of copper, 62·847; water, 15·454; sp. gr. 4·2—4·3;—*Octahedral arseniate of copper*, of a sky-blue or verdigris-green colour, consisting of arsenic acid, 49·00; oxide of copper, 14·00; and water, 35·00;—*Oblique prismatic arseniate of copper*, of a bluish-black, composed of oxide of copper, 54; arsenic acid, 30; water, 16; sp. gr. 4·1—4·28;—*Phosphate of copper* occurs crystallized, and in radiated masses, consisting of phosphoric acid, 28·7; oxide of copper, 63·6; water, 7·4;—*Pyrites of copper*, of a copper-red or tombac-brown colour, containing from 19 to 23 per cent. of sulphur, 7 to 18 per cent. of iron, and from 58 to 61 of copper;—*Red oxide of copper*, of a crimson-red colour, containing about 70 per cent. of copper, and 10 of oxygen; sp. gr. 5·6—6·1;—*Rhomboidal arseniate of copper*, of an emerald-green colour; its constituents from 39 to 58 per cent. of oxide of copper; 21 to 43 of arsenic acid; water, 17 to 21: sp. gr. 2·5—2·6;—*Right prismatic arseniate of copper*, of an olive green, passing into liver-brown colour; composed of about 60 per cent. of copper and 40 of arsenic acid;—*Seleniuret of copper*, consisting of copper, 64; and silenium, 40;—*Sulphuret of Copper*, of a lead or iron-grey colour, containing about 80 per cent. of copper, 12 to 20 of sulphur, and a little iron;—*Sulphate of copper, Blue vitriol*, of a sky-blue colour, consisting of oxide of copper, 32·13; sulphuric acid, 31·57; water, 36·30;—*Velvet-blue copper*, a compound of oxide of copper, sulphuric acid, silica, and zinc.

Cop'peras (Ital.), sulphate of iron, or green vitriol.

Cop'rolites (Gr. *kopros* fæces, and *lithos* a stone), in geology, the petrified fæces of fishes, reptiles, and other primeval animals, which occur abundantly in the lias and coal formations.

Cora'cinæ, in ornithology, a sub-family of the Corvidæ, or Fruit Crows, of which the Coracina is the type; tribe Conirostres.

Cor'aco-brach'ialis (Lat.), in anatomy, a muscle situated in the superior part of the arm, whose use is to raise the arm upwards and forwards.

Cor'acoid (Gr. *like a raven's beak*), in anatomy, a term applied to certain processes; as, the *coracoid processes* of the scapula; the *coracoid ligament*, by which the superior border of the scapula is converted into a foramen.—*Coraco-radial* is an epithet applied to the *biceps flexor cubiti* muscle, as attached to the *coracoid process* of the scapula and the radius.

Coral, a general term for all calcareous marine products secreted by polypi.—*Corallia* is a family of corticiferous Polyparia, in which the animals are hydriform, with internal ovaria.

Corallif'eri (*coral*, and Lat. *fero* to bear), in zoology, an order of Zoophytes; the calcareous secretions of marine animals called Polypi.

Cor'alline (Ital.), in natural history, a zoophyte, in which each polypus is contained in a horny shell; also the animal which secretes coral.

Cor'allite (*coral*, and Gr. *lithos* a stone), a mineral substance or petrifaction in the form of coral.

Coral Rag, in geology, a calcareous coralliferous deposit in the neighbourhood of Calne, constituting a member of the oolitic formation.

Coran'to (Ital.), in music, a certain air, consisting of three crotchets in a bar.

Corbeils (Lat. *a basket*), in fortification, little baskets of earth set upon the parapets to shelter the men in firing on the besiegers.—In architecture, sculptured baskets of flowers or fruit, sometimes placed on the heads of caryatides; a term also applied to the bell of the Corinthian capital.

Corbels, in Gothic castellated edifices, a row of stones projecting from the wall to support the parapet.—*Corbel table* is a series of semicircular arches, which cut one another in a wall, supported by timbers with their ends projecting out, and carved into heads, faces, lions' heads, &c.

Cordate, or **Cor'dated** (Lat. *cordatus*), in botany, having the shape of a heart; often prefixed to words to denote a heart-shape; as, cordate-reniform, cordate-triangular, cordate-roundish, cordate-oblong, cordate-sagittate, cordate-auriculate, cordate-orbicular, cordate-lanceolate, cordate-peltate.

Cordia'ceæ, in botany, a nat. order of exogenous plants, of which the Cordea, a genus of trees with drupaceous fruit, is the type.

Cordon, in military science, a line or series of military posts.—In fortification, a row of stones jutting out before the base of a parapet.

Cor Hydræ and **Cor Leonis,** in astronomy, stars of the first magnitude, the one in the constellation Hydra, and the other in the constellation Leo.

Corian'drum (Gr. *koris* a bug, so called from the fetid smell of the leaves), in botany, a tribe of umbelliferous annual plants, of which the Coriandrum is the type. The seeds of *C. sativum* are used by distillers in flavouring spirits, and by confectioners for incrusting with sugar. They are also used in spices, and to qualify the taste of senna.

Coriaria'ceæ (Lat. *corium* a hide), in botany, a nat. order of hypogynous Exogens, of which the Coriaria is the type. They are natives of Europe, Peru, Chili, and New Zealand. *C. myrtifolia* is a species used in dyeing black.

Corin'thian, one of the five orders of architecture.

Coriu'do, a genus of reptiles belonging to the family Chelonidæ, the common Turtle. It is found from 6 to 7 feet long, and weighs from 7 to 8 cwt.

Co'rium (Lat.), in anatomy, the true skin lying beneath the cuticle.

Corm (Gr. *a stem*), in botany, a thickened underground stem.

Corn-brash, in geology, a calcareous deposit overlying the Bath oolite, which is very rich in marine bivalves and Echinodermata.

Cor'nea (Lat. *cornu* a horn), in botany, a nat. order of umbellated Exogens, of which Cornus, or Dogwood, is the type.—In physiology, a part of the eye, so called from its resembling transparent horn.

Cornel, in botany, a tree, the *Cornus mas*, which furnishes a hard wood, used for wheel-work, wedges, &c.

Corne'lian, in mineralogy, a siliceous stone of a reddish-white colour; a variety of calcedony, or agate, much used in seal-engraving. The flesh-coloured variety is termed *Carnelian*, and the horn-like variety is named *Cornelian*.

Cornice (Fr.), in architecture, any moulded projection; the upper division or moulding of an entablature, or any part of a building.—In artillery, *Cornice ring* is the next ring from the muzzle.

Cornstone, in geology, a limestone found in the old red sandstone formation.

Cornu Am'monis (Lat.), the name of the shells called Ammonites.

Cornu'bianite (Lat. *Cornubia*, Cornwall), in mineralogy, a dark slaty rock, abundant in Cornwall.

Cornu'tus (Lat. *horn-shaped*), in zoology and botany, a term used to designate various species of animals or plants.

Corol'la (Lat. *a little crown*), in botany, the innermost of the envelopes by which the organs of fructification in flowers are covered.

Corollifio'ræ (Lat. *corolla*, and *flores* flowers), in botany, a sub-class of the dicotyledonous plants, in which the petals are united together, and inserted in the receptacle.

Coro'na (Lat. *a crown*), in science, a term of varied application.—In astronomy, the *Corona Borealis* is a constellation of the northern hemisphere, known as the Northern Crown or Garland; the *Corona Australis* is a constellation of the southern hemisphere, known as the Southern Crown.—In architecture, the *Corona* is the brow of the cornice which projects over the bed-mouldings to throw off the water, forming a division between the cymatium and crown members and the lower division of the cornice.—In botany, the term is applied to the crown-like cup which is found at the orifice of the tube in the corolla of the narcissus and other flowers.—In odontology, *Corona dentes* is the exposed part of a tooth which projects beyond the alveolus and gum.

Cor'onary (Lat. *corona*), in anatomy, a term applied to vessels, nerves, &c., from their surrounding the parts like a crown; as, the coronary arteries of the heart, &c.

Coronil'leæ (Lat. *corona*), in botany, a division of the leguminous tribe of plants, Hedysareæ, with the flowers disposed in umbels.

Cor'posant (corrupted from Sp. *cuerpo santo*, holy body), in electricity, a luminous phenomenon or volatile meteor, sometimes observable in stormy nights about the rigging and masts of a ship.

Corpus'cular (Lat. *corpusculum* an atom), relating to corpuscles, or atoms.—*Corpuscular philosophy* is the system of nature which professes to account for natural phenomena by the minute particles of matter.—*Corpuscular action* is the influence or power which atoms or particles exercise on each other.

Cor'ridor (Fr.), in architecture and fortification, a covert-way; an open passage, or gallery, leading to different apartments, sometimes lying round the whole compass of the fortifications of a place.

Corro'sive Sub'limate, the bichloride of mercury, a deadly poison.

Cor'rugated Iron (Lat. *corrugatus* wrinkled), in mechanical science, wrinkled or fluted iron which has been galvanized or painted; used for roofing, and other building purposes.

Corruga'tor (Lat. *corrugo* to wrinkle), in anatomy, a muscle that contracts or corrugates the forehead.

Cortex (Lat. *bark*). *Cortex Peruvianus*, or Peruvian bark, is the Cinchona of medicine.

Cor'tical (Lat.). In anatomy, *cortical substance* is the exterior part of the brain.

Corticif'era (Lat. *cortex* and *fero* to bear), a name given to a family of Polyparia.

Corun'dum (Ind.), a crystallized reddish-coloured mineral, or adamantine spar, of extreme hardness. It consists of alumina, silica, and oxide of iron. There are four species:—Spinel, or dodecahedral corundum; Automolite, or octahedral corundum; Sapphire and Ruby, or rhombohedral corundum; Chrysoberyl, or prismatic corundum.

Cor'vidæ (Lat. *corvus* a crow), a family of conirostral birds, the Crows, in which the bill is strong, and slightly cultirostral.—*Corvinæ* are a sub-family of the Corvidæ, of which Corvus is the genus and type, consisting of various species; as, *Corvus corax*, or Raven; *C. corone*, or Carrien Crow; *C. cornix*, or Hooded Crow; *C. monedula*, or Jackdaw; *C. frugilegus*, or Rook.

Coryban'tiasm (Gr.), in pathology, a state of frenzy, in which the patient is subject to mental illusions and fantastic visions.

Coryla'ceæ (Lat. *corylus* the hazel), in botany, a nat. order of exogenous plants, the Mastworts, of which the Corylus is the type. It comprises the hazel-nut, the beech, Spanish chestnut, &c.

Corymb (Lat. *corymbus* a bunch), in botany, a raceme, in which the stalks of the lower leaves are larger than those of the under.

Corymbif'eræ, a nat. order of Compositæ, comprehending most of the Tubifloræ of De Candolle.

Cor'ypha (Gr. *a summit*), in botany, the name of the Fan Palm, of the order Palmaceæ, which grows to the height of 100 feet, with fan-shaped leaves, some of them about 20 feet long.

Coryphæ'nidæ (Gr. *koryphaios* a leader), a family of acanthopterygious fishes, of which the Coryphæna is the type.

Cosine (Lat.), in mathematics, the sine of the complement of the arc of a circle.

Cos'mical (Gr. *kosmos* the world), in astronomy, the rising or setting with the sun; relating to the whole system of heavenly bodies.

Cosmog'ony (Gr.), in physiology, the science of the earth's origin and formation.

Cosmog'raphy (Gr.), a description of

the universe, or of the several parts of the visible world.

Cosmol'ogy (Gr.), the science of the globe, its structure, and its parts.

Cosmora'ma (Gr. *kosmos*, and *orao* to view), a picturesque exhibition of the world, or of its various parts, represented as of their natural size.

Cos'mosphere (Gr. *kosmos*, and *sphaira* a sphere), an apparatus for showing the relative position of the earth and fixed stars at any given time.

Coss (Ind.), a measure of distance in India, about a mile and a half in length on the average. The standard coss is in some places 35 to a degree; in others 37½, 40, 45; whilst the common coss varies from 1 to 2½ British miles.

Costate (Lat. *costa* a rib), in botany, a term to indicate the presence of only one rib in a leaf.

Costean'ing, in mining, the searching for mineral lodes by sinking pits or driving adits.

Co-tan'gent (Lat.), in geometry, the tangent of an arc, which is the complement of another to 90°.

Cotise (Fr. *côté* side), in heraldry, a bendlet, reduced one-half, and borne on each side of the bend.—*Brande.*

Cot'tidæ (Gr. *kotte*, from the large size of their heads), a family of fishes, the Bull-heads, or Miller's Thumbs, of which Cottus is the type; tribe, Canthileptes, or Mail-cheeks.

Cot'unite, a mineral, so called from M. Cotunia, which occurs in extremely minute acicular crystals in the crater of Vesuvius. It consists of lead and muriatic acid; sp. gr. 2·89.

Cot'yle (Gr. *a cavity*), in anatomy, the hollow in the ilium which receives the head of the femur, or thigh-bone.

Cotyle'don (Gr.), in botany, the lobe that nourishes the seed of a plant; thus, when the embryo has one leaf only, it is termed *monocotyledonous*, and when it has two leaves *dicotyledonous*. —In anatomy, *Cotyledons* are the cup-shaped vascular productions of the chorion in ruminating animals, which serve the office of a placenta.—*Cotyledoneæ* is a term used for cotyledonous plants, now more generally termed Vasculares, including the Exogens and the Endogens.

Cotyl'iform (Gr. *kotyle*), in physics, an epithet applied to such organs as have a rotate figure.—*Cotyloid* is applied to the cup-shaped form of the acetabulum, or cavity of the hip-bone, which receives the head of the thigh-bone.

Couch'ant (Fr.), in heraldry, lying down with the head erect.

Cou'marin, the name of certain odoriferous substances obtained from the Tonka bean and the seed of the *Dipteryx odorata.*

Coun'termine (Lat. *contra*, and *mine*), in fortification and military science, a gallery and well sunk and driven till they meet the enemy's mine, to prevent its intended effects.

Coun'termure (Lat. *contra*, and *murus* a wall), in fortification, a wall raised behind another wall to defend the place after a breach is made.

Countersa'lient (Lat. *contra* against, and *salio* to leap), in heraldry, is when two beasts are represented as leaping from each other.

Coun'terscarp, in fortification, the slope of the exterior side of the ditch towards the country. The term is sometimes applied to the whole covert-way, with its parapet and glacis. — *Angle of the counterscarp* is that made by its two sides meeting.

Countervalla'tion, in fortification, a chain of redoubts raised about a fortress to prevent sorties of the garrison, the works being often united by a line of parapets.

Coup de Soleil (Fr.), in pathology, a disease produced by exposure of the head to the sun's rays.

Coupe-gorge (Fr. *cut-throat*), in military tactics, a position which affords an enemy so many advantages that the troops who occupy it must either surrender or be cut to pieces.

Cou'pure (Fr.), in fortification, a ditch dug to prevent a besieging army getting too close to the walls of a fortified town or place. — *Coupures* are passages cut through the glacis in the re-entering angle of the covert-way, to facilitate the sallies of the besieged.

Course, a term of frequent use in practical science and the arts. It constitutes the elements of any art or science explained in methodical arrangement; as, a course of chemistry, medicine, anatomy, &c. — In architecture, *Course* is a continued range of stones, level or of the same height, throughout the whole length of the building, and not interrupted by any aperture.—*Course of a plinth* is its continuity in the face of the wall.— *Course of the face of an arch* is the face of the arch stones, whose joints radiate to the centre.—*Bond course,* stones which are inserted into the wall farther than either of the adjacent courses, for the purpose of binding the wall together. — In navigation, *Course* is that point of the compass or horizon which a ship steers on, or the angle which the rhumb line on which it sails makes with the meridian.—The *Course* of a ship is a term applied to the principal sails; as, the mainsail, foresail, mizzen, mizzen staysail, &c.

Coursers (Lat. *cursores*), in ornithology, an order of birds which, from the smallness of their wings, are incapable of flight, but from the length and strength of their legs, possess great power of running; as, the ostrich, the cassowary, &c.

Cou'zeranite, a greyish-black mineral, occurring in small crystals in the Pyrenees, consisting of silica, alumina, lime, potash, soda, and magnesia.

Covert-way, in fortification, a space of ground on the outer edge of the ditch, level with the surrounding country, and ranging round the works; it is protected by the glacis, or sloping bank of earth extending to the level country.

Cow Tree, in botany, the Galactodendron, or Milk tree, of S. America, which yields, from incisions cut in the bark, a substance similar to the first milk of the cow after calving; the milk being found, on analysis, to contain about 30 per cent. of galactin.

Crab, a term of frequent occurrence in practical science and the arts.—In zoology, it is a name given to the decapod Crustaceans of the family Brachiura.—In botany, it is the fruit of the *Pyrus acerba*, or Wild Apple.—In mechanics, it is a kind of portable windlass, or machine, for raising weights, or otherwise exerting great force, by winding a rope round a horizontal barrel. It is also a machine fixed in the ground at the lower end of rope-walks, used for stretching the yarn to its fullest extent before it is worked into strands.—In marine affairs, the *Crab* is a kind of wooden pillar, whose lower end being let down through a ship's deck, rests upon a socket like the capstan. It is employed to wind in the cable, or to purchase any other weighty matter which requires a great mechanical power.—In astronomy, the *Crab* is one of the signs of the zodiac.

Crabron'idæ, in entomology, a family of hymenopterous stinging insects, the Hornets, of which Crabro is the genus and type.—*Crabronites* are a section of the same family.

Cra'cidæ (Gr. *kraxo* to vociferate), in ornithology, a family of large gallinaceous birds of America, the Alectors, of which the Crax is the type.

Cradling, in architecture, a term applied to the timbers in arched ceilings and coves, on which the laths and plaster are to be laid.

Crag (Gael.), in geology, a reddish deposit of the older pliocene period, which rests in some places on the London clay, and more extensively on the chalk beds.

Cram'ming, a familiar term in the universities and other institutions for the act of preparing a student to pass an examination.

Cramp (Germ. *krampf*), in pathology, a painful contraction or spasm of one or more muscles, generally of the lower extremities, and sometimes of the stomach.—*Cramp-fish* is the *Raia torpedo*, or Electric Ray, of Linnæus, which, when touched, gives an electric shock.

Cramp-iron, in architecture and building, a piece of iron or other metal bent at each end, and used in masonry for fastening the stonework together.

Crane (Sax. *cran*), in mechanics, a machine for raising heavy weights by means of a rope or chain, acted on by a windlass, and passing over a pulley at the extremity of a projecting jib.—In marine affairs, *Crane lines* are lines going from the upper end of the spritsail-topmast to the middle of the forestays, which serve to keep the spritsail-topmast upright and steady.—*Crane's-bill* is the name of an instrument used in surgery.

Cranich'idæ, in botany, a family of plants of the tribe Neotteæ, of which Cranichis is the genus and type; order Orchidaceæ.

Craniog'nomy (Gr. *index to the skull*), the doctrine or science which teaches that the characteristics of the mind or disposition may be known by the conformation of the skull.

Craniol'ogy (Gr. *kranion* the skull, and *logos* a treatise), in physiology, the art of discovering the faculties from the formation of the skull; the doctrine of *Phrenology* (which see).

Craniom'etry (Gr. *kranion*, and *metron* measure), the art of measuring the skulls of animals, for the purpose of ascertaining their distinguishing characteristics.—*Craniometer* is an instrument for measuring the dimensions of the skull; a kind of compasses or calipers, also adapted for measuring the breadth or thickness of any article.

Cranios'copy (Gr. *kranion*, and *skopeo* to examine), art of examining and determining the animal characteristics. Dr. Prichard has characterized the primitive forms of the skull according to the width of the *bregma*, or space between the parietal bones—(1), the *steno-bregmate*, the narrow or Ethiopian variety;—(2), the *meso-bregmate*, the middle or Caucasian variety;—(3), the *platy-bregmate*, the broad or Mongolian variety. (See *Phrenology*.)

Cra'nium (Gr. and Lat.), in physiology, that portion of the head which forms the great cavity containing the brain: the skull. It is composed of eight distinct bones, viz., the *os frontis*, the two *ossa parietalia*, the two *ossa tempora*, the *os occipitum*, the *os ethmoides*, and the *os sphenoides*.

Crank (Gael. *crangaid*), in mechanical science, the end of an axis bent twice at right angles, or an iron rod so bent attached to an axis, serving as a handle by which to turn it, as the *crank* of a grindstone; a contrivance for changing circular into alternate motion, or the reverse, as "the crank of a steam-engine:" an instrument for changing the direction of motion in a bell-wire.—*Crank-wheel*, in rope-making, is a machine for the spinning of lines, &c., fixed on an iron spindle, or axis, with a handle to turn it by.

Crasis (Gr. *mixture*), in physiology and medicine, a term applied to a due mixture or temperature of the body, when there is such an admixture of their constituent parts as to constitute a healthy condition.

Crass (Lat. *crassus*, thick or gross), in natural history, a word used as a prefix to numerous genera and species of animals and vegetables, which uniformly denotes thickness; as, *Crassicollis*, thick-necked. The following terms are in frequent use:—*Crassiceps*, thick-headed; *crassicornis*, thick-horned; *crassicostus*, thick-ribbed; *crassidentes*, thick-toothed; *crassifolius*, thick-leaved; *crassilabrus*, thick-lipped; *crassinervius*, having thick nervures or veins in the leaves; *crassipes*, large-footed; *crassipennis*, thick-winged; *crassipetalus*, having thick petals; *crassirostris*, thick-beaked; *crassispinna*, thick-spined; *crassisquamatus*, thick-scaled.

Crassamen'tum, or **Cras'sament** (Lat. *crassus* thick), in physiology, the thick or red portion of the blood, as distinct from the serum, or thin portion; the fibrin, which forms the clot.

Crassula'ceæ (Lat. *crassus*), in botany, a nat. order of plants, the House-leeks, consisting of succulent shrubs or herbs, of which Crassula is the type and genus.

Crassum Intesti'num (Lat.), in anatomy, the large intestine.

Cratæ'gus (Gr. *strength*), in botany, a genus of thorny shrubs, the Hawthorn.

Crater (Gr.), the mouth of a volcano.—In astrology, a constellation in the southern hemisphere.

Crateroi'dea (Gr. *cup-like*), in botany, a family of Lichens.

Crateropod'inæ (Gr. *long-legged*), in ornithology, a family of birds distinguished by the length and strength of their limbs,—the Long-legged Thrushes or Babblers, of which the Crateropus is the type; order, Dentirostres.

Craw-fish (Fr.), the fresh-water Lobster, the *Astacus fluviatilis* of naturalists.

Crax. (See *Cracidæ*.)

Crayon (Fr.), a chalk pencil of different colours and substances, either natural or artificial. The principal native crayons are black, white, and red. The best white is a pure chalk obtained in France. The red is a chalk or clay coloured by the peroxide of iron. Artificial crayons are composed of different coloured earths and other pigments, rolled into solid sticks with some tenacious substance.

Cre'asote (Gr. *flesh-preserver*), an oily liquid obtained from wood-tar, consisting of carbon, oxygen, and hydrogen, and so named from its property of preserving animal substances.

Cre'atin (Gr. *kreas* flesh), a crystallizable substance obtained from muscular fibre.

Cremai'llere (Fr.), in fortification, an indented zigzag line.

Cremas'ter (Gr. *kremao* to suspend), in anatomy, a muscle which springs from the lower edge of the internal oblique muscle of the abdomen.

Cremolob'idæ (Gr. *krema*, and *lobos* a pod), in botany, a family of cruciferous plants, of which Cremolobus is the type.

Cremo'na (Ital.), a superior kind of violin, first made at Cremona, in Italy.

Crenate, or **Crena'ted** (Lat. *crenatus* notched), in botany, applied to leaves with superficial rounded divisions at their edges, or when notched with indentations. Thus they assume different specific names: when notches are angular, the term *crenate-angular* is used; when full of round notches, *crenulate*; when serrated, *crenately-serrated*, *crenate-serrate*, or simply *serrated*; when so deeply indented as to appear lobed, *crenately-lobed*; and when toothed, *crenate-toothed*.

Crenaux (Fr.) in fortification, small openings or loopholes, made through the walls of a fortified town or place, which are extremely narrow towards the enemy, and wide within.

Crenila'brus (Lat. *crena* a slit, and *labrum* a lip), an extensive genus of acanthopterygious fishes, of the family Labridæ. Four species have been found off the British coast : the Gilt-Head, or Golden Maid, *C. tinca;* the Goldfinny, *C. corymbicus;* the Gibbous Wrasse, *C. gibbus;* and the Scale-rayed Wrasse, *C. leusias.*

Crep'itant (Lat. *crackling*), in pathology, an epithet applied to the crackling sound during respiration in the pneumonia and œdema of the lungs.

Crepus'cular, Crepus'culus (Lat. *glimmering*), a state between light and darkness.—In zoology, the term *Crepuscularia* is applied to divers animals which issue from their retreat on the approach of evening twilight, as in many species of the owl and the Lepidoptera, the latter embracing the families Zygænidæ, Sphingidæ, Sesiidæ, Œgeriidæ.

Crepus'cule (Lat. *twilight*), the time from the first dawn of the morning and the last remains of daylight.

Crescen'do (Ital.) in music, denotes the gradual swelling of the notes over which it is placed, marked thus <.

Crescent (Lat. *crescens* increasing), in astronomy, a term applied to the new moon when receding from the sun.—In heraldry, a bearing in the form of a new moon.—In architecture, a series of buildings disposed as the arc of a circle.

Crescentia'ceæ (Lat. *crescens*), in botany, a nat. order of perigynous Exogens, consisting of small trees with clustered leaves, of which Crescentia (the Calabash) is the genus and type.

Cress (Germ. *kresse*), in botany, plants of the genus Nasturtium; the Watercress, *N. officiale*, and the *N. amphibium*, being indigenous to this country : order Cruciferæ.

Cre'tinism (Fr.), a species of idiotism, with which the goitrous inhabitants of the Alpine valleys are afflicted. The *goître* is a wen or swelling on the throat.

Creux (pron. *kru*,—Fr. *deep*), a term used by carvers and engravers for cuttings beneath the surface of the plate.

Crich'tonite (named from *Crichton*), a bluish-black mineral of a brilliant metallic lustre, occurring in small crystals in the form of acute rhomboids.

Cricos'tome (Gr. *krikos* a circle, and *stoma* a mouth), in malacology, a family of shells, comprising all the turbinated univalves, with a perfectly round aperture.

Crinoi'deans (Gr. *lily-like*), in zoology, an order of lily-shaped Zoophytes, consisting of animals with a round, oval, or angular column, composed of numerous articulating joints, sup-

porting at its summit a series of plates or joints, which form a cuplike body. The small plates which constitute the skeletons of these animals often form entire beds of limestone, familiarly known as St. Cuthbert's beads.

Criocer'atites (Gr. *ram's horn*), a genus of fossil Cephalopods, allied to the Ammonite, the shells of which are discoidally spiral.

Criocer'idæ (Gr. *ram's horn*), a family of coleopterous insects, of the section Tetramera, of which the Crioceris is the type and genus.

Crista (Lat. *a crest*), in anatomy, a name given to certain processes and parts of bones, as the *crista ilii*, a process of the ethmoid bone, so called from its resemblance to a cock's comb.

Crista'cea (Lat. *crista*), a family of polythalamous Cephalopods, in which the shell is semi-discoid, globular, or spheroidal.

Crochet (Fr.), a kind of figured ornamental needlework.

Crocodil'ians (Gr. *krokodeilos*), a section of the Lizard family, Varanidæ, of which the Crocodilus, or Crocodile, a large saurian reptile, is the type and genus. There are twelve species of crocodiles extant; viz., eight true crocodiles, three alligators, and one gavial.

Croc'olite (Lat. *crocus* saffron, and *lithos* a stone), one of the zoolites, and a variety of the mineral natrolite.

Crocus, a name applied to any mineral which has been calcined into a red or deep yellow powder; as, *Crocus martis*, the peroxide of iron ; *Crocus metallorum*, oxide of antimony, &c.

Cronsted'ite, a mineral containing silex and iron ; sp. gr. 3·3.

Cropping-out, in geology and mining, the appearance of a seam or lode of metal near the surface.

Crosette (Fr.), in architecture, a truss, or console, in the flank of an architrave of a door or window; also the small projecting piece in archstones which hang upon the adjacent stones.

Cross (Welsh *croes*), in heraldry, the meeting of two horizontal lines with two perpendicular ones, so as to make two right angles in the form of a cross.—In architecture, there are two kinds of crosses in use; the one styled the *Greek cross*, and the other the *Latin cross.—Cross-quarters* is an ornament of cruciform tracery.—*Cross-vaulting* is the intersection of two or more simple vaults of archwork.—*Cross-springers*, in the pointed style of architecture, are the ribs that spring from the diagonals of the piers or pillars.—*Cross-beam* is a large beam going from wall to wall, or a girder that holds the sides of a house together.—In naval architecture, *Cross-spales* are pieces of timber placed across the ship, and nailed to the frames, securing both sides of the ship together till the knees are bolted.—*Cross-trees* are pieces of timber, supported by the cheeks and trestle-trees, at the upper ends of the lower and top masts.—*Cross-staff* is an instrument used formerly by mariners in taking the meridian altitude of the sun or stars.—*Cross-bar shot* is a bullet with an iron bar passing through it, and standing out a few inches on each side.—*Cross-garnets* are hinges which have a cross-piece on one side of the joint, and a long strap on the other.—In mining, *Cross-course* is a lode or vein which intersects another lode; *Cross-cut*, a lode level driven at right angles.—*Cross-wort*, a name given to plants of various genera.

Crotal'idæ (Gr. *krotalon* a rattle), in herpetology, a family of poisonous serpents, of which the Crotalus, or Rattlesnake, is the type, in which the upper jaw is furnished with poisonous fangs; order Ophides.—*Crotalophorus* is the name of a sub-genus of Rattlesnakes.

Crotchet (Fr.), in music, a note or character equal to two quavers, or half a minim.

Croton (Gr.) in botany, a genus of plants, one species of which yields the powerful drug *Croton oil*, and another species the Cascarilla bark of commerce; order Euphorbiaceæ, of which Crotoneæ is a family.—*Crotonic acid* is an acid obtained from croton oil, which is highly poisonous.

Croup (Sax. *hreopan*), in pathology, inflammation of the air-tubes, which produces a false membrane, and endangers life.

Crown (Fr. *couronne*), in architecture, the upper member of a cornice, including the corona.—*Crown-post* is the trust-post that sustains the tie-beam and rafters of a roof.—In fortification, an outwork having a large gorge, intended to enclose a rising ground.—In geometry, a plane ring included between two concentric perimeters.—In heraldry, the representation of that ornament, to express the dignity of persons.—In astronomy, a name for two constellations, termed *Borealis* and *Meridionalis*.—*Crown-wheel of a watch* is the upper wheel, which, by its motion, drives the balance.—*Crown* or *Contrate wheel* is a wheel the teeth of which are at right angles to the plane of the wheel.—Among jewellers, the upper part of the rose-diamond.

Crowning, in architecture, that which crowns any decoration, as a cornice or pediment.

Crow's-bill, in surgery, an instrument used for extracting bullets, or other foreign substances, from a wound.—*Crow's-feet* is an instrument with four points used in war for arresting the progress of cavalry by wounding the horses' hoofs.

Cru'cial (Lat. *cross-like*), in experimental science, applied to a searching inquiry.

Cru'cible, a melting-pot for chemical operations; a small conical vessel used by chemists, founders, and others, for holding ores, metallic or other substances, necessary to be subjected to strong heat for fusion. It requires to be made of some material not easily acted upon by corrosive liquids, and capable of enduring a very strong and continued action of fire.

Crucif'eræ (Lat. *cross-bearing*), in botany, a nat. order of plants, consisting of annual, biennial, and perennial herbs.

Crucite (Lat. *crux* a cross), in mineralogy, a red oxide of iron, crystallized in the shape of a cross.

Crura'lis (Lat. *crus* the leg), in anatomy, a muscle situated in the fore part of the thigh, springing from between the two trochanters and the os femoris, and inserted in the upper part of the patella.

Crypt (Gr. *krypto* to hide), in anatomy, applied to some of the minute cavities or simple glands of mucous membranes.

Cryptoga'mia (Gr. *kryptos*, and *gamos* marriage), an order of plants in which the distinction of sex is not obvious.

Cryptop'oda (Gr. *hidden feet*), in malacology, a division of the brachyourous or short-tailed Crustacea.

Cryptorhyn'chides (Gr. *hidden snout*), a family of coleopterous insects, consisting of about twenty-four genera, of which the Cryptorhynchus is the type.

Crystal (Gr. *krystallos*), in mineralogy, an inorganic body, which, by the operation of chemical affinity, has assumed the form of a regular body. Every perfect crystal is bounded by plane surfaces, which are called its faces; the straight line formed by the intersection of two faces is called an edge; the meeting of three or more edges in a point forms a solid angle.—*Crystallina* is an alkaloid obtained from *Indigofera tinctoria*, the Indigo plant.—*Crystalline* is an epithet applied to a lens of the eye.—*Crystal-*

lite is a name given to whinstone cooled slowly after fusion.—*Crystallography* is the science which describes crystals.

Crystalliza'tion (Gr. *krystallos*), in mineralogy, the process by which the particles of liquid and gaseous bodies attach themselves during conversion into solids to other bodies, so as to form symmetrical crystals.

Ctenoï'deans (Gr. *like a comb*), an order of fishes according to the arrangement of Agassiz.

Cube (Gr. *kubos*), in geometry and mathematics, a regular solid body with six equal sides, each of which is a square.—In arithmetic, the product of a number multiplied into itself, and that product multiplied by the same number; as, $4 \times 4 = 16 \times 4 = 64$, the cube of four.—*Cube root*, the number or quantity of which, multiplied by itself, and then into the product, produces the cube; 4, in the preceding example, being the cube root of 64.—*Cubic number* is a number produced by multiplying a number into itself twice; thus, 27 is a cubic number—because 3 multiplied by 3, and the product afterwards by 3, makes 27.—In algebra, *Cubic equation* is that in which the unknown quantity rises to the third or cubic degree of power.

Cubit (Lat. *cubitus*), in anatomy, the forearm; the *os cubiti* being the large bone of the forearm; the *cubital nerve*, the ulnar nerve; the *cubital artery*, the ulnar artery.

Cu'culus (Lat.), a migrating genus of passerine birds; the Cuckoo.

Cucurbita'ceæ (Lat.), a nat. order of diclinous Exogens, the Gourds, of which the Cucurbita is the type.

Cultiros'tres (Lat. *culter* a knife, and *rostrum* a beak), in ornithology, a family of Wading birds, distinguished by their strong bills.

Cul'verin (Fr.), a long slender piece of ordnance.

Culvert, a conduit or arched drain for the conveyance of water under canals or roads.

Cum'brian System, in geology, the name of the slate or graywacke system, most remarkably developed in Cumberland.

Cumin'idæ, or **Cumin'eæ** (Arab. and Heb.), a family of plants of the nat. order Umbelliferæ, partaking of the distinctive characters of Cuminum, a plant which is cultivated in the south of Europe and in all Asia Minor for its seeds, which have a bitterish warm taste. (Isa. xxviii. 27.)

Cum'mingtonite, a greyish-white mineral found at Cummington, in Massachusetts, occurring in fine needles, forming tufts of crystals. It consists of soda, silica, protoxide of iron, and protoxide of manganese: sp. gr. 3·26.

Cu'mulo-stra'tus (Lat.), in meteorology, a cloud formed by the junction of two clouds.

Cunette (Fr.), in fortification, a deep trench sunk along the middle of a dry moat.

Cunonia'ceæ, in botany, a nat. order of trees or shrubs, natives of the southern hemisphere, of which Cunonia is the type.

Cupel (Lat. *cupella*), in metallurgy, a shallow earthen vessel, resembling a cup, used in assaying precious metals. It is made of the phosphate of lime, and absorbs metallic bodies when changed by fire into a fluid scoria, but retains them as long as they continue in their metallic state.—*Cupel-dust* is the powder used in purifying metals.—*Cupellation* is the act of refining gold or silver by means of a cupel.

Cu'pola (Sp. and Ital.), in architecture, the round top of a dome; a spherical vault.

Cupping-glass, a glass vessel like a cup, to be applied to the skin before and after scarification.

Cupres'seæ (Lat. *cupressus* the cypress), a sub-order of the Pinaceæ, or Pine trees, of which the Cupressus is the type.

Cu'pula (Lat. *a little cup*), in botany, a collection of minute scaly bracteas connected at their base, and forming a cup, by which the flowers of certain plants are surrounded, as in the acorn or hazel-nut.

Curculion'idæ (Lat. *curculio* a weevil), a family of coleopterous insects, the Weevils, of which the Curculio is the type and genus. Of this family there are enumerated 4,089 species, distributed through 404 genera. The common Nut Weevil is a familiar example of this extensive family.

Curcu'ma (Arab.), in botany, a genus of plants, including the Turmeric plant, belonging to the order Zingiberaceæ. —*C. longa*, or Turmeric plant, is an herbaceous fleshy-rooted plant, found wild in various parts of the East Indies, and cultivated for its aromatic qualities.—*Curcumine* is the colouring matter obtained from the roots of the *C. longa*.—*Curcuma paper* is paper stained with a decoction of turmeric acid, and used by chemists as a test of free alkali, by the action of which it is stained brown.

Curette (Fr.), in surgery, an instrument

shaped like a little scoop, used in taking away the opaque matter that may be left after extracting a cataract from the eye.

Currents (Lat. *currens* running or flowing). In navigation, a *sea current* is an ocean mass of water in continued motion, and in a certain direction, sometimes extending for several thousand miles, with an average breadth of two or three hundred miles, as the current of the Mexican gulf.—Currents are also certain settings of the stream, by which floating bodies are compelled to alter their course or velocity, according to the direction of the current.—In electricity, the *electrical current* is the passage of the electric fluid from one pole of an apparatus to the other.

Curry, in cookery, a highly-spiced East Indian mixture.—*Curry powder* is a condiment of which the ingredients are chiefly turmeric, coriander seed, Cayenne, black pepper, cumin, mushroom powder, &c. The mushroom powder is the source of flavour in meat, and consequently restores what the process of cooking has dissipated.

Curso'ria (Lat. *cursores* runners), in entomology, a family of insects of the order Orthoptera, peculiarly adapted for running.

Curtain (Sp. and Ital.), in fortification, that portion of the wall or rampart which lies between two bastions, and connects their flanks, behind which the soldiers fire upon the invading force.

Curtate (Lat. *curtatus* shortened), in astronomy, an epithet applied to the distance of a heavenly body from the sun, reduced to the plane of the ecliptic.—In geometry, a term sometimes applied to a line projected orthographically upon a plane.—*Curtation* is the interval between a planet's distance from the sun and the curtate distance.

Curvilin'ear (Lat. *curve-lined*), in geometry, an epithet relating to curves or curved lines; and in natural history the following combinations occur:—*Curvicaulis*, bent in the stem; *curvicaudus*, curve-tailed; *curvicollis*, curved in the neck; *curvicostatus*, marked with small bent ribs; *curvidens*, having curved teeth; *curviflorus*, having a curved corolla; *curvifolius*, having reflecting leaves; *curvinervis*, having the nervures curved; *curvipedes*, bent in the limbs; *curvirostris*, curved in the beak.

Cuscuta'ceæ (Arab.), in botany, a nat. order of monopetalous Exogens, the Dodders, of which Cuscuta is the genus and type.

Cushion, in electricity, that part of an electric machine which presses against the plate or glass cylinder.

Cusp (Lat. *a pointed end*), in mathematics, a term applied to branches of different curves that appear to end in a point, as the horns of the moon; or a spear-shaped ornament appended to some arches, or to the heads of pointed arch windows.

Cus'pidate, Cus'pidated (Lat. *cuspis*, the point of a weapon), in botany, a term applied to those leaves which terminate in a bristly point, as the *Loranthus cuspidatus*.

Cuspida'ti (Lat. *cuspis*), in anatomy, the canine or sharp-pointed teeth.

Cut Glass, in the arts, fine flint glass, cut with sharp edges, which have been shaped by cutting instead of moulding.

Cu'ticle (Lat. *cuticula*), in anatomy, the exterior membranous covering of the body; the epidermis, or scarf-skin. —In botany, the thin, and generally colourless, pellicle which covers the exterior of plants, and which is easily detached from the vegetable structure.

Cutis (Lat.), in anatomy, the dermis, or true skin, as distinguished from the cuticle, or scarf-skin. It is abundantly supplied with blood-vessels and nerves.

Cuttle-bone, the dorsal plate of the cuttle-fish, formerly sold in the shops as an absorbent.

Cy'anate (Gr. *kyanos* dark blue), in chemistry, a salt formed by the combination of cyanic acid with a salifiable base.

Cya'nea (Gr. *kyanos*), in botany, a genus of blue flowering plants, natives of the Sandwich Islands; order Lobeliaceæ.—The Greek word *kyanos* (blue) forms a prefix to numerous species in natural history; as, *cyanicornis*, having blue antennæ, or horns; *cyanicterus*, blue and yellow; *cyanipes*, blue-legged; *cyanirostris*, blue-beaked; *cyanocarpus*, blue-seeded; *cyanocephalus*, blue-headed; *cyanocollis*, blue-throated; *cyanogastra*, blue-bellied; *cyanogynus*, having blue styles; *cyanomelas*, blue and black; *cyanothphyctis*, covered with blue pustules; *cyanopus*, blue-footed; *cyanopyrra*, blue and rose-coloured; *cyanotis*, blue-eared; *cyanurus*, blue-tailed.

Cyan'ic Acid, an acid formed of 26 equivalents of cyanogen + 8 of oxygen = 34.

Cyanide, a compound of cyanic acid with a salifiable base, from which various compounds are formed; as, *Cyanide of ammonia*, in bright crystalline plates; *Cyanide of cobalt*, a whitish-brown precipitate; *Cyanide of iron,* a grey insoluble powder; *Sesquicyanite of iron; Bicyanide of mercury,* crystallized in colourless transparent masses, highly poisonous; *Percyanide of gold; Cyanide of palladium; Cyanide of silver; Cyanide of zinc,* a brilliant white tasteless powder.

Cyanite (Gr. *kyanos*), a mineral of a bluish-green colour, which occurs in a crystallized state; composed of alumina, silica, iron, and lime.

Cyanogen (Gr. *kyanos,* and *gennao* to produce, from its being an essential ingredient of Prussian blue), in chemistry, a bicarbonate of azote or nitrogen, composed of 12 equivalents of carbon and 14 of nitrogen. It is a gas of a strong and peculiar odour; with hydrogen it produces hydrocyanic or prussic acid; and with the metals cyanurets or cyanides; with oxygen it forms cyanic acid.

Cyanometer (Gr. *kyanos,* and *metron* a measure), an instrument for ascertaining the depth of the blue tint of the atmosphere.

Cyanopathy (Gr. *blue disease*), in pathology, an affection in which the whole surface of the body exhibits a blue or purple colour, known as the Blue Disease.

Cyanotype (Gr.), a process of taking solar portraits in Prussian blue by a wash of cyanogen on prepared paper.

Cyanurate (Gr. *kyanos*), a salt formed with cyanuric acid and a salifiable base.—*Cyanurate of ammonia,* composed of 1 equivalent of hydrated cyanuric acid, 1 of ammonia, and 1 of water;—*Cyanurate of potassa,* in white acicular crystals;—*Cyanurate of silver,* a white precipitate.

Cyanuret, a compound of cyanogen.

Cyanuric Acid, in chemistry, an acid in the form of small colourless prismatic crystals; it is inodorous, and slightly soluble in water; it consists of cyanogen 3, oxygen 3, and water 7.

Cyathea (Gr. *kyathos* a cup), in botany, a family of plants of the order Polypodiaceæ, of which Cyathea, a genus of ferns, is the type.

Cycadeaceæ (Gr.), in botany, a nat. order of the class Gymnospermia, of which the Cycas is the type.

Cycadites, fossil plants allied to the Cycas and Zamia.

Cycle (Gr. *kyklos* a circle), in chronology, a series of years, in which, after a certain round has passed, a similar course commences.

Cyclo, in natural history, is a prefix of very general use in connection with words implying *circularity,* or *round-*

ness. The following and other similar compounds frequently occur:—*Cyclocarpus,* round-seeded; *cyclogaster,* round-bellied; *cyclonotus,* having a circle round the back; *cyclophyllus,* round-leaved; *cyclopterus,* round-winged or finned; *cyclorama,* a circular view represented in painting; *cyclothelis,* having circular papillæ; *cyclospermus,* round-seeded; *cyclostomus,* round-mouthed.

Cyclica (Gr. *kyklos*), a family of coleopterous insects, comprising the Tortoise, Beetles, &c.

Cyclobranchians (Gr. *round gills*), an order of Mollusca, in which the organs of respiration are branchial; they form the eighth order of the Gasteropods of Cuvier.

Cycloid (Gr. *like a circle*), in mathematics, a geometrical curve traced out by any point of a circle rolling on a straight line.

Cycloideans (Gr. *appearing round*), one of the great orders of fishes, distinguished by their scales being round, as in the salmon.

Cyclometry (Gr. *circle-measuring*), the art of measuring circles or cycles.

Cyclone (Gr. *kykloo* to encircle), a violent rotatory wind.

Cyclopædia (Gr. *kyklos,* and *padeia* instruction), a work which contains an account of the arts and sciences, or of any particular department of literature.

Cyclopteridæ (Gr. *round-finned*), a family of cartilaginous fishes, the Lump-suckers, of which Cyclopterus is the type.

Cyclosis (Gr.), motion in a circle.—In botany, a term applied to the circulating motion of the vital fluids in plants.

Cygnus (Lat. *a swan*), in astronomy, a constellation in the northern hemisphere, the bright stars in which, with those of Lyra and Aquila, form a remarkable triangle.—In ornithology, the Swan (*Cygnus*) is a well-known genus of natatorial birds belonging to the Anatidæ, or Duck family. The tame swan, *C. mansuetus,* is a native of Asia and eastern Europe, and is chiefly kept as an ornament for the waters of our parks and pleasure-grounds.

Cylinder (Gr. *kylindros*), a long circular body of uniform dimensions, with two equal ends parallel to each other.—The *Cylinder of a steam-engine* is that part of the engine in which the piston moves, the motion being produced by the alternate admission and condensation of steam from the boiler.—In natural history, the word *cylinder* forms a prefix to various compounds; as, *cylindricornis*, having the horns or antennæ cylindrical; *cylindriflorus*, having the flowers of a cylindrical shape; *cylindrocarpus*, having cylinder-shaped seed; *cylindroides*, like a cylinder.

Cyma, or **Cyma'tium** (Lat.), in architecture, the upper moulding of a cornice, of an undulating character. In botany, a form of inflorescence consisting of a solitary flower.

Cyme (Gr. *kyma* a wave), in botany, a kind of inflorescence or panicle.

Cynailu'rus (Gr. *a dog-cat*), in zoology, the hunting leopards of Africa and India.

Cynan'che (Gr.), in nosology, a disease of the throat; a species of quinsy.

Cynan'thropy, (Gr. *kuon* dog, and *anthropos* a man), in pathology, a species of madness, during which the patient imagines himself transformed into a dog.

Cynarrho'don (Gr. *kyon*, and *rhodon* a rose), in botany, the ovary of the rose.

Cynip'sides (Lat. *the dog-fly*), a tribe of hymenopterous insects, which, like the Ichneumons, are parasitical in the larva state; the Cynips, or Gall-fly, is the type and genus.

Cynorex'ia (Gr.), an insatiable or canine appetite.

Cyn'osure (Gr. *dog's-tail*), in astronomy, a constellation of seven stars near the north pole; generally called Ursa Minor, or Charles's Wain.

Cypera'ceæ (Lat. *cyperus*), in botany, a nat. order of endogenous plants, the Sedges, of which Cyperus is the type and genus.

Cypræ'idæ (Lat. *Cypria*, one of the names of Venus), a family of marine Gasteropods, the Cowries, of which Cypræa is the type and genus.—*Cypraina* is a sub-family of the Cowries.

Cypress (Lat.), the common name of the plants of the genus Cupressus; order Pinaceæ.—*Cypress turpentine*, a turpentine obtained by wounding the bark of the tree *Pistacia terebinthus*.

Cypri'næ, a sub-family of the Salmonidæ, including the Carps, &c.

Cyprine, a mineral, a cupreous variety of idocrase, of a fine blue tinge.

Cyprin'idæ, a family of malacopterygious fishes, of which Cyprinus, the common Carp, is the genus. It frequents ponds, lakes, and rivers.

Cyrilla'ceæ, in botany, a nat. order of hypogynous Exogens, consisting of shrubs with evergreen leaves, of which the Cyrilla, so called in honour of Professor Cyrilli, of Naples, is the type and genus.

Cyrtan'dreæ (Gr. *kyrtos* a curve, and *andros* a male), in botany, a tribe of plants of the order Gesneriaceæ, of which Cyrtandria is the type and genus.

Cyst (Gr. *kystis* a bladder), in pathology, a term applied to small sacs or bladders, containing matter of different sorts in disease.

Cystibran'chians (Gr. *kystis*, and *branchia* gills), a family of Crustaceans, whose organs of respiration are lodged in vesicular cavities.

Cystine, a kind of calculus formed in the human bladder.

Cystis (Gr.), in anatomy, the bladder. —*Cystitis*, inflammation of the bladder.—*Cystocele*, hernia of the bladder.—*Cystotomia*, the operation of cutting the bladder for the extraction of a calculus.—*Cystic*, an epithet frequently applied to the bladder; as, the *cystic duct*, which leads from the gall-bladder.—*Cystic oxide*, a species of calculus, sometimes existing in the bladder.

Cytina'ceæ, in botany, an order of the Rhizogens of Lindley.

Cyt'isus (Gr. and Lat.), in botany, a genus of ornamental trees and shrubs with yellow flowers. The common Broom and Pea tree (*C. laburnum*) are well-known British species.

Cyt'oblast (Gr. *kytos* a cell, and *blastos* a germ), in botany, the nucleus cellule, or assimilative force from which the organic cell is developed. These nuclei appear like dark spots, which may be seen in the fluids of the growing parts of all plants.—*Brande*.

Cytoblaste'ma (Gr.), in physiology, the viscid fluid in which animal and vegetable cells are produced, and by which they are held together.

Cytogen'esis (Gr. *kytos*, and *genesis* origin), in physiology, the development of cells in animal and vegetable structures.

D.

Da Capo (Ital.), in music, a phrase denoting a repetition from the beginning.

Dacryoblennorrhœ'a (Gr. *dakryo* to weep, *blenna* mucus, and *rheo* to flow), in pathology, a flow of mucus mingled with tears.

Dacryohæmorrhy'sis (Gr. *dakryo*, and *aima* blood), in pathology, a discharge of tears mingled with blood.

Dacryo'ma (Gr.) in pathology, a diseased state of the lachrymal duct of the eye.

Dactyliog'raphy (Gr. *daktylios* a ring, and *grapho* to engrave), the art of engraving on gems.

Dactylol'ogy (Gr. *daktylos* a finger) the art of communicating ideas by spelling words with the fingers.

Dactylon'omy (Gr. *daktylos*, and *nomos* a rule), the art of numbering with the fingers.

Dactylop'terus (Gr. *daktylos*, and *pteros* a wing or fin), in ichthyology, a genus of fishes covered with large scales, and the head long and flattened; fam. Loricata.

Dado (Ital.), in architecture, the part in the middle of the pedestal between the base and cornice.

Dæda'lian (from *Dædalus*, of Greek mythology), artificial; resembling a labyrinth.

Dæ'dalous (Gr.), in botany, having a margin with various windings and turnings; of a beautiful and delicate texture, as applied to leaves.

Dæmonoma'nia. (See *Demonomania*.)

Daguerre'otype (Fr.), a process invented by Daguerre, by which images from the lens of a camera obscura are fixed on metal plates.

Dahlia (from *Dahl*, the Swedish botanist), a genus of composite flowers, comprising many varieties.—*Dahline* is a chemical substance extracted from dahlia roots.

Daisy (Sax. *the day's eye*), a perennial plant and flower of the genus Bellis, of which there are many varieties; as, *B. perennis*, the cultivated variety; *B. hortensis*, garden or large double-flowered; *B. fistulosa*, double-quilled; *B. prolifera*, or hen-and-chickens: these are British species.

Dalber'gieæ (from *Dalberg*, the Swedish botanist), in botany, a tribe of leguminous plants, of which the Dalbergia is the type; sub-order Papilionaceæ.

Da'lian Problem, in mathematics, the duplication of the cube, or the process of finding the side of a cube double that of another one.

Damask Steel (from *Damascus*, where it was first made), in the arts, a fine kind of steel from the Levant, of a streaky mottled appearance, used in the manufacture of the best sword and scimitar blades.—*Damaskeening* is the art of adorning steel or iron with inlaid gold or silver, chiefly used for sword-blades or locks of pistols.

Dammar Pine, in botany, the name of two large coniferous trees, the *Dammara orientalis* and the *D. australis*.—*Dammarin* is a resinous substance obtained from the Dammar pine.—*Dammar*, or *Damar*, is a mixture of the yellowish oil produced from incisions made in the trunk of the tree *Comarium microcarpum* and Chinese varnish.

Dan'ae, in astronomy, one of the newly-discovered planets, first observed by Goldsmidt in 1860.

Danæa'ceæ (from *Dana*, the Italian botanist), an order of fern-like Acrogens, of which the Danæa is the type; they are all tropical plants.

Danoet'té (Fr.) in heraldry, the outline of a bordure or ordinary largely indented.

Dan'delion (Fr. *dent-de-lion*), a composite plant with a yellow flower, the *Leontodon taraxacum*, which has powerful diuretic qualities.

Da'ourite, in mineralogy, the rubellite, a variety of red schorl.

Daphne, in botany, the name of the Spurge Laurel, an evergreen shrub, common in Britain, France, and other parts of Europe.—In astronomy, the name of one of the newly-discovered planets, first observed in 1856.

Daphnin, in chemistry, the bitter principle of the *Daphne mezereum*, or Spurge Laurel.

Dasygas'trie (Gr. *hairy-bellied*), in entomology, a division and extensive group of the Bee family, including those solitary bees which have a hirsute venter, by which they carry their provisions.

Das'ypus (Gr. *hairy-footed*), in zoology, a genus of ant-eaters, the Armadillos, which are enveloped in shelly plates; order Edentata.

Dasys (Gr.), in natural history, a very useful prefix, signifying *hairy*, which frequently occurs in the definitions of genera or species; as, *dasyanthus*, having the corolla hairy; *dasycarpus*, having hairy seeds; *dasycaulon*, having a hairy stem; *dasyglottis*, having the legumes hairy; *dasypus*, hairy-footed; *dasypleurus*, having both sides ciliated, &c.

Dasyu'rus (Gr. *hairy-tailed*), in zoology, a genus of marsupial animals, the Brush-tailed Opossums, which are carnivorous.

Dath'olite (Gr. *dasyno* to thicken, and *lithos* a stone), a vitreous mineral composed of silica, lime, and boracic acid, not transparent, whence its name.

Datum, *pl.* **Data** (Lat.), a thing given in logical and mathematical premises; a proposition or truth granted or admitted. — *Datum-line*, in civil engineering, is the base or horizontal line of a section, from which heights and depths are calculated.

Datu'ria, a vegetable alkali obtained from the stramony, or thorn-apple.—*Daturine* is the active and poisonous principle of the thorn-apple.

Dau'cidæ, in botany, a tribe of the Umbelliferæ, of which Daucus, the Carrot, is the type and genus.—The cultivated carrot is the *D. sativa* of botanists.

Davyne (so called in honour ot Sir H. Davy), a yellowish transparent mineral ejected from Vesuvius; its constituents being silica, alumina, lime, iron, and water; sp. gr. 2'4.

Day (Sax. *dæg;* Lat. *dies*), an astronomical period, which depends upon the interval between two transits over the meridian of any point in the heavens, real or imaginary. But the only days distinguished by that name in astronomy are the *sidereal day*, the *real solar day*, and the *mean solar day.*—The *sidereal day* is the interval between two transits of the same fixed star, which is divided into twenty-four sidereal hours.—The *real solar day* is the interval between two moons or transits of the sun over the meridian.—The *mean solar day* is the average of all the real solar days.—The Babylonians commenced the day at sunrising, the Jews at sun-setting, and the Egyptians at midnight, as do many modern nations: the British, French, Spanish, Americans, &c.—In the computation of time, the *civil* or *mean solar day* is the time employed by the earth in revolving on its axis, 365·2425 of such revolutions constituting a mean Gregorian year: with most of the modern nations it commences at midnight, and consists of 24h. 3m. 56s., 55 of sidereal time.— *Solar days* are not always of equal length: 1st, from the unequal velocity of the earth in its orbit, that velocity being greater in winter than in summer; and 2nd, from the obliquity of the ecliptic.—A *sidereal day*, the day universally adopted by astronomers in their observations, is the time that elapses between two successive culminations of the same star.

Death's-head Moth, a term applied to the *Sphinx atropos*, the largest moth in Europe, so named from the figure of a human skull being distinctly marked upon its thorax; fam. Spingidæ.

Death-watch, in entomology, the name of a small beetle, the Anobium, which inhabits old wooden furniture, and makes a ticking noise like the beat of a watch, superstitiously imagined to portend the approach of death.

Debac'le (Fr. *a breaking up*), in geology, applied to the pristine deluge; a violent torrent or rushing of waters, which, overcoming all opposing barriers, carries with it stones, rocks, and other fragments, spreading them in all directions.

Deblai (Fr.), in fortification, the excavation formed by removing earth for the construction of parapets.

Débris (Fr.) in geology, fragments of rocks, detached from the summits and sides of mountains; ruins.

Deca (Gr.), a prefix in compound words, signifying *ten*.

Dec'agon (Gr. *deka*, and *gonia* an angle), in geometry, a plane figure with ten sides and ten angles. If the sides and angles are all equal, the figure is a regular *decagon*, and may be inscribed in a circle.—In fortification, a polygon figure with ten sides and as many angles.

Decagyn'ia (Gr. *deka*, and *gyne* a female), in botany, an order in the tenth class of the Linnæan system, including those plants which have ten pistils, or female organs of fructification.

Decahe'dron (Gr. *deka*, and *hedra* a side), in geometry, a figure or body having ten sides.

Decalcifica'tion (Lat. *de*, and *calx* chalk), in odontology, or dentistry, the removing of the hardening element of the teeth by chemical influence.

Dec'alitre (Fr.), a measure of ten litres; 1¾ English pint.

Dec'ametre (Gr. *deka*, and *metron* a measure), a French measure of ten mètres, nearly equal to 393 inches.

Decan'dria (Gr. *deka*, and *aner* a male or stamen), in the Linnæan system ot botany, a term applied to those plants which have ten male organs, or stamens. It embraces a considerable number of natural orders, ot which the leguminous plants are the most important. The orders are—*D. monogynia*, ten stamens, one style, as in the pea; *D. digynia*, ten stamens, two styles; *D. trigynia*, ten stamens, three styles; *D. pentagynia*, ten stamens, five styles; *D. decagynia*, ten stamens, ten styles.

Decaphyl'lous (Gr. *ten-leaved*), in botany, applied to a corolla of ten petals, or to a calyx of ten segments.

Dec'apods (Gr. *ten-footed*), an order of Crustaceæ, comprising those with ten feet, as the Crab, Lobster, Shrimp, &c.—*Decapodal*, having ten feet.

Decarboniza'tion (Lat. *de*, and *carbon*) the process of freeing a substance of its carbon.

Dec'astyle (Gr. *deka*, and *stylos* a column), in architecture, an edifice with a portico of ten columns.

Decay (Lat *de*, and *cado* to fall), in

physics, a slow decomposition of moist organic matter exposed to air, by means of oxygen, without sensible increase of heat.

Decem (Lat. *ten*), in natural history, a prefix to numerous species, signifying *ten*; as, *decemdentus*, ten-toothed; *decemfidus*, ten-cleft; *decemlocularis*, ten-celled; *decemmaculata*, ten-spotted; *decempunctatus*, marked with ten coloured points.

Dec'igramme (Fr.), the tenth of a gramme.

Decili'tre (Fr.), the tenth of a litre, ⅕ of an English pint.

Dec'imals (Lat. *decem* ten), that branch of arithmetical science which treats of decimal fractions, or such fractions as have ten, or some multiple of ten, for a denominator; thus, two-tenths would be written ·2; two hundredths, ·02, and so on.

Decime (Fr.), a copper coin in France of ten centimes, and nearly equal to one penny.

Dec'imetre (Fr.), the tenth part of the mètre, nearly four English inches.

Decli'nal (Lat. *declino* to bend down), in geology, a term applied to the slope of strata from an axis.

Declina'tion (Lat.), in astronomy, the *Declination of a celestial body* is the angular distance from the equator;— *Declination circles* are small circles of the sphere parallel to the equator, in which the stars perform their apparent diurnal revolutions.—In magnetism, *Declination of the magnetic needle* is the deviation of the axis of a magnetic needle from the astronomical meridian.—In dialling, *Declination of a wall or vertical plane* is an arch of the horizon, comprehended either between the plane and the prime vertical, when it is counted from east to west, or between the plane and the meridian, when it is counted from north to south.

Declina'tor (Lat.), an instrument used in dialling for taking the declination and inclination of a plane; and also in astronomy for observing the declination of the stars.—*Decliner* is a term applied to a dial which cuts either the plane of the prime vertical circle, or the plane of the horizon obliquely.

Decoc'tion (Lat. *a boiling*), the act of boiling a substance in water for the purpose of extracting its virtues.— In pharmacy, it is a term in very general use, denoting the solution of the active principles of vegetables obtained by boiling them in water. There are various officinal decoctions, as chamomile, aloes, marshmallows, guaiacum, cinchona, &c.,

which may be classed into simple and compound preparations. The principal *Simple decoctions* consist of D. *althæa officinalis*, decoction of marshmallows, used as an emollient fomentation; D. *anthemidis nobilis*, decoction of chamomile; D. *cinchonæ*, decoction of cinchona; D. *cydonia*, decoction of quince seed; D. *daphnis mezerei*, decoction of mezereon; D. *digitalis*, decoction of foxglove; D. *dulcamara*, decoction of woody nightshade; D. *glycyrrhizæ*, decoction of liquorice; D. *hæmatoxyli*, decoction of logwood; D. *hordei*, decoction of barley; D. *lichenis*, decoction of Iceland moss, or liverwort; D. *lobeliæ*, a purgative decoction; D. *papaveris*, decoction of poppy; D. *quercus*, decoction of oak bark; D. *sarsaparillæ*, decoction of sarsaparilla; D. *taraxaci*, decoction of dandelion.— Among the *Compound decoctions* may be enumerated—D. *aloes compositum*, decoction of aloes; D. *guaiaci compositum*, decoction of guaiacum; D. *hordei compositum*, decoction of barley; D. *malvæ compositum*, decoction of mallow; D. *sarsaparilla compositum*, decoction of sarsaparilla.

Decomposi'tion (Lat. *de*, and *compono* to put together), in physics, the separation of a body into its constituent elements.

Decus'sated (Lat. *crossed at right angles*), in botany, applied to leaves of various plants arranged in pairs, which alternately cross each other at angles.

Decusso'rium (Lat. *decusso*, to divide crossways), in surgery, an instrument used for pressing gently on the dura mater, causing an evacuation of the pus collected between the cranium and that membrane, through the perforation made by the trepan.

De'dalous. (See *Dædalous*.)

Dedola'tion (Lat. *chipping*), in surgery, the action of cutting so as to inflict an oblique wound.

Defæca'tion (Lat. *de*, and *fæces* dregs), in sanitary economy, the expulsion of adventitious matter; the purification from dregs.

Defila'ting, in military science, that part of fortification which is to determine the heights or directions of the lines of rampart or parapet, so that the interior of the work may not be incommoded by a fire directed towards it from such commanding eminences.

Deflec'tion, in mathematics, a term applied to the distance by which a curve departs from another curve, or from a straight line. It is also applied to any continuous change of direction.

Defolia'tion (Lat. *de*, and *folia* leaves), in botany, a term applied to the fall or shedding of leaves in the autumnal season.

Degluti'tion (Lat. *de*, and *glutio* to swallow), the act of swallowing through the agency of the pharynx and the œsophagus.

Degrada'tion (Lat.), in geology, the wearing away of banks or rocks by the action of water or other causes.— In painting, an obscuring or lessening the appearance of distant objects in a landscape in the same manner as they would appear to the eye placed at that distance from them.

Degree, in geometry, the division of a circle, the 360th part of its circumference; each degree being divided into sixty other parts, called minutes, and each of these again into sixty seconds; thus, in geography, a *degree of latitude* is the 360th part of the earth's surface north or south of the equator, and a *degree of longitude* the same part of the surface east or west of any given meridian.—In arithmetic, a *degree* consists of three figures; thus, 270, 360, compose two *degrees*. Also, a division, space, or interval marked on a mathematical or other instrument, as on a thermometer or barometer. —In algebra, a *degree* is a term applied to equations, to distinguish the highest power of the unknown quantity; thus, if the index of that power be three or four, the equation is respectively of the third or fourth *degree*.—In music, *degree* is an interval of sound, marked by a line on the scale.

Dehis'cence (Lat. *dehisco* to gape), in botany, a term applied to the opening of the capsules of plants, and also to the cells of anthers emitting pollen, &c.

Deinothe'rium (Gr. *a terrible beast*), in geology, a name given to the fossil remains of certain gigantic Pachydermata, remarkable for enormous tusks projecting from the lower jaw.

Delesser'iæ (in honour of M. Delessert), in botany, a sub-order of the Ceramaceæ, or Rose-tangles, of which the Delesseria is the type.

De'liac (from the city of *Delos*), in the fine arts, a term applied to beautiful silver and bronze; a kind of sculptured vase.

Delima'ceæ (Lat. *delimo* to file), a tribe of plants belonging to the nat. order Dilleniaceæ, of which Delima, a climbing shrub, is the type.

Deliques'cence (Lat. *de*, and *liquesco* to melt), in physiology, the process by which saline matters attract water from the air, and thus become melted.

Deliq'uium (Lat. a liquefying), in pathology, a fainting or swooning; syncope.—In chemistry, a melting or dissolution in the air.

Delir'ium (Lat.), in pathology, a wild and bewildered state of mind; symptomatic derangement.—*Delirium tremens*, a disease of the brain, or of the nervous system, accompanied with delirium and trembling, generally resulting from the excessive use of alcoholic spirits.

Delites'cence (Lat.), in pathology, the sudden subsidence of a tumour, or of general inflammation.

Delphin'idæ (Lat. *delphinus* a dolphin), in ichthyology, a family of cetaceous animals (the Dolphin tribe), which are characterized by the moderate size of the head, and the presence of teeth in both jaws.

Delta (Gr. Δ), in geology, a term applied to the alluvial deposits formed between the diverging mouths of a river, as the Delta of the Nile.

Deltoid (like the Greek letter Δ), in botany, shaped like a delta, or rhomb; in anatomy, an epithet applied to a muscle of the shoulder which serves to lift the arm; the deltoides.

Demen'tia (Lat.), in pathology, a form of mental alienation sometimes met with in aged persons.

Demephitiza'tion, the act of purifying from mephitic or foul air.

Demi (Fr.), a prefix used in composition, signifying *half*, as *demilune*: it corresponds with the Greek *hemi* and the Latin *semi*, which are frequently used in the composition of scientific names, especially those of Greek or Latin origin.

Demi-bas'tion (Fr.), in fortification, the part of a crown work which has one face and one flank cut off by the capital.

Dem'icross, in astronomy, an instrument for taking the altitude of the sun and stars.

Demicul'verin (Fr.), in gunnery, a large piece of ordnance.

Demidis'tance (Fr.), in fortification, the distance between the outward polygons and the flank.

Dem'igorge (Fr.), in fortification, that part of the polygon which remains after the flank is raised, and goes from the curtain to the angle of the polygon.

Dem'ilune (Fr. *a half-moon*), in fortification, an outwork consisting of two faces and flanks.

Dem'iquaver, in music, a note corresponding to half a quaver.—*Demi-

semiquaver is the shortest note in music, and only equal to half a demi-quaver.

Demi-relie've (Ital.), in sculpture, half-relief.

Demi'tone, in music, a semitone, or interval of half a tone.

Demonoma'nia (Gr. *daimon* a demon, and *mania* madness), in pathology, a species of frenzy or mental illusion, in which the patient fancies himself to be possessed by demons, or under their malign influence.

Demot'ic (Gr. *demos* the people), applied to the alphabet used by the people, as distinguished from that used by the hierarchal order, as among the Egyptians.

De'nary (Lat.), in the science of numbers, having the number 10 as the characteristic.

Den'drachate (Gr. *dendron* a tree, and *achates* agate), in mineralogy, a species of agate, in which there are delineations of ferns, trees, mosses, &c. The colouring matter of this mineral is dendritic manganese.

Dendrite (Gr. *dendron*), an arborescent mineral or stone, in or on which are the figures of trees or shrubs.—*Dendritic*, veined like the leaves of a tree, or having the resemblance of ferns, mosses, or trees.

Dendron forms a useful prefix to various compounds connected with natural history; as, *Dendrob'ates*, a genus of birds, the True Woodpeckers, of the family Picidæ;—*Dendro'bium*, a genus of plants of the order Orchidaceæ, natives of Australia and the East Indies;—*Dendrochi'rus*, a genus of fishes, of the order Scorpenidæ;—*Dendrocit'ta*, a genus of Indian birds of the Crow family;—*Dendrocolap'tes* and *Den'drocops*, genera of birds belonging to the True Creepers, of the family Certhiadæ;—*Dendrocyg'na*, a genus of aquatic birds, the True Ducks, of the family Anatidæ;—*Dendro'dus*, in palæontology, a genus of placoid fishes of the red sandstone formation, found in the county of Moray;—*Dendrolitha'ria*, a class of Corallines which assume an arborescent appearance;—*Den'droma*, a genus of birds belonging to the Tree-runners;—*Den'dromus*, a genus of birds belonging to the True Woodpeckers;—*Dendrones'sa*, the Tree Duck;—*Dendroides, Dendroph'agus*, and *Dendroph'ilus*, the names of coleopterous insects found beneath the bark of trees, &c.

Den'droid (Gr. *dendron*, and *eidos* resemblance), having an arborescent appearance, like the leaves or branches of a tree.

Den'drolite (Gr. *dendron*, and *lithos* a stone), in geology, a fossil plant, or part of a plant.

Dendrol'ogy, or **Dendrog'raphy** (Gr. *dendron*), in botany, a dissertation on, or description of, trees; whence *Dendrologist*, a writer on, or cultivator of, trees.

Dendrom'eter (Gr.), an instrument for measuring the diameter and height of trees.

Den'dromys (Gr. *tree mouse*), an African genus of rodents.

Den'drophis (Gr. *a tree serpent*), a serpent of a long, slender body.

Deneb (Arab.), a bright star in the tail of the Lion.

Denom'inator (Lat.), in vulgar fractions, the number below the numerator, as 4 in ¼; but in decimals the denominator is not written, but expressed by a dot; as ·5 denotes 5 parts in 10, or half.

Dens, *pl.* **Dentes** (Lat.), in anatomy, the teeth of animals, which are organs of mastication and destruction possessed by the Mammifers, Fishes, and Reptiles.—In man, the *dentes*, or teeth, are thirty-two in number, sixteen in each jaw, consisting of four incisors, or cutting teeth, two canine teeth, four bicuspid, or lesser molar teeth, and six molars, or great molars, occupying the farther parts of the alveolar arch (*Dunglison*).—In natural history, the following compounds of *dens, dentis*, occur:—*Denticollis*, having the neck or corselet dentated; *denticornis*, having dentated antennæ; *dentipede*, having the feet or limbs with a small spine or tooth, as in *Buprestis dentipes.*—*Dentalite*, or fossil *Dentalium*, a genus of shells which occur in the galt and greensand of the chalk formation, and in tertiary strata.

Dental For'mula (Lat.), a prescribed formula for denoting the number of the different kinds of teeth in an animal.

Den'tary (Lat. *dentes* teeth), in the head of fishes and reptiles, a bone that supports the teeth.

Denta'ta (Lat.), in anatomy, a name given to the second vertebra of the spinal column, from a tooth-like process which occurs in it.

Den'tate, or **Denta'ted** (Lat. *dentes*), in natural history, having tooth-like processes, or the margin of anything divided into incisions resembling teeth.—In botany, *Dentately* forms the following adverbial combinations:—*Dentately lobed*, toothed so deep as to appear lobed; *dentately pinnatifid*, appearing pinnatifid; *dentately runcinate*, appearing runcinate; *dentately serrated*, having the margin divided into incisions resembling a saw; *dentately sinuated*, having the margin slightly toothed. Sometimes the adverb *Denticulately* occurs, from the term *Denticulate*, slightly toothed; as, *denticulately serrated* resembling the edge of a fine saw; *denticulately ciliated*, having the margin so finely toothed as to appear edged with hairs; *denticulately scabrous*, having very small teeth.

Den'ticle (Lat. *dentes*), in odontology, a little tooth, or projection like a tooth.

Dentic'ulate (Lat.), having small teeth, or projections like teeth.

Den'tifrice (Lat. *dens*, and *fricare* to rub), a powder for cleaning the teeth.

Den'ticule, in architecture, is the flat, projecting part of a cornice on which dentils are cut.—*Denticulation* is the state of being notched, or set with small teeth or tooth-like prominences.

Dentils (Lat. *dentes* teeth), in architecture, the small square projections resembling teeth in the bed-mouldings of cornices in the Ionic, Corinthian, Composite, and occasionally Doric orders. In the Grecian orders they are not used under modillions.

Dentine (Lat. *dentes*), in dentistry, that part of a tooth known as ivory.

Dentiros'tres, or **Dentiros'ters** (Lat. *dens*, and *rostrum* a beak), in ornithology, a tribe of the order Insessores, or Perching birds, so named from a notch near the tip of the beak in the upper mandible.

Denti'tion, or **Dentila'tion** (Lat.), the period at which the teeth are formed within the jaws, and protruded through the gums.—*Dentize* is to renew the teeth, or have them renewed.

Denuda'tion (Lat. from *nudus* bare), in geology, the laying of rocks bare by the washing away of the superficial deposits.—In surgical pathology, the condition of a part deprived of its natural envelopes.

Deob'struent (Lat. *de*, and *obstruo* to obstruct), in medicine, that which removes obstructions, and opens the natural passages of the fluids of the body, as the pores and lacteal vessels.

Deodoriza'tion (Lat. *de*, and *odor* smell), in chemistry and sanitary economy, the art or process of deodorizing, or neutralizing unpleasant smells; thus, quicklime deodorizes night-soil, and chloride of lime deodorizes infectious or febrile miasmata.

Deoxida'tion, or **Deoxygena'tion** (Lat. *de*, and *oxygen*), in chemistry, the operation of depriving of oxygen; the partial or total abstraction of oxygen from any body.

Dephlegma'tion (*de*, and Gr. *phlegm*), the clearing spirits and acids of aqueous matter by evaporation or distillation.

Dephlogistica'tion (*de*, and Gr. *phlogistos* burnt), the abstracting of phlogiston, or the supposed principle of inflammability.—*Dephlogisticated air* was the name applied by Dr. Priestley to oxygen.

Depil'atory (Lat. *depilo* to strip off), any application, such as lime and orpiment, for stripping off the hair of an animal body.

Deple'tion (Lat. *depleo* to empty), in surgery, the act of emptying the animal vessels by blood-letting or medicine.

Deploy (Fr.), in military science, the expansion of a body of troops, so as to present a large front, to extend a line of small depth, whether an army, a division, or a battalion, which has been previously formed in one or more columns.

Depolariza'tion, in natural philosophy, the act of depriving of polarity, as the rays of light.

Depos'it (Lat. *depositum*), in geology, matter laid or thrown down after being suspended in or carried along by water, as the mud, gravel, stones, &c., at the bottom of a river, lake, or sea.

Depres'sion (Lat.), in cosmology, *depression of the pole of the earth* is a problem which arises from the spherical figure of the earth; thus, when a person sails or travels towards the equator, he is said to depress the pole, because as many degrees as he approaches nearer the equator, so many degrees will the pole be nearer the horizon.—In astronomy, the *depression of the sun* is its distance at any time below the horizon, measured by an arc of the vertical circle.—In navigation and nautical astronomy, the *depression* or *dip of the horizon* is the depression or dipping of the visible horizon below the true horizontal plane, arising from the eye of the observer not being placed on the same level with the surface of the sea, but at some distance above it. —In algebra, *depression of equations* is the reduction of equations to a lower degree, by dividing them by one or more of their component factors.

Depura'tion, or **Depuri'tion** (Lat. *depuro* to purify, or make clean), in medicine, the removal of impurities from the humours of the animal body; purification.—*Depurator* is the name of a machine for cleansing and preparing cotton for spinning.

Derby Spar, in mineralogy, a beautiful variety of the fluate of lime (fluorspar), which occurs in cubical crystals of a variegated colour.

Dermabran'chiates (Gr. *skin-gills*), in zoology, a family of Gasteropods, or Snails, of which the Dermabrancha is the type. The branchiæ, or respiratory organs, consist of thin membranous plates, or ramified skin.

Dermaneu'ral (Gr. *derma* the skin, and *neuron* a nerve), in ichthyology, an epithet applied to the upper row of spines on the back of a fish, from their connection with the skin, and their protection of the nervous system.

Dermap'terans (Gr. *skin-wings*), in entomology, an order of insects, comprehending those genera which have the elytra horizontal and entirely coriaceous, the two membranous wings being folded longitudinally.

Der'matine (Gr. *derma* skin-like coating), a dark olive-green mineral, found in Saxony, which occurs in thin coatings, as well as in reniform masses: sp. gr. 2·136.

Dermatol'ogy, or **Dermatog'raphy** (Gr. *derma* skin), in pathology, a treatise on the skin and its diseases.—*Dermatomy* is the anatomy of the skin.—*Dermatologist* is one who writes and treats on the skin and its diseases.

Derma Skel'eton (Gr. *a skin-skeleton*), in physiology, the external covering of many invertebrated animals.

Dermis'tidæ (Gr. *derma*, and *esthio* to eat), in entomology, a family of coleopterous insects, of which Dermistes is the type; so named from its ravages on dead bodies and stuffed animals.

Descen'sion (Lat.), in astronomy, the calculation of a setting body with relation to a right sphere.—*Oblique descension* is an arc of the equinoctial, intercepted between the next equinoctial point and the horizon, passing through the centre of the object, at its setting, in an oblique sphere.—*Right descension* is an arc of the equinoctial, intercepted between the next equinoctial point and the intersection of the meridian, passing through the centre of the object, at its setting, in a right sphere (*Bouvier*).—*Descension of a sign* is an arc of the equator, which sets with such a sign or part of the zodiac, or any planet in it.

Descent (Lat. *descensus*), in physics, the motion of a body towards the centre of the earth, according to the law of gravity. The laws of descent have been thus defined:—Bodies in an unresisting medium have a uniformly accelerated velocity;—When the action of gravity is uniform, the space passed over in a given time is exactly one-half of that which would be passed over in the same time by the velocity acquired at the end of the time if continued uniformly;—The spaces passed over in different times are proportioned to the squares of the velocities or the squares of the times;—The time of the oblique descent of a body down any chord of a circle, drawn from the highest or lowest point of the circle, is equal to the descent through the diameter of the circle;—The times of descent through all arcs of the same cycloid are equal;—A heavy body falling to the earth by its own gravity is found to descend through $16\frac{1}{8}$ feet in the first second, $32\frac{1}{4}$ in the second second, $64\frac{1}{2}$ in the third, and so on.—*Craig*.

Desic'cative (Lat. *de*, and *siccus* dry), in pharmacy, a preparation which dries up the matter or secretions discharged from wounds, membranes, ulcers, &c.

Desmid'ieæ (Gr. *desmos* a band), in botany, a sub-order of the Diatomaceæ, or Brittleworts, of which the Desmidium is the type and genus.

Desmine (Gr. *desme* a bundle), a mineral formed in fasciculated tufts in the lavas of extinct volcanoes.

Desmog'raphy, **Desmol'ogy** (Gr. *desmos* a band), in anatomy, a description of, or treatise on, the ligaments of the body.

Desquama'tion (Lat. *de*, and *squama* a scale), a throwing off in scales.

Desuda'tion (Lat. *sweating*), in pathology, an eruption of small pimples resembling millet seeds, which sometimes occurs on the skin of children.

Detach'ment (Fr.), in naval operations, a number of ships selected from a fleet, and sent on separate services.—In military science, a certain number of men, squadrons of horse, regiments or companies of infantry, selected from the main body of an army for the performance of some particular duty.

Deter'sive (Ital.), in pharmacy, a medicine which has the power of carrying off foul secretions or cleansing ulcers.

Detona'ting Powder (Lat. *detono* to explode), in chemistry, a preparation of fulminating mercury, silver, or other compounds, which detonates when struck or heated.—*Detonating tube* is a strong glass tube used by chemists for the detonation of gaseous bodies.

Detri'tus (Lat. *worn*), in geology, the disintegrated materials of the earth's surface; the waste or matter worn off rocks, &c.

Detrunca'tion (Fr.), in midwifery, the separation of the trunk of the fœtus from the head, the latter remaining *in utero.*

Deu'tero, or **Deuto** (Gr. *deuteros* second), a term used in chemistry when two equivalents of any substance are combined with one of another.

Deuterohydrog'uret, in chemistry, a compound of two equivalents of hydrogen with one of some other element.

Deuteropa'thia (Gr. *deuteros*, and *pathos* suffering), a sympathetic affection of one part with another.

Deutox'ide, in chemistry, a body in the second degree of oxidation.

Devitrifica'tion (Lat. *de*, and *vitrum* glass), the act of converting glass into a grey opaque substance.

Devo'nian System, in geology, a name given to the palæozoic strata of North and South Devon, considered as coeval with the old red sandstone of Herefordshire. The rocks of South Devon probably belong to the newer old red sandstone deposits.

Dew-point, in natural philosophy, that degree of temperature in the atmosphere which causes the dew to be deposited.—*Dew-worm* is a large variety of the Earth-worm, which appears aboveground when moist with dew.

Dew-retting, in chemical science, the exposure of flax in the bleaching-grounds to the action of the dew, rain, or snow, to effect by maceration the decomposition of the gum or resin which coats the fibre.

Dexter (Lat. *right hand*), a term used in heraldry to denote the right side of a shield or coat of arms.

Dextral (Lat. *dexter*), in conchology, an epithet applied to univalve shells which have their turns or convolutions from left to right when placed in a perpendicular position, with the apex downwards. Sinister or reverse shells are contrary.

Dextrine (Lat. *dexter*), the gummy or soluble matter into which the interior substance of starch is convertible by diastase, or by certain acids.

Diabe'tes (Gr. *passing through*), in pathology, an immoderate discharge of urine, of which there are two species, *D. insipidus*, from the insipid nature of the urine; and *D. mellitus*, from the urine containing abundance of a peculiar saccharine matter.

Diabro'sis (Gr. *corrosion*), in surgery, the action of corrosive substances which possess a property intermediate between caustics and escharotics.

Diacaus'tic (Gr. *dia* through, and *kaio* to burn), in surgery, a system of cauterizing by refraction, as when the solar rays are made by a burning-lens to act on the animal organism.—In geometry, the *Diacaustic curve* is the caustic curve by refraction.

Diache'nium (Gr. *dia*, and *achanes* gaping) in botany, a simple fruit, formed by the ovary adhering to the calyx, which, on ripening, separates into two cells.

Diach'ylon (Gr. *dia*, and *chylos* juice), in surgery, the name of common plaster made by boiling hydrated oxide of lead with olive oil.

Diaco'dium (*dia*, and *kodia* a poppy), in the materia medica, a preparation of the poppy.

Diac'ope (Gr. *a cutting off*), in surgery, a longitudinal fissure or fracture of the cranial bone, or an oblique cut of the cranial integuments.—In ichthyology, the name of a beautiful genus of fishes which inhabit the Indian seas; fam. Chætodonidæ.

Diacous'tics (Gr. *dia*, and *akouo* to hear), that branch of physical science which treats of the properties of refracted sounds; diaphonics.

Diadel'phia (Gr. *dia*, and *delphys* the womb), in botany, a class of plants which have their stamens united in two parcels.

Diadex'is (Gr. *a transference*), in pathology, a translation of the humours of the body from one place to another.

Diaglyph'ic (Gr.), in sculpture, &c., applied to objects sunk into the general surface.

Diagno'sis, Diagnos'tic (Gr. *distinguishing*), in pathology, the sign or symptom by which a disease is known or distinguished from others.

Diag'onal (Gr. *dia*, and *gonia* an angle), a straight line drawn through a square or other rectilineal figure.

Diag'onite (Gr.), in mineralogy, a name for Brewsterite.

Di'agram (Gr.), a geometrical figure or scheme.

Di'agraph (Gr.), an instrument used in perspective.

Diagraph'ics (Gr. *dia*, and *graphe* description), the art of design or drawing.

Di'allage (Gr. *difference*), a mineral of a brilliant green colour, with a silky or pearly lustre. It consists of silica, alumina, lime, magnesia, oxide of chrome, and oxide of iron: sp. gr. 3'0.

Di'alling, the art of constructing dials. —*Dialling lines* or *scales* are graduated lines or rules made to facilitate the construction of dials. In Scotland, the term is used by miners for the use of the mining compass.

Dial'ogite, a mineral of a rose-red colour, with a laminar structure and vitreous lustre; a carbonate of manganese.

Dialu'ric (Gr. *dia*, and *ouron* urine), appertaining to the urine.—*Dialuric acid* is a newly-discovered acid, produced in combination with ammonia by the decomposition of alloxatin.

Dial'ysis (Gr. *dia*, and *luo* to loosen), in pathology, loss of strength; exhaustion; weakness of the limbs.—In surgery, solution of continuity.

Diamagnet'ic (Gr. *dia*, and *magnet*), in natural philosophy, a term applied to a class of substances which, under the influence of magnetism, take a position, when freely suspended, at right angles to the magnetic meridian.

Diamag'netism (Gr.), a peculiar property of many bodies, which are repelled by sufficiently powerful electro-magnets, and take a position at right angles to the magnetic equator.

Diam'eter (Gr. *dia*, and *metron* measure), in geometry and mathematics, a right line drawn through the centre of a circle; the measure across the shaft of a column.

Di'amond (Fr.), the most valuable and the hardest of all precious stones or gems. It is pure carbon; and its primitive crystals are the regular octahedron, which reflects all the light falling on its posterior surface at an angle of incidence greater than 24° 13', whence its great brilliancy is derived. The diamond has various tints of colour; sometimes of a yellowish, bluish, or rose-red tinge, though sometimes perfectly colourless. The largest diamond known is said to have belonged to the Emperor of Brazil; but the celebrated Koh-i-noor diamond, which passed from the hands of the Mogul princes to the possession of Queen Victoria, is among the most valuable in Europe.—In geometry, diamond is the name of a quadrangular or rhomboidal figure.—*Diamond beetle* is the popular name of the *Entimus nobilis*, a beautiful coleopterous insect, belonging to the family Curculionidæ.

Dia'na, Tree of, is a term applied to the arborescent form of the crystallized silver, which becomes separated when mercury is put into a solution of the nitrate of silver.

Dian'dria (Gr. *dis* two, and *andres* males), in botany, one of the classes of Linnæus, which comprehends those plants with two stamens.

Diapa'son (Gr. *dia*, and *pason* of all), in music, a chord which includes all tones; the interval of the octave, so called because it includes all admitted musical sounds. It is also used to denote the compass of any voice or instrument:—

"From heavenly harmony
This universal frame began
From harmony to harmony,
Through all the compass of the notes
  it ran,
The *diapason* closing full in man."
Dryden.

A scale by which musical-instrument makers adjust the bore of their pipes.

Diapede'sis (Gr. *a leaping through*), in animal physiology, the escape or transudation of blood through the coats of any vessel.

Diapensia'ceæ (Gr.), in botany, a nat. order of perigynous Exogens, of which the Diapensia is the type.

Diaphon'ics (Gr. *dia*, and *phone* sound), in acoustics, the science or doctrine of refracted sounds.

Diaphore'sis (Gr. *dispersion*), augmented perspiration, or elimination of the humours of the body through the pores of the skin.—*Diaphoretic*, causing perspiration.

Di'aphragm (Gr. *dia*, and *phrasso* to fence in), in anatomy, the midriff, or large muscular organ situated between the thorax or chest and the abdomen, forming a movable partition between those two cavities. It is imperfectly developed in birds, and in the lower animals it does not exist.—*Diaphragmatitis* is inflammation of the diaphragm.

Diaph'ysis (Gr.), in anatomy, the state of growing between; a term applied to the body or central portion of the long bones.

Diapla'sis (Gr.), the replacing of a luxated or fractured bone in its proper situation.

Diapnot'ic (Gr. *respiration*), in materia medica, applied to remedies which operate by promoting gentle respiration.

Diapoph'ysis (Gr. *a growing from*), in anatomy, the transverse process of a vertebra in the archetype skeleton.

Diarrhœ'a (Gr. *a purging*), in pathology, a copious alvine evacuation; a flux of the bowels, arising from various causes, but generally from food or drink of too stimulating a nature. There are various species of diarrhœa: as, *D. biliosa*, bilious;—*D. crapulosa* (Lat. *crapula* surfeit);—*D. mucosa*, mucous;—*D. cœliaca*, cœliac passion, when the food passes off in a white liquid state like chyle;—*D. verminosa*, from worms.

Diarthro'sis (Gr. *dia*, and *arthron* a

joint), in anatomy, a movable joint; an articulation admitting of motion in various directions.—*Diarthrodial*, having free motion in the articulation of the joints.

Di'aspose (Gr. *to scatter*), a laminated mineral of a pearly shining lustre, consisting of alumina and water; when exposed to heat, it precipitates with violence, is dispersed (whence its name), and splits into small brilliant scales.

Di'astase (Gr. *dia*, and *istemi* to set), a vegetable principle extracted from crushed malt, analogous to gluten. It is by the action of this small portion of diastase that the starch of the barley is converted into sugar in the first stage of brewing, preparatory to the fermentation by which ale or malt spirits are obtained.

Dias'tasis (Gr. *separation*), in surgery, the separation of two bones previously in contact, or of the pieces of a fractured bone.

Diaste'ma (Gr. *an interval*, or *fissure*), in zoology, the space which occurs in animal dentition when the canine teeth are wanting, as in the class of Rodents.—The following compounds have been used by physiologists as applying to monstrosities or organic irregularities, when characterized by a fissure or longitudinal division of some particular part of the animal body:— *Diastemato-cephalia*, of the brain; *diastemato-caulia*, of the trunk of the body; *diastemato-cheilia*, of the lip; *diastemato-crania*, of the skull; *diastemato-cystia*, of the bladder; *diastemato-gastria*, of the parietes of the belly; *diastemato-glossia*, of the tongue; *diastemato-gnathia*, of the jaws; *diastemato-metria*, of the womb; *diastemato-pylia*, of the pelvis; *diastemato-rachia*, of the spine; *diastemato-rhenia*, of the nose; *diastemato-stophylia*, of the uvula; *diastemato-sternia*, of the sternum; *diastematria*, of the intestinal canal.

Diastim'eter (Gr. *distance measurer*), a philosophical instrument for measuring distances.

Dias'tole (Gr. *diastello* to separate), in physiology, the opening or dilatation of the heart after contraction.

Di'astyle (Gr. *dia*, and *stylos* a column), in architecture, that mode of intercolumniation in the arrangement of pillars where the space between the columns consists of three or four diameters.

Diather'mal, or **Diather'matous** (Gr. *dia*, and *therma* heat), a term applied to those transparent bodies which suffer the radiation of heat to pass through them, as in the case of rock salt, &c.

Diath'esis (Gr.), in pathology, the state of the body or constitution in which there is a predisposition to particular diseases.

Diatoma'ceæ (Gr. *a separating*), in natural history, a genus of minute Algæ, of which the Diatoma is the genus. They are of a very heterogeneous character, consisting of crystalline fragmentary bodies, flat, stiff, and brittle, usually nestling in slime, uniting into various forms, and then separating again. Dr. Lindley says that "they seem to form the extreme limits of the vegetable and animal kingdoms. Their regular form, and the power of separating into distinct particles which most of them have, are almost as much the attributes of the mineral as of the animal or vegetable kingdom. Agardh includes them among plants; Kützing asserts that their life is as much animal as vegetable."—*Diatomous*, in mineralogy, applied to those crystals which have one distinct diagonal cleavage.

Diaton'ic (Gr. *dia*, and *tonos* a tone), a term applied to the natural scale of music, including both tones and semitones, proceeding by degrees.

Diazo'ma (Gr. *dia*, and *zoma* a cincture), in zoology, a genus of the Ascidia, in which the species dispose themselves circularly or in rays, so as to form one or more stelliform systems.

Diboth'rians (Gr. *dis* double, and *bothrion* a pit), in natural history, a division of the Entozoa, including those tape-worms of the family Bothriocephala which have not more than two pits or fossæ on the head.

Dibran'chia (Gr. *double gills*), in malacology, a class of the Cirripeds.

Dibran'chiates (Gr. *ut supra*), an order of the Cephalopods, which are furnished with two gills, and an apparatus for secreting and discharging an inky fluid.

Dic'erates (Gr. *double-horned*), in malacology, a family of Mollusca, comprehending such Gasteropods as have the head furnished with two tentacula.

Dichæ'tæ (Gr.), a subdivision of the apterous insects, consisting of two families, the Athericera and the Pupipara.

Dichlamyd'eous (Gr. *double covering*), in botany, having calyx and corolla.

Dichot'omy (Gr. *occurring in pairs*), in natural history, an artificial arrangement of natural objects into pairs.— In botany, branching by constant forking, as when the stem or vein of a plant divides into two branches, each branch dividing into two others. —*Dichotomous*, occurring in pairs at the nervures in the wings of certain insects, and in the veins of certain ferns.

Di'chroism (Gr. *double-coloured*), in optics, the property of some crystallized bodies of appearing under two distinct colours, according to the direction in which light is transmitted through a body, as in the muriate of palladium, which appears of a deep red colour along the axis, and of a lively green when viewed in a transverse direction.

Dichromat'ic (Gr. *dis* double, and *chroma* colour) having or producing two colours.

Dic'linate (Gr. *dis*, and *klino* to incline), an epithet applied to crystals in which two of the axes are obliquely inclined.

Dicotyle'dons (Gr. *dis*, and *kotyledon* a seed-lobe or seed-leaf), in botany, a class of Exogens, the first grand division of the vegetable kingdom, whose seeds in germinating divide into two lobes; the stem being increased by external layers, with an evident distinction between wood and bark.—*Dicotyledonous*, having two seed-leaves.

Dicot'yles, in zoology, a genus of hogs, the Peccary.

Dic'roite, a mineral of a blue and shining colour, which occurs in gneiss and granite, and consists of silver, alumina, magnesia, oxide of iron, and manganese.

Dicrot'ic (Gr. *dis*, and *kroyo* to strike), in pathology, having a double pulsation.

Dicruri'næ (Gr. *dis*, and *oura* a tail), in ornithology, a sub-family of fly-catching birds, the Drongo Shrikes, of which the Dicrurus is the type.

Dict'yogens (Gr. *diktyon* a net, so called from the reticulated nature of the leaves), a class of plants intermediate between Exogens and Endogens, in which the root of the wood is a solid concentric circle.

Dictyot'idæ (Gr. *diktyon*, and *otis* an ear), in botany, a tribe of Fuci, of which the Dictyota is the type.

In natural history, the following compounds, connected with *dis* or *dicho*, two or double, are of frequent occurrence:—*Dicarpus*, two-seeded; *dicephalus*, two-headed; *diceratus*, two-horned, or having two antennæ; *dichopetalus*, having two petals; *dichopterous*, two-winged; *dichrous*, two-coloured; *dichrurus*, having a two-coloured tail; *diclinus*, two-bedded, or having the sexes separate; *diccocus*, two-seeded; *dictyocarpus*, (Gr. *diktyon*, a net), having reticulated fruit; *dictyodes*, net-like, reticulated; *dictyorhizus*, having a

reticulated root; *dictyoptera*, having reticulated wings.

Dicyn'odon (Gr. *double canine-toothed*), in zoology, a genus of reptiles with no teeth in the upper jaw, except two long tusks in sockets curved downwards.

Didac'tyle (Gr. *dis*, and *daktylos* a finger), in natural history, applied to two-fingered or double-toed animals; as to the ruminants among quadrupeds, the ostrich among birds, and the amphiuma among reptiles.

Didecahe'dral (Gr.) in crystallography, applied to ten-sided prisms with five-sided summits.

Didel'phidæ (Gr. *dis*, and *delphys* a womb), in zoology, a family of the Marsupialia, including the Opossums, Kangaroos, and other species of the genus Didelphis, which are possessed, as the name implies, of an external abdominal pouch or sac, in which the fœtus is placed after a short period of uterine gestation, and where it remains suspended to the nipple by its mouth until sufficiently matured to come forth into the air.

Didodecahe'dral (Gr. *dis* double, *dodeka* twelve, and *hedra* sides), in crystallography, having the form of a dodecahedral or twelve-sided prism, with hexahedral or six-sided summits.

Did'ymous, in botany, growing in pairs or twins.

Didyna'mia (Gr. *double power*), the fourteenth class of plants in the Linnæan system, which have four uneven stamens. The class is divided into two orders, the Gymnospermia, including those genera the ovary of which splits into four seed-like lobes, and the Angiospermia, those which have the seed enclosed in a pericarp of some kind. To this artificial class belong the Verbena, Scrophularia, Bignonia, Acantha, and their cognate genera.

Dielec'tric (Gr.), in natural philosophy, a body which has not the power of transmitting the electric influence through itself.

Dietet'ics (Gr. *diaitetikos* relating to diet), that part of medical science which relates to food or diet, and teaches us to adapt the quantity and quality of particular kinds of food to suit the state or power of the digestive organs.

Differen'tial, an infinitely small quantity.—*Differential calculus*, a term applied to one of the most important branches of the higher mathematics. It is the method of finding the ratios of the differences of variable magnitudes, on the supposition that these differences become infinitely small.

Diffu'sion (Lat.). In chemistry, the *diffusion of gases* is a term applied to two gaseous bodies which do not act chemically upon each other; but when mixed together in any relative proportions, they diffuse themselves through each other, and become intimately blended—the heavier one not falling, nor the lighter one floating.

Digas'tric (Gr. *double-bellied*), in anatomy, a term applied to a double muscle, situated between the mastoid process and the lower jaw, its office being to pull the lower jaw backwards and downwards.

Digest (Lat. *digestum*), in chemistry, to expose any body to a gentle heat in a boiler or matrass, as a preparation for chemical operations.

Diges'ter (Lat. *digestum*), in the materia medica, a medicine that aids digestion.—In chemistry, a strong vessel of copper or iron, with a lid tightly fitted and furnished with a safety-valve, in which bodies may be subjected to high pressure from steam.

Diges'tion (Lat.), in physiology, the process by which the nutritive parts of food in the animal system are rendered available for nutrition.—It is also a term chemically applied to the operation of exposing bodies to a gentle heat, to prepare them for some action on each other; or the slow action of a solvent on any substance.

Diges'tive (Lat.), in pathology, any medicine or preparation which increases the tone of the stomach and aids digestion.—In surgery, an application which ripens an ulcer or wound, or disposes it to suppurate.

Digit (Lat. *digitus* a finger), a finger's breadth;—three-fourths of an inch;—the twelfth part of the diameter of the sun or moon;—one of the ten symbols or figures by which all numbers are expressed.

Digita'lis (Lat.), in botany, a biennial plant, used medicinally to diminish the frequency of the pulse and the irritability of the system; the foxglove.—*Digitalia*, a vegetable alkali procured from the *Digitalis purpurea*.

Digita'tion (Lat.), in anatomy, finger-like processes, as exhibited in various muscles, as the *serratus magnus*, &c.

Digit'igrades (Lat. *digitus*, and *gradior* to tread), in zoology, a name applied to those quadrupeds which, while walking, move only on the extremity of the toes, as in the genera Canis, Felis, and Mustela.

Diglyph (Gr. *dis*, and *glypho* to carve), in architecture, an ornament which has two channels sunk in, while the *triglyph* has three.

Digyn'ia (Gr. *dis*, and *gyne* a female), in botany, the Linnæan system for plants with two styles, or a single style deeply cleft into two parts.—*Digynious*, having two styles or female organs of fructification.

Dihe'dron (Gr.), a solid figure with two sides or surfaces.—*Dihedral*, having two sides.

Dihexahe'dral (Gr.), in crystallography, having the form of a hexahedral prism with trihedral summits.

Dike (Sax. *dic*; Swed. *dike*), in geology, a wall of mineral matter cutting through strata in a vertical or inclined direction. It differs from a vein in being generally of greater dimensions, and in being seldom ramified.

Dillenia'ceæ (in honour of Professor Dillenius), in botany, a nat. order of plants, consisting of evergreen trees, or climbing plants, of which the Dillenia is the type.

Dill Oil, a yellow oil obtained from the seeds of the *Anethum graveolens*, which are carminative and stimulant.

Dil'uent (Lat. *diluo* to wash away), making thin; weakening in intensity.

Dilu'vium (Lat.), in geology, the superficial deposits of clay, sand, and gravel, often containing shells and bones of Mammalia, which lie far from their original sites, of which no satisfactory solution has yet been given.—*Diluvial*, produced by the Deluge.

Dime'rans (Gr. *dis*, and *meros* the thigh), a section of coleopterous insects which have only two joints in each tarsus.

Dimerocri'nites (Gr. *dimeris* divided, and *krinon* a lily), a genus of Crinoideans, of which the finger-joints are in two rows.

Dimeroso'mata (Gr. *a divided body*), in entomology, an order of Arachnidans, or Spiders, whose bodies are divided into two segments.

Dimor'phism (Gr. *double forms*), in mineralogy, the property of assuming two forms under different circumstances: thus sulphur assumes one form when crystallizing at a high temperature, and another wholly different when becoming solid at the ordinary temperature.—*Dimorphous*, assuming different forms.

Dimya'ria (Gr. *double muscle*), in malacology, the name of such bivalvular Mollusca as are furnished with two abductor muscles.

Dinor'nis, or **Deinor'nis** (Gr. *deinos* and *ornis* a terrible bird), in ornithology, a genus of extinct aquatic birds of a gigantic size, of the family Struthionidæ, somewhat resembling the ostrich, and formerly inhabiting New Zealand.

Dinosau'ria (Gr. *deinos* and *sauros*, a terrible lizard), in zoology, a class of gigantic fossil animals of the Saurian or Lizard tribe.

Dinothe'rium. (See *Deinotherium*.)

Diœ'cia (Gr. *a double dweller*), a class of plants which have male flowers on one plant, and female flowers on another; it forms the twenty-second class in the Linnæan system.

Diona'a (from one of the names of Venus), a genus of very curious plants, commonly known as Venus's Fly-trap, the leaves of which have a peculiar motion, by which insects are entrapped; order Droseraceæ.

Diop'side (Gr. *diopsis* transparent), in mineralogy, a variety of pyroxene. It occurs in pale green prismatic crystals. A specimen from Piedmont contained silica, lime, magnesia, oxides of manganese, and iron.

Di'optase (Gr. *dioptomai* to look through), a mineral of a fine emerald-green colour, consisting of oxide of copper, silica, water, and protoxide of iron: sp. gr. 3'2.

Diop'tra (Gr.), an instrument for measuring altitudes.

Diop'trics (Gr.), that part of optics which treats of refracted vision, or the different refractions of light in passing through different media.— *Dioptric*, relating to the science of refracted light.

Diora'ma (Gr. *seeing through*), a mode of painting and scenic exhibition, which is so arranged as to receive shades of light and various hues by means of movable blinds, and thus produce a complete optical illusion.

Di'orite (Gr.), in mineralogy, a variety of greenstone.

Diarrho'sis (Gr.), in pathology, the dissolution of the solids of the animal body, and their evacuation by the urinary passages.

Diarthro'sis (Gr.), in surgery, the reduction of a fractured or dislocated bone.

Dioscorea'ceæ, in botany, a nat. order of plants belonging to the class Dictyogens, of which Dioscorea is the type.

Diox'ide (Gr. *dis* double, and *oxide*), in chemistry, a compound of oxidation; when the second degree of oxidation is formed of single equivalents, and the lowest oxide consists of two equivalents of the + element, one of an oxide, and one of oxygen, the compound is called a *dioxide*.

Diox'ylite (Gr. *dis* double, *oxys* sharp, and *lithos* a stone), a salt of lead,

consisting of the carbonate and sulphate of lead.

Dip, in electricity and magnetism, the angle which the magnetic needle, when freely poised, makes with the plane of the horizon.—In geology, the inclination of a stratum or bend from the horizon.

Dipet'alous (Gr.), in botany, having two flower-leaves or petals.

Diphthe'ria, or **Diphtheri'tis** (Gr. *a double membrane*), a throat disease, the angina pellicularis, accompanied by the formation of a false membrane.

Diphyl'leus (Gr. *double-leaved*), in botany, having two leaves, as a calyx, &c.

Diphy'odonta (Gr. *dis* double, *phyo* to produce, and *odontes* teeth), in zoology, animals which produce two sets of teeth in succession.

Dipla, or **Diplo**, a prefix to numerous scientific words, derived from the Greek word *diploos* (double); as, *diplogenic* (producing two substances), *diplozoon* (double-bodied), &c.

Diplei'doscope (Gr. *viewing a double form*), an instrument for observing the transit of the sun over the meridian by day, or of the stars by night, so as to correct a timekeeper.

Dip'loë (Gr. *double*), in anatomy, the cellular structure which separates the two tables of the skull.—In botany, the cellular substance of a leaf.

Diplomat'ics (Gr.), the science of deciphering ancient writings, literary and public documents, letters, decrees, charters, and codicils, to ascertain their authenticity, signatures, &c. — *Diploma*, a letter or writing conferring some privileges or degree, as in medicine or law.

Diploneu'rans (Gr. *double nerves*), a vertebrated division of the animal kingdom, so named from their having two nervous systems, the ganglionic and the cerebro-spinal.

Diplo'pia (Gr. *double-sighted*), a disease of the eye which causes a person to see an object double.

Diplop'tera (Gr. *double-winged*), in entomology, a division of stinging hymenopterous insects, consisting of Wasps, which have the upper wings doubled up when at rest.

Diplozo'on (Gr. *double animal*), a singular parasitic worm, which has the appearance of two bodies, and infests the gills of the bream.

Dipneumo'nians (Gr. *double lungs*), in entomology, a section of Araneidæ, or Spiders, comprehending those with two pulmonary sacs.

Dipping, in geology, the interruption of

a vein of ore, or of a mineral stratum sloping downwards.—The *Dipping-needle*, in magnetism and navigation, is an instrument which dips or inclines to the earth, and shows the magnetic inclination at the different points of the earth's surface. In the equatorial regions the needle takes a horizontal position; but as we recede from the equator towards either pole, it dips or inclines one end to the earth, the north end as we proceed northward, and the south end as we proceed southward, and the further north or south we proceed, the greater is the dip or inclination.—*Craig.*

Diprismat'ic (Gr. *doubly prismatic*), in mineralogy, having cleavages parallel to the sides of a four-sided vertical prism, and, at the same time, to a horizontal prism.

Dipsaca'cea (Gr. *thirstiness*), in botany, a nat. order of plants, consisting of exogenous shrubs or herbs, of which the Dipsacus, or Teazel, is the genus and type.

Dipso'sis (Gr. *thirst*), in pathology, a morbid degree of extreme thirst.

Dip'tera, or **Dip'terans** (Gr. *double-winged*), in entomology, a class of insects comprising such as have two membranous wings attached to the mesothorax.—*Dipterous*, an epithet applied to insects with two wings.

Diptera'cea, or **Dipterocarpa'cea** (Gr. *double-winged*, and *karpos* fruit), in botany, a nat. order of hypogynous Exogens, consisting of gigantic trees with showy flowers, of which the Dipterocarpus is the type and genus; native of India.

Dipteryg'ians (Gr. *two-finned*), in ichthyology, a family of fishes furnished with two fins only.

Dipyre (Gr. *doubly burnt*), a very curious mineral occurring in the Western Pyrenees in slender, indistinctly-formed prisms, of a greyish or reddish-white colour. It consists of silica, alumina, lime, and water: sp. gr. 2·7.

Direc'trix (Lat.), in geometry, a straight line perpendicular to the axis of a conic section.

Dir'igent (Lat.), in geometry, a term applied to the line of motion along which a describent line is carried in the generation of any plane or solid figure.

Di Salto (Ital.), in music, a motion by skips, not by degrees. The degrees and skips of melody are both called by the general term *interval*, which is the distance between two sounds, or their difference in respect of pitch.

Disc, or **Disk** (Lat. *discus*), in optics, the magnitude of a telescope-glass, or width of its aperture.—In astronomy, the body and face of the sun or moon, or of a planet, as it appears to us on the earth, or the body and face of the earth, as it would appear to a spectator in the moon.

Discoid, or **Discoid'al** (Gr. *resembling a disc or quoit*), in botany, a term applied to plants, or the organs of plants, which have two flattened surfaces, with a circular border.—In conchology, univalve shells are said to be *discoid* when their spires are vertically convoluted on the same plane.—In Composite plants, the heads of the flowers are said to be *discoid* when the florets are all tubular.—*Discoidea*, in geology, is a genus of fossil Echinodermata, found in the chalk, oolitic, and greensand formations.

Discord, in music, dissonance of sounds; a combination of sounds which are inharmonious, and disagreeable to the ear.

Discrete (Lat.) In the science of numbers, *Discrete proportion* is when the ratio of two or more pairs of numbers or quantities is the same, but there is not the same proportion between all the numbers; as, 3 : 6 : : 8 : 16, 3 bearing the same proportion to 6 as 8 does to 16; but 3 is not to 6 as 6 to 8.

Discu'tient (Lat.), in surgery, an application which disperses a tumour or any coagulated fluid in the body.

Disdiapa'son, in music, a compound concord in the quadruple ratio of 4 : 1 or 8 : 2.—*Disdiapason diapente* is a concord in a sextuple ratio of 1 : 6.—*Disdiapason semidiapente* is a compound concord in the proportion of 16 : 3.—*Disdiapason ditone* is a compound consonance in the proportion of 10 : 2.—*Disdiapason semiditone* is a compound concord in the proportion of 24 : 5.

Disinfect'ants (Lat.), in chemistry, certain applications which neutralize or destroy miasmatic infections.

Disintegra'tion (Lat. *not entire*), the act of breaking up or separating integrant parts of a substance, not by chemical action.

Disoxida'tion, in chemistry, the process of freeing from oxygen by disengaging it from a substance.

Disper'mous (Gr.), in botany, containing only two seeds.

Disper'sion (Lat. *a scattering*), in optics, the separation of the coloured rays of light in passing through a prism, varying according to the refracting power of the material of which the prism is composed.

Disrup'tion (Lat. *a rending asunder*), in geology, a displacement of the crust of the earth; earthquakes, volcanoes, or other disturbing causes.

Dissec'tion (Lat.), in anatomy, the operation of cutting off the constituent parts of an animal body, for the purpose of critical examination as to the structure and use of its parts.

Dissep'iment (Lat. *dis*, and *sepes* a hedge), in botany, a partition in an ovary or fruit.

Dissolu'tion (Lat.), in pathology, *Dissolution of the blood* is a state of the blood which does not allow it to coagulate when cooling after leaving the body, as in cases of malignant febrile diseases.

Dissol'vent (Lat.), in pathology, a solvent, or any medicine capable of dissolving concretions or calculi of the body.

Distance, in military science, a term of frequent occurrence; thus, it often denotes the relative space left between men standing under arms in rank, or the interval which appears between those ranks, &c.—The *Distance of divisions* is the number of paces, of thirty inches each, comprised in the front of any division or body.—In fortification, *Distance of the bastion* is a term applied to the exterior polygon.

Distem'per, in painting, a method of tempering paint with oil, or mixing colours with something besides oil and water.

Distichi'asis (Gr. *dis*, and *stichos* a row), in pathology, a double row of eyelashes, by the innermost of which the eyeball is irritated and inflamed.

Dis'tichous (Gr. *double row*), in botany, having flowers arranged in two opposite rows.

Distil'late (Lat. *distillo* to distil), in chemistry, a fluid distilled and found in the receiver of a distilling apparatus.

Distilla'tion (Lat.), in chemistry, a process by which heat is applied to certain substances in covered vessels of a particular form in order to separate their more volatile constituents into vapour; and for condensing them immediately by cold into the liquid state in a distinct vessel, called a refrigerator.

Distor'tion (Lat. *twisting out of shape*), in optics, the change in the form of an image depending on the form of the lens.

Distribu'tion (Lat.), in architecture, the disposing of the several parts of a building according to the rules of art and science.—In natural philosophy, *Distribution of electricity* is a term applied to the densities of the electrical fluid in different bodies placed so as to act electrically upon one another, or in different parts of the same body.

Disul'phuret, in chemistry, a sulphuret, containing two equivalents of the sulphur to one of the base.

Ditetrahe'dral (Gr.), in crystallography, having the form of a tetrahedral prism with dihedral summits.

Ditone (Gr. *dis*, and *tonos* tone), in music, an interval comprehending two tones; the proportion of the sounds that form the ditone is 4 : 5, and that of the semiditone 5 : 6.

Ditrichot'omous (Gr.), in botany, having the stems of a plant continually dividing into double or treble ramifications; sometimes applied to a panicle of flowers.

Ditrig'lyph (Gr. *twice treble division*), in the Doric order of architecture, an arrangement of intercolumniations by which two triglyphs are obtained in the frieze between the triglyphs that stand over the columns.

Diu'resis (Gr. *dia*, and *ouron* urine), in pathology, an increased flow of urine. —*Diuretic*, increasing the secretion of urine.

Diur'ni (Lat. *diurnus* daily), in natural history, a term variously applied : in entomology, to a family of lepidopterous insects, from their flying chiefly during the day; and in ornithology, to a section of the Accipitres, or birds of prey.

Divarica'tion (Lat. *to straddle apart*), in botany and physiology, a branching at an obtuse angle; a forking; a crossing or intersection of fibres at different angles.

Diver'gence (Lat.), in natural history, the condition of two lines or organs emanating and branching from a common point or centre.—In optics, *Divergent rays* are those which, going from a point of the visible object, are dispersed, and continually depart one from another in proportion as they are removed from the object.

Divertimen'to, in music, a short, pleasant composition, vocal or instrumental, written in a light and familiar style.—*Dr. Busby*.

Diving Bell, in hydrostatical science, an apparatus consisting of a bottomless chest of cast-iron, into which men are placed, and supplied with air by means of an air-pump through a flexible tube, the air in the apparatus preventing the water from ascending into it, as in the case of an inverted tumbler immersed in water.

Doc'imacy (Gr. *dokimasia*), in materia medica, a process for determining the purity of medicines.—In medical jurisprudence, it is a term applied to a series of tests to which the lungs of a new-born child are subjected, for the purpose of determining whether it has respired after birth or not.—In metallurgy and chemistry, the art of testing and assaying the purity of metallic bodies.

Docimol'ogy (Gr.), a treatise on the art of assaying or examining metallic bodies, &c. (See *Docimacy*.)

Do'deca (Gr.), a prefix to compound words, signifying twelve.

Dodec'agon (Gr. *twelve-angled*), in geometry and mathematics, a figure of twelve angles or sides. The area of a *dodecagon* is three times the square of the radius of a circle inscribed in it, or 11·1961524 of the square on the side.

Dodecagyn'ia (Gr.), the Linnæan name for any order of plants in which the number of pistils is twelve.

Dodecahe'dral (Gr. *twelve-sided*), in geometry, consisting of twelve equal sides.—In mineralogy, *Dodecahedral corundum* is one of the names of the mineral spinel, the colours of which are blue, brown, black, green, and white. It consists of alumina, silica, magnesia, oxide of iron, and lime.—*Dodecahedral garnet* is a species of the garnet, of which there are ten sub-species.—*Dodecahedral mercury* is a mixture of mercury and silver which occurs in quicksilver mines with cinnabar.

Dodecahe'dron (Gr. *twelve-sided*), in crystallography, a figure with twelve sides, either triangular, quadrangular, or pentagonal.

Dodecan'dria (Gr. *dodeka*, and *andres* males), a class of plants in the Linnæan system having twelve stamens.—*Dodecandrian* is an epithet applied to plants that have twelve to nineteen stamens.—*Dodecapetalous*, having twelve petals.

Dodec'astyle (Gr.), in architecture, a building that has twelve columns in front.

Dolab'riform (Lat. *dolabra* an axe, and *forma*), in botany, an epithet applied to certain fleshy leaves which are straight at the front, taper at the base, and compressed, dilated, rounded, and thinned away at the upper back end, so as to appear axe-shaped. —In zoology, shaped like a hatchet, as the foot of certain bivalves.

Dol'erite, in mineralogy, a variety of trap rock, consisting of augite and Labrador spar.

Dollar (Swed. Dan. and Germ. *daler*, or *thaler*), in the science of numismatology, a silver coin of different States, of the average value of 4*s*. 2*d*. The *dollar* is coined in various States,

but the general type of the whole is the Spanish dollar, which is minted at the rate of 8½ to the Castilian mark (= 3550½ troy grains) of silver. The dollar is still minted at the rate of 8½ to the mark in all the Spanish-American republics except the Columbian. That of the United States is of nearly the same value, 4*s*. 2⅙*d*., containing 371¼ grains of pure silver. —*Cycl. of Commerce*.

Dolly, in mining, a perforated board placed over a tub containing the ore to be washed.

Dol'omite, in mineralogy, a variety of magnesian limestone which occurs in mountain masses, sometimes slaty and translucent on the edges. It constitutes a portion of the Apennines. Compact dolomite is snow-white and very hard. It consists of carbonate of lime and carbonate of magnesia. —*Dolomitic marble* is a variety of dolomite of a white colour, occurring in small granular concretions.

Dol'orite, in mineralogy, a variety of trap rock.

Doric (from *Doris*, in ancient Greece), in architecture, the *Doric order* is the second of the five orders, being that between the Tuscan and the Ionic. Temples of this order were usually dedicated to Juno, Minerva, Mars, and Hercules. Its proportions are: the height of the column, including the capital and base, sixteen modules, which, divided into eight parts, give two for the architrave, three for the frieze, and three for the cornice.

Doris (Gr.), in astronomy, the name of a planet or asteroid, first noticed by Goldschmidt in 1857.

Dorsal (Lat. *dorsum* a back), in natural history, an epithet of frequent occurrence, applying to the back, and often used as a prefix to scientific compounds.

Dorsibran'chiates (Lat. *back-gills*), in ichthyology, an order of the Annelids, in which the branchiæ are equally distributed along the whole of the body.

Dorsocer'vical Region (Lat. *dorsum*, and *cervix* the neck), in anatomy, the region at the back part of the head.

Dosol'ogy (Gr. *dosis* that which is given, and *logos* a discourse), a discourse or treatise on the proper administration of doses of medicine.

Dossil (old Fr.), in surgery, a nodule or lump of lint to be laid on a sore.

Double, a term of frequent use in connection with art and science.—In music, *Double octave* is an interval composed of fifteen notes in diatonic progression;—*Double-bass* is a large musical instrument of the viol kind.

—In navigation and seamanship, *Double-banked* is having two opposite oars managed by rowers on the same bench, or having two men to the same oar.

Doublet (Fr.), in optics, a magnifying glass, consisting of a combination of two plane convex lenses. — In lapidary work, a counterfeit stone, composed of two pieces of crystal, and sometimes glass, softened together with their proper colours between them, that they may have the same appearance to the eye as if the whole substance of the crystal had been tinged with these colours. —*Craig.*

Douche (Fr.), in therapeutics, the name given to a shock of a column of fluid on the body, of a nature, temperature, and volume determined by the circumstances of the case.

Doucine (Fr.), in architecture, a moulding, convex below and concave above, which serves as a cymatium to a cornice.

Dover's Powder, in pharmacy, a compound of ipecacuanha, opium, and sulphate of potash; an excellent sedative and sudorific.

Dovetail Joint, in anatomy, the serrated articulation or suture of the bones of the skull, &c.

Draco (Gr. and Lat. *a dragon*), in zoology, a genus of saurian reptiles (the Dragons), which are distinguished by a development of the gular skin, or expansive membranes on the sides of the body.—In entomology, the name of an insect found in India and Africa, and distinguished from the Lizard tribe merely by having a broad lateral membrane, strengthened by radii or bony processes. It lives among trees, and is able, by means of the membrane, to spring from tree to tree.—In meteorology, *Draco volans* is a term applied to a meteor in cold marshy countries, consisting of phosphuretted or carburetted hydrogen, which, in certain excitements and combinations, becomes luminous.

Dra'cole, in chemistry, an oil obtained by heating draconic acid with baryta. —*Draconic acid* is obtained by treating the essence of tarragon with nitric acid.

Draco'nin (Lat. *draco*), the colouring matter contained in the resinous substance called *dragon's blood*.

Draeon'tic, in astronomy, belonging to that space of time in which the moon performs one entire revolution.— *Crabbe.*

Dracun'culus (Lat. *a little dragon*), in zoology, a small worm (sometimes called the Guinea-worm) in the muscular parts of the legs and arms.

Dragan'tin, the name of a mucilage obtained from gum tragacanth.

Dragon (Gr.), in zoology, a genus of Saurian reptiles, characterized by two wing-like projections of the skin. —In architecture, a term applied to a horizontal piece of timber on which the angle rafters of a roof pitch.

Dragon Fly, the common name of the neuropterous insects belonging to the genus Agrion or Libellula.

Dragon's Blood, the indurated drops from the cut wood of the tree *Pterocarpus draco*.

Dragon's Head and Tail, in astronomy, the nodes of the planets, or the two points in which the orbits of the planets intersect the ecliptic.

Drain Traps, in the arts, certain contrivances for preventing the escape of foul air from drains, but admitting the water into them.

Drastic (Gr. *effective*), in pharmacy, an epithet applied to medicines which are powerful and rapid in their operations and effects.

Draught Com'passes, in engineering and the arts, compasses with movable points, used for drawing the finer lines in mechanical plans, &c.

Dredging Machine, in excavation, an engine used for taking up mud or gravel from the bottom of rivers or docks.

Dressing, among type-founders, a process by which they dress the casting of letters for the use of printers by scraping and bearding, &c.—In agriculture, manure spread over land.— In joinery, *Dressings* is a term applied to the architraves, and to all sorts of mouldings beyond the naked walls or ceilings.

Drift (Dan. and Sax. *drifan*), in geology, a term applied to the diluvian formation of the earth's crust.—In mining, a passage cut out under the earth between shaft and shaft, or turn and turn.—In architecture, the horizontal force or tendency which an arch exerts to overset the piers.— In navigation, the angle which the line of a ship's motion makes with the nearest meridian when she drives with her side to the wind and waves, and is not governed by the helm.

Dropsy (Gr. *hydor* water, and *opsis* appearance), an unnatural appearance of water in any part of the body.

Dropwort, in botany, a British flowering herb of the order Spiræaceæ, sometimes called Queen of the Meadow.

Drosera'ceæ (Gr. *droseros* dewy), in bo-

-tany, a nat. order of herbaceous Exogens, of which the Drosera, or Sun-dew, is the type.

Drosom'eter (Gr. *drosos* dew, and *metron*), in natural philosophy, an instrument for measuring the quantity of dew which collects on the surface of a body exposed to open air during the night.

Drug (Fr. *drogue*), in pharmacy, any substance, vegetable, animal, or mineral, which is used in the composition or preparation of medicines; the general name of substances used in medicine, and compounded by apothecaries and physicians.

Drum (Dutch *trom*), in architecture, the upright part of a cupola, either above or below a dome; also the solid part or base of the Corinthian and Composite columns.—In mechanics, a sort of short cylinder revolving on an axis, generally for the purpose of turning several small wheels, by means of straps passing round its periphery.—In anatomy, the *drum of the ear* is the tympanum, or barrel of the ear; the hollow part of the ear, behind the membrane of the tympanum. The latter is a tense membrane, which closes the external passage of the ear, and receives the vibrations of the air.

Drummond Light, (from the inventor, Lieut. Drummond), a very intense light, produced by throwing a stream of oxygen gas and another of hydrogen gas, brought into union, in an ignited state upon a ball of lime.

Drupa'ceœ (Lat. *drupa* the seed of the olive), in botany, a nat. order of rosal exogenous plants, with polypetalous regular flowers, and a drupaceous fruit. (See *Drupe*.)

Drupe (Lat. *drupa*), in botany, a superior, indehiscent, one-celled fruit, consisting of a succulent rind, and containing a hard stone in the centre, as the cherry, plum, or peach.—*Drupaceous*, bearing fruit in the shape of a drupe.

Drying Oil, in the arts, a term applied to linseed and other oils which have been heated with oxide of lead, and form the basis of many useful paints and varnishes.

Dry-pile, in electricity, a galvanic apparatus, in which the plates are separated by layers of farinaceous paste mixed with common salt.

Dry-rot, a disease which attacks wood, and destroys the cohesion of its parts, usually attributed to the attacks of fungi, especially the *Polyporus destructor*. Various scientific processes have been carried into operation for preserving timber from dry-rot, the most prominent of which is that of

kyanizing (so called from *Kyan*, the discoverer), by the application of corrosive sublimate, the perchloride of mercury. The timber is immersed in the solution thus prepared, when the primary element of fermentation is neutralized, and the fibre of the wood rendered imperishable.

Duct (Lat. *ductus* a canal or aqueduct), in anatomy and botany, a term of very extensive application, as signifying a tube or vessel for conveying a fluid, especially the arterial or venous blood, or the secretions of the animal system, or the juices of plants, &c. In the anatomical structure of man the following are the principal ducts:—*D. arteriosus*, a tube which, in the fœtus, joins the pulmonary artery with the aorta;—*Ducts of* Belini, the orifices of the uriniferous canals of the kidneys;—*D. communis choledochus*, the bile duct, formed by the junction of the cystic and hepatic;—*D. cysticus*, the duct which leads from the neck of the gall-bladder to join the hepatic;—*D. hepaticus*, the duct which results from the conjunction of the proper ducts of the liver;—*D. incisorius*, a continuation of the foramen incisivum between the palatine processes into the nose;—*D. ejaculatorius*, a duct within the prostate gland, opening into the urethra;—*D. nasal*, or *lacrymal*, a duct continued from the lachrymal sac, and opening into the nose;—*D. pancreaticus*, the pancreatic duct, which joins the gall duct at its entrance into the duodenum;—*D. of Steno*, the excretory duct of the parotid gland;—*D. thoracicus*, the great trunk formed by the junction of the absorbent vessels;—*D. venosus*, a branch which in the fœtus joins the left vena hepatica with the umbilical vein.

Ductilim'eter (Gr.), an instrument for comparing the ductility of lead, tin, and other metals.

Dudley Limestone, in geology, a calcareous deposit belonging to the silurian system, occurring near Dudley, equivalent to the Wenlock limestone. It contains about one hundred and twenty species of fossil shells, fourteen crustaceans, and one annelid.—*Penny Cyclop.*

Dugong, in zoology, a large cetaceous herbivorous animal which inhabits the Indian Ocean, and is frequently confounded with the Manatus. It is the *Halicore dugong* of Cuvier, or the Sea-cow.

Dulcama'ra (Lat.), the Bitter-sweet, or *Solanum dulcamara* of botanists. The roots and stalks, on being chewed, first produce a sensation of bitterness, which is soon succeeded by a degree of sweetness—hence the name.

Dul'cimer (Lat. *dulcis* sweet), in music, an instrument the strings of which are made of brass, and struck with little sticks, which produce an agreeable and lively kind of music.

Dune (Sax. *a low hill*), in geology, a bank of drifted and movable sand, frequently met with on the sea-coast.

Duodec'imals (Lat. *duodecim* twelve), in the science of arithmetic, a method of ascertaining the number of square feet and square inches in a rectangular whose sides are given in feet and inches, called *cross multiplication*.

Duode'num (Lat. *twelve inches*), in anatomy, the first division of the small intestine, immediately following the stomach, in man twelve finger-breadths in length.—*Duodenary*, increasing in a twelve-fold proportion.

Du'picho (Sp.), an elastic bitumen, obtained in Brazil from the roots of the *Siphonia elastica*.

Du'plicable (Lat. *duplex* double), in geometry, *Duplicate ratio* is the ratio of the squares of two quantities, or the square of their ratio.—*Duplication of the cube* is the finding the side of a cube of twice the solid contents of a given cube.

Du'plicature, in anatomy, is a term applied to the reflections of a membrane upon itself.

Dura Mater (Lat. *hard mother*), in anatomy, the exterior of the three membranes which envelop the encephalon, and which lines the vertebral canal and the cranial cavity.

Dura'men (Lat. *stability*), in botany, the central layers or heart-wood of exogenous trees. It is merely the sap-wood, solidified by the infusion of certain secretions into the interior of the cells and tubes of which such wood is composed.

Dutch, an epithet of frequent occurrence in botany, and the arts; as, *Dutch elm*, the *Ulma tuberosa* of botanical science;—*Dutch myrtle*, the plant *Myrica gale* of Linnæus; order Myricaceæ;—*Dutch pink*, a colour obtained from the plant *Reseda luteola;* order Resedaceæ;—*Dutch rush*, the *Equisetum hymenale* of botanists;—*Dutch drops*, the balsam of turpentine;—*Dutchman's laudanum*, the name given to a tincture of the flowers of *Passiflora rubra*, or red passion-flower, formed by infusion of wine or spirits.—*Dutch gold*, in metallurgy, an alloy of zinc and copper.—In the arts, we have *Dutch clinkers*, long, narrow bricks imported from Holland; and *Dutch tiles*, ornamental tiles glazed and painted.

Dyke, in geology and mining, an intersection in the strata of rocks.

Dynam'eter (Gr. *a power measurer*), in optics, an instrument for determining the magnifying power of telescopes.

Dynam'ics, the science of moving powers, or of matter in motion, or of the motion of bodies that mutually act upon one another.

Dys (Gr. *bad* or *ill*), is a prefix to numerous terms connected with pathology, expressive of an irregular or diseased state of the body; as, *Dysarthritis*, irregular gout;—*Dysarthresis*, faulty articulation of a joint;—*Dyscataposis*, difficulty of swallowing;—*Dyscholia*, a morbid condition or depravation of bile;—*Dyschræa*, a morbid alteration or change of the colour of the skin;—*Dyschylia*, a morbid condition of the chyle;—*Dyschymia*, a morbid condition of the chyme;—*Dyscinesia*, difficulty of motion from rheumatism or paralysis;—*Dyscœlia*, habitual suffering in the bowels;—*Dyscopria*, a bad condition of the fæces;—*Dyscrasy*, a bad admixture or depraved condition of the animal fluids;—*Dysdacria*, a morbid condition of the tears;—*Dyseccrisis*, deficient or defective excretion;—*Dysecoia*, difficulty of hearing;—*Dysgenesia*, lesion in the organs of generation;—*Dysgeusia*, depravation of the sense of taste;—*Dyshaphia*, lesion of the sense of touch;—*Dyshæmia*, depraved condition of the blood;—*Dyshydria*, a morbid state of the perspiration;—*Dyslalia*, difficult articulation of words;—*Dysmenia*, difficult or retarded menstruation;—*Dysodia*, a disease characterized by fetid emanations;—*Dysopsy*, dimness of sight;—*Dysorexy*, want of appetite;—*Dysphagy*, difficulty of digestion;—*Dysphony*, difficulty in speaking;—*Dyspnœa*, difficulty of breathing;—*Dysthetic*, relating to a morbid state of the blood-vessels;—*Dysthymia*, depression of spirits;—*Dystonia*, a morbid alteration of the tone of any structure or organ of the body;—*Dysury*, difficulty of voiding urine.

Dysæsthe'sia (Gr. *dys*), in pathology, impaired feeling, or a tendency to insensibility.

Dys'clasite (Gr. *dys*, and *klasis* imperfect fracture), a mineral which occurs in white masses, exhibiting considerable transparency, and having an opalescent appearance. It consists of potash, soda, silica, lime, water, oxide of iron, and oxide of manganese: sp. gr. 2·362.

Dysentery (Gr. *dys*, and *enteron* an intestine), in pathology, a painful disease, often epidemic, attended with fever, and with frequent mucous or bloody evacuations.

Dyspep'sia, Dyspep'sy (Gr. *indigestion*), in pathology, a state of the stomach in which its functions are disordered.

—*Dyspeptic*, a person afflicted with bad digestion.

Dystom'ic (Gr. *dys*, and *tome* a section), in mineralogy, having an imperfect fracture or cleavage.

Dytis'cidæ (Gr. *dytiskos* diving), in entomology, a tribe of aquatic coleopterous insects, of which the genus Dytiscus is the type; the tribe comprehends eighteen genera.

E.

Eagle Stone, in mineralogy, a variety of clay ironstone (ætites); so called from an old opinion that it had dropped from some eagle's nest.

Eagle Wood, in botany, a highly fragrant Oriental wood.

Earth (Sax. *eorth*; Germ. *erde*), the name of the world or planet which we inhabit; the terraqueous globe; a region.—In chemistry, any species of earthy matter; a body or substance composed of oxygen and a base of metallic oxide. By ancient philosophers *earth* was termed an element; and, in popular language, we still hear of the four elements—fire, air, earth, and water.—In astronomy, the earth, as a planet, is the third in order from the sun, round which it performs a revolution once a year, or in 365 days, 6 hours, 9 minutes, 6·9 seconds, revolving at the same time on its axis every twenty-four hours. Its equatorial diameter is nearly 7,925 miles, and its polar diameter about 7,856. Its mean distance from the sun is about 95,000,000 miles.

Earth Fall, in geology, the name given to a natural phenomenon, from which a portion of the earth's surface is elevated by some subterraneous force, then cleft asunder, and the earth suddenly depressed, when the space becomes occupied with water.

Earth Flax, in mineralogy, a flexible, fibrous, and elastic mineral substance, consisting of long parallel filaments.

Earth Nut, in botany, a term applied to various underground productions, as the *Conopodium flexuosum*, the round tubes of *Cyprus rotundus*, the subterranean pods of *Arachis hypogæa*, &c.

Earthquake, in cosmography, a shaking or violent agitation of the earth, and one of the most formidable phenomena of nature, sometimes producing immense rents that engulf large tracts of country, villages, and towns. Mounts Ætna and Vesuvius are the most formidable in Europe, and their destructiveness often terrible.

Earthy Fracture applies to a mineral when the fracture is rough, with minute elevations and depressions.

Ear Trumpet, in acoustics, an instrument or trumpet used to aid defective hearing by collecting and concentrating the waves of sound, so that they may strike upon the tympanum with increased force.

Easel (Germ. *esel*), in painting, the frame on which the artist rests his picture while at work.—*Easel-pieces* are the smaller pieces, either portraits or landscapes, which are painted on the easel, as distinguished from those which are drawn on walls, ceilings, &c.

Eau de Cologne (Fr. *Cologne water*), in cosmetics and perfumery, a kind of liquid perfume originally prepared at Cologne. As a substitute for the original article, Dr. Ure gives the following:—Alcohol, 1 pint; of the oils of bergamot, orange-peel, and rosemary, each 1 drachm; bruised cardamom seeds, 1 drachm; orange-flower water, 1 pint; distil 1 pint from a water-bath. — In science, there are a variety of preparations which have received French names;—as, *Eau de Javelle*, bleaching liquid, or the aqua alkalina oxymuriatica; —*Eau de Luce*, a compound of the essential oil of amber and the volatile alkali;—*Eau de Rabel*, one part of sulphuric acid to three of rectified spirit of wine.

Ebena'ceæ (Heb. *ebn*, and Gr. *ebenos*), in botany, a nat. order of exogenous trees and shrubs, the wood of which is as heavy and hard as ebony; so called from *Diospyros ebenum*, the True Ebony.

Ebony. (See *Ebenaceæ*.)

Ebur'na (Lat. *ebur* ivory), in malacology, a genus of spiral univalve Mollusca, in which the shell is smooth, the body whorl ventricose, and the intestines grooved. It belongs to the sub-family Eburninæ, of the family Turbinellidæ.

Eburna'tion (Lat.), in pathology, the excessive deposition of compact osseous matter which sometimes takes place in the diseased state of bones.

Eburnifica'tion (Lat. *ebur*), the conversion of substances in objects which have the appearance or characters of ivory, arising from an inordinate accumulation of the phosphate of lime.

Eccen'tric (Lat. *deviating from a centre*), in geometry, a term applied to a circle not having the same centre with another circle, and consequently not parallel, in opposition to concentric, having a common centre.—*Eccentricity*, in astronomy, is the distance of the centre of a planet's orbit from the centre of the sun.

Ecchymo'sis (Gr. *ekcheo* to pour out), extravasation of blood, causing livid spots or blotches, generally the result of blows or bruises.

Eccoprot'ic (Gr. *ex*, and *kopron* excrement), having the quality of promoting alvine discharges; a medicine which purges gently; a mild cathartic,

Eccre'sis (Gr.), in pathology, the excretion of perspirable matter from the lungs and fæces.

Eccrinol'ogy (Gr. *ekkrino* to separate from, and *logos* a discourse), in anatomy and physiology, a treatise on the secretions of the animal body.

Ec'dysis (Gr. *expiation*), in natural history, a casting off of the old skin, unaccompanied by any variation of form, or by the development of any new members.

Ech'elon (Fr. *by steps*), in military science, the position of an army in the form of steps, or with one division more advanced than another.

Echid'na (Gr. *echinos* a hedgehog), in zoology, a genus of spring quadrupeds, the Porcupine Ant-eaters, natives of Australia; order Edentata.

Echim'ys (Gr. *echinos*, and *mys* a rat), in zoology, the Spring rats, which have strong spines mixed with the hair on the back; order Rodentia.

Echin'idæ (Gr. *echinos*), in zoology, a family of radiated animals, comprehending those known under the name of Sea-urchins, Sea-eggs, &c., of which there are various genera and species.

Echinoder'mata, or **Echin'oderms** (Gr. *echinos*, and *derma* skin), in zoology, a class of Radiata which are armed with movable or articulated spines. The class is divided into two orders: the first constitutes the Pedicellata,

and embraces the Star-fishes, the Sea-urchins, the Holothuriæ, &c.; the second order, Apoda, are without the vesicular feet of the other, and are allied to the Holothuriæ.

Echi'nus (Gr. *a hedgehog* or *sea-urchin*), a genus of the Echinodermata, which have the body invested by a shell composed of angular pieces that join each other exactly, and are perforated by innumerable holes, for the transmission of the membranous feet. — *Echinus* forms a prefix to numerous compound words connected with botany and zoology, signifying *spiny, lamellar*, or *prickly*. — In architecture, a term equivalent to the ovalo or quarter-round; but it is only properly so named when carved with eggs.—In botany, *Echinus* is applied to a genus of plants, of the order Euphorbiaceæ.

Echo (Gr. *sound*), in acoustics, the repercussion of sound. — *Echometry* is the art of measuring the duration of sounds.—*Echometer* is an instrument for measuring the duration of sounds; also the art of constructing vaults to produce echoes.

Eclamp'sy (Gr. *vivid light*), in pathology, a flashing of light symptomatic of epilepsy; the epilepsy of a child.

Eclipsa'reon (Lat. *eclipsis*), in astronomy, an instrument for showing the phenomena of eclipses.

Eclipse (Lat.), obscuration of the light of a heavenly body by the intervention of another body. An eclipse of the sun is caused by the intervention of the moon, which totally or partially hides the sun's disc; an eclipse of the moon is occasioned by the shadow of the earth, which falls on it, and obscures it in whole or in part.

Eclip'tic (Lat.), in astronomy, an imaginary great circle of the heavens, in which the sun appears to perform his annual revolution.—*Ecliptic limits* are the greatest distances at which the moon can be from her nodes, in order that an eclipse of the sun or moon may happen.

Econom'ics, or **Econ'omy** (Lat. *economia*, from Gr. *oikos* a dwelling, and *nomos* law), the science of household affairs, or of domestic management. — In physiology, the laws which govern the organization of plants and animals; the order and connection of the phenomena exhibited by organized bodies, as, "animal economy," "vegetable economy," &c.—*Political economy* is the science which investigates the circumstances most favourable to the production of national wealth, and the laws which determine its distribution among the different ranks and orders of society.—*Maude*.

Eoos'sines, a sort of grey limestone.

Eoos'tate, in botany, having no nerves on the leaf.

Ecoutes (Fr.), in fortification, small galleries made at equal distances in front of the glacis.

Eoplex'ia (Gr.), in pathology, a kind of stupor arising from a blow, or from sudden consternation.

Eo'ptome (Gr. *a fall* or *dislocation*), in pathology, a term synonymous with luxation; also the elimination of gangrenous parts, expulsion of the placenta, prolapsus of the womb, and descent of the intestine or omentum in hernia.

Eopyreu'ma (Gr.), in surgery, a state of perfect suppuration, or suppuration itself.

Ecsarco'ma (Gr.), in surgery, a fleshy excrescence or sarcoma.

Ec'stasy (Gr. *ekstasis*), in pathology, a species of catalepsy, when the patient remembers the ideas he had during the paroxysms when the fit is over.—*Ecstatic* is an epithet applied to a state of ecstasy

Eothy'ma (Gr.), in pathology, a cutaneous eruption, characterized by pimples or large round pustules upon an indurated and highly-inflamed base.—*Dunglison*.

Ecto, a Greek prefix to compound words, signifying *outside*.

Ecto'pia (Gr.), in pathology, the morbid change of the situation of a part.

Ectrim'ma (Gr.), in pathology, ulceration of the skin in those parts of the body in contact with the blood.

Ectro'pium (Gr. *ektrepo*), an unnatural eversion of the eyelids.

Ectrot'ic (Gr.), producing abortion.

Ectylot'ic (Gr.), in medicine, having a tendency to remove callosities or indurations of the skin.

Ecze'ma (Gr. *a boiling out*), in pathology, an eruption of the skin, consisting of small vesicles, sometimes mistaken for the itch.

Eden'tates (Lat. *without teeth*), in zoology, an extensive order of the class Mammalia, comprehending those unguicolated quadrupeds which have no front teeth. They are divided into three tribes, the Tardigrada, the ordinary Edentata, and the Monotremata: the Sloths, Ant-eaters, and the Ornithorhynchus are examples.—*Edentates* is also a name given to a sub-order of the Cetacea, including the two genera Balæna and Balænoptera, the Toothless or Whalebone whales.

Ed'ingtonite, the name of a mineral found in the Kilpatrick hills of Dum-

bartonshire—a variety of felspar; so named in honour of Mr. T. Edington, of Glasgow. It occurs in small greyish-white crystals, and consists of silica, alumina, lime, water, and alkali : sp. gr. 2·7—2·75.

Educ'tion Pipe, the pipe from the exhaust passage of the cylinder to the condenser.

Edul'corant (Lat. *making sweet*), in pharmacy, a medicine which purifies the fluids of the system by depriving them of their acidities or other disagreeable qualities.—*Edulcoration*, in chemistry, is the science of rendering substances more mild by freeing them from salts, acids, or other impurities.

Effec'tion (Lat.), in geometry, an effect of a general proposition. The term is also used in reference to problems which, when they are deducible from or founded upon some general propositions, are called the geometrical *effections* of them.

Efflores'cence (Lat. *production of flowers*), the pulverization of minerals or crystals on exposure to the air.—In chemistry, the formation of a mealy powder on the surface of certain bodies, occasioned either by decomposition or drying, often the result of the formation of minute spicular crystals.—In pathology, an eruption or redness of the skin.

Efflu'vium, pl. **Efflu'via** (Lat. *effluo* to flow out), in physics, the minute and often invisible particles which exude from terrestrial or putrefying bodies, as the odour or smell of plants, or the noxious exhalations from diseased bodies, or putrefying animal or vegetable substances.

Effodien'tia (Lat. *effodio* to dig), in zoology, a family of edentate animals, so called from their digging habits.

Effrac'ture (Lat. *a breaking open*), in surgery, a fracture, with depression of the cranial bones.

Effu'sion (Lat. *a pouring out*), in pathology, the pouring out or extravasation of a fluid into a visceral cavity, or into the areolæ of the cellular tissue.

Eft, an old Saxon word, applied, in natural history, to the different species of batrachian lizards found in Great Britain; as, *Lacerta palustris*, or Warty Eft; *L. aquaticus*, or Water Eft; and *L. vulgaris*, or Brown Eft.

Eg'eran, in mineralogy, a variety of garnet found at Egeran, in Bohemia.

Ege'ria, in astronomy, the name of one of the newly-discovered planets, first observed by De Gasparin in 1850. Its mean distance from the sun is

245,889,000 miles, and the time of its periodical revolution is four years and fifty-one days.

Eg'lantine, in botany, the English name of the *Rosa rubiginosa* of Linnæus, known as the Sweet-brier; order Rosaceæ.

Egret, in natural history, a fowl of the heron kind; a feather of the fowl; the down of thistles; a species of monkey.

Egyp'tian Blue, in chemistry, a bright-coloured pigment, produced by the hydrated protoxide of copper, mixed with a small quantity of iron.

Ehretia'ceæ (from *Ehret*, the French botanist), a nat. order of exogenous plants, mostly tropical, of which Ehretia is the type.

Eider Duck, in ornithology, a species of duck found in the Orkneys, much valued for its down.

Ei'dograph (Gr. *fac-simile drawing*), an instrument to copy drawings.

Eidoura'nion (Gr. *eidos*, and *ouranion* heaven), a machine for representing the heavenly bodies.

Ekeber'gite, a transparent mineral of a vitreous or resinous lustre, consisting of soda, silica, alumina, lime, protoxide of iron, and water: sp. gr. 2·74.

Elæagna'ceæ (Gr. *olive*), in botany, a nat. order of exogenous plants, consisting of trees and shrubs, of which the Elæagnus is the type and genus.

Elæod'ic Acid, in chemistry, a compound produced during the saponification of castor-oil.

Elai'den (Gr. *elaion* oil), in chemistry, a fatty matter produced by the action of nitric acid upon castor and other oils.

Elaid'ic Acid, an acid, the result of the action of nitrate of mercury.

Ela'idine, in chemistry, a substance resembling stearine, which results from the action of hyponitric acid upon olive, almond, and other oils.

Ela'in, in chemistry, the oily principle of solid fats. That portion of fat or oil which remains in a liquid state when pressed out of hog's lard or other solid fats.

Elaiom'eter (Gr. *elaion* oil, and *metron* a measure), an instrument used for discovering adulteration in olive-oil.

Elal'dehyde, a chemical product obtained when pure aldehyde is kept long, and loses its solubility in water.

Ela'olite (Gr. *oil-stone*), a mineral of a dark green or brick-red colour, consisting of silica, alumina, lime, potash, soda, and oxide of iron: sp. gr. 2·54.

El'aphus (Gr. *elaphas*, a stag), a genus

of ruminating animals (the True Stags), of the family Cervidæ.

Elap'sinæ (Lat.), in herpetology, a subfamily of serpents, of the family Coluberidæ.

Elasmothe'rium (Gr. *elasmos* a plate, and *therion*, a wild beast), in palæzoology, a genus of extinct Pachyderms, intermediate between the elephant and the horse.

Elas'tic (Sp. *elastico*), springing back to its original form.—In mechanical science, *Elastic curve* is a figure assumed by an elastic plate or lamina, one end of which is fixed horizontally in a vertical plane, and the other loaded with a weight which by its gravity has a tendency to bend the plate.—*Elastic bands*, consisting of braces, belts, &c., are made with threads of caoutchouc, either naked or covered.—*Elastic gums* is a general name given to those vegetable extracts, such as gutta percha and caoutchouc, which may be elongated by heat, &c.

Elastic'ity is the inherent property in bodies, by which they recover their former figure or state after external pressure, tension, or distortion.

Elater'idæ (Gr. *elater* an impeller), in entomology, a family of coleopterous insects, of which the Elater is the genus.

Elate'rite (Gr. *elate*), a mineral pitch, a massive variety of bitumen.

Elate'rium (Gr.), the Squirting Cucumber, of the order Cucurbitaceæ.—*Extract of elaterium* is gathered from this plant before it ripens, the juice being gently expressed, when a green sediment is deposited, which is collected and dried: one-eighth of a grain operates as a drastic purge.

Elatina'ceæ (Gr. *elate* a fir), in botany, a nat. order of Exogens (the Water Peppers), of which the Elatine is the genus.

Elatrom'eter (Gr. *elater*, and *metron* a measure), in physics, an instrument for measuring the degree of diversity or rarefaction of air contained in the receiver of an air-pump.

Elec'tric (Gr. *elektron* amber), a term applied to any body capable of exhibiting electricity by means of friction or otherwise,—*Electricity* being a property in bodies, when excited by friction, of attracting or repelling light bodies.

Electric is a term of varied application connected with the science of electricity.—*Electric current* is the transmission of electricity from a body overcharged to one that is undercharged, through the agency of metallic wires or conductors.—*Electric aura* is a current of electrified air, employed as a mild stimulant in electrifying sensitive parts, as the ear or the eye.—*Electric telegraph* is a mode of transmitting messages and intelligence by means of electricity over wires, either for long or short distances.—*Electric wire* is the popular name for the wires of the magnetic telegraph.—*Electric column* is a sort of electric pile invented by De Luc, composed of thin plates of different metals, with paper interposed between them.—*Electric fishes*, when touched, produce an electric shock; the most remarkable of which is the *Torpedo gymnotus*.

Electro is a useful prefix to different inventions of recent introduction; as, *Electro-chemistry*, the science which explains the phenomena of the decomposing power of electric currents.—*Electro-magnetism*, that branch of electrical science which explains the phenomena of the action of a voltaic current on the magnetic needle.—*Electro-gilding*, a mode of gilding copper or silver by the agency of voltaic electricity.—*Electro-magnetic telegraph*, an apparatus for conveying intelligence by means of electricity moving between two places on iron wires.—*Electro-metallurgy*, the art of decomposing metals from solutions of their salts by the voltaic current. —*Electro-telegraphic*, belonging to the electro-magnetic telegraph, or by its means.

Elec'trode (Gr. *odos* a way), the termination of an electric battery, by which the electricity passes into or from the fluid in which it is placed.

Elec'tro-dynam'ic (Gr. *dynamis* power), relating to electricity in motion.

Electrol'ogy (Gr.), the department of physical science which treats of electricity.

Elec'trolyte (Gr. *elektron*, and *luo* to loosen), a substance susceptible of direct decomposition by the action of the electric current.

Electrom'eter (Gr. *elektron*, and *metron* a measure), an instrument for measuring the quantity or intensity of electricity, or its quality; or an instrument for discharging it from a jar.—*Electromotor* is an apparatus for moving the electric fluid.

Elec'tro-neg'ative, having negative electricity.

Electroph'orus (Gr. *elektron*, and *phero* to bear), an instrument for conveying electricity. It consists of a flat cake of resin, having a plate of brass, with a glass handle placed upon it. The resin is rendered negatively electrical by friction, and the brass plate becomes electro-polar by induction. The brass plate, if touched by the finger whilst lying upon the resin, and lifted off by its glass handle, gives a spark of positive electricity.—*Craig*.

Elec'tro-plate (Gr. *elektron*, and *plate*), a precipitation of silver or gold on a surface of copper or other metal.—*Electro-plating* is a process by which a pattern, cast in alloy or white metal, is transferred to a tank or trough, and subjected to galvanic agency. In the tank is a chemical solution of silver; and the wires of a galvanic battery are so arranged that the current, in completing its circuit, must necessarily pass through the solution. The result is, the solution is decomposed, and a fine film of metallic silver is deposited on the surfaces of the articles suspended in the trough.—*Penny Cyclop*.

Elec'troscope (Gr. *elektron*, and *skopeo* to view), an instrument by which electrical attraction and repulsion are rendered apparent, as in the gold-leaf electrometer.

Elec'trotint (Gr. *elektron*), the art of etching by galvanic process, in which a composition of white-lead, lard, olive-oil, lamp-black, and turpentine is used.

Elec'trotype (Gr. *elektron*), a method of taking reverse fac-similes of medals, coins, pages of type, &c., by means of voltaic electricity.

Elec'trum (Lat. from Gr. *elektron*), in mineralogy, a variety of gold ore, of a pale colour, generally known as argentiferous gold ore.

Elec'tuary (Lat.), in materia medica, a powder mixed with syrup, so as to be of the consistency of honey.

El'ement (Lat.), in physics, an atom, an ingredient, a minute particle, the primary or constituent principle of anything;—in the plural, the first principles of any art or science. — Popularly, *earth, air, water*, and *fire* are called the *four elements*, because they were formerly deemed first principles.—In a chemical sense, an atom, or the minutest particle of matter, which cannot be divided by chemical analysis, and therefore considered as a simple substance, as hydrogen, oxygen, nitrogen, &c. There are fifty-five elementary or simple substances at present known. Five of these exist in a separate state as gases—namely, oxygen, hydrogen, chlorine, nitrogen, and fluorine; the last, however, of these has not yet been obtained in a separate state, and is only known to be a distinct substance from the qualities of the compounds it forms with other matter. Seven are non-metallic solids and liquids — namely, sulphur, phosphorus, selenium, boron, carbon, bromine, and iodine; of these, the last two, bromine and iodine, are either gaseous, liquid, or solid, according to the temperature. Sulphur, phosphorus, selenium, boron, and carbon are solids, but differ from the remaining substances in being non-conductors of electricity.

El'emi, in pharmacy, the resinous exudation of the plant *Amyris elemini-fera*, of which the compound *Elemi ointment* is a preparation.

Elephanti'asis (Gr. *elephas* an elephant), in pathology, a species of leprosy; a disease which affects the lower extremities, so as to occasion swelling, with roughness and scales upon the skin, when the limb sometimes attains an enormous size, which has occasioned it to be compared to the foot of the elephant.

El'ephas (Gr. *an elephant*), in zoology, an important genus of proboscidean Pachyderms, which is the largest of terrestrial Mammalia.

Eleva'tion (Lat.), a term of frequent use in the arts and sciences.—In architecture, it is a front view of a building or object drawn to a scale, without regard to perspective.—In gunnery, it is the angle which the chase of a cannon or mortar, or the axis of the hollow cylinder, makes with the plane of the horizon.—In astronomy, it is the distance of a heavenly body above the horizon, or the arc of a vertical circle intercepted between it and the horizon. — In dialling, it is the angle which the style makes with the substylar line.

Eleva'tor (Lat.), in anatomy, a muscle that raises any part to which it is attached; also a surgical instrument for raising depressed portions of the skull.

Elgin Marbles, in archæology and the arts, a valuable collection of ancient reliefs, statues, &c., which formed the decorations of the Parthenon at Athens, and are now preserved in the British Museum. They were sent to England in 1812 by Lord Elgin, then ambassadoi at Constantinople, and purchased by the British Government in 1816.

Elimina'tion (Lat. *a thrusting out*), in algebra, the process of reducing a number of equations, containing certain letters, to a smaller number, in which one or more letters shall not be found.

Eliqua'tion (Lat. *eliquo* to fuse), in metallurgy and chemistry, the operation by which a more fusible substance is separated from one that is less so, by means of a degree of heat sufficient to melt the one and not the other.

Elixa'tion (Lat.), in pharmacy, the process of extracting the virtues of ingredients by stewing or boiling.

Elix'ir (Arab. *eliksir* essence), in pharmacy, a term applied to many compound tinctures made by a solution of various pharmaceutical substances in alcohol, and analogous to compound alcoholic tinctures. Of the different elixirs the following may be enumerated as the principal:—*Elixir paregoricum*, or Tinctura camphoræ compositæ; — *E. proprietatis*, the Elixir of Nature, or Tinctura aloes composita; — *E. sacrum*, Sacred Elixir, or Tinctura rhei et aloes;— *E. salutis*, Elixir of Health, or Tinctura sennæ;—*E. stomachicum*, Stomachic Elixir, or Tinctura gentianæ compositæ;—*E. vitrioli*, Acidum sulphuricum aromaticum;—*E. longevi-tas*, an aromatic tincture with aloes; —*E. arthritic*, a mixture of the tinctures of aloes, guaiacum, and myrrh.

Elk, in geology, a gigantic species of fallow-deer, found fossil in Ireland and the Isle of Man—now extinct.— *Elk-wood* is a name given to the soft, spongy wood of the *Magnolia umbrella*.

Ellag'ic Acid, in chemistry, an acid extracted from the gall-nut, along with gallic acid. The two acids separate from the aqueous infusion in the state of a yellowish crystalline mass; they are then separated by boiling water, which dissolves the gallic acid, and leaves the ellagic unacted upon.

Ellebo'rine, a resin obtained from the *Helleborus hymenalis*, of an extremely acrid taste.

Ellip'sis (Gr.), in geometry, an oval figure produced from the section of a cone by a plane cutting both sides of it, but not parallel to the base.— *Ellipsograph* is an instrument for describing ellipses.—*Ellipsoid* is an elliptical spheroid produced by the revolution of an ellipse about either axis.

Ellipsolith'es (Gr. *elleipsis*, and *lithos* a stone), in geology, a name applied to certain fossil Cephalopods existing in the carboniferous limestone.

Ellipsostom'ata (Gr. *elleipsis*, and *stoma* a mouth), a family of Mollusca, the shells of which have elliptical apertures.

Ellip'tic Com'passes, in mathematics, an instrument used for describing an ellipsis.

Ellipti'city, in mathematics and cosmography, a term applied to the figure of the earth, which means the fraction which the excess of the axis major over the axis minor of an ellipse is to the axis minor itself.—*Elliptoid*, in geometry, is an infinite or indefinite ellipse defined by an indefinite equation.

Elm (Sax.), a noble forest tree, the Ulmus of botanists, the timber of which is very hard, and particularly useful in mill-work.

Elmin'thes (Gr.), in vermiology, a name given to small intestinal worms.

Elo'des (Gr. *elos* a swamp), in pathology, a term applied to sweating sickness.

Elonga'tion (Lat.), in surgery, the lengthening of a limb from disease or injury of the articulation above; also the extension practised in the reduction of a dislocated or fractured bone. —In astronomy, the recess or digression of a planet from the sun, with respect to an eye supposed to see from our earth. The term is chiefly used in speaking of Venus and Mercury; the arc of a great circle, intercepted between either of these planets and the sun, being called the *elongation* of that planet from the sun.

Elydor'ic (Gr. *elaion* oil, and *hydor* water), in painting, a term applied to a species of painting, by which the freshness of water-colours and the mellowness of oil-painting are produced.

El'ytron (Gr. *a sheath*), in entomology, the coriaceous covering or wing-case sheaths which protect the inferior or membranous wings of coleopterous and orthopterous insects; a term also applied to the scales which invest the dorsum of Annelides.—In anatomy, *Elytroides* is applied to the tunica vaginalis.

Emar'ginate, or **Emar'ginated** (Lat. *emarginatus*), in conchology, a term applied to a shell without a margin, or when the edges, instead of being level, are hollowed out.—In botany, applied to a leaf having a small acute notch at the summit.

Embat'tled, in heraldry, having the outline of a shield resembling a battlement.

Emberi'zidæ (Lat.), in ornithology, a family of small birds (the Buntings), of which Emberiza is the type and genus.

Embla'zon, in heraldry, to adorn with signs armorial, or with figures of heraldry.—*Emblazoner* is one that emblazons, or displays with pomp; a herald.

Embra'sure (Fr.), in fortification, an opening in the wall or parapet of a fort, through which the guns are fired.—In gunnery, a piece of iron which grasps the trunnions of a piece of ordnance, when it is raised upon the boring machine.

Embroca'tion (Gr. *embrocho* to moisten), in surgery, the liquid or lotion with which an affected part is rubbed or washed; the act of moistening and rubbing a diseased part.

Em'bryo (Gr.), in physiology, the offspring in the womb before it becomes a fœtus; the rudiments of anything yet imperfectly formed.—In botany, the vegetable fœtus, a fleshy body occupying the interior of a seed, and constituting the rudiment of a future plant.—*Embryo buds* is a term botanically applied to those spheroidal solid bodies, resembling woody nodules, which are formed in the bark of trees, and capable, under favouring circumstances, of throwing out branches.—*Embryonic sac* is a small vesicle frequently found in plants at the apex of the nucleus of the ovules, and when the embryo is formed.— *Embryology*, a treatise on embryos.— *Embryotomy*, the operation of cutting the embryo or fœtus out of the womb.

Em'erald (Fr. *émeraude*), in mineralogy, a precious stone of a beautiful green colour, much esteemed in ornamental jewellery, the finest specimens of which are obtained from Peru. It occurs in prismatic crystals, and consists of silica, alumina, glucina, and oxide of chromium.—*Emerald green* is the name of a beautiful light green pigment.

Emer'sion (Lat.), in astronomy, the reappearance of a star which has been hid by the rays of the sun, or by an eclipse.

Em'ery (Fr. *émeri*), in mineralogy, a variety of corundum employed in cutting gems. It usually occurs in masses of a black or bluish-grey colour, and is extensively used in polishing metals and valuable minerals. It consists of alumina, silica, and oxide of iron: sp. gr. $3\cdot66$.— *Emery paper* is a rough scouring paper prepared from the mineral.

Emet'ic (Ital. *emetico*), a medicine which produces vomiting.—*Emetic tartar* is a triple salt, composed of antimony, potassa, and tartaric acid. —*Emeto-cathartic* is an epithet applied to such medicines as produce vomiting and purging.—*Emetology*, a treatise on vomiting and emetics.

Em'etine (Gr. *emeo* to vomit), in medicine, a substance obtained from ipecacuanha, which acts as a powerful emetic.

Em'issory, in physiology, an epithet applied to those ducts which convey fluids to certain veins.

Emmen'agogue (Gr. *emmenia* menstruation, and *agogos*), in pharmacy, a medicine for promoting menstrual discharge.—*Emmenology* is a treatise on the subject.

Emolles'cence (Lat. *a softening*), in metallurgy, the softening of a metal when beginning to melt; the lowest degree of fusibility.

Empais'tic (Gr. *stamped* or *embossed*), in the arts, a kind of inlaid work, which bears some resemblance to the modern buhl, and consists of inlaid threads or pieces of different metals impressed into other metals.

Empale'ment (Port. *empalar*), in military science, the act of enclosing, fencing, or fortifying with stakes.—In heraldry, the conjunction of coats of arms pale-wise.

Empetra'ceæ (Gr. *en*, and *petros* a stone), in botany, a nat. order of exogenous plants (the Crowberries), common in the Highlands of Scotland, where they are eaten.

Emphrac'tic (Gr.), in pathology, a substance which stops up the pores of the skin.

Em'phyma (Gr. *inflation*), a sarcomatous tumour.

Emphyse'ma, in physiology, a collection of air in a cellular membrane, rendering the part tense and elastic.

Empir'ic (Gr.), one who practises from experience only, and not from theory or acquired skill; an ignorant physician; a quack.—*Empirical*, relating to empiricism unwarranted by science.—*Empiricism*, the practice of medicine without a regular education; quackery.

Emplas'tic (Gr.), in pathology, a constipating medicine; an epithet applied to topical remedies which adhere like plaster to the surface on which they are laid.

Emprosthoto'nia (Gr. *emprosthen* anterior, and *teino* to draw), in pathology, that variety of tetanus in which the body is drawn forward by the permanent contraction of the muscles.

Empye'ma (Gr.), in pathology, a collection of blood or pus in the pleura, or in some cavity of the body.—*Empyocele* is a collection of pus in the testes or tunica vaginalis.

Empyreu'ma (Gr.), the burnt smell and acrid taste produced by the distillation of alkaline or oily substances.—*Empyreumatic* is a term applied to the smell or taste of burnt substances.

Emunc'tory (Lat. *emungo* to drain off), in anatomy, an organ which gives issue to matters which ought to be excreted.

Em'ydæ (Gr. *emys* a tortoise), in zoology, a family of the order Chelonides, comprising the River Turtles, of which Emys is the type and genus.—*Emydines* is a section of the family.

Emydosau'rians (Gr. *emys*, and *sauros* saurian), an order of reptiles embracing the Crocodiles.

Enaliosau'rians (Gr. *sea-lizards*), in palæontology, a group of extinct marine Saurians, which were furnished with paddles like those of a whale, and had the head and trunk of a crocodile.

Enallostegæ (Gr. *enallos* changeable, and *stege* a chamber), a family of foraminiferous Cephalopods.

Enam'el (Fr.), in mineralogy, a substance partly vitrified, or in which the granular appearance is destroyed.—In the arts, a semi-transparent opaque glass; the art of painting with vitrifiable colours on metal plates. The enamel which is the simplest, and combines with all others, is an oxide made by calcining together about 30 parts of tin to 100 of lead. To every 4 parts of this add 4 parts of sand and 1 of sea-salt, and melt them together. A blue colour is given by a very little of the oxide of cobalt; a yellow, by the sulphate of silver; a green, by the deutoxide of copper; red, by the protoxide of copper; black, by the protoxide of iron; and violet, by the protoxide of manganese (*Dict. of Art and Science*).—In dentistry, a term applied to the smooth, hard substance which covers the crown of a tooth.—*Enamelled cards* are cards covered on one side with a coating of white-lead and size, and a gloss imparted to them by highly polished steel rollers.—*Enamel-painting on lava* is a new style of painting applicable to monumental decoration, the material consisting of lava and stone.

Enan'thesis (Gr. *inflorescence*), an eruption of the skin from internal disease.

Enarthro'sis (Gr. *en*, and *arthron* a joint), in anatomy, a species of diarthrosis; the insertion of the head of one bone into the cavity of another; a ball-and-socket joint.

Encan'this (Gr. *kanthos* the angle of the eye), a small tumour or excrescence growing from the inner angle of the eye.

Encau'ma (Gr.), in pathology, an ulcer of the corner of the eye.

Encaus'tic (Gr.), the art of enamelling; a method of painting in burnt wax.—*Encaustic tile*, a variegated paving-tile, on which patterns have been formed in coloured clays on the ordinary buff tile, and fired, which brings out the colours more vividly.

Enceinte (Fr.), in fortification, an enclosure; ground enclosed with a fortification.

Encephalelco'sis (Gr. *en*, *kephale* the head or brain, and *elcosis* ulceration), ulceration of the brain.—In pathology there are various compounds formed from the Greek words *en* and *kephale*, appertaining to the brain; as, *Encephalalgia*, deep-seated headache;—*Encephalic*, situated in the head;—*Encephalitis*, inflammation of the brain;—*Encephalocele*, hernia of the brain;—*Encephalon*, the contents of the cranium;—*Encephalotomy*, dissection of the brain;—*Encephaloid*, resembling the matter of the brain;—*Encephalopathia*, disease of the brain;—*Encephalophyma*, a tumour of the brain;—*Encephalorrhagia*, hæmorrhage of the brain;—*Encephaloscopia*, inspection of the brain;—*Encephalosismus*, concussion of the brain.

Enchy'ma (Gr.), in physiology, that which is poured upon.

Enchymo'nia (Gr.), in physiology, a spontaneous ecchymosis or extravasation of blood from some internal cause, as a violent emotion of the mind.

Encké's Comet, in astronomy, one of the periodic comets which have been ascertained as belonging to the solar system, revolving round the sun in about 1,200 days, within the orbit of Jupiter.

Enclave'ment (Fr.), in obstetrics, the infraction of the head of the fœtus in the superior aperture of the pelvis of the female.

Encœlial'gia (Gr. *egkoilia* the intestines, and *algos* pain), pain or inflammation in the bowels.

En'cope (Gr.), in surgery, a wound or incision made with a cutting instrument.

En'crinite (Gr. *krinon* a lily), a species of fossil Zoophyte. Encrinites are the petrified radiated remains of the Stone-lilies, or lily-shaped animals.

Encyclopæ'dia (Gr. *en*, *kyklos* a circle, and *paideia* learning), in literature, a complete circle of the sciences; a dictionary of arts, science, and literature; a general system of knowledge and instruction.—*Encyclopædist*, one who compiles or assists in the compilation of an encyclopædia.

Encys'ted (Gr. *en*, and *kystos* a bladder), in physiology, consisting of a fluid enclosed in a vesicle or bag.—*Encystis*, an encysted tumour.

Endec'agon (Gr. *endeka* eleven), a plane geometrical figure bounded by eleven sides.

Endecan'dria, an order of plants with eleven stamens.

Endecaphyl'lous (Gr. *endeka*, and *phyllon* a leaf), in botany, having a winged leaf composed of eleven leaflets.

Endeix'is (Gr.), in pathology, an indication of diseases.

Endem'ic (Gr. *en*, and *demos* the people), peculiar to a country; applied especially to diseases arising from local causes; an endemic disease.

Endo, or **Endon** (Gr. *within*), in botany, a prefix in the compounding of scientific words, denoting inner or internal growth.

Endobranchia'ta (Gr. *with inner gills*), a family of the Annelids, with organs of respiration situated internally.

Endocardi'tis (Gr.), inflammation of the heart.

Endocar'dium (Gr. *endon*, and *kardia* the heart), a membrane which lines the interior of the heart.

En'docarp (Gr.), the inner membrane of fruit.

Endogastri'tis (Gr. *endon*, and *gaster* the belly), inflammation of the internal membrane of the stomach.

En'dogens (Gr. *producing within*), a primary class of plants which increase in diameter internally; the second class of the first grand division of the vegetable kingdom.—*Endogenous*, of the nature of Endogens.

Endophyl'lous (Gr. *endon*, and *phyllon* a leaf), in botany, enclosed within a sheath.

Endopleu'ra (Gr. *endon*, and *pleura* a membrane), in botany, the internal integument of a seed; the membrane which lines the lungs.

Endorhi'za (Gr. *endon*, and *rhiza* a root), in botany, the embryo of an endogenous plant.

Endosiph'onite (Gr. *endon*, and *siphon* a pipe), a fossil Cephalopod found in the Cambrian rocks.

En'dosis (Gr.), the intermission of a fever.

Endosmo'sis (Gr. *endon*, and *osmos* impulsion), in physiology, the attraction, through an animal or vegetable membrane, of a thin fluid by a denser one.

En'dosperm (Gr. *endon*, and *sperma* seed), the farinaceous albumen of seeds.

Ene'ma (Gr. *eniemi* to go into), in surgery, a medicine injected into the rectum; a clyster.

En'filade (Fr.), in military science, a passage running in a straight line, or that which lies in the direction of a line; as a verb, to pierce or rake with shot in a right line.

En'gidites, in entomology, a family of coleopterous insects whose bodies are elliptical or oval.

Engine (Fr.), in mechanical science, a machine for throwing water or propelling a vessel or car by steam.—*Engineer* is one who manages engines, particularly a steam-engine.—*Engineering* is the art or science of an engineer. — *Engineman* is the person who superintends or manages an engine on railways, steamboats, or any public works.—A *Military Engineer* forms and directs the engines and works necessary for offence and defence.—A *Civil Engineer* is one who constructs canals, railroads, docks, harbours, aqueducts, or other public works.—A *Mining Engineer* is one employed in the construction of plans, and directing the working of mines, coal-pits, &c.

Engrail (Fr.), in heraldry, to indent in curved lines, or make ragged at the edges.—*Engrailment*, the ring of dots round the border of a medal.

Engra'ver, in the graphic art, one who cuts designs in metal or wood, from which fac-simile impressions are produced.

Enhy'drite (Gr. *en*, and *hydor* water), in mineralogy, a rock-stone or other mineral enclosing water, as *enhydrous* quartz.

Enmanché (Fr. *manche* a sleeve), in heraldry, representing a sleeve; sleeved.

En'neagon (Gr. *nine-angled*), in geometry, a figure with nine sides or angles.

Ennean'dria (Gr. *nine stamens*), in botany, an order of plants, including such as have nine stamens, according to the sexual system of Linnæus.—*Enneapetalous*, having nine petals;—*Enneapyllous*, having nine leaflets;—*Enneasepalous*, having nine sepals; — *Enneaspermous*, having nine seeds.

En'siform (Lat. *ensis* a sword, and *forma*), in botany, having the shape of a sword.—In natural history there are various compounds with *ensis*, denoting resemblance to a sword; as, *Ensicaudatus*, having the tail sword-shaped;—*Ensiferus*, having appendages of a sword-like shape, as in the long, straight branches of *Alcyonum ensiferum;—Ensifolius*, having sword-shaped leaves; — *Ensirostris*, having the beak sword-shaped.

En'statine, a mineral, the basilicate of magnesia, which is augite in crystallization, and bears some resemblance to scapolite.

Entab'lature (Sp. and Fr.), in architecture, the whole of a story of a building which is above the columns, consisting of the *Architrave*, which rests immediately on the column; the *Frieze*, next over the architrave, being the middle member; and the *Cornice*, which is the uppermost part.

Enter'adene (Gr. *enteron* an intestine, and *aden* a gland), in anatomy, an intestinal gland. — *Enteradenography*, an anatomical description of the intestinal glands.

En'teric (Gr. *enteron* within), relating to the intestines.—In anatomical science, *enteron* forms various combinations with terms connected with the intestines ; as, *Enteralgia*, pain in the bowels;—*Enteritis*, inflammation of the bowels; — *Enterocele*, hernia of the intestines;—*Entero-epiplocele*, a rupture in which a part of the intestine is protruded ;—*Enterogastrocele*, ventral or abdominal hernia ;—*Enterohydrocele*, a watery rupture ;—*Enterolith*, a stone in the stomach or bowels ; — *Enterology*, a treatise on the intestines or bowels ;—*Enteromphalos*, an umbilical or navel rupture ;—*Enteroscheocele*, a rupture of the intestines ;—*Enterotome*, a surgical instrument used for operating in the intestines ;—*Enterotomy*, dissection of the intestines ; in surgery, incision of the bowels for the removal of strangulation.

Enthelmin'thes (Gr. *entos* within, and *elminthos* a worm), in pathology, intestinal worms.

Ento is a Greek prefix to numerous scientific words, signifying the *inner side*.

Entom'oline (Gr. *entoma* insects), a principle contained in the integuments of insects.

Entom'olite (Gr. *a stone insect*), petrifaction of an insect.

Entomol'ogy (Gr.), that part of zoology which treats of insects.

Entomoph'agous (Gr.), feeding on insects. — *Entomophaga*, a tribe of marsupial quadrupeds, comprehending Opossums, Bandicoots, &c.

Entomostom'ata (Gr.), a family of univalve shells.

Entomos'tracan (Gr.), a crustacean having a thin shell.

Enton'ic (Gr. *en*, and *tonos* tone), relating to phlogistic diathesis, or a morbid increase of vital power and strength of action in the circulating system.

Entozo'on (Gr. *entos* within, and *zoon* an animal), a worm or animal living embedded in some part of another.—The *Entozoa* form the second class of the Radiata of Cuvier's arrangement.

Enuclea'tion (Lat. *a taking out*), in

surgery, a mode of extirpation of tumours, through a simple incision of the skin, by cautious isolation with the finger from the surrounding cellular structure.

Enu'resis (Gr.), in pathology, iucontinence of urine.

Enzoot'ic (Gr. *en* in, and *zoon* an animal), appertaining to the disease called *Enzootia,* which attacks the different animals of a country.—*Report of the Privy Council on Public Health and Diseases of Cattle.*

E'ocene (Gr. *eos* the dawn, and *kainos* recent), in geology, the first of the three subdivisions into which the tertiary period of the earth is divided. The strata of the London and Paris basins consist of Eocene deposits. Deshayes enumerates 1,238 species of fossil shells as belonging to the eocene group, forty-two of which are all that can be identified with living species.

Eol'ipile (Gr. *Æolus,* and *pila* a ball), an instrument consisting of a hollow metal tube, for exhibiting the elastic power of steam by filling the ball with water and heating it.

Epacrida'ceæ (Gr. *epi,* and *akros* summit), in botany, a nat. order of monopetalous Exogens, of which Epacris is the type and genus, and so named from inhabiting the tops of hills.

Epact (Gr. *epaktos* additional), in chronological science, the difference between solar and lunar time. The excess of the solar year above the lunar is 11 days; or the epact of any year expresses the number of days from the last new moon of the old year, which was the beginning of the present lunar year, to the 1st of January. To adjust the lunar year to the solar through the whole of 19 years, 12 of them must consist of 12 synodical months each, and 7 of 13, by adding a month of 30 days to every year when the epact would exceed 30, and a month of 29 days to the last year of the cycle, which makes in all 209 days, *i.e.* 19 × 11.

Epaule (Fr.), in fortification, the shoulder of a bastion ; the angle made by the flank and face.

Epaule'ment (Fr.), in fortification, a side-work hastily raised to cover men or cannon, and made of gabions, fascines, or bags of earth.

Eph'elis (Gr. *epi,* and *helos* the sun), in pathology, a disease resulting from exposure to the rays of the sun.

Ephem'era (Gr. *living for a day*), in pathology, a fever which continues a day. — In entomology, an insect of the family Ephemerinæ, that lives only one day.

Ephem'eris, *pl.* **Ephemer'ides** (Gr.), in astronomy, an account of the daily positions of the planets or heavenly orbs ; a table, or collection of tables, exhibiting the places of the planets every day at noon.

Ephial'tis (Gr.), the nightmare.

Ephip'pion (Gr. *ephippios* on a horse), in anatomy, a term applied to the sella turcica of the sphenoid bones. —In botany, a genus of plants of the order Orchidaceæ.—In zoology, a genus of dipterous insects.

Epi, a Greek prefix to numerous scientific words, denoting *on* or *upon.*

Epicar'ides (Gr. *epi,* and *karis* a crustacean), in zoology, a family of the Isopoda.

Ep'icarp, in botany, the external layer of the pericarp.

Epiceras'tic (Gr.), a medicine to soften sharp humours.

Epicho'rian (Gr. *chorion* the skin), the deciduous membrane of the fœtus.

Epicra'nium (Gr.), in anatomy, a term usually applied to the occipito-frontalis muscle.

Ep'icycle (Gr. *kyklos* a circle), in geometry, a circle within another circle ; a small orbit carried round a larger one.

Epicy'cloid (Gr. *like a circle*), in geometry, a curve line generated by the revolution of a point in the circumference of a circle.

Epidem'ic (Gr. *on the people*), a disease which attacks many persons at the same time.

Epider'mis (Gr. *derma* the skin), the cuticle or scarf-skin of a man's body ; the bark or exterior coating of a plant.—*Epidermic,* relating to the skin or bark of a plant.

Ep'idote (Gr.), a crystallized mineral.

Epidro'mis (Gr.), a rushing of fluids to any part.

Epigas'tric (Gr. *gaster* the stomach), denoting the part situated near the abdomen.

Epigas'trocele (Gr.), hernia of the stomach.

Epiglot'tis (Gr. *glotta* the tongue), the fifth cartilage of the larynx.

Epigraph'ics (Gr. *graphe* writing), the science of inscriptions, and the art of deciphering them.

Ep'ilepsy (Gr. *a seizing upon*), in pathology, the falling sickness ; a disease which causes loss of sensation.— *Epileptics,* medicines for epileptic patients.

Epime'las (Gr.), in mineralogy, a white precious stone.

Epior'nis (Gr. *epi,* and *ornithos* a bird), the name of a gigantic fossil bird, at one time living in Madagascar, its eggs being six times larger than those of the ostrich.

Epipas'tic (Gr.), in pathology, applied to those remedies which affect the skin.

Epipedom'etry (Gr. *pous* a foot, and *metron* a measure), the measurement of figures that stand upon the same base.

Epiph'ora (Gr.), in pathology, an impetuous flux of the humours.

Epiphyllosper'mous (Gr. *phyllon* a leaf, and *sperma* seed), in botany, having the seeds at the back of the leaves, as ferns.

Epiphyl'lous (Gr.), in botany, growing upon a leaf.

Ep'iphyte (Gr. *phyton* a plant), a plant found growing upon other vegetables or trees.

Epip'loon (Gr. *floating on*), in anatomy, the caul or loose membrane of the abdomen; the omentum.—From this word the following combinations have been formed by anatomists:—*Epiplo-cystoscheocele*, scrotal hernia formed by omentum and bladder; *epiplo-ischiocele*, hernia formed by omentum through the ischiatic notch; *epiplo - merocele*, femoral hernia formed by omentum; *epiplo-sarcomphalus*, umbilical hernia formed by indurated and enlarged omentum.

Ep'isomite (Gr.), the native sulphate of magnesia.

Epispas'tics (Gr.), medicines to draw blisters.

Ep'isperm (Gr.), the integuments of a seed.

Episthot'onos (Gr. *epithen* forward, and *teino* to bend), a spasmodic affection by which the body is bent forward.

Epistil'bite (Gr.), a crystallized mineral, consisting of soda, silica, alumina, lime, and water; sp. gr. 2·2.

Epith'ysis (Gr.), a sort of articulation of the bones by accretion.

Epizo'ans (Gr. *epi*, and *zoon* an animal), in zoology, a class of parasitic animals which infest fishes, &c.

Epizoot'ic (Gr.), in geology, having animal remains annexed.

Epizo'oty (Gr.), a murrain or pestilential disease among cattle.

Epoch, or **Ep'ocha** (Lat.), a point of time fixed or rendered remarkable by some historical event.

Eprouvette' (Fr.), a machine for proving the strength of gunpowder.

Epsom Salts, a species of crystallized purgative salts, consisting of sulphate of magnesia.

Epu'lis (Gr. *epi*, and *oula* the gums), in pathology, a tubercle on the gums,

which loosens the teeth, and occasionally becomes cancerous.

Epulot'ic (Gr.), in medicine, a cicatrizing medicament.

Epura'tion (Lat.), the act of purifying.

Equant, in astronomy, an imaginary circle introduced for the purpose of determining the motions of the planets.

Equa'tion (Lat.), in algebra, the expression of the same value or quantity in different terms, denoted by the sign ($=$) between them; thus, if the question is concerning two numbers, they may be called x and y, and the conditions from which they are to be investigated must be expressed by equations, thus:—If it be required that the sum of two numbers sought be 60, that condition is thus expressed, $x + y = 60$. If their difference must be 24, then $x - y = 24$. If their product is to be 96, then $xy = 96$.—In astronomy and chronology, *Equation of time* is the reduction of the apparent time or motion of the sun to equable, mean, or true time. — In arithmetic, *Equation of payments* is the finding the time to pay several debts at once which are due at different dates, and bearing no interest till after the time of payment.

Equa'tor (Lat.), in cosmography and ouranology, a great circle of the celestial sphere, of which the plane is perpendicular to the axis of the earth's diurnal motion. — In geography, a great circle of the terrestrial sphere, which divides the earth into northern and southern hemispheres.

Equato'rial (Lat.), pertaining to the equator; an instrument for directing a telescope upon any celestial object, and keeping it in view for any length of time, notwithstanding the diurnal motion.

Equian'gular (Lat.), in geometry, having equal angles; an epithet applied to figures whose angles are all equal, as in a parallelogram, a square, or equilateral triangle.

Equilib'rium (Lat.), in mechanics, equality of weight; equipoise.

Equimul'tiple (Lat.), any number or quantity multiplied by the same number as another.

Equinoc'tial (Lat.), the great line or circle of the celestial sphere, commonly called the *equator*. (See *Equator* and *Equinox*.)—*Equinoctial colure* is the great circle which passes from the poles of the world through the equinoctial points.—*Equinoctial points*, the two great points in which the equator and ecliptic cross each other, the one in the first point of

Aries, and the other in the first point of Libra.

Eq'uinox (Lat. *æquus*, and *nox* night), the intersection of the equator and ecliptic; the precise time in which the sun enters the first point of Aries or Libra, when the days and nights are equal. The problem of the equinoxes, and the apparent changes in the positions of the heavenly bodies, have been matters of interesting speculation in all ages. From a series of observations made by the astronomer Hipparchus, at Alexandria, B.C. 161 to 127, it was discovered that the point of the autumnal equinox was about 6° to the eastward of the star Spica Virginis, which, 150 years before, was about 8° east of the star. On this authority he demonstrated that the equinoctial points were not fixed in the heavens, but move to the westward about 1° in 75 years. In 1750 the autumnal equinox was observed to be 20° 21′ westward of Spica Virginis. This motion is called the Precession of the Equinoxes, because by it the time and place of the sun's equinoctial station precede the usual calculations.—The *Vernal equinox* is that intersection of the equator and the ecliptic in which the sun is when about to rise into the northern hemisphere; the *Autumnal equinox* being that in which the sun is when about to sink into the southern hemisphere.

Equiseta'ceæ (Lat. *horse-tailed*), in botany, a nat. order of Exogens, of which the Equisetum, or Horse-tail, is the type and only genus.—In chemistry, *Equisetic* is applied to an acid obtained from the *Equisetum fluviatile*.

Equiv'alent (Lat.), a thing of the same weight or value.—In chemistry, the proportion in which the various chemical bodies unite, oxygen or hydrogen being assumed as unity. Under the article *Atomic Theory* is given a table of equivalents, assuming hydrogen as unity, to which the reader is referred.

Equus (Lat.), in zoology, the scientific name of the genus Horse, a quadruped of which there are various species; as, *E. caballus*, or Common horse; *E. hemionus*, or Tartary horse; *E. asinus*, the Ass; *E. zebra*, the Zebra; *E. quagga*, the Quagga; *E. montana*, the Onagga, an African species, smaller than the ass.

Era (Lat.), in chronology, a certain period of time, containing a given number of years, or a point from which any number of years is begun to be counted; as, the Christian *era*. It differs from *epoch*, which is a certain point of time fixed by historians and chronologists.

Era'to, in astronomy, the name of one of the newly-discovered planets, first observed in 1860.

Er'bium, in mineralogy, a metal recently discovered in ores of yttrium.

Erec'tile Tissue, in anatomy, a peculiar kind of tissue, which is susceptible of active turgescence by an increased flow of blood, as in the corpus cavernosum of the penis.

Eremacau'sis (Gr. *eremos* lonely, and *kausos* burning), a change which vegetables undergo after death; putrefaction.

Er'ethism (Gr. *erethizo* to excite), in pathology, an irritable state of the constitution.—*Erethistic*, relating to erethism.

Ergot (Fr.), in anatomy, a medullary cavity in the ventral of the brain, composed of cortical substances.—In agriculture, a disease of the rye, which in medicine produces a stimulating effect on the uterus.—In farriery, a stub, like a piece of soft horn, about the size of a chestnut, situated behind and below the pastern joint.—*Ergotine* is a narcotic and poisonous substance, obtained as a brown powder, of a pungent and bitter taste, in the ergot of rye.—*Ergotism*, in pathology, is a morbid affection produced on the human system by the ergot of rye, the chief symptoms of which are gangrene of the fingers and toes, sometimes of the hands and feet.

Erica'ceæ (Lat. *erica* heath), in botany, a nat. order of hypogynous Exogens (the Heaths, or Heathworts), of which Erica is the genus and type. —*Ericidæ* is a tribe of the Heaths in which the fruit is multilocular.

E'rinite (from *Erin*, one of the names of Ireland), a mineral occurring in masses; colour emerald green, consisting of oxide of copper, alumina, arsenic acid, and water: sp. gr. ′4.

Eriocaula'ceæ (Gr. *erion* wool, and *kaulon* a stalk), in botany, a nat. order of Exogens (the Pipeworts), consisting of perennial marsh plants, of which the Eriocaulon is the type and genus.

Eriom'eter (Gr. *erion*, and *metron* a measure), in optics, an instrument for measuring the diameters of minute particles and fibres, by ascertaining the diameter of any one of the series of rings which they produce.

Er'lanite (from *Erla*, in Saxony), a mineral of a light green or grey colour, with a white streak, consisting of silica, alumina, lime, soda, magnesia, peroxide of iron, and oxide of manganese: sp. gr. 3·0.

Er'mine (Fr.), in natural history, an animal about the size of a squirrel, a species of polecat, valued for its fur. —In heraldry, *Ermine* is represented by a white field or fur with black spots, and is supposed to denote the linings of mantles and robes.

Erotyl'idæ (Gr. *erotylos* amatory), a family of monilicorn coleopterous insects, of which Erotylos is the type and genus.

Erpetol'ogy (Gr. *erpetos* a reptile), a treatise on reptiles.

Erran'tes (Lat. *errans* wandering), a family of Annelids, consisting of several tribes and numerous genera; they are all marine animals, and generally dwell beneath stones, or are buried in the sand.

Errat'ic (Lat. *not fixed*), in geology, *Erratic blocks* is a term used for those transported boulders which are so largely and so confusedly mixed up in what is termed the Diluvium.

Erup'tion (Lat.), in pathology, an efflorescence of the skin; an acute cutaneous disease.

Erycin'idæ (from *Erycina*, a name of Venus), in entomology, a family of beautiful lepidopterous insects, containing the genera Erycina, Polyommatus, and Thecla.

Erysip'elas (Gr. *eryo* to draw, and *pelas* adjoining), in pathology, an inflammatory disease of the skin, vulgarly called *Rose*, from its redness. It is generally attended with vesications on the afflicted part, and with symptomatic fever. Its species are *E. phlegmonodes*, phlegmonous; *E. œdematodes*, edematose; *E. gangrene*, gangrenous; *E. erraticum*, wandering.

Erythe'ma (Gr. *erythros* red), in pathology, a morbid redness of the skin, generally terminating in scales, and sometimes in gangrene. The different species are *E. fugax*, fugacious; *E. læve*, smooth; *E. marginatum*, marginated; *E. papulatum*, papulated; *E. tuberculatum*, tuberculated; *E. nodosum*, nodose; *E. intertrigo*, fret or erosion of the skin.

Erythrolit'mine (Gr. *erythros*, and *litmus*), in chemistry, a red substance obtained from litmus. It is soluble in hot alcohol, and dissolves in alkalies with a blue colour.

Er'ythros (Gr. *red*), a prefix to numerous Latinized adjectives which occur in natural history, denoting *redness*, or some of its forms; as, *erythrinus*, red or nearly red; *erythrocarpus*, having red seeds; *erythroceras*, having red antennæ; *erythropectinus*, having antennæ pectinated and ferruginous in appearance; *erythrogaster*, having a red abdomen; *erythrogrammus*, marked with red rays; *erythroleucus*, being red and white; *erythrolophus*, having a red crest or tuft; *erythromelas*, red and black; *erythronotus*, having a red back; *erythrophthalmus*, having red eyes; *erythrophyllus*, having red leaves; *erythropterus*, having red wings; *erythropygius*, having a red croup; *erythroramphus*, having a red beak; *erythrorhynchus*, having a red snout; *erythrosomus*, having a red body; *erythrospermus*, having red seeds; *erythrostomus*, having a red mouth; *erythrothorax*, having a red breast.

Erythroxyla'ceæ (Gr. *erythros* red), in botany, a nat. order of hypogynous Exogens, of which the Erythroxylon is the type and genus. The wood and the juice of the fruit are generally *red*, whence the name.

Escalade' (Fr.), in military science, the act of scaling the walls of a fortification by the use of scaling-ladders.

Escape'ment (Fr.), in horology, that part of the mechanism of a watch or clock by which the circulating motion of the wheels is converted into a vibrating motion.

Escarp (Fr.), in fortification, the side of a ditch forming the exterior of a rampart.—*Escarpment*, in geology, is the abrupt face of a ridge of high land.

Eschar (Gr.), in pathology, a crust or scab made by a burn or some caustic application.—*Escharotic* is a term applied to a caustic application.

Escutch'eon (Fr.), in heraldry, a shield of a family on which arms are emblazoned.

Esophagot'omy (Gr. *oisophagos* the throat, and *temno* to cut), in surgery, the operation of making an incision into the œsophagus, for the purpose of removing any foreign substance.

Esoph'agus, or **Œsoph'agus** (Gr. *oiso*, and *phago* to eat), in anatomy, the passage leading from the pharynx to the stomach, by which the food is conveyed.

Esplanade' (Fr.), in fortification, the sloping of the parapet of the counterscarp, or covert-way, towards the open country; a glacis.

Esquisse (Fr.), in painting, a slight sketch of a picture.

Estacade' (Sp. and Fr.), in military science, a dike constructed with piles to impede an enemy; a stoccade.

Esthet'ics (Gr.), the science of sensations, which deduces from nature and taste the rules and principles of art; the science which treats of the beautiful in nature and art.

Ete'sian (Lat.), in physicology, an epithet applied to certain winds which blow at particular times of the year.—*Etesian* winds are yearly or anniversary winds, answering to the monsoons of the East Indies.

Ethal, in chemistry, a substance formed by the saponification of spermaceti.

Ether (Gr. *aither*), in physics, an element supposed to be much finer and rarer than air, and to occupy the heavenly space from the termination of the atmosphere.—In chemistry, a highly volatile, fragrant, inflammable, and intoxicating liquid, produced by distilling equal weights of sulphuric acid and alcohol. The different *ethers* are—the acetic, oxalic, chloric, hydriotic, hydrochloric, hydrobromic, sulphuric, methylic, muriatic, carbonic, cyanic, benzoic, and chlorobenzoic.—*Etherification* is the process of producing ether by the union of an alcohol and an acid.—*Ethereum*, or *Etherine*, is a carburetted hydrogen.

Ethics (Lat. *ethicus*), the science of moral philosophy, which treats of human actions and mental affections.

Ethion'ic Acid, a bisulphate of ether.

Eth'moid (Gr. *like a sieve*), in anatomy, one of the eight bones composing the cranium, situated in the os frontis.

Ethnog'raphy (Gr. *ethnos* a nation, and *graphe* description), the science that describes the different races of mankind, or the different nations.—*Ethnology* is a treatise on them.

Ethule (Gr. *aither* and *ule* matter), in chemistry, the elementary carbon and hydrogen of ether. It is the hypothetical base or radicle of the ethers. With oxygen, *ethule* forms ether, the oxide of *ethule*. Alcohol is the hydrate oxide of *ethule*.

Etiol'ogy (Gr. *aitia* cause, and *logos* discourse), that branch of pathology which treats on the causes of disease.

Eu, a Greek particle prefixed to numerous words connected with science and art, and signifying *good* or *well*; as, *Euaimia*, a healthy condition of the blood.—*Euchylia*, in physiology, a healthy condition of the chyle.

Euchlore (Gr. *eu*, and *chloros* green), in mineralogy, having a distinct green colour.

Eu'chlorine (Gr.), the oxide of chlorine.

Eu'chlorite (Gr.), a mineral containing water and copper.

Eu'chroite (Gr.), a mineral of a light emerald-green colour, containing copper and arsenic.

Eu'chrome (Gr.), a compound of zinc and euchloric acid.

Eu'chymy (Gr.), a good state of the humours of the body.

Eu'clase (Gr. *eu*, and *klao* to break), a very rare mineral, brought in small greenish crystals from S. America.

Eu'crasy, a good temperament, or healthy state.—*Eupepsy*, a good digestion.—*Euphlogia*, in pathology, a healthy kind of inflammation.

Eudiom'etry (Gr.), the art of ascertaining the salubrity of the air.—*Eudiometer* is an instrument to measure the purity of gas.

Eudy'alite (Gr.), a mineral found both crystallized and massive.

Euge'nia (Gr.), in astronomy, the name of one of the newly-discovered planets, first observed by Goldschmidt in 1857.

Eu'kairite (Gr.), a seleniuret of silver and copper.

Eu'lebrite (Gr.), a seleniuret of zinc.

Eumen'idæ (Lat. *the Furies*), a family of hymenopterous insects.

Euno'mia (Gr.), the name of one of the newly-discovered planets, first observed in 1851.

Eu'phonon (Gr. *eu*, and *phone* sound), a musical instrument of great sweetness and power.

Euphorbia'ceæ, a nat. order of Exogens, of which Euphorbium is the type.

Euphros'yne (Gr.), the name of one of the newly-discovered planets, first observed in 1854.

Euplexop'tera (Gr.), in entomology, an order of insects comprehending the Earwigs.

Euroc'lydon (Gr. *euros* the east wind, and *klydon* a wave), a dangerous easterly wind in the Mediterranean.

Euro'pa, the name of one of the newly-discovered planets, first observed in 1858.

Eu'rythmy (Gr. *eu*, and *rhythmos* harmony), in architecture, just harmony of the parts of a building.—In medicine, regularity of the pulse.

Eusta'chian (from *Eustachius* the discoverer), in anatomy, denoting a tube which runs from the inner tympanum of the ear to the nostrils, and supplies the drum of the ear with air.

Eustyle (Gr.), in architecture, the position of columns in an edifice.

Euter'pe, in astronomy, the name of one of the newly-discovered planets.

Eux'enite (Gr.), a Norwegian mineral.

Evaporom'eter (Lat.), an instrument to ascertain the quantity of evaporation in a given time.

Ever'ticule, Evertic'ulum (Lat. *everto* to turn out), in surgery, an instrument used for clearing the bladder from calculous particles.

Ev'olute (Lat. *e* and *volutus*, unrolled), a curve formed by the end of thread unwound from another curve, the radius or curvature of which is constantly increasing.

Evolu'tion (Lat.), the act of unrolling or unfolding.—In geometry, the unfolding or opening of a curve.—In arithmetic, the extraction of roots of any power.—In military tactics, movements by which the disposition of troops is changed.—In algebra, *evolution* is the reverse of involution, as, 4 is the root of 16, and 12 the root of 144.—In physiology, the theory of generation, in which the germ is held to pre-exist in the parent, and each part to be unfolded and expanded, but not actually formed, by the act of procreation.

Exæ'resis (Gr. *exaireo* to remove or take out), that part of surgery which relates to the removal of morbid or superfluous parts of the body.

Exan'thema, or **Exan'thesis** (Gr.), in pathology, an efflorescence or eruption of the skin; a rash.—*Exanthemata* denotes a certain class of diseases, under which are comprehended the genera Rubeola, Scarlatina, Urticaria, Purpura, Rosolea, and Erythema.—*Exanthematology* is a treatise on eruptive fevers.

Excitomo'tary (Lat.), in physiology, causing motion in animal bodies independent of sensation or volition.—*Brande.*

Exentera'tion (Lat. from Gr. *enteros*), the act of taking out the bowels.

Exergue (Fr.), in numismatics, the basis of a coin or medal, which usually gives the date, place, &c., of the coin.

Exfœta'tion (Lat. *ex*, and *fœtus*), imperfect fœtation in some organ exterior to the uterus.

Exin'tine, in botany, a membrane situated between the extine and the intine in the pollen of the yew, juniper, cypress, &c.

Exo, a Greek preposition of very frequent use in scientific terms to denote *outside of*, or *outward*; as, *Exo-skeleton*, &c.

Exogastri'tis (Gr. *exo*, and *gaster* the stomach), inflammation of the external membrane of the stomach.

Ex'ogen (Gr. *exo* out, and *gennao* to grow), in botany, a plant or tree which increases in diameter by the addition of new wood to the outside of the old wood. *Exogens* are the first class of the grand division of the vegetable kingdom. The term *Dicotyledons* is also applied to this class.

Exom'phalos (Gr. *omphalos* the navel), hernia or rupture at or near the navel.

Exophthal'mia (Lat. from Gr. *ophthalmos* the eye), the protrusion of the eyeball from the orbit.

Exophyl'lous (Gr. *exo*, and *phyllon* a leaf), in botany, naked, as the leaves of Exogens.

Exorhi'zæ (Gr. *exo*, and *rhiza* a root), in botany, plants whose radicles elongate downward.

Exos'mose (Gr. *ex*, and *osmos* impulsion), in anatomy, the passage of one fluid to another through a membrane from within.

Exos'tome (Gr. *exo*, and *stoma* a mouth), in botany, a passage through the outer integument of an ovule.

Exosto'sis (Gr.), in anatomy, an unnatural protuberance or tumour of the bone.

Exot'ic (Gr. *exotikos* foreign), in botany, foreign; not produced at home; an epithet applied, in natural history and materia medica, to animals, plants, and medical agents, the product of foreign countries; a plant of foreign origin.

Expectora'tion (Lat. *ex*, and *pectus* the breast), the discharge of mucous or other fluids accumulated on the surface of the bronchial membrane; the matter expectorated.—*Expectorant* is a medicine promoting expectoration.

Exper'iment (Lat.), in physiology, a term applied to the venesection of animals for the purpose of making discoveries in the structure and functions of their various organs.—In pathology and medical jurisprudence, a trial made on a man or other animal with a new medical agent or alimentary substance, in order to determine its operation or properties.—*Experimental philosophy* comprehends those branches of science the deductions in which are founded on experiment. The principal experimental science is chemistry; but there are many others, as optics, pneumatics, hydrostatics, electricity, magnetism, &c.—*Experimentum crucis* (experiment of the cross) is a term applied in science to any leading or decisive experiment subjected to the severest tests; or such an experiment as leads to the true knowledge of things sought after, in the same manner as the cross on the highway directs the traveller in his course.

Expo'nent (Lat.), in algebra, the index of a power, as 2 is the exponent of 8^2, and 4 the index of x^4. The *exponent* of the ratio or proportion between two numbers or quantities is the quotient arising when the antecedent is divided by the consequent.—*Exponential calculus*, in fluxions, is the method of differencing or finding the fluxions of exponential qualities.—*Exponential curve* is a curve the nature of which is defined or expressed by an exponential equation.—*Exponential equation* is one in which is contained an exponential quantity, as the equation $a^3 = b$, or $x^n = a, a$, &c.—*Exponential quality* is that whose power is a variable quantity, as the expression a^n, or x^x.—*Exponential quantities* are of several degrees: a^x of the first order x^{xy} of the second, and so on.

Expressed Oil, in chemistry, an oil obtained by the mechanical operation of pressing or squeezing, instead of by boiling; thus castor, olive, almond, and cocoa-nut oils are obtained by being expressed.

Expres'sivo, Espres'sivo (Ital.), in music, a term indicating that the movement or passage over which it is placed is to be performed with expression.

Exten'sor (Lat. *ex*, and *tendo* to stretch out), a term applied to certain muscles, whose property is to stretch out.

Extine, in botany, the outer coat of the pollen grain.

Extract (Lat. *extractum*), in pharmacy, the product of the evaporation of a fluid obtained by the expression of either animal or vegetable substances. In chemistry, a peculiar substance supposed to form the active principle of the vegetable in which it occurs.—Of the numerous extracts used in the pharmaceutical laboratory the following may be enumerated, in alphabetical order, as among the principal ones:—*Extractum aconiti*, extract of aconite; *E. aloes purificatum*, purified extract of aloes; *E. anthemidis*, extract of chamomile; *E. belladonnæ*, extract of belladonna; *E. cinchonæ*, extract of bark; *E. cinchonæ resinosum*, resinous extract of bark; *E. colchici aceticum*, acetic extract of meadow saffron; *E. colchici cormi*, extract of the cormus, or meadow saffron; *E. colocynthidis*, extract of colocynth; *E. colocynthidis compositum*, extractum catharticum; *E. conii*, extract of hemlock; *E. digitalis*, extract of foxglove; *E. elaterii*, extract of elaterium; *E. gentianæ*, extract of gentian; *E. glycyrrhizæ*, extract of liquorice; *E. hæmatoxyli*, extract of logwood; *E. hyoscyami*, extract of henbane; *E. jalapæ*, extract of jalap; *E. lactucæ*, extract of lettuce; *E. lupuli, E. humuli*, extract of hops; *E. opii purificatum*,

extract of opium; *E. papaveris*, extract of white poppy; *E. pareiræ*, extract of pareira; *E. rhei*, extract of rhubarb; *E. rutæ*, extract of rue; *E. sarsaparillæ*, extract of sarsaparilla; *E. stramonii*, extract of thorn-apple; *E. taraxaci*, extract of dandelion.

Extrac'tion (Lat.), in surgery, an operation by which foreign or diseased parts are removed by the natural or by artificial openings, as a bone from the œsophagus, or a calculus from the bladder.—In chemistry, the art of separating a simple or compound substance from a body of which it is a component part.—*Extraction of roots*, in arithmetic and algebra, is an operation which consists in finding a certain root of a number or algebraic symbol; as, 7 is the root of 49, and x is the root of x^2.

Extra'dos (Sp. or Fr.), in architecture, the exterior curve of an arch.

Extra-u'terine, in midwifery, an epithet applied to those cases of pregnancy in which the fœtus is contained in some organ exterior to the uterus.

Extravasa'tion (Lat. *extra* and *vas*, out of the vessel), in pathology, the escape of the animal fluids, especially of blood or serum, from their natural vessels, and their consequent effusion into the meshes of the adjoining tissue.

Exulcera'tion (Lat.), in surgery, the process of ulceration caused by some caustic or irritating application.

Exu'viæ (Lat.), the cast skin of animals, or whatever is put off or shed and left by animals or plants.—In geology, the remains of natural objects deposited during the changes of the earth's crust.—*Exuviation* is the casting or throwing off the skins of certain animals; the process by which the Crustacea throw off their old shells.

Eye (Sax. *eag*), the organ of sight or vision; the most important feature of animal organization; the globe or ball, movable in the orbit, chiefly consisting of the *cornea*, the *sclerotica*, and the *retina*—the external parts being the *eyebrows*, the *eyelid*, and the *eyelashes*. The *Cornea* is a small segment of a small sphere; the *Sclerotica* is a fibrous membrane of great firmness, which gives form and support to the eyeball; the *Retina* is the expansion of the optic nerve lining the choroid.—In architecture, *eye* is a general term, signifying the centre of a part;—*the eye of a pediment* is a circular window in its centre;—*the eye of a dome*, the horizontal aperture on its summit, usually covered with a lantern;—*the eye of a volute*, the circle at the centre, from the circumference of which the spiral line commences.— In horticulture, *eye* is a term applied to the leaf-bud, from which some other individual plant may be propagated.

Eye-bolt, in nautical science or art, a bar of iron, or bolt, with an eye at one end, formed to be driven into the deck or sides of a ship, the eye being left out, to hook tackles or fasten ropes to.

Eye-glass, or **Eye-piece**, in telescopes, the glass next the eye; the lens, or combination of lenses, in a microscope to which the eye is applied.

F.

Faba'ceæ (Lat. *faba* a bean), in botany, a nat. order of herbaceous plants, of which the Faba, or common esculent bean, is the type and genus.

Fabra'rum Aqua (Lat. *smiths' water*), a name applied to a chalybeate produced by quenching red-hot iron in water; commonly known as forge-water.

Façade (Fr.), in architecture, the elevation or front view of an edifice.

Face (Fr. from Lat. *facies*), a term of frequent use in practical science and the arts.—In zoology and anatomy, it applies to the anterior portion of the head of a mammiferous animal. The face of birds comprehends the cheek, temples, eyes, forehead, and vertex; and the face of insects is that part between the prothorax and the proboscis. — In military tactics, *face* means the side of a battalion when formed into a square. — In fortification, the *face of a bastion* is formed of two sides extending from the sides of a salient angle;—*face prolonged* is that part of the line of defence which is between the angle of the shoulder and the curtain;—*face of a place* is the front, comprehended between the flanked angles of the two neighbouring bastions, composed of a curtain, two flanks, and two faces. —In gunnery, the *face of a gun* is the superficies of the metal at the extremity of the muzzle.—In mechanics, *face* is applied to the part of a cogged wheel which impels another wheel.—*Face-guard* is a wire-gauze mask to defend the face from accident in various chemical and manufacturing experiments.

Facet (Fr. *facette* a little face). The minute face of a diamond or other crystal.—In zoology, *facets* are the compound eyes of insects, composed of an innumerable assemblage of eyelets or lenses, called *facet-eyes*, each eyelet being a *facet*. — In anatomy, a small circumscribed portion of the surface of a bone, as the articular surface. — In architecture, the *facets* of a column are the flat projections between the flutings.

Facial (Lat. *facies* the face), in phrenology, the *facial angle* is an angle formed by the concurrence of two ideal lines, one perpendicular and the other horizontal.—In anatomy, the *facial bones* are thirteen in number, exclusive of the teeth. The *facial artery* is a branch of the external carotid, which passes over the lower jaw, and distributes its ramifications to the face and palate. The *facial nerve* rises from the lower and lateral parts of the pons varolii, and quitting the cranium, enters the aquæductus Fallopii, and after supplying the muscles to the internal ear, &c., is distributed in three principal divisions of the face, termed the *facial* muscles.

Facies (Lat. *the face*), in anatomy, the anterior part of the skull, forming cavities of the orbits, nose, and mouth. —In zoology, the general aspect or external appearance of an animal as it appears on a casual or first view.

Facing, in architecture, that part of the work in a building seen by the spectator; more particularly that better sort of material used to mask an inferior. — In carpentry, the wooden covering of the sides of windows, doors, &c., in the inside of rooms. — In plaster-work, the last layer of fine plaster or stucco on walls.—In the evolutions of military science, the different movements of the men to the right, left, &c.; also the name given to the lappets, cuffs, and collars of a regimental uniform.

Factors, in the science of arithmetic, the multiplicand and the multiplier, or those numbers by the multiplication of which another is produced; thus 4 and 6 are the factors of 24, and in algebra *a* and *y* are the factors of *ay*.

Faculæ (Lat. *facula* a little torch), in astronomy, a name applied to those spots on the surface of the sun which appear brighter than the rest; the darker spots are termed *maculæ*.

Faculty (Lat.), in the Universities, a

term applied to the masters and professors of the sciences; as, the *faculty of arts*, which includes humanity and the philosophy of theology, law, and physics. The degrees conferred by the faculties are those of Bachelor, Master, and Doctor. The term is more especially applied to the body of physicians.

Fæ'culæ. (See *Facula.*)

Fahl'erz, Fahl'ore, in mineralogy, a grey copper ore.

Fahl'unite, in mineralogy, a hydrated silicate of alumina, found at Fahlun, in Sweden.

Fah'renheit, a thermometrical scale, so called from the inventor. (See *Thermometer.*)

Faience (Fr.), pottery embellished with painted designs, manufactured at Faenza.

Fairy Beads, in geology, a name applied to the small perforated and radiated vertebræ, or plates, of the fossil Crinoidia, sometimes called *St. Cuthbert's Beads*, which occur so abundantly in the shales and limestones of the carboniferous or mountain limestone formation. — *Fairy Stones* is a name given to the fossil remains of Echinus, Cedaris, &c.

Falcif'eri (Lat. *falx* a sickle), in fossilology, the name of a group of Ammonites.

Falcon'idæ (Lat. *falco* a falcon), in ornithology, a family of Raptores, or rapacious birds, comprehending Eagles, Hawks, Kites, &c., of which the Falco is the type and genus.—In heraldry, falcons are generally represented with bells on their legs.— *Falconinæ* are a sub-family of the Falconidæ.

Falling Sluice, in hydraulics, a sluice contrived to fall of itself, and augment the water-way, on the increase of a flood in a mill-dam or river.—*Falling star*, an igneous meteor which appears to fall rapidly to the earth.— *Falling-star tube*, an electrical experiment made to imitate a falling star by means of a glass tube, four or five feet in length, with a small ball inside of it at each end.

Fallo'pian (from *Fallopius*, the discoverer), in anatomy, an epithet applied to two tubes or ducts arising from the uterus.

Falset'to (Ital.), in music, a note that does not belong to the natural compass of voice; an artificial manner of singing, produced by tightening the ligaments of the glottis, and thus extending the vocal compass about an octave higher.

Faltranck, in pharmacy, a mixture of several aromatic plants, used as a vulnerary medicine.

Faluns, in geology, a series of deposits belonging to the middle tertiary or miocene period. They contain a great number of animal remains of the mastodon, rhinoceros, palæotherium, the tapir, and various Mammalia, besides a great number of extinct and recent shells.

Falx (Lat. *a sickle*), in anatomy, a term applied to certain membranous processes which have a form resembling that of a scythe or sickle; as, *falx cerebri*, a process of the dura mater.

Fam'ily, in natural history, a certain group of genera with similar characteristics. By some naturalists the term is synonymous with Order. In mathematics, it expresses a congeries of several kinds of curves, all of which are defined by the same equation.

Fan Palm, in botany, the Talipot tree of the East Indies, which grows to an enormous height, with a straight cylindrical trunk, and is one of the most magnificent of the Palm tribes.

Fanta'sia (Ital.), in music, a fantastical air, or piece of instrumental music, in which the composer, instead of being confined to the rules of art, is allowed to yield himself to the vagaries of imagination.

Fantocci'ni [-tohene] (Ital.), dramatic representations in which puppets are substituted for human performers.

Farcy (Fr.), a disease of horses, of a leprous, loathsome character.

Farding-bag, in physiology, the first stomach of a cow or other ruminating animal, where green food lies till it is chewed over again.

Fari'na (Lat.), the nutritive powder obtained from the seeds of corn, grasses, or other leguminous plants The term is sometimes used for the pollen which occurs in the anthers of plants.—*Farinaceous*, pertaining to meal, or to mealy plants.—*Farinose*, reducible to farina by trituration.—In botany, an epithet applied to such parts of plants as are covered with a fine mealy powder.

Fas'cia (Lat. *a belt* or *bandage*), in architecture, a broad fillet, band, or face, used sometimes by itself, and sometimes in combination with mouldings. Architraves are often divided into two or three fasciæ, each of which projects slightly beyond that which is immediately below it.—In astronomy, the belt across a planet, as the belts of Jupiter.—In anatomy, a term applied to any aponeurotic expansion of muscular fibre by which certain parts are bound together. The principal fasciæ are the *Fascia cerebriformis*, a small web of cellular substance which stretches over the inguinal glands;—*F. iliaca*, which covers the inner surface of the iliac and psoas muscles;—*F. infundibuliformis*, a portion of the cellular membrane, of a funnel shape, which passes down the spermatic cord;—*F. lata*, a thick and strong tendinous muscle, surrounding the muscles of the thigh; —*F. propria*, the cellular envelope of a hernial sac;—*F. superficialis*, a very thin layer of cellular membrane, which covers the abdominal muscles.

Fas'ciated (Lat. *fascia*), in botany, a term applied to the branches, peduncles, and petioles of plants, when they exhibit, through malformation, a fillet-like shape, consequent on several of them uniting together.—In zoology, the Latin adjectives *fasciatus, fasciolaris, fasciolatus*, designate such species as are marked on the back with a broad-coloured line or band.

Fascicula'ted (Lat. *fasciculus*), in botany, an epithet applied to the leaves, flowers, filaments, spines, branches, and roots of plants, when united in fascicles.

Fascic'ulite (Lat. *fasciculus*), in geology, a variety of fibrous hornblende, the fibres being arranged in a fasciculated manner.

Fascic'ulus (Lat. *a little bundle* or *fascicle*), in botany, a form of inflorescence, when many flowers or small stalks spring from one point. When the little stalks come only from about the apex of the peduncle, and not from its whole length, a fascicle is called a *corymb*; when they do not come from a common point, an *umbel*; and when its principal division is not umbellate, a *cyme*.

Fascine (Lat. *fascia* a band), in military operations, a fagot, or bundle of fagots, for raising batteries, filling ditches, &c.

Fas'saite (from *Fassa*, in the Tyrol), in mineralogy, a variety of augite.

Fata Morga'na (Ital.), a meteoric phenomenon nearly allied to the mirage, an atmospheric refraction frequently observed between the coasts of Sicily and Calabria. It consists of an optical deception, in which the images of houses, castles, and other objects in the adjoining landscapes are fantastically represented, sometimes in the water, and sometimes in the air.

Fats, in commercial science, a general term for those solid oily substances found in the animal and vegetable kingdoms.

Fauces (Lat. *the jaws*), in anatomy, the posterior parts of the mouth; the space surrounding the velum palati, the uvula, and the tonsils.

Fault (Lat. *fallo* to deceive), in geology, an interruption in the continuity of strata.

Fauna (Lat.), in zoology, the various kinds of animals peculiar to a country.

Fausse-braye, in fortification, a low rampart.

Fausses Eaux (Fr. *false waters*), in physiology, a term for water discharged from the uterus during pregnancy.

Faux Jour (Fr. *false light*), in the fine arts, a term denoting that a picture is so placed that the light falls upon it from a different direction than that in which the painter has represented it as coming in the picture.

Favus (Lat. *a honey-comb*), in pathology, a disease of the skin; the scald head.

Feather Edges, in architecture, made thin at one edge.

Feb'rifuge (Lat. *dispelling fever*), in therapeutics, a medicine which has the power of subduing or mitigating fever.

Febris (Lat. from *ferveo* to be heated), in pathology, a class of diseases characterized by excessive heat or continued thirstiness. The medical faculty distinguish the principal kinds of fever by the terms *Continued, Intermittent*, and *Remittent*. *Continued* is applied to Common fever (Synochus) and Typhus;—*Intermittent* to Quotidian fever, in which the paroxysms recur daily; the Tertian Assodes, or Hungarica, in which they occur each second day; and the Quartan, in which they recur each third day;—the *Remittent* is a class distinguished by remissions and exacerbations, instead of distinct intervals and paroxysms.—The other fevers are the Gastric, or Choleric, Hay, Hectic, Puerperal, Bilious, or Yellow, Sweating, Milk, Miliary, Scarlet, Hospital, Marsh, Plague, Measles, Small-pox, &c.

Fec'ula (Lat.), a pulverulent matter obtained from plants; farina; starch.

Feed-pipe, in hydraulics, a pipe for supplying water to a steam-engine boiler, or to a pump.—*Feed-pump*, the force-pump for supplying the boilers of steam-engines with water.

Fe'lidæ (Lat. *felis* a cat), in zoology, the Cat family, of which the genus Felis is the type. Besides the Cat, this family, according to Linnæus, includes the Lions, Tigers, Lynxes, and Leopards; but Dr. Leach arranged the Lions under the generic term *Leo*.

Felsite, a talcose mineral or jade rock.

Felspar, a siliceous mineral, which forms a constituent part of sienite and granite, and which, next to quartz, is the most abundant in the mineral world. It occurs crystallized and massive, and is composed of silica, alumina, potash, lime, and oxide of iron : sp. gr. 2·3. According to Professor Jamieson, felspar is divided into five species; namely, *rhombohedral felspar*, or nepheline; *prismatic felspar*, or common felspar; *tetarto-prismatic felspar*, or scapolite; *polychromic*, or Labrador felspar; and *pyramidal felspar*, or meionite.—*Felspathic*, of the nature of felspar.

Felt (Sax.), in the arts, a cloth or stuff made of wool and hair, fulled or wrought into a compact substance by rolling and pressure with lees or size.

Female (Fr. *femelle*), in botany, a female plant, or flower, which has pistils, but no stamens, or male organs of reproduction.—In zoology, the she-animal which conceives and brings forth young.—In mechanics, a *female screw* is the spiral-threaded cavity in which the male screw works.

Femur (Lat. *the thigh bone*), in anatomy, the first bone of the leg from the pelvis.—In architecture, the interstitial space between the channels of the triglyph of the Doric order.—*Brande*.

Fenes'tra (Lat. *a window*), in anatomy, a term applied to two small openings in the bones of the ear. — *Fenestral*, having openings like a window.

Feræ (Lat. *wild beasts*), in zoology, a class of Mammalia which are mostly beasts of prey, the Carnassiers of Cuvier. According to Swainson they constitute an order including the families Felidæ, Phocidæ, Sorecidæ, Delphidæ, and Mustelæ.—*Feral*, or *Ferine*, is an epithet applied to such animals as are wild and savage.

Fer'gusonite, a crystallized compound of columbic acid and yttria, consisting of oxide of tantalum, yttria, zirconia, oxide of cerium, oxide of tin, oxide of uranium, and oxide of iron : sp. gr. 5·8.

Fermenta'tion (Lat.), in physics, a gaseous change that takes place in certain substances, which is of three kinds: *vinous*, producing alcohol; the *acetous*, producing vinegar; and the *putrefactive*, giving rise to various fetid products.—*Putrefactive*

fermentation is that spontaneous decay and decomposition of animal and vegetable matter which is unaccompanied with the production of alcohol or acetic acid.

Ferns. (See *Filices*.)—*Fern-root* is the root of the male fern, occasionally given in medicine as a vermifuge.

Fero'nia, the name of one of the newly-discovered planets, first observed by Peters in 1861.

Ferret'to (Lat. *ferrum* iron), a substance used in colouring glass ; copper calcined with white vitriol.—*Francis*.

Ferric (Lat. *ferrum*), extracted from iron.—*Ferric acid*, the acid of iron.

Ferro, or **Ferri** (Lat. *ferrum*), a prefix of frequent occurrence in scientific terms, signifying *iron*, or properties appertaining thereto.—*Ferricalcite* is a species of calcareous earth having much iron in it.—*Ferrilite*, a variety of basalt.—*Ferrocyanate, Ferrocyanide, Ferroprussiate*, a compound of cyanogen and iron.—*Ferrocyanic*, noting an acid formed by a union of hydrocyanic acid and protoxide of iron.—*Ferrotype*, a term applied to certain chemical agents used in photography.—*Ferrugo*, a disease of plants, commonly known as *rust*.

Fer'ulæ (Lat. *a rod*), in surgery, consisting of splinters or chips of different matter, as of wood, bark, leather, paper, &c., applied to bones that have been disjointed when they are set again.

Fesse (Fr. from Lat. *fascia*), in heraldry, one of the ordinaries, consisting of a band or girdle.—*Fesse point* is the centre of the escutcheon. —*Parti per fesse*, a parting across on the middle of the shield, from side to side, through the *fesse* point.

Feta'tion, or **Fœta'tion** (Lat. *fœtus*), in physiology, the forming or natural growth of a fœtus in the womb.

Fetus. (See *Fœtus*.)

Fibril'læ (Lat. *fibra* a fibre), in botany, the minute subdivisions of the root of a plant.

Fibrine, in chemistry, a white fibrous substance, obtained from coagulated blood. Fibrine, both vegetable and animal, is a most important element of animal nutrition. It differs from albumen in containing less sulphur ; and caseine differs from both in containing no phosphorus.

Fib'rolite (Lat. *fibra*, and Gr. *lithos* a stone), a mineral of a dingy grey colour and fibrous texture, consisting of silica, alumina, and iron.

Fib'ula (Lat.), in anatomy, a long outer bone of the leg, so named on account of its connecting and giving firmness to other parts.

Field (Sax.), in heraldry, the entire surface of a shield.—In military science, *Field colours* are small flags used to mark out the ground for the squadrons or battalions. — *Field-pieces* are cannons of small calibre, consisting of from three to twelve-pounders, carried along with an army in the field.—*Field officer*, a military officer above the rank of captain —*Field Marshal*, an officer of the highest military rank.—*Field-works*, in fortification, are works thrown up by an army while engaged in besieging a town, or by the besieged in defence of the place, or sometimes by an army to strengthen a position. — *Field-staff* is a weapon carried by gunners, about the length of a halberd, with a spear at the end, having on each side ears screwed on, like the cock of a matchlock, where lighted matches are contained.

Fifth (Sax.), in music, an interval, and, with the exception of the octave, the most perfect of concords. Musicians specify three kinds of fifths; viz. the Perfect Fifth (C—G), composed of three tones and a semitone; the Flat or Diminished Fifth, termed also the Imperfect Fifth (B—F), composed of two whole tones and two semitones; and the Extreme or Superfluous Fifth (C—G♯), composed of four whole tones.—In anatomy, the *fifth pair of nerves* is the largest pair connected with the brain.

Figure (Lat. *figura*), in the science of arithmetic and numbers, a certain character by which we denote any number which can be expressed by the use of the nine digits and the cipher.—In geometry, a space bounded on all sides, either by lines or planes; a diagram.—In painting and design, the lines and colours which form the representation of any animal, but more particularly of the human form.—In dancing, the several steps which the dancer makes, as marking certain figures on the floor. —*Figure-stone*, a mineral, the bildstein.—*Figure-weaving*, the process of weaving patterns or designs.

Fil'aments, in anatomy, those fine threads of which the nerves, skin, and flesh are composed.

Fil'ices (Lat. *filix* a fern), in botany, an important order of plants, the Ferns, which form the Filical alliance of Lindley's "Vegetable Kingdom," according to the following arrangement:—1st, the Ophioglossaceæ, or Adders' Tongues, in which the spore-cases are ringless, distinct, and two-valved; 2nd, Polypodiaceæ, or True Ferns, in which the spore-cases are ringed, dorsal, or marginal; 3rd, the Danæaceæ, in which the spore-cases are ringless, dorsal, and connate. The species of the Filices are rather numerous, and are usually denoted by *filix* or *fili*, as a prefix, thus: —*Filicaulis*, having a thread-like stem; *filicornis*, having thread-like antennæ; *filiferus*, having filamentous processes or appendages; *filifolius*, having thread-like leaves, *filiformis*, occurring in the form of a thread; *filigerous*, bearing filaments.

Fillet (Lat. *filum* a thread), in architecture, a small square moulding, much used in entablatures. — In joinery and carpentry, any small scantling less than battens. — In heraldry, a kind of orle or bordure, containing only a third or fourth part of the breadth of the common bordure.

Fillings, in the art or science of brewing, a term for prepared wort, which is added in small quantities to casks of ale to cleanse it.

Filter (Fr.), in chemistry, a strainer, used for rendering fluids transparent by separating suspended impurities. —*Filtering cup* is a pneumatic apparatus for the purpose of showing that if the pressure of the atmosphere be removed from an under surface, the pressure which remains on the surface above has the effect of forcing a fluid readily through the pores of such substances as it could not otherwise penetrate.—*Filtering machine*, any contrivance by which liquids may be filtered.—*Filtering stone*, any porous stone, such as oolite or sandstone, through which water is filtered.—*Filtering paper*, any paper unsized and sufficiently porous to admit water to pass through it.

Filtra'tion (Fr.), in chemical operations, the process by which liquids or fluids are separated from substances mechanically suspended in them, or colouring matters in a state of solution are separated.

Fim'bria (Lat. *a fringe*), in botany, the fringe-like ring of the operculum of mosses, by the elastic power of which the operculum is displaced.— In anatomy, a term applied to the fringe-like extremity of the Fallopian tubes.

Fina'le (Ital. from Lat. *finis* the end), in music, the concluding passage in a concerted piece, by which the acts of an opera conclude; the last movement of a concerto or symphony.

Fin'gering, in music, the art of applying the fingers to a musical instrument so as skilfully to produce the notes intended.—*Finger-board* is the board at the neck of a violin, guitar, or the like, where the fingers act on the strings; also the whole range of keys, white and black, of a piano-forte or organ.

Fir (Sax. *furh*), in botany, the name of several species of forest trees belonging to the genera Abies and Pinus. The genus Abies is divided into four sections : the *Silvers*, which have the leaves growing singly round the branches; the *Spruces*, the leaves of which also grow singly round the branches; the *Larches*, which have the leaves growing in clusters; the *Cedars*, the leaves of which are evergreen, and arranged in clusters.

Fire (Sax. *fyr*), in physics, the igneous element; the light and heat extricated from a body during its combustion; popularly, one of the four elements; a word forming various compounds connected with science and art; as, *Fire-arms*, arms charged with powder and balls, as guns, pistols, &c. ;—*Fire-ball*, a ball filled with combustibles ;—*Fire-blast*, a species of blast affecting plants or fruit trees ; —*Fire-brake*, a will-o'-the-wisp ;— *Fire-brand*, a piece of wood kindled or partly burnt ;—*Fire-brick*, a very hard kind of brick used for lining furnaces, &c. ;—*Fire-clay*, in geology, a variety of clay, common in the strata of the coal formation, from which fire-brick and other articles are manufactured ;—*Fire-cock*, a cock or plug to let out water from the main pipes to extinguish fire ; —*Fire-damp*, carburetted hydrogen gas in coal mines ;—*Fire-drake*, a fiery meteor ; a kind of firework ;— *Fire-engine*, a machine for throwing water to extinguish fires ;—*Fire-escape*, a machine to escape from fire ;—*Fire-fly*, an insect which emits, at night, a vivid light ;—*Fire-plug*, a stopple in a pipe which supplies water in case of fire ;—*Fire-pot*, an earthen pot to enclose a grenade ;— *Fire-pump*, a force-pump erected in a populous place for the extinguishing of fires ;—*Fire-ship*, a ship filled with combustibles to send against an enemy ;—*Fire-tower*, a sort of lighthouse ;—*Firework* or *Fireworks*, preparations of sulphur, nitre, and charcoal, to be fired for amusement. (See *Pyrotechny*.)

Fire-stone, in geology, a metallic fossil ; a kind of pyrites, which stands great heat when exposed to the action of fire. It is an arenaceo-argillaceous deposit of a greyish-green colour, composed of marl and grains of silicate of iron. The transition from the marl to the fire-stone is in many localities so gradual, that the chalk marl may be said to repose immediately on the galt.

Firing, in farriery, the process of cautery.

Fir'mament (Lat.), in ouranology, the great sphere of the fixed stars ; the most remote of all the celestial spheres ; the ethereal vault of heaven. —In Scripture, *firmament* denotes the great arch or expanse over our heads, in which are placed the atmosphere and the clouds, and in which the stars appear to be placed. According to ancient astronomers, it was supposed to have two motions— a diurnal one, given to it by the *primum mobile*, from east to west about the poles of the ecliptic ; and another opposite motion from west to east, which last it finishes, according to Tycho, in 25,412 years ; in which time the fixed stars, as shown by the precession of the equinoxes, return to the same points in which they were at the beginning. Cicero calls this the *magnus annus*.

Fish (Sax. *fisc*), in ichthyology, a vertebrated, oviparous animal that inhabits the water, and breathes by the means of branchiæ, or gills ; having one auricle and one ventricle to the heart, cold red blood, and extremities made for swimming (*Agassiz*).— In popular language, the term fish is erroneously applied to the Cetacea, which are Mammalia, and breathe by lungs. Craw-fish, crab-fish, and shell-fish are terms also used in common phraseology for the Crustaceans and testaceous Mollusca.—In navigation, *fish* is a machine employed to hoist and draw up the flukes of the ship's anchor towards the top of the bow, in order to stow it after it has been catted.—*Fish-gig* is an instrument used to strike fish at sea, particularly dolphins.

Fissip'ara, or **Fissipa'rism** (Lat. *fissus* divided, and *pario* to bring forth), in zoology a term applied to those animals which propagate by spontaneous fission, having an inherent power of self-support and growth, as in the Polypi, Infusoria, and certain worms. —*Fissiparous*, an epithet applied to a generation or production by a spontaneous division of the body of the parent into two or more parts.

Fissipen'næ (Lat. *fissus*, and *penna* a wing), in entomology, a section of nocturnal lepidopterous insects, in which the wings are split longitudinally.

Fissiros'tris (Lat. *fissus*, and *rostrum* a beak), in ornithology, a tribe of Perching birds, in which the gape of the mouth is very wide. They feed on insects taken during flight: order Insessores.

Fissu'ra (Lat.), in anatomy, *fissura silvii* is the fissure which separates the anterior and middle lobes of the cerebrum.—*F. umbilicalis*, the groove of the umbilical vein.

Fis'tuca (Lat.), in mechanics, a pile-driving implement raised by pulleys, and guided in its descent to fall on the head of a pile so as to drive it into the ground, being what is called by the workmen a *monkey*.

Fis'tula (Lat. *a pipe*), in pathology, a long, sinuous, pipe-like ulcer.—*Fistula in ano* is a fistula which penetrates into the cellular substance about the anus, or into the rectum itself;—*F. in perinæo*, fistula in the course of the perinæum, from which it sometimes extends to the urethra, bladder, vagina, or rectum;—*F. lacrymalis*, fistula penetrating into the lachrymal sac;—*F. salivary*, fistula penetrating into the parotid duct from a wound or ulcer.

Fistular'idæ (Lat. *fistula*), in ichthyology, a family of malacopterygious fishes, of which the Fistularia, or Tobacco-pipe fish, is the type and genus.

Fistu'lidans (Lat. *fistula*), in ichthyology, a tribe of the Echinodermata, whose bodies are in the shape of a long cylindrical tube.

Fit (Fr. *vite* quick), in pathology, a sudden attack, paroxysm, or exacerbation of a distemper; a sudden and violent attack of any disease, particularly if attended with convulsions, as an epileptic *fit*; any sudden or temporary affection.

Fitchy (Fr. *fiché* fixed), in heraldry, a term applied to a cross when the lower branch ends in a sharp point, as if intended to be fixed in the ground.

Fixed, an epithet of frequent application in chemistry, astronomy, &c.—In chemistry, *fixed bodies* are substances which bear great heat without evaporation or volatilization.—*Fixed air* is applied to carbonic acid gas, and *fixed alkalies* to soda and potash.—*Fixed oils* are the common greasy oils which do not evaporate except at a very high temperature: they are generally obtained by expression, and are termed *fixed* in contradistinction to the *volatile* oils. —In astronomy, *fixed stars* are such stars as invariably retain the same apparent position and distance from each other; they are supposed to be suns similar to our own, some of them of much greater magnitude, and to form centres around which other spheres revolve.—*Fixed signs* is a term sometimes applied to the signs Taurus (♉), Leo (♌), Scorpio (♏), and Aquarius (♒); the seasons being considered as less variable when the sun is in these constellations.

Flabella'ria (Lat. *flabellum* a fan), in fossil botany, a genus of plants allied or belonging to the Palm tribe, having the leaves petiolated, flabelliform, and plaited at the base. A genus of Polyfers (the Fan-coral), the coralline structures of which occur in large foliaceous expansions, formed of corneous threads enveloped in a calcareous crust.—From the Latin term *flabellum* a fan, a variety of species in natural history are formed; as, *flabelliformis*, fan-shaped; *flabellipes*, having fan-shaped feet; *flabellifolius*, having fan-shaped leaves.

Flacourtia'ceæ (from *Flacourt*, a French naturalist), in botany, a nat. order of hypogynous Exogens, belonging to the Violal alliance of Lindley, of which the Flacourtia, a shrub with pretty white flowers, is the type and genus.

Flagil'læ (Lat. a *whip* or *twig*), in botany, a name applied to runners without leaves.

Flame (Lat. *flamma*), in physics, inflammable gas in a state of combustion, as it ascends in a stream from a burning body; a thin flame of white-hot vapour.—*Flame* and *blaze* are both ignited vapour, produced by the application of fire.

Flange, in railway economy, a ledge or rim raised on a rail, or on the tire of a wheel, for the purpose of confining the wheel within certain limits.

Flank (Fr. *flanc*), in fortification, any part of a work which defends another along the outside of its parapet; such as the *flank of the bastion*, that part which joins the face to the curtain; *oblique flank*, that part of the curtain from which the face of the opposite bastion may be discovered; *retired* or *covered flank*, the platform of the casement which lies hid in the bastion.—*Flank razant* is the point from which the line of defence commences. — In military science, *flank* is the side of an army or battalion from the point to the rear, of which there are different kinds; as, the *inward flank*, in manœuvring, the first file or the left of a division, subdivision, or section; *outward flank*, the extreme file on right or left of a division; *leading flank*, the first battalion, division, &c., which conducts the attack; *flank files*, the first two men on the right, and the last two on the left ; *flank company*, a certain number of men drawn up on the right or left of a battalion ; *flank en potence*, any part of the right or left wing formed at a right angle with the line.—In architecture, the side of a building or of a wall which adjoins the front.

Flashe, a sluice made on navigable rivers for the purpose of raising the water over shoals, &c., while vessels are passing.

Flashings, in architecture, pieces of lead or other metal let into the joints of a wall.

Flasques (Fr.), in gunnery, the two checks of the carriage of a great gun.

Flat (Dutch), in music, a tone depressed half a note below a natural one, expressed by a character in the form of ♭.—*Flat fifth* is the interval of a fifth depressed by a flat.

Flat'idæ (Fr. *plat*), in entomology, a family of hemipterous insects, belonging to the Cicadæ, or Singing insects. (See *Fulgora*.)

Flavi (Lat. *flavus* yellow), in natural history, a prefix often used in the definition of species, and more especially in ornithology; as, *flavicaudatus*, yellow-tailed; *flavicollis*, yellow-necked; *flavicornis*, having yellow antennæ; *flavigastris*, yellow-bellied; *flavipalpis*, having yellow palpi; *flavipes*, yellow-footed; *flavipennis*, yellow-plumed; *flavirostris*, yellow-beaked; *flavisquamis*, yellow-scaled; *flavitarsis*, having the tarsi of a yellow colour; *flaviventris*, having a yellow belly; *flavipterus*, yellow-winged.

Flax (Sax. *flax*), in botany, an annual plant, the *Linum usitatissimum* of botanists, of which the finest thread is made, and woven into linen cloth.—*Flax-weed* is the *Linaria vulgaris* of botanists; order Scrophulariaceæ. (See *Phormium*.)— *Flax-comb*, an implement with which the fibres of flax are cleansed.—*Flax-dresser*, one who prepares flax for the use of the spinner.

Fleam, in surgery and farriery, an instrument used for letting blood or bleeding cattle.

Flesh (Sax. *flæsc*), in zoology, the muscular part or softer solids of an animal body, as distinguished from bones and fluids, as the muscles, glands, fat, &c.—In chemistry, *flesh* is defined as the muscular tissue or fibre of the animal economy, chiefly composed of fibrine, mixed with blood, membrane, nervous matter, and fat.—*Dried flesh*, when analyzed, gives the same formula as dried blood, viz.—$C_{48}H_{39}N_6O_{15}$. —In botany, *flesh* is a term applied to the soft pulpy substance of fruit, or to that part of a root which is fit to be eaten, as the turnip, &c.

Fleur-de-lis (Fr.), in blazonry, a flower which resembles an iris, three of which constituted the ancient bearing in the arms of France.

Fleury, Fleurette, in heraldry, a term for a cross.

Flex'ible (Lat.), an epithet applied to various terms in natural history; as, *flexible sulphuret of silver*, a rare mineral, occurring in tubular crystals, and consisting of silver, sulphur, and iron.—As a Latinized adjective (*flexilis*), it denotes various species in natural history; as, *flexicaulis*, having a flexible stem; *flexifolius*, having flexible leaves; *flexipes*, having flexible peduncles.

Flexion (Lat.), in anatomy, the action of the flexor muscles, or the condition of an organ bent by those muscles.—*Flexor* is a term applied to certain muscles which serve to bend the parts to which they are attached, in opposition to the extensors, which serve to stretch them.— In comparative anatomy, *Flexura* is the joint between the anti-brachium and carpus, usually called the fore-knee of the horse, analogous to the wrist in man.

Flint (Sax.), in mineralogy, a hard siliceous stone; a sub-species of quartz found in considerable abundance in nodules and layers in chalk rocks. It breaks into wedge-shaped fragments, and when struck with steel elicits sparks of fire. It consists of silica, alumina, oxide of iron, and water: sp. gr. 2·7.—*Flint glass*, a superior kind of glass or crystal, consisting of silicic acid, oxide of lead, and potassa.—*Flinty slate* differs from common slate in containing a larger proportion of siliceous earth. When flinty slate ceases to have the slaty structure it becomes hornstone. If it contains crystals of felspar, it becomes hornstone porphyry.

Floats, in steam navigation, the boards fixed on the paddle-wheels of steamers, and to undershot water-wheels, by which they act.

Flocci (Lat. *locks of wool*), in botany, the woolly filaments often found mixed with sporules of Fungi of the tribe Gasteromycetes, and also to the external filaments of the Byssaceæ.

Floccilla'tion (Lat.), in pathology, the act of picking the bed-clothes; an alarming symptom in acute diseases.

Floccus (Lat.), in zoology, the long tuft of flaccid hair which terminates the tail of the Mammalia.

Flookan, in mineralogy, the name of a slimy kind of clay or earth.—In mining, the deviation or shifting of a lode or vein by a cleft, &c.

Flora (Lat. *a flower*), the botany of a particular country; a catalogue of flowering plants.—*Floral envelopes*, a term applied to the corolla, calyx, and bracts which envelop the inner parts of a flower.—*Florascope*, an optical instrument for examining flowers.—*Floret*, a small monopetalous flower, many of which, as in the Compositæ, enclosed in one calyx or perianth, form a compound flower. —*Floriculture*, in horticulture, the culture of flowers.

Flora (Lat. from the goddess *Flora*), in astronomy, the name of one of the newly-discovered planets, first observed by Hind in 1847. Its mean distance from the sun is 209,930,000 miles, and the time of its periodical revolution three years and fifty-one days.

Florin (Ital.), in numismatology, a term applied to different silver coins current in various parts of Europe, and first coined at Florence, whence the name. The imperial florin, an integer of account in the Austrian empire, is worth about 2*s.* o$\frac{1}{2}$*d.* sterling; the Dutch florin, or guilder, is equal to 1*s.* 8*d.* sterling; the florin is also a German gold coin, worth about 6*s.* 11*d.* It is likewise the name of a British silver coin, the tenth of a pound sterling, and worth two shillings, first minted in 1849, and now in general circulation.

Flos (Lat.), in chemistry, the more subtile parts of bodies separated from what is grosser.—*Flos ferri* (flower of iron), in mineralogy, is a variety of arragonite. It occurs in little cylinders, and takes its name from its being found in veins of sparry iron.

Floss (Lat. *flos*), in botany, a downy substance observed on the husks of certain fruits.

Flower (Lat. *flos, floris*), in botany, that part of a plant which contains the organs of fructification. A flower, when complete, is furnished with a calyx, corolla, stamens, and pistils; the stamens carrying the anthers, or male organs of reproduction, and the pistils the stigmas, or female organs, by which the pollen, or impregnating

dust, is conveyed into the ovary, or seed-vessel.—*Flower-stalk* is the peduncle of a plant, or the stem which supports the fructification.—*Flower-head* is that mode of inflorescence in which all the flowers are sessile, as in the daisy.—In pyrotechnics, a particular kind of firework, which, when ignited, throws out a fountain of vivid florescent-looking sparks.

Flowers (Lat. *flores*), in chemistry, a term applied to certain light flocculent substances obtained by distillation;—*Flowers of antimony*, a white vapour which rises during the combustion of antimony, and condenses on cool surfaces, generally in the form of shining needles;—*Flowers of sulphur* are the crystalline grains which collect in the receiver during the process of the sublimation of common sulphur.—In the arts, *Artificial flowers* are imitations of nature for personal decoration, &c., which are skilfully manufactured from wax, linen, paper, feathers, shells, &c.; and the artists are called *Flowermakers* or *Florists*.—In physiology, a term applied to the catamenial discharge.

Fluate, in chemistry and mineralogy, a salt compounded of fluoric acid and a base.—*Fluates* are compounds of metallic oxides, earths, and alkalies with fluoric acids.

Flu'cerine (Lat. *fluor* a stream, and *cerium*), the neutral fluate of cerium, a Swedish mineral, occurring in six-sided prisms, in plates, and in amorphous masses, consisting of oxide of cerium, yttria, and fluoric acid: sp. gr. 4·7.

Flu'ellite, a mineral compounded of fluoric acid and alumina; the fluate of alumina.

Flu'gelman (Germ.), in military science, a well-drilled soldier, who gives the time in the manual and platoon exercises.

Fluke, in navigation, the broad part or arm of an anchor which takes hold of the ground.—*Fluke-worm* is a worm that infests the liver of sheep; a species of Entozoa.

Fluobo'rate (*fluor* and *borax*), a compound of fluoboric acid with a base.

Fluobor'ic Acid Gas, in chemistry, a colourless gas obtained by heating to redness a mixture of dry boracic acid and powdered fluor-spar.—*Fluosilicic acid gas* is a gas obtained by applying a gentle heat to 1 part of powdered fluor-spar, 1 of silica, and 2 of sulphuric acid in a retort.

Fluophos'phate, a compound of fluoric and phosphoric acids.

Fluor, or **Fluor Spar** (Lat. *fluor* a stream), in chemistry, fluate of lime, a mineral, of which there are three varieties, the compact, the crystallized, and the foliated. It consists of lime and fluoric acid. — *Fluor albus*, a disorder to which females are subjected at all ages, but more particularly in the prime of life, consisting of an irregular discharge of impure mucid humour. (See *Leucorrhœa*.)

Flu'oride, in chemistry, a compound of fluorine with another elementary body.

Flu'orine (Lat. *fluor*), a substance obtained from fluor-spar and other minerals. Its odour resembles chlorine and burnt sugar. Its equivalent is 18·68: sp. gr. 1·29. The compounds of fluorine are :—*Fluoric acid* = 3 atoms of fluorine + 1 of boron, equiv. 66·98; *Hydrofluoric acid* = 1 atom of fluorine + 1 of hydrogen, equiv. 19·68; *Fluosilicic acid* = 3 atoms of fluorine + 1 of silicon, equiv. 78·58.

Fluviooli'næ (Lat. *river frequenters*), in ornithology, a sub-fam. of birds (the Water-caps); fam. Musicapidæ.

Flu'vio-marine (Lat. *fluvius* a river, and *mare* the sea), in geology, an epithet applied to such formations as have been deposited by the agency of rivers at the bottom of the sea, at a greater or less distance from their embouchures.

Flux (Lat. *fluxus*, from *fluo* to flow), in mineralogy or metallurgy, any substance used to promote the fluxion of minerals or metals.—In pathology, a disease attended by violent secretion from the bowels ; a kind of dysentery. —*Black flux*, in chemistry, a mixture of carbonate of potash and charcoal, which remains when tartar is deflagrated with half its weight of nitre ;— *White flux* is the name given when an equal weight of nitre is used, and the whole of the charcoal is burned off, and carbonate of potash remains. —In physics, *flux and reflux of the tide* are the regular and periodical motions of the sea, which happen twice in 24 hours 48 minutes.

Fluxion (Lat. *fluxus* a flowing), the analysis of fluxions and fluents.—In chemistry, the running of metals into a fluid state. — In mathematics, a method of calculation based on the idea of motion. The method of fluxions differs from that of the differential calculus in no respect but that of notation.

Flying Buttress, in architecture, a buttress in the form of an arch, springing from a solid mass of masonry, and abutting against the springing of another arch, which rises from the upper points of abutment of the first.—*Flying bridge*, in military science, is a bridge of pontoons.—*Flying pinion*, in horology, is that part of a clock which is furnished with a fly or fan, by which it beats the air, and checks the rapidity of the descent of the weight attached to the striking portion of the machinery.

Fly Powder, a mixture of white oxide and metallic arsenic, obtained from the spontaneous sublimation of the cakes of the arsenic of commerce, used to kill flies.

Focus (Lat.), in optics, the point of convergence to which the rays of light are collected by a lens. The focal length is its distance from the lens.— In geometry, the *focus* of a parabola is a point in the axis which has this property, that a radius drawn from any point in the curve makes the same angle with the tangent at that point that the tangent makes with the axis. In the ellipse, the two foci are situated at equal distances from the centre.

Fœ'tus (Lat.), a perfectly-formed child in the womb. In the early stage of uterine gestation the young is called the embryo.

Fog (Icel. *fag*), in meteorology, dense watery vapour exhaled from the earth, and often collected in thick dark masses when there is no wind to disperse it.

Foil (Norm. *afolee*), in architecture, a term applied to those leaf-like forms seen in Gothic windows, niches, crests, battlements, &c. They are distinguished by the number of them combined, so as to form a figure, by the names trefoil, quatrefoil, cinquefoil, &c.—In jewellery, a thin leaf of metal, artistically placed under a precious stone, in order to increase its brilliancy, or give it an agreeable and different colour.

Folia'ceæ (Lat. *foliatus* leaved), in botany, the first class of the order Cellulares, including those cryptogamous plants which are furnished with leaves, embracing the Ferns, Horse-tails, Club-mosses, and Marsileas.—*Foliation* is the vernation or leaving of plants.

Folia'ta, **Fo'liated** (Lat. *foliatus*), in geometry, an epithet for a curve of the second order, expressed by the equation $x^3 + y^3 = axy$, which is one of the defective hyperbolas.—In conchology, occurring in thin laminæ or leaves, when the edges of the shelly layers are not compact.—In mineralogy, *foliated* is applied to minerals consisting of plates or thin layers.—*Foliated coal* is a species of lamellar black coal distinguished for its jetty lustre and easy frangibility. —In architecture, adorned with trefoils and leaf-like ornaments.

Fol'liole (Lat. *folliculus* a little bag), in botany, a capsule which splits on one side only.—In anatomy, a small secreting gland.—*Folliculated*, having or producing follicular seed-vessels.

Fo'mahaut (Arab.), in astronomy, a star of the first magnitude in the constellation Aquarius.

Fon'tanel (Fr.), in physiology, the opening of the skull of infants, which exists at birth between the frontal and parietal bones, and is subsequently closed by osseous deposit.

Footings, in architecture, the lower part of a brick or stone wall, in which the bricks or stones project beyond the general surface.

For'alites (Lat. *foro* to bore, and Gr. *lithos* a stone), in geology, tube-like markings in sandstones and other geological strata, which appear like burrows of vermicular animals.

Fora'men (Lat. *foro* to pierce), in anatomy, a perforation or opening by which the blood-vessels or nerves penetrate through the bones. The principal foramina, or foramens, are thus enumerated by Hoblyn and others:—*Foramen cæcum*, the *blind hole*, which is situated at the root of the spine of the frontal bone;—*F. incisivum*, the opening immediately behind the front teeth;—*F. magnum occipitis*, the great opening at the under and fore part of the occipital bone;—*F. ovale*, an opening situated in the partition which separates the right and left auricles in the foetus;—*F. rotundum*, the round aperture of the internal ear;—*F. supra-orbitarium*, the upper orbitary hole, situated on the ridge over which the eyebrow is placed.— The term *foramen* is also applied to numerous little holes of the cribriform plate; to several openings—the *round*, the *oval*, the *spinal*—of the sphenoid bone; to certain holes—the *mastoid*, the *stylo-mastoid*, the *videan*, the *glenoid*—of the temporal bones; to the opening (*malar*) through which the malar nerve passes; to the opening (*infra orbitar*) for the passage of nerves to the face; to the groove (*palato-maxillary*) through which the palatine nerve and vessels proceed to the palate; to another opening (the *palatine*) which transmits branches of the same to the soft palate; and to two openings at the base of the cranium, called respectively the *anterior* and *posterior lacerated foramen*.

Foraminif'era (Lat. *foramen*), in conchology, an order of foraminated, polythalamous, internal shells, which have no siphuncle or chamber beyond their last partition. They are divided by D'Aubigny into five families, with numerous genera; they are chiefly microscopic. — *Foraminiferous*, in physiology, having holes or perforations; an epithet applied to the Foraminifera.

Force (Fr.), in physics, the impelling power produced by the action of material bodies.—In mechanics, the power which produces motion, or a change in motion.—*Equilibrium of forces* is the composition or resolution of forces, or the conspiring or opposing of forces, so as to balance one another, and keep the body in a state of equilibrium or at rest.—*Force-pump* or *Forcing-pump* is a pump capable of driving a stream of water above the pump-barrel by compressed air.

Forceps (Lat.), in mechanical science, a general name for tools constructed on the principles of pliers or fine pincers.—In surgery, an instrument for extracting the foetus. The *artery* or *dissecting forceps* is used in dissection, for taking up the mouths of arteries, &c.

Forcer, in mechanical science, a solid piston applied to pumps for the purpose of producing a constant stream, or for raising water to a greater height than can be obtained by atmospheric pressure.

Forcing-pit, in horticulture, a pit of wood or masonry sunk in the earth for containing the fermenting materials used to produce bottom heat in forcing plants.

Forest Marble, in geology, the name of that series of the lower oolitic formation which consists of a coarse and shelly oolite.

Forfic'ula (Lat.), a genus of orthopterous insects, of which the common Earwig is the type.

Form, or **Forme**, in typography, an assemblage of pages or lines of type, arranged in order, and ready for printing; the whole being enclosed in an iron chase, within which it is firmly locked by a number of small wedges of wood, called *quoins*.—In phrenology, a power of the mind, according to Dr. Gall, indicated on the sides of the *crista galli*; its functions, in a healthy state, being a facility for the recollection of persons and objects.

Forma'tion (Lat.), in geology, any assemblage of rocks, alluvial deposits, or sedimentary strata referred to a common origin or period (*Lyell*).—The term properly signifies a series of rocks, usually passing gradually into each other, and the whole being considered as belonging to a certain period of geological time. A geological formation may consist of rocks entirely dissimilar, as the coal, shale, ironstone, and sandstone of the coal formation; or the chalk, flints, and sands of the chalk formation.

Formic Acid (Lat. *formica* an ant), in chemistry, an acid derived from ants—a sour liquid which they eject when irritated. It may be obtained artificially by distilling, in a large retort, a mixture of 2 parts of tartaric acid, 3 of peroxide of manganese, and 3 of sulphuric acid, diluted with 5 of water.—*Formiate* is a salt formed by the union of formic acid with a base.

Formica'tion (Lat.), in pathology, a certain creeping sensation affecting the skin, like the crawling of ants.

Formic'idæ (Lat. *formica* an ant), in entomology, an extensive family of hymenopterous insects, of which the Formica is the type and genus.—Five species are enumerated as belonging to Britain, viz., the hill ant, *F. rufa;* the jet ant, *F. fuliginosa;* the red ant, *F. rubra;* the common yellow ant, *F. flava;* and the small black ant, *F. fusca.*

Formobenzo'ic Acid, in chemistry, an acid forming a white granular powder, prepared by dissolving bitter oil of almonds in water, adding hydrochloric acid, and evaporating in a gentle heat.

For'mula (Lat.), a term of frequent application in the different sciences.—In chemistry, a concise mode of exhibiting by symbols the results of chemical changes (*Brande*); thus, the formula of common salt (chloride of sodium), is Na + Ch, or NaCl.—In medicine, a prescription; the mode of preparing medicines (*Hoblyn*).—In mathematics, a theorem, or general rule or expression for solving certain particular cases of some problem; as,

$$\sqrt{ax-x^2}$$

is the formula or generic value of the ordinate to a circle whose diameter is d and absciss x (*Craig*).—*Formule*, in chemistry, is a hypothetical radicle, the formula of which is C_2H; *i.e.* 2 atoms of carbon and 1 of hydrogen.

Fornix (Lat. *an arch*), in conchology, the excavated part of a shell beneath the umbo.—In anatomy, a part of the corpus callosum of the brain, which,

when viewed in a particular direction, has something like the appearance of a Gothic arch.

Fors'terite, a mineral which forms small brilliant crystals, found at Vesuvius; so called in honour of Mr. Forster.

Fort, or **Fortress** (Lat. *fortis* strong), in military science, a small fortified place, environed on all sides with a moat, rampart, and parapet.—*A royal fort* is a fortification having at least twenty-six fathoms for the line of defence.—*Fortalice* is the name of a small fortress, formerly reckoned in Scottish law as *inter regalia.*

Forte (Ital.), in music, a direction to sing or play with force or tone.

Fortifica'tion (Lat.), the science of military architecture; the art of constructing such works of defence as may best enable the besieged to withstand the attacks of an assailing force.

Fortu'na (Lat.), in astronomy, the name of one of the newly-discovered planets, first observed by Hind in 1852. Its mean distance from the sun is 233,810,000 miles, and the time of its periodical revolution three years and three hundred days.

Forzan'do (Ital.), in music, a word used to indicate that notes are to be boldly struck and continued.

Foss, Fossa, Fosse (Lat.), in fortification, a ditch or moat full of water.—In anatomy, an osseous cavity with perforation. In the human skeleton there are various fossæ; as, *Fossa hyaloidea*, the cup-like excavation of the vitreous humour in which the crystalline lens is embedded;—*F. lacrymalis*, a depression in the frontal bone for the reception of the lachrymal gland;—*F. navicularis*, the dilatation towards the extremity of the spongy portion of the urethra;—*F. ovalis*, the oval depression presented by the septum of the right auricle, &c.—*Fosse-way*, one of the great Roman roads through England, which extended from the coast of Lincolnshire to that of Devonshire.

Fossil (Lat. *fossilis*, from *fodio* to dig), a substance dug out of the earth, as petrified plants, shells, bones, &c.; organic remains of animals and plants found in the different geological strata of the earth's crust.—*Fossilization* is the process of conversion into a fossil, or petrifaction.—*Fossilology* is the science of fossils, or a treatise on them.

Fosso'res (Lat. *fossor* a digger), in entomology, a group of insects which excavate cells for their eggs in wood or earth; the second family of Hymenoptera, which are armed with a sting, and furnished with wings.

Fougade, or **Fougasse** (Fr.), in fortification, a little well-like mine filled with combustibles to blow up a fort.

Fount, Fountain (Lat. *fons*), the head or source of a river; an artificial spring.—*Glass fountain* is a pneumatic instrument, consisting of a glass vessel and a tube within it, for the purpose of showing the elasticity of the air.

Fourchette (Fr.), in ornithology, the bone formed by the junction of the clavicles; commonly called the merry-thought.

Fourneau (Fr.), in military engineering, the chamber of a mine in which the powder is lodged.

Fourth, in music, an interval enumerated among the discords. The minor or lesser *fourth* consists of five semitones; but the *fourth* sharp, or greater, consists of six semitones.—In anatomy, *fourth pair of nerves* is a term applied to the nervi pathetici.

Fovil'la (Lat. *foveo* to nourish), in botany, a fine substance emitted from the pollen of flowers.

Fowler's Solution, in chemistry, a solution of the arseniate of potassa, coloured and flavoured by the compound spirit of lavender.

Fraches (Fr.), in glass-blowing, a name applied to the flat iron pans into which the glass vessels, already formed, are put into the lower oven over the working furnace.

Fraction (Lat.), in arithmetic and algebra, a broken number which consists of a part or parts of any number considered as a unity. The parts of a unit or whole are expressed by two numbers with a line between them, as $\frac{1}{2}$, $\frac{1}{4}$; and, in *decimal fractions*, by a period placed before it, as ·5, ·8: the upper figure of a vulgar fraction is called its numerator, and the under its denominator.

Fracture (Lat. *fractura*), in mineralogy, the uneven or irregular surface which a mineral exhibits when broken. When the surface is perfectly smooth, it is termed *cleavage*: fractures are earthy, granular, splintery, conchoidal, &c.—In surgery, fracture is a break in a bone, when crushed or broken by some external violence; a *simple fracture* is where a bone is broken only in one part; a *compound fracture* is when two bones contiguous to each other are broken; a *complicated fracture* is one attended with a train of symptoms, as a wound or ulcer.

Frænum, Fræ'nulum (Lat. *a bridle*), in

anatomy, a membrane or string by which one organ is connected with another; as, *Frænum epiglottidis*, the ligament which connects the epiglottis with the root of the tongue and os hyoides;—*F. linguæ*, a fold of the mucous membrane of the mouth which binds down the tongue;—*F. preputii*, a fold of integument connecting the prepuce with the glans penis.

Fraise (Fr.), in fortification, a range of horizontal stakes for the purposes of defence, consisting of pointed stakes six or seven feet long, driven horizontally or inclined into the intrenchments of a camp, half-moon, &c.

Frambœ'sia (Fr. *framboise*, a raspberry), in pathology, a contagious disease (the Yaws), which is epidemic in certain parts of Africa and the West India Islands.

Francoa'ceæ (from *Dr. Franco*, of Valentia), in botany, a nat. order of hypogynous Exogens, of which the Francoa, a plant of Chili, is the genus and type.

Frankenia'ceæ (from *Frankenius*, professor of botany at Upsal), a nat. order of hypogynous Exogens, of which the Frankenia, or Sea-heath, is the type.

Frank'incense, a gum resin, used as a perfume, which exudes from a species of fir; supposed to be the olibanum of commerce.

Frank'linite (from the celebrated *Benj. Franklin*), a mineral found in grains or granulated masses, associated with the red oxide of zinc and other minerals. It consists of peroxide of iron, oxide of zinc, and red oxide of manganese: sp. gr. 4·87.—*Thomson*.

Frax'inin (Lat. *fraxinus* an ash), in chemistry, a neutral principle obtained from the ash tree, which has neither an acid nor alkaline reaction.

Freestone, a species of free-working sandstone or oolite, commonly used in building.

Freezing (Sax. *frysan*), in physics, the mutation of a fluid body into a solid state by the abstraction of heat.—*Freezing point* is that point or degree of cold at which certain fluids begin to freeze, as indicated by Fahrenheit's thermometer, which is 32° above zero for water, and 40° below zero for quicksilver.—*Freezing mixture* is a preparation for congealing water or other fluids. Thus an equal mixture of snow or pounded ice and salt sinks the thermometer to 30°; equal parts of nitrate of ammonia and water make it sink to 46°; and muriate of lime 3 parts, and snow or ice 2 parts, sink it to 80°, or, from the freezing point to 48° below zero. Freezing mixtures are also made by the rapid solution of salts, without the use of snow or ice.

Fresco (Ital. *shadiness*), in the arts, a method of painting on fresh plaster by which the colours sink in and become durable.

Fret, or **Fretto** (Swed. *frata*), in music, that stop of a musical instrument which causes or regulates the vibrations of the strings.—In architecture, a kind of knot of two small fillets interlaced;—*Fret-work*, that kind of work which is adorned with frets, and sometimes used to fill up and enrich flat empty spaces, but principally in roofs fretted over with plaster-work.—In heraldry, a bearing composed of six bars crossed and variously interlaced.

Friction (Lat.), in therapeutics, the art of rubbing any part of the surface of the body with the hand or brush, or with oil or ointment.—In mechanics, the act of rubbing the surface of one body against that of another;—*Friction rollers* are small cylinders fixed between the axis on which a pulley turns, and the pulley itself, the hollow axis of the latter being made larger in order to receive them;—*Friction balls*, a mechanical contrivance for moving heavy weights round a centre, as in cutting a block of marble.

Frieze (Fr.), in architecture, a large flat member, which separates the architrave from the cornice.—In the Doric order, the frieze is always ornamented with triglyphs and sculptures.—In the Corinthian and Composite orders the frieze is variously decorated, according to the taste or skill of the architect.

Fringillidæ (Lat.), in ornithology, a family of the Conirostres (the Finches), of which the Fringilla, or Chaffinch, is the type. This family includes the Linnets, Sparrows, Bullfinches, Goldfinches, Buntings, Larks, &c.;—*Fringillinæ*, is a sub-family of the Fringillidæ, comprehending the Ground-finches;—*Fringillaceous*, pertaining to the Finches.

Frond (Lat. *frons* a leaf), in botany, a green, leafy branch; the leaf of a fern or palm. The herbaceous parts of flowerless plants are called *fronds*. —In surgery, a bandage chiefly employed in wounds and diseases of the nose and chin, or in fracture of the jaw. — *Frondescence* is the precise month and season of the year when each species unfolds its leaves.— *Frondiparous*, in botany, is an epithet applied to the fruits which

produce leaves from their upper part.

Frons (Lat.), in zoology, the region of the cranium between the orbits and the vertex.

Frontal (Lat.), in anatomy, a term applied to parts connected with the anterior region or frontal part of the head; as, *arteria frontalis* (frontal artery), an artery which forms a branch of the ophthalmia; *bosses frontales*, two eminences, one situated on each side of the external surface of the frontal bone; *cresta frontalis*, a crest situated at the interior extremity of the frontal groove; *musculus frontalis*, a muscle in the anterior hollow of the occipito-frontalis; *os frontalis*, the bone situated at the anterior part of the cranium; *sutura frontalis*, the suture which divides the os frontalis in the fœtus.—*Craig*.

Frost (Sax.), in physics, the temperature of air which occasions the congelation of water, when the thermometer sinks to or below 32° Fahrenheit. (See *Freezing*.)

Fructescence (Lat. *fructus* fruit), the precise time when the fruit of a plant arrives at maturity.—*Fructification* is the act of fructifying, which consists of the following parts, viz.: the calyx, corolla, stamen, pistil, pericarp, seed, and receptacle.

Fruit (Lat. *fructus*), in botany, a term properly applied to the ovarium of a fruit plant when it has attained maturity; generally speaking, *fruit* is whatever the earth produces for the nourishment of animals; the product of a tree or plant in which the seeds are contained, or which is taken for food.

Frustum (Lat.), in geometry, the part of a solid body next to the base, left by cutting off the top by a plane parallel to the base.—The *frustum of a cone* is the part cut off from a cone, which does not contain the vertex;—*Frustum of a pyramid*, that part which remains after the top is cut off by a line parallel to the base; —*Frustum of a globe or sphere* is any part of it which is cut off by a plane.

Fucaceae (Lat. *fucus* paint), in botany, a nat. order of Algæ (the Seawracks), of which Fucus is the genus. They are generally inhabitants of the ocean.—*Fuceæ* are a sub-order of the Fucaceæ, in which the frond is polysiphonous, and often bladdery. —*Fucoid*, resembling sea-weed.

Fugata (Ital.), in music, compositions written in the style of fugues.

Fugue (Ital. *flying*), in music, a composition in which the different parts follow and repeat each other.

Fulcrum (Lat. a *prop*), in botany, the support of a plant ; a stipula.—In mechanics, the support or prop on which a lever rests.

Ful'gora (Lat. *fulgor* brightness), in entomology, a genus of Moth Cicadas (the Lantern-fly), which emit light in the dark ; fam. Flatidæ.

Ful'gurite (Lat. *fulgor*), in meteorology, a tube of vitrified sand, supposed to be formed by a stroke of lightning on a sandy plain, &c. ; a term used to designate any mineral with marks of fusion, supposed to be from the action of lightning, as implied by the word.

Fuliguli'næ (Lat. *fuligo* blackness), in ornithology, a sub-family of the Anatidæ (the Sea-ducks), distinguished from the River-ducks by the broadness of the hinder toe.

Fuller's Earth, in mineralogy, a species of marl, having the property of absorbing grease.

Fulmin'ic Acid, in chemistry, an acid produced by the action of nitric acid on alcohol in the presence of a salt of silver or mercury, and forming a kind of very explosive salts.

Fumar'amide, a snow-white powder formed by the action of aqua ammoniæ on fumarate of oxide of ethule.

Fumaria'ceæ (Lat. *fumus* smoke), in botany, a nat. order of thalamifloral Exogens (the Fumeworts of Lindley), consisting of herbaceous plants, of which the Fumaria is the type and genus.

Fu'marolles (Fr. from Lat. *fumus* smoke), in volcanic districts, those crevices in the earth from which steam and boiling fluids are emitted.

Fungi (Lat. *fungus* a mushroom), in botany, an extensive nat. order of cellular and flowerless plants propagated in brown spores. That part in which the reproductive organs are placed is called the *hymenium* ; the hollow base from which the stipe or stem arises is called the *volva*, or *wrapper* ; the upper part is the *cap*, or *pileus*, the inferior radiating surface of which is called the *gills*, or *laminæ*.

Fungic'olæ (Lat. *fungus*, and *colo* to inhabit), in entomology, a family of coleopterous insects.

Fungus (Lat.), in surgical pathology, a spongy excrescence or soft cancer, being an unnatural and morbid growth. —*Fungoid*, like a fungus.—*Fungous*, consisting of or representing mushrooms.

Fu'nicle (Lat. *funiculus* a little rope),

in botany, a stalk which attaches the seed to the placenta.

Funis (Lat. *a rope*), in anatomy, the umbilical cord, or navel string.

Furfur (Lat. *bran*), in pathology, disease of the skin, in which the cuticle falls off in small scales like bran or meal.

Furibon'do (Ital.), in music, a word applied to movements intended to be performed with energy.

Furio'so (Ital.), in music, with great energy.

Fur'niture (Fr.), in typography, the materials for keeping the pages bound together, and regulating the proper margin. — In architecture, brass-work of locks, knobs of doors, window shutters, &c.

Furun'cle (Lat.), in pathology, an inflammatory tumour, commonly called a *boil*.

Fusarole' (Ital.), in architecture, a moulding placed under the echinus in the Doric, Ionic, and Composite capitals.

Fuse, in mining and blasting, a short metal tube charged with an explosive composition, and having a slow match attached, for firing a blast-charge or bomb-shell.—In military science, a tube fixed in the bore of a shell for exploding.

Fusees (Fr.), in horology, a cylinder, or part of a watch round which the chain winds.—In gunnery, that part of a bomb or grenade which makes it take fire.

Fusel Oil (Germ. *fusel*), in chemistry, a deleterious component of alcohol, used in the manufacture of fruit essences. — *Fuselol* is an oil of potato spirit, which is colourless, and possesses a strong and nauseous odour.

Fusi'næ (Lat. *fusus* a spindle), in malacology, a sub-family of Mollusca (the Spindle-shells), of which Fusus is the type and genus ; fam. Turbinellidæ.

Fusing Point, in metallurgy, the degree of heat at which liquefaction takes place.

Fusion (Lat.), in metallurgy, the degree of heat at which a solid substance melts. Of the common metals the degrees of heat are—tin, 442° ; bismuth, 497° ; lead, 612° ; zinc, 773° ; silver, 1173° ; copper, 1996° ; gold, 2016° ; cast-iron, 2786°.

Fustic, a wood of the tree *Morus tinctoria*, used in dyeing yellow ; chiefly brought from the West Indies.

Futtocks, in navigation, the timbers of a ship between the floor timbers and the top ones. — *Futtock shrouds*, small shrouds.

G.

Ga'bio, in mineralogy, the aggregate of saussurite and diallage.

Ga'bion (Fr.), in fortification, a large wicker basket filled with earth, to shelter the men from the enemy's fire.—*Gabionnade* is a bulwark of gabions.

Ga'bionite, in mineralogy, a foliated scapolite, of a greyish-green colour, found in Norway, consisting of alumina, magnesia, potash and soda, protoxide of iron and manganese, and water: sp. gr. 3·0.

Gad'idæ (Lat. *gadus*), in ichthyology, a family of malacopterygious fishes (the Cod-fishes), of which the Gadus is the type and genus.

Gadol'inite (from *M. Gadolin*, the discoverer), a rare hard mineral, of an iron-black colour, composed of yttria, glucina, protoxide of cerium, protoxide of iron, and silica; sp. gr. 4·2.

Gahnite, in mineralogy, a greenish hard metal.

Gaiement (Fr. *gaie* lively), in music, a word denoting that the movement to which it is prefixed is to be performed in a lively, cheerful style.

Galac'tia, or **Galactirrhœ'a** (Gr. *galaktos*, from *gala* milk, and *rheo* to flow), a morbid overflowing of milk.

Galac'tic Circle, in astronomy, the circle at right angles to the diameter, forming the galactic pole.—The *Galactic Poles* are the opposite points of the celestial sphere, round which the stars are most scattered.

Galac'tine (Gr. *of milk*), in chemistry, a milky and waxy substance.

Galac'tite (Gr.), in mineralogy, a whitish fossil substance.

Galactoden'dron (Gr.), in botany, the Milk tree, or Cow tree.

Galac'togogues (Gr.), medicines which promote the secretion and flow of milk from the breast.

Galactom'eter (Gr. *gala* milk, and *metron* a measure), an instrument to ascertain the quality of milk; a lactometer.

Galactopo'sia (Gr.), the method by which diseases are attempted to be cured by milk.—From *galaktos*, of milk, we have *Galactopyra*, milk fever;—*Galactosis*, secretion of milk;—*Galacturia*, discharge of a milk-like fluid by the urinary passages.

Gal'axy (Gr. *galaxias*), in astronomy, the milky way; a luminous tract or zone, seen in the evening encompassing the heavens.

Gale'na (Lat.), in mineralogy, a native sulphuret of lead.

Gall (Sax. *gealla*), in physiology and animal economy, the bile, which is a bitter, yellowish-green fluid secreted in the liver.—*Gall-stone* is a calcareous concretion, or calculus, formed in the gall-bladder.—*Gall-bladder* is a small membranous sac, which receives the bile from the liver. —*Gall-ducts*, in anatomy, the ducts or canals which convey the bile from the liver —*Gall-nuts* are powerfully astringent, and used in dyeing and ink-making.

Gallate (from *gall*), in chemistry, a neutral salt formed from the union of gallic acid with a base.

Gal'lery (Fr.), in fortification, a covered walk across a ditch in a besieged town, made of strong planks, and covered with earth.—In architecture, a long, narrow room, the width of which is at least three times less than its length, by which proportion it is distinguished from a saloon.—In mining, a narrow passage or branch of a mine carried on underground to a work designed to be blown up.

Gallic (from *gall*), derived from galls, or oak-apples.—*Gallic acid* is an acid obtained in fine white needles from gall-nuts moistened, bruised, and exposed for four or five weeks to a temperature of about 80°.

Gallic'olæ (Lat. *galla* a gall-nut, and *colo* to inhabit), in entomology, a family of hymenopterous insects, whose larvæ inhabit gall-nuts.

Gallina'ceæ, or **Galli'næ** (Lat. *gallus* a cock), in ornithology, an order of birds, of which the domestic Cock (*Gallus*) is the type, including Fowls, Pheasants, Grouse, &c.

Gallinsec'ta, a family of hemipterous insects—Gall-insects.

Gal'loper, in gunnery, a carriage that bears a gun of a pound-and-a-half ball.

Gallotan'nic Acid (Lat. *galla* gall, and *tannin* astringent), the pure tannin of nut-galls, employed for chemical purposes.

Galt. (See *Gault*.)

Gal'vanism (from *Galvani*, the discoverer), in physical science, that branch of electricity in which electrical phenomena are exhibited without the aid of friction, and a chemical action takes place from the contact of certain metallic and other bodies.—A *galvanic battery* consists of any arrangement of galvanic circles, made so as to produce an effect greater than a simple circle could occasion.—*Galvanometer*, an instrument constructed for the purpose of detecting the presence of feeble electro-chemical currents.—*Galvanoscope*, an apparatus for ascertaining the direction in which the pole of a magnetic needle is moved by a galvanic current.—*Galvanized iron*, iron tinned by a peculiar patent process, by which it is rendered less liable to oxidation from moisture. —*Galvano-plastic*, same as electro-metallurgic.

Gamboge, a vegetable gum resin used in the arts as a bright yellow pigment, especially in miniature and water-colour paintings. It is also used in medicine as an emetic and purgative hydrogogue.

Gammari'na (Gr. *gammaron* a lobster), in entomology, a family of amphipodous Crustaceans (the Sandhoppers), of which the genus Gammarus is the type.—*Gammarolite* is a fossil lobster or crab.

Gamut (Gr. *gamma*), in music, a scale on which musical notes are disposed in their several orders.

Gan'glion (Gr.), in anatomy, an enlargement in the course of a nerve —a small mass of nervous matter resembling a knot; a tumour in the sheath of a tendon.—In surgical pathology, a hard, indolent, globular swelling, situated in the course of an extensor tendon, and formed by viscid albuminous fluid, generally contained in a cyst.

Gangrene (Fr.), in pathology, mortification of living flesh, or of some portion of a living animal;—*Gangrenous*, intimating mortification.

Ganocoph'ala (Gr. *bright-headed*), in geology, an order of fossil reptiles, with polished horny plates covering the head.

Ganoi'dians (Gr. *ganos* splendour, and *eidos* appearance), in ichthyology and fossilology, an order of fishes which have angular scales composed of bony or horny plates, covered with a thick plate of enamel. This order contains about sixty genera, most of which are extinct.

Garbe (Sax. *garba*), in heraldry, a sheaf of any kind of grain, borne in several coats of arms.

Gar'ganine, an extract of madder, prepared in France by means of sulphuric acid.

Garnet (Ital. *granato*), a crystallized mineral of a reddish colour, of which there are many species. The precious garnet is found in dodecahedrons, in mica slate, amongst the oldest or primary rocks in many parts of the world. It is harder than quartz, and

consists of nearly equal parts of silex, alumina, and oxide of iron, with traces of manganese. Common garnets are more opaque, of a duller colour, and less hard than the precious garnet, though harder than quartz.

Garrot (Fr.), in surgery, a small cylinder of wood, employed to tighten the circular band by which the artery of a limb is compressed, for the purpose of suspending the blood in hæmorrhage from amputation or otherwise.

Garruli'næ (Lat. *garrulus* chattering), in ornithology, the Jays, a sub-family of the Corvidæ, or Crows, of which the Garrulus is the type.

Garrya'ceæ (from *Nich. Garry*), in botany, a nat. order of declinous Exogens, consisting of shrubs without stipules, of which the Garrya is the type.

Gas, *pl.* **Gases** (Fr.), in chemistry, an aëriform fluid; a term applied to all permanently elastic fluids or airs differing from atmospheric air; a body, the constituent particles of which have so expanded by heat as to become aëriform. Of the different gases, four of them are simple substances—oxygen, hydrogen, nitrogen, and chlorine. The rest are more or less compound; as carbonic acid gas is a compound of oxygen and carbon. The gases which are inflammable are hydrogen and all its compounds, carbonous oxide, and cyanogen. Those which more or less support combustion are oxygen, protoxide of nitrogen, chlorine, and its oxides. Some gases emit an odour which is insupportable, and often characteristic. In Graham's "Elements of Chemistry" the following analyses of gases are given, which exhibit the distinctive properties of oxygen, nitrogen, protoxide of nitrogen, deutoxide of nitrogen, hydrogen, carbonic oxide, and carbonic acid:—

Gases soluble in water.—Carbonic acid: solution disturbs lime-water;—Protoxide of nitrogen: does not disturb water.

Gases which support combustion. —Oxygen;—Protoxide of nitrogen. —Carbonic oxide: product of combustion disturbs lime-water;—Hydrogen: does not disturb water.

Gases which extinguish combustion.—Deutoxide of nitrogen: forms brown fumes with oxygen;—Nitrogen: does not.

Gas is applied in a variety of ways, and the word forms a compound allied to numerous words connected with science and art.—*Portable* or *coal gas*, after its manufacture, is compressed by a condensing or force-pump into strong vessels prepared to receive it. These vessels being portable, the gas may thus be used where required, at any distance from the gas-works.—*Gas apparatus* consists of the furnaces, retorts, pipes, valves, purifying machine, lime machine, gasometers, gas meters, governors, &c., used in the manufacture, the purifying, and the supply of gases, particularly of coal gas.—*Gas-burner* is the jet or contrivance fixed to the end of a gas-pipe for the purpose of separating and diffusing the flame. — The *Gas hydraulic main* is the large pipe or tube into which the tubes leading from the various retorts are fixed, and which conveys the gas to the tar vessel or cistern in which it is cooled and purified from any undecomposed tar.— *Gas main* consists of the principal pipes which conduct the gas from the gas-works to the places where it is to be consumed.—*Gas-light* is the light afforded by the combustion of carburetted hydrogen gas, as procured by the distillation of coal, oil, tar, &c.; it is therefore called *coal gas, oil gas,* &c. — *Gas-meter,* a simple but ingenious mechanical contrivance, the design of which is to measure and record the quantity of gas passing through a pipe in any given time.— *Gas-works.* The manufactory at which coal gas is made for public purposes, together with the whole machinery and apparatus, is included under this term.

Gas'alier, a gas-burner for containing several lights; answering the same purpose as a *chandelier* for candles.

Gas'elier, an apparatus for making aërated waters.

Gasom'etry (*gas,* and Gr. *metron* a measure), the art and science of measuring gas.—*Gasometer* is a reservoir in gas-works, into which the purified gas is received; also an instrument for measuring gas;—sometimes termed a *gas-meter.*

Gas'oscope (*gas,* and Gr. *skopeo* to view), an apparatus for indicating the presence of carburetted or hydrogen gas in mines, buildings, &c.

Gasteromyce'tes (Gr. *gaster* the belly, and *mykos* a mushroom), in botany, an order or tribe of Fungi, in which the hymenium is closed in a pericardium.

Gasterop'oda, or **Gas'teropods** (Gr. *gaster,* and *podes* feet), in zoology, the third class of Mollusca, that crawl upon a fleshy disc situated under the belly, which serves them as feet. The Limax, or Slug, is an example of the class. The Gasteropods are divided by Cuvier into nine orders, viz.: the Pulmonea, the Nudibranchiata, the Inferobranchiata, the Tectibranchiata, the Heteropoda, the Pectinibranchiata, the Tubulibranchiata, the Scutibranchiata, and the Cyclobranchiata.

Gastric (Gr. *gaster* the belly), in physiology, an epithet applying to the stomach or belly.—*Gastric juice* is the thin pellucid liquid which for the dilution of food) distils from certain glands in the stomach.

Gaster, or *gastro,* in medical science, is a prefix much used in the composition of terms connected with that important organ of the animal economy, the *stomach,* or the region of the belly—as shown by the following list :—*Gastrocele,* hernia in the stomach; *gastro-cephalitis,* co-existent inflammation of the stomach and the substance or membranes of the brain; *gastro-cholecystitis,* inflammation of the stomach and gall-bladder; *gastro-colic,* an epithet applied to designate organs and blood-vessels which are alike connected with, and distributed upon, the stomach and colon; *gastro-colititis,* inflammation of the large intestine; *gastro-cystitis,* inflammation of the stomach and urinary bladder; *gastro-dermitis,* inflammation of the stomach and skin; *gastro-duodenalis,* pertaining to vessels which belong to, or are distributed over, the stomach and duodenum; *gastro-duodentitis,* co-existent inflammation of the stomach and duodenum; *gastro-dynia,* pain in the stomach, same as *gasteralgia; gastro-encephalitis,* inflammation of the stomach and the brain; *gastro-enteritis,* simultaneous inflammation of the stomach and small intestines; *gastro-piploric,* pertaining alike to the stomach and omentum; *gastro-epiploitis,* simultaneous inflammation of the stomach and omentum; *gastro-hypatic,* belonging to, or connected with, the stomach and the liver; *gastro-hepatitis,* simultaneous inflammation of the stomach and the liver; *gastro-hysterotomia,* the abdominal Cæsarian operation; *gastro-inflammatory,* an epithet applied to a combination of inflammatory and gastric fever; *gastro-intestinal,* applied to diseases simultaneously implicating the stomach and intestines; *gastro-metritis,* complicated inflammation of the stomach and womb; *gastro-mucosus,* applied to fevers in which gastric irritation is complicated with inordinate secretion of mucus; *gastro-nephritis*, a complication of gastritis with nephritis; *gastro-œsophagitis*, simultaneous inflammation of the stomach and gullet; *gastro-pericarditis*, inflammation of the stomach and pericardium; *gastro-peritoneum*, inflammation of the stomach and peritoneum; *gastro-pharyngitis*, inflammation of the stomach and pharynx; *gastro-pleuritis*, a complication of gastritis with pleurisy; *gastro-pneumonia*, a complication of gastritis and pneumonia; *gastro-pyloric*, belonging to the pyloric artery; *gastro-splenic*, pertaining to the stomach and spleen; *gastro-splenitis*, gastric irritation with painful tumefaction of the spleen; *gastro-adynamic*, applied to a fever in which the gastric are complicated with adynamic symptoms; *gastro-ataxic*, applied to a fever in which the gastric are complicated with the ataxic symptoms; *gastro-arachnoiditis*, co-existent inflammation of the stomach and the arachnoid membrane of the brain; *gastro-bronchitis*, inflammation of the stomach and bronchia.—*Craig.*

Gastril'oquist (Gr. *gaster*, and Lat. *loquor* to speak), one who speaks from his belly or stomach, or who so modifies his voice as to appear to come from another person;—a ventriloquist

Gastri'tis (Gr.), inflammation of the intestines, or more especially the stomach.

Gastror'aphy (Gr. *gaster*, and *rapto* to sew), in surgery, the sewing up of wounds of the abdomen.

Gastrorrha'gia (Gr. *gaster*, and *regnymi* to burst out), gastric hæmorrhage; exudation of blood from the internal surface of the stomach.

Gastrot'omy (Gr. *gaster*, and *tome* incision), in surgery, the operation of cutting open the belly; an incision of the stomach for extracting some foreign body introduced into it through the œsophagus; also an incision of the abdominal parietes for the purpose of extracting a fœtus.

Gauge (Fr.), a standard of measure; a term of frequent application in the arts and sciences; as, *gauge-of-way* is the width between the rails on a railway; the broad gauge being 7 feet, and the narrow gauge 4 feet 7½ inches. — *Gauge-cock*, a cock commonly attached to steam-boilers, for the purpose of ascertaining the height of water in them.—*Pressure-gauge*, an instrument to determine the pressure exerted in hydrostatic or pneumatic machines,

as the hydrostatic press, the air-pump, steam-engine, &c. — *Gauge-point*, in gauging, the diameter of a cylinder, whose altitude is 1 inch, and its contents equal to those of a given measure.—*Rain-gauge*, an instrument for measuring the quantity of water which falls from the clouds at any given place.—*Sea-gauge*, an instrument for finding the depth of the sea.—*Gauge-point of a solid* is used to denote the diameter of that circle, or the diagonal of that square, whose area is expressed by the same number as is equal to the number of cubic inches in the solid.—*Siphon-gauge*, a name given to any gauge which is made in the form of a siphon, that is, with two legs bent upon each other, such as that of the steam-gauge, the condenser-gauge, &c.—Among letter-founders, *gauge* is a piece of hard wood variously notched, used to adjust the dimensions, slopes, &c., of the various sorts of letters.

Gauging, in practical science, the art of measuring the capacities of vessels of any shape or form. — The *gauging rod*, or *gauging rule*, is adopted for the purpose of measuring the contents of any vessel. The latter is a kind of sliding rule about 12 inches long, particularly adapted for the purposes of gauging: it has four faces or sides, which are furnished with sliding pieces running in grooves. The lines upon them are mostly logarithmic ones, or distances which are proportional to the logarithms of the numbers placed at the head. — *Gauger* is an officer whose business it is to measure and ascertain the contents of vessels or casks, generally for revenue purposes.

Gault, in geology, a stiff marl or black clay; an intermediate deposit, which divides the upper from the lower members of the greensand formation, and contains numerous organic remains.

Gaylussite (from *Gay-Lussac*, the French chemist), a white crystallized mineral disseminated in clay, and consisting of carbonic acid, soda, lime, water, and alumina: sp. gr. 1·92; H = 2·0—3·0.

Gazon (Fr.), in fortification, a turf or piece of earth covered with grass, for lining the faces of parapets.

Geat (Dutch), in metallurgy, the orifice through which the metal runs into the mould.

Geckot'idæ (from *gecko*, the Indian name), a family of platydactile or broad-toed Saurians, the Geckos, divided by Cuvier into eight sub-genera.

Gel'atine (Ital.), an animal substance of the consistence of jelly, obtained by boiling with water the soft and solid parts, as the muscles, cartilages, bones, tendons, &c. The coarser forms of gelatine, obtained from hoofs, hides, &c., are called *glue*; that from the skin and finer membranes, *size*; and when obtained from air-bladders and other membranes of fish, *isinglass*.

Gelatino'si, the name of the gelatinous Polypi, whose bodies are gelatinous, and more or less conical.

Gem (Lat. *gemma*), in mineralogy, a precious stone cut by the lapidary, and used for ornamental purposes. The principal gems are the diamond, ruby, emerald, amethyst, onyx, calcedony, jasper, rock crystal, topaz, cornelian, and blood-stones. These are the natural or real gems; but there are others of an inferior character artificially produced; and these are called *artificial gems*, which are usually made of a very fusible, transparent, and dense glass or paste, containing a large proportion of oxide of lead, the colours being given by a skilful admixture of the metallic oxides. — In botany, *gems* are the leaf-buds, or frondous germination of a plant, to distinguish it from flower-buds.

Gemina'tion (Lat. *doubling*), in botany, a term applied to the parts or organs of plants which are disposed in pairs from the same point.

Gem'ini (Lat.), in astronomy, the twins, Castor and Pollux; the third sign in the zodiac, into which the sun enters on the 21st of May.

Gemmæ (Lat.), in botany, leaf-buds, as distinguished from the flower-buds.

Gemmip'ares (Lat. *gemma* a bud, and *pario* to bring forth), animals which propagate as vegetables by buds, as the fresh-water Polypi.

Gen'erant (Lat. *producing*), in physics, the power or principle that produces; thus, a circle which revolves rapidly on any diameter generates a sphere; a line moved steadily along forms a surface; the circle and line are therefore generants. — In mathematics, a line is generated by a point, a solid by a surface, and so on. In the fluxional analysis, all kinds of quantities are supposed to be generated by the motion of other quantities.

Genera'tion (Lat.), in geometry, *generation*, or *genesis*, is the production of a geometrical figure or quantity. — In physiology, it is the collective name of all those vital operations engaged in the production of an organized being. In the Mammifera, it comprehends conception, pregnancy, parturition, and lactation.

Genera'tor (Lat.), in music, the principal sound or sounds by which others are produced.

Gener'ic (Lat. *genus* a kind), in natural history, pertaining to a genus; distinguishing a genus from a species.

Genesiol'ogy (Gr. *genesis* first production, and *logos* a discourse), in physiology, a treatise on the origin and first production of animals.

Gen'esis (Gr. *generation*), in geometry, the formation of a line, plane, or solid by the motion or flux of another. —*Genetic*, pertaining to the origin of a thing, or its mode of production.

Ge'nia (Gr. *geneion* the chin), in anatomy, a word used in the composition of terms to indicate the muscles, &c., connected with the chin.

Gen'itals (Lat.), in physiology, the sexual organs.—In botany, the stamens and styles of generation.

Gen'ouillère (Fr.), in fortification, that part of the parapet of a battery which remains above the platform, and under the gun, after the opening of the embrasure has been made.

Gentiana'ceæ (Lat.), in botany, a nat. order of corollifloral herbaceous Exogens, of which the Gentian, a pretty flowering plant, is the type and genus.—*Gentianin* is the bitter principle of gentian.

Genus, *pl.* **Gen'era** (Lat.), in natural history, a distinct class of beings, or group of animals or plants, which exhibit a certain degree of analogy, and are each connected by peculiarities of structure. Each genus is subdivided into different species or varieties; and whenever any natural object cannot be referred to a known species, it is made to constitute a genus. All species connected with the genus have the same name preceding the specific or distinguishing term; as, *Equus caballus*, the horse; *Equus asinus*, the ass.—In music, the general name for any scale, as the *diatonic genus* and *chromatic genus*.

Geocen'tric (Gr. *ge* the earth, and *kentron* a centre), in astronomy, having the earth for a centre; but the planets moving round the sun as a centre are not geocentric; yet we speak of their geocentric places, latitudes, longitudes, &c., meaning thereby as they appear when viewed from the earth's centre.

Geoc'ronite (Gr.), a mineral containing lead, sulphur, antimony, arsenic, &c.

Geocy'clic (Gr. *ge*, and *kyklos* a circle), encircling the earth periodically.

Geode (Gr.), earthstone; a nodule of ironstone with internal cavities.

Geode'sia, or **Geod'esy** (Gr. *ge*, and *daio* to divide), the division or geometry of the earth; land-surveying.

Geog'nosy (Gr. *ge*, and *gnosis* knowledge), a knowledge of the substances that compose the earth or its crust.

Geog'ony (Gr. *ge*, and *gone* birth), the doctrine of the formation of the earth; geology.

Geog'raphy (Gr. *ge*, and *graphe* description), a description of the earth, according to the divisions of its surface, natural or artificial, together with its productions and inhabitants; a book containing a description of the earth.

Geol'ogy (Gr. *ge*, and *logos* a discourse), that part of natural philosophy which treats of the formation and structure of the earth beneath its surface, and the changes it has undergone. Geology is the history of the primeval conditions of our planet, as illustrated in the monuments of change which exhibit themselves on and beneath the surface of the earth. It is, in fact, the great history of Nature, which classifies, by means of existing monuments, the various rocks and strata of the earth's crust, according to their comparative ages, and treats of the different races of animals and plants which characterise the mundane formations or systems deposited by water during the lapse of countless ages. Geologists have reduced the grand divisions, in which the aqueous systems have been classed, into a perfectly intelligible form, of which the annexed is a summary—commencing with the unstratified rocks, the primary formations of the great globe itself:—1. PRIMARY FORMATIONS, consisting of schists of various kinds, limestones, graywacke, mica slate, gneiss, &c.; a few organic remains in the newest beds only. Igneous rocks of many sorts, such as granite, porphyry, greenstone, basalt, and traps of various kinds, produced at different eras, occur in each system;—2. The *Silurian System*, the upper and lower consisting of sandstones (often micaceous), limestones (abounding in the oldest types of organic life), and slates;—3. The *Devonian* or *Old Red Sandstone System*, consisting of sandstones (often red), cornstones, and shales, with extinct fishes, &c.;—4. *Carboniferous System*, consisting of the coal formation, carboniferous or mountain limestone—organic remains—all extinct. —5. SECONDARY FORMATIONS, consist-

ing of the chalk, greensand, oolite, lias, new red sandstone, with their subordinate beds, all abounding in organic remains, chiefly marine—all extinct. — 6. TERTIARY or SUPRA-CRETACEOUS FORMATIONS, composed chiefly of clays, sands, gravels, and limestones, containing a mixture of extinct and recent animal remains, and distinguished by the presence of those of numerous Mammalia, extinct and recent;—7. Recent deposits of clay, sand, gravel, limestones, &c., from existing rivers, lakes, &c., formed during the historical era, and sometimes containing the remains of man or of his works.

Geom'etry (Gr. *ge*, and *metron* a measure), the science which treats of and explains the properties of figured space, and the proportions, properties, and measurement of lines and surfaces.—In architecture, *Geometrical elevation* is a design for any part of a building drawn according to the rules of geometry, as opposed to the *perspective* or *natural* elevation.—*Geometrical staircase* is a term applied to a staircase when the stairs are supported only by being inserted in the wall at one end, with a continued range of balusters at the other. —In arithmetic, *Geometrical progression* is when a series of numbers are in geometrical proportion, and have a common ratio or multiplier; thus, multiply 1 by 2, and the number produced by 2 again, and the second result by 2, the numbers resulting will consequently be in geometrical progression. The series will, of course, be 1, 2, 4, 8, 16, 32.

Geon'omy (Gr. *ge*, and *nomos* law), the science of physical laws.

Geopon'ics (Gr. *ge*, and *ponos* labour), the science or art of cultivating the earth; agriculture, or rural economy.

Geora'ma (Gr. *ge*, and *orao* to see), a hollow sphere which interiorly exhibits a complete geographical view of the earth's surface.

Geos'copy (Gr. *ge*, and *skopeo* to view), a knowledge of the nature and qualities of soil gained by viewing it.

Geosele'nic (Gr.), relating to the earth and moon.

Geothermom'eter (Gr. *ge*, and *therma* warmth), an instrument for measuring the warmth of the earth, or ascertaining the degree of heat contained in the earth at different places, especially in artesian wells, mines, &c.

German Silver, in metallurgy, an alloy or mixture of copper, zinc, and other metal.—*German steel*, a metal made of pig or white plate iron, in forges where charcoal is used for fuel.

Ger'minal Membrane, in physiology, the membrane formed of cells, which immediately surrounds the ovum or egg after segmentation.

Gesneria'ceæ (from *Gesner*, of Zurich), in botany, a nat. order of corollifloral Exogens, consisting of herbs or shrubs, of which Gesneria is the type and genus.

Geysers (Icel. *roaring*), certain fountains in Iceland, doubtless of volcanic origin, which spout forth boiling water. The jet of the great geyser is said to have been observed to rise 550 feet. One of the small geysers was observed by Mr. Henderson, in 1815, to project a stone to the height of 200 feet.

Giant's Causeway, in geology, a remarkable basaltic formation in the northern coast of the county of Antrim.

Gibbon, in zoology, the long-armed ape, and a general name given to all the species of the Hylobates. The largest of the group is black, and an inhabitant of Sumatra.

Gibbous (Lat. *gibbosus*), in astronomy, an epithet applied to the enlightened portion of the moon when more than half-full, when the dark part appears falcated, or horned, and the light part convex.—In botany, the term is applied to leaves, petals, &c., when irregularly swelled on one side, or both, as the corolla of the Foxglove. —In natural history, *gibbosus* forms a prefix to the various compounds signifying *bunch-like*; as, *gibbiflorus*, having gibbous flowers; *gibbipennis*, having the elytra swelled out, oval, and globular; *gibbirostris*, having a beak or snout of a protuberant shape; *gibbifolius*, having the leaves of a boss-like form.

Gibbsite, a white-greenish mineral found in Massachusetts, which occurs in stalactitial masses, and consists of alumina, water, silica, and peroxide of iron: sp. gr. 2'4.

Gie'seckite (from *Sir C. Giesecke*, its discoverer), a brownish crystallized mineral found in Greenland, consisting of silica, alumina, magnesia, protoxide of iron, protoxide of manganese, potash, and volatile matter: sp. gr. 2'83.

Gil'bertite (from *Davies Gilbert*), a laminated whitish mineral, composed of plates lying irregularly on each other; constituents, silica, alumina, lime, magnesia, protoxide of iron, and water: sp. gr. 2'64.

Gilliesia'ceæ (from *Dr. Gillies*), a nat. order of liliaceous plants, of which Gilliesia is the genus.

Gills (Swed. *gæl*), the apertures for breathing in fishes, consisting of cartilaginous or bony arches attached to the bones of the head. The water has admission by the opening of the gills, and acts upon the blood as it circulates in the fibrils.

Gimbals, or **Gimbols** (Lat. *gemellus* a pair), in navigation, brass rings used in suspending the mariner's compass, by means of which the card is kept in a horizontal position, notwithstanding the motion of the vessel.

Gim'bleting, in navigation, a term denoting the turning of an anchor round by the stock, so that the motion resembles the turning of a gimblet.

Gin (Fr.), in mechanical science, a term applied to different machines for raising heavy weights, driving piles, cleaning cotton, &c.—*Ginning* is the operation by which the seeds of cotton are separated from the filaments by means of the apparatus called a *cotton gin*.

Girth, the circumference of a body. In measuring a tree, the term is used as the fourth part of the circumference, on account of the use made of it. The square of the fourth part is considered, in this case, as equal to the area of the section of the tree; which square, therefore, multiplied by the length of the tree, gives the solid contents.

Gismon'dine (in honour of the mineralogist *Gismondi*), a mineral occurring at Capo de Bove, near Rome, in white translucent crystals, consisting of silica, alumina, lime, magnesia, oxide of iron, and oxide of manganese: sp. gr. 2'16.

Giusto (Ital.), in music, a term signifying that the movement before which it is written is to be performed in a steady, equal, and just time.— *Busby*.

Gla'cier, *pl.* **Gla'ciers** (Fr. from Lat. *glacies* ice), in physiology, a term applied to a vast accumulation of ice and snow, found in the valleys and slopes of lofty mountains; the Alpine glaciers occupying a space of 1,484 square miles, and the vertical thickness ranging from 100 to 600 feet.— *Glacialist*, an adherent to the glacial theory of geologists.

Glacis (Fr.), in fortification, a sloping bank of earth, extending from the parapet of a counterscarp to the level country.

Gland (Lat. *glans*, *glandis* an acorn), in anatomy, an organ of the body in which secretion is carried on, and which consists of a congeries of blood-vessels, nerves, and absorbents. — *Glands* are divided into three principal classes:—1. The *absorbent glands*, which form a part of the absorbent system;—2. The *servent glands*, whose office is to separate the various secretory and excretory fluids of the blood;—3. *Vascular glands*, consisting of a congeries of arteries and veins, but without any opening internally.—*Glans penis* is the vascular body which forms the apex of the penis.—In botany, a gland is any superficial callosity.—*Lenticular glands* are brown oval spots observed on the bark of many plants, especially willows, indicating points from which the roots will appear, if the branch be placed in circumstances favourable for their production.

Glanders, in farriery, a distemper of the glands in horses, in which corrupt matter runs from the nose.

Glass (Sax. *glaes*), in the arts, a transparent, impermeable, brittle substance, formed by fusing sand with fixed alkalies; that which is made of glass.—*Glass-house* is a manufactory in which silex or flint dust and fixed alkalies are subjected in furnaces to such an amount of heat as to render them fluid, which, when cold, constitute glass.—*Glasses*, spectacles.

Glau'berite, a crystallized mineral which occurs in rock salt, consisting of sulphate of soda and sulphate of lime: sp. gr. 2·80; H = 2·5.

Glauber Salt (from *John Glauber*, a German chemist), in chemistry, a native sulphate of soda, a substance which occurs as a mineral body in a state of efflorescence, the primary form of the crystal being an oblique prism. It is found in the salt mines of Germany, Switzerland, and France: sp. gr. 1·47.

Glau'colite (Gr. *blue stone*), in mineralogy, a silicate of alumina and lime of a greenish-blue colour, consisting of silica, alumina, lime, potash, soda, and magnesia: sp. gr. 2·7—3·2.

Glauco'ma (Gr.), in pathology, a disease of the eyes, giving a bluish-green colour to the vitreous humour.

Glau'conite (Gr. *glaukos* sea-green), in geology, an argillaceous marl, sometimes containing a mixture of greensand.

Glaucop'inæ (Gr. *blue-eyed*), in ornithology, a sub-family of the Corvidæ (the Wattle Crows), of which the Glaucopis is the type.

Glaucus (Gr. *sea-green*), a genus of nudibranchiate Mollusca, which constitutes the type of a family, the Glaucidæ, which are marine, gelatinous, and elongated.

Glazing, in painting, a term applied to transparent or semi-transparent colours passed thinly over other colours to modify their effect.

Gleichenia'ceæ, in botany, a tribe of Ferns, of which the Gleichenia is the type; order Polypodiaceæ.

Glenoid (Gr. *glene* a hollow, and *eidos* resemblance), in anatomy, the name of a bone or part having a shallow cavity, as the socket of the shoulder joint.

Gliding, in music, a term applied by flute-players to the action of sliding the finger from off the hole it has been employed in stopping, by which the ear is imperceptibly led to the succeeding note.—*Busby*.

Globe (Lat. *globus*), a spherical solid body; the terraqueous ball; the earth, or world; an artificial sphere made of metal, plaster, paper, &c., on the surface of which a map of the earth, or of the celestial constellations, is delineated, the one being called the *terrestrial*, the other the *celestial* globe.—*Globular projection* is a kind of map in which the eye is supposed to be distant from the globe, represented in whole or in part by onehalf of the chord of an arc of 90°. —In navigation, *globular sailing* is the sailing from one place to another over the arc of a great circle, or the shortest distance between two places.

Globule (Lat. *globulus* a little globe), a small particle of matter of a spherical form.—In physiology, the small microscopic particles of blood which float in a transparent serum.

Glob'uline, in botany, a green globule lying among the cells of cellular tissue, first pointed out by Turpin, a French phytotomist. The term is also applied to an albuminous compound existing with hæmatosine in the globules of the blood.

Glossan'thrax (Gr. *glossa* the tongue, and *anthrax* a carbuncle), a form of anthrax, or blain, to which horses and cattle are subject, characterized by the development of malignant carbuncle in the mouth, and especially on the tongue.

Glossi'tis (Gr.), in pathology, inflammation of the tongue.

Glos'socele (Gr.), protrusion of the tongue.

Glosso-epiglot'tic (Gr. *glossa* and *epiglottis*), an epithet applied to the muscles which pass from the tongue to the epiglottis.

Glossog'raphy, **Glossol'ogy** (Gr.), in anatomy, a description of, or discourse on, the tongue.

Glot'talite, a whitish vitreous mineral, discovered in the trap formation near Port Glasgow, consisting of silica, lime, alumina, peroxide of iron, and water : sp. gr. 2·18.

Glucic Acid, an acid obtained from the solution of grape sugar saturated with baryta and lime.

Glucí'na, or **Glucine** (Gr. *glykys* sweet), a white earth or powder found in the beryl and emerald.

Glucin'ium, **Gluci'num**, or **Gly'cium**, the metallic base of glucina.

Glue (Lat. *gluten*), a cement made by boiling some animal substance to a jelly.

Glu'males, in botany, an extensive class of endogenous plants, given by Lindley to his Glumal alliance. It comprises the orders Graminaceæ, Cyperaceæ, Desvauxiaceæ, Restiaceæ, and Eriocaulaceæ.

Glume (Lat. *gluma*), in botany, one of the bracts of grasses ; the calyx and corolla of corn and grasses ; the husk or chaff of grain.

Gluten (Lat.), a viscid elastic substance found in wheat and other grains.

Glu'teus (Gr. *gloutos* the buttocks), in anatomy, the name of certain large muscles on which we sit ; hence we have the term *gluteal* applied to the posterior iliac artery, to the lymphatics, which have the same distribution as that artery, and to a nerve distributed to the gluteal muscles.

Glyc'erine (Gr.), a sweet substance extracted from fatty materials.

Glyph (Gr. *glypho* to carve), in architecture, a vertically-sunken channel ; a channel in a Doric frieze.

Glyph'ograph (Gr. *glypho*, and *graphe* writing), an engraved plate formed in relief by the electrotype process. —*Glyphographer* is an engraver or worker in glyphography.

Glyphog'raphy, or **Galvan'oglyphy** (Gr. *glypho*), in the arts, a process for producing engravings in relief at a much less cost than wood engravings, and with all the convenience of printing with letter-press. A drawing is etched on a zinc plate coated with varnish, as in the ordinary process of etching. Several coats of ink are spread over the plate by a small composition roller, which are only deposited on those parts where the varnish has not been cut through by the graver. When the incisions are thus rendered deep enough, the plate is placed in connection with a galvanic battery, and another plate is formed from the deposition of sulphate of copper, or blue vitriol, in which the hollows of the engraving are produced in relief. —*Supp. to Craig's Dicty.*

Glyptics (Gr.), the art of engraving figures on precious stones.

Glyp'todon (Gr. *glypho*, and *odontes* teeth), an extinct gigantic quadruped, belonging to the family of Armadilloes.

Glyptog'raphy (Gr. *glypho*, and *graphe* description), a description of the art of engraving upon gems.

Glyptothe'ca (Gr. *glypho*, and *theke* a deposit), a building or room for the preservation of works of sculpture.

Gmel'inite, a reddish-white mineral (the Hydrolite), consisting of soda, silica, alumina, lime, and water : sp. gr. 2·1.

Gnathi'tis (Gr.), inflammation of the lower jaw or cheek.

Gneiss (Germ.), in geology, a stratified primary rock, composed of the same materials as granite ; a species of granite of lamellar or slaty texture.

Gneta'ceæ, in botany, a nat. order of Gymnogens (Joint Firs), consisting of small trees or shrubs.

Gnomiomet'rical (Gr. *gnomon* an index, and *metron* a measure), in optics, measuring the angles of crystals, strata, &c., by reflection.

Gnomon (Gr. *an index*), the hand, style, or pin of a dial ; an apparatus for ascertaining astronomical altitudes.—*Gnomon of a globe*, the index of the hour circle.

Gnomon'ics (Gr.), the art of constructing dials to show the hour of the day by the shadow of a gnomon.—*Gnomonology* is a treatise on dialling

Go'bidæ (Lat.), a family of malacopterygious fishes, of which the Gobius, or Gudgeon, is the type.—*Gobianæ* is a sub-family or division of the Gobies.

Godfrey's Cordial, in pharmacy, a kind of soothing syrup, composed of sassafras, caraway, coriander, and anise seeds infused in water, with tincture of opium and treacle added.

Godroon (Fr.), in architecture, an inverted fluting, bending, or cabling, used in various ornaments and members.

Go'ethite, a German mineral of a brownish colour. Its constituents are peroxide of iron, oxide of manganese, and water.

Goggles (Welsh *gogeln*), in surgery, optical instruments for curing squinting. They are short conical tubes, with a thin plate of ivory fixed in tubes near their anterior extremities. Through the centre of each of these plates is a small circular hole for the transmission of the rays of light.—*Goggles* are also blinds for horses that are apt to take fright.

Goître (Fr.), a tumour on the throat ; the bronchocele.

Gold (Sax.), a precious metal, of a bright yellow colour and of the sp. gr.

19·3; it is the most valuable and the most ductile of all the metals, and is used by all civilized nations as a standard of value. It occurs in regular veins in primary rocks; but the greatest quantity is obtained from alluvial soils, and in beds and sands of rivers. It is so malleable that it may be beaten into a leaf 280,000th of an inch in thickness, and so ductile that a single grain may be drawn into 500 feet of wire. Gold unites with most other metals, and with sulphur, ammonia, &c. It fuses at 2016°. Its equivalent is 199·2; symbol, Au.—*Standard gold* is an alloy of 11 parts of pure gold and 1 of copper; its sp. gr. is 17·157. 1 lb. troy produces 46·71 sovereigns.—*Gold amalgam* is a yellowish-white mineral, a mixture of gold and quicksilver; chiefly found in California.—*Gold-beating* is a process by which the gold is brought to a state of extremely thin leaves, much used in the arts, and in various kinds of gilding. — *Goldbeaters' skin* is an extremely fine membrane between which goldbeaters lay the leaves of their metal while they beat it.—*Gold fields* are the auriferous deposits and diggings in Australia, California, and other localities.—*Gold foil* is thin sheets of gold, used by dentists and others. — *Gold size*, a glue of a golden colour, a thin tenacious varnish used by gilders.

Golden, made or consisting of gold; a term applied to anything of acknowledged value; as, *Golden number*, in chronology, is the number reckoned from 1 to 19, showing what year in the lunar cycle any given year is.—*Golden rule*, in arithmetic, the rule of three, so called from its great utility in arithmetical science. — *Golden pheasant* is one of the most magnificent birds seen in our aviaries. It is the *Phasianus picus* of Linnæus.

Goniom'etry (Gr. *gonia* an angle, and *metron* a measure), in mechanical science, the art or method of measuring angles.—*Goniometer* is an instrument used in measuring them, particularly those formed by the facets of mineral crystals. It consists of a brass circle graduated on the edge, and furnished with a vernier, by which the divisions may be read to a minute.

Gon'ocele (Gr. *gone* semen, and *kele* hernia), in pathology, a tumefaction of the spermatic cord.

Gonorrhœ'a (Gr. *gone*, and *rheo* to flow), in pathology, a morbid running of venereal taint.

Gorge (Fr.), in fortification, the entrance of a bastion, or other outwork, consisting of the distance or space between the extremities of the two faces, as between the faces of a half-moon, redoubt, or bastion.—In architecture, a cavetto or concave moulding, the narrowest part of the Tuscan and Doric capitals, between the astragal, above the shaft of the pillar, and the annulets.

Gorget (Fr. *gorgette*), in surgery, an instrument used in the operation of lithotomy.

Gossan, in mining, a term applied to the oxide of iron and quartz, an ochreous mineral substance, which frequently occurs in mineral lodes at shallow depths.

Gossyp'ium (Gr. from Arab. *goz* a soft substance), in botany, a most important genus of plants (the Cotton tree), from the capsules of which is produced the down used in the manufacture of cotton yarns and cloths.

Gothic Architecture, a style in which pointed arches of greater height than breadth, and a profusion of ornaments, in imitation of leaves and flowers, are the principal characteristics. It began to flourish during the middle ages, and is still continued in our ecclesiastical architecture.

Goulard, in pharmacy, an extract of sugar of lead, used for inflammations.

Gov'ernor, in mechanical science, a contrivance for maintaining uniform velocity with varying resistance.

Gowan, in geology decomposed granite.

Gowt, or **Go'ut**, in engineering, a sluice used in embankments for letting out water.

Grace Note, in music, any note added as an ornamental flourish.

Graddo (It.), in music, a word applied to the notes moving by conjoint intervals.

Gra'dient (Lat. *gradus* a step, descent), the proportionate ascent or descent of the several planes on a railroad; thus, an inclined plane 2 miles in length, with a total fall of 18 feet, is described as having a *gradient* of 9 feet per mile.

Grad'uate (Ital. *graduare* to step forward), in literature and the arts, one who has received a degree in a college or university, or from some professional incorporated society.—*Graduation*, regular progression; act of graduating.

Gradua'tor (Lat. *gradus*), in physics, a contrivance for accelerating spontaneous evaporation; also an instrument for dividing any right line or curve into equal portions.

Gradua'tion, in astronomy, the division of circular arcs into degrees, minutes, &c.

Grafting (Fr. *greffe*), in the science of horticulture, the art or process of inserting the scion of one tree into the stock of another, so as to make it produce fruit of the same kind and quality as that of the tree from which the graft was taken.

Graining, in painting, the art of imitating the grain and colours of woods and marbles by means of either oil or water colours.

Grains of Paradise, the seeds of a species of Amomum, spice, or pepper.

Grakles, in ornithology a name applied to the sub-family Lamprotortinæ; ram. Corvidæ.

Grallato'res, or **Grallæ** (Lat. *gralla* stilts), in ornithology, the fourth order of birds, the Waders. The families of this order are the *Ardeadæ*, or Herons; the *Charadriadæ*, or Plovers; the *Scolopacidæ*, or Sandpipers and Snipes; the *Rallidæ*, or Rails; and the *Tantalidæ*, or Ibices. It comprises all such species as live both on the land and the sea, and to which the one element is as essential as the other.

Gramin'eæ (Lat. *gramen* grass), in botany, an order of Endogens (the Grasses), consisting of evergreen herbs, with narrow and undivided leaves.

Graminiv'orous (Lat. *gramen*, and *voro* to devour), an epithet applied to those animals which subsist entirely on vegetable food, while those which live on flesh alone are called *carnivorous*. In natural history, the following words occur, as designating species : — *Graminous*, grass-like; *graminicolus*, growing among dry stubble, or in corn-fields; *graminifolius*, having grass-like leaves; *graminiform*, resembling grass.

Grammar (Gr. *gramma*, a letter), the art of speaking and writing a language correctly; the science which has for its object the laws regulating human language; the elementary parts of learning, or of any science. Grammar is divided into four parts, Orthography, Etymology, Syntax, and Prosody.

Gram'matite, in mineralogy, a variety of hornblende, found in the primary rocks.

Gramme (Fr.), a French weight equal to 15·444 grains.

Grampus, a fierce and voracious Cetacean, the *Delphinus orca*, which sometimes attains the length of 25 feet.

Gran'atite (Lat. *granum* a grain), a precious stone, a reddish-brown mineral, occurring in primary rocks in many parts of Scotland and America, consisting of alumina, silica, oxide of iron, oxide of manganese, and lime.

Gran Gusto (Ital.), in painting, a term expressive of something very extraordinary in a picture, and calculated to surprise.—In music, an expression applied to any high-wrought composition.—With *grandis* (grand), the following compounds occur in natural history to designate species :— *Grandiflorus*, large-flowered; *grandifolius*, large-leaved; *grandidentatus*, furnished with large teeth.

Granite (Fr. from Lat. *granum* a grain), in mineralogy, a hard and durable rock or stone; a crystalline aggregate of quartz, felspar, and mica. Granite is a plutonic rock that seems to have been consolidated from a state of fusion at a considerable depth beneath the surface of the earth, and to have been denuded and raised to the surface during the lapse of time, so as now to form the summits of lofty mountains. Granite is said to be *porphyritic* when large crystals of felspar are disseminated through the mass; *sienitic*, when hornblende supplies the place of mica; *chloritic*, when chlorite supplies the place of mica, &c.—*Granitic aggregate* is a granular compound, consisting of two or more simple minerals, among which only *one* of the essential ingredients of granite is present. Among the granitic aggregates may be enumerated combinations of quartz and hornblende, —quartz and actinolite, — felspar and schorl,—mica and hornblende, —quartz, hornblende, and garnet, —quartz, hornblende, and epidote, &c.—*Granitine* is an aggregate of three mineral constituents, one or more differing from those which compose granite.—*Graphic granite* is a variety of granite composed of felspar and quartz, so arranged as to produce an imperfect laminar structure. When a section of graphic granite is made at right angles to the alternations of the constituent minerals, broken lines, resembling Hebrew characters, present themselves; hence its derivation.

Graniv'oræ (Lat. *grain-eaters*), an order of Insessorial birds which feed on grains.

Gran'ular Limestone, in mineralogy, a variety of limestone, consisting of small grains or minute crystals. It is of different colours; and the white variety is used as statuary marble.

Granula'tion (Lat.), in pathology, firm, rounded, or ovoid, glistening, semi-transparent tumours, resembling in figure and volume a millet-seed or pea.—In chemistry, an operation by which metallic substances are reduced into small grains for the purpose of facilitating their combination with other substances.

Granu'liform, in mineralogy, having an irregular granular structure.

Gran'ulite (Lat. *granum*, and Gr. *lithos* a stone), in mineralogy, a rock consisting of felspar and quartz.

Graphic Mi'croscope, an instrument for the purpose of depicting, on the principle of reflection, the objects represented by the microscope.

Graphic Tellu'rium, or **Graphic Gold**, a mineral of a steel-grey colour, approaching to tin-white. Its constituents are tellurium, gold, and silver.

Graphiol'ogy, (Gr. *grapho* to write, and *logos* a discourse), a treatise on written characters.

Graphite (Gr. *grapho*), a form of mineral carbon; the substance of which pencils are made.

Graph'olite (Gr.), a species of slate proper for writing on.

Graphom'eter (Gr.), a surveying instrument; a graduated semicircle. Its use is to observe any angle, the vertex of which is at the centre of the instrument in any plane, and to find how many degrees it contains.

Grap'tolite (Gr. *graptos* painted, and *lithos* a stone), a genus of fossil Zoophytes or Protozoa.

Graptol'ithus (Gr.), a stone having the appearance of drawings, maps, ruins, &c.

Grass. (See *Graminea*.)

Gravel, in medicine, a disease occasioned by the concretion of calculi in the kidneys and bladder.—In mineralogy, small stones, generally deposited on the beds of rivers or the seashore, from the consolidation of which, in former periods, the conglomerates of the various formations take place.

Gravim'eter (Lat. *gravitas* gravity, and *metor* to measure), an instrument for ascertaining the specific gravity of bodies.

Gravita'tion (Lat.), the act of tending to the centre; the mutual tendency which all bodies in nature have to approach each other. (See *Gravity*.)

Grav'ity.—*Specific gravity* is the weight of the matter of any body, compared with the weight of an equal bulk of pure water, taken as a standard. Thus, if a body when immersed in fluid loses just as much of its weight as is equal to the weight of a given volume of the fluid, and the weight lost in water be made the divisor of the weight in air, the quotient gives the specific gravity. The instrument used is called the *hydrostatic balance*. One cubic foot of rain-water weighs exactly 1,000 ozs. avoirdupois; hence the relative weight of other bodies is easily referred to this standard; and hence gold, when hammered, weighs 19·362, which is its specific gravity.—*Centre of gravity* is that point at which all the weight of a mass might be collected without disturbing the equilibrium of any system of which the mass forms a part. When a body is suspended by a string, and allowed to find its position of rest, the centre of gravity is in the line of the string.

Graystone. (See *Greystone*.)

Graywacke (Germ. *grey stone*), in mineralogy, a term applied to some of the lowest secondary strata; a kind of arenaceous rock.

Grazio'so (Ital.), in music, with elegance and grace.

Great Sixth, in music, a term applied to the chord of the fifth and sixth, when the fifth is perfect, and the sixth major.—*Busby*.

Greek Fire, an artificial fire which burnt under water, and was formerly used in war, especially between the Christians and the Saracens. It was either poured from the ramparts in large boilers, or launched in red-hot balls of stone and iron, or darted in arrows and javelins twisted round with flax and tow saturated with it; sometimes it was blown through long tubes of copper placed on the prow of a galley or fireship. The old French writer Joinville says:—"It sometimes came flying through the air like a winged long-tailed dragon, about the thickness of a hogshead, with a report of thunder, and the velocity of lightning, dispelling the darkness of the night by its deadly illumination."

Green, a term which forms a prefix to many important words connected with science and art.—*Green earth* is a variety of chloritic earth which occurs in the vesicular cavities of some amygdaloids: it constitutes the *mountain green* of painters.—*Brunswick green* is made by saturating cold water with muriated ammonia, and adding three times as much copper clippings as ammonia. The muriate of ammonia is decomposed by the copper, which is itself corroded and converted into a green oxide.—*Green vitriol*, the sulphate of iron, consisting of 1 atom of the protoxide of iron, and 1 atom of sulphuric acid. The crystals contain 7 atoms of water.—*Sheele's green* is an arseniate of copper. — *Mineral green* is a subcarbonate of copper.

Green'obite, a mineral of a deep rose-red colour, consisting of silica, oxide of titanium, lime, and protoxide of manganese: sp. gr. 3·44.

Green'ockite (in honour of *Lord Greenock*), a hard, crystallized mineral, a native sulphate of cadmium, consisting of sulphur 22·56, and cadmium 77·30: sp. gr. 4·84.

Greensand, in geology, arenaceous beds of the tertiary formation of the cretaceous system, so termed from its abounding with small grains of chlorite.

Greenstone, in mineralogy, a variety of trap; an igneous rock in which felspar is combined with augite or hornblende. It sometimes occurs of great extent and thickness.

Grego'rian Chant is choral music according to eight church modes arranged by Pope Gregory I.

Grego'rian Tel'escope, a reflecting telescope invented by Professor Gregory, of St. Andrew's.

Grenade, in military science, a hollow globe or ball of iron filled with gunpowder for explosion.

Gren'atite, a mineral; the Staurolite.

Gressu'ra (Lat. *gradior* to proceed), in anatomy, the perinæum, which proceeds from the anus to the pudendum.

Greystone, in geology, a term applied to certain volcanic rocks, composed of felspar, augite, or iron and hornblende.

Groin (Goth. *grein*), in architecture, the line formed by the intersection of two arches which cross each other at any angle.—*Groined ceiling* is a ceiling formed by three or more curved surfaces, so that every two may make a groin, all the groins terminating at one extremity in a common point.—In engineering, *groin* is a wooden breakwater to retain sand or mud thrown up by the tide.

Grossula'ceæ (Lat.), in botany, a nat. order of exogenous plants, of which the Grossularia, or Gooseberry, is the type; it consists of only one genus, Ribes.

Grossula'ria (Lat.), in mineralogy, a green garnet.—In botany, a species of gooseberry.—*Grossularite*, a species of green-coloured garnet, consisting of silica, alumina, lime, oxide of iron, and oxide of manganese: sp. gr. 3·37.

Gros'suline, a peculiar principle obtained from gooseberries and other fruits.

Ground, in the fine arts, a word of varied application.—In painting, it is the first layer of colour on which the figures or other objects are painted. —In sculpture, it is the surface from which, *in relievo*, the figures rise.— In architecture, it is used to denote the face of the scenery or country round a building. — *Ground plan*, the plan of the story of a house level with the surface of the ground, or a few steps above it. — *Ground plates* are the outermost pieces of timber which lie near the ground.

Gryphæ'a (Lat. *gryps* a griffin), in fossilology, a genus of shells of the Oyster family.

Gryphite, in conchology, a fossil bivalve shell.

Grypho'sis (Gr. *grypos* incurved), in physiology, a growing inwards of the nails.

Guérite (Fr.), in fortification, a small tower for holding a sentinel.

Guilloche (Fr.), in architecture, an ornament in the form of two or more bands twisting over each other, so as to repeat the same figure, in a continued series, by the spiral returning of the bands.

Guinea, an English denomination of money, of the value of 21*s.*, first coined of gold brought from *Guinea;* now disused; but the word is of frequent occurrence in botany and zoology. — *Guinea-corn*, a vegetable growing on the coast of Africa.—*Guinea-deer*, a small quadruped.—*Guinea-fowl*, a fowl from the coast of Guinea.—*Guinea-grass*, a valuable plant or grass.—*Guinea-hen*, a domestic African fowl.— *Guinea-pepper*, the seeds of Amomum, from Africa.—*Guinea-pig*, a small Brazilian animal.—*Guinea-wheat*, the plant *Zea mays.*—*Guinea-worm*, the *Filaria Medinensis* of Gmelin—a worm which proves a considerable pest in warm countries, by insinuating itself under the skin.

Guitar (Span.), a stringed musical instrument much used in Spain and Italy.

Gules (Fr.), in heraldry, *red*, represented in engravings by straight perpendicular lines.

Gum (Lat.), a concrete vegetable substance, soluble in water, which exudes from certain trees, and hardens on the surface. There is a great variety of gums, which are of vast utility in the different branches of art and science.—The principal of them are here enumerated in alphabetical order:—*Gum ammoniacum*, the produce of the Persian tree *Dorema ammoniacum;*—*Gum animé*, the resinous produce of the West Indian tree *Hymenæa courbaril;*—*Gum ara-*

bic, the concrete juice which exudes from several species of Acacia;—*Gum copal*, the resinous produce of the Mexican tree *Elaphrium excelsum*;—*Gum cistus*, a secretion of several species of plants of the genus Cistus;—*Gum elastic* (see *Caoutchouc*);—*Gum-elemi tree*, a tall tree, full of resinous fragrant juice;—*Gum galbanum*, the produce of the Syrian plant *Galbanum officinale*;—*Gum juniper*, a concreted resin which exudes in white tears from the *Juniperus communis*;—*Gum lac*, the resinous produce of the East Indian tree *Butea frondosa*; also the resinous produce of an insect which deposits its eggs on the branches of a tree called *bihar*;—*Gum of starch*, the soluble substance of fecula;—*Gum resin*, the concrete juice of certain plants, partly soluble in water and partly in alcohol, consisting of aloes, asafœtida, bdellium, galbanum, gamboge, guaiac, myrrh, olibanum, opoponax, sacacolla, scammony, and styrax;—*Gum senegal*, the produce of the tree *Acacia Senegal*;—*Gum tragacanth*, the produce of the plant *Astragalus tragacantha*; —*Gum tree* is the popular name of the Black Gum, of the genus Nyssa, one of the largest trees of the Southern States of America;—*Gum-water* is a distillation from gum, especially from gum arabic.

Gumma (Lat.), in pathology, a soft tumour resembling *gum*.

Gun (Welsh *gwn*), in military science, a general term for all species of fire-arms, as muskets, rifles, carbines, ordnances, &c., the principal of which are the *Muzzle-loading* and *Breech-loading guns*, the latter comprehending the *Needle Gun* (which see). —*Gunpowder* is a mixture of 5 parts of nitre, 1 of sulphur, and 5 of charcoal, finely powdered and very accurately blended.—*Gun-cotton* is a preparation of cotton by steeping it in nitric or nitro-sulphuric acid, and afterwards washing it, by which it acquires the explosive properties of gunpowder.—*Gun-barrel*, the metallic tube of a gun.—*Gun-boat*, a boat for carrying cannon.—*Gun-lock*, the lock of a gun.—*Gun-metal*, an alloy of copper and tin.

Gunter's Chain, in surveying, a chain for measuring land, so called from Gunter, the inventor; its length is 66 feet, and it is divided into 100 links, of 7·92 inches each.—*Gunter's line* is a logarithmic line engraved on scales, sectors, &c.—*Gunter's quadrant* is an astronomical instrument for finding the hour of the day,

&c.—*Gunter's scale* is a scale having various lines and angles engraved on it, and used for resolving questions in navigation.

Gusto'so (Ital. *tastefully*), in music, a term signifying that the movement before which it is written is to be performed in a finished style.

Gutta, *pl.* **Guttæ** (Lat. *a drop*), a term applied to medical prescriptions, written gt. or *pl.* gtt.; as, *gutta anodyna*, the anodyne drop, a solution of acetate of morphia; *gutta myra*, the black or Lancashire drop.—In pathology, *gutta opaca* is cataract;—*Gutta serena*, amaurosis;—*Gutta rosacea*, rosy drop.—In architecture, *Guttæ* are small ornaments resembling drops, used in the Doric entablature on the under side of the mutules of the cornice, and beneath the tænia of the architrave under the triglyphs.

Gutt'ifer (Lat. *gutta*), a plant yielding gum or resin.

Guttifera'ceæ (Lat. *gutta*, and *fero* to bear), a nat. order of exogenous plants which yield resinous juices.

Gut'tural (Lat. *guttur* the throat), in music, an epithet given to that tone and style of intonation which the Italians call "singing in the throat."

Gymna'sium (Gr. *gymnos* naked), formerly, a place for athletic exercises; at present, any place of exercise.— *Gymnastics* is the science of performing gymnastic exercises; the gymnastic art.

Gymnodon'tes (Gr. *gymnos*, and *odontes* teeth), in ichthyology, the name of a family of malacopterygious fishes, of the order Plectognathes.

Gymno'tus (Gr. *gymnos*, and *notos* the back), a genus of apodal fishes, with eel-shaped bodies, of which the Electricus has the remarkable property of communicating an electric shock to the person touching it; fam. Sternarchidæ.

Gynan'dria (Gr. *gyne* a female, and *andres* men), a class of plants (the twentieth class of Linnæus) which have their stamens and pistils consolidated into a single body.

Gypsum (Gr. *gypsos*), native sulphate of lime, commonly known as plaster of Paris, extensively used in the plastic arts. It occurs in the new red sandstone of England and Germany, and in the tertiary rocks of the neighbourhood of Paris, &c. It consists of 1 atom of sulphuric acid, 1 of lime, and 2 of water: sp. gr. 2·32.

Gyra'tion (Lat. *a whirling round*).— *Circle of gyration* is the circle described by the centre of gyration around an axis or a point of suspension (*Brande*). — *Centre of gyration* is a point at any such distance from the axis, that the moment of inertia would not be altered.

if the whole mass were collected at that point.

Gy'roscope (Gr. *gyros*, and *skopeo* to view), an instrument to illustrate the principles of circular motion.

H.

Haar'kies (Germ.), in mineralogy, a native sulphuret of nickel; capillary pyrites in very delicate acicular crystals.

Hab'itat (Lat. *habito* to inhabit), in zoology and physiology, the natural locality or abode of an animal or plant.

Hack'berry, in botany, the popular name of the *Celtis occidentalis*, an ornamental tree of N. America, the wood of which is hard and close-grained.

Hack'ia, in botany, a hard and valuable kind of wood, growing in Demerara, and known as *Lignum vitæ*.

Hæma-, Hæmo-, (Gr. *haima* blood), in physiology, a prefix to many compound words connected with or signifying *blood*; as, *Hæmadynamometer*, an instrument for measuring the force of the flow of blood in the arterial vessels; —*Hæmapophysis*, a term applied to the parts projecting from a vertebra; —*Hæmastatics*, that department of physiology which treats of the laws that regulate the movements of the blood in the vessels of the animal system;—*Hæmatemesis*, the vomiting of blood from the stomach;—*Hæmatine*, or *Hæmatosine*, the colouring matter of the blood;—*Hæmatocele*, an effusion of blood into the scrotum;— *Hæmatocrya*, a term applied to cold-blooded vertebrated animals;—*Hæmatoid*, of the nature or appearance of blood;—*Hæmatosis*, hæmorrhage or flux of blood;—*Hæmatotherma*, warm-blooded vertebrated animals; —*Hæmoptysis*, disease of spitting blood;—*Hæmostatic*, arresting the flow of blood.

Hæmal (Gr.), in anatomy, relating to blood; an epithet applied to the arch proceeding from a vertebra which encloses and protects the organs of circulation.

Hæ'matite (Gr. *haima*), in mineralogy, native oxide of iron.

Hæmatol'ogy (Gr.), a treatise on the nature and properties of blood.

Hæmatom'phalum (Gr. *haima*, and *omphalos* the navel), in pathology, hernia of the navel, with a bloody serum contained in the sac, or exhibiting on its surface many varicose veins.

Hæmatosco'pia (Gr. *blood-inspection*), an examination of the qualities of the blood when drawn from a vein.

Hæmatox'yline (Gr.), the colouring matter of the wood of the *Hæmatoxylon Campeachianum*, or logwood, a well-known dye-stuff.

Hæmatu'ria (Gr. *haima*, and *ourion* urine), in pathology, the voiding of bloody urine.

Hæmodora'ceæ (Gr. *haima* blood, from its red-coloured roots), a nat. order of plants, allied to the Narcissus tribe, of which Hæmodorum is the genus.

Hæmop'tysis (Gr. *haima*, and *ptyo* to spit), in pathology, the spitting or coughing up of blood, produced sometimes by an over-fulness of blood in vessels of the lungs, or by rupture in consequence of ulceration.

Haidin'gerite, in mineralogy, an arseniate of lime, white and transparent, with a vitreous lustre: sp. gr. 2·84.

Hair, in botany, long expansions of the cuticle, intended to protect the surface of a plant.—*Hair-grass* is the common name of the grass Aira, of which there are numerous species.— *Hair-salt*, in mineralogy, is the native sulphate of magnesia.

Half-moon, in fortification, an outwork composed of two faces forming a salient angle, whose gorge is in the form of a crescent or half-moon.

Half-pike, in military and naval matters, a defensive weapon, so called from its being shorter than the ordinary pike.

Haliot'idæ (Gr. *als* the sea, and *otis* of the ear), a family of the gasteropodous Mollusca, of which the Haliotis, or Ear-shell, is the type.

Hal'itus (Lat. *a breathing*), the odour or vapours which escape from blood.

Hal'leylite, a mineral with a waxy lustre, whose constituents are silica, alumina, and water.

Halo, a luminous circle sometimes appearing round the heavenly bodies, but more especially the sun and moon.

Hal'ogens (Gr. *als* salt, and *gennao* to produce), substances which, by combination with a metal, produce saline compounds, such as chlorine and iodine.

Haloid (Gr. *like salt*), in chemistry, an

epithet applied to a class of chemical combinations composed of two elementary compounds, one or both of which are analogous in composition to sea-salt.

Halora'geæ (Gr. *als* the sea, and *rax* a berry), an order of exogenous plants, the Hippurids.

Hal'teres (Gr.), in entomology, two organs in the Diptera consisting of cylindrical filaments, terminating in a club extremity, one arising from each side of the thorax, in the situation of which the second pair of wings in the Diptera originate.

Hamamelid'eæ, in botany, a nat. order of umbelliferous Exogens, of which the Hamamelis, or Witch-hazel, is the type.

Hand (Sax.), in anatomy, the organ of prehension in man and the mammalia; it consists of—1. the *carpus*, or wrist, which is composed of eight bones, viz. the *scaphoid*, or boat-shaped; the *semilunar*, or half-moon; the *cuneiform*, or wedge-like; the *pisiform*, or pea-like; the *trapezium*, or four-sided; the *trapezoid*, like the former; the *os magnum*, or large bone; the *unciform*, or hook-like.—2. The *metacarpus*, or the four bones constituting the palm and back of the hand.—3. The *digiti*, or fingers, consisting of twelve bones, arranged in three phalanges, or rows.—4. The *pollex*, or thumb, consisting of three bones.

Harbour, in the art or science of glass-blowing, a technical name for a large chest, to hold the mixed ingredients previous to their being put in the pot for fusion.

Hardness, a term of frequent use to express the qualities of particular minerals; and this can be done almost with scientific exactitude. Mineralogists have formed a scale which affords an approximation in estimating the hardness of minerals; and according to this, the degree of hardness is expressed in numbers, from the softness of Talc (1), to the hardness of Diamond (10); thus:— 1, Talc, white or greenish; 2, rock-salt, pure and cleavable; and gypsum, uncrystallized and semitranslucent; 3, calcareous spar, cleavable; 4, fluor-spar, which cleaves perfectly; 5, apatite, the asparagus stone from Salzburg; 6, adularia; 7, rock-crystal, limpid and transparent; 8, topaz; 9, corundum, with smooth fractured faces; 10, diamond. Any mineral which neither scratches nor is scratched by any one of the substances above named is stated to possess the degree of hardness expressed by the number opposite that mineral. Thus, supposing a body neither to scratch nor to be scratched by fluor-spar, its hardness is represented by 4; but if it should scratch fluor-spar, and not apatite, then its hardness is stated to be from 4 to 5.

Har'maline, a peculiar substance discovered in the seeds of the plant *Peganum harmula*. It may be used as a yellow dye, and by oxidation be made to yield a magnificent red dye-stuff. Formula, $C_{24}H_{13}N_2O$.

Harmo'nia, in astronomy, the name of one of the newly-discovered planets, first observed in 1856.—In anatomy, a form of articulation in which the surfaces of bones are merely placed in opposition to each other, so as not to allow motion.

Harmon'icon, a peculiar form of musical glasses invented by Dr. Franklin, whence the notes are obtained by striking with a cork on pieces of glass, which differ in size, and are loosely suspended, so as to admit of vibrating sounds.

Harmon'ics, the doctrine or science of musical sounds.—*Harmonic proportion* is a series of quantities in which any three adjoining terms being taken, the difference between the first and second is to the difference between the second and third as the first is to the third.—*Harmonic triad* is the chord of a note, consisting of a third and perfect fifth.

Harmon'iphon (Gr.), a musical instrument played with keys like a pianoforte.

Harmonom'eter (Gr.), an instrument for measuring the harmonic relations of sounds.

Har'mony, in music, the just adaptation of parts to each other, according to musical sounds; melody.

Har'motone (Gr. *harmos* a joint, and *temno* to divide), a white mineral, the Staurolite, or Cross-stone, the crystals of which intersect each other. The constituents are silica, alumina, lime, protoxide of iron, and water: sp. gr. 2·40; H = 4·25.

Harpal'idæ (Gr. *harpaleos* greedy), in entomology, an extensive family of coleopterous insects, of which the Harpalus is the type.

Hartall, orpiment, an oxide of arsenic, used as a yellow paint.

Hartshorn, in pharmacy, the horn of the common stag, which obtains a place in the pharmacopœia because it contains less earthy matter and more gelatine than other bones;— *Spirit of hartshorn*, a volatile spirit, obtained by the distillation of the horn of the hart (see *Ammonia*);—

Red hartshorn, Lavender drops, Spiritus lavendulæ compositus;—*Salt of hartshorn*, a solid carbonate of ammonia.

Harvest Moon, the lunation in the season of harvest, which occurs about the time of the autumnal equinox.

Hat'chetine, (from *Hatchet*, the eminent chemist), a bituminous mineral or mountain-tallow, found at Merthyr Tydvil, in S. Wales.

Hatching, the maturing of fecundated eggs by natural or artificial heat, so as to produce the young birds.—In drawing and engraving, *hatching* is the making of lines with a pen, pencil, or graver, the intersecting of such lines with others is termed *cross* or *counter-hatching.* —In heraldry, *hatching* is much used to denote the several colours of a shield.

Hau'rient (Lat. *haurio* to drink), in heraldry, an epithet applied to fishes when represented in a perpendicular position, as if sucking in the air.

Haus'manite (Germ.), a manganesian mineral found in the Hartz, which occurs massive and granular; its constituents are red oxide of manganese, oxygen, water, baryta, and silica: sp. gr. 4·8; H = 5·0—5·5.

Haustella'ta (Lat. *haustellum* a sucker), in entomology, one of a numerous class of insects which have the oral apparatus adapted for suction.

Haustel'lum, the suctorial organ of the Haustellata.

Hauyne, (from *Hauy*, the distinguished French mineralogist), a blue mineral found in granular or spherical masses. It is harder than quartz, and consists of potash, silica, alumina, lime, oxide of iron, sulphuric acid, and water: sp. gr. 2·68—3·0.

Haver'sian Canals, in anatomy, small longitudinal canals in the substance of bones, so called from the name of Dr. Havers, who first discovered them.

Hawthorn (Sax. *haw* the fruit, and *thorn*), the English name of several species of the genus Cratægus.—*C. oxycanthus* is the well-known hedge-plant of Great Britain; order Pomaceæ.

Hay'denite, a mineral resembling chabasite, discovered by Dr. Hayden.

Hay'essine, in chemistry, the borate of lime, used in the manufacture of glass, and so called from its discoverer, Mr. Hayes.

Hazel (Sax.), the popular name of plants of the genus Corylus.—*C. avellana* produces the common hazel-nut.

Heart (Sax. *heort*), in anatomy, the most important organ of the viscera of mammiferous and other animals. It is the muscle which is the seat of life in the animal system. In man, it is situated in the thorax, on the anterior part of the diaphragm. Internally it is divided into the two ventricles, right and left, which are separated from each other by a fleshy septum, called the *septum cordis.* The cavities adhering to the base are, from their resemblance in form, called the *auricles.* Each ventricle has two orifices—the one auricular, through which the blood enters; the other arterious, through which it passes out. The vessels of the heart are distinguished into common and proper. The common are—the aorta, arising from the left ventricle; the pulmonary artery, from the right ventricle; the four pulmonary veins, which terminate in the left auricle; the two venæ cavæ, which empty themselves into the right auricle. The proper vessels are—the coronary arteries, which arise from the aorta, and are distributed on the heart, and the coronary veins.

Heat (Sax.), in physiology, the sensation caused by a hot body, or the cause of that sensation.—In chemistry, the supposed matter or cause of heat, termed *caloric*, which, if material, is an imponderable subtile fluid, the particles of which repel each other, and are attracted by all other substances, either by direct contact or radiation.—*Animal heat* is the heat consequent on respiration and digestion in the bodies of animals, produced in the system of each by the oxygen of the atmosphere combining with the carbon of the blood, and forming carbonic acid gas.—In mechanics, the term is applied to that degree of heat which is required for iron-work, namely, the blood-red heat, the smallest degree; the flame, or white heat, the second degree; and the sparkling, or welding heat, which is the strongest degree.

Hebe, in astronomy, the name of one of the newly-discovered planets, first observed by Hencke in 1847. Its mean distance from the sun is 231,350,000 miles; and the time of its periodical revolution is 3 years and 284 days.—In natural history, the word *hebe* frequently occurs in the definition of species, and signifies *pubescence ;* as, *hebeanthus*, having pubescent or downy flowers; *hebecarpus*, having downy seeds; *hebecladus*, having downy branches; *hebegynus*, having the ovary pubescent; *hebepetalus*, having downy petals.

Hectare, a French measure, consisting of 10,000 square mètres, or 11960·33 English square yards.

Hectic (Gr. *hexis* habit), in pathology, a form of fever arising from local irritation in a feeble constitution.

Hec'togramme (Fr.), a French weight of 100 grammes = 3·2 ounces troy.

Hec'tolitre (Fr.), a French measure of capacity, containing 100 litres = 22 English imperial gallons.

Hec'tomètre (Fr.), a French linear measure of 100 mètres = 328 English feet.

Hedenber'gite, a species of mineral, of a greenish-black colour, with a shining lustre. Its constituents are—silica, lime, magnesia, and protoxide of iron: sp. gr. 3·154; H = 3·5.

He'dyphane (Gr. *hedys* pleasing, and *phaneo* to appear), a white or greyish mineral, consisting of oxide of lead and lime.

Hel'enine, in mineralogy, a substance obtained in white crystals from the plant *Inula helenium*. Formula, $C_{14}H_{19}O_{12}$.

He'liac, or **Heli'acal** (Gr. *helios*), relating to the sun.—In astronomy, a star is said to rise *heliacally* when, after being in conjunction with the sun, it rises so as to be visible.

Helian'thes (Gr. *helios* the sun, and *anthos* a flower), in botany, a suborder of the Compositæ, of which Helianthus, or Sunflower, is the type.

Helianthoi'da (Gr.), an order of Polypes resembling a sunflower.

Hel'icoid (Gr.), in geometry, a parabolic spiral or curve line.

Helicom'etry (Gr.), in geometry, the art of measuring spiral lines on a plane.

Heliocen'tric (Gr.), in astronomy, relating to the sun's centre.—*Heliocentric longitude* is the angle formed at the sun's centre by the projection of the radius vector of a planet on the ecliptic, with a line drawn from the sun's centre to the first point of Aries.—*Dr. Henry.*

Heliochromy (Gr.), the process by which photographic pictures in their natural colours are obtained.

Heliog'raphy (Gr.), a description of the sun.

Heliom'eter (Gr.), a micrometer for measuring the diameters of the sun, moon, and planets.

He'lioscope (Gr.), a telescope for making observations of the sun without dazzling the eyes.

He'liostat (Gr.), in optics, an instrument used to fix the position of the solar rays.

He'liotrope (Gr.), in mineralogy, a deep green, siliceous mineral, with red spots.—In astronomy, an instrument to reflect light.—In botany, a plant that turns towards the sun; the Turnsole.

Helispher'ic (Gr.), winding spirally round the pole of the sphere; noting the rhumb line in navigation.

Helix, *pl.* **Hel'ices** (Gr.), a spiral line; the smaller scroll or volute in a Corinthian capital.

Helminthachor'ton (Gr. *helmins* a worm, and *chorton* food), in botany, Corsican wormwood, celebrated for its vermifuge properties.

Helmin'thia, Helmin'thagogue (Gr.), a medicine for expelling worms.

Helmin'tholite (Gr.), fossil remains of worms.

Helminthol'ogy (Gr.), the natural history of worms.

Helminthop'yra (Gr.), worm disease.

Helminthos'tachys (Gr.), a brown-yellow flowering plant; order Ophioglossaceæ.

Helop'idæ (Gr. *Helops*, one of the genera), a family of coleopterous insects.

Helo'sis (Gr. *heilio* to turn), an eversion of the eyelids; a spasmodic distortion from convulsion of the muscles of the eye.

Helvin, a crystallized mineral, of which the primary form is a cube. Its constituents are—silica, glucine, alumina, glucina, protoxide of manganese, protoxide of iron, and sulphuret of manganese: sp. gr. 0·166; H = 6·0—6·5.

He'matherms (Gr. *haima* blood, and *therme* heat), a name given to animals possessed of warm blood.

Hem'atine (Gr.), the colouring principle of logwood.

Hem'atite (Gr.), the blood-stone; a kind of ironstone; a native oxide of iron.

Hematol'ogy (Gr.), science of the blood.

Hemato'sine (Gr.), one of the proximate principles of the blood.

Hemeralo'pia (Gr. *hemera* a day, and *ops* the eye), in pathology, a disease which prevents distinct vision in broad daylight.

Hemerapa'thia (Gr. *hemera*, and *pathos* disease), in pathology, certain states of disease or affections which are observed only by day, or which last only one day.

Hemerobi'idæ (Gr. *a day's life*), in entomology, a family of neuropterous insects, the Hemerobians, of which the Hemerobius is the type.

Hemerocal'les (Gr. *hemera*, and *kalos* beautiful), in botany, a tribe of the Liliaceæ, or Day-lilies, assimilating to the Tulips.

Hemi, a Greek prefix signifying *half*, equivalent to *demi* and *semi*; frequently used as a prefix in composition.

Hemicra'nia, Hem'icrany (Gr.), a pain in one side of the forehead.

Hem'icycle (Gr. *hemi*, and *kyklos* a circle), in architecture, a semicircle used to denote vaults of the cradle form, and arches or sweeps of vaults constituting a semicircle.

Hemihe′dral (Gr.), in mineralogy, a term applied to a crystal with half of the similar edges or angles similarly replaced.

Hemiolog′amous (Gr.), in botany, applied to Grasses having some florets neuter and some hermaphrodite.

Hemio′pia (Gr. *hemi*, and *ops* the eye), a disease obscuring part of an object from sight.

Hem′iplegy (Gr. *hemi*, and *plesso* to strike), a paralysis of one side of the body.

Hemiprismat′ic (Gr.), in mineralogy, applied to such combinations of crystals as only show half of the faces.

Hemip′tera (Gr. *hemi*, and *pteron* a wing), a class of insects having the upper wings half-crustaceous and half-membranous.

Hem′isphere (Gr.), a map or projection of half the terrestrial globe.—In astronomy, one half of the mundane sphere. The equator divides the sphere into two equal parts; that on the north is called the *northern hemisphere*, the other the *southern*. So the horizon divides the sphere into the *upper* and *lower hemispheres*.

Hem′itone (Gr.), in music, a semitone or half-note.

Hemi′trope (Gr.), in mineralogy, having two parts.

Hemlock, a poisonous biennial plant. —*Hemlock Spruce*, the *Abies Canadensis*.

Hem′orrhage (Gr. *haima*, and *rhegnymi* to burst), a flux of blood from the bursting of a vessel.

Hem′orrhoids (Gr. *haima*, and *rheo* to flow), in pathology, the piles.

Hemp (Sax. *hænep*), in botany, a plant of whose fibres ropes and coarse linen are made.—*Bengal hemp* is the coarse fibre of the plant *Crotalaria juncea*.—*Hemp Agrimony* is the plant *Eupatorium cannabinum*.

Hendec′agon (Gr.), in geometry, a figure of eleven angles.

Henna, a plant whose leaves are used by Oriental women to stain their nails.

Hepar (Gr.), the liver.—*Hepar sulphuris*, liver of sulphur; a combination of sulphur with an alkali.

Hepatal′gia (Gr.), pain of the liver.

Hepat′ic (Gr. *hepar*), in pathology and anatomy, an epithet applying to the liver; as, *Hepatic artery* and *hepatic duct*, situated between the lobes of the liver;—*Hepatic glands*, those glands which receive the lymphatic glands of the liver;—*Hepatic plexus* is connected with the hepatic vessels and the vena portæ;—*Hepatic*

cinnabar, a dark-coloured steel-grey variety of cinnabar, the Mercure sulphur of Hauy;—*Hepatic pyrites*, or *hepatic sulphuret of iron*, a variety of prismatic iron pyrites of a yellow colour;—*Hepatic flux*, a form of dysentery, accompanied with copious discharges of bilious matter.

Hepat′icæ (Gr. *hepar*), in botany, one of the groups of Dr. Lindley's Muscal alliance; comprising the orders Ricciaceæ, Marchantiaceæ, Jungermanniaceæ, and Equisitaceæ.

Hepatirrhœ′a (Gr. *hepar*, and *rheo* to flow), in pathology, an intestinal flux.

Hepatisa′tion (Lat.), in pathology, conversion of the lungs into a liver-like substance.

Hep′atite (Gr.), in mineralogy, a variety of heavy-spar, distinguished by its emitting a fetid smell when rubbed.

Hepati′tis (Gr.), inflammation of the liver.

He′pato- (Gr.), in anatomy, a prefix to numerous words, signifying *connection with the liver*.

Hep′atocele (Gr.), hernia of the liver.

Hepatogas′tric (Gr.), belonging to the liver and stomach.

Hepatog′raphy (Gr. *hepar*, and *graphe* to describe), in anatomy, a description of the liver.

Hepatol′ogy (Gr.), a treatise on the liver.

Hepial′idæ, a family of lepidopterous insects, of the section Nocturna, of which the Hepialus, or Ghost-moth, is the type.

Hep′tagon (Gr. *hepta* seven, and *gonia* an angle), in geometry, a figure of seven angles.—In fortification, a place with seven defensive bastions. —*Heptahedron*, a solid figure with seven sides.

Heptagyn′ia (Gr. *hepta*, and *gyne* a female), in botany, an order in the Linnæan system, which comprehends plants whose flowers have seven pistils.—*Heptandrian*, having seven stamens.

Heptahexahe′dral, in mineralogy, presenting seven ranges of faces, one above another, each range containing six faces.

Heptas′tichous (Gr. *hepta*, and *stichos*, a row), in botany, applied to the arrangement of leaves in seven spiral rows, the eighth leaf in the series being placed above the first.

Her′aldry, the science of conventional distinctions impressed on shields, banners, &c.

Herbiv′ora (Lat. *herba*, and *voro* to eat), in zoology, animals that feed on grass; a name applied by Cuvier to a family of the Cetacea, including the Lamantins, the Dugongs, and the Stellerus.

Herboriza'tion, botanical researches; the appearance of plants in fossils.

Her'cules, in astronomy, one of the constellations of the northern hemisphere, situated between Draco, Bootes, Lyra, and Ophiuchus.

Her'derite, in mineralogy, a variety of fluor-spar, found in the form of a rhombic prism.

Her'ison (Fr.), in fortification, a beam armed with iron spikes, and used as a barrier.

Hermaph'rodite (Gr. *hermes*, and *Aphrodite* Venus), partaking of both male and female natures in the same individual.

Hermeneu'tics (Gr.), the science of interpreting the Scriptures or other works in the learned languages.

Hermet'ic, Hermet'ical, chemical; completely closing. When a vessel is perfectly closed by fusing its extremity or mouth, it is said to be *hermetically* sealed.

Her'nia (Lat.), a rupture; a tumour arising from the protrusion of a part of the intestines.—*Herniotomy*, the operation for hernia.

Herpes (Gr.), a cutaneous eruption or disease.

Herpetol'ogy (Gr.), that branch of natural history which treats of reptiles.

Her'rerite, a translucent mineral, consisting of carbonic acid, peroxide of nickel, and tellurium.

Herschel, in astronomy, the planet Georgium Sidus, so called in honour of its discoverer, Sir W. Herschel.

Her'schelite, a white translucent mineral, which occurs in six-sided prisms, and consists of potash, silica, and alumina: sp. gr. 2·11; H = 4·5.

Herse (Fr.), in fortification, a portcullis in the form of a harrow, set with iron spikes.

Her'sillon, in fortification and the military science, a plank or beam whose sides are set with spikes or nails, to incommode and retard the march of an enemy.

Hespe'ria, the name of one of the newly-discovered planets, first observed in 1861.

Hesper'idæ (Gr. *hesperos* evening), a family of lepidopterous insects (Hesperian Butterflies), of which Hesperia is the type; tribe Nocturidæ.

Hes'tia, the name of one of the newly-discovered planets, first observed by Goldschmidt in 1857.

Hetero- (Gr.). (See *Heteros*.)

Heterocer'cal (Gr. *heteros* irregular, and *kerkos* a tail), in ichthyology, a term applied to fishes in which the tail or caudal fin is unsymmetrical.

Heterogan'gliate (Gr. *heteros* different, and *ganglion* a knot of nerves), in anatomy, having the nervous ganglia scattered unsystematically; more especially applied to the invertebrate molluscous animals.

Heterog'ena (Gr. *heteros*, and *gyne* a female), in entomology, a family of hymenopterous insects.

Heterogen'esis (Gr. *heteros*, and *genos* kind), the production of a different kind or species in the animal or vegetable kingdom.

Heterom'era (Gr.), a section of coleopterous insects, consisting of four groups—the Melasoma, Taxicornes, Stenelytra, and Trachelides.

Heterop'athy (Gr.), the practice of attempting to remove one disease by inducing a different one; the opposite of homœopathy.

Het'eropod (Gr.), an order of Gasteropods.

Het'eropode (Gr.), an animal with finny feet.

Heterop'tics (Gr.), false optics.

Het'eros, a Greek word used as a prefix in many words, usually signifying *otherwise, different in kind, not regular*.

Heteros'cian (Gr. *heteros*, and *skia* shadow), having the shadow at noon always one way.

Heterot'amous (Gr.), in mineralogy, having a different cleavage.

Het'erozite, a mineral containing phosphoric acid and iron.

Heu'landite, in mineralogy, a hemiprismatic Zeolite of various colours; its constituents are—silica, alumina, and potash: sp. gr. 2·20; H = 3·5—4·0.

Hex'agon (Gr. *hex* six, and *gonia* an angle), in geometry, a figure of six sides and six angles.

Hexagyn'ia (Gr. *hex*, and *gyne*, a female), a Linnæan order of plants having six pistils.

Hexahe'dron (Gr.), in geometry, a body of six sides; a cube.

Hexan'dria (Gr.), the sixth class in the botanical system of Linnæus, including such plants as have six stamens.—*Hexandrous*, having six stamens.

Hex'apod (Gr.), having six feet.

Hex'astyle (Gr.), in architecture, a building having six columns in the portico.

Hexoctahe'dron (Gr.), a solid containing under forty-eight equal triangular faces.

Hiber'nate (Lat. *hibernus* wintry), to pass the winter in a torpid state, as some animals do.

Hidrot'ics (Gr.), medicines which produce perspiration.

Hieroglyph'ics (Gr. *hieros* sacred, and *glyphe* carving), picture-writing, consisting of figures of animals, plants,

&c., as found sculptured or painted on Egyptian obelisks, temples, &c.—*Hierography*, sacred writing.—*Hierology*, a treatise on sacred things.—*Hierophant*, an interpreter of hieroglyphics, or sacred things.

High-pressure Engine, a steam-engine in which the steam is not condensed, but admitted into the cylinder at a very high temperature.

Hilum (Lat.), in pathology, a small blackish tumour formed by protrusion of the iris through a breach of the cornea.—In botany, the mark on the seed when separated from the placenta.

Hippocam'pus (Gr.), in anatomy, a term applied to two productions of medullary substance in the lateral ventricle of the brain.

Hippocasta'neæ (Gr. *horse-chestnuts*), in botany, a tribe of the order Sapindaceæ.

Hippocratea'ceæ, in botany, an order of plants consisting of arborescent or climbing trees, of which Hippocratea, so called from Hippocrates, is the type.

Hip'polith (Gr. *hippos* a horse, and *lithos* a stone), a stone found in the intestines or stomach of the horse.

Hip'pomane (Gr.), an excrescence on the forehead of a foal.

Hippopathol'ogy (Gr.), pathology of the horse; treatise on veterinary medicine.

Hipposteol'ogy (Gr. *hippos*, and *osteologia*), a treatise on the anatomy of the horse.

Hippu'ric (Gr. *hippos*, and *ourion* urine), relating to the urine of horses.—*Hippuric acid* is a compound obtained from the urine of the horse when mixed with muriatic acid.

Hip'purites (Gr. *hippos*, and *oura* a tail), in fossilology, a genus of plants in the chalk formation representing a horse's tail.

Hippus (Gr.), in pathology, an alternate dilatation and constriction of the pupil of the eye, resulting from a spasmodic affection of the iris.

Hirsu'tus, or Hirtus (Lat. *hairy*), a term of frequent occurrence in the definition of species in natural history, signifying *hairy*, or *prickly*; as, *Hirticaudis*, hairy-tailed, or having the extremity of the wing-covers thickly set with hairs; *hirticollis*, hairy-necked; *hirticornis*, having hairy antennæ; *hirtiflorus*, having hairy flowers; *hirtipes*, hairy-footed.

Hirudin'idæ (Lat. *hirudo* a leech), a family of apodous Annelids, of which the Hirudo is the type and genus.

Hirundin'idæ (Lat.), in ornithology, a family of birds of the Fissirostral tribe, of which the Hirundo, or Swallow, is the type.

Hisin'gerite, a black mineral, consisting of protoxide of iron, silica, alumina, oxide of manganese, and water: sp. gr. 3·04.

His'pidæ (Lat. *hispidus* bristly), a family of coleopterous insects, of which Hispa is the type; tribe Monilicornes.

Hister'idæ (Lat.), a family of coleopterous insects, of which Hister is the type; tribe Lamellicornes.

Histog'eny (Gr. *histos* a tissue, and *gennao* to produce), in anatomy, the formation of organic tissues; from which we form the words—*Histography*, a description of the organic tissues; *Histology*, doctrine of the organic tissues; and *Histonomy*, the laws of organic tissues.

Historiog'raphy (Gr. *historia*, and *grapho* to write), the art or science of writing history.

His'tory (Gr. *historia*). (See *Natural History*.)

Hol'etra (Gr. *holos* whole, and *etron* the abdomen), an order of Arachnides, or Spiders, in which the abdomen is closely joined to the thorax.

Ho'libut, the flat-fish *Pleuronectes hyppoglossus*, which sometimes weighs from three to four hundred pounds.

Hollow Square, in military science, a body of infantry drawn up with an empty space in the middle for the colours, drums, and baggage, and facing the enemy in every direction.

Holmite, in mineralogy, a variety of the carbonate of lime, consisting of lime, carbonic acid, oxide of iron, silica, alumina, and water.

Holohe'dral (Gr. *holos* whole, and *hedron* a side), in mineralogy, a term applied to a crystal with all the similar edges or angles similarly replaced.

Holom'eter (Gr.), a mathematical instrument for taking measures.

Holophan'erous (Gr.), an epithet applied to the metamorphosis of insects when complete.

Homalin'eæ (Gr. *homalos* regular), in botany, a nat. order of exogenous plants, consisting of trees or shrubs, of which the Homalium is the type.

Homilet'ics (Gr. *social*), the science which teaches the principles of adapting the discourses of the pulpit to the spiritual benefit of the hearers.

Homo, in zoology, the Lat. for *man*, who constitutes the class and only genus and species of the order *Bimana*.

Homœo- (Gr. *homoios* similar), a prefix in compound words signifying *similarity*, but not identity.

Homœop'athy (Gr. *homoios*, and *pa-*

thos disease), in pathology and therapeutics, the theory of curing diseases with very minute doses of medicine; the doctrine that diseases are cured by medicines which have the power to cause similar diseases in healthy persons.

Homog'amous (Gr.), in botany, having hermaphrodite florets.

Homogang'liate (Gr.), having the nervous ganglia arranged symmetrically.

Homoge'nea (Gr. *homos* the same, and *genea* birth), an order of Infusoria, the bodies of which present neither viscera nor complication.

Homoge'neous (Gr. *homogenes*), of the same kind or nature; consisting of similar parts, or of elements of the like nature.

Homogen'esis (Gr.), in botany and zoology, the production of a similar kind or species.

Hom'ograph (Gr.), in military science, a system of telegraphic signals by means of a white handkerchief.

Homol'ogous (Gr. *homos*, and *logos* ratio), in geometry, the sides of similar figures which are proportional to each other are said to be homologous.

Hom'ologue (Gr.), in anatomy, the same part or organ differing in form or functions.

Homol'ogy (Gr.), the doctrine of similar parts or proportions.

Homomor'phous (Gr. *homos*, and *morphe* change), in entomology, an epithet expressing similarity of form, applied to certain insects, of which the larva is like the perfect insect, but wingless.

Homoph'onous (Gr.), in music, having the same pitch.

Homop'oda (Gr. *homos*, and *podes* feet), a section of amphipodous Crustaceans with numerous feet, all terminating with a point or hook.

Homop'tera (Gr.), having the four wings alike.

Homot'onous (Gr.), in pathology, a term applied to fevers, in which the symptoms exhibit the same intensity throughout their progress.

Hom'otype (Gr. *homos*, and *typos* a type), a part homologous with another in a series.

Hone (Swed. *hen*), a sort of fine whetstone for sharpening fine-edged instruments, as lancets, razors, &c.

Honora'rium (Lat.), a fee given to a professor of a university, or to a professional gentleman for his services.

Hopeite (from *Dr. Hope*, professor of chemistry), a white transparent mineral, crystallized in prisms: sp. gr. 2·76; H = 2·5.

Ho'rary (Lat. *hora* an hour), in astro-

nomy, the horary motion of the sun or a planet is the arc which it describes in one hour.

Hordei'a (Lat. *hordeum* barley), a peculiar vegetable product found in barley; a yellowish powder insoluble in water.

Hori'zon (Gr.), the line that terminates the view when the eye is carried round in a level direction; this is called the *sensible horizon*. The *rational horizon* is an imaginary great circle, whose plane passes through the centre of the earth, and whose poles are the zenith and nadir. —*Artificial horizon* is an instrument used in connection with the quadrant or sextant for obtaining the altitude of a heavenly body, to procure which, a perfectly horizontal reflective surface is necessary.—*Horizontal projection* is the projection made on a plane parallel to the horizon. This may be understood perspectively or orthographically, according as the projecting rays are directed to a given point.—*Horizontal line*, in perspective, is such an imaginary line in a picture as is parallel to the horizon, and at the height of the eye. It therefore passes through the centre of the picture.

Horn (Swed.), in zoology, a hard, semitransparent, pointed substance which grows on the heads of some quadrupeds.—In music, a brass wind instrument of a spiral form.—In architecture, a term sometimes applied to the Ionic volute, which has the appearance of a ram's horn.

Hornblende, a mineral of a darkish green colour, abounding in oxide of iron, and generally coarse and laminar. It consists of silica, magnesia, lime, alumina, protoxide of iron, and fluoric acid, and scratches glass: sp. gr. 3·15—3·38.—*Hornblende schist* is a metamorphic slate, in which hornblende is an ingredient.

Horn Ore, in mineralogy, a species of silver ore of a pearl-grey colour, consisting of silver, muriatic acid, sulphuric acid, oxide of iron, alumina, and lime· sp. gr. 4·8.—*Horn silver*, the native chloride of silver.

Hornstone, in mineralogy, a variety of quartz of a horn-like appearance.— *Hornstone porphyry*, a variety of porphyry of a red or blackish colour, with a splintery or conchoidal fracture.

Horn-work, in fortification, an outwork having angular points or horns, usually situated in advance of the principal works of a place, and composed of two demibastions, joined by a curtain.

Horog'raphy (Lat. from Gr. *hora* an hour, and *graphe* description), the art or science of constructing dials, or drawing hour-lines.

Hor'ologe (Gr.), a machine or instrument for measuring time.

Horol'ogy (Gr.), an explanation of the method of measuring hours; the art of constructing time-pieces.

Horom'etry (Gr.), the art of measuring hours.

Hor'oscope (Gr.), in astrology, a figure or scheme of the hours or twelve signs of the zodiac, from which observations are professed to be made of the aspect of the heavenly bodies.

Horse. (See *Equus*.)—*Horse-shoe magnet*, an artificial magnet in the shape of a horse-shoe.

Horse-whim, in mechanical science, a machine for raising ore from a mineshaft, usually worked by a horse.

Horticul'ture (Lat.), the culture of kitchen-gardens, orchards, or flowerbeds.—*Horticulturist*, one skilled in gardening and floriculture.

Hortus Siccus (Lat.), a collection of dried plants.

Hot-pressing, in mechanical science, the application of heat, in conjunction with mechanical pressure, for the purpose of giving a smooth and glossy surface to paper, linen, &c.

Hour (Gr. *hora*), in the measurement of time, the twenty-fourth part of a natural day; the space of sixty minutes. —In angular measure, it is the twenty-fourth part of a circle or complete revolution = 15°.—The time indicated by a chronometer or other time-piece.

Hour Circle, in cosmography, a term applied to any great circle that passes through the two poles; the hour of the day being known when that circle is ascertained upon which the sun is for the time being. Hourcircles are drawn on the globe at 15° distant from each other on the equator.

How'itzer (Germ.), in gunnery, a piece of ordnance intermediate between the gun and the mortar.

Humate (Lat. *humus* the ground), a compound of humic acid with a base.

Humbold'tilite (from *Humboldt*, the great naturalist), a vitreous, transparent mineral, found in the lavas of Vesuvius, consisting of silica, lime, magnesia, alumina, and protoxide of iron: sp. gr. 3·104.—*Humboldtine* is a mineral found in the moor coal of Bohemia, which is composed of oxalic acid and protoxide of iron.

Humec'tant (Lat.), in therapeutics, an epithet applying to remedies which are supposed to augment the fluidity of the blood.—*Humectantia* are medicines for moistening and softening. —*Humectation*, in pharmacy, is the preparation of medicine by steeping it in water for a given time.

Hu'mero-cu'bital (Lat.), in anatomy, the brachial internal muscle which extends from the humerus to the cubitus.

Hu'merus (Lat.), in anatomy, the arm from the shoulder to the ulnus, or elbow; the arm-bone, which articulates with the scapula.—*Humeral*, belonging to the humerus.

Humine (Lat. *humus*), in chemistry, the black nutritive matter of vegetables, consisting of carbon united with oxygen.

Humiria'ceæ, in botany, a nat. order of exogenous plants, consisting of trees flowing with balsam, of which the Humirium is the genus.

Humite (from *Sir A. Hume*), a mineral found in yellow-brown or colourless crystals.

Hu'moral (Lat.), in pathology, relating to the humours of the body.—*Humoral pathology*, a system in medicine which attributes all the diseases to morbid changes in the humours, or fluid parts of the body.

Humours (Lat. *humeo* to be wet), in physiology, cutaneous eruptions, or the moisture of the body.—The humours of the eye are the aqueous, or watery; the crystalline, or icy; and the vitreous. The first two contain about 80 per cent. of albumen, muriate, acetate of soda, and animal matter; the last, besides the usual salts, 36 per cent. of a peculiar matter like albumen.

Hu'mulus (Lat. *humus*), a genus of climbing plants (the Hop), used in the making of beer.

Humus (Lat. *vegetable mould*), a pulverulent brown substance formed by the action of air on solid animal or vegetable matter.

Hurdles, in fortification, twigs of willows or osiers interwoven, sustained by long stakes, and made in the figure of an oblong square.

Hu'realite, a crystallized mineral, with a vitreous lustre, whose constituents are phosphoric acid, protoxide of iron, protoxide of manganese, and water: sp. gr. 2·270.

Hu'ronite, the name of a yellowish-green mineral which occurs in boulder stones in the neighbourhood of Lake Huron; its constituents are silica, alumina, protoxide of iron, lime, magnesia, and water: sp. gr. 2·86; H = 2·25.

Hurtoir (Fr.), in fortification, a piece of timber placed at the head of the platform next to the interior stone of the parapet, for the purpose of preventing the wheels of the gun-carriages from rolling upon the interior stone.

Hy′acinth (Gr.), a plant with a beautiful flower; a yellow, brown, or reddish mineral or gem.

Hyacin′thine, a brown or greenish mineral in eight-sided prisms.

Hy′ades (Gr.), in astronomy, a small constellation of five stars in the face of Taurus.

Hy′aline (Gr.), like glass; transparent.

Hy′alite, a grey variety of uncleavable quartz.

Hyali′tis (Gr.), inflammation of the hyaloid membrane of the eye.

Hy′aloid (Gr.), in anatomy, applied to a transparent membrane.

Hyalosid′erite (Gr.), a variety of chrysolite, with a vitreous lustre and metallic surfaces. Its constituents are silica, alumina, lime, magnesia, protoxide of iron, soda, and potash: sp. gr. 2·875; H = 5·5.

Hyb′odonta (Gr. *hybos* a hump, and *odontes* teeth), in fossilology, a subfamily of extinct sharks. Their fossil remains commence with the coal formation, and terminate with the commencement of the chalk.

Hybrid (Gr.), the offspring of two plants or animals of different varieties or species.

Hydar′thrus (Gr. *hydor* water, and *arthron* a joint), in surgery, a white swelling of the joints.

Hy′datid (Gr. *hydatis* a watery vesicle), a small worm, a genus of Entozoa, which is formed like a bladder, and infests the entrails of the human body; an insect in the skull of sheep. —In pathology, a term applied to all encysted humours containing an aqueous fluid.

Hy′datoid (Gr.), in physiology, an epithet applied to the aqueous humour of the eye, and to the pellucid membrane by which the two chambers of that organ are invested.

Hydra (Gr.), in zoology, a genus of gelatinous Polypi, the entire organization of which consists of a small gelatinous horn, the edges being provided with filaments that act as tentacula; order Gelatinosi.

Hydrac′id (Gr. *hydor* water), in chemistry, an acid containing hydrogen.

Hy′dragogue (Gr. *hydor*, and *ago* to expel), a violent cathartic to expel watery secretions.

Hydral (Gr.), in botany, a term applied to an alliance of plants consisting of unisexual aquatic Endogens, with perfect or imperfect flowers. The Hydral alliance comprises the orders

Hydrocharidaceæ, Naiadaceæ, and Zosteraceæ.

Hydrant (Gr.), a pipe by which water is raised and discharged from the main conduit of an aqueduct.

Hydrar′go-chloride (Gr. *hydrargyros* mercury), in chemistry, a compound of bichloride of mercury with another chloride.

Hydrar′gyllite (Gr.), in mineralogy, a native phosphate of alumina.

Hydrar′sine (Gr.), an ethereal volatile product of a fetid smell.

Hydrate (Gr.), a compound in definite proportions of a metallic oxide with water.

Hydrau′licon (Gr.), a musical instrument acted upon by water; a water-organ.

Hydrau′lics (Gr.), that branch of hydrodynamics which treats of fluids in motion, and of conveying water through pipes; the science of the motion of fluids, and the construction of all kinds of machines relating thereto. —*Hydraulic Press*, in mechanical science, a machine in which powerful pressure is produced by water forced into a cylinder, and therein acting on a piston which raises a table on which the material to be pressed is placed.

Hy′driodate (Gr.), in chemistry, a salt formed by hydriodic acid with a base.

Hydriod′ic (Gr.), noting an acid composed of hydrogen and iodine.

Hydrobo′racite (Gr.), a mineral of a whitish colour, with red spots, consisting of lime, magnesia, boracic acid, and water: sp. gr. 1·9.

Hydrobro′macite (Gr.), a mineral of a brightish colour.

Hydrobro′mic, in chemistry, composed of hydrogen and bromine.

Hydrocanthar′idæ (Gr. *hydor*, and *cantharis* a scarab), in entomology, a family of coleopterous insects.

Hydrocar′bon, **Hydrocar′buret**, a compound of hydrogen and carbon.

Hydrocar′bonate, carburetted hydrogen gas.

Hydrocarbon′ic, an epithet used to denote an inflammable gas.

Hydrocar′dia (Gr. *hydor*, and *kardia* the heart), in pathology, dropsy of the pericardium.

Hy′drocele (Gr.), a collection of serous fluid in the scrotum or spermatic cord.

Hydroceph′alus (Gr. *hydor*, and *kephale* the head), dropsy of the brain, or water in the head.

Hydrocharida′ceæ, in botany, a nat. order of plants.

Hydrochem′istry, that department of chemistry which relates more especially to water and other fluids.

Hydrochlo′rate, in chemistry, a supposed compound of hydrochloric acid with a base.

Hydrochlor'io, noting an acid commonly called *muriatic acid*.

Hydrocor'isæ (Gr. *hydor*, and *koris* a bug), in entomology, a tribe of hemipterous insects, including the Water Scorpions, *Nepidæ*, and the Boatmen, *Notonectidæ*.

Hydrocotyl'eæ (Gr.), in botany, a tribe of umbelliferous plants, of the suborder Orthospermæa, of which the Hydrocotyle, or Pennywort, is the type.

Hydrocy'anate, a supposed compound of hydrocyanic acid with a base.

Hydrocyan'io, a term applied to an acid whose base is hydrogen, and its acidifying principle cyanogen.

Hydrodynam'ics (Gr.), the science which applies the principles of dynamics to determine the conditions of motion or rest in fluid bodies. It comprises hydrostatics and hydraulics.

Hydroflu'ate, in chemistry, a supposed compound of hydrofluoric acid and a base.

Hy'drogen (Gr.), a colourless, tasteless gas, which, combined with oxygen, produces water ; it is the lightest body in nature, and hence the best material for filling balloons. Its equivalent is 1 ; symb. H. With oxygen it constitutes water—hence the name.

Hydrog'raphy (Gr.), the science or description of the watery part of the terraqueous globe.

Hydrog'uret, a compound of hydrogen with a metal.

Hy'drolite (Gr. *water-stone*), a white crystallized mineral, consisting of silica, alumina, peroxide of iron, potash, and water : sp. gr. 2·054 ; H = 4·00.

Hydrol'ogy (Gr. *hydor*, and *logos* a discourse), the knowledge of the nature and properties of water.

Hydromet'ridæ (Gr. *hydor*, and *metron* a measure), in entomology, a family of Geocorisæ, or Land-bugs, of aquatic habits, frequenting the surface of water.

Hydromet'rograph (Gr.), an instrument for measuring and recording the quantity of water discharged in a given time.

Hydrom'etry (Gr.), the art of determining the specific gravity of liquids, and thence the strength of spirituous liquors.—*Hydrometer*, an instrument for measuring the specific gravity, &c., of fluids.

Hydrom'phalus (Gr. *hydor*, and *omphalos* the navel), a tumour formed by accumulation of serum in the sac of umbilical hernia ; or simply distention of the navel by the fluid of ascites.

Hydrono'sis (Gr. *water-disease*), in pathology, a kind of sweating sickness ; ephemeral fevers, with violent perspiration.

Hydro-oxal'io Acid, a peculiar acid formed during the action of nitric acid on sugar, gum, and other substances.

Hydrop'athy (Gr. *hydor*, and *pathos* suffering), in pathology, the water-cure, or the method of curing diseases by water.

Hydropericar'dium (Gr.), an unnatural accumulation of watery fluid in the sac of the heart.

Hydroperitonæ'um (Gr.), dropsy of the peritonæum.

Hydropersulphu'rio Acid, a compound of two equivalents of sulphur and one of hydrogen.

Hy'drophane (Gr.), a variety of opal, which is white and opaque when dry, but transparent in water.

Hydroph'ides (Gr.), water-serpents, whose jaws are furnished with poisonous fangs ; order Orphides.

Hydrophil'idæ, a family of coleopterous insects.

Hydropho'bia (Gr.), in pathology, a preternatural dread of water, a symptom of canine madness.

Hydroph'thalmy (Gr.), in pathology, a disease in the eye, which causes it almost to start out of the socket.

Hydrophylla'ceæ, a nat. order of exogenous plants.

Hy'drophyte (Gr. *hydor*, and *phyton* a plant), a variety of serpentine.

Hydrophytol'ogy (Gr.), a treatise on water-plants.

Hydropneumat'io (Gr.), an epithet given to a vessel of water, used for the collection of gases in chemical experiments.

Hydrops (Gr. *hydor*, and *opsis* appearance), a generic term in nosology, comprehending every morbid accumulation of serum in cysts and cavities of adventitious formation.

Hy'dropsy (Gr.), in pathology, a disease of extravasated water ; the dropsy.

Hy'dropult (Gr. *hydor*, and Lat. *pello* to force), a machine for throwing water by hand-power, used as a garden-engine or fire-annihilator, and applicable to all the purposes for which a hydrant or force-pump is required.

Hydror'achis (Gr. *hydor*, and *rachis* the spine), a collection of serum in the membranes of the spinal cord.

Hy'drosalts, salts, the acid or base of which is a compound containing hydrogen as one of its elements.

Hydrosar'cocele (Gr. *hydor*, *sarx* flesh, and *kele* a hernial tumour), a swelling formed by dropsy of the tunica vaginalis.

Hydrose'lenates, in chemistry, a family of salts formed by a combination of hydroselenic acid with salifiable bases.

Hy′drostat (Gr.), an apparatus for preventing the explosion of steam-engines.

Hydrostat′ics (Gr. *hydor*, and *statikos* standing), the science which explains the equilibrium and pressure of water and other fluids; the art of weighing fluids.—*Hydrostatic paradox* is a term often used to designate that principle in hydrostatics by which a very small quantity of water may be made to overcome a very great weight. —*Hydrostatic balance* is a machine for weighing substances in water, for the purpose of ascertaining their specific gravities.—*Hydrostatic press* (commonly called *Bramah's press*) is a machine by which an enormous amount of pressure may be obtained through the medium of water.

Hydrosul′phurets, in chemistry, a genus of salts, resulting from the combination of hydrosulphuric acid with salifiable bases.

Hydrotel′lurates, a genus of salts, resulting from the combination of an acid composed of hydrogen and tellurium with salifiable base.

Hydrotho′rax (Gr.), dropsy in the chest.

Hydrot′ic (Gr.), medicine to expel water or phlegm.

Hydroti′tis (Gr. *hydor*, and *ous, otis* the ear), in pathology, dropsy of the ear.

Hydroxan′thate, a compound of hydroxanthic acid with a base.

Hydroxan′thic, an acid formed by the action of alkalies on the deutosulphuret of carbon.

Hydrox′ide, a metallic hydrate.

Hy′druret (Gr.), a combination of hydrogen destitute of acidity.

Hydrus (Gr.), a genus of ophidian reptiles, the Water-snake.—In astronomy, a constellation in the southern hemisphere.

Hyetom′eter (Gr.), a rain gauge.

Hyge′ia, the name of one of the newly-discovered planets, first observed by De Gasparin in 1853. Its mean distance from the sun is 300,340,000 miles, and the time of its periodical revolution 5 years and 215 days.

Hy′geine, Hy′giene (Gr.), that branch of medicine which relates to the means of preserving health.

Hygro- (Gr.), a prefix to compound words implying *moisture.*

Hygrobleph′aric (Gr.), in anatomy, an epithet applied to the excretory ducts, and their orifices, of the lachrymal gland.

Hygrol′ogy (Gr. *hygros*, and *logos* a discourse), in pathology, the doctrine of the humours or fluids of the body.

Hygrom′etry (Gr.), the art of measuring the moisture of the atmosphere.— *Hygrometer*, an instrument to measure the degrees of moisture or dryness of the atmosphere.

Hy′groscope (Gr. *hygros*, and *skopeo* to view), an instrument to show the moisture and dryness of the air.

Hygrostat′ics (Gr.), the measuring of degrees of moisture.

Hyleosau′rus (Gr. *hyle* a wood, and *saurus* a lizard), an extinct gigantic genus of reptiles, the fossil remains of which exist in the Wealden strata of Sussex.

Hy′lobates (Gr. *hyle*, and *baino* to walk), in zoology, a genus of Quadrumana, the Gibbons, or Long-armed Apes.

Hymenol′ogy (Gr. *hymen* a membrane, and *logos* a discourse), in anatomy, a treatise on, and dissection of, the membranes of the animal system.

Hymenomyce′tes (Gr. *hymen*, and *mykes* a mushroom), an order or tribe of Fungi.

Hymenop′tera (Gr. *hymen*, and *pteron* a wing), in entomology, a term applied to insects like the Bee.

Hymenop′teran (Gr.), a mandibulate insect, having four membranous wings.

Hyoglos′sus (Gr.), in anatomy, a term applied to a muscle which extends from the hyoid bone to the tongue.

Hyoid, resembling the Greek letter *v*; and, in anatomy, applied to the bone which supports the tongue, from its shape.

Hyoscya′mia (Gr.), in chemistry, a vegetable alkali.—*Hyoscyamus*, Henbane. —*Hyoscyamine*, the active principle of henbane.

Hypapoph′ysis (Gr.), an apophysis of a vertebra growing downward.

Hypar′gyrite, an ore of silver.

Hyper, a Greek prefix, implying *over, beyond, excess.* In the compound terms of chemistry it corresponds with *super.*

Hyperæsthe′sia (Gr. *hyper* and *aisthanomai* to feel), in pathology, excessive sensibility.

Hyper′bola (Gr.), in geometry, a curve formed by cutting a cone in a direction parallel to its axis.—*Hyperbolic conoid* or *hyperboloid*, a solid formed by the revolution of an hyperbola about its axis.

Hypercathar′sis (Gr. *hyper*, and *kathairo* to cleanse), excessive purgation.

Hy′percrisis (Gr.), the crisis of a disease; a violent critical effort of evacuation.

Hyperica′ceæ, an order of herbaceous exogenous plants.

Hypericin′eæ (Gr.), in botany, a nat. order of exogenous plants, usually herbaceous, of which the Hypericum,

or St. John's Wort, is the genus and type.

Hypermyriora'ma (Gr.), an exhibition consisting of innumerable views.

Hyperox'ygenized, supersaturated with oxygen.

Hypersaroo'sis (Gr.), proud flesh.

Hy'persthene (Gr. *hyper*, and *sthenos*, strength), Labrador hornblende, a mineral of a greenish-black colour, whose constituents are silica, magnesia, protoxide of iron, lime, and water: sp. gr. 3·3; H = 4·75.

Hypersthe'nia (Gr.), in physiology, excess of vital power.

Hyper'trophy (Gr.), a morbid enlargement of any part of the body.

Hyperzoodyna'mia (Gr. *hyper*, *zoos* living, and *dynamis* power), excessive augmentation of force in the animal economy.

Hyphomyce'tes (Gr.) *hyphos* a crown, and *mykos* a mushroom), an order of Fungi, in which the spores generally quaternate on distinct sporophores.

Hypnot'ics (Gr.), in the materia medica, a medicine tending to produce sleep.

Hypo, a Greek prepositive, frequently used to denote *excess*.

Hyp'ocaust (Gr. *hypo*, and *kaio* to burn), in architecture, a vaulted apartment from which heat is distributed to other rooms by means of earthen tubes.

Hypochon'dria (Gr.), in anatomy, the part of the abdomen, on both sides, that lies under the spurious ribs.

Hypochon'driac (Gr.), one who is morbidly melancholy.

Hypochondri'asis (Gr.), the hypochondriac affection; melancholy; disordered imagination.

Hypochon'drium (Gr. *hypochondrion*), the hypochondriac region.

Hypoder'mic (Gr.), introducing medicines under the skin.

Hypogas'tric (Gr.), seated in the lower part of the belly.

Hypogas'trocele (Gr.), a rupture of the lower belly.

Hyp'ogeal, Hypoge'ous (Gr.), in botany, epithets denoting all parts in plants growing under ground.

Hyp'ogene (Gr.), in mineralogy, relating to a class of rocks commonly called *primary* rocks.

Hypoglot'tis (Gr. *the tongue*), in anatomy, a name given to two glands of the tongue.—In pathology, an inflammation or ulceration under the tongue, called also *Ranula*.

Hyponi'trites, in chemistry, a genus of salts, resulting from the combination of hyponitrous acid with salifiable bases; formula N + 3 O, or NO₃.

Hyponi'trous Acid, an acid composed of nitrogen and oxygen.

Hypophos'phite, a compound of hypophosphorous acid and a salifiable base.

Hypoph'ysis (Gr.), a gland and sac in the brain.

Hypo'pium, a deposition of matter in the anterior chamber of the eye.

Hyposul'phate, a compound of hyposulphuric acid and a base.—*Hyposulphite*, a compound of hyposulphurous acid with a base.

Hyposul'pho-Ben'zoates, a genus of salts formed by the combination of hyposulpho-benzoic acid with salifiable bases.

Hyposulphu'ric Acid, a compound of sulphur and oxygen.

Hyposul'phurous Acid, an acid constituted of 2 atoms of sulphur, 16 × 2 = 32, and 2 of oxygen, 8 × 2 = 16, its equivalent being 48.

Hypoth'enuse (Gr.), in geometry, the longest side of a right-angled triangle, or the line that subtends the right angle.

Hypoxida'ceæ (Gr.), in botany, an order of narcissal Endogens.

Hypozo'ic (Gr.), in geology, a term applied to the primary rocks in which no organic remains have been discovered.

Hypsom'etry (Gr.), the art of measuring heights of the earth's surface.

Hyri'anæ, in malacology, a sub-family of the Unionidæ, of which the Hyria, a bivalved Mollusc, is the genus.

Hys'tatite, a titaniferous iron ore.

Hysteran'thous (Gr.), in botany, applied to those plants the leaves of which expand after the opening of the flowers.

Hyste'ria (Gr. *hystera* the womb), a species of neurosis or nervous disease, which generally attacks unmarried women from the age of 15 to 35.

Hyster'ics, fits peculiar to women.

Hyster'ocele (Gr.), a rupture of the womb.

Hysteropto'sis (Gr.), a falling down of the womb; prolapsus uteri.

Hysterorrhœ'a (Gr.), a discharge of blood or mucus from the womb.

Hyster'oscope (Gr.), an instrument whereby a view of the os uteri in the living subject may be obtained.

Hysterot'omy (Gr.), dissection of the womb.

Hystric'idæ (Gr. *hys* a pig, and *thrix* a bristle), in zoology, a family of mammiferous animals, of which the genus Hystrix, or Porcupine, is the type.

I.

Iatro- (Gr. *iatros* a physician), in medical science, a prefix to compound words, signifying a connection with physicians or medicine.—*Iatrophic acid*, the acrid principle of croton oil.—*Iatrolept*, one who cures by anointing.

Io, in chemistry, a termination affixed to those acids which contain in combination the highest known quantity of the acidifying principle.

Ice (Sax.), water or other liquid solidified by cold; water becoming solid at 32° Fahrenheit.—*Icebergs* are vast bodies of ice, among the most remarkable of which are those of Spitzbergen. Some of these icebergs are the creation of ages, and receive annually additional bulk by the falling of snow and of rain, which often instantly freezes, and more than repairs the loss occasioned by the influence of the sun.—*Icefloe* is an aggregated mass of floating ice, frequent in the northern seas, and very dangerous to navigation.

Iceland Spar, in mineralogy, a pure variety of calcareous spar or carbonate of lime, remarkable for its clearness, and the beautiful double refraction which it exhibits.

Ice Spar, a mineral of a whitish-grey colour, consisting of silica, alumina, potash, lime, peroxide of iron, and water: sp. gr. 4·32; H = 3.

Ichneu'mones, a tribe of parasitical hymenopterous insects.

Ich'nites (Gr. *ichnos* a footprint), in geology, fossil footprints of animals. —*Ichnolite* is a stone retaining the impression of fossil footmarks.

Ichnog'raphy (Gr.), in perspective, the view of anything cut off by a plane parallel to the horizon.—In architecture, a transverse or horizontal section of a building, exhibiting the plot of the whole edifice, and of the several apartments in any story.— Among painters the word is used to describe images or ancient statues of marble and copper, of busts and semibusts, of paintings in fresco, or mosaic works.

Ichnol'ogy (Gr.), the science of fossil footprints.

Ichor (Gr.), a thin and sanious fluid, which escapes from wounds or sores, and irritates or inflames the parts over which it flows.

Ichthyocol'la (Gr. *ichthys* a fish, and *kollos* glue), the scientific name of isinglass, a very pure form of gelatine, prepared from certain parts of the entrails of several fish. Good isinglass is free from smell or taste, and perfectly soluble in boiling water.

Ichthyodor'ulites (Gr. *ichthys*, *doru* a spear, and *lithos* a stone), in geology and ichthyology, a name for the fossil spines of fishes.

Ich'thyolite (Gr. *a fish stone*), a stone containing the petrifaction of a fish or any of its parts.

Ichthyol'ogy (Gr.), the science or knowledge of fishes; that department of natural history which treats of the structure, habits, and classification of fishes.—*Ichthyotomy*, the anatomy of fishes.

Ichthyophthal'mite (Gr. *ichthys*, and *ophthalmos* the eye), a mineral of pearly lustre; the fish-eye stone.

Ichthyopteryg'ia (Gr. *ichthys*, and *pteryx* a fin), an order of fossil reptiles with limbs like fins, formed for swimming.

Ichthyosau'rus (Gr. *ichthys*, and *sauros* a lizard), in palæontology, an extinct marine animal, the Fish-lizard.

Ichthyo'sis (Gr.), in pathology, a roughness and thickening of the skin, portions of which become scaly, and occasionally corneous, with a tendency to excrescences.

I'cica Resin, in botany, the name of those useful resinous exudations of S. America, where the Icica trees occur, and furnish the valuable resins, carana, elemi, and tacamahaca.

Ic'terus (Gr.), in pathology, the jaundice.—*Icteric*, affected with jaundice.

Iconog'raphy (Gr. *eikon* an image, and *grapho* to write), in the fine arts, a description of statues and similar monuments of ancient art.

Icosahe'dron (Gr.), in geometry, a regular solid, consisting of twenty triangular pyramids, whose vertices meet in the centre of a sphere, which is supposed to surround it, and therefore have their height and bases equal.

Icosan'dria (Gr.), the twelfth Linnæan class, comprising such plants as have twenty or more stamens inserted in the calyx.

Idæ, or **Ides**, a Greek termination, employed in natural history to denote a certain order or class of animals to which the termination *ida* or *ides* is affixed.

Ide, in chemistry, a termination for certain compounds which are not acid; as oxides, chlorides, &c.

Ide'alism, in metaphysical science, the theory or system which makes everything consist in ideas, and denies the existence of material bodies.—*Ideology* is a treatise on ideas, or the science of mind.

Idioleo'tric (Gr. *idios* peculiar), having the property of manifesting electricity on friction.

Idiop'athy (Gr.), in pathology, a primary disease, not consequent on other morbid affections.

Idiosyn'crasy (Gr. *a peculiar mingling*), in physiology, a peculiarity of temperament or constitution, which predisposes persons to the attacks of certain disorders from which others are exempt.

Id'ocrase (Gr. *seeing a mixture*), a mineral of various shades of brown and green, with a vitreous lustre, consisting of silica, alumina, protoxide of iron, lime, and magnesia: sp. gr. 3·34; H = 6.

Id'rialine, a mineral substance, composed of 18 parts of carbon and 1 of hydrogen.

Ignis Fat'uus (Lat. *a deceptive fire*), a luminous meteor seen in summer nights in marshy places; Jack-a-lantern; Will-with-the-wisp. The general opinion is, that this light is produced by the decomposition of animal or vegetable matter, or by the evolution of gases which spontaneously inflame in the atmosphere.

Iguan'idæ, a family of Saurian reptiles, of which Iguana is the type and genus.

Iguan'odon (Gr.), in geology, an extinct Saurian reptile of enormous size. The remains of one discovered in Tilgate Forest measured 70 feet from the snout to the tip of the tail; the head was 4½ feet in length; the tail, 13 feet; height of the body, 9 feet; its circumference, 14½ feet; length of the thigh and leg, 8 feet 2 inches. (*Dr. Mantel*). The Wealden formation, which contains the remains of these more than gigantic tenants of a former world, is overlaid by the chalk rocks of England, and is a fresh-water deposit.

Il'ia (Lat.), in anatomy, the small intestines; that part of the abdomen which contains the intestines.—*Iliac*, relating to the lower bowels, or *ilia*.—In pathology, the *iliac passion* is a spasmodic and dangerous colic.—*Iliacus internus* is a thick, broad, and radiated muscle, which is situated in the pelvis, upon the inner surface of the ilium, which is the last portion of the small intestine, so named from its convolutions.—*Ilium os*, the haunch bone.

Illecebra'ceæ (Lat. *illicio* to allure), in botany, a nat. order of exogenous herbaceous plants (the Knotworts),

of which the Illecebrum, a pretty flowering plant, is the type.

Il'menite, in mineralogy, a variety of iron ore, of a dark brown colour, consisting of titanic acid, peroxide of iron, protoxide of iron, protoxide of manganese, and magnesia: sp. gr. 4·76; H = 5·75.

Immer'sion (Lat.), in astronomy, the disappearance of any celestial object behind another, or its shadow. Thus, in the eclipse of one of Jupiter's satellites, the immersion takes place when the satellite disappears behind the body of the planet, or enters into the planet's shadow; and in an occultation of a planet or fixed star by the moon, the immersion is the disappearance of the star or planet behind the body of the moon, and its reappearance is called its emersion.

Impact (Lat.), in mechanical science, the action of one body upon another, to put the latter, if at rest, in motion, or if in motion, to increase, retard, or alter its direction. The point against which the impelling body acts is called the *point of impact*.

Impasta'tion, in sculpture, the mixture of different matters bound together by means of cements, capable of resisting the action of fire or air.

Imperato'rine, in chemistry, a peculiar acrid substance extracted by ether from the root of *Imperatoria ostruthium*. It forms long transparent crystals.

Impe'rial (Lat.), in architecture, an epithet sometimes applied to the Moorish or Saracenic dome, particularly when it tapers towards the top, and is more than ordinarily spread out below.—*Imperial Medals* were such medals or coins which were struck after the conclusion of the Roman republican era, and until the fall of the Eastern empire.—At the present time *Imperial* is the name of a gold coin of different dates and values, current in Russia for ten roubles, or nearly £1 13*s*.

Impeti'go (Lat.), in pathology, a cutaneous eruption, consisting of clustering pustules of a yellow colour and very itchy, and terminating in a scaly crust, intersected with cracks.

In'uline, a vegetable product, resembling starch, obtained from the roots of *Inula hellenium* by boiling them in water.

In'cidence (Lat. *falling on*). In dynamics and optics, the angle of incidence is the angle made by a ray of light falling on an object with a line drawn perpendicularly to the surface struck.

Incinera'tion (Lat.), in pharmacy, the process by which a vegetable or animal substance is reduced to ashes for pharmaceutical use.

Inclina'tion (Lat.), in mathematics, the tendency or inclination of two planes or two lines towards each other, so as to form an angle.—*Inclination of the axis of the earth* is the angle which it makes with the plane of the ecliptic, or the angle between the planes of the equator and ecliptic, which is 23° 28'.—*Inclination of meridians*, in dialling, is the angle that the hour line on the globe, which is perpendicular with the dial-plate, makes with the meridian.—*Inclination of a planet*, an arc or angle comprehended between the ecliptic and the plane of a planet in its orbit.

Inclined Plane, in mechanical science, a sloping plane, or a plane that forms an oblique angle with the horizon.

Inclinom'eter (Lat. *inclino* to bend, and Gr. *metron* a measure), an apparatus for determining the vertical element of the magnetic force.

Inclu'sa (Lat.), a family of testaceous Mollusca.

Incommen'surable (Lat.), not to be reduced to any common measure.—In geometry, a term applied to homogeneous magnitudes which have no common measure.—*Incommensurable numbers* are such as have no common divisor that will divide them both equally.

Incras'sate (Lat. *crassus* thick), in pharmacy, to make fluids thicker by evaporating the thinner parts, and making fluids thicker by the mixture of other substances less fluid.

In'crement (Lat.), in mathematics, a small but finite increase of a variable quantity.

Incrusta'tion (Lat.), in chemistry, the disposition of stone-like molecules on the surface of bodies exposed to the action of waters impregnated with calcareous salts.—In anatomy, the development of osseous plates in the organic tissues, from age or chronic inflammation.—In architecture and sculpture, a work fixed with cement or cramp-irons into notches made to receive it.

Incuba'tion (Lat.), in pathology, the period intervening between the development of a disease and the impression of the causes by which it has been produced.—In zoology, the action commonly exercised by birds of sitting on their eggs, in order to develop the contained embryo.

Incum'bent (Lat.), in entomology, a term applied to the wings of insects, when the one lies over the other.—

In botany, the anthers of plants are said to be incumbent when so attached that the lower part is in contact with the filament and petals, and so disposed as to lie one over the other.

Indehis'cent (Lat. *not gaping*), in botany, applied to fruits which do not split open, as the apple.

Indent'ed (Lat. *in*, and *dentes* teeth). In fortification, *indented line* is a serrated line forming several angles, so that one side defends another.

Indeter'minate (Lat.). In algebra, *indeterminate analysis* is a branch which has for its object the investigation of problems that admit of an infinite number of different solutions.—*Indeterminate coefficient* is a method of analysis of very extensive application in the higher mathematics.

Index, *pl.* **In'dexes**, and in mathematics **In'dices** (Lat. *an indicator*), in music, a character or director at the end of a stave to direct to the first note of the next stave.—In arithmetic and algebra it is used as an exponent.—In optics it expresses the constant ratio which exists between the sines of the angles of incidence and refraction.—*Index of a globe* is a little style fitted on to the north pole, and turning round with it, pointing to certain divisions in the hour circle.

In'dian Corn, in botany, the valuable produce of the plant *Zea mays*, called *Maize* by the South Americans. There are many varieties, one of which, the *Zea curagua*, or Valparaiso Cross-corn, is held in a sort of religious veneration.—*Indian Cress* is the common name of the plants of the genus Tropæolum.—*Indian ink*, called also *China ink*, is an ink manufactured in China, and imported into this country in square cakes. It is used as a water-colour, and in linear drawings.—*Indian red*, a variety of ochre—a fine purple earth, of compact texture, and great specific gravity.

In'dianite, a greyish shining mineral found in the Indian Carnatic, in masses of a foliated structure.

Indica'tor (Lat.), applied to the muscle which extends the forefinger.

In'dicolite (*indigo*, and Gr. *lithos* a stone), an indigo-coloured mineral, a variety of tourmaline or schorl, found in Sweden.

Indic'tion (Lat.), in chronology, a cycle of fifteen years, instituted by Constantine the Great.

Indigof'era (Ind. *indigo*, and Lat. *fero* to bear), a genus of leguminous plants, the flowers of which are purple, blue, or white, and disposed in racemes; sub-order Papilionaceæ.

Indigot'ic, in chemistry, noting an acid obtained from indigo when it is gradually added to boiling nitric acid, previously diluted with 12 or 15 parts of water. It forms fine colourless or yellowish-white needles.

In'digotine, a pure blue indigo, forming about four-tenths of the indigo of commerce.

Indivis'ibles, in geometry, are the elementary parts or principles into which a body or figure may be resolved; elements infinitely small.

Induc'tion (Lat.), in electricity, that condition of an electrified substance which, when opposed to another, causes the latter to acquire, under certain circumstances, an opposite electric state upon the surface opposed to the inducing body, and is rendered electro-polar.

Inductom'eter (Lat. and Gr.), an instrument for measuring the force of electrical induction.

Indu'plicate (Lat.), in botany, having the margins bent abruptly inward.

Indu'siæ (Lat. *a covering*), in zoology, a case or covering of certain larvæ.— *Indusial*, composed of indusiæ.— *Indusial limestone*, a name given to a certain limestone from its containing the indusiæ, or cases, of the larvæ of Phryganea.

Indu'sium (Lat.), in entomology, the case or covering of certain larvæ.— In botany, the membrane which encloses the thecæ in ferns.

Inen'chyma (Gr.), in botany, a term applied to those tissues which consist of cells with spinal fibres.

Iner'tia (Lat. *inert*), in obstetrics, inertion or failure of the uterine constrictions at the time they are necessary for expelling the fœtus.—In physics, the quality by virtue of which matter is incapable of spontaneous change.

Inescut'cheon, in heraldry, a species of ordinary, being an escutcheon placed upon the fess point, and containing the third part when charged, and the fifth when otherwise.

In'fantry (Fr.), in military science, the foot-soldiers of an army.—*Infantry exercise* applies to the use of the firelock, and practice of the manœuvres for regiments of foot, according to military regulations established by authority.

Infec'tion (Lat.), in pathology, the propagation of disease through the medium of the air, distinguished from *contagion*, which results from absolute contact with a diseased person, or with the substances which have been contaminated by him.

Inferobranchia'ta (Gr. *branchia* gills), an order of gasteropod Mollusca, which have their branchiæ not placed on the back, but in two long series of laminæ situated on the two sides of the body.

Infiltra'tion (Lat.), in pathology, an infusion of fluid into the areolæ of a structure, and especially of the cellular tissue.

Inflamma'tion (Lat.), in pathology, a redness and swelling on any part of the animal body, caused by excessive action of the blood, and usually attended with painful and febrile symptoms.

Inflec'tion (Lat. *a bending*), in optics, the effect produced by the edges of an opaque body on the light passing in contact with them, by which the rays are bent out of their course.

Influen'za (Ital.), in pathology, a febrile epidemic catarrh, prevalent at certain seasons.

Infra (Lat. *within* or *beneath*), a prepositive particle, often prefixed to scientific terms; as, *Infra-costal*, beneath the ribs;—*Infra-maxillary*, beneath the jaw;—*Infra-orbital*, beneath the orbit;—*Infra-spinous*, beneath the spinal process.

Infundibu'liform (Lat. *funnel-shaped*) in botany, applied to a monopetalous corolla, with an inversely conical border springing from a tube.

Infundib'ulum (Lat. *infundo* to pour in), in anatomy, a small cavity of the cochlea, at the termination of the modiolus. —*Infundibula* are the membranous tubes which embrace the mammillæ of the kidneys.

Infuso'ria (Lat.), in entomology, microscopic insects, or minute animalcules found in water as well as in moist atmosphere and other situations, and constituting the last and lowest link in the animal kingdom. The great entomologist Ehrenberg has ascertained that the Infusoria, which have hitherto been considered as scarcely organized, have an internal structure resembling that of the higher animals, viz., muscles, intestines, eyes, nerves, and organs of reproduction. Their powers of reproduction are so great, that, from one individual, a million were produced in ten days; on the eleventh, twelve millions; and on the twelfth day, sixteen millions. Ehrenberg has described and figured more than five hundred species, and has found them in fog, rain, and snow.

Inges'ta (Lat.), in pathology, a term applied to different kinds of nutriment taken into the system.

Inglu'vies (Lat. *a crop*), in ornithology,

the crop or dilatation of the œsophagus of granivorous birds, in which the food is accumulated and macerated, but not digested.

In'guina (Lat.), in anatomy, belonging to the groin; as, *Inguinal hernia*, hernia of the groin;—*Inguinal glands*, glands situated in the groin;—*Inguino-cutaneus*, the anterior branch of the first lumbar nerve.

Inhab'itiveness, in phrenology, the organ which gives the love of particular regions or countries, or, in other words, the love of home. It is also termed *concentrativeness*.

Inha'ler, in pathology, a contrivance for breathing or drawing warm steam into the lungs, as a remedy for coughs and catarrhal complaints.

In'ion (Gr. *is, inis* a sinew), in anatomy, the ridge of the occiput.

Ink (Dutch *inkt*), a fluid, or semi-substance, of various colours, used for writing or printing. The processes for making inks are various, some of which are of a purely scientific nature. According to Brande, the ordinary *black writing ink* consists of the tannogallate of iron, suspended in water by gum arabic—the colour being deepened and improved by the addition of a little logwood —*Blue ink* is produced from sulphate of indigo.—*Red ink* is a solution of alum coloured with Brazil wood.—*Marking* or *indelible ink* is a solution of nitrate of silver. — *Sympathetic inks* are compounds which, when written with, remain invisible till heated, as solutions of cobalt, &c. — *Printing ink* is made from boiled linseed or nut oil, burned and mixed with lamp-black and soap. For coloured inks various pigments are used, as red-lead, vermilion, &c. —*Ink stones* are a sort of small round stones, of white, red, grey, yellow, or black colour, containing a quantity of native martial vitriol, from which they derive the property of making ink, and hence their name. They are almost entirely soluble in water.

Innomina'tus (Lat. *without a name*), in anatomy, an epithet applied to various parts, for which it was found difficult to give a distinctive appellation; as, *Arteria innominata*, that branch given off to the right by the arch of the aorta, which subsequently divides into the carotid and subclavian;—*Nervi innominati*, a name formerly given to the fifth pair of nerves;—*Os innominatum*, a bone composed of three portions; viz., the ilium, or haunch-bone; the ischium, or hip-bone; and the os pubis, or share-bone.

Inocula'tion (Lat.), in anatomy, the practice of communicating a disease, especially the small-pox, by inserting contagious matter. The insertion of the virus of the cow-pox is called *vaccination*.—In horticulture, *inoculation* is the act or practice of inserting buds of one plant upon the stock of another.—In agriculture, the *inoculation of grass lands* is the turning a ploughed field into a meadow.

Inoscula'tion (Lat.), in anatomy, union by junction of the extremities, as in arteries or veins.

Insaliva'tion (Lat.), in physiology, the admixture of saliva with the aliment during the act of mastication.

Insconced (Fr.), in military science, a term used when any part of an army has fortified itself with a sconce, or small work, in order to defend some pass.

Insect (Lat. *in*, and *seco* to cut), a numerous class of invertebrate animals, whose bodies are composed of three distinct parts joined together, with three pairs of feet, and generally wings.

Inser'tion (Lat.), in pathology, the same as inoculation.—In anatomy and botany, the intimate attachment of one part or organ to another, as the insertion of a ligament, muscle, or its tendon into a bone; or, in botany, that of a corolla, stamen, pistil, leaf, or ovary into any determinate point of a plant.

Insesso'res (Lat. *perchers*), in ornithology, an order of birds which habitually perch on trees.

Insist (Fr. *insister*), in geometry, an angle is said to *insist* upon the arc of the circle intercepted between the two lines which contain the angle.

In Situ (Lat.), in mineralogy, a term frequently applied to minerals when found in their original bed or stratum.

Instinct (Lat. *instinguo* to urge on), in physics, the power by which animals are directed unerringly to do whatever is necessary for their preservation and the continuance of their species.

In'sulator (Lat.), in electricity, a non-conductor, by which the electric current is insulated.

Intagl'io (Ital. *intagliare* to carve), in sculpture and gem-engraving, a stone in which the subject is hollowed out, so that an impression from it would present the appearance of a bas-relief.

In'teger (Lat. *entire*), in arithmetic, a whole number, as distinct from a fraction. — *Integral calculus*, in mathematics, is the reverse of the *differential calculus*, and corresponds with the inverse method of fluxions.

Integuma'tion (Lat. *intego* to cover), in

physiology, that which treats of the integuments of animals or plants.

Inter, a Latin preposition signifying *between* or *among*, and used as a prefix to numerous words connected with anatomy and physiology; as, *Interauricular*, applied to the septum between the auricles of the heart in the fœtus;—*Intercervical*, situated between the cervical vertebræ;—*Interclavular ligament*, a ligament which, passing transversely across the sternum, connects the heads of the two clavicles;—*Intercostal*, applied to certain muscles, blood-vessels, arteries, and nerves, which are situated or distributed between the ribs;—*Intercurrent*, applied to fevers or other diseases which occur sporadically in the midst of an epidemic;—*Interlateri-costal*, applied to the external intercostal muscles;—*Interlobular*, applied to the great fissure which separates the anterior from the middle lobe of the brain;—*Intermaxillary bone*, an osseous piece which exists between the superior maxillary bones of certain adult mammifera, and also of those of the human fœtus, and receives the superior incisor teeth;—*Interosseous*, applied to various parts and organs situated between the bones;—*Interparietal bone*, a cranial bone situated, in the mammifera, between the parietal frontal and superior occipital bones;—*Interpleuri-costal*, applied to the internal costal muscles;—*Interscapular*, applied to the region situated between the scapulæ;—*Interspinales cervicis*, six small muscles situated between the spinous processes of the neck;—*Intervertebral*, situated between the bodies of the vertebræ, as the invertebral ligaments, or fibro-cartilages.—*Craig.*

Interax'is (Lat.), in architecture, the space between the axis in columnar erections. "Doors, windows, niches, and the like, are placed centrally in the *interaxis.*"—*Gwilt.*

Intercolumnia'tion (Lat.), in architecture, the distance between two columns measured at the lower part of their shafts.

Intercos'tal (Lat.), in anatomy, applied to the muscles, arteries, veins, and nerves situated between the ribs.

Interganglion'ic (Lat. and Gr.), in anatomy, lying or extending between ganglions.

Inte'rior (Lat.). In geometry, *Interior angle* is an angle formed within any figure by two straight-lined parts of the perimeter or boundary of the figure. The term is also applied to the two angles formed by two parallel lines, when cut on each side of the intersecting line.

Intermit'tent (Lat.), in pathology, an epithet applied to a fever or other disease, the paroxysms of which recur at fixed or uncertain periods; also, to a pulse which, after some vibration, is observed to stop for a short time.

Intermodil'lion (Lat.), in architecture, the space between two modillions.—*Interpilaster* is the interval between two pilasters.

Interneural (Lat. *inter*, and Gr. *neuron* nerve),) lying between neural processes in vertebræ.

Interscen'dant (Lat.), in algebra, interscendant quantities are when the exponents of their powers are irrational.

Intersec'tion (Lat.), in mathematics, the cutting of one line or plane by another.

Inter-tie, in architecture, a horizontal piece of timber framed between two posts to keep them together.

Intertri'go (Lat.), in pathology, a species of erythema, superinduced by acidity of the fæcal or urinary evacuations.

In'tervale, in geology, an alluvial deposit on the bank of a river.

Intestina'lia (Lat.), in zoology, a class of animals which infest the interior of other animal bodies.

Intes'tines (Lat.), in anatomy, a convoluted muscular canal, contained in the abdominal cavity, and extending from the stomach to the anus. They are distinguished into two portions, the small and the large; the former divided into duodenum, jejunum, and ilium; and the latter into cæcum, colon, and rectum.

Intona'tion (Lat.), in speaking, reading, or singing, the modulation of the human voice.—In music, the action of sounding the notes of the scale with the voice or an instrument, compared with another voice or instrument.

Intor'sion (Lat.), in botany, the bending of any portion of a plant towards one side or the other.

Intra'dos (Ital.), in architecture, the interior and lower line or curve of an arch in contradistinction to the *extrados*, or upper curve.

Intra-u'terine (Lat. *inter*, and *uterus* the womb), within the uterus or womb.

Introrse (Lat.), in botany, applied to anthers which open on the side next the pistil.

Introsuscep'tion, or **Intussuscep'tion** (Lat. *intus* within, and *suscipere* to receive), in anatomy, the act whereby substances about to undergo the process of assimilation are introduced into the interior of organized bodies, to be absorbed for the purposes of nutrition.

In'uline, a peculiar vegetable substance extracted from elecampane.

Inverse (Lat. *inverted*), in arithmetic and algebra, *Inverse proportion* is the rule of three, or proportion, applied in a reverse or contrary order.—*Inverse ratio* is the ratio of the reciprocals of two numbers.—*Inverse method of tangents* is the method of finding the curve belonging to a given tangent, as opposed to the direct method.—*Inversion*, in mathematics, is the inverting of the terms of a proportion by changing the antecedents into consequents, and the consequents into antecedents.—In music, the change of position either of a chord or a subject.—In pathology, *Inversio uteri* is that state of the uterus in which it is turned inside out.

Invertebra'ta (Lat. *invertebrates*), in zoology, an important division of the animal kingdom, including all those animals which are not possessed of a vertebra', or backbone.

Invol'ucel (Lat. dimin. of *involucrum*), in botany, a partial involucrum.

Involu'crum (Lat. *a wrapper*), in botany, a term applied to the bracteas which surround the flowers of umbelliferous plants.

Involu'tion (Lat.), in arithmetic and mathematics, the raising of quantities from their roots to any powers assigned.

I'odal (Gr.), an oleaginous liquid.

I'odate (Gr. *iodes* violet colour), a salt composed of iodine, oxygen, and a base.

Iod'ic, I'odous (Gr.), noting an acid containing iodine and oxygen.

I'odide (Gr.), a compound of iodine and a metal.

I'odine (Gr.), a substance of a bluish-black colour and metallic lustre. It is one of the elementary bodies obtained from certain marine plants. It is incombustible, but, in combination with several other bodies, it exhibits the phenomena of combustion. Like chloride, it destroys vegetable colours.

I'odism (Gr.), in medicine, a morbid condition sometimes produced by the use of iodine.

Iod'uret (Gr.), a combustible compound substance containing iodine.

I'olite (Gr. *iodes*, and *lithos* a stone), a mineral of a violet colour, which occurs massive and crystallized in six-sided prisms. Its constituents are silica, alumina, magnesia, oxide of iron, and manganese: sp. gr. 2·56; $H = 7·0—7·5$.

Ion'ic, relating to one of the five orders of architecture, whose distinguishing feature is the volute of the capital.

Ions, the elements into which a body is separated when subjected to electro-chemical decomposition.

Ipecacuan'ha, in materia medica, the root of the plant *Cephaelis ipecacuanha*, imported from Brazil, and used as a powerful emetic. There are several varieties.

Ire'ne (Gr.), in astronomy, the name of one of the newly-discovered planets, first observed by Hind in 1851. Its mean distance from the sun is 246,540,000 miles, and the time of its periodical revolution is 4 years and 57 days.

Irida'ceæ, Irid eæ (Gr. *iris* the rainbow), in botany, a nat. order of narcissal Endogens, consisting of herbaceous plants, of which the Iris, or Fleur-de-lis, is the type.

Irid'ium (Gr. *iris*), in mineralogy, a whitish-coloured metal found in the ore of platinum: sp. gr. 18.—*Iridosmine* is a natural alloy of iridium and osmium, consisting of iridium, osmium, and iron: sp. gr. 18·25—19·5; $H = 4·5$.

Iris (Gr. *the rainbow*), in anatomy, the ring-shaped diaphragm which surrounds the pupil of the eye, so called from being coloured.—*Iris*, in astronomy, one of the newly-discovered planets, first observed by Hind in 1847; its mean distance from the sun being 227,550,000 miles, and the time of its periodical revolution 3 years and 250 days.

Irish Moss, in botany, the name of a marine plant brought from Ireland, obtained from the *Chondrus crispus*. Being of an emollient and demulcent property, it is used medicinally, and for various economic purposes.

Iri'tis (Gr. *iris*), in surgery, inflammation of the iris of the eye.

Iron (Sax. *iren*), the most general and useful of the metals, extremely hard, yet fusible and malleable. It is exceedingly ductile, and distinguished from every other metal by its magnetic properties: sp. gr. 7·6—7·8. All acids act upon iron, and nitric acid oxidizes it with great vehemence. It is capable of combining with a number of metals, but it does not unite with lead or bismuth, and very feebly with mercury.

Iron forms a prefix to a variety of terms connected with science and the arts; as, *Iron-flint*, a variety of quartz, presenting several shades of red and yellow ;—*Iron-glance*, a pure peroxide of iron, in the proportion of iron 69·34 to oxygen 30·66: sp. gr. 5·0—5·3; H = 5·5—6·5 ;—*Iron-liquor*, acetate of iron, used as a mordant by dyers ;--*Iron ore*, an oxide of iron ; —*Ironstone*, an ore of iron, of which there are several varieties ;—*Iron pyrites*, a mineral of a brass-yellow colour, approaching to bronze yellow. It is very abundant in nature, and occurs disseminated in rocks, veins, and beds, investing other minerals, and often enclosed in them. It is composed of 2 atoms of sulphur and 1 of iron. The varieties are—Hepatic Pyrites, Arsenical Iron Pyrites, Auriferous Iron Pyrites, White Pyrites, Magnetic Iron Pyrites, Prismatical Iron Pyrites.

I'sagon (Gr.), in mathematics, a figure with equal angles.

I'satine, in chemistry, a compound body obtained from indigo when it is oxidized by means of sulphuric acid and bichromate of potash. It forms hyacinth or orange-red crystals of a brilliant lustre.—*Isatyde* is a yellowish-white powder, obtained when isatine is dissolved in hydrosulphuret of ammonia: formula, $C_{16}H_6NO_3$.

Isa'tis (Gr. *isazo* to render equal), in botany, a genus of tall, cruciferous herbs, the Woad, all the species of which furnish a blue dye like indigo ; type of the order Cuciferæ.

Ischiad'ic (Gr. *ischion* the hip), in anatomy, relating to the hip, or the parts adjacent.—The *Ischiadic artery* is a branch of the internal iliac, which passes out at the ischiadic foramen, between the puriform and gemelli muscles, in company with the great sciatic nerve. It is distributed within the pelvis to the rectum and the internal obturator, puriform, coccygeal, and levator ani muscles.

Ischial'gia (Gr. *ischion* and *algos* pain), in pathology, pain about the coxa-femoral articulation, or in the course of the ischiatic nerve.

Is'chiocele (Gr. *ischion*), in pathology, hernia formed by the protrusion of the viscera through the great ischiatic foramen.

The following names have been given to muscles, nerves, &c., connected with the *ischium*, which are here presented in alphabetical order: —*Ischio-clitorianus*, the nerves of the clitoris—a branch of the pudic ; *Ischio-clitorideus*, the erector clitoridis ;—*Ischio-coccygeus*, the muscle more generally called *coccygeus* ;— *Ischio-femoralis*, or the *Abductor magnus femoris* ;—*Ischio-femoro-*

peroneus, the biceps femoris.—*Ischio-perinealis*, the transversus perinei muscle ;—*Ischio-popliti-tibial*, the semi-membranosus muscle ;—*Ischio-prætibialis*, the semi-tendinous muscle; -*Ischio-prostaticus*, a name given to the muscular fibres ;—*Ischio-trochanteriani*, the gemelli muscles.

Ischoblen'nia (Gr. *ischo* to suppress, and *blenna* mucus), in pathology, suppression of the mucous discharges, to which the following terms have been applied:—*Ischoilia*, suppression of fæces ; constipation ; *Ischogalactia*, suppression of milk ;—*Ischolochia*, suppression of lochial discharge;— *Ischomenia*, suppression of menstrual discharge ;—*Ischopyosia*, suppression of an habitual purulent secretion.

Is'chury (Gr.), a stoppage or suppression of urine.

I'serine, in mineralogy, an oxide of titanium.

I'singlass, a pure form of gelatine, prepared from the entrails of certain fresh-water fishes ; a name applied to mica.

Isis, the name of one of the newly-discovered planets, first observed by Pogson in 1856.

Iso, in scientific terms, a Greek prefix, signifying *equal*: as, *Isochromatic*, in optics, having the same colours.— *Isochromatic lines* are those coloured rings which appear when a pencil of polarized light is transmitted along the axis of a crystal, as mica or nitre, and is received in the eye after passing through a plate of tourmaline.— *Isobarometric*, in meteorology, applied to the mean difference between the monthly extremes of the barometer.— *Isodynamic*, of equal power, as applied to the earth's surface in which the magnetic forces are equal.—*Isogonic*, having equal angles, applied to the declinations of the magnetic needle.— *Isotheral*, having the same mean summer temperature. — *Isothere*, an imaginary line connecting those places on the earth which have the same mean summer temperature.

Isom'erism (Gr.), identity of elements and proportions, but different properties.

Isomor'phism (Gr.), the quality of assuming the same crystalline form, though composed of different elements or proximate principles, yet with the same number of equivalents.

Isoperimet'rical (Gr.), in geometry, having equal boundaries, as equal perimeters or circumferences.—*Isoperimetry* is the science of figures which have equal perimeters or boundaries.

Isop'oda, or **I'sopods** (Gr.), in malacology, an order of aquatic Crustaceans, characterized by having uniformly fourteen equal feet, unguiculated, and without any vesicular appendage at their base.

I'sopyre (Gr. *isos*, and *pyros* fire), in mineralogy, a silicate of alumina, lime, and peroxide of iron.

Isos'celes (Gr.), in geometry, having two legs or sides equal, as a triangle.

Isother'mal (Gr. *isos*, and *therma* heat), having equal heat or temperature.—*Isothermal lines* are imaginary lines which pass through those points on the surface of the earth at which the mean annual temperature is the same.—*Isothermal zones* are spaces on opposite sides of the equator, having the same mean temperature, and bounded by correspondent isothermal lines.

Isthmi'tis (Gr.), inflammation of the fauces.

Isthmus (Gr. *isthmos*), a neck of land joining a peninsula to the main land. —In anatomy, that which divides the cavity of the mouth from that of the pharynx.

Ite, in chemical terms, a termination used to indicate that a saline compound is formed by an acid ending in *ous;* thus, the sulphur*ites* are formed by sulphur*ous* acids with bases, while the sulph*ates* are formed by sulphur*ic* acid with the same bases.

Itis (Gr.), in pathology, a termination affixed to the name of the organ affected, implying a state of inflammation.

Itt'nerite (after *M. von Ittner*), a bluish mineral, consisting of silica, alumina, lime, soda, peroxide of iron, and water: sp. gr. 2·38; H = 7·0.

Itt'ria, Ytt'ria, a non-acid compound of the metal ittrium or yttrium with oxygen.

Ix'odes, the name of a genus of parasitical Acari found on the skins of domestic quadrupeds.

Ix'olite (Gr. *ixos* bird-lime, and *lithos* a stone), a mineral of a greasy lustre, found in bituminous coal.

J.

Jaca Tree, in botany, the name of a Bread-fruit tree, the *Artocarpus integrifolia*, a native of the East Indies.

Jacinth (Lat.), a species of pellucid gem.

Jack, in mechanical science, an implement for raising great weights, of which there are various kinds; as, the *Kitchen Jack*, in which weight is applied as a power to overcome friction, and a uniform motion obtained by means of a fly-wheel;—*Jack-in-the-Box*, a large male screw turning in a female one, which forms the upper part of a strong wooden box, shaped like the frustum of a pyramid. It is used by means of levers passing through holes in it.—In architecture, *jack timbers* are a row of timbers, which, being intercepted by other pieces, are shorter than the others.

Jacobs' Membrane (from *Dr. Jacobs*, the discoverer), in physiology, a serous membrane or layer of the retina in the eye.

Jacquard Loom, an ingenious piece of mechanism, invented in 1800 by M. Jacquard, of Lyons, which entirely superseded the use of draw-boys in the weaving of textile manufactures with figured patterns.

Jamaci'na, a vegetable alkaline principle obtained from the Cabbage-bark tree, *Geoffroya Jamaicensis*.

Jame'sonite (from *Professor Jamieson*), a crystallized mineral of a steel colour, consisting of sulphur, lead, copper, iron, and antimony: sp. gr. 5·56; H = 2—25.

Janca Tree, Poison-wood, the *Amyris foxifera* of Wildenow.

Japon'ic Acid, an acid obtained from catechine when exposed to the air with caustic alkalies.

Jasmina'ceæ (Gr. *ia* a violet, and *osme* smell), a nat. order of exogenous plants, consisting of twining shrubs of which the Jasminum, or Jasmine, is the type: often called Jessamine.

Jasper, in mineralogy, a siliceous mineral of various colours used in jewellery.

Jau'lignite, a mineral resin obtained from the lignite of juline.

Jaundice (Fr. *jaune* yellow), in pathology, a disease accompanied by a suffusion of bile, giving the eyes and skin a yellow hue, and making things appear yellow to the patient.

Jazel, in mineralogy, a precious stone of an azure colour.

Jef'fersonite (in honour of *President Jefferson*), in mineralogy, a variety of the pyroxene, a dark green foliated variety of augite.

Jeju'num (Lat. *empty*), in anatomy, a part of the small intestines, reaching from the duodenum to the ilium.

Jessant, in heraldry, an epithet applied to a lion or other beast when erected over two or more colours.

Jet (Fr. *jayet*), in mineralogy, a very

beautiful fossil, of a fine deep black colour; a variety of coal of a very compact texture, susceptible of a high polish; used for the manufacture of trinkets.—*Jet-lustre* is a Bohemian black-lead for polishing grates.—In military tactics, *jet* is the movement of any body pushed forward by main force.

Jettee, Jetty (Fr.), in architecture, a border round the stilts under a pier; in bridges, a projection in building; a mole projecting into the sea.

Jewel (Fr. *joyau*), an ornament of dress; a precious stone.

Jews' Frank'incense, a resin obtained from the plant *Styrax officinale.*

Jigging, in mining, the process of sorting ore by passing it through a wire-bottomed sieve.

Joggles, in architecture and masonry, joints of hard stones or other masses so indented that the adjacent stones fit into the indentations.

Johan'nite, in mineralogy, a sulphate of the protoxide of uranium, of a grass-green colour: sp. gr. 3·19; H = 2·5.

Join'ery, in mechanical science, the art of fitting and joining pieces of timber in the construction of utensils or parts of a building, so as to form one entire piece.

Jointer, in architecture and bricklaying, a crooked piece of iron forming two curves of contrary flexure by its edges on each side, and used for drawing, by the aid of the jointing-rule, the coursing and vertical points of the work.—*Jointing-rule* is a straight-edge used by bricklayers for regulating the direction and course of the jointer in the horizontal and vertical joints of brickwork.

Jugate (Lat. *juga* a yoke), in botany, a term applied to the leaflet pairs in compound leaves.

Ju'gular (Lat. *jugulum* the throat), pertaining to the throat or neck.—*Jugular veins* are the veins which bring the blood from the head down the sides of the neck. By their union with the subclavian vein, they form the superior vena cava, which terminates in the superior part of the right auricle of the heart.—*Jugulars,* in ichthyology, comprehend that class of fishes which are distinguished by having ventral fins anterior to the pectorals.

Jujubes, in the materia medica, a fruit of the pulpy kind, produced on a tree which Linnæus considers as a species of Rhamnus.

Julep (Arab.), in medicine, a mucilaginous mixture.

Julus, in botany, a catkin; an inflorescence of the Willow, Hazel, &c.

Junca'cee (Lat. *juncus* a rush), in botany, a nat. order of endogenous herbaceous plants, of which Juncus, the Rush, is the type.

Juncagin'ee, in botany, an order of alismal Endogens (Arrow-grass), consisting of aquatic plants.

Jungermannia'cee (from *Jungermann,* a German botanist), in botany, a nat. order of Acrogens, consisting of creeping moss-like plants, of which Jungermannia is the genus and type.

Jun'kerite, a crystallized mineral of a yellow-grey colour, consisting of protoxide of iron, carbonic acid, silica, and manganese: sp. gr. 3·8; H = 3·81.

Ju'piter, in astronomy, the largest planet of the solar system, which is attended by four satellites. Its equatorial diameter is 1,086 times that of the earth, or upwards of 86,000 miles. Its mean distance from the sun is 490,000,000 miles. It revolves on its axis in 9 hours 55 min. 49 sec.

Juras'sic, in geology, a term applied to the oolitic system, and so called from its occurrence in the Jura mountains of Switzerland.

Jure'ma Bark, an astringent bark obtained from the *Acacia jurema* of Brazil.

Juwan'za, in botany, the name of the Camel's Thorn (*Alhagi Maurorum*), which furnishes the manna of the desert, and is used for making screens, &c.

K.

Kak'odule (Gr. *bad smell*), in chemistry, a compound radical body, the formula of which is $C_4H_6As_2$: symb. Kd. Oxide of kakodule, or alkarsine, has a formula of $C_4H_6As_2O = KdO$.—*Kakodylic,* composed of kakodule, as *kakodylic acid.*

Kak'oxene (Gr. *kakos* bad, and *oxys* sharp), a mineral with red or brown radiated crystals.

Kalei'dophone (Gr. *a sweet sound*), an instrument which gives forth sweet-sounding vibrations.

Kalei'doscope (Gr. *a beautiful view*), an optical instrument or toy, which exhibits a great variety of beautiful colours and symmetrical forms.

Kali (Arab.), a plant, the ashes of which are used in making glass; hence the word *alkali.*

Kangaroo', in zoology, a marsupial quadruped of Australia, having short fore legs, and long hind legs, on which it leaps.

Ka'olin (Chinese), in mineralogy, a fine species of porcelain clay, composed of silica and alumina from decomposed felspar. There is a large tract of this substance found at St. Austel, in Cornwall.

Kar'pholite (Gr. *a shrivelled stone*), in mineralogy, a hydrated silicate of alumina and manganese, in stellated crystals, consisting of silica, alumina, oxide of manganese, oxide of iron, lime, fluoric acid, and water : sp. gr. 2·93.

Karphosid'erite (Gr. *shrivelled steel*), a hydrated phosphate of iron.

Kathetom'eter (Gr. *kathelos* perpendicular), an instrument for measuring perpendicular heights.

Keesh, in metallurgy, the flakes of the carburet of iron.

Kelænone'sian (Gr. *kelainos* black, and *nesos* an island), in ethnology, an epithet applied to the dark-coloured inhabitants of the Pacific Islands.

Kelp, the alkaline calcined ashes of the weed used in the manufacture of glass and soap, but barilla is the article now chiefly employed.

Kepler's Laws, in astronomy, the laws of planetary motion laid down by Kepler, by which are established the important principles that the planets each describe ellipses, of which the sun is the centre ; and that squares of lines of the revolutions of the planets are as the cubes of their mean distances from the sun.

Ker'asine (Gr. *keras* a horn), a mineral of a yellowish colour, the primary crystal of which is a rectangular four-sided prism. Its constituents are oxide of lead, muriatic acid, and carbonic acid : sp. gr. 6 ; $H = 3\cdot0$.

Kerate (Gr.), in mineralogy, a substance of a corneous nature. Kerates are not metallic, but it is a name applied to an order of earthy minerals : sp. gr. 5·5—6·5.

Kerati'asis (Gr. *keras*), in pathology, a horn-like excrescence developed on the forehead or temple.

Keratonyx'is (Gr. *keras*, and *nyxis* a puncture), in surgery, the operation of couching, performed by introducing a needle through the cornea of the eye, and depressing or breaking the opaque lens.

Kerat'ophite (Gr. *keras*, and *phyton* a plant), a name given to a horny Zoophyte.

Kermes (Arab.), a small insect, used as a scarlet dye.—*Kermes mineral*, a reddish mineral.

Ker'osene, a liquid hydrocarbonate, obtained from a kind of bituminous shale in New Brunswick.

Keuper (Germ.), in geology, the upper portion of the new red sandstone formation.

Key (Sax. *cæg*), a term applied to different branches of science.—In music, the particular diatonic scale in which a composition begins and ends, and which more or less prevails in a given piece of music.—*Key-board* consists of the series of tenors in a keyed instrument, the keys being coloured black and white.—In hydrography, a ledge or lay of sunken rocks, applied more particularly to certain rocks, called the *keys*, in the West Indies. —*Key-stone* is a term applied to the middle voussoir in the arch of a bridge, or the arch-stone over the centre of the arch.

Kil'lenite, a mineral of a greenish and brownish yellow, so named from occurring in granite veins at Killeny, near Dublin ; it consists of silica, alumina, potash, oxide of iron, and water : sp. gr. 2·69 ; $H = 4\cdot0$.

Kil'ogram, a French weight, equal to 2 lbs. 3 ozs. 5 drs.

Kil'olitre, a French measure of 1,000 litres, or 264 gallons.

Kil'omètre, a French itinerary measure of a thousand mètres, or about five furlongs.

Kim'meridge Clay, in mineralogy, a greyish yellow and blue clay of the oolite formation.

Kinet'ics (Gr. *kineo* to move), that part of mechanical science which treats of motion without reference to the forces producing it.

King-post, in architecture, the middle post of an assemblage of trussed framing for supporting or suspending the beam at the middle and lower end of the struts.

King's Yellow, the name given to orpiment, or the yellow sulphuret of arsenic, when used as a pigment.

Kingwood, in commerce, one of the most beautiful of the hard woods imported from Brazil.

Kinic Acid, a vegetable acid discovered in cinchona bark, and sometimes called cinchonic acid ; it reddens litmus. Its compounds are kinates of quina and cinchona, lime, potash, soda, &c.—*Kinoyle* is a sublimate obtained in yellow needles when a kinate is distilled.

Kir'wanite, a dark, olive-green mineral, found in cavities of basalt on the north-east coast of Ireland. Its constituents are silica, protoxide of iron, lime, alumina, and water : sp. gr. 2·94 ; $H = 2$.

Klinkstone, in geology, a basaltic stone, of the fletz trap formation.

Klinom'eter (Gr.), in geology, an instrument for measuring the inclination of stratified rocks, &c.

Kneb'elite, a greyish, opaque mineral of glistening lustre, consisting of silica, protoxide of iron, and protoxide of manganese.

Knee (Germ. *knæ*), in anatomy, the articulation of the leg bones and thigh.—*Knee-pan* is a little round bone on the fore part of the knee joint, attached by a strong ligament to the upper end of the tibia.—In architecture, a piece of timber bent artificially, on which another piece is received to relieve any given weight, or resist any particular strain.

Knor'ria, certain fragments of stone found in the coal formation, which have the appearance of branches of yew.

Kob'elite, in mineralogy, a sulphuret of lead and bismuth.

Kon'ilite (Gr. *konia* dust, and *lithos* stone), the name of a siliceous mineral.

Kou'pholite (Gr. *kouphos* light, and *lithos*), in mineralogy, a species of zeolite or prehnite, of a green colour, from the Pyrenees.

Kre'osote. (See *Creasote*.)

Krekid'olite (Gr. *krokis* woof, and *lithos*), an opaque mineral of a bluish colour, consisting of silica, protoxide of iron, protoxide of manganese, magnesia, lime, soda, and water: sp. gr. 3·2; H = 4.

Kry'olite, in mineralogy, a hydrated fluate of alumina and soda.

Krys'taline, the name of a salifiable base.

Kungoo, a red powder produced by steeping turmeric root in an alkali.

Kunkur, a variety of nodular limestone found in India.

Kupferschief'er (Germ. *copper slate*), in geology, the copper slate of Thuringia, a low member of the magnesia limestone series.

Ky'anite, a bluish mineral, found both massive and in regular crystals.

Ky'anize (from *Mr. Kyan*, the inventor), to preserve timber from the dry-rot, by the use of a solution of corrosive sublimate (perchloride of mercury). The timber is immersed in the solution, by which process the primary element of fermentation is neutralized, and the fibre of the wood rendered indestructible.

L.

Lab'danum, a resin which exudes from the plant *Cistus Creticus*.

Label, in Gothic architecture, a term applied to the drip-stone, or projecting moulding over windows, door-ways, &c.

La'biate, La'biated (Lat. *labium* a lip), in botany, applied to certains, plant so named from the order Labiatæ, in which the divisions of the corollas resemble *lips*; the Mint, Rosemary, and Thyme are familiar examples.

La'bium (Lat. *a lip*), in entomology, the lower lip of insects.—In conchology, the inner lip of the shell.

Lab'oratory (Fr.), a place fitted up for chemical investigations and experiments; a chemist's lecture-room.—In military affairs, a place where fireworks are prepared for actual service and experiment.

Lab'radorite, Labrador spar; a beautiful variety of opalescent felspar from Labrador, consisting of silica and alumina, lime, soda, and oxide of iron: sp. gr. 2·7; H = 6·0.

Lab'ridæ (Lat. *labrum* a lip), in ichthyology, a genus of acanthopterygious fishes, covered with large scales, of which Labrus is the genus.

Labri'næ (Lat.), a sub-family of the Chætodonidæ, of which Labrus is one of the genera.

Labur'num (Lat.), in botany, the common name of the *Cytisus alpinus* and *C. laburnum*.

Lab'yrinth (Gr.), in anatomy, the internal part of the ear.—In metallurgy, a series of troughs attached to a stamping-mill, through which a current of water passes.—*Labyrinth fret*, in architecture, is a fret with many turnings in the form of a labyrinth.

Labyrin'thodon (Gr. *labyrinth*, and *odontes* teeth), an extinct genus of reptiles, supposed to have been one of the Batrachian order, found in the new red sandstone formation.

Lac, a resinous substance considered as a gum, but inflammable, and not soluble in water. The commercial varieties are *stick-lac*, *seed-lac*, and *shell-lac*, the last being the purest. The great consumption of lac is in the manufacture of dye-stuffs, sealing-wax, and of certain varnishes and lacquers.—*Lac-dye* and *lac-lake*, the name given to two preparations of lac imported into this country in small cubic cakes.—*Laccic acid* is a yellow and crystallizable acid obtained from stick-lac.—*Laccine*, a brittle, yellow substance obtained from shell-lac.

Lacer'ta (Lat. *a lizard*), in zoology, a genus of slender-tongued Lizards.—In astronomy, a constellation of the northern hemisphere.

Lacer'tidæ (Lat.), in herpetology, a family of the order Sauria, including the genera Lacerta and Monitor.

Lacertil'ia (Lat.), an order of reptiles, of which the Lizard is the type.

Lach'rymal Canals, in physiology, the ducts which convey the tears from the eye to the nasal ducts.—*Lachrymal ducts* are the small tubes which convey the tears from the lachrymal glands to the eyes. — *Lachrymal gland*, the gland which secretes the tears.

Lacquer, a yellow varnish, consisting chiefly of a solution of pale shell-lac in alcohol, and applied to tin, brass, and other metals to preserve them from tarnishing, and to improve their colour.—*Lacquered ware* are those articles varnished with lacquer.

Lacrimo'so (Ital.), in music, a term signifying that the passage is to be performed in a plaintive and sorrowful manner.

Lac'tarine (Lat. *lac* milk), in the arts, a preparation of caseine from milk, extensively used by calico-printers.—*Lactine* is a sweetish substance existing in milk.

Lactates (Lat. *lac*), salts formed of lactic acid with a salifiable base. In the neutral lactates the hydratic water of the acid is replaced by one equivalent of metallic oxide.

Lac'teals (Lat.), in anatomy, the absorbents of the mesentery, which convey the milky fluid from the small intestines into the thoracic duct.

Lactine, a sweetish substance existing in milk ; sugar of milk.

Lactom'eter (Lat. *lac*, and Gr. *metron* a measure), a glass tube for ascertaining the proportion of cream and milk, and also for determining the specific gravity of milk.

Lac'toscope (Lat. *lac*, and Gr. *skopeo* to view), an optical instrument for ascertaining the opacity of milk and the richness of cream.

Lactua'rium (Lat.), the inspissated milky juice of the *Lactuca virosa*,.or Acid Lettuce.—*Lactucic acid* is the name of the acid found in the juice of the plant.—*Lactucine* is the active principle of the Lactuarium, which forms yellowish, indistinct crystals, that have a strong, persistent, bitter taste.

Lacu'næ(Lat. *gaps*), in anatomy, small cavities in some of the mucous mem-

branes, in which the process of secretion is carried on.

Lacu'nar (Lat.),in architecture, a ceiling or soffit with hollow ornamentation.

Lacunose' (Lat. *lacunosus* dotted or pitted), in botany and zoology, having depressions or excavations on the surface.

Lacus'trine (Lat. *belonging to a lake*).—*Lacustrine deposits*, in geology, are certain fresh-water beds deposited by lakes, and confined to the more recent formations.

Ladle, in gunnery, a copper instrument used for drawing the charge of a great gun ; also a long staff with a hollow place at the end of it, which will hold as much as the proper charge of the piece of ordnance it belongs to.

Læmod'ipoda(Gr. *laimos* the throat, and *podes* feet), in malacology, an order of Crustacea, in which the head is confluent with the first segment of the thorax, and supports the four anterior feet.

Lætit'ia, the name of one of the newly-discovered planets, first observed in 1856.

Lagoph'thalmy (Gr. *lagos* a hare, and *ophthalmos* an eye), a disease of the eye, in which it cannot be shut, but remains open during sleep, as in the case of the hare.

Lake (Germ. *lache*, from Lat. *lacus*), in painting, a red water-colour ; a term applied to certain colours produced by the combination of vegetable colouring matter with the peroxide of tin, and with similar oxides, which are intermediate between acids and alkalies.

Lamboid, or **Lamboi'dal** (Gr. *lambda*), in anatomy, an epithet which designates, from its similarity to the Greek letter Λ, the suture which unites the occipital and parietal bones, now more correctly termed the *occipito-parietal suture*.

Lamellibran'chiates (Lat. *lamella* a thin plate, and *branchiæ* gills), an order of Mollusca, in which the branchiæ occur in the form of large semicircular layers.

Lamel'licorns (Lat. *lamella*, and *cornea* a horn), in entomology, a family of pentamerous Coleoptera, in which the antennæ are inserted into a deep fossula, under the lateral margin of the head.—*Cuvier*.

Lamelliros'trals (Lat. *lamella*, and *rostrum* a beak), in ornithology, a tribe of swimming birds, the fourth in Cuvier's system.

Lam'idæ, a family of coleopterous insects, of which the Lamia is the type.

Lam'inar, arranged in plates or scales.

Lamp (Lat. *lampas*).—*Safety lamp* is a lamp invented by Sir Humphry Davy to prevent the explosion of fire-damp or inflammable air in coal mines.

Lamp-black (Lat. *fuligo lampadum*), a species of charcoal, of which the finest sort is produced by collecting the smoke from a lamp ; but it is generally obtained by burning resinous substances in furnaces, and collecting the soot produced on cloths in a close chamber.

Lamprotorni'næ (Gr. *lampros* brilliant, and *ornithos* a bird), in ornithology, a family of Sturnidæ, or Starlings (the Grackles), of which the Lamprotornis is the type.

Lampyr'idæ (Gr. *lampyris* the glow-worm), a family of Serricornes, of which the Lampyris, a genus of coleopterous insects, is the type. The light which it diffuses is of a lambent, electric, greenish colour, which the insect can vary or suspend at pleasure.

Lanark'ite, in mineralogy, a sulpho-carbonate of lead found at Leadhills, in Lanarkshire, of a greenish or greyish colour: sp. gr. 8·8 ; H = 2—5.

Lan'caster Gun, a piece of ordnance with an oval bore and a very long range ; so named after the inventor.

Lan'ceolate, or **Lan'ceolated** (Lat. *lanceolatus*), in botany, shaped like a lance.—In entomology, applied to an insect when the base is not so broad as the centre, and the lateral margins gradually taper to the apex.—In conchology, applied to a shell of an oblong shape, and tapering gradually to each end.

Lancet (Fr.), a small, pointed, surgical instrument, used for letting blood, &c.—*Lancet-arch*, in architecture, an arch, the head of which is like the point of a lancet, and usually applied to long, narrow windows.

Land (Sax., Gothic, Swed., &c.), the solid matter which constitutes the fixed part of the surface of the globe. It forms a prefix to a variety of scientific compounds ; as, *Land-springs*, sources of water which only come into action after heavy rains ; —*Land-flood*, an overflowing of land by water ;—*Land-slip*, part of an eminence which slips down in consequence of being undermined, and its support swept away ;—*Land-scurvy*, an affection consisting of circular spots, stripes, and patches, scattered over the arms, thighs, and trunk—the *Purpura hæmorrhagica* ;—*Landrail*, the migratory bird *Rallus crex*, called also the Corncrake, from its peculiar cry ;—*Land-force*, an army or body of troops serving on land.

Landscape Gardening, in horticulture, the art of scientifically laying out grounds so as to produce the effect of natural landscape.

Landsturm (Germ.), in military affairs, a local militia of Prussia, which is never called from its own district but in case of actual invasion.

Langrage, Langrel, in naval warfare, a kind of chain-shot, formed of bolts, nails, &c., tied together.

Languen'te (Ital.), in music, noting a soft and languishing manner.

Laniar'iform (Lat. *lanio* to tear), shaped like the canine teeth of carnivorous animals.

Lan'idæ, in ornithology, a family of birds known by the name of Shrikes, of which Lanius, the Butcher Bird, is the type.

Lanta'nium (Gr. *lanthano*), in mineralogy, a metallic substance associated with the oxide of cerium.

Lantern (Fr.), in architecture, a little turret or drum-shaped erection on the top of a dome.—*Lantern-wheel*, in mechanics, is a kind of pinion, having cylindrical teeth or bars, called trundles or spindles, on which the teeth of the main wheel acts.—*Magic lantern* is an optical instrument, by which little painted images are represented so much magnified as to be accounted the effect of magic by the ignorant.

Lanu'go (Lat.), the first hair produced in the fœtus.

Lanyard, in nautology, a piece of line or rope for fastening the tackle of a ship.

Lap'arocele (Gr. *lapara* the loins, and *kele* hernia), in pathology, a rupture through the side of the belly.

Lapidifica'tion (Lat. *lapis* a stone, and *fio* to become). conversion into stone.

Lapil'li (Lat. *little stones*), in geology, small volcanic cinders.

Lapis (Lat. *a stone*), a term applied to various mineral substances, and from which there is a variety of scientific formations ; as, *Lapis Armenius*, Armenian stone, from which the colour called *blue bice* is prepared ;—*L. ætites*, eagle-stone, a variety of iron ore ;—*L. bezoar*, a concretion found in the stomachs of certain animals : the *L. bezoar factitius* consists of equal parts of Armenian bole and dried blood, with mucilage of gum tragacanth ;—*L. calaminaris*, calamine, impure carbonate of zinc ; —*L. calcareus*, limestone, consisting of carbonic acid and lime ;—*L. carpionum*, a quadrangular flat bone ; —*L. contrayerva*, the pulvis contrayervæ compositus ;—*L. dentalis*, dentalium ;—*L. divinus*, lapis ophthalmicus, nitrate of potassa;—*L. hæmatitis,* blood-stone ; — *L. Hibernicus,* Irish slate ;—*L. lazuli, L. cæruleus, L. cyanus,* azure-stone ; a mineral from which the blue colour *ultramarine* is prepared ;—*L. Lydius,* Lydian stone; a species of flinty slate ;—*L. manati,* manati-stone, the tooth of the sea-cow ;—*L. medicamentosus,* a preparation of alum, litharge, Armenian bole, colcothar, vitriol, and vinegar, boiled to a strong consistence ;—*L. nephriticus,* a mineral, of which there are two kinds—common nephrite and axe-stone ; — *L. petracorius,* perigord-stone, used to colour glass black ;— *L. prunellæ,* sal prunellæ ; — *L. pumex,* pumice-stone, which swims upon water.

Laq'ueus Gut'teris (Lat.), in pathology, a malignant inflammation of the tonsils.

Larboard, in nautology, the left-hand side to a person on shipboard looking towards the head; opposed to *starboard.—Larboard tack,* so called when a ship is close hauled, with the wind on her larboard side.

Largo (Ital.), in music, a slow movement, one degree quicker than *adagio.—Larghetto* is a movement a little quicker than *largo.*

Lar'idæ (Lat.), a sub-family of aquatic birds, of which the Larus, or Common Gull, is the type ; fam. Alcadæ.

Lar'mier (Fr.), in comparative anatomy, a membranous sac which secretes a thick, blackish, and unctuous fluid, situated in an infra-orbitary depression of the maxillary bone.—In architecture, the flat jutting part of a cornice.

Lar'ridæ, in entomology, a family of hymenopterous insects, of the section Fossores, of which Larrus is the type.

Larva, *pl.* **Larvæ** (Lat.), a flying insect in a masked or caterpillar state; the second state of the insect.

Laryngis'mus (Gr. *larynx*), spasmodic action of the larynx.—*Laryngitis,* inflammation of the larynx.—*Laryngotomy,* operation of opening the larynx.

Larynx (Gr.), in anatomy, the upper part of the trachea, a cartilaginous cavity, the superior opening of which is called the *glottis.*

Lateen Sail, in nautology, a triangular sail used by small vessels in the Mediterranean and Eastern seas.

Latent (Lat. *lying concealed*), in pathology, a term applied to diseases of obscure diagnosis;—in botany, to the vegetable embryo when described only by adventitious causes;—in chemis-

try, when so intimately combined with bodies that its presence is not indicated by the thermometer.—*Latent heat* is that which is insensible to the thermometer, upon which the liquid and aëriform state of bodies depend.

Lat'erite (Lat. *later, lateris* a brick), a mineral substance which forms an important ingredient in hydraulic cement.

Latex (Lat.), in botany, the vital fluid of vegetables.

Lat'itude (Lat.), in geography, the distance of a place from the equator, north or south.—In astronomy, the distance of a star north or south of the ecliptic.

Lat'robite, a translucent mineral of a pale red colour, consisting of silica, alumina, lime, oxide of manganese, magnesia, potash, and water: sp. gr. 2·7—2·8; H = 5·0—6·0.

Lau'danum (Lat.), in medicine, an extract of opium, tinctura opii.

Laughing Gas, nitrous oxide, or protoxide of nitrogen, so called from the laughter it produces when inhaled.

Lau'monite, a soft mineral of a yellowish colour and pearly lustre, consisting of silica, alumina, lime, and water: sp. gr. 2·3.

Laura'ceæ (Lat.), a nat. order of Exogens, or evergreens, consisting of shrubs and trees, of which Laurus (the Laurel) is the genus. Laurel is the popular name of the two species of Cerasus—*C. Lusitanica* and *C. lauro-cerasus,* the Cherry or Common Laurel: order Amygdaleæ. —*Laurel-water* is a distilled water from the leaves of *Prunus lauro-cerasus.*

Lava (Ital.), a stream of melted minerals discharged by volcanoes, and which flows down, and sometimes bursts through, the sides of volcanoes during an eruption.

Laven'duline, a vitreous mineral, consisting of silica, alumina, lime, potash, and oxide of manganese: sp. gr. 2·7—2·8 ; H = 5·0—6·0.

Laxa'tor (Lat. *laxo* to loosen), in anatomy, a term applied to certain muscles which relax, or make loose.

Laz'ulite, a vitreous mineral of a pale blue colour of various shades ; the lapis-lazuli, or azure-stone, consisting of phosphoric acid, alumina, magnesia, silica, protoxide of iron, and water: sp. gr. 3 ; H = 5—5·5.

Lead, in mineralogy, a soft, ductile, heavy metal, of a dull whitish colour, with a cast of blue: sp. gr. 11·38; equiv. 103·6; symb. Pb. The following are some of the chemical compounds of lead :—Dinoxide = 213·2 ;

peroxide = 119·6; protoxide = 111·6; sesquioxide = 231·2; chloride = 139·02; iodide = 229·9; bromide = 182·0; fluoride = 122·28; sulphuret = 119·7.—*Leads*, in letter-press printing, are pieces of type-metal cast to specific thicknesses and lengths, lower than the types, so that they may leave an open space where placed. — *Lead pencil*, an instrument for drawing or making lines, made of plumbago, or black-lead.—*Lead-shot*, shot manufactured from lead.—*Lead-spar*, a sulphate of lead.—*Lead-wort*, the common name for several species of plants belonging to the order Plumbagineæ.

Leda, in astronomy, the name of one of the newly-discovered planets, first observed by Chacornac in 1856. Its mean distance from the sun is 263,480,000 miles, and the time of its periodical revolution 4 years and 202 days.

Leel'ite, a silico-aluminous mineral, tinged by oxide of manganese: sp. gr. 2·60.

Lega'to (Ital.), in music, a term denoting that one note is tied to another, as indicated by these marks ⌒ ⌣.

Leggia'dro (Ital.), in music, a term denoting that the passage is to be performed in a brisk and lively manner.

Legume, Legu'men (Lat. *pulse*), in botany, any kind of fruit like the pod of a pea which opens at the back and front.

Lehun'tite (in honour of *Captain Le Hunt*), a flesh-coloured mineral; a compact zeolite, consisting of silica, alumina, soda, lime, and water: sp. gr. 1·95; H = 3·75.

Lemma (Gr.), in geometry and mathematics, an assumption, or preparatory proposition, for the purpose of facilitating the demonstration of a theorem.

Lemming, the Lapland Marmot, a rodent quadruped as large as a rat, with black and yellow fur. The Lemmings are very abundant in the north of Europe, and on the shores of the Arctic Sea, and are remarkable for their occasional migrations in immense numbers, during which they march in a straight line across rivers, lakes, &c.

Lem'nian, an epithet applied to a kind of siliceous earth found in the island of Lemnos.

Lemnis'cate, in geometry, a curve in the form of the figure 8.

Lemon, an acid fruit of the Lemon tree, the *Citrus medica*, of Persia.—*Essential salt of lemon*, the binoxalate of potash, used in removing moulds and stains from linen.

Lemu'ridæ (Lat.), in zoology, a family of quadrumanous animals, of which the Lemur is the type and genus.

Lens (Lat.), in physics, any transparent medium of certain forms.—In optics, a thin piece of glass, or other transparent substance, having on both sides polished spherical surfaces, which have the property of changing the direction of the rays of light passing through it. There are various forms of lens; as, the *convex lens*, which converges the rays; the *concave*, which disperses them; the *plano-convex*, having one surface plane and the other convex; the *double convex*, having both sides convex; the *plano-concave*, having one surface plane and the other concave; the *double concave*, having two concave surfaces; the *meniscus*, having one side concave and the other convex. The plural, *lenses*, is a general term applied to magnifying-glasses for conveying light to a focus in a telescope and other optical instruments.

Len'tement (Fr.), in music, a word signifying that the movement to which it is prefixed is to be slowly performed.

Lentibula'reæ (Lat.), in botany, a nat. order of exogenous plants, living in water or marshes, of which the Lentibularia is the genus.

Lentic'ular (Lat. *lens*), doubly convex; of the form of a lens.—In mineralogy, *lenticular ore* is the octahedral arseniate of copper.—In anatomy, the term is applied to a ganglion of the head situated on the external side of the optic nerve; and also to the papillæ situated at the posterior part of the tongue, which are from nine to fifteen in number, of the size of a large mustard seed.

Lenti'go (Lat.), a freckly eruption upon the skin.

Lentil (Fr.), a plant of the Vetch kind; a sort of pulse with orbicular seeds.

Len'zinite, in mineralogy, a hydrated silicate of alumina, white and translucent, consisting of silica, alumina, and water: sp. gr. 1·8—2·10; H = 1·5.

Leo (Lat.), in astronomy, the Lion; the fifth sign of the zodiac, consisting of fifty-nine stars.

Leonhar'dite, a mineral resembling laumonite.

Lep'adites (Gr. *lepas* a limpet), a family of Cirripeds (the Goose Barnacles), of which Lepas is a genus.

Lepidoden'dron (Gr. *lepis* a scale, and *dendron* a tree), a genus of fossil plants found in coal formations.

Lepido'ganoid (Gr.), in geology the

name of a sub-order of fossilized ganoid fishes.

Lepidolep′ridæ (Gr. *rough-scaled*), a family of fishes, the Ribbons.

Lep′idolite (Gr. *lepis*, and *lithos* a stone), a mineral of pinkish colour and granular texture.

Lepidop′tera (Gr. *lepis*, and *pteron* a wing), in entomology, an order of insects having four wings, as the Butterfly and Moth.

Lepiphyl′lum (Gr.), in geology, a fossil leaf which occurs in coal formations.

Lepor′idæ (Lat. *lepus* a hare), in zoology, a family of rodent animals, as the Hare.

Lepra, or **Lep′rosy** (Lat.), a loathsome disease of the skin.

Lep′tides (Gr.), a sub-family of dipterous insects, of which Leptis is the genus.

Leptostom′inæ (Gr. *slender-mouthed*), a sub-division of the Cuculidæ, or Long-billed Cuckoos, of which the Leptostoma is the genus.

Leto, the name of one of the newly-discovered planets, first observed by Luther in 1861.

Leucæ′mia (Gr.), in pathology, whiteness of blood.

Leuchtenber′gite, a mineral of a yellowish colour and pearly lustre. Its constituents are silica, alumina, magnesia, peroxide of iron, lime, and water : sp. gr. 2·97.

Leucine (Gr. *leukos* white), in chemistry, a white pulverulent substance obtained by sulphuric acid acting on muscular fibre.

Leucite (Gr. *leukos*), a white volcanic mineral, consisting of silica, alumina, potash, and oxide of iron : sp. gr. 2·48 ; H = 5·5—6·0.

Leucocythæ′mia (Gr. *leukos*, *kytos* a cell, and *haima* blood), in pathology, a diseased state of the body, which is characterized by an excess of white particles in the blood.

Leuco′ma (Gr.), a white opacity of the cornea of the eye.

Leu′cophane (Gr. *whitish appearance*), a mineral found in Norway imperfectly crystallized, of a pale greenish colour and vitreous lustre; its constituents being silica, glucina, lime, fluorine, sodium, protoxide of manganese, and potassium : sp. gr. 2·97 ; H = 3·50—3·75.

Leucophleg′macy (Gr.), a dropsical habit.

Leucopy′ria (Gr. *leukos*, and *pyr* fever), in pathology, hectic fever.

Leucop′yrite (Gr.), arsenical pyrites.

Leucorrhœ′a (Gr. *leukos*, and *rheo* to flow), in pathology, fluor albus, commonly known as the whites.

Leucothe′a, in astronomy, the name of one of the newly-discovered planets, first observed by Luther in 1855. Its mean distance from the sun is 276,960,000 miles, and its periodical revolution 4 years and 340 days.

Leva′tor (Lat.), in anatomy, a muscle that lifts up some part, as the lip or the eyelid ; the name also of a surgical instrument for raising up a depressed part, as of the skull.—Of the *Levator muscles*, the principal are the *Levator labii inferioris*, a muscle of the mouth situated below the lips ;—*Levator labii superioris*, a muscle of the mouth and lips that raises the upper lip towards the orbit, and a little outwards ;—*Levator oculi*, the rectus superior oculi ;—*Levator palati*, a muscle situated between the lower jaw and the os hyodes, laterally.—*Levator palpebræ superioris*, a proper muscle of the upper eyelid.—*Levator scapulæ*, a muscle situated on the posterior part of the neck ;—*Levator anguli oris*, a muscle situated above the mouth, which draws the corner of it upwards, and makes that part of the cheek opposite to the chin prominent, as in smiling ;—*Levator ani*, a muscle of the rectum, which rises from the os pubis, within the pelvis ;—*Levator ani parvus*, the transverse muscle of the perinæum.

Level, in surveying and the science of practical geometry, an instrument which shows the direction of a straight line parallel to the plane of the horizon.—A *spirit-level* is a glass tube filled generally with spirit of wine, the bubble in which, when the tube is placed horizontally, occupies the upper part.—The *artillery foot-level* and *gunner's level-bender*, the line and plummet of the common level, with a scale for showing the inclination of a straight line to the horizon.—*Levelling* is the art of determining the depressions or heights of points on the ground, with respect to a spheroidal surface coinciding nearly with that of the earth.—*Levelling staves* are instruments used with the spirit-level for supporting a mark, and showing, at the same time, its height above the ground.

Lever (Fr. *levier*, Ital. *leva*), in mechanics, a bar, or inflexible rod, for raising a great weight by turning on a fulcrum or prop ; the second power in mechanical science.—*Universal lever* is a machine formed by the combination of the lever with the wheel and axis.—*Lever boards* are a set of boards to fasten so that they may be turned at any angle to admit any proportion of light or air that may be required.—*Lever watch* is a watch with a lever balance.

Levyne (from *Mr. Levy*, the crystallographer), in mineralogy, a crystallized, hydrated alumino-silicate of lime and soda: sp. gr. 2·15; H = 4·0.

Leyden Jar, in electricity, a glass phial or jar coated inside with some conducting substance, for the purpose of being charged and used in making experiments.

Lias, in geology, the lowest portion of the oolitic formation, composed of clayey limestone, bluish clays, and bituminous shales.

Libavius, the bichloride of tin, a liquor used in calico-printing; prepared by dissolving tin in aqua regia.

Libellu'lidæ (Lat.), in entomology, a family of neuropterous insects, of which the Libellula, or Dragon-fly, is the type.

Lib'eral Arts, those arts which depend more on intellectual exertion and refined taste, as distinguished from those which require great manual labour, as the mechanical arts.

Libeth'enite (from *Libethen*, in Hungary), a dark green crystallized mineral, whose constituents are phosphoric acid, oxide of copper, and water: sp. gr. 3·6; H = 4·0.

Libra (Lat. *a balance*), in astronomy, a constellation of the zodiac, surrounded by Scorpio, Ophiuchus, Virgo, Centaurus, and Lupus. The constellation is so named because the sun is in this sign at the autumnal equinox, when the days and nights are equal.

Libra'tion (Lat.), in astronomy, an apparent irregularity of the moon's motion, by which she appears to librate about her axis.

Libret'to (Ital.), a little book containing the words of an opera.

Lichen (Gr.), in botany, an order of plants of very low organization, which grow on the bark of trees, on rocks, and on the ground.—In pathology, an eruption of the skin; a cutaneous distemper.

Lich'enine, a vegetable product obtained from a species of lichen.

Lichenog'raphy (Gr.), in botany, a description of lichens.

Lichnite, the name of a brilliant white marble obtained from the island of Paros.

Life-boat, in nautology, a boat constructed with great strength, to resist violent shocks, and possessing great buoyancy.—*Life-buoy*, a buoy with a mast to render it conspicuous, to be thrown into the sea upon a man's falling overboard.

Lig'ament (Lat.), in anatomy, a strong elastic membrane or substance connecting the extremities of the movable bones.—In conchology, an external substance, generally of a compact fibrous texture, by which the two valves of bivalvular shells are united.

Lig'ature (Lat.), in music, a binding, indicated by a curved line, thus ⌒. In vocal music, all the notes which are set to one syllable are bound by a ligature.

Light (Sax. *lyht*), in physics, that ethereal agent of the presence of which we are informed by the sensibility of the visual organs. From recent discoveries of the properties of light, especially its polarization, it is found that the phenomena of light by which we are surrounded depend on the undulations of a highly attenuated fluid, or ether, universally diffused through the regions of space, which, when acted on by luminous bodies, is thrown into a succession of waves.—In painting, *light* means that part the most illuminated, and which is the medium by which objects are discerned.—*Light equation* is a term applied by astronomers to the time employed by light to traverse the solar system, when phenomena are not seen at the moment of their happening. The first object in astronomical prediction is the finding the absolute moment of time at which a phenomenon occurs; the next is to apply a correction, which gives the time at which it is seen at the place for which the prediction is made. This correction is called the *light equation.*—*Light-balls*, in military science, are hollow cases filled with a combustible composition, which, being thrown by night in a burning state from mortars, or in some cases from the hand, serve to discover the working parties or troops of the enemy.

Lightning, in physics, the flash that precedes thunder; an electric phenomenon produced by the passage of electricity between one cloud and another, or between a cloud and the earth.

Lights, in military science, a term variously applied; thus, *Blue-lights* are used for signals, &c., and will burn half a minute, their material consisting of saltpetre, sulphur, and red orpiment;—*Stevens's long lights*, of the same materials, are made of brown paper, and are of the same diameter as the compound signal-rocket.

Lignine (Lat. *lignum* wood), the proximate chemical principle of wood; the fibre of wood, forming about 95 per cent. of barked wood, and the chief ingredient of cotton, linen, and paper.

Lignite (Lat.), in mineralogy, fossil wood carbonized, and converted into a kind of coal.

Lignum Vitæ (Lat. *wood of life*), in botany, a very hard and close-grained wood, of the plant *Guaiacum officinale*, remarkable for the direction of its fibres, each layer of which crosses the preceding diagonally.

Lig'ula (Lat. *a tie*), in botany, a membranous appendage at the apex of the sheathing petiole of grasses.—In entomology, the lower lip of insects; also, the name of a genus of Entozoa, forming the family Cestoidea.—*Ligulated* flowers, in botany, are such as have a monopetalous slit on one side, and open flat, as in the Dandelion.

Lig'urite (from *Liguria*, in Italy), a yellowish-green mineral, which occurs in talcose rock, and is said to form a gem superior to chrysolite. Its constituents are silica, alumina, lime, magnesia, oxide of iron, and oxide of manganese: sp. gr. 3·47; H = 5·0—6·0.

Li'lalite, a mineral of a lilac colour.

Lil'asine, a chemical principle discovered in lilac.

Lilia'ceæ, a nat. order of Endogens, containing many of the most beautiful floral plants of that class of the vegetable kingdom, of which the Lilium, or Lily, is the type.—The varieties are numerous; as, *Lily of the Valley*, a species of Convallaria; *Lily Daffodil, Lily Hyacinth, Lily Pink, Lily Thorn*, &c.

Lily En'crinite, in geology, the fossil zoophyte, one of the most beautiful of the Crinoidean family, found in the Muschelkalk; so termed from the resemblance it bears to the head of a lily when the arms are folded.

Lima'cians (Lat. *limax* a snail), a name comprehending the genera of Slugs.—*Limacineæ*, a family of Terrestrial Snails, comprehending the various genera—Succinea, Bulimus, Achintina, Clausilia, Pupa, Anastoma, Hilex, Helicolimax, Testacella, Parmacella, Limacella, Limax, and Onchidium.

Limb (Sax. *lim*), in astronomy, a term applied to the edge of a planet.

Limbers, in the artillery service, two-wheel carriages having boxes for ammunition.

Lime (Sax. *lim*), in mineralogy, a calcareous earth, the oxide of calcium, obtained by exposing limestone to a red heat, and used in making mortar and other cements. Lime is fusible only by the heat of a galvanic battery or a gas blow-pipe. It is exceedingly caustic, and when water is cast on it great heat is produced. The water unites with lime, and forms a hydrate.—*Lime-water* is an aqueous solution of lime.—In botany, *Lime* is the name of the *Citrus limetta*.—*Lime tree* is the *Tilia Europæa*, or Linden tree.

Limestone, in mineralogy, a stone of which lime is made. (See *Lime*.)

Limnæ'idæ (Gr. *limne* a marsh), a family of fresh-water Molluscs, of which Limnæa is the genus.

Lim'onite a brown iron ore.

Lim'ulus (Lat. *limus* mud), in zoology, a genus of Entomostraca. The Limuli are known by the name of King-crabs, or Molucca-crabs.

Lina'ceæ (Lat. *linum* flax), in botany, a nat. order of exogenous plants, composed of herbs or shrubs, of which Linum is the genus.

Lin'arite (from *Linares*, in Spain), a vitreous mineral of a deep azure colour, the cupreous sulphate of lead: sp. gr. 5·3—5·4; H = 2·5—3·0.

Lin'ea (Lat.), in anatomy, a term of frequent application; as, *Linea alba*, a white line extending from the ensiform cartilage to the pubes, formed by the meeting of the tendons of the abdominal muscles;—*Linea innominata*, an elevated line formed by a part of the brim of the pelvis;—*Linea transversales*, transverse tendinous lines passing from the linea semicucularis to the linea alba.

Lin'eæ, a nat. order of exogenous plants, composed of herbs or shrubs bearing different-coloured fugacious petals.

Lin'ear (Lat. *linearis*), consisting of lines.—In mathematics, *linear numbers* are such as have relation to length only, like a number which represents one side of a plane figure. If the plane figure be a square linear figure it is called a *root*.—In the integral calculus, *linear equations* are those in which the unknown quantity is only of the first degree.—In drawing and painting, *linear perspective* is that which regards only the positions, magnitudes, and forms of objects.—In botany, the term is applied to narrow leaves when they are of equal breadth throughout.

Lines, in fortification, a series of field-works connected by means of curtains, or long straight walls, as the Chatham Lines.—*Lines* are most commonly made to shut up an avenue or entrance to some place, and are distinguished into *lines of approach, of defence, of communication, contravallation*, &c.—In military science, *line* is a term applied to the regular troops, in distinction from other establishments of a military nature. All numbered and marching regiments are called the *line*, in distinction from the militia, volunteers, fencibles, yeomanry, marines, &c.—*Line of battle* is the disposition of an army prepared for battle An army is commonly drawn up in three lines—the *van*, the *main body*, and the *rear-guard*.—In navigation, *line* is used in different senses and applications at sea, denoting—1, the arrangement or order in which a fleet of ships-of-war is disposed to engage an enemy;—2, a general name for the small ropes used in a ship.—In geography and astronomy, *horizontal line* is a line drawn parallel to the horizon on any part of the earth.—The *equinoctial line* is a great circle on the earth's surface, exactly at the distance of 90° from each of the poles.—*Meridian line* is an imaginary circle drawn through the two poles of the earth.—In geology, *line of dip* is the declivity of strata from a horizontal line.—In mechanics, *line of centres* is a line drawn from the centre of one wheel to the centre of another, when their circumferences touch each other.—*A ship of the line* is a ship of war large enough to have a place in the line of battle.—In heraldry, *lines* are the figures used in armorial bearings to divide the shield into different parts, and to compose different figures.—In music, *Leger lines* are those lines which are added above or beneath the five lines composing the stave, for the reception of such notes as are too high or too low to be placed upon or within the regular stave.

Linguis'tics (Lat. *lingua* the tongue), the science which treats of the origin, various senses, and application of words.

Lin'iment, in pharmacy, a remedy for external use by means of friction, ordinarily composed of oil, soap, or camphor and ammonia.

Link, a term applied to Gunter's chain for the measurement of land. This chain extends to 100 links, each measuring 7·92 inches; the entire length being 4 poles, or 64 feet.

Linstock, in gunnery, a pointed staff or stock holding some lint, and so forming a match used by gunners in firing a cannon.

Lintel (Sp.), in architecture, a horizontal piece of stone or timber over a door, window, or other opening, to discharge the superincumbent weight.

Lion (see *Leo*), in geology, fossil remains of the extinct lion. *Felis spelæa*, and others of the Cat tribe as large as lions, occur in the tertiary formation of Europe.—In heraldry, the *Lion of England* is a lion passant regardant.—In botany, *Lion's-mouth*, *Lion's-paw*, *Lion's-tail*, *Lion's-tooth*, are the names of plants or herbs.

Liqua'tion (Lat. *a melting*), in metallurgy, the process of separating, by a regulated heat, an easily-fusible metal from one less fusible, with which it is combined.

Liquor (Lat. *a fluid substance*).—*Liquor of flints* is a solution of silicated potash.—*Liquor of Libavius* is bichloride of tin.

Lir'iconite, the name of a blue crystallized mineral, chiefly consisting of copper and arsenic.

Litharge (Gr. *lithos* a stone, and *argyros* silver), semi-vitrified oxide of lead, usually produced in the purification of silver from lead. It is not only employed in medicine, but in the various arts of pottery, painting, glass-making, &c.

Lith'ia, an alkaline substance found in the mineral petalite and other lapideous bodies.—*Lithiate* is a salt formed from lithic acid and a base.

Lith'ium (Gr. *lithos*), the metallic base of lithia, the oxide of which was discovered in 1817, in the iron mine of Uto, in Sweden.

Litho, a Greek prefix to various compound words, denoting *stone*.

Lithochrom'ics (Gr. *lithos*, and *chroma* colour), the art of printing coloured pictures from drawings on stone.

Lithocol'la (Gr.), a cement for writing on stone.

Lithoden'dron (Gr.), a term applied to coral.

Lithod'omi (Gr. *lithos*, and *domos* a habitation), molluscous animals which bore into, and lodge themselves in, solid rocks.

Lithogen'esy (Gr. *lithos*, and *gennao* to produce), the science which treats of the origin and history of minerals.

Lith'oglyph (Gr. *lithos*, and *glypho* to engrave), the art of engraving on precious stones.—*Lithoglyphite* is a stone which presents the appearance of being engraved.

Lith'ogogue (Gr. *lithos*, and *ago* to expel), in pathology, a remedy for expelling the calculi from the urinary passages.

Lith'ograph (Gr. *lithos*, and *grapho* to write), a print from a drawing on stone.

Lithog'raphy (Gr.), the art of engraving, drawing, and printing on stone, by a chemical process which depends on the mutual antipathy of oil and water, and the power of the stone to imbibe either with equal avidity.

Lithol'abus (Gr. *lithos*, and *labe* seizure), an instrument for extracting the tsone in the operation of lithotomy.

Lithol'ogy (Gr. *lithos*, and *logos* a discourse), the natural history of stones.

Lith'omarge, in mineralogy, a variety of talc. Its constituents are silica, alumina, oxide of iron, chloride of sodium, and water.

Lithontrip'tic (Gr. *lithos*, and *tripsis* wearing away), medicines to dissolve the stone in the kidney or bladder.

Lithontrip'tor (Gr.), an instrument for breaking stones or calculi in the bladder.

Lithoph'agi (Gr. *lithos*, and *phago* to eat), animals that eat stones.

Litho-photog'raphy (Gr.), printing from photographs on stone.

Lith'ophyte (Gr. *lithos*, and *phyton* a plant), a tribe of Polypi with a fixed internal axis of stony consistency.

Lithostro'tion (Gr. *paved with stones*), a sort of fossil madrepore.

Lith'otint (Gr. *lithos*, and Eng. *tint*), a tint obtained by a brush used on the lithographic stone instead of a crayon.

Lith'otome (Gr. *cut stone*), a stone so formed naturally as to appear cut artificially.

Lithot'omy (Gr. *lithos*, and *temno* to cut), the art or practice of cutting into the bladder for the removal of stone.

Lithot'rity (Gr. *stone-crushing*), the operation of breaking or bruising the stone in the bladder.

Lithox'ylite, petrified wood.

Litmus, a lichen used in dyeing; a blue liquid colour obtained from the orchil.

Lit'uites (Lat. *lituus* a trumpet), in geology, a group of fossil Cephalopods, found in the silurian and older formations.

Lixiv'ium (Lat. *lix* ash-wood), an alkaline salt in solution; lye.

Llandel'lo Formation, in geology, the lowest series of the silurian system.

Lla'nos (Sp.), a term applied to those extensive plains which extend along the banks of the river Orinoco, in S. America.

Loadstar, the pole-star; the Cynosure.

Loadstone, an oxide of iron; the magnet by which the needle of the mariner's compass is directed.

Lo'boite, in mineralogy, a species of idocrase.

Loch'ia (Gr.), in pathology, evacuations which follow childbirth. — *Lochiorrhagia*, a profuse flow of the lochia.

Loc'ulament (Lat.), in botany, the cell in the pericarp of a plant, in which the seed is lodged.

Locust (Lat.), in entomology, a migratory devouring insect of the order Orthoptera, of which there are various species.—In botany, a tree of several varieties.

Lode, in mining, a mineral or metallic vein.

Logan, in geology, a large rock so balanced as to be easily moved; a rocking stone, of which there are some curious specimens in Cornwall.

Logania'ceæ (from *James Logan* the botanist), in botany, a nat. order of dichlamydeous Exogens, of which Logania is the type.

Log'arithm (Gr. *logos*, and *arithmos* number), a rational number, or a number having a ratio or proportion to another number.—*Logarithms* are a series of numbers in arithmetical progression, answering to another series of numbers in geometrical progression.—*Logistic logarithms* are certain logarithms of sexagesimal numbers or fractions used in astronomical calculations. The logistic logarithm of any number of seconds is the difference between the common logarithm of that number and the logarithm of 3,600, the number of seconds in a degree.—*Logarithmic curve* is a curve in which the subtangent is the same at every point.

Log-board, in nautical science, a table or board containing an account of a ship's way measured by the log.— *Log-book* is a register into which are transcribed the contents of the logboard, &c. — *Log-glass* is a half-minute sand-glass used for timing the speed of sailing.—*Log-line*, a line of about 150 fathoms, fastened to the log.

Logic (Ital. *logica*, from Gr. *logos* discourse), the science or art of reasoning, or the science of the laws of thought, and the correct or just connection of ideas. —*Logician* is a teacher or professor of logic, or one versed in logic.

Logis'tic (Gr. *logos*), an epithet applied to certain logarithms of sexagesimal numbers or fractions used in astronomical calculations.—*Logistic spiral*, in mathematics, is a spiral line whose radii everywhere make equal angles with the tangents.

Logog'raphy (Gr. *logos*, and *grapho* to write), the science or art of taking down the words of an orator without having recourse to short-hand; also a method of printing in which whole words in type are used instead of single letters.

Logom'eter (Gr.), a scale for measuring chemical equivalents.

Log'otype (Gr.), in typography, two or more letters cast in one piece, as fl, ff, &c.

Lohooh (Arab.), in pathology, a medicine of a consistence between a soft electuary and a syrup.

Loimol'ogy (Gr. *loimos* plague), the doctrine of pestilential diseases.

Loimop'yra (Gr. *loimos*, and *pyr* fever), pestilential fever.

Lom'onite, a mineral of the Zeolite family.

London Clay, in geology, a tertiary formation developed under and around the city of London, and constituting the London basin.

Longi (Lat. *longus* long), in compound words, a prefix signifying *length*.

Long'icorns (Lat. *long-horned*), a family of tetrametrous Coleoptera, remarkable for the length of their antennæ.

Longim'etry (Lat. *longus*, and Gr. *metron* a measure), in surveying, the art of measuring distances.

Longipal'pi (Lat. *long feelers*), in entomology, a family of short-winged Beetles, in which the maxillary palpi are nearly as long as the head.

Longipen'nes (Lat. *long-winged*), in ornithology, a term applied to a family of oceanic birds remarkable for their long wings, as the Albatross, Petrel, &c.

Longiros'ters (Lat. *long-beaked*), in ornithology, a family of Wading birds, distinguished, as in the Snipes, for the extreme length of the bill.

Longis'simus Dorsi (Lat.), in anatomy, a muscle of the back which assists in keeping the spinal column erect.

Lon'gitude (Lat. *length*), in geography, the circumference of the earth, measured east and west; the distance of any part of the earth, to the east or west, from a meridian, or from any place, estimated in degrees.—In astronomy, the distance of a heavenly body from the first degree of Aries, reckoned on the ecliptic.—*Heliocentric-longitude* is the longitude of a planet as seen from the sun.—*Geocentric longitude* is the longitude of a planet seen from the earth; that is, the point of the ecliptic to which it perpendicularly corresponds, as seen from the centre of the earth.

Long Primer, in typography, a sort of type intermediate between small pica and bourgeois.

Longus Colli (Lat.), in anatomy, a pair of muscles in the neck. When one contracts it moves the neck to one side, and when they both act the neck is bent forward.

Loopers, in entomology, the larvæ of certain species of moths, which form a loop when crawling.

Lophobran'chiate (Gr.), in ichthyology, a term applied to an order of fishes with gills arranged in tufts.

Lorantha'ceæ (Gr. *loron* a thong, and *anthos* a flower), in botany, a nat. order of parasitical exogenous shrubs.

Loria'næ, in ornithology, a sub-family of the Psittacidæ, or Parrots, the Lories, of which the Lorius is the type.

Loricari'næ (Lat. *lorica* a coat of mail), in ichthyology, a sub-family of the Silures, or Cat-fish, whose bodies are mailed with large osseous plates.

Lotus (Lat.), the Water-lily of the Nile.

Low Pressure, a term applied to a steam-engine, the motive force of which is produced by forming a vacuum within the cylinder by drawing off the steam into another vessel called the *condenser*, and there condensing it.

Low Wines, in distillation, the product obtained by a single distillation of molasses, or of fermented saccharine and spirituous liquid.

Loxa Bark, in botany, a pale Peruvian bark, the product of *Cinchona condaminea*.

Loxi'adæ, in ornithology, a family of Perching birds, the Cross-bills.

Loxodrom'ics (Gr. *loxos* oblique, and *dromos* course), the art of oblique sailing by the rhomb, which always makes an equal angle with every meridian.

Lozenge (Fr.), in geometry, an oblique-angled parallelogram, or rhomb.—In pathology, a form of medicine to be held in the mouth till melted.—In heraldry, a bearing in the shape of a parallelogram.—*Lozengy*, having the field or charge covered with lozenges.

Lucern (Fr.), in botany, a valuable species of Trefoil belonging to the genus Medicago, which is excellent food for cattle.

Lucer'nal Mi'croscope (Lat. *lucerna* a lamp), an instrument adapted to exhibit objects of a magnified size upon a screen, being illuminated by means of a lamp, and the rest of the apartment being kept dark.

Lucerni'næ (Lat. *lucerna*), a sub-family of the Helicidæ, or Testaceous Snails, including the Lamp Snails, or Land Volutes.

Lucim'eter (Lat. and Gr. *a light measurer*), an apparatus for measuring the intensity of light; a photometer.

Lucul'lite, in mineralogy, a variety of black limestone, often polished for ornamental purposes.

Lumachel' (Ital.), in mineralogy, a calcareous stone composed of shells and coral conglutinated.

Lumba'go (Lat.), in pathology, pain in the loins; a rheumatic affection of the muscles about the loins.

Lum'brical (Lat. *worm-like*), in anatomy, applied to small muscles in the hands and feet.

Luna Cor'nea (Lat.), in chemistry, a muriate of silver.

Lunar (Lat. *lunaris*), orbed like the moon.—*Lunar cycle*, in astronomy, is the period of time after which the new moons return on the same days of the year (*Brande*).—*Lunar observation* is an observation of the moon's distance from a star, for the purposes of finding the longitude.—*Lunar rainbow* is a rainbow occasioned by the reflection of the light of the moon.—*Lunar theory*, the deduction of the motion of a planet from the law of gravitation.—*Lunar year* is the period of twelve lunar months, or 354 days, 8 hours, 48 minutes, and 34 seconds.—*Lunar month* is the time in which the moon completes a revolution about the earth; the synodic month.

Luna'tion (Lat.), in astronomy, the time from one new moon to another.

Lunette (Fr. from Lat. *luna*), in fortification, a small half-moon, or work similar to a ravelin.—In architecture, an aperture for the admission of light.—In optics, a kind of glasses.

Luniso'lar (Lat.), combining the motions or revolutions of the sun and moon.—A *lunisolar period* is that after which the eclipses again return in the same order; a term applied to a period of 532 years, which is found by multiplying the cycle of the sun by that of the moon.

Lu'nistice (Lat. *luna* the moon, and *sto* to stand), in astronomy, the furthest point of the moon's northing or southing.

Lu'nula (Lat. *a little moon*), in physiology, a term applied to that portion of the human nail near the root which is whiter than the rest.

Lu'puline, the bitter and active principle contained in the hop.

Lupus (Lat. *a wolf*), in pathology, a virulent disease characterized by its tendency to destructive ulceration of the parts it attacks.

Lute, Luting (Lat. *lutum*), in chemistry, a sort of paste or clay with which chemists close up their vessels, and used especially for connecting retorts and receivers, so as to prevent the escape either of the vapour or gases generated during distillation or sublimation.

Lute'tia (Lat. *Paris*), in astronomy, the name of one of the newly-discovered planets, first observed by Goldschmidt in 1854; its mean distance from the sun is 232,240,000 miles, and the time of its periodical revolution 3 years and 292 days.

Luthern, in architecture, a sort of window over the cornice in the inclined plane of the roof of a building.

Luxa'tion (Lat.), in pathology, dislocation or displacement of the articular extremities of the bones, resulting from the infliction of external violence, or destruction of the cartilages or articular ligaments by inflammation.

Lycan'thropy (Gr. *lykos* a wolf, and *anthropos* a man), a kind of madness in which men howl like wolves.

Lyce'um (Lat. from Gr. *lykeion*), a literary seminary; an association for lectures on science or literature.

Lycodon'tes (Gr. *lykos*, and *odontes* teeth), in geology, a name given to certain fossil teeth, supposed to be those of a kind of wolf-fish.

Lycopodia'ceæ (Gr. *lykos*, and *podes* feet), in botany, a nat. order of Acrogens, consisting of moss-like plants, of which Lycopodium, or Club-moss, is the type.

Lye, in chemistry, a solution of alkali in water, particularly applied to dissolved potash.

Lyenceph'ala (Gr. *lyo* to loosen, and *enkephale* the brain), in physics, a term applied to the lowest group of Mammalia.

Lymph (Lat. *a stream*), in anatomy, a transparent, colourless liquid, which, after its removal from the body, separates into a clear fluid.—*Lymphatic* is an absorbent vessel which carries lymph from all parts of the body.—*Lympheurism*, a morbid dilatation of the lymphatic vessels.—*Lymphography*, a treatise on the lymphatic vessels.

Lyra (Lat.), in astronomy, a northern constellation, the Lyre, surrounded by Cygnus, Aquila, Hercules, and the head of Draco.

Lyssa (Gr.), in pathology, canine madness.

Lyte'rian, indicating the solution or termination of a disease.

Lythra'ceæ, a nat. order of saxafragal Exogens, of which the Lythrum, or Purple Loosestrife, is the type.

M.

The letter **M** is in frequent use as an initial for various terms in science, literature, and art.—In astronomy, it stands for *meridiem*, or mid-day; hence A.M., *ante meridiem* (morning), and P.M., *post meridiem* (afternoon).—In medical prescriptions, M. stands for *misce* (mix), or *mixtura* (a mixture).—A.M. or M.A. stands for *artium magister*, master of arts; M.D. for *medicinæ doctor*, doctor of medicine; A.M. for *anno mundi*, in the year of the world; MS. for *manuscript*. — As a numeral, M stands for a thousand; and, with a dash over it, for a million.

Macad'amizing, an improved system of paving with small broken stones that bind with the earth, and form a solid, smooth mass; first introduced by Mr. Macadam.

Macera'tion (Lat.), in chemistry, the art of softening and dissolving away by steeping in a fluid.

Machic'olated (Fr. from Gr. *machomai* to fight), in architecture, having parapets projecting beyond the faces of the walls, and supported by arches. —*Machicolation* is an opening or aperture in the parapet of a fortified building.

Mach'icoulis (Gr.), in fortification, a projecting balcony or parapet, with holes for firing through.

Machine (Fr. from Lat. *machina*), in mechanical science, any invention or work in which one part contributes to the motion of another.—*Machinery* is a combination of mechanical powers, so constructed as to regulate force and motion; a term applied to machines in general.

Macig'no (Ital.), in mineralogy, a hard, siliceous sandstone.

Mack'erel Gale, in navigation, a strong breeze.—*Mackerel sky*, a sky streaked or marked like a mackerel.

Macle, a mineral found in prismatic crystals.

Maclure'ite, a mineral of a yellowish colour and vitreous lustre.

Macro (Gr. *makros* large), a prefix to numerous scientific words, signifiying *largeness*.

Macroceph'alus (Gr. *large-headed*), in botany, applied to embryos of which the two cotyledons grow together.

Ma.xrocer'cinæ (Gr. *makros*, and *kerkos* a curve, in allusion to the upper mandible), a sub-family of the Psittacidæ, or Parrots, distinguished for the gaudiness of their plumage, of which the Macrocercus, or Macaw, is the type and genus.

Mac'rocosm (Gr. *makros*, and *kosmos* world), the great or whole world, or visible system.

Macrodac'tyli (Gr. *long-fingered*), a family of birds furnished with very long toes.

Macrodiag'onal (Gr.), the longer of the diagonals of a rhombic prism.

Macrom'eter (Gr.), an instrument for measuring the distance of inaccessible bodies by means of two reflectors.

Macrop'nea (Gr.), in pathology, that state of the breathing in which the respiration is deep.

Macrop'odous (Gr. *makros*, and *podes* feet), applied to a family of crustacean invertebrate animals.

Macrotrach'ia (Gr. *large-throated*), in conchology, a tribe of the order Dythra, or bivalve shells; it comprehends the families Pholidæ, Myadæ, Tellinidæ, Chamidæ, and Saxicavidæ.

Macrou'rans (Gr. *long-tailed*), a family of Decapods, the Long-tailed Crustaceans, including the Lobster and all of the same kind.

Mac'ulæ (Lat.), in pathology, spotted discolorations on the surface of the body.—In astronomy, dark spots on the surfaces of the sun, moon, and some of the planets.

Mad'repores (Fr. *madré* spotted, and Lat. *pora* a pore), a general name for Corals with star-shaped cavities.

Mad'reporite, in mineralogy, a species of columnar carbonate of lime.

Maesto'so (Ital.), in music, a term denoting that the passage is to be played with majesty and strength.

Mae'stricht Beds, in geology, the uppermost group of the cretaceous or chalk formation, as it occurs near Maestricht.

Mag'deburgh Hemispheres, in physicology, an apparatus for illustrating atmospheric pressure, consisting of two hollow brass hemispheres fitted together, which, after the withdrawal of the air, cannot be separated.

Magellan'ic Clouds (from *Magellan*, the circumnavigator), in astronomy, those conspicuous nebulæ of stars seen in the southern hemisphere, two of them about 12° or 13° from the south pole, and the third more distant.

Magic (from the ancient *Magi*), the art of producing wonderful effects through the supposed agency of supernatural beings, though the means formerly adopted are now familiar to the votaries of science.

Magic Lantern, an optical instrument, by means of which small painted figures are magnified at pleasure on the walls of a dark room.

Magis'tral, in military science, the tracing or guiding line in fortification, the first laid down in the work or on paper, and from which the position of all the other works is determined. In field fortification, the crest-line of the parapet is the *magistral;* in permanent fortification, the *cordon,* or coping of the gudie-line, is the guide.—*Milit. Cycl.*

Magma (Lat.), a crude mixture of mineral or organic matters in a thin, pasty state.

Magne'sia (Gr.), a white, earthy substance used in medicine, and obtained by exposing its hydrated carbonate to a red heat.—*Magnesium* is the metallic base of magnesia.—*Magnesite* is the carbonate of magnesia.—*Magnesia alum* is a mineral of a snow-white colour and shining lustre, found at Cape Verd, and consisting of sulphates of alumina, magnesia, and manganese, chloride of potassium, and water.—*Magnesian limestone,* in geology, consists of a series of beds occurring in some places above the coal measures.—*Magnesian pharmacolite* is a mineral of a dirty-white or honey-yellow colour, consisting of arsenic acid, lime, magnesia, protoxide of manganese, and iron: sp. gr. 2·52; H — 6—7.

Magnet (from *Magnesia,* in Asia Minor, where first observed), the loadstone. —In mineralogy, one of the oxides of iron, which attracts iron, and possesses the property of pointing itself in a certain direction, and also of communicating this property to iron and steel bars. Magnets are of two kinds, *natural* and *artificial;* the latter are known as bar magnets and horse-shoe magnets. If of a single bar, it is a *single* magnet; if of several joined together, a *compound* magnet. Two points at or near the ends are called the *poles,* and the whole power of the magnet seems concentrated in these points; one is called the *north* pole, and the other the *south* pole.

Magnetic Battery, a battery formed of several magnets, with all their poles similarly disposed.—*Magnetic equator* is a line round the earth, everywhere equally distant from both magnetic poles; and here the magnetic needle does not dip, but stands horizontal, being equally attracted to both the terrestrial magnetic poles.—*Mag-*

netic dip is a property of the magnetic needle of inclining one of its poles towards the earth. It differs in different latitudes. The dip at London is about 69° 12′; over the magnetic poles the dip is 90°; at a line around the earth, forming an equator to these poles, there is no dip.—*Magnetic declination,* synonymous with the variation of the compass, which indicates the deviation of the magnetic needle from the true geographical meridian.—*Magnetic needle,* a small artificial magnet balanced on its centre, so that it may direct itself as influenced by terrestrial magnetism. —*Magnetic induction* is the power which a magnet has of communicating the qualities which it possesses to bars of iron or steel placed near it, although not in contact —*Magnetic poles* are two points of the earth to which the poles of an artificial magnet always tend; that in the northern hemisphere is called the *north* pole, and the antipode to this is called the *south* pole. The north pole is situated in the north-eastern part of Hudson's Bay, at about 80° west longitude and 60° north latitude.

Mag'netism (Fr.), the science which investigates the phenomena presented by natural and artificial magnets.— *Terrestrial magnetism,* that property of the earth from which the magnetism of the ordinary magnets, the direction of the magnetic needle, and other phenomena are derived, and upon which they necessarily depend.

Magne'to-electric'ity, that branch of natural philosophy established on the fact that magnetism and electricity have certain principles in common.

Magnetom'eter (Gr.), an instrument to ascertain the force of magnetism.

Magne'to-mo'tor, a voltaic series of two or more large plates, employed to exhibit electro-magnetic phenomena.

Magnolia'ceæ (from *M. Magnol,* of Montpelier), in botany, a nat. order of exogenous plants, of which the Magnolia, a highly-ornamental tree, is the type and genus.

Maia, the name of one of the newly-discovered planets, first observed by Tuttle in 1861.

Main (Sax. *magn*), in nautical science, a prefix to various terms; as, *Mainboom,* the spar of a small vessel on which the mainsail is extended;— *Mainsail,* the sail of the mainmast; —*Main-sheet,* the rope attached to the lower corner of the mainsail;— *Mainyard,* the yard on which the mainsail is extended, supported by the mainmast; —*Mainmast,* the principal mast in a ship ;—*Main-tackle*, a large strong tackle, hooked occasionally upon the main pendant, and used for various purposes, particularly in securing the mast, by setting up the rigging, stays, &c. ;—*Maintop*, the top of the mainmast of a ship or brig.

Major (Lat. *greater*), in logic, the first proposition of a syllogism.—In military matters, a field officer next in rank above a captain and below a lieutenant-colonel.

Major-general, a military officer next to a lieutenant-general.

Malac'ca Bean, in botany, the fruit of the *Anacardium Indicum* or *orientale*. It resembles the Cashew nut. —*Malacca-root*, the root of the *Sagittaria alexipharmaca*, or *Arundo Indica*, a West Indian plant.

Mal'achite, in mineralogy, native carbonate of copper, either blue or green.—*Green malachite* occurs in mammillary masses, consisting of concentric layers.—*Blue malachite* is found both in crystals and as an incrustation.

Mal'aco- (Gr. *malakos*), a prefix in compound words, signifying *softness*.

Mal'acolite, a variety of green augite.

Malacol'ogy (Gr. *malakos*, and *logos* a discourse), the natural history of molluscous animals, or of shells and shell-fish.

Malacopteryg'ii (Gr. *soft-finned*), the second great division of osseous fishes, the species of which are distinguished by all the rays of the fins being soft and cartilaginous. It consists of three sections—the Abdominales, Sub-brachiales, and Apodes. —*Malacopterygious*, applied to fishes with soft fins.

Malacos'teon (Gr.), in pathology, softness of bones.

Malacos'traca (Gr. *malakos*, and *ostrakon* a shell), the first section of the Crustacea, according to Cuvier's arrangement, containing the five orders, Decapoda, Stomapoda, Læmopoda, Amphipoda, and Isopoda.—*Malacostracous*, pertaining to Malacostraca. —*Malacostracology*, the science of Crustacea.

Mala'ria (Ital.), an exhalation from marshy districts; a noxious exhalation.

Malate (Lat. *malum* an apple), a salt from malic acid with a base.

Malda'nian, in zoology, a family of sedentary Annelids.

Malesherbia'ceæ (from *M. Malesherbes*, of Paris), in botany, a nat. order of exogenous plants, of which the Malesherbia is the type.

Mallea'ceæ, in conchology, a family of Mollusca, which comprehends a variety of genera ; as the Posidonia, Crenatula, Perna, Malleus, Gervillia, Cotillus, and Avicula.

Mal'leoli (Lat.), in military science, bundles of wood, made of combustible materials, for setting on fire at night, to discover the position of an enemy.

Maltha (Gr.), in mineralogy, a soft glutinous substance which smells like pitch ; mineral pitch.

Malva'ceæ (Lat. *malva*), in botany, a nat. order of exogenous plants, of which the Malva, or Mallow tree, is the genus.

Mamma'lia (Lat. *mamma* a teat or breast of a female), in zoology, the first grand division of vertebrated animals which suckle their young.— *Mammalogy* is the science of mammiferous animals.

Mammoth, a fossil elephant of immense size, the bones of one of which were discovered buried in ice in the north of Russia.

Man, *pl.* **Men** (Sax.), in zoology and natural history, the great epitome of all science and art ; the sole specific example of the only genus Homo, as contained in Cuvier's order Bimana. The great naturalist, Blumenbach, divides this species into five varieties. —1. The *Caucasian* variety, which includes all the ancient and modern Europeans, except the Fins ; the former and present inhabitants of Western Asia, as far as the River Oby, the Caspian Sea, and the Ganges (that is, the Assyrians, Medes, and Chaldeans ; the Sarmatians, Scythians, and Parthians ; the Philistines, Phœnicians, Jews, and the inhabitants of Syria generally ; the Tartars, properly so called ; the tribes actually occupying the chain of the Caucasus ; the Georgians, Circassians, Mingrelians, and Armenians ; the Turks, Persians, Arabians, Afghauns, and Hindoos of high castes), and the Northern Africans, the Egyptians, Abyssinians, and Guanches.—2. The *Mongolian* variety, which includes the tribes of Central and Northern Asia ; as the Mongolians, Calmucks, and Buriats ; the Mantchoos, Da-urians, Tungooses, and Coreans ; the Samoides, Yukagers, Koriacs, Tschuktschi, and Kamtschadales ; the Chinese and Japanese, the inhabitants of Tibet and Bootan, of Tonquin, Cochin-China, Ava, Pegu, Cambodia, Laes, and Siam ; the Finnish races of Northern Europe, as the Laplanders and the tribes of Esquimaux.—3. The *Ethiopian* variety, comprehending all the nations of Africa not included in the first variety.—4. The

American variety, including all the native Americans except the Esquimaux.—5. The *Malay* variety, which includes the inhabitants of Malacca, Sumatra, Java, Borneo, Celebes, and the adjacent Asiatic Islands; of the Molucca, Ladrone, Philippine, Marian, and Caroline groups; of New Holland, Van Diemen's Land, New Guinea, New Zealand, and of all the islands of the South Sea.—Cuvier's arrangement, however, differs from that of Blumenbach; he distinguishes only three principal divisions—the Caucasian, the Mongolian, and the Ethiopian; leaving the Malay and American varieties as doubtful.

Man'akin, in ornithology, a group of small birds remarkable for richness of plumage; order Ampelidæ.

Mandibula'ta, Mandib'ulates (Lat. *mandibulum* a jaw), in entomology, a class of insects which preserve their organs of mastication in their last stage of metamorphosis.

Manège (Fr.), a place where horsemanship is taught, or horses trained.

Manganese', a black mineral; a metal of grey colour, hard, brittle, and difficult of fusion.

Man'ganite, a mineral composed chiefly of an oxide of manganese; its constituents are manganese, oxygen, and water: sp. gr. 4.33.

Mangel-wurzel (Germ.), in botany, the *Beta vulgaris*, or Field Beet, extensively cultivated for feeding cattle.

Mangif'era (Ind. *mango* a fruit), in botany, a general name for the Mango trees of the East Indies, the fruit of which is very highly esteemed; order Terebinthaceæ.

Mangrove, a tree which forms dense groves in the tropics; also a plant which grows in and near salt water; order Rhizophoraceæ.

Manheim Gold, an alloy, consisting of 3 parts of copper and 1 of gold.

Man'ifold Writer (Sax. *manigfeald* multiplied), an apparatus for producing duplicate copies of letters or other documents, by a stylus, upon thin tracing-paper, interleaved with a blackened paper; sometimes called a *manifold* by the reporters of the press, with whom it is in general use.

Manna (Heb.), a saccharine substance that exudes from the bark of the *Fraxinus ornus*. At first the manna resembles drops of honey, but soon thickens into solid grains.—*Mannite* is a peculiar kind of sugar obtained from manna; it is composed of hydrogen, carbon, and oxygen.

Manœu'vre (Fr.).—In military science, *manœuvres of war* consist in habituating the soldier to a variety of evolutions, to accustom him to different movements, and to render his mind familiar with the nature of every principle of offensive or defensive operations.

Manom'eter (Gr. *manos* rarefied, and *metron* a measure), an instrument for measuring the rarefaction of elastic fluids.

Man'talet, Mantlet (Sax.), in fortification, a kind of movable parapet for sheltering the gunners from the fire of the assailants.

Mantis'sa, the decimal part of a logarithm.

Mantle, in zoology, the skin of molluscous animals which covers in the viscera and other parts of the body.

Mantling, in heraldry, the ornamental drapery around coats of arms.

Manu'brium (Lat. *a handle*), in anatomy, a term applied to the upper part of the sternum.

Map (Sp. *mapa*), a geographical picture or delineation of any portion of land and water; a representation of the earth, or any part of it, in which the lines of latitude and longitude, and the relative positions of countries, kingdoms, states, mountains, rivers, seas, &c., are represented.—*Mapping* is the art of delineating maps.

Maple, the name of trees and shrubs belonging to the genus Acer.

Mar'abou Feathers (Fr.), the under tail-coverts of the *Ciconia argala* and *C. maraboue*.

Maranta'ceæ (from *Maranti*, a Venetian physician), in botany, a nat. order of endogenous plants, of which the Maranta, or Arrowroot, is the type.

Maras'mus (Gr.), in pathology, a wasting of the body; atrophy.

Marble (Fr.), a carbonate of lime, or calcareous rock, of many varieties, extensively used for statues, busts, mantel-pieces, monuments, pillars, &c. There are three grand divisions of marbles:—1. Marbles of one plain colour, comprising the various shades from white to black;—2. Marbles of two colours, which are very varied;—3. Marbles variegated with many colours, several of which are very beautiful.—Parian marble is white, large-grained, and translucent. The marble of Carrara has a finer grain and closer texture, and is now usually employed by statuaries. In England, marbles abound in the counties of Derby, Devon, and Anglesea. In Scotland, they are found in Sutherlandshire and Argyleshire; in Ireland, at Kilkenny and other places.

Marbled Paper, paper veined or stained for covering boxes, books, or walls.

Marc (Fr.), the refuse or cake after expressing the oil or juice from fruits or seeds, as of apples, olives, &c., mostly used for manure.

Mar'casite, in mineralogy, a variety of iron pyrites; a term applied to a substance having metallic particles in it, called by the Cornish miners *mundic*.

Mar'celine (from *St. Marcel*, in Piedmont), a mineral of a greenish-black colour and vitreous lustre, consisting of silica, oxide of manganese, oxide of iron, and alumina.

Marcgravia'ceæ (in honour of *Marcgrave*, the German naturalist), in botany, a nat. order of exogenous plants, of which the Marcgravia is the type.

Marchantia'ceæ (in honour of *Marchant*, of Paris), a nat. order of plants, of which the Marchantia, or Liverwort, is the type.

Mar'garamide, a substance obtained from ammonial soap.

Mar'garate, a salt formed of margaric acid and a base.

Margar'ic, **Margarit'ic**, in chemistry, noting a fatty acid prepared from hog's lard and potash.

Mar'garite (Gr. *a pearl*), in mineralogy, pearl mica, a thinly-laminated mineral of a greyish, reddish, or yellowish-white colour: sp. gr. 3·0; H = 3·5—4·5.

Mar'garon, in chemistry, a solid fatty matter, obtained by distilling margaric acid with excess of lime.

Mar'ginate, **Mar'ginated** (Lat. *marginatus*), in conchology, denoting a prominent margin or border.—In entomology, an epithet used when the sharp edge is marginated on the outside, and surrounds the surface with a narrow border.

Marine Chair, a machine contrived for enabling the spectator to view the satellites of Jupiter in the open sea. —*Marine engine*, a steam-engine for use in ships at sea.

Mark (Sp. *marco*), a term applied to a money of account in Hamburg, Lubeck, Denmark, and Norway; also to a weight, used chiefly for gold and silver, in different parts of the Continent, varying from about 3,500 to 3,700 troy grains.

Marking Ink, an indelible ink for marking linen, usually made by dissolving a drachm of fused nitrate of silver in half an ounce of distilled water.

Marl, in mineralogy, a sort of calcareous earth compounded of carbonate of lime and clay.

Marline, in nautology, a small line used for winding round ropes.—*Mar-line-spike*, a piece of iron used in splicing small ropes.

Marlstone, in geology, a calcareous and irony stratum.

Marmite, in mineralogy, a black sulphuret of zinc.

Mar'molite, in mineralogy, the silicate of magnesia, consisting of silica, magnesia, lime, and water: sp. gr. 2·47; H = 3·5.

Mar'quetry (Fr.), inlaid work, consisting of different pieces of divers coloured woods; parquetry.

Mars (Lat.), in astronomy, the fourth planet in the order of distance from the sun. Its mean diameter is 4,398 miles; distance from the sun 142,000,000 miles; period of revolution round the sun, 686 days, 23 hours, 30 min., 39 sec.

Marsupia'lia, in zoology, a class of animals, the females of which are furnished with a *marsupium* or pouch for carrying their young, as in the Opossum or Kangaroo.—*Marsupial*, in anatomy, is a term applied to the obturator internus, from its purse-like shape.

Martel'lo (Ital.), an epithet applied to circular towers, some of which may still be seen on different parts of the British coast.

Mar'tial (Lat. *Mars*), in mineralogy, *martial ethiops* is the protoxide of iron, obtained by moistening iron filings slightly with water and exposing them for a day or two in the air, when a quantity of black or protoxide is formed upon the surface.

Mascag'nin, in mineralogy, native sulphate of ammonia, found in volcanic districts.

Mascle, in heraldry, a bearing in the form of a lozenge perforated.

Massil'ia, in astronomy, the name of one of the newly-discovered planets, first observed by De Gasparis in 1852. Its mean distance from the sun is 229,598,000 miles, and the time of its periodical revolution 3 years and 269 days.

Mast (Sax. *mast*), a long piece of timber raised nearly perpendicularly to the keel of a vessel, to support the yards or gaffs on which the sails are extended. In ship-building there are three principal masts:—(1) the *main-mast*, the largest mast in a ship, standing nearly in midships between stem and stern;—(2) the *foremast*, the next in size to the mainmast, which stands near the stem of a ship, and carries the foresail and foretopsail-yard;—(3) the *mizen-mast*, the smallest mast, which stands about half-way between the mainmast and the stern. *Jury-mast* is a yard set up instead of a mast which has been broken down by a storm. There are different names applied to different parts of the mast; as, *lower mast*, the lowest part of the mast;—*topmast*, that which is raised at the head or top of the lower mast;—*topgallant mast* is a smaller mast than the preceding, to which it is raised;—*topgallant - royal mast* is smaller than the preceding, and is usually elevated through irons at the head of the topgallant mast.

Mas'taoine, a soft, elastic substance, which has all the characteristics of caoutchouc when moist.

Mastic (Fr.), a gum or peculiar resin which exudes from the lentisk tree, used in plastering walls, and in varnishing.—In architecture, a kind of mortar or cement.

Masti'tis (Gr. *mastos* the breast), in pathology, inflammation of the breast in women.

Mas'todon (Gr. *mastos*, and *odontes* teeth, from the mammillated projections of the teeth), a huge, mammiferous, pachydermatous, extinct quadruped, allied to the elephant, and exceeding it in size, known only by its fossil remains. — *Mastodon-saurus*, a gigantic extinct saurian.

Mater (Lat. *mother*), in anatomy, a term applied to the membranes of the brain, as the *dura mater* and the *pia mater.*

Mate'ria Med'ica (Lat.), in medical science, that branch which treats of the articles employed in the practice of medicine, and explains the nature and mode of action of those substances which are had recourse to for the restoration of health.

Mate'rialism, the theory that the material universe is self-existent and self-directed, and that the functions of life, sensation, and thought arise out of modifications of matter; a doctrine which denies the existence of a spiritual or unnatural principle in man, as distinct from matter.

Mathemat'ics (Gr. *mathesis* learning), that science which treats of agnitude and number, or of whatever can be measured or numbered.—*Pure mathematics* is where geometrical magnitude or numbers are the subject of investigation.—*Mixed mathematics* is where the deductions thus made are from relations obtained by observation and experiment, and constitute what is called *physical science.*

Mattock, in military art, an implement used by the pioneers of an army, which resembles a pickaxe, but has two broad edges instead of points.

Mausole'um (Lat.), a magnificent tomb or monument, so called from *Mausolus*, King of Caria, to whose memory it was raised by his wife Artemisia, 353 B.C. Hence all sepulchral structures of importance are called mausoleums.

Maxil'læ (Lat.), in entomology, a name applied to the lower jaw of insects.

Maximilia'na, in astronomy, one of the newly discovered plants.

Max'imum (Lat.), the greatest quantity or degree attainable.—*Maxima et minima*, in geometry, are the greatest and the least quantities of a variable quantity, the method of finding which is by what is termed *methodus de maximis et minimis.*

Masol'ogy (Gr. *mazos* the breast, and *logos* a discourse), the science of mammiferous animals.

Mean (Sax. *mæne*), an epithet of frequent occurrence in scientific phraseology.—In mathematics, *mean* is that quantity which has an intermediate value between several others, formed according to any assigned law of succession: the *arithmetical mean* is formed by dividing all the quantities by their number; the *geometrical mean* is the middle term of a duplicate ratio, or continued proportion, and three terms.—In astronomy, *mean distance* of a planet from the sun is an arithmetical mean between the planet's greatest and least distance; *mean motion* is that by which a planet is supposed to move equably in its orbit; *mean time*, that which is measured by an equable motion; *mean conjunction*, or *opposition*, is when the mean place of the sun is in conjunction or opposition.

Meandri'na, a genus of hemispherical, lamelliferous corals, the Brain Coral, so named from the labyrinthine form of the cavities and ridges, which resemble the convolutions of the brain.

Measles, in pathology, the Rubeola, a contagious disease, usually characterized by small red spots; also a disease in swine and trees.

Measure (Fr.), the entire extent or dimensions of an object, including length, breadth, and thickness.—The *measure of a line* is its length compared with some determinate line, such as a mile, foot, inch, &c.—The *measure of a surface* is the number of square miles, feet, inches, &c., contained on it.—The *measure of a solid* is the number of cubic inches, feet, &c., it contains.—The *measure of an angle* is the number of degrees, minutes, &c., contained in the arc of a circle comprised between the two legs which form the angle, the angular point being the centre.—*Measure of velocity*, the space uniformly passed over by a moving body in a given time.

Meat Biscuit, in the culinary art, a concentrated preparation of meat pounded and dried, then mixed with meal, and baked.

Mecca Balsam, a fine oleo-resin, obtained from the Balsamodendron Gileadensis.

Mechan'ics (Gr. and Lat. *machina*, a machine), that science in natural philosophy which treats of forces and powers, and their actions on bodies by the intervention of machinery; the science of the laws of matter and motion, as applied to the construction of machines. The term *mechanics* of late years has been extended to the motion and equilibrium of all bodies, whether solid, fluid, or aëriform, and has been employed to comprehend the sciences of hydrodynamics and pneumatics.—*Mechanical philosophy* is the science of mechanics applied to physical inquiries, or, on the other hand, the application of the laws of general science to the improvement and construction of machinery.—The *six mechanical powers* are the lever, wheel and axle, pulley, inclined plane, wedge, and screw.—*Mechanical force* is the power of any machine or mechanical contrivance. It is, in fact, the measure of all other force, as it bears reference to the effect produced: thus steam, water, man, and horse power are all represented by the amount of mechanical force they can exert.

Mechlo'ic, in chemistry, noting an acid formed by passing chlorine gas over fused meconine.

Mec'onate, a salt formed of meconic acid and a base.

Mec'onine, a white, fusible substance obtained from opium.

Meco'nium (Gr. *mekon* a poppy), the juice of the white poppy; opium; the first fæces of children.

Me'dian (Lat. *medius*), in anatomy, situated in the middle of the body.

Me'diant (Lat. *medius*), in music, the chord which is a major or minor third higher than the key-note.

Mediasti'num (Lat.), in anatomy, the duplicature of the pleura, which divides the cavity of the thorax into two parts.

Med'icament (Lat.), anything used in healing; a topical application.

Med'icate (Lat.), to tincture or impregnate with anything medicinal.

Med'icine (Lat.), that branch of physic which relates to the healing of diseases; the science of the preservation of health, and the cure of diseases. It is divided into practical, theoretical, and forensic. *Practical medicine* is divided into four branches —surgery, physic, midwifery, and therapeutics. *Theoretical medicine* is divided into anatomy, pathology, and physiology. *Forensic medicine* consists in the application of the principles of medical science to the administration of justice and the preservation of the public health.

Me'dium (Lat.), that through which a body not in contact with another must pass to reach it.—In optics, any substance through which light is transmitted.—In logic, the medium or mean term of a syllogism.—In fencing, the preparatory guard of the broadsword or sabre, which consists in presenting the sword in a perpendicular line with the centre of the object opposed.

Medul'la (Lat.), in anatomy, the marrow in the cavities of the bones.—In botany, the pith of plants.—*Medullary rays*, in botany, are the vertical plates of cellular tissue which radiate from the stem of exogenous plants through the wood to the bark.

Modu'sidæ, a family of Acalephans, known commonly by the name of Sea-nettles or Sea-blubbers.

Medu'sidans, gelatinous radiate animals, which float or swim in the sea, of which the Medusa is the genus.

Meer'schaum, (Germ. *foam of the sea*), a silicated, soft, magnesian mineral, used in manufacturing tobacco-pipes.

Mega- (Gr. *megas*), a prefix in compound words, denoting *largeness of size*.

Mega'ceros (Gr. *large-horned*), in geology, the fossil Deer of the British Isles; the Irish Elk.

Meg'acosm (Gr. *megas*, and *kosmos* world), the great world, as distinguished from *microcosm*.

Megalodon'tes (Gr. *large-toothed*), a family of coleopterous insects.

Meg'alonyx (Gr. *megas*, and *onyx* a claw), in geology, a large extinct Mammal.

Megalop'tera (Gr.), a family of neuropterous insects.

Megalosau'rus (Gr.), in geology, a fossil gigantic amphibious animal of the Saurian tribe.

Meg'amètre (Gr.), an instrument for determining longitude by measurement of the stars.

Meganyc'terans (Gr. *megas*, and *nycteris* a bat), a tribe of the order Cheiroptera, including the largest species of Bats.

Megapodi'idæ, in ornithology, a family of rasorial birds, the Great-foots, with the feet very large.

Meg'ascope (Gr.), an optical instrument for examining large bodies.

Megathe'rioid (Gr.), one of a family of extinct mammiferous quadrupeds.

Megathe'rium (Gr. *a great beast*), in geology, a large extinct animal found in S. America.

Megrim (Fr.), in pathology, a violent intermitting pain affecting one side of the head ; vertigo.

Meibo'mian, in anatomy, noting glands situated at the edge of the eyelids.

Mei'onite (Gr.), in mineralogy, a greyish-white felspar.

Melæ'na (Gr.), a discharge of black blood, in consequence of the presence of acid.

Melain (Gr. *melas* black), the colouring matter of the ink of the cuttle-fish.

Melam, a substance consisting of carbon, nitrogen, and hydrogen.

Melam'pyrine, a substance containing neutral crystals.

Melan'agogue (Gr. *melas*, and *ago* to drive), a medicine for expelling black bile, choler, or melancholy.

Melania'næ, a sub-family of the Turbidæ, the Black Snails, in which the shells are spiral.

Mel'anite, in mineralogy, a species of black garnet.

Melanoch'roite, a Siberian mineral of a hyacinthine or orange-red colour, nearly opaque. It consists of oxide of lead and chromic acid : sp. gr. 5·75.

Melano'sis (Gr.), in pathology, a malignant disease, characterized by deposition of black matter.

Melan'terite, a native sulphate of iron.

Melantha'ceæ, an order of liliaceous Endogens.

Mel'aphyre, a variety of black porphyry.

Melas'ma (Gr.), a disease of aged persons, in which a black spot appears upon the skin, and forms a foul ulcer.

Melaso'ma (Gr. *melas*, and *soma* a body), the name of a family of heteromerous Coleoptera, consisting of black or cinerous-coloured Beetles, mostly apterous, and frequently with soldered elytra.

Melastoma'ceæ, a nat. order of exogenous plants, of which the Melastoma is the type.

Melia'ceæ, in botany, a nat. order of exogenous plants.

Melice'ris (Gr. *meli* honey, and *keros* wax), in pathology, an encysted tumour, the contents of which resemble honey and wax.

Meliphag'idæ (*Meliphaga* one of the genera), a genus of tenuirostral birds, Honey-suckers.

Mellate, in chemistry, a salt formed of mellitic acid and a base.

Mel'litate, in chemistry, a compound of mellitic acid and a base.

Mellite, **Mel'lilite**, in mineralogy, the honey-stone, a yellow crystallized mineral.

Melo'sis (Gr.), in surgery, the art of probing a wound.

Melpom'ene, the name of one of the newly-discovered planets, first observed by Hind in 1852. Its mean distance from the sun is 218,930,000 miles.

Membrane (Lat.), in physiology, the expansion of any of the tissues of the body into a thin layer.—Membranes are of different kinds ; as, *Membrana pupillaris*, the membrane which covers the pupil of the eye of the fœtus before the sixth month ;—*Membrana nictitans*, a thin membrane which serves to defend the eyes of birds and beasts from dust, &c. ;—*Membrana tympani*, the drum of the ear ; the membrane which separates the internal from the external ear ;—*Membrana urinaria*, the urinary coat belonging to the fœtus in the womb ; — *Membrana adiposa*, the membrane which contains the fat, and serves as one of the integuments of the body.—*Membranology* is that branch of anatomy which treats of the membranes of the body.

Memo'ria Tech'nica (Lat.), artificial or technical memory.

Men'achanite (from *Menachan*, in Cornwall), the ferruginous oxide of titanium.

Mengite, a mineral of a hyacinth or brick-red colour and vitreous lustre, found at Miask, in Siberia. Its constituents are phosphoric acid, peroxide of cerium, oxide of lanthanium, thorina, peroxide of tin, protoxide of manganese, and lime : sp. gr. 4·92 ; H = 5·0.

Men'ilite, a kind of semi-opal found at Menil Montant, near Paris.

Menin'ges (Gr.), in anatomy, two membranes that envelop the brain, called the *pia mater* and *dura mater*.—*Meningitis* is inflammation of the membranes of the brain.

Menin'go-phalanx, in surgery, an instrument for the protection of the cerebral membranes during the operation of the trephine on a diseased or fractured skull.

Meningorrhœ'a (Gr. *menigx* the membrane of the brain, and *rheo* to flow), extravasation of the blood on or between the cerebral membranes.

Meningo'sis (Gr.), in anatomy, the union of osseous pieces by the intervention of membrane, as exhibited in the cranial bones of the fœtus.

Menis′cus (Gr. *meniskos* a crescent), in optics, a lens convex on one side, and concave on the other.

Menisperma′ceæ (Gr. *mene* the moon, and *sperma* seed), a nat. order of exogenous plants, of which Menispermum is the genus.

Menisper′mate, a compound of menispermic acid and a salifiable base. —The *menispermic acid* is obtained from the seeds of the *Cocculus Indicus*.

Menisper′mina, a vegetable alkali extracted from the *Cocculus Indicus*.

Menisper′mine, a tasteless, white, opaque, crystalline, alkaloid.

Menses (Gr. *menos* a month), in physiology, the monthly flow of blood which takes place in women, and in others of the female Mammifera, by the organs of generation.

Men′struum (Lat.), a fluid substance which dissolves a solid body ; a solvent.

Mensura′tion (Lat.), in geometry, the art or act of ascertaining the extension, solidity, and capacity of bodies by measuring lines and angles.

Mentag′ra (Lat.), an herpetic eruption of the skin.

Mephi′tis (Lat.), a noxious exhalation, particularly applied to carbonic acid gas.

Mercap′tan, in chemistry, a liquid composed of sulphur, carbon, and hydrogen.

Merca′tor′s Chart, in geography, a projection of the globe of the earth *in plano*.—In navigation, *Mercator′s sailing* is the science of finding upon a plane the way of a ship on a course assigned, the meridians being all parallel, and the parallels of latitudes being straight lines.

Mer′cury, in astronomy, the planet nearest the sun, from which he is distant about 36,000,000 miles. His mean sidereal revolution is performed in 78·969258 mean solar days. His diameter is about 3,140 miles. He revolves on his axis in 24 hours, 5 min., 28 sec.—In mineralogy, a white metal which is fluid at common temperatures ; quicksilver. Its specific gravity is 13·5 ; its equivalent is 200. Formula, Hg, from the Latin *hydrargyrum*.

Merid′ian (Lat. *mid-day*), in astronomy and geography, an imaginary great circle of the sphere, passing through the earth′s axis and the zenith of the spectator, dividing the sphere into two hemispheres, eastern and western, and crossing the equinoctial at right angles. In geography, the meridians are as numerous as the places on the earth, and the first meridian is that from which the reckoning commences. This is fixed differently by different nations, the capital of each country being mostly chosen as the first meridian for their respective globes. In all our English maps and globes, the meridian of England is that circle which passes through London and the poles of the earth, and from which our longitude is reckoned.—*Meridional distance* is the difference of the longitude between the meridian under which the ship is at present, and any other she was under before.

Meri′no (Sp.), a species of sheep noted for the fineness of their wool.

Merismat′ic (Gr. *merizo* to divide), in zoology, multiplying by division.

Merlin, in military phraseology, a handspike.

Merlon (Fr.), in fortification, the part of a parapet included between two embrasures.

Merop′idans, a family of insessorial birds, of which the Merops, or Bee-eater, is the type.

Meros (Gr.), in architecture, the plane face between the channels in the triglyphs of the Doric order.

Mes′entery (Gr. *mesos* middle, and *enteron* intestine), in anatomy, a membrane by which the intestines are attached to the vertebræ.

Me′sial (Gr.), in anatomy, applied to a longitudinal line dividing the body into two equal parts.

Mes′merism (in honour of *Ant. Mesmer*, of Vienna) another term for animal magnetism ; an agent (as taught by its advocates) by which one person can communicate certain influences at will to the mind of the person mesmerized, or put into a state of sleep, in which questions are answered.—*Mesmerization* is the act of producing the mesmeric state.

Mes′ocarp (Gr.), in botany, the middle of the three layers in fruit.

Mesoco′lon (Gr.), in anatomy, the mesentery of the colon.

Mesogas′tric (Gr. *mesos*, and *gaster* the belly), in anatomy, occupying the umbilical region.

Mesole (Gr.), a mineral which occurs massive, globular, or reniform.

Mesoleu′cos (Gr.), a precious stone, black, with a streak of white in the middle.

Mes′olite (Gr.), in mineralogy, a hydrated silicate of alumina, lime, and soda.

Mesolog′arithm (Gr.), a logarithm of the cotangent, or differential logarithm.

Mesom′elas (Gr.), a precious stone with a black vein parting every colour in the midst.

Mesompha'lion (Gr.), in anatomy, the middle navel.

Mesotho'rax (Gr.), the middle thorax or trunk of an insect.

Mes'otype (Gr.), a hydrated silicate of alumina and soda.

Mesozo'ic (Gr. *mesos* and *zoe*, middle life), in geology, an epithet applied to the middle period of the earth's crust as relates to animal remains.

Mesto (Ital.), in music, a term signifying that a piece is to be played in the pathetic style.

Meta (Gr.), a prefix to compound words, signifying *beyond*.

Metabo'lians (Gr. *metabole* change), in entomology, a class of insects that undergoes a metamorphosis.

Metacar'pus (Gr. *meta*, and *karpos* the wrist), that part of the hand between the wrist and the fingers.

Metagal'late, a salt formed from meta-gallic acid and a base.

Metagen'esis (Gr. *meta*, and *gennao* to reproduce), in zoology, the changes of form which the representative of a species undergoes in passing from an imperfect to a more perfect state.

Metal (Fr. from Lat. *metallum*), an undecompounded body of peculiar lustre, insoluble in water, fusible by heat, and capable, in the state of an oxide, of uniting with acids, and forming with them metallic salts. Metals are distinguished, in different degrees, by malleability, ductility, fusibility, tenacity, elasticity, and crystalline texture. Gold, silver, iron, copper, mercury, lead, and tin were known to the ancients from the earliest periods. Gold and silver were called *noble* metals; the rest *base* metals. The following is a list of the metals, arranged according to the order of time when they were first discovered :—

	A.D.
Antimony	1400
Zinc	1520
Bismuth	16th century
Arsenic and Cobalt	1733
Platinum	1741
Nickel	1751
Manganese	1774
Tungsten	1781
Tellurium	1782
Molybdenum	1782
Uranium	1789
Titanium	1791
Chromium	1797
Columbium	1802
Palladium and Rhodium	1803
Iridium	1803
Osmium	1803
Cerium	1804
Potassium, Sodium Ba-	
rium, Strontium, and	
Calcium	1807
Cadmium	1818
Lithium	1818
Selenium	1818
Silicium and Zirconium	1824
Aluminium, Glucinium, and Yttrium	1828
Thorium and Magnesium	1829

These metals are distinguished into different classes, which have been thus arranged by Hoblyn :—1. *Metallic bases of the alkalies*, viz., potassium, sodium, and lithium. The oxides are termed *alkalies*, and the metallic bases *alkaline* or *alkaligenous* metals.—2. *Metallic bases of the alkaline earths*, viz., barium, strontium, calcium, and magnesium, and their oxides are termed *alkaline earths*. — 3. *Metallic bases of the earths*, viz., aluminium, zirconium, glucinium, silicium, yttrium, and thorium.—4. Metals yielding oxides, which are *neutral salifiable bases*, viz., gold, silver, mercury, copper, lead, iron, tin, platinum, palladium, nickel, cadmium, zinc, bismuth, antimony, cobalt, and manganese.—5. Metals which are *acidifiable* by combination with oxygen, viz., tellurium, arsenic, chromium, molybdenum, tungsten, columbium, and selenium.—6. *Metals magnetic*, viz., iron, nickel, and cobalt. Metals are termed *native* when found in an uncombined form; *mineralized*, when combined with other bodies; compounds of two or more metals, except mercury, are called *alloys*, and possess the characteristic properties of pure metals; those of mercury with other metals are called *amalgams*. Metals are the best reflectors of caloric, and the worst radiators.— (*Gray, Ure, Hoblyn.*)

Met'alling, an engineering term for stone and other material applied to give firmness and solidity to roads and railways.

Metalloch'romy (Gr. *chromos* colour), art of colouring metals.

Metallog'raphy (Gr.), a description of metals.

Met'alloid, in chemistry, a non-metallic, inflammable body, as sulphur, phosphorus, &c.; applied also to the metallic bases of the fixed alkalies.

Met'allurgy (Gr.), the art of working metals, or separating them from their ores.

Metamor'phic (Gr.), in geology, changeable, as applied to a class of stratified primary rocks. — *Metamorphism* is the state of being metamorphic.

Metaphys'ics (Gr. *meta*, and *physis*

nature), the philosophy of mind, as distinguished from that of matter; a speculative science, which soars beyond the bounds of actual experience. The science has been divided into six parts—ontology, cosmology, anthropophosy, psychology, pneumatology, and metaphysical theology.

Metas'tasis (Gr. *meta*, and *stasis* standing), the removal of the seat of a disease from one place to another.

Metatar'sus (Gr.), the sole of the foot between the toes and the ankle.

Me'teor (Gr. *meteora* things in the air), any natural phenomenon in the atmosphere or clouds; a fiery or luminous body occasionally seen moving rapidly through the atmosphere.—*Meteors* may be divided into classes according to their nature or origin. Thus winds, whirlwinds, &c., are *aërial* meteors; dews, fogs, rain, snow, and other depositions or disturbances of the water of the atmosphere, are called *aqueous* meteors. Many arise from the refraction or reflection of light from the aqueous particles suspended in the air; these are called *luminous* meteors—such are halo, mirage, rainbow, &c.; while those that present the appearance and phenomena of combustion are *igneous* meteors—such are falling stars, lightning, &c.—*Meteorology* is the science of the atmosphere, and its various phenomena.

Met'eorite, or **Meteor'olite** (Gr. *meteoros*, and *lithos* a stone), a solid substance or body falling from the high regions of the atmosphere; a meteoric stone.

Meteoros'copy (Gr. *meteoros*, and *skopeo* to view), that part of astronomy which treats of the difference of the remote heavenly bodies, their distances, &c.—*Meteoroscope* is an instrument for taking the magnitude and distances of the heavenly bodies.

Methyl (Gr. *methu* wine, and *yle* material), in chemistry, a compound of carbon and hydrogen.

Meth'ylated Spirit (Gr. *methu*), spirit of wine 5½ per cent. over proof, mixed with wood naphtha, or methylic spirit.

Meth'ylene (Gr.), in chemistry, a highly volatile and inflammable liquid compound of carbon and hydrogen.

Met'oche (Gr.), in architecture, the space between two dentils.

Met'ope (Gr.), in architecture, a square space between triglyphs in the frieze of the Doric order.

Metral'gia (Gr. *meter* the womb, and *algos*), pain in the womb.

Metrans'trophe (Gr.), inversion of the womb.

Metri'tis (Gr.), inflammation of the womb.

Met'rocele (Gr.), hernia of the womb.

Metrol'ogy (Gr. *metron* measure, and *logos* discourse), a treatise on weights and measures.

Met'ronome (Gr.), in music, an instrument for determining the movements of musical compositions.

Metron'omy (Gr. *metron*, and *nomos* law), the measuring of time by an instrument.

Metrorrha'gia (Gr. *meter*, and *segnymi* to burst forth), hæmorrhage of the womb.

Metrot'omy (Gr.), incision of the womb.

Mezza-voce (Ital.), in music, an expression denoting that the movement is to be sung or played with moderate strength.

Mezzo-relievo (Ital.), middle or demi-relief.

Mez'zotint, Mezzotin'to (Ital.), a kind of engraving on copper, resembling drawings in Indian ink.

Miasm, Mias'ma, *pl.* **Mias'mata**, a noxious particle, substance, or exhalation floating in the air.

Mica (Gr. *shining*), a mineral generally found in thin transparent laminæ; one of the ingredients of granite, gneiss, and mica slate.

Mica Schist, in mineralogy, one of the lowest stratified rocks, composed of quartz and mica.

Mi'chaelite, in mineralogy, a variety of opal.

Micro- (Gr. *mikros*), a prefix to compound words, signifying *smallness*.

Mi'crocosm (Gr. *mikros*, and *kosmos* world), the little world; man considered as an epitome of the macrocosm, or the great world.

Microg'raphy (Gr.), the description of such objects as are too minute to be seen without the help of a microscope.

Mi'crolite (Gr. *a minute stone*), a mineral having very small crystals.

Microl'ogy (Gr.), a treatise on microscopic animals and plants.

Microm'eter (Gr.), an instrument applied to telescopes and microscopes for measuring very small distances.

Microphon'ics (Gr.), the science of magnifying low sounds.

Mi'croscope (Gr. *mikros*, and *skopeo* to view), an optical instrument which enables us to examine objects too minute to be seen by the naked eye.

Micros'mic Salt, in chemistry, a triple salt of soda, ammonia, and phosphoric acid.

Micros'copy (Gr.), the art by which small objects are made to appear large.

Micturi'tion (Lat.), the voiding of urine.

Mid'dletonite, a mineral found between layers of coal.

Midrib, in botany, the principal vein of

a leaf, which runs from the stem to the point.

Midriff, in anatomy, the diaphragm; the membrane which separates the heart and lungs from the stomach and lower venter.

Mi'emite, magnesian carbonate of lime.

Milia'ria (Lat. *milium* millet), in pathology, miliary fever, a disease attended by an eruption resembling millet seed.

Milk (Sax. *melce*), in zoology, a fluid secreted in the breasts or udders of mammiferous animals, and with which such animals feed their young. —In botany, it is the emulsion or juice of plants.—*Woman's milk* contains butter or fatty matter, 4·5 per cent.; sugar of milk, 3·5.—*Cow's milk* contains cream, 4·6; butter or fatty matter, 2·68; caseum, 8·95; sugar of milk, 3·60.

Milky Way, in astronomy, a broad and irregular starry zone or galaxy that surrounds the heavens; a great luminous band that stretches from horizon to horizon, and which, when traced with diligence and mapped down, is found to form a zone completely surrounding the whole sphere, almost in a great circle. This remarkable belt has maintained, from the earliest ages, the same relative position among the stars; and when examined through telescopes, is found to consist entirely of stars, scattered by millions, like glittering dust on the face of the general heavens.

Mill (Sax.), an engine or machine for grinding grain, fruit, or other substances, whose action depends chiefly on circular motion; as, a bark-*mill*, cotton - *mill*, flour-*mill*, oil - *mill*, saw-*mill*, &c.

Mil'legram (Fr.), a thousandth part of a gramme in French measure.

Mil'leped (Lat.), an insect having a great many feet; the Wood-louse.

Millepor'idæ (Lat. *mille* a thousand, and Gr. *poros* a pore), the name of an extensive family of stone - making Polypes.

Mil'leporite, in geology, fossil millepores.

Mil'lilitre (Fr.), in French measure, a thousandth part of a litre.

Mil'limètre (Fr.), a thousandth part of a mètre.

Millstone, the stone of a mill which crushes the substance to be ground, chiefly used for grinding grain.— *Millstone grit*, in geology, is a group of strata which, when present, occurs between the mountain limestone and the coal formation, of which it is a subordinate member.

Milt (Sax.), in anatomy, a viscus situated in the left hypochondrium, under the diaphragm; the spleen.

Mim'etene, the mineral arseniate of lead.

Mimo'seæ (Gr. *mimos* a mimic), in botany, an order of leguminous plants, of which the Mimosa, or Sensitive-plant, is the type.

Mine (Fr.), a subterraneous work or excavation for obtaining metals, metallic ores, or other mineral substances; also, an excavation for lodging gunpowder in order to blow up something above. — *Military mines* are excavations made in the rampart of a fortress, or under ground, in order to contain gunpowder, by which, on being exploded, the rampart may be breached, or any works of the enemy above the mine, or near it, may be destroyed.

Min'eral (Fr. from Low Lat.), a body destitute of organization, and which naturally exists within the earth or on its surface; a term including all inorganic substances.—*Mineral*, as an epithet, has various applications. —*Mineral kingdom* is a term applied to the third grand division of natural objects, embracing all inorganic substances whatever. — *Mineral acids* comprehend the nitric, sulphuric, hydrochloric, chromic, and numerous other acids.—*Mineral salts* are salts found native, being formed by the mineral acids with bases.—*Mineral waters* are waters impregnated with mineral substances.—*Mineral caoutchouc* is a variety of bitumen, intermediate between the harder and softer kinds.—*Mineral charcoal* is a fibrous variety of non-bituminous mineral coal.—*Mineral green* is carbonate of copper.—*Mineral adipocere* is a fatty bituminous substance which occurs in the argillaceous iron ore of Merthyr, in Wales.

Mineral'ogy (*mineral*, and Gr. *logos* a discourse), the science which teaches the proportions, composition, and relations of mineral bodies, and the art of distinguishing and describing them.

Minim (Lat.), in music, half a semibreve, and double that of a crotchet.

Min'ium (Lat.), in painting, red oxide of lead, a compound substance procured by exposing the protoxide of lead to the long-continued action of heat and air, by which it acquires more oxygen, and becomes of a fine red colour.

Min'uend (Lat.), in arithmetic, the number from which another number is to be subtracted.

Minus (Lat.), in algebra, a term signifying *less;* noting the sign of subtraction thus (—); as, 10 — 6 = 4.

Minus'cule (Lat.), a small or minute sort of character used in MSS. in the middle ages.

Mi'ocene (Gr. *meion* less, and *kainos* recent), in geology, relating to the second division of the tertiary epoch. The miocene strata contain an admixture of the extinct genera of lacustrine Mammalia of the eocene period, with the earliest forms of genera which exist at the present day.

Mirab'ilite, the efflorescence on the soil among salt springs.

Mirage (Fr.), in meteorology, an optical illusion, presenting an image of water in sandy deserts, or of a village in a desert, as if built on a lake.

Miscar'riage, in pathology, the expulsion of the fœtus from the uterus within six weeks after conception. If it occurs before six months, it is called *abortion;* and if during any part of the three months before the completion of the natural term, *premature labour.*

Mistu'ra (Lat.), in pharmacy, a fluid composed of two or more ingredients, mostly contracted in prescriptions; thus, *f. mis.* means, let a mixture be made.

Mith'ridate, in medicine, a confection. —In botany, common mustard.

Mitral (Gr. *mitra* a mitre), in anatomy, applied to the valves of the left ventricle of the heart.

Mitra'næ, in conchology, a sub-family of Volutidæ, or Volutes.

Mnemon'ics, Mnemotech'ny (Gr. *mneme* memory), the science of improving the memory by artificial means.

Mnemos'yne, the name of one of the newly-discovered planets, first observed by Luther in 1859.

Mocha Stone, in mineralogy, the moss agate.

Modera'to (Ital.), in music, noting a moderate time, neither quick nor slow.

Modil'lion (Fr.), in architecture, an ornament, sometimes square on its profile, and sometimes scroll-shaped, placed under the cornice of a building; a console or bracket.

Module (Fr. from Lat. *modulus*), in architecture, a measure taken for regulating the proportions of an order, or the dispositions of the whole building; the diameter or semi-diameter of the column at the bottom of the shaft has usually been selected by architects as their *module.*

Mohsite (from *Mohs,* the celebrated mineralogist), in mineralogy, the crystallized titanite of iron.

Moineau (Fr.), a small, flat bastion raised in front of an intended fortification.

Mola'res (Lat.), in anatomy, a term applied to the double teeth, the grinders. —*Molares glandulæ* are two salivary glands, situated on each side of the mouth, between the masseter and buccinator muscles, the excretory ducts of which open near the last dens molaris.

Mole (Lat.), in engineering, a massive work of masonry or stones, placed in the sea by means of coffer-dams, extended either in a right line or in an arc of a circle, before a port, which it serves to close, and to defend the vessels therein from the impetuosity of the waves.—In pathology, a mass of fleshy matter growing in the uterus.

Mol'ecule (Lat.), a very minute particle of matter; an atom; a corpuscle.—*Integral molecule,* in mineralogy, is the last particle into which the nucleus of a crystal can be mechanically divided.

Mollusc, *pl.* **Mollus'ca** (Lat. *mollis* soft), a molluscous animal, with a soft, invertebrated body and no internal skeleton, but furnished with respiratory and circulating organs, and a nervous system. The Mollusca constitute an important division of the animal kingdom, and are divided into six classes—the Cephalopoda, Pteropoda, Acephala, Brachiopoda, and Cirrhipoda, or Cirropods.

Molto (Ital. from Lat. *multum*), in music, a word generally used in combination by way of augmentation; as, *molto allegro,* very quick; *molto adagio,* very slow, &c.

Molyb'date (Gr. *molybdaina* lead), a salt composed of molybdic acid and a base.—*Molybdate of lead* is a mineral which occurs crystallized and massive; it consists of oxide of lead, molybdic acid, and oxide of iron.

Molybde'na, Molyb'den (Gr.), a mineral ore, which is a common sulphate of molybdenum.

Molyb'denite (Gr.), a mineral containing molybdenum.

Molybde'num (Gr.), a sort of brittle metal, mineralized by sulphur.

Molyb'dic Acid, in chemistry, an acid formed by oxidizing the binoxide of molybdenum with nitric acid, and forming a fine white powder.

Molyb'do-sul'phuret, a combination of molybdenum with sulphur.

Momen'tum (Lat.), in mechanical science, the force possessed by matter in motion, or the quantity of motion in a moving body.

Mon-, or **Mono-** (Gr. *monos*), a prefix in compound words, signifying *single* or *only one.*

Monad (Gr. *monos*), an ultimate atom; a primary constituent of matter.

Mon'adelph (Gr. *a single brother*), in botany, a plant whose stamens are united into one parcel by filaments.—In the Linnæan system, *Monadelphia* is a class of plants consisting of those which have hermaphrodite flowers, and have the filaments cohering in a tube.

Monadel'phon (Gr.), in botany, a stamen of which the filaments are combined into a single mass.

Monan'dria (Gr. *monos*, and *aner, andros* a male or stamen), in botany, the first class of plants in the Linnæan system, having only one stamen.—*Monandrian*, belonging to the class Monandria.

Mon'azite, a reddish-brown mineral.

Mongo'lian, in ethnology, a term applied to a class of mankind who have the Mongols and the Chinese as the type.

Monkey Wrench, in mechanical science, a spanner with a movable jaw.

Monobas'ic (Gr.), in chemistry, having only a single atom of base.

Mon'ochord (Gr.), in music, an instrument of one string, used for the purpose of ascertaining and demonstrating the relative proportions of musical sounds.

Mon'ochrome (Gr. *monos*, and *chroma* colour), a painting executed in a single colour.

Mon'ocle (Fr.), a reading-glass for one eye.

Monocli'nate (Gr.), in mineralogy, a term applied to crystals in which one of the axes is obliquely inclined.

Monocotyle'don (Gr.), a plant having only one seed-lobe; an Endogen.

Mon'odelph (Gr. *one womb*), in zoology, a Mammal which brings forth its young in so mature a state as not to require the protection of a pouch.

Monœ'cian (Gr. *monos*, and *oikos* dwelling), a class of plants which have the stamens and pistils in separate flowers of the same plant.

Mon'ogam (Gr. *monos*, and *gamos* marriage), in botany, a plant that has a simple flower, though the anthers are united.

Mono'gram (Gr. *single letter*), one character or cipher in writing; an abbreviation of a name by means of a cipher or figure composed of an intertexture of letters.

Mon'ogyn (Gr. *one female*), a plant having only one style or stigma.—*Monogynia* is the name of the first order in each of the first thirteen classes in the botanical system of Linnæus.

Mon'olith (Gr. *a single stone*), an obelisk or monument formed of a single stone.

Monoma'nia (Gr.), in pathology, insanity upon one particular subject.

Monome (Fr.), in algebra, an expression composed of a single term, or a series of factors, all of which are single terms.

Monome'rans (Gr. *monos*, and *meros* limb), in entomology, a section of coleopterous insects, including those in which the tarsi were supposed to be formed by a single joint.

Monop'teron (Gr. *one-winged*), a temple or edifice consisting of a circular colonnade supporting a dome.—*Monopteral*, having only a single wing.

Mon'otremes (Gr. *monos*, and *trema* a hole), in zoology, a family of edentate Mammalia, with one external aperture for the passage of the semen, urine, and other excrements. It consists of two genera, the Echidna and Ornithorhynchus.

Monotrig'lyph (Gr.), in architecture, such an intercolumniation in the Doric order as brings only one triglyph over it.

Monotropa'ceæ (Gr. *monos*, and *trepo* to turn), in botany, a nat. order of Exogens, the Rape Firs, of which Monotropa is the genus.

Monsoon, in physicology, a modification of the trade winds in the Eastern seas.

Month (Sax. *monath*, from *mona* the moon), a division of time regulated by the course of the moon and the sun.—The *lunar month* is the time from one new moon to another, or 29 days, 12 hours, 44 min., 3 sec.—A *solar month* is the time in which the sun runs through one entire sign of the zodiac, the mean quantity of which is 30 days, 10 hours, 29 min., 5 sec.

Montmar'trite, in mineralogy, a compound of the sulphate and carbonate of lime, found at Montmartre, near Paris.

Moon (Sax. *mona*), in astronomy, one of the heavenly bodies; the satellite of the earth, round which she revolves as a centre. Her sidereal revolution is in 27 days, 7 hours, 43 min.; her synodical revolution is 29 days, 12 hours, 44 min., 3 sec.; her mean distance from the earth, about 237,000 miles. The rotation on her axis is uniform, and is performed in the same time as her revolution in her orbit, whence she always presents nearly the same face to the earth.—*Half-moon*, in fortification, is an outwork resembling a crescent in form.

Moonstone, in mineralogy, a variety of adularia, or resplendent felspar.

Moorstone, in mineralogy, a whitish kind of granite, existing in Cornwall and other parts of England, found useful in the coarser kinds of building.

Moraine (Fr.), in geology, an accumulation of sandstone and other débris found at the bases and along the ravines of glaciers.

Morbid Anat'omy, the study of the alterations produced in the bodily structure by disease.

Morbus (Lat.), in pathology, a disease or disordered action of any part of the animal organization. Hoblyn has enumerated the following list of diseases to which the human frame is liable :—*Morbus arcuatus*, the jaundice ; — *M. caducus*, falling sickness ;—*M. interpellatus*, a disease attended with irregular or uncertain paroxysms ;—*M. cæruleus*, cyanosis ; blue disease ;—*M. cardiacus*, typhus fever ;—*M. coxarius*, disease of the hips ;—*M. gallicus*, framboesia, or yaws ;—*M. niger*, melæna ; black disease ;—*M. pedicularis*, lousy disease;—*M. pilaris*, hairworm disease ; —*M. regius*, jaundice ; king's evil ;— *M. rubulus*, framboesia, or yaws ;— *M. sitibundus*, diabetes ; thirst disease ;—*M. sudatorius*, sweating sickness ; — *Morbi pathetici*, morositates ; depraved appetites, and morbid changes in the feelings and propensities.

Mordant (Lat. *mordeo* to bite), a substance used in dyeing, which combines with and fixes colours.

Moren'do (Ital.), in music, a term indicating a style of performance in which the tones of the voices or instruments are to be gradually softened, or made to die away.

Moresque (Fr. from Ital. *moresco*), in architecture and painting, the style used by the Arabs and Moors, in which foliage, fruits, flowers, &c., are combined by springing out of each other, but without any figure of man or animal.

Mor'oxite (Lat. *morus* the mulberry), in mineralogy, a native phosphate of lime of a mulberry colour.

Morox'ylate, a salt formed of moroxylic acid and a base.

Moroxyl'io, noting an acid procured from the white mulberry.

Mor'phia, Morphine (from *Morpheus*, the god of slumber), in chemistry, the narcotic principle of opium.

Morphol'ogy (Gr. *morphe* form, and *logos* discourse), in botany, the science which treats of the metamorphosis of organs.

Morsus Diab'oli (Lat. *the devil's bite*), in anatomy, a term applied to the jagged ends of the Fallopian tubes.

Mortar (Fr. from Lat. *mortuarium*), in the chemical laboratory, a strong vessel in which substances are pounded and pulverized with a pestle ;—a short, wide piece of ordnance for throwing shells, bombs, grape-shot, &c. ;—cement for the junction of stones and bricks, usually made of lime, sand, and water.—*Mortar-piece*, a sort of short, thick cannon.—*Hydraulic mortar* is a cement which acquires but little solidity in the air, but becomes extremely hard under water. The poorer kinds of limestone are burnt, ground, mixed with water and sand, and immediately applied to the work.

Mortifica'tion (Lat.), in pathology, the state of being mortified, or the loss of vitality in some part of the body. The particular stages of mortification are designated by the terms—1. *Gangrene*, or the incipient stage ;— 2. *Sphacelus*, or complete mortification ;—3. *Slough*, or the technical term for the fibrous, senseless substance resulting from sphacelus ;— 4. *Necrosis*, or death of the bones ;— 5. *Hospital gangrene*, or the combination of humid gangrene with phagedenic ulceration ;—6. *Pustule maligne*, or carbuncle, supposed by some to originate in horned cattle ;— 7. *Gangrenous ergotism*, necrosis ustiliginea scu epidemica.

Mosa'io (Ital. *mosaico*), in the fine arts, a species of representation of objects by means of very minute pieces of coloured glass, or of stones or pebbles of different colours, carefully inlaid.—In architecture, *mosaic work* is the inlaying of pavements, walls, &c., with small dies of different coloured stones or glass in regular figures, to represent historical objects.—*Mosaic gold*, bisulphuret of tin, a yellow, flaky substance, sometimes employed in ornamental japan work.

Mosan'drite, a greyish-brown mineral. —(*Dana.*)

Mososau'rus (Lat. *Mosa* the river Meuse, and Gr. *sauros* a lizard), in geology, the name of a gigantic aquatic saurian, the remains of which are found in the chalk formation near Maestricht, in Belgium.

Mos'chidæ (Lat. *moschus* musk), a family of Ruminants of the Deer kind, of which Moschus, the Musk Deer, is the type.

Moss (Sax.), a family of plants with leafy stems and narrow, simple leaves; any minute, small-leaved cryptogamic plant. The Mosses form the Muscales or Muscal Alliance of Lindley, and embrace the Hepaticæ and the Musci.

Motet (Fr.), in music, a composition consisting of from one to eight parts.

Mother-of-pearl, in conchology, the shell in which pearls are generated. It is the hard, silvery, brilliant, internal layer of several kinds of shells, particularly of the oyster tribe. Mother-of-pearl is brittle and very delicate to work, but it may be fashioned by saws, files, and drills, with the aid sometimes of a corrosive acid.

Motion (Lat.), in physics and dynamics, the act of moving or changing position in space.—The *laws of motion* are thus illustrated by Sir Isaac Newton :—1st, every body perseveres in its state of rest or uniform motion in a right line, until a change is effected by the agency of some external force ; 2nd, any change effected in the quiescence or motion of a body is in the direction of the force impressed, and is proportional to it in quantity ; 3rd, action and reaction are equal and in contrary directions.—*Natural motion* is that which arises from the effect of gravitation, or of the centrifugal force.—*Relative motion* is the alteration of places between two objects in motion relatively to each other.—*Quantity of motion*, in mechanics, the product of the mass or moving body by the velocity. In animal physiology, this may be distinguished as —1. The *voluntary*, the spontaneous act of the will ; a function attached to the *brain ;* — 2. The *excited*, as the closure of the larynx on the contact of acrid vapours ; of the pharynx on that of the food, &c., a function of the *medulla ;* — 3. That of *irritability*, as the action of the heart, the intestinal canal, &c., a function of the *muscular fibre ;*—in vegetable physiology, as the vascular circulation, which exists in plants as well as in animals ; and the muscular movement, which may be observed—1. In the *bud*, as it spreads its leaves ; 2. In the *flower-bud*, as it throws back its petals and its calyx ; 3. In the *stamens*, when at the period of fecundation they bend towards the pistil which they surround ; 4. In the corolla of the *Great Nightshade*, when it closes itself against the rays of the sun, and opens to the freshness of the night air ; 5. In the *Convolvulus*, which, on the contrary, shuts its flowers in the evening, and expands them again in the morning ; 6. In the *Acacias*, which fold up their leaves during the night, and open them during the day ; or, 7. In the *Mimosa pudica*, which recoils, as if by an electric impulse, from the slightest touch (*Raspail*).—*Motive*

power is the propelling force by which motion is obtained.

Moto (Ital. from Lat. *motus*), in music, a term signifying that a composition is to be played or sung with agitation and emphasis.

Mouldings, in architecture, carving, &c., a term applied to all the varieties of outline or contour given to the surfaces or edges of the various subordinate parts of buildings.

Mountain Blue, in mineralogy, a species of blue malachite, or blue copper ore. Carbonate of copper occurs regularly crystallized in scopiform or stellular concretions, radiated, and also curved lamellar.

Mountain Limestone, in geology, the carboniferous limestone, a formation intermediate between the old red sandstone and the coal measures.

Mountain Soap, in mineralogy, a variety of green earth of a brownish or blackish colour. It is massive, dull, smooth, and soapy to the touch. Its constituents are silica, alumina, oxide of iron, lime, and water.

Mountain Tallow, a mineral soluble in alkali, which is found in Scotland.

Moussue (Fr.), in heraldry, the name of a cross which is rounded at the ends.

Mucic (Lat. *mucus*), in chemistry, obtained from gum, as *mucic acid*.—*Mucite* is a substance in which mucic acid is combined with something else.

Mu'cilage (Fr. from Lat. *mucus*), the liquor which lubricates certain parts of animal bodies.—In chemistry, one of the proximate elements of vegetables.

Muco'so-sac'charine, in chemistry, partaking of the qualities of mucilage and sugar.

Mucous Membrane, in anatomy, a membrane secreting mucus, and lining internal passages and other cavities.

Mucus (Lat.), in anatomy, the slimy substance effused on the surface of the membranes covering the inner surface of the body.

Mu'darine (from the plant *Mudar*), in chemistry, a peculiar principle, having the property of softening by cold, and hardening by heat.

Mugil'lidæ (Lat. *mugil* a mullet), a family of acanthopterygious fishes, the Mullets.

Muller-glass, in mineralogy, the common name of the hyolite. It has a glassy lustre, and is as hard as quartz.

Mul'licite, a bluish-black mineral with a vitreous lustre, consisting of phosphoric acid, protoxide of iron, and water.

Mult-, Multum (Lat. *much* or *many*), forming a useful prefix to numerous scientific terms ; as, *Multangular*, hav-

Q

ing many angles ;—*Multifid*, having many divisions ;—*Multiform*, having many forms or appearances ;—*Multilocular*, having many cells ;—*Multipartite*, divided into many parts or lobes ; — *Multipedes*, insects with many feet ; — *Multispiral*, having many spiral coils ;—*Multivalve*, in malacology, animals or shells with more than two valves ;—*Multungulate*, in zoology, having the hoof divided into more than two parts.

Mul'tiple (Lat.), in arithmetic, a number which exactly contains another number several times; as 12 is a *multiple* of 3.

Multiplica'tion (Lat.), in arithmetic, the process of finding the amount of a given number or quantity, called the *multiplicand*, when repeated a certain number of times, expressed by the *multiplier*. Multiplication is either simple or compound : simple multiplication is when the proposed quantities are integers or whole numbers ; compound multiplication implies that one of them is a compound quantity; that is, one consisting of several denominations, as pounds, shillings, and pence.—*Multiplication table* is a small table containing the product of all the simple digits, and onwards up to 12 times 12.

Mul'tiplying-glass, a kind of lens presenting a number of plane surfaces.

Mumps, in pathology, an inflammation of the parotid glands ; a disease in which the glands about the throat and jaws are swelled.

Mundic, in mineralogy, a Cornish name for iron pyrites.

Muni'tion (Lat.), materials for war or for commerce ; stores of all kinds for a fort, an army, or navy.—*Munition ships*, ships freighted with the necessary naval and military stores for hostile operations.

Mural (Lat. *relating to a wall*), in astronomy, *mural arch* is a walled arch situated exactly in the plane of the meridian, for placing a quadrant, sextant, &c., to observe the meridian altitude of the heavenly bodies.— *Mural circle* or *quadrant*, an instrument used for measuring angles.

Mur'chisonite (in honour of the celebrated geologist *Murchison*), in mineralogy, a variety of crystallized felspar, found in the new red sandstone near Exeter. It consists of silica, potash, and alumina.

Murex (Lat.), in conchology, a Mollusc having a univalve spiral shell, noted for its purple dye.—*Murexide*, the purpurate of ammonia.

Mu'liacite, in chemistry, an anhydrous

sulphate of lime, containing a little common salt.

Mu'riates (Lat. *muria* sea - salt or brine), in chemistry, salts composed of muriatic acid and a base.— *Muriate of soda* is common salt.— *Muriate of iron*, formerly known as ferrum salitum.—*Muriate of potash*, formerly known by the name of regenerated sea-salt, &c. — *Muriatic acid* is an acid obtained from common salt.

Muric'idæ (Lat. *murex*), in zoology, a family of carnivorous Gasteropods (the Murexes and Whelks), of the tribe Zoophaga.—*Muricinæ* is a subfamily of the Muricidæ.

Mu'ricite, in mineralogy, the fossil remains of Muricidæ.

Mu'ridæ (Lat. *mus* a mouse), a family of Rodents, of which the genus Mus is the type.—*Murines* are a tribe of Rodents, containing the families Muridæ, Aroicolidæ, and Sciuridæ.

Musa'ceæ, Musæ, a nat. order of lofty, stemless trees, with leaves sheathing at the base, and forming a kind of spurious stem, often very large.

Muschel (Germ.), in mineralogy, a limestone of the red sandstone group.— *Muschel-kalk* is a calcareous rock containing organic remains.

Mus'cidæ (Lat. *musca* a fly), a family of dipterous insects, of which the common House Fly (Musca) is the type.

Mus'cites (Lat. *muscus* moss), in geology, fossil plants of the Moss family.

Muscle (Lat. *mus*), a fleshy fibre susceptible of contraction and relaxation. The muscles are the instruments of motion in animal bodies, acting voluntarily or involuntarily.

Muscol'ogy (Lat. *muscus*), that part of botany which treats of Mosses.

Mus'culite, in geology, a petrified mussel or shell.

Musette (Fr.), in music, the name of an air or melody, the characteristics of which are softness and sweetness.

Muse'um (Lat.), a collection of curious objects in nature and art ; a building or room for such a collection.

Musophag'idæ (Gr. *musa* the plantain tree, and *phago* to eat), a family of birds, the Plantain-eaters. — *Musophaginæ*, a sub-family of the Plantain-eaters.

Mussite, in mineralogy, a variety of augite of a pale green.

Mustel'idæ (Lat. *mustela* the weasel), in zoology, a family of carnivorous quadrupeds, embracing the Weasels, Polecats, Martens, &c.—*Mustelinæ*, a sub-family of the Mustelidæ.

Mutage, a process used for arresting the progress of fermentation in the must of grapes.

Nematoneu'ra (Gr. *nema*, and *neuron* a nerve), a division of the Radiata, including such animals of that class as have the nervous filaments distinctly traceable.

Nemo'cera (Gr. *nema*, and *keras* a horn), in entomology, a section of dipterous insects with filiform or thread-like antennæ.

Neoco'mian (Gr.), in geology, a term applied to the greensand formation.

Neora'ma (Gr. *neos* new, and *orao* to see), an optical machine representing the interior of a large building.

Neozo'ic (Gr. *neos*, and *zoon* an animal), in geology, a term denoting new animality, and applied to a dvision of the fossiliferous strata.

Nepen'the (Gr. *removing sorrow*), a drug that drives away all pain.

Nepen'thes (Gr.), in botany, a name applied to the Pitcher-plant, which forms the order Nepenthaceæ.

Nephral'gia (Gr. *nephros* the kidney, and *algos* pain), a disease of the kidneys.

Nephrelmin'thic (Gr. *nephros*, and *elminthos* a worm), in pathology, a term applied to diseases which result from the presence of worms in the kidney.

Nephrite (Gr.), a hard, tough mineral, of greenish colour, composed chiefly of silica.

Nephrit'ic (Gr.), in pathology, a medicine for diseases of the kidneys or for the stone.

Nephri'tis (Gr.), an inflammation of the kidneys.

Neph'rocele (Gr.), hernia of the kidneys.

Nephrol'ogy (Gr.), a treatise on the kidneys.

Nephrot'omy (Gr.), in surgery, the operation of extracting the stone from the kidneys.

Neptune, one of the most distant of the newly-discovered planets, first observed by Le Verrier and Adams in 1846. Its mean distance from the sun is 2,864,000,000 miles, and its periodical revolution 164 years, 26 days, and 17 hours.

Neptu'nian, in geology, a term applied to stratified rocks, or those which have been deposited by water.—*Neptunist* is a name applied to the geologists of the school of Werner, who believed all old rocks to have been of aqueous origin.

Nereid'ian, in zoology, a class of Annellidans, of which the genus Nereis is the type.

Ner'itinæ, a family of the Naticidæ, the Nerits, the shells of which are globose.

Nerves (Lat. *nervi*, from Gr. *neuron*), in physiology, the important organs of sensation and motion, which proceed from the brain or spinal marrow to all parts of the body. The nervous system has been divided into four different branches, consisting of the cerebral nerves, the spinal nerves, the respiratory nerves, and the sympathetic nerves.—1. The *Cerebral nerves*, or those rising from the brain, are thus enumerated and classified by Willis:—The first pair, or olfactory nerve, expanding upon the membrane of the nose; the second pair, or optic nerve, terminating in the retina of the eye; the third pair, or motores oculorum, distributed to the muscles of the eye; the fourth pair, or trochleares, distributed to the superior oblique muscle of the eye; the fifth pair, trigemini, or trifacial nerve, the grand sensitive nerve of the head and face. This nerve consists of the large, or ganglionic portion, or trifacial, the sentient and organic nerve of the face; the minor, or ganglionic portion, or masticatory, the nerve of motion in the temporal, masseter, buccinator, pterygoids, &c.; the sixth pair, or abducentes, distributed to the external rectus muscle of the eye; the seventh pair includes the portio mollis, or auditory, and the portio dura, or facial, the nerve of motion and expression; the eighth pair, or grand respiratory nerve, comprises the glosso-pharyngeal, the par vagum, and the spinal accessory; the ninth pair, or lingual nerve, the muscular nerve of the tongue, the hypoglossal, sub-lingual, or gustatory nerve.— 2. The *Spinal nerves*, or those arising from the spinal marrow, are distinguished into the cervical nerves—nine pairs: the first of these is enumerated by Willis as the tenth nerve of the head, and called sub-occipital, from its situation; the last four cervical, and the first dorsal nerves, furnish the axillary plexus. The dorsal nerves, twelve pairs; the lumbar nerves, five pairs; the sacral nerves, six pairs.—3. The *Respiratory nerves*, which arise from the medulla oblongata, are—the fourth, or pathetici; the portio dura of the seventh, or facial; the glosso-pharyngeal nerve; the par vagum, and the nervus ad par vagum accessorius; the phrenic nerve; the external respiratory; the fifth, and certain spinal nerves, with the par vagum, should be distinguished as exciters of respiration, the rest being motors.—4. The *Sympathetic nerve* is a collection of ganglia and branches connected with the sixth nerve, a portion of the fifth, the portio dura, the eighth, ninth, and

· all the spinal nerves. It is, in fact a collection of branches from almost every nerve in the frame.—*Craig*.

Nervine, in pathology, a medicine for nervous affections. — In botany, the venous system of leaves.

Neural'gia (Gr. *neuron*, and *algos* pain), in pathology, an acute painful affection of the nerves.

Neurapoph'ysis (Gr. *neuron*, and *apophyo* to grow from), in anatomy, a portion of bone projecting from a vertebra.

Neuras'theny (Gr.), nervous debility.

Neurilem'ma (Gr. *neuron*, and *lemma* a membrane), in anatomy, the membrane which invests the substance of the nerves, and forms for each filament a distinct sheath.

Neurine (Gr.), the substance which constitutes the nerves.

Neuri'tis (Gr.), inflammation of the nerves.

Neurog'raphy, **Neurol'ogy** (Gr. *neuron*, and *graphe* description), that part of animal physiology which describes or treats of the nerves.

Neurop'athy (Gr.), in pathology, nervous affection.

Neurop'tera (Gr. *neuron*, and *pteron* a wing), a genus of insects without a sting, having four membranaceous, articulated wings.

Neuro'sis (Gr.), a morbid affection of the nervous system.

Neuro-skel'eton (Gr.), in anatomy, the deep-seated bones of the vetebral skeleton.

Neurot'ics (Gr.), medicines for the nerves.

Neurot'omy (Gr. *neuron*, and *temno* to cut), the anatomy or cutting of the nerves.

Neuro'ma (Gr. *neuron*), in pathology, a tumour in the course of a nerve.

Neutral (Lat.), in chemistry, an epithet applied to salts composed of an acid and a base in such proportions that they exactly destroy each other's properties.—In botany, applied to flowers having neither stamens nor pistils.—*Neutralization* is the process by which an acid is combined with a base in such proportions as to render inert the properties of both.

Nickel, a whitish metal, malleably ductile, and very hard, which occurs in all meteoric iron, and which, like iron, may be rendered magnetic: sp. gr. 9·0.—*Nickel-glance*, or *sulpho-arseniuret of nickel*, occurs massive, with a granular structure and uneven fracture: sp. gr. 6·129.

Nic'otine (so called from *Jean Nicot*, who first introduced it into France), an oil or principle extracted from tobacco.

Nic'titate (Lat. *to wink*).—*Nictitating membrane* is a fold of skin with which birds cover their eyes.

Niel'lo (Ital.), a method of engraving on gold or silver plate, the lines of which are filled permanently with black enamel ; an art extensively practised by the Romans and modern Italians.

Nigrine, in mineralogy, a silico-calcareous oxide of titanium.

Nimbus (Lat. *a cloud*), in meteorology, the rain-cloud.—In painting and sculpture, a circular disc round the heads of divinities, sovereigns, and saints ; an aureola.

Ni'obe, one of the newly-discovered planets, first observed by Luther in 1861.

Nio'bium, a metal discovered in columbite.

Nitidula'reæ (Lat. *nitidus* clean), a tribe of coleopterous insects, of which Nitidula is the type ; fam. Clavicornes.

Nitraria'ceæ, in botany, a nat. order of exogenous plants, of which the Nitraria is the type.

Nitrate, in chemistry, a salt formed of nitric acid and a base.—*Nitrate of silver* is prepared by saturating pure nitric acid with pure silver, evaporating the solution, and crystallizing the nitrate. Properly prepared, it forms an excellent indelible ink for writing on linen with a pen.—*Nitratine* is the nitrate of soda.

Nitre (Fr. from Gr. *nitron*), in chemistry, nitrate of potassa, or potash ; called also saltpetre.—*Nitric acid*, or *aquafortis*, is a heavy liquid of a yellow colour, composed of 30 parts of nitrogen and 70 of oxygen.—*Nitric oxide* is a gas fatal to animal life. —*Nitrite* is a salt formed of nitrous acid and a base.

Nitroben'zide, a yellowish liquid obtained from benzine and nitric acid.

Ni'trogen (Gr. *nitron*, and *gennao* to produce), in chemistry, a simple gaseous body, which forms a constituent part of nitric acid, and has received the name of *azote*, from its being unrespirable, and incapable of supporting animal life. It is rather lighter than common air ; its equivalent is 14. It combines with oxygen in five proportions, giving the formulæ to the nitrous oxide of NO ; nitric oxide, NO_2 ; hyponitrous acid, NO_3 ; nitrous acid, NO_4 ; nitric acid, NO_5.

Nitrome'ter (Gr.), an instrument for ascertaining the quality or value of nitre.

Nitromuriat'ic, nitric and muriatic acid combined.

Nitronaph'thalase, a compound resulting from the action of nitric acid on naphthaline.

Nitrous, partaking of nitre.—*Nitrous* acid has less of oxygen than *nitric* acid.

Ni'turet, a body consisting of oxygen, hydrogen, and carbon, with one atom of nitrogen.

Noctilioni'næ (Lat. *nox* night), in entomology, a family of the Vespertilionidæ, of which the Noctilio, a genus of Bats, is the type.

Noc'tograph (Gr.), a writing frame for the blind.

Noctur'na (Lat. *nox*), the Moth Butterflies, comprehending the third family of the Lepidoptera.

Node (Lat. *nodus* a knot), in surgery, a hard tumour upon a bone, which is often attended by caries or necrosis.—In astronomy, the two points in which the orbit of a planet intersects the plane of the ecliptic; a point or hole in the gnomon of a dial which indicates the hour by its light, as the gnomon does by its shadow.—In geometry, a small oval figure.

Nogging, in architecture, a partition framed of timber scantlings, with interstices filled by bricks.

Noma (Gr. *nomo* to corrode), in pathology, an ulcer which attacks the skin and cheek or vulva of young girls. It appears in the form of red and somewhat livid spots, and in a few days becomes gangrenous.

Nomad, in physics, an atom, or very minute particle.

Nombril (Fr.), in heraldry, the centre of an escutcheon.

Nome (Gr.), in algebra, a simple quantity affixed to some other quantity.

No'menclature (Lat.), the language or terms peculiar to science or art.

Nonages'imal (Lat. *the ninetieth*), in astronomy, *nonagesimal degree* is the ninetieth degree of the ecliptic, reckoned from either of the points in which it is intersected, being the highest at any instant. It is used in calculating the parallaxes of the moon.

Non'agon (Gr. *nine-angled*), in geometry, a plane figure having nine angles.

Non-conduc'tor (Lat.), in physics, a substance that does not conduct or transmit; particularly one that does not conduct the electric fluid.

Non'descript (Lat. *not yet described*), in zoology, botany, &c., anything not yet classed or described.

Non-elec'tric (Lat.), in physics, a substance not electric, but which conducts the electric fluid.

Non'tronite, in mineralogy, a silicate of iron found in small nodules, of a yellowish-green colour, so called from Nontron, in France, where it occurs. Its constituents are silver,

peroxide of iron, alumina, magnesia, clay, and water.

Non'upla (Ital.), in music, the appellation appropriate to a quick species of time, consisting of nine crotchets or nine quavers in a bar, and the beating of which is performed by two falls and one elevation of the hand.

Normal (Lat. *norma* a rule), according to rule or principle.—*Normal schools* are schools for training schoolmasters.

Norroy (Fr.), in heraldry, the title of the third of the three kings-at-arms, or provincial heralds.

North Pole, in astronomy, an imaginary point in the northern hemisphere, 90° from the equator.—*North star* is the north polar star.

Norway Ragstone, a coarse variety of whetstone.

Nosing, in architecture, the moulding upon the upper edge of a step.

Nosol'ogy (Gr. *nosos* disease, and *logos* a discourse), the doctrine of diseases, or their classification and nomenclature.

Nostal'gia (Gr. *nosteo* to return, and *algos* grief), in pathology, home-sickness.

Nostrum (Lat.), a quack medicine kept for profit in the hands of the inventor.

Notacan'thinæ (Gr. *notos* the back, and *akantha* a spine), a sub-family of the Neidæ, consisting of those genera which have the body anguilliform and much compressed, of which the Notacanthus is the type.

Notal'gia (Gr. *notos*, and *algos* pain), in pathology, pain in the back.

No'tochord (Gr. *notos*, and *chorde* a chord), in anatomy, a term applied to the gelatinous column which forms the primary condition of the spine in vertebrate animals.

Notorhi'zal (Gr. *notos*, and *rhiza* a root), in botany, an epithet applied to the radicle in the embryonic plant on the back of the cotyledons.

Novac'ulite (Lat. *novacula* a razor), an argillaceous stone used for hones and whetstones.

Nubec'ula (Lat. *a little cloud*), in astronomy, a name given to the Magellanic clouds, or two extensive nebulous patches of clouds.—In pathology, a small speck on the corner of the eye.

Nu'cleus (Lat. *a kernel*), in physiology, a body about which matter is collected in animal and vegetable cells.—In astronomy, the bright central spot sometimes seen in the misty matter forming the head of a comet.

Nudibrach'iate (Lat. *nudus* naked, and *brachia* an arm), having naked arms; a term applied to those Polypi whose tentacles are not covered with cilia.

Nudibranchia'ta (Lat. *nudus*, and *branchiæ* gills), in malacology, the second order of the class Gasteropoda, consisting of Mollusca without shells, and having their branchiæ exposed on some part of the back.

Nugget (Sc. *a lump*, as a *nugget* of sugar, &c.), in mining, a term applied to a lump of gold taken from the mine in its natural state, either *in situ* or *in transitu*. The largest specimens have been found in the gold-diggings of Victoria, in Australia, one of which weighed 134 lbs., the pure gold weighing 126 lbs.

Number (Fr. from Lat. *numerus*), in arithmetical and mathematical science, an assemblage of two or more units.—*Cardinal numbers* are those which express the quantity of units, as 1, 2, 3, 4, &c., whereas *ordinal numbers* are those which express order, as 1st, 2nd, 3rd, &c.—*Compound number*, one divisible by some other number besides unity; as 12, which is divided by 2, 3, 4, and 6.—*Cubic number* is the product of a square number by its root.—*Whole numbers* are otherwise called integers.

Nu'meral (Lat.), relating to, or consisting of, a number. The *numeral letters* are the seven Roman capitals, I, V, X, L, C, D, M; the *numeral figures*, 1, 2, 3, 4, 5, 6, 7, 8, 9, and 0.—*Numeral algebra*, those cases in which numerals are employed, in contradistinction to literal, or where letters are used.

Numera'tion (Lat. *numero* to number), the first rule in arithmetic.

Nu'merator (Lat.), in arithmetic, the numerator of a fraction is that number which stands above the line, as 7 is the numerator of $\frac{7}{8}$. The whole fraction bears the same proportion to the whole number 1 as this numerator bears to the lower figure.

Numismat'ics, **Numismatol'ogy** (Lat. *numisma* a coin), the science of coins and medals.

Num'mulite (Lat. *nummus* money), an extinct molluscous animal, of a thin, lenticular shape, having some resemblance to a coin.

Nus'sierite (from its occurring at *Nussière*, in France), in mineralogy, a phosphate of lead and lime, of a greenish colour, with a feeble or greasy lustre: sp. gr. 5·04; H = 4·0.

Nuta'tion (Lat.), in astronomy, a tremulous motion of the axis of the earth, by which its inclination to the plane of the ecliptic is continually varying, being in its annual revolution twice inclined to the ecliptic, and as often returning to its former position.

Nut Pine, in botany, a new species of Pine (the *Pinus monophyllus*) from the Rocky Mountains, the seeds of which, as obtained from the cones, afford the principal food of some of the Indian tribes.

Nu'triment, or **Nutri'tion** (Lat. *nutrio* to nourish), in physiology, that which nourishes and sustains the vital functions, having for its object the sustenance, increment, and reparation of animal and vegetable bodies, by assimilation of the nutritive principles of the respective parts.

Nut'talite (in honour of *Professor Nuttall*), a mineral associated with calcspar, occurring in prismatic crystals of vitreous lustre. Its constituents are silica, alumina, lime, potash, protoxide of iron, and water: sp. gr. 2·7; H = 4.5.

Nyctalo'pia (Gr. *nyx* the night, *alaomai* to grope about, and *ops* the eye), a defect of vision, in which the patient can see better by night than by day.

Nymph (Gr.), in entomology, the second stage of a metabolian insect.

Nympha'ceæ (Gr.), in zoology, a family of bivalve Mollusca.

Nymphæa'ceæ (Gr.), in botany, a nat. order of Endogens, consisting of floating aquatic plants, of which Nymphæa, or Water-lily, is the type.

Nymphip'ara (Gr.), a family of dipterous insects.

Nysa, in astronomy, one of the newly-discovered planets, first observed by Goldschmidt in 1857.

Nysson'idæ (Gr. *nysso* to sting), in entomology, a family of hymenopterous insects, containing the genera Astata, Nysson, Oxybelus, Nitella, and Pison.

O.

Oakum (Sax.), loose hemp, obtained by untwisting old ropes, with which, being mingled with pitch, leaks are stopped.

Obbliga'to (Ital.), in music, a term signifying composed on purpose for the particular instrument named.

Obcor'date (Lat. *ob* against, and *cor* the heart), in botany, a term applied to leaves shaped like a heart, with the apex next the stem.

Ob'elisk (Gr. from *obelos* a needle), a lofty, quadrangular, monolithic column, diminishing upwards.

Object-glass, the glass of a telescope or microscope which is nearest to the object and farthest from the eye.

Oblate (Lat.), in mathematics, an epithet applied to a spheroid which is made by the revolution of an ellipse about the smaller of the two axes.—*Oblate spheroid* is a sphere flattened at the poles, or such a sphere as is produced by the revolution of an ellipse about its shorter axis.

Oblique (Fr.), in military science, a term of varied application ; as, *Oblique position* is a position taken in oblique direction from the original line of formation ;—*Oblique fire* or *defence* is that which is under too great an angle, as is generally the defence of the second flank, which can never be so good as a defence in front ;—*Oblique deployment* is a term applied to the component parts of a column when extending into line, and when they deviate to the right or left for the purpose of taking up an oblique position.—*Oblique radius* is a line extending from the centre to the exterior side of a polygon.—*To oblique*, in military evolutions, is to move forward to the right or left by stepping sideways in either of those directions, according to the words of command.

Oblong (Fr.), in geometry, a rectangular or quadrangular figure longer than broad.

Ob'olite Grit, in geology, the lower silurian sandstone of Russia and Sweden, so called from the abundance of shells of the Obolus, a brachiopod Mollusc.

Ob'ovate (Lat.), reversely ovate, the broad end of the egg being uppermost.

Observ'atory (Lat.), a building constructed for astronomical observations.

Obsid'ian (Lat.), a mineral of a green or brownish colour (the *obsidianus lapis* of the Romans) ; a volcanic substance resembling common green bottle glass. It consists of silica, alumina, potash or soda, oxide of iron, and lime : sp. gr. 3·34 ; H = 6—7.

Obstet'rics (Lat. *obstetrix* a midwife), in medical science, the art of delivering women in childbirth.—*Obstetrician* is one who practises obstetrics ; a man-midwife.

Obtun'dent (Lat. *obtundo* to blunt), in pharmacy, a mucilaginous or oily medicine to deaden pain.

Obtuse (Lat. *not pointed*).—In mathematics, an *obtuse angle* is an angle containing more than 90°.

Obverse, in numismatics, the side of a coin or medal that has the face or head upon it, the other side being the *reverse*.

Ob'volute (Lat. *ob*, and *volvo* to roll), in botany, applied to an arrangement of leaves in buds.

Oc'ciput (Lat.), in anatomy, the hinder part of the head, or that part of the skull which forms the hind part.

Ocean (Lat.), the vast body of salt water which encompasses the great divisions of the earth. The ocean, inland seas, &c., cover an area of 147,800,000 square miles.

Ochna'ceæ (Gr. *ochne* the wild pear), in botany, a nat. order of exogenous plants, abounding in a watery juice, of which the Ochna is the genus and type.

Ochre (Gr. *ochros* yellow), a variety of clay ; the hydrated sesquioxide of iron, an earth used in painting, in which the oxide of iron is the colouring matter.

Oct-, or **Octo-** (Lat. and Gr.), a prefix in compound words, signifying *eight*.

Oc'tachord (Gr. *okto*, and *chorde* a chord), an instrument or system of eight sounds.

Oc'tagon (Gr. *okto*, and *gonia* an angle), in geometry, a figure of eight sides and eight angles.—In fortification, a place which has eight bastions or sides.

Octagyn'ia (Gr. *okto*, and *gyne* a female), an order of plants in the Linnæan system having eight pistils.

Octahe'dral (Gr. *okto*, and *hedra* a base), having eight equal sides.

Octahe'drite (Gr.), the pyramidal ore of titanium.

Octahe'dron (Gr.), one of the five regular solids, the surface of which consists of eight equal and equilateral triangles.

Octan'dria, Octan'drian (Gr. *okto*, and *andres* males), a class of plants in the Linnæan system having eight stamens.

Octan'gular (Lat.), having eight angles.

Octant (Lat. *octo*), in astronomy, the eighth part of a circle.—In astrology, an aspect or position. The moon is said to be in her *octants* when she is at 45°, 135°, and 315° from her conjunctions.

Oc'tave (Fr. from Lat. *octavus*), in music, an harmonic interval containing five tones and two semitones ; the eighth note of the scale, the most perfect of scales and most perfect of concords. The octave embraces all the primitive sounds, namely, all the original tones and semitones.

Octil'lion, in numeration, the number produced by involving a million to the eighth power.

Octode'imo (Lat.), a book in which a sheet is folded into eighteen leaves.

Oc'topod (Gr. *okto*, and *podes* feet), an animal having eight feet.

Oc'tostyle (Gr. *okto*, and *stylos* a column), in architecture, a portico or the face of a building having eight columns.

Od'erite, in mineralogy, a variety of black mica.

Odom'eter (Gr. *a road measurer*), an instrument attached to the wheel of a carriage for measuring distances.

Odom'etry (Gr.), the measurement of distances.

Od'ontalgy (Gr. *odous* a tooth, and *algos* pain), the toothache.

Odon'talite (Gr. *odous*, and *lithos* a stone), a fossil tooth or bone.

Odon'tograph (Gr.), an instrument to measure or design the teeth of wheels.

Odontog'raphy, **Odontol'ogy** (Gr.), the anatomy or science of the teeth.

Œde'ma (Gr.), in pathology, a tumour; a collection of water in the cellular membranes.

Œnan'thic (Gr. *oinos* wine, and *anthos* a flower), noting an acid obtained from œnanthic ether; an oily liquid which gives to wine its characteristic odour.

Œr'stedito, a crystallized mineral of a brown colour and splendent lustre. Its constituents are titanate of zirconia, silica, lime, magnesia, protoxide of iron, and water: sp. gr. 3·62 ; H= 1·5.

Œsoph'agus (Gr.), the canal leading from the pharynx ; the short cavity at the back of the mouth to the stomach ; the gullet.—*Œsophagitis*, inflammation of the œsophagus.—*Œsophagotomy*, operation of cutting into the œsophagus to extract a foreign body.

Œs'tridæ (Gr. *oistros*), in entomology, a family of dipterous insects, of which the Œstrus, or Gadfly, is the type.

Ogee (Fr.), in architecture, a particular kind of moulding.

Ogive (Fr.), a rib in a Gothic vault, that crosses diagonally from angle to angle.

Ogyg'ian (from *Ogyges*, king of Attica), relating to a great inundation which is stated to have occurred in the reign of that sovereign, about 1764 years B.C.

Oil (Lat. *oleum*), an unctuous juice expressed from animal or vegetable substances.—The *fixed oils* are compounds of carbon, hydrogen, and oxygen ;—the *volatile oils* are obtained by distilling certain vegetables with water.—*Oil of vitriol*, the old name of sulphuric acid.—*Oil-bag*, a gland in animals containing oil.—*Oil-cloth*, a cloth or canvas having on one side a thick coat of oil-paint.—*Oil-colour*, a colour made by grinding a coloured substance in oil.

Oi'sanite, in mineralogy, an ore of titanium.

O'kenite, a translucent mineral found at Dico Island, in Greenland ; the Dysclasite. Its constituents are silica, lime, and water.

Olaca'ceæ (Gr. *a furrow*), in botany, a nat. order of exogenous plants, of which Olax is the genus and type.

Old Red Sandstone, in geology, a series interposed between the mountain limestone and the silurian rocks.

Olea'ceæ (Gr. *olea* the olive), a nat. order of plants belonging to the Solanal alliance of Lindley, of which the Olea is the type.

O'leate (Lat. *oleum* oil), in chemistry, a salt formed of oleic acid.

Olef'iant, in chemistry, relating to a gas which, combined with chlorine, produces a compound resembling oil.

O'leic, in chemistry, noting an acid derived from a soap made by digesting hog's lard in potash lye.

O'leine, in chemistry, a fusible oil expressed from fat.

O'leon, in chemistry, a substance obtained by distilling oleic acid mixed with lime.

Olfac'tory Nerves (Lat. *olfacio* to smell), the first pair of nerves proceeding directly from the brain, being the nerves of smelling.

Oleom'eter (Lat. *oleum*, and Gr. *metron* a measure), an instrument for ascertaining the purity and weight of oil.

Oleo-resin, a mixture of a terebinthinate oil and a resin.

Olib'anum (Gr.), a gum resin, the frankincense of the ancients.

Olive (Fr.), in botany, the fruit of the tree from which *olive oil* is produced.

Ol'ivenite, in mineralogy, an ore of copper of an olive-green colour. It consists of oxide of copper, phosphoric acid, and water.

Ol'ivile, a crystalline substance obtained from the gum of the olive tree.

Ol'ivine, in mineralogy, a variety of chrysolite.

Oliv'inæ (Lat. *oliva*), in conchology, a sub-family of the Volutidæ, the shells of which are smooth and slightly polished. The Oliva, or Olive shell, a genus of marine Mollusca, is the genus and type.

Olym'pia, one of the recently-discovered planets, first observed by Chacornac in 1860.

Oma'sum (Lat.), in comparative anatomy, the third stomach of ruminant animals.

Omen'tum (Lat.), in anatomy, a fold of the peritoneal membrane covering the intestines in front.

Om'phacine (Gr. *omphakinos*, unripe

fruit), a juice or oil extracted from green olives.

Om'phacite (Gr.), a green variety of augite.

Om'phazit, in mineralogy, a variety of pyroxene.

Ontol'ogy (Gr. *ontos* being, and *logos* a discourse), the science of existence in itself, or its ultimate grounds and conditions ; metaphysics.

Onyx (Gr.), in mineralogy, a precious stone; a regularly-banded agate, much prized for cameos.—In pathology, an abscess on the cornea of the eye

O'olite (Gr. *oos* an egg, and *lithos* a stone), in mineralogy, a species of limestone, composed of globules clustered together.

Oolit'ic (Gr.), composed of or resembling oolites.—On the continent of Europe (says Tomlinson) the *oolitic* system is known as *Jura kalk* and *Calcaire Jurassique*, from the conspicuous development of the strata in the Jura Mountains.

Opal (Lat.), in mineralogy, a hard white mineral, the hydrate of silica, remarkable for its iridescent reflection of light. There are many varieties, as Fire Opal, Hydrophane, Common Opal, Semi-opal, Wood Opal, Casholong Jasper, Menilite, Hyalite, Geyserite.

Open, in military science, a term frequently used in contradistinction to *close* ; as, *open column, open distances, open order*, &c.—In fortification, *open flank* is that part of the flank which is covered by the orillon. —*Opening of trenches* is the first breaking of ground by the besiegers, in order to carry on their approaches towards the place.

Op'era (Ital. from Lat. *opera*), a musical drama, in which the music forms an essential part. — *Opera-glass* is a small perspective glass or telescope used in theatres, operas, &c.

Oper'culum (Lat.), in botany, a cover; the lid of the theca of a moss.

Ophical'cic (Gr. *ophis* a serpent, and Lat. *calx* chalk), a rock composed of marble and serpentine.

Oph'icleide (Gr. *ophis*, and *kleis* a key), a musical wind instrument used in the orchestra and in military bands.

Ophid'ians (Gr. *ophis*), an order of reptiles including all the serpentine species.

Ophid'ion (Gr. *ophis*), a sea-fish resembling a serpent.

Ophid'inæ, a sub-family of the Gymnetres, or Ribbon-fishes, of which the Ophidion is the type.

O'phiolite (Gr. *ophis*, and *lithos* a stone), the mineral serpentine.

Ophiol'ogy (Gr.), that part of natural history which treats of reptiles or serpents.

Ophion'idæ (Gr.), a family of coleopterous insects, belonging to the tribe Ichneumonides.

Ophite, Ophi'tes (Gr. *ophis*), in mineralogy, the serpentine stone.

Ophthal'mia (Gr. *ophthalmos* the eye), inflammation of the eye.

Ophthalmoblennorrhœ'a (Gr. *ophthalmos*, *blenna* mucus, and *rheo* to flow), a puriform discharge from the eyelids.

Ophthal'mocele (Gr. *ophthalmos*, and *kele* hernia), extraordinary protrusion of the eye.

Ophthalmog'raphy, Ophthalmol'ogy (Gr.), a description of, or treatise on, the eye.

Ophthalmos'copy (Gr. *ophthalmos*, and *skopeo* to inspect), a branch of physiognomy limited to the observation of the eyes. — *Ophthalmoscope*, an instrument for examining the interior of the eye.

Ophthalmot'omy (Gr.), the dissection of the eye.

Oph'thalmy (Gr.), an inflammation of the eye, or of parts connected with it.

O'piane (Fr.), the pure narcotic principle of opium.

O'piate (Lat. from *opium*), a medicine producing sleep.

Opisthot'onos (Gr. *opisthen* backward, and *teino* to bend), a convulsive affection of several muscles, by which the body is bent rigidly backward.

O'pium (Lat.), the inspissated or concrete juice of a species of poppy.

Opobal'sam (Gr. *opos* juice, and *balsamon* balm), a balsam of Peru ; one of the names of the balm of Gilead or Mecca, the produce of the tree *Balsamodendron opobalsamum.*

Opodel'doc, a liniment made by dissolving soap in alcohol, with the addition of camphor and volatile oils.

Opop'anax (Gr. *opos, pan* all, and *akos* a remedy), a gum resin of an acrid taste, resembling gum ammoniac.

Opos'sum (Ind.), an American marsupial quadruped, characterized by the abdominal pouch of the female.

Opsiom'eter (Gr. *opsis* vision, and *metron* a measure), an instrument for measuring the extent of distinct vision in different persons.

Optics (Gr. *optikos*, from *ops* the eye), that branch of physical science which treats of light and vision.— *Optic axis*, a ray of light passing through the centre of the eye, or falling perpendicularly on it.—*Optic angle*, the angle included or contained between the two rays of light drawn from the extreme points of an object.—*Optic nerves*, the second pair of nerves arising from the thalami nervorum, and perforating the bulb of the eye.—*Optic inequality*, in astronomy, an apparent irregularity in the motions of very distant bodies, so called.—*Optician* is one skilled in optics, who makes or sells optical glasses or spectacles.

Op'time (Lat. *optimus* the best), a term applied in the University of Cambridge to those who hold the highest rank as scholars.

Op'timism (Lat.), the doctrine that everything is ordered for the best.

Optom'eter (Gr.), in optics, an instrument for measuring the limits of distinct vision.

Orato'rio (Ital.), in music, a sacred musical composition.

Orbic'ulates (Lat. *orbis* round), a tribe of Crustaceans, of the family Brachyura.

Orbit (Lat. *orbis*), in astronomy, the line or path which any celestial body describes by its revolution.—In optics, the cavity in which the eyeball is embedded.—In ornithology, the skin which surrounds the eye of a bird.

Or'bito-sphenoid (Gr.), in anatomy, an epithet applied to the lesser wing of the sphenoid bone.

Or'chel, a mineral resembling alum.

Or'chestra (Gr.), a place appropriated to musicians, or to the performers in a concert.

Orchida'ceæ (Gr.), in botany, a nat. order of exogenous plants, of which the Orchis is the type.

Orchil, in botany, a species of lichen, and a dye which the plant yields.

Orcine, in chemistry, a crystallizable colouring principle obtained from a species of lichen.

Order (Lat. *ordo* method), a term of extensive application in the arts and sciences.—In natural history, it is the subdivision of a class, containing tribes, genera, and species.—In architecture, it is the rule of proportion which is to be observed in the construction of any building. The leading parts which constitute the order in architecture are the column and the entablature. The column is divided into a shaft, a base, and a capital; the entablature into a cornice, frieze, and architrave. The five principal orders are Doric, Ionic, Corinthian, Tuscan, and Composite, three of which are Greek—the Doric, Ionic, and Corinthian; and two Roman or Italian—the Tuscan and the Composite. Besides these there are the *Attic order*, the pilaster of an attic; *Caryatic order*, in which the entablature is supported by the figures of women instead of columns; *Persian order*, in which the entablature is supported by the figures of men instead of columns. —In military science, *order of battle* is the arrangement and disposition of the different parts of an army, according to the nature of the ground, for the purpose of engaging an enemy, by giving or receiving an attack, or in order to be reviewed, &c.

Or'dinary (Lat.), in heraldry, a portion of an escutcheon contained between the straight and other lines. The heraldic ordinaries are divided into two classes—the honourable, or greater ordinaries, and the subordinate, or lesser. The honourable ordinaries are—the chief, pale, bend, bend sinister, fesse, bar, chevron, cross, and saltire. The subordinates are—the bordure, orle, tressure, inescutcheon, canton, quarter billet, gyson, pile, flanche, lozenge, fusil, rustre, mascle, fret roundle, and gutté.

Ordnance (Fr.), cannon, applied to all sorts of great guns used in war.

Ore (Sax.), a mineral body or substance from which metal is extracted; metal yet in its fossil state.

Organ'ic (Fr. from Lat. *organicus*), consisting of various parts co-operating with each other.—*Organic bodies* are such as have organs, on the action of which depend their growth and perfection.—*Organic disease*, a disease affecting the organs.—*Organic remains* are fossil remains of organized bodies.

Organog'raphy (Lat. and Gr.), in botany, a description of the organs or structure of plants.

Organol'ogy (Lat. and Gr.), in botany, that branch of physiology which treats in particular of the different organs of animals.

Organ Stop, in music, the stop of an organ, or a collection of pipes which run through the compass of the instrument.

Or'ganon (Gr.), an instrument; a machine for facilitating labour in architecture and the arts.

Orgues (Fr.), in fortification, long, thick pieces of timber, forming a portcullis for the defence of a gate.

Orichalcum (Lat.), a metallic substance resembling gold.

O'riel (Old Fr. *oriol*), in architecture, a bay-window beyond the wall, and supported upon brackets.

Ori'on, in astronomy, a constellation of the southern hemisphere.

Orismol'ogy (Gr. *orismos* a term), in natural history, that branch which relates to the technical terms of the science; glossology.

Orle (Fr.), in heraldry, an ordinary in the form of a fillet round a shield.

Or'molu (Fr.), gilded brass.

Ornithol'ogy (Gr. *ornis* a bird, and *logos* a discourse), that branch of natural history which treats of the structure, habits, and classification of birds. According to Linnæus, they are divided into six orders ; viz., *Accipitres*, or Birds of Prey ; the *Picæ* ; the *Anseres*, or Swimming Birds ; the *Grallæ*, or Waders ; the *Gallinæ* ; and the *Passeres*. Swainson adopts the following orders :— *Raptores*, Birds of Prey ; *Insessores*, Perchers ; *Scansores*, Climbers ; *Rasores*, Scratchers ; *Grallatores*, Waders ; *Natatores*, Swimmers.— *Ornitholites* are the fossil footprints of birds.

Ornithorhyn'chus (Gr. *ornis*, and *rhynchos* a beak), a genus of Mammals found in Australia, whose mouth resembles the bill of a duck.

Orobancha'ceæ (Gr. *orobos* a vetch, and *ancho* to strangle), in botany, a nat. order of exogenous plants, of which the Orobanche, or Broomrape, is the type.

Orog'raphy, Orol'ogy (Gr. *oros* a mountain), a description of, or treatise on, mountains, as to their geological structure, relations, &c.

Orontia'ceæ (Gr.), in botany, an order of herbaceous endogenous plants, of which the Orontium is the type.

Or'piment (Lat.), a yellow sulphuret of arsenic ; a pigment.

Or'rery (in honour of *Lord Orrery*), in astronomy, a machine for representing the motions and relative distances of the heavenly bodies.

Or'thidæ (Gr. *orthos* straight, and *eidos* form), a family of nocturnal lepidopterous insects ; the Spinning Hawk Moths.

Orthodrom'ics, or **Or'thodromy** (Gr. *orthos*, and *dromos* a course), the art of sailing on the arc of some great circle, which is the shortest distance between any two points on the surface of the globe.

Or'thogon (Gr.), in geometry, a rightangled figure.

Orthop'edy (Gr. *orthos*, and *podes* feet), in surgery, the art of curing or remedying deformities in the limbs of children.

Orthoplo'ceæ (Gr. *orthos* and *ploke*, right folding together), in botany, a sub-order of cruciferous plants.

Orthopnœ'a (Gr. *orthos* and *pnoe*, right breathing), in pathology, a difficulty of breathing, which can only be performed when the patient is in an erect position.

Orthop'tera, Orthop'teran (Gr. *orthos*, and *ptera* wings), an order of insects, comprising Cockroaches, Crickets, Grasshoppers, &c.

Oryctog'nosy (Gr. *oryktos* a fossil, and *gnosis* knowledge), that branch of mineralogy which has for its object the arrangement and classification of minerals.

Oryctol'ogy (Gr. *oryktos*, and *logos* discourse), that branch of zoological science which treats of fossil organic remains, or the nomenclature of minerals.

Os (Lat.), a bone.—*Ossicle*, a small bone.

Os (Lat. *os, oris* a mouth), in anatomy, an opening of parts, either internal or external ; as, *os uteri*, the orifice of the uterus ; *os externum*, the entrance to the vagina.

Os'cheocele (Gr. *osche* the scrotum, and *kele* a tumour), in surgery, a scrotal hernia or rupture.—*Oschitis*, inflammation of the scrotum.

Oscillato'ria (Lat.), a group of minute filamentous organized beings, which have oscillatory motions ; a genus of Algæ, so named from their oscillatory motions.

Oscula'tion (Lat. *act of kissing*), in geometry, the contact between any curve and a circle which has the same curvature as the given curve at the point of contact.—*Osculatorius*, in anatomy, is an epithet applied to the sphincter muscle of the lips, so called because by it the act of kissing is performed.

Os'mazome (Gr. *osme*, smell, and *zomos* broth), a brownish - yellow animal substance, obtained by digesting cold water on muscular fibre, and then treating it with pure alcohol.

Os'mium (Gr.), a metallic substance found associated with the ore of platinum.

Os'mose (Gr.), the process by which fluids and gases pass through membranes.

Osmunda'ceæ, a family of Polypodiaceæ, of which Osmunda, a genus of Ferns, is the type.

Osphresiol'ogy (Gr. *osphresis* sense of smelling, and *logos* a discourse), a treatise on olfaction and odours, or the sense of smelling.

Osservan'za (Ital.), in music, a term implying that the movement at the beginning of which it is written is to be executed with scrupulous exactness.

Ostag'ra (Lat. *os* a bone), in surgery, a forceps used for extracting the fragments of broken bone.

Osteal'gia (Lat. and Gr.), pain in the bones.

Osteine (Fr.), the tissue of bone.

Ostei'tis (Gr.), osseous inflammation.

Os'teocele (Gr. *osteon* bone, and *kele* hernia), a hernia in which the sac is cartilaginous and bony.

Osteocol′la (Gr. *osteon*, and *kolla* glue), an incrustating carbonate of lime; an inferior kind of glue.

Os′teocope (Gr. *osteon*, and *kopos* weariness), in pathology, pain in the bones, or in the nerves and membranes that encompass them.

Osteoden′tine (Gr.), a structure formed in teeth resembling bone.

Osteog′eny (Gr.), the formation or growth of bone.

Osteog′raphy (Gr.), a description of the bones.

Os′teolite (Gr.), a fossil petrified bone.

Osteol′ogy (Gr.), a treatise on the bones.

Os′teophyte (Gr.), a bony tumour or projection.

Osteosarco′ma (Gr. *osteon*, and *sarx* flesh), a conversion of the bone into a mass resembling flesh.

Osteot′omy (Gr. *osteon*, and *temno* to cut), the dissection of bones.

Os′teotrite (Gr.), an instrument for removing diseased bones.

Osteozoa′ria (Gr. *osteon*, and *zoon* an animal), in zoology, a name for vertebrate animals.

Osthex′y (Gr.), ossification of parts of the body.

Osti′tis (Gr.), inflammation of the bones.

Ostra′ceæ, or **Ostra′cidæ** (Lat. *ostrea* an oyster), a family of bivalvular Mollusca.

Ostrap′oda (Lat. *ostrea*), in malacology, an order of Crustacea which have the body enclosed in a bivalve shell.

Otacous′tic (Gr. *ous, otos* the ear. and *akouo* to hear), assisting the sense of hearing.

Otacous′ticon, an ear-trumpet.

Otal′gia, Otal′gy (Gr.), pain in the ear; the earache.

Ota′ria (Gr.), those animals of the Seal family which have external ears.

Oti′tis (Gr.), in pathology, inflammation of the ear.

Ot′ocrane (Gr.), that portion of the skull connected with the organ of hearing.

Otog′raphy (Gr.), in anatomy, a description of the ear.

Ot′oliths (Gr. *otos*, and *lithos* a stone), small masses of carbonate of lime contained in the labyrinth of the ear.

Otol′ogy (Gr.), a treatise on the ear.

Otoplas′tice (Gr.), in surgery, an operation for restoring the ear.

Ot′oscope (Gr. *otos*, and *skopeo* to view), an instrument for listening to the sound passing through the tympanum in diseased states of the ear.

Otot′omy (Gr. *otos*, and *temno* to cut), dissection and preparation of the organs of hearing.

Ourol′ogy, Ouros′copy (Gr. *ouron* urine), in pathology, the judging of diseases from examining the urine.

Ous, in chemistry, a termination implying that the compound has a smaller quantity of oxygen than that whose name ends in *ic*; as in sulphur*ous* and sulphur*ic*.

Outwing, in military science, to extend the flanks of an army or line in action so as to gain an advantageous position against the right or left wing of an enemy.

Ova (Lat.), in architecture, the egg-shaped ornaments carved on the contour of the ovolo.

O′vary (Lat. *ovarium*), in anatomy, an organ containing the female ova, or in which impregnation is performed.—In botany, a hollow case enclosing ovules or young seeds.

O′verture (Fr.), in music, the introductory passage prefixed to an opera or oratorio.

O′viduct (Lat. *ovum* an egg, and *ductus* a passage), a canal or duct through which the ovum passes, after impregnation, from the ovary to the uterus. In the human subject, the oviducts are called the *Fallopian tubes*.

Ovig′erous (Lat. *egg-bearing*), in zoology, an epithet applied to certain receptacles in which the eggs are received after they have been excluded from the formative organs of the ovum, as the long pouches appended to the hinder part of the body in many of the Entomostracans and parasite Crustacea.

Ovip′arous (Lat.), producing eggs.

Ovipos′itor (Lat.), in entomology, the instrument by which an insect conducts its eggs to their appropriate nidus.

O′visac (Lat. *ovum*, and *saccus* a sack), the cavity in the ovary which immediately contains the ovum. In the Mammifera it forms the corpus luteum after the ovum has been expelled.

O′volo (Ital.), in architecture, a convex moulding, the profile and sweep of which, in the Ionic and Corinthian capitals, are usually the quadrant of a circle, or quarter-round.

Ovo-vivip′arous (Lat. *producing eggs alive*), an epithet applied to animals which, like the Salamander and the Viper, never lay eggs, but hatch them in the body.

Ovule, or **O′vulum** (Lat.), in botany, the seed before it is perfect.

Ovuli′næ (Lat. *ovum*), in malacology, a sub-family of the Cowries, the shells of which are smooth and polished, of which Ovula is the genus; order Gasteropoda.

Ovum, *pl.* **Ova** (Lat. *an egg*), in physiology, the capsule containing the prolific germ of animals; thus the egg of a bird, the vesicles found in the ovarium in Mammifera, and the spawn of fishes, are all ova.

Ox'alate (Gr. *oxys* sharp), in chemistry, a salt formed by a combination of oxalic acid with a base.

Oxal'ic Acid (Gr. *oxys*), a poisonous acid, often called *salts of sorrel*, extensively used as a bleaching material.

Oxalida'ceæ (Gr.), in botany, an order of exogenous plants, of which Oxalis, or Wood-sorrel, is the type.

Ox'amide (Gr.), in chemistry, a substance obtained by heating oxalate of ammonia in a retort.

Oxida'tion (Lat.), in chemistry, the process of converting metals or other substances into an oxide by the combination of a certain portion of oxygen.

Oxide (Gr. *oxys*), in chemistry, the combination of a metal with oxygen without being in the state of an acid. There are different degrees of oxidation; thus we have black and white oxide of mercury; and in chemical nomenclature the terms protoxide, deutoxide, tritoxide, &c., are employed to denote the first, second, third, &c., degrees of oxidation.

Oxy-, or **Oxi-** (Gr.), in chemistry, an important prefix to compound words, signifying that oxygen enters into the composition of the substance named.

Ox'ygen (Gr. *oxys*, and *gennao*, to generate), in chemistry, an elementary gaseous body which generates acids and oxides, and constitutes the vital part of atmospheric air. Oxygen is the most extensively diffused substance in nature, forming 21 per cent. by volume of the atmosphere, and eight-ninths by weight of the waters of the globe. It is the great supporter of life and combustion,

and, in combination with other substances, it forms oxides and acids.—*Oxyhydrogen* is an epithet applied to the *oxyhydrogen blowpipe*, an instrument by which one volume of oxygen is consumed with two of hydrogen, in passing through a small aperture, producing an intense heat.—*Oxyhydrogen microscope*, an instrument resembling a magic lantern, but in which the light is formed by the action of hydrogen thrown in an ignited state upon a cylinder of lime.—*Craig.*

Ox'ygon (Gr. *oxys*, and *gonia* an angle), a term applied in geometry to figures in which all the angles are acute.

Ox'yiodine, in chemistry, a compound of the chloriodic and oxyodic acids.

Ox'ymel (Gr. *oxys*, and *meli* honey), a mixture of honey and vinegar, sometimes made the vehicle of medicine, as oxymel of squills.

Oxymu'riate, in chemistry, a salt formed of oxymuriatic acid and a base.—*Oxymuriate of lime* is chloride of lime, highly esteemed as a bleaching compound.

Oxyph'ony (Gr. *oxys*, and *phone* voice), in pathology, an unnatural shrillness of the voice, indicative of inflammation or spasm of the larynx.

Ox'ysalt (Gr. *oxys*), a salt with which oxygen is combined.

Oxysul'phuret (Gr. *oxys*), in chemistry, a combination of sulphur with a metallic oxide.

Ozæ'na (Gr.), in pathology, a nasal ulceration, which discharges a fetid purulent matter, sometimes accompanied with caries of the bones.

Ozone (Gr.), a modification of oxygen produced by electrical action.—*Ozonometer* is an instrument for detecting the presence and quantity of ozone.

P.

P, as an abbreviation, stands for P.M. (*post meridiem*); M.P., Member of Parliament; and P.S., postscript.

Pacchio'nian Bodies (from *Pacchioni*, the Italian anatomist), in anatomy, small fleshy-like elevations formed on the external surface of the dura mater.

Pachyder'mata, or **Pach'yderms** (Gr. *thick-skinned*), a name applied by Cuvier to the seventh order of the mammiferous quadrupeds, including the Elephant, Hippopotamus, Rhinoceros, Tapir, Swine, Horse, and many extinct genera.

Pacin'ian Bodies (from *Pacini*, the Italian anatomist), in anatomy, minute oval bodies attached to the

extremities of the nerves of the hand and foot.

Pagu'rian (Lat. *pagurus* a crab), a macrurous decapod Crustacean; a kind of Crab-fish.

Paixhan Gun, in military science, a howitzer for throwing shells, so named from Paixhan, its inventor.

Palæo- (Gr.), a prefix to compound words, signifying *ancient*.

Palæog'raphy. (See *Paleography*.)

Palæontol'ogy. (See *Paleontology*.)

Palæozo'ic. (See *Paleozoic*.)

Palæozol'ogy (Gr. *palaios* old, *zoe* life, and *logos* a discourse), that branch of palæontology which describes fossil animal remains.

Paleog'raphy (Gr. *palaios*, and *graphe* description), the art or science of deciphering ancient inscriptions; ancient writings collectively.

Paleol'ogy (Gr.), a treatise on, or the science of, antiquities.

Paleontol'ogy (Gr. *palaios*, and *ontos* existence), the science that treats of fossil remains, both animal and vegetable.

Paleosau'rus (Gr. *ancient lizard*), a fossil reptile found in the magnesian limestone of the Permian system.

Paleothe'rium (Gr. *palaios*, and *therion* a wild beast), in geology, a genus of extinct Pachyderms found in the fossil state.

Paleozo'ic (Gr. *palaios*, and *zoe* life), in geology, a term applied to the lowest fossiliferous strata.

Pal'impsest (Gr. *palin* again, and *psao* to rub), a parchment or manuscript re-written upon.

Palingene'sia (Gr. *palin*, and *genesis* birth), a new or second birth.

Pal'isade, Palisa'do (Fr.), in fortification, a defence formed by pales or stakes driven into the ground and sharpened at the top.

Palla'dium (Lat.), in mineralogy, a whitish metal, very hard, but ductile and malleable.

Pallas, in astronomy, a small planet or asteroid discovered in 1802.

Palliobranchia'ta (Lat. *pallium* a mantle, and Gr. *branchia* gills) a class of molluscous invertebrate animals, with the branchiæ arranged on the inner surface of the mantle.

Pal'lium (Lat.), in zoology, the fleshy covering which lines the interior of the shells of bivalve Mollusca.

Palma'ceæ (Lat.), a nat. order of endogenous plants, of which the Palm is the type.—*Palm oil* is an article used in the manufacture of soap, ointments, &c. It is chiefly imported from the west coast of Africa, where it is principally obtained from the tree *Elais Guineensis*.

Pal'macites (Lat. *palma* a palm tree), in fossilology, the remains that bear an analogy or resemblance to the existing Palms.

Pal'mapedes, or **Pal'mapeds** (Lat. *palma* the hand, and *pedes* feet), swimming web-footed birds, the Anseres of Linnæus.

Palmar (Lat. *palma*), in anatomy, relating to the palm of the hand.—*Palmares* is the name given to two muscles of the hand.

Palmate, in chemistry, a salt formed of palmic acid and a base.—In botany, shaped like a palm.

Palmine, in chemistry, a substance obtained from castor-oil by treatment with nitric acid.—*Palmic* is an acid obtained from palmine.

Pal'miped (Lat.), web-footed; fin-footed; applied to birds. A swimming bird.

Palo-di-vac'ca, the Cow tree, a native of the Caraccas, from which a vegetable milk, or glutinous or milky sap, is obtained by incision.

Palp, in entomology, a jointed sensiferous organ of an insect.

Pampas, a name given to extensive plains in South America.

Pampre (Fr.), in sculpture, an ornament consisting of vine-leaves and grapes.

Pan-, Pant-, or **Panto-** (Gr. *pan* all), a prefix in compound words, signifying *all* or *everything*.

Panace'a (Lat. from Gr. *pan*, and *akeomai* to cure), a medicine professing to cure all sorts of diseases; a herb, called also *All-heal*.

Pan'creas (Gr. *pan*, and *kreas* flesh), in anatomy, a glandular viscus of the abdomen, situated under and behind the stomach; the sweetbread. Its secreted fluid is conveyed by an excretory duct, which opens with or near the cysto-hepatic into the duodenum.—*Pancreatico-duodenal*, an epithet applied to certain blood-vessels distributed on the pancreas and duodenum.—*Pancreatitis*, inflammation of the pancreas.

Pandana'ceæ (Malay), in botany, an order of endogenous plants, consisting of trees or bushes, with imbricated leaves, of which the Pandanus is the type.

Pande'an Pipes (Gr.), a musical wind instrument.

Pandect (Lat.), a treatise that comprehends the whole of any science.

Pandem'ic (Gr. *pan*, and *demos* a people), in pathology, incident to a whole people.

Pandicula'tion (Lat.), in pathology, the restlessness and yawning that accompany the cold fits of an intermittent fever.

Pando'ra, one of the newly-discovered planets, first observed by Searle in 1858.

Pandu'riform (Lat. *pandura* a fiddle), in botany, an epithet applied to leaves which are contracted in the middle, and broad at each end, like a fiddle.

Pan'icle (Lat.), a form of inflorescence; a raceme bearing branches of flowers.

Panope'a, one of the recently-discovered planets, first observed by Goldschmidt in 1861.

Panop'ticon (Gr. *pan*, and *optomai* to see), a prison so constructed that the inspector may see the prisoners at all times without being seen himself.

Panora'ma (Gr. *pan*, and *orao* to see), a picture presenting from a central point a view of objects in every direction.

Panphar'macon (Gr.), a universal medicine.

Panstereora'ma (Gr. *pan*, *stereos* solid, and *orao* to see), a model of a town or country in cork, pasteboard, or other substance.

Pantech'nicon (Gr. *pan*, and *techne* art), a place in which every species of workmanship is collected and exposed for sale.

Pantochronom'eter (Gr. *pan*, and *chrono-metron* time-measurer), an astronomical instrument, which is a combination of the compass, the sun-dial, and the universal time-dial.

Pan'tograph (Gr. *pan*, and *grapho* to write), a mathematical instrument for copying all sorts of drawings and designs.

Pantog'raphy (Gr.), a complete description; an entire view of a thing.

Pantol'ogy (Gr.), a treatise on universal instruction.

Pantom'eter (Gr. *pan*, and *metron* a measure), an instrument for measuring angles, elevations, &c.

Papavera'ceæ (Lat.), a nat. order of exogenous plants, of which the Papaver, or Poppy, is the type.

Papaya'ceæ (Malabar), in botany, a nat. order of plants without branches, of which the Papaw tree, the common name of the tree *Carica papaya*, is the type.

Papier-mâché (Fr.), articles manufactured of paper reduced to pulp.

Papiliona'ceæ (Lat. *papilio* a butterfly, from the disposition of the petals resembling a butterfly), in botany, a sub-order of Leguminosæ.

Papiliona'ceous (Lat. *papilio*), in entomology, relating to or resembling the butterfly.—In botany, consisting of a standard, wings, and keel, like a pea-flower; noting a class of plants, as Beans, Peas, and other Pulse.

Papilion'idæ (Lat.), in entomology, a family of the Diurnal Butterflies.

Papilion'ides (Lat.), in entomology, a tribe of lepidopterous insects, consisting of the families Papilionidæ, Nymphalidæ, Satyridæ, Erycinidæ, and the Hesperidæ.

Papil'la (Lat.), in anatomy, a nipple or teat.

Pap'ula (Lat.), in pathology, an eruption on the skin.

Papyroc'racy (Lat. *papyrus* paper, and Gr. *kratos* power), the power of paper money, as bank-notes, bills of exchange, &c., representing national wealth.

Papy'rus (Lat.), an Egyptian reed or bulrush, used by the ancients for forming a substance to write upon.

Para- (Gr.), a prefix used in compound words, signifying *close to* or *beyond*.

Parab'ola (Gr. *para*, and *ballo* to cast), in geometry, one of the conic sections, formed by the intersection of the cone by a plane parallel to one of its sides.—*Parabolic*, having the form of a parabola.—*Parabolism*, in algebra, a reduction to an equivalent state.—*Paraboloid*, in geometry, a higher order of parabola; a parabolic conoid.

Paracel'sist, a follower of Paracelsus in medical quackery, physics, and mystical science.

Paracente'sis (Gr. *para*, and *kenteo* to pierce), in surgery, the operation of tapping any of the cavities of the body for the purpose of withdrawing the contained fluid.

Paracen'tric (Gr. *para*, and *kentron* a centre), in geometry, noting a sort of curve line.

Par'achute (Gr. *para*, and Fr. *chute* a fall), an apparatus attached to a balloon, which resembles a common umbrella.

Paracyan'ogen (Gr.), in chemistry, a brown, solid matter, obtained by decomposing cyanuret of mercury by heat.

Paradisi'adæ, in ornithology, a sub-family of the Trochilidæ (Birds of Paradise), remarkable for the beauty of their plumage.

Par'ados (Sp.), in military science, an elevation of earth behind fortified places, to secure them from sudden attack.

Par'affine (Lat. *parum* and *affinis*, but little affinity), in chemistry, a fine, clear-burning oil, derived from the distillation of wood-tar.

Par'allax (Gr. *para*, and *allasso* to change), in astronomy, a change of place or aspect; the difference between the *apparent* place of a celestial object and its *true* place.

Par'allel (Gr. *para*, and *allelon* one another), in geometry, a line equally distant throughout from another line.—*Parallels*, in fortification, are wide trenches, so constructed as to afford the besieging troops a free covered communication between their various batteries and approaches.—*Parallels of declination*, in astronomy, are small circles of the sphere parallel to the equator.—*Parallels of altitude*, in geography, are small circles of the sphere parallel to the horizon.—*Parallels of latitude* are small circles on the terrestrial sphere parallel to the equator.—*Parallel sailing*, in navigation, sailing on a parallel of latitude, or circle parallel to the equator.—*Parallel ruler* is a mathematical instrument formed of two equal rulers, connected by two cross-bars or blades, movable about joints, so that while the distance between the two rulers is increased and diminished, their edges always remain parallel.

Parallel'ogram (Gr. *parallelos* parallel, and *gramma* a letter), in geometry, a right-lined quadrilateral figure, whose opposite sides are parallel and equal.

Parallelopi'ped (Gr.), a solid figure or body comprehended under six parallelograms, the opposite sides of which are equal and parallel.

Paral'ysis (Gr. *a loosening from*), a sudden loss of power or motion in the body, or a part of it ; a palsy.

Paramagnet'ic (Gr. *para*, and *magnes* a magnet), a term applied to bodies which are attracted by both poles of the magnet.

Param'eter (Gr. *para*, and *metron* a measure), in geometry, a constant straight line, belonging to each of the three conic sections.

Paranaph'thaline (Gr.), a substance resembling naphthaline.

Par'apet (Ital. *parapetto*), in fortification, a breastwork, wall, or screen, raised on the extreme edge of a rampart or other work, throughout which embrasures or openings are cut for cannon to fire through.

Paraphimo'sis (Gr.), in pathology, a disease of the glans penis by contraction of the prepuce.

Parapho'nia (Gr.), an alteration of the voice.

Paraphreni'tis (Gr. *para*, and *phrenitis* frenzy), in pathology, an inflammation of the diaphragm ; delirium.

Paraple'gia (Gr. *para*, and *plege* a stroke), in pathology, a paralysis of the lower half of the body.

Paraselo'ne (Gr. *para*, and *selene* the moon), a mock moon ; a meteor in a watery cloud resembling the moon.

Paraton'nerre (Gr. *para*, and Fr. *tonnerre* thunder) a lightning conductor ; a pointed metallic rod.

Paregor'ic (Gr. *paregorikos* soothing), an assuaging medicinal preparation ; anodyne.

Paren'chyma (Gr. *para*, and *chymos* juice), the cellular tissues of animals and vegetables ; the pith of plants.

Parget (Lat.), plaster laid upon roofs of houses ; gypsum, or plaster of Paris.

Parhe'lion, Parhe'lium (Gr. *para*, and *helios* the sun), a meteor appearing as a very bright light near the sun ; a mock sun.

Paria'næ (Lat. *parum* but little), in ornithology, a sub-family of the Sylviadæ, of which the Parus, or Titmouse, is the type.

Parie'tal (Lat. *paries* a wall), noting two lateral bones of the cranium.

Park of Artillery, train of artillery belonging to an army.

Paronych'ia (Gr. *para*, and *onyx* a claw), in pathology, whitlow ; phlegmonous inflammation of the dense cellular tissue which enters into the composition of the fingers.

Paro'tis (Gr. *para*, and *ous, otos* the ear), in anatomy, a gland under the ear which secretes saliva ; in pathology, a tumour in the parotid gland.—*Parotitis*, inflammation of the parotid gland ; the mumps.

Parthen'ope, one of the newly-discovered planets, first observed by De Gasparis in 1850. Its mean distance from the sun is 233,610,000 miles ; and its periodical revolution is 3 years and 306 days.

Parturi'tion (Lat. *parturio* to bring forth), act of bringing forth young ; childbirth.

Paru'lis (Gr. *para*, and *oulon* the gum), in pathology, a gum-boil.

Pasig'raphy (Gr. *pas* universal, and *grapho* to write), a universal language, designed to be spoken and written by all nations ; a subject which has exercised the genius of Liebnitz and other distinguished philosophers.

Passade (Fr.), in the manège, a turn or course of a horse backward or forward.

Pas'seres (Lat. *passer* a sparrow), an order of birds which includes the Sparrow, Swallow, Blackbird, and numerous other small birds.—*Passerine*, belonging to the order Passeres, of which the Sparrow is the type.

Pastil (Lat.), in pharmacy, a preparation composed chiefly of sugar and mucilage.—Among painters, a roll of paste made up of various colours with gum-water, for the purpose of making crayons.

Patare'ra, a small swivel piece of artillery.

Patel'la (Lat. *patina* a pan) in anatomy, the cap of the knee.—In ichthyology, a univalve shell-fish.—*Patellite* is the fossil remains of the patella.

Pathog'eny (Gr. *pathos* disease, and *genesis* generation), in pathology, the production and development of disease.

Pathog'nomy (Gr. *pathos*, and *gnome* signs of), the science of the signs by which the state of the passions is indicated. — *Pathognomic*, pertaining to the signs which would characterize a disease.

Pathol'ogy (Gr. *pathos*, and *logos* a discourse), the doctrine of diseases, together with their causes, effects, and differences ; a treatise on diseases.

Pat'ina (Lat.), in numismatics, the fine rust with which coins become covered by age, when lying in certain soils.

Pattée (Norm. Fr.), in heraldry, a cross, small in the middle and wide at the ends.

Pavon'idæ (Lat. *pavo* a peacock), a family of rasorial birds, including the Peacocks and Pheasants, in which the tail is much developed and of singular beauty.—*Pavo*, the Peacock, is the type and genus.

Pav'onine (Lat. *pavo*), in painting, resembling the tail of a peacock.

Pearl (Fr.), a whitish, hard, smooth substance, of a peculiar lustre, consisting of concentric layers of a fine, iridescent, compact nacre, formed in certain bivalve shells, particularly in the pearl oyster, *Meleagrinea margaritifera*. They are identical in composition with the nacre or internal coating of the shell. to which they most frequently adhere, which is thence called mother-of-pearl.—In surgery, a film in the eye.—*Pearl-white* is a sub-nitrate of bismuth, obtained by pouring the nitre of that metal into a diluted solution of sea-salt, by which a beautiful light white powder is obtained.—*Pearl-sinter*, a volcanic mineral of a siliceous nature, usually found in tufa.—*Pearl-ash* is an impure carbonate of soda.

Pearl Spar, a crystallized mineral of a pearly lustre, consisting of carbon, lime, magnesia, oxide of iron, and oxide of manganese: sp. gr. 2·83.—*Pearl-stone*, a variety of obsidian; a silicate of alumina, of a pearly lustre.

Pea-stone, in mineralogy, a variety of limestone.

Pebble (Sax. *pabol*), in mineralogy, a rounded nodule, especially of siliceous minerals, &c.; a transparent rock-crystal or quartz, used instead of glass for spectacles.—*Pebble-crystal*, a crystal in the form of nodules.

Pech'blende (Germ.), in mineralogy, an ore of uranium.

Pec'ora (Lat.), in the Linnæan system, the fifth order of Mammalia.

Pectate, in chemistry, a salt composed of pectic acid and a base.

Pecten (Lat. *a comb*), a vascular membrane in the eyes of birds; a genus of bivalve shells; the Clam.

Pectic, in chemistry, relating to pectine; noting an acid found in many vegetables.

Pec'tinal (Lat. *pecten*), a fish whose bones resemble the teeth of a comb.

Pec'tinate (Lat. *pecten*), in botany, formed like the teeth of a comb.

Pectine (Gr. *pektos* congealed), the gelatinizing principle of certain vegetables, such as currants, apples, &c.

Pectinibran'chiates (Lat. *pecten*, and *branchiæ* gills), in natural history, the sixth order of Gasteropods according to Cuvier's arrangement. It comprehends nearly the whole of the spiral univalves, and many shells simply conical. It is so named from the respiratory organs of the animals consisting of branchiæ composed of laminæ, united in the form of combs.

Pec'tolite (Lat. *pecten*, and Gr. *lithos* a stone), a mineral of a greyish colour, consisting of silica, lime, soda, potash, alumina, oxide of iron, and water: sp. gr. 2·69; H = 4·5.

Pec'toral (Lat. *pectus* the breast), a medicine for diseases of the breast.

Pectoril'oquy (Lat. *pectus*, and *loquor* to speak), a phenomenon in the state of diseased lungs, ascertained by means of the stethoscope.

Ped'estal (Fr.), in architecture, the foot, base, or substruction of a column, statue, pillar, or wall.

Ped'icle (Lat. *pedes* feet), in botany, the footstalk which supports one flower.

Pedicula'tion (Lat.), louse disease.

Pedic'ulus (Lat. *a louse*), a genus of apterous parasitical insects which infest the human body, and that of other animals.

Ped'iluvy (Lat. *pedes*, and *lavo* to wash), a foot-bath.

Ped'iment (Lat.), in architecture, the triangular ornament over the entablature of a building.

Ped'ipalp (Lat. *pedes*, and *palpo* to feel), in zoology, an order of animals or reptiles which includes the Scorpions.

Pedom'eter (Lat. *pes*, and Gr. *metron* a measure), an instrument for ascertaining the distance a man travels.

Pedun'cle (Lat. *pedunculus*), the flower-stalk of a plant.

Peg'asus, a constellation in the northern hemisphere, containing eighty-nine stars.

Peg'matite (Gr. *pegma* anything fastened together), in mineralogy, a primitive granite rock; a fine-grained compound of felspar and quartz.

Pel'iom, Pelio'ma (Gr. *pelioma* blueness), in mineralogy, a variety of iolite.—In pathology, a livid spot or bruise.

Pella'gra (Lat. *pellis* the skin, and *æger* sick), a disease chiefly affecting the skin, somewhat resembling elephantiasis.

Pellet (Lat.), shreds used as pellets in dressing wounds.—In architecture, a Gothic ornament.—In heraldry, little black roundels or balls, otherwise termed ogresses and gemstones, worn on armorial bearings.

Pel'licle (Lat. *pellis*), in chemistry, a

film of salt or other substance which forms on the surface of liquors.

Pel'litory, in pharmacy, the root of the Spanish Chamomile, called Pellitory of Spain; a perennial medicinal plant.

Pelok'onite (Gr. *pelos* black, and *konis* powder), a bluish-black, vitreous mineral, found in China: sp. gr. 2·56; H = 3.

Peltate, or **Pel'tated** (Lat. *pelta* a shield), in botany, applied to a leaf when the petiole is fixed in the disc instead of the margin, like the handle of a shield.

Pelvis (Lat. *a basin*), in anatomy, the lower part of the abdomen.—*Pelvimeter*, an instrument for measuring the female pelvis.—*Pelvis renum* is a membranous bag that receives the urine, and pours it into the bladder. —*Pelvis cerebri*, the infundibulum in the brain.

Pem'mican, meat or food cooked and prepared for use in long voyages or journeys.

Pemphi'gus (Gr. *a small blister*), in pathology, a disease of the skin, consisting of an eruption of blisters.

Penæa'ceæ, in botany, a nat. order of endogenous plants, belonging to the Rhamnal alliance of Lindley, of which the Penæa is the type.

Pencil of Rays, in optics, a collection of rays of light radiating from or converging to a common point.

Pendant (Fr. from Lat. *pendens* hanging), in Gothic architecture, an ornamented piece of stone or timber hanging from the roof.—*Pendentive* is a spandrel or triangular space between the arch-headed walls supporting a dome.

Pen'dulum (Lat. *pendens*), any heavy body so suspended that it may vibrate or swing backwards and forwards about some fixed point.—*Compensation pendulum* is a pendulum which is so constructed that it always retains precisely the same length, counteracting the effects of heat and cold.

Penguin, in ornithology, the common name of the birds of the family Alcadæ, which belong to the genera Aptenodytes, Spheniscus, and Eudypes. The wings resemble fins, and though not fitted for flight, assist them in their rapid divings and evolutions under water.

Pen'niform (Lat. *penna* a feather), in anatomy, applied to the muscles of which the fibres pass out on each side from a central tendon.

Penol'ogy (Lat. *pœna* punishment, and Gr. *logos* discourse), the science which treats of public punishments as they affect the community.

Pente- (Gr.), a common prefix to compound words, signifying *five*.

Pentac'rinite (Gr. *pente*, and *krinon* a lily), a fossil animal resembling the star-fish.

Pen'tagon (Gr. *pente*, and *gonia* an angle), a plane figure having five angles.

Pen'tagraph (Gr. *pente*, and *grapho* to write), an instrument with five points for copying designs.

Pentagyn'ia (Gr. *pente*, and *gyne* a female), an order of plants which have five pistils.

Pentahe'dron (Gr.), a figure having five sides.

Pentahexahe'dral (Gr.), in crystallography, exhibiting five ranges of faces one above another, each range containing six faces.

Pentam'erans (Gr. *five-jointed*), a section of coleopterous insects, including those species which have five joints on the tarsus of each leg.

Pentan'dria (Gr. *pente*, and *andres* males), a class of plants in the system of Linnæus which have hermaphrodite flowers, with five stamens or male organs of reproduction.

Pentan'gular (Gr.), having five corners or angles.

Pentapet'alous, Pentaphyl'lous (Gr.), in botany, having five petals or leaves.

Pen'tastyle (Gr.), in architecture, a building having five columns in front.

Pentatom'idæ (Gr. *pente*, and *tome* a section), a group of hemipterous insects, the Wood-bugs, of which the Pentatoma is the type.

Penum'bra (Lat. *pene* almost, and *umbra* a shade), in astronomy, an imperfect shadow.—In painting, the boundary of light and shade.

Peperi'no (Ital.), a kind of volcanic rock, composed of sand, cinders, &c., cemented together.

Pep'sine (Gr. *pepto* to digest), the active principle of the gastric juice.— *Peptic*, promoting digestion.

Per- (Lat.), a prefix of frequent use in compound words, signifying *through, very, in excess*.

Peram'bulator (Lat. *perambulo* to walk about), a machine for measuring distances on roads; a light vehicle used by nursery-maids for children.

Perbisul'phate, in chemistry, a sulphate with two proportions of sulphuric acid.

Percar'buretted, in chemistry, combined with a maximum of carbon.

Perchlo'rate, in chemistry, a salt composed of perchloric acid and a base.

Perchlo'ric, in chemistry, an epithet applied to chloric acid when chlorine is combined with a maximum of oxygen.

Perchlo′ride, in chemistry, a compound of an excess of chlorine with a base.

Perennibran′chiates (Lat. *perennial gills*), in zoology, a division of the batrachian reptiles, such as the Siren, Monopome, and Proteus.

Peri-, a prefix to scientific words of Greek origin, signifying *around* or *about*.

Per′ianth (Gr. *peri*, and *anthos* a flower), a collection of floral envelopes, among which the calyx cannot be distinguished.

Perib′olus (Gr. *peri*, and *bole* a throw), a court or enclosure round a temple.

Pericar′dium (Gr. *about the heart*), a thin membrane, or membranous sac, which surrounds the heart.—*Pericarditis*, in pathology, inflammation of the pericardium.

Per′icarp (Gr. *around the seed*), the shell or covering of a fruit.

Perichæ′tium (Gr.), in mosses, the leaves at the base of the stalk.

Perichon′drium (Gr. *peri*, and *chondros* cartilage), the membrane that covers a cartilage.

Pericra′nium (Gr.), a membrane that covers the skull.

Per′iderm (Gr. *peri*, and *derma* skin), in botany, the outer layer of bark.

Peridodecahe′dral (Gr.), having twelve sides all round; applied to a crystal.

Per′idot, in mineralogy, the prismatic chrysolite.

Per′idrome (Gr. *peri*, and *dromos* a course), a gallery or an alley between columns or walls.

Per′igee, Perige′um (Gr. *near the earth*), that point of the moon's orbit which is nearest to the earth; opposed to *Apogee*.

Per′igord; an ore of manganese.

Perig′ynous (Gr. *peri*, and *gyne* a female), growing from the sides of a calyx. When the stamens grow out of the corolla, calyx, or perianth, or are not in any way joined to the seed-vessel, they are said to be *perigynous*.

Perihe′lion (Gr. *near the sun*), the point in the orbit of a planet or comet which is nearest the sun.

Perihexahe′dral (Gr.), applied to a crystal whose primitive form has four sides, and its secondary six.

Perim′eter (Gr.), the circuit or boundary of a plane figure.

Perioctahe′dral (Gr.), applied to a crystal whose primitive form has four sides, and its secondary eight.

Perioe′ci (Gr. *peri*, and *oikos* dwelling), people who live under the same parallel of latitude, but in opposite meridians, so that when it is noon with one, it is midnight with the other.

Perios′teum (Gr. *peri*, and *osteon* a bone), a fibrous membrane which invests the bones.—*Periostitis*, in pathology, inflammation of the periosteum.

Periph′ery (Gr. *carrying round*), circumference of a circle or other curvilinear figure.

Per′iplus (Gr.), circumnavigation.

Peripneu′mony (Gr.), inflammation of the lungs.

Peripolyg′onal (Gr.), having many sides.

Perip′tery (Gr. *peri*, and *pteron* a wing), a building surrounded with a row of columns.

Peris′cii (Gr. *peri*, and *skia* a shadow), people whose shadows move all round, as the inhabitants within the arctic and antarctic circles.

Per′iscope (Gr.), a view all round.

Per′isperm (Gr. *peri*, and *sperma* seed), the albumen of a seed.

Peristal′tic (Gr. *peristello* to involve), in anatomy, applied to the vermicular motion of the intestines, produced by the contractions of successive portions.

Peris′terite, a variety of felspar.

Per′istome (Gr. *round the mouth*), a set of processes surrounding the orifice of the theca of a moss.

Per′istyle (Gr. *peri*, and *stylos* a column), a building encompassed with interior columns, or a circular range of pillars.

Perisys′tole (Gr. *peri*, and *systole* contraction), the pause that ensues on the contraction of the heart before the diastole or dilatation can follow.

Perit′amous (Gr. *peri*, and *temno* to cut), in mineralogy, cleaving in more directions than one parallel to the axis.

Peritone′um (Gr. *peri*, and *toneo* to extend), the membrane which envelops the abdominal viscera, and lines the cavity of the abdomen.

Peritro′chium (Gr. *peri*, and *trochos* a wheel), a circular frame of wood fixed upon a cylinder or axle, round which a rope is wound; and the wheel and cylinder being movable about a common axis, a power applied to the wheel will raise a weight attached to the rope with so much the greater advantage.

Per′linæ (Lat.), a sub-family of hymenopterous insects, of which Perla is the genus.

Permuta′tion (Lat. *permuto* to change), in algebra, the arrangement of any determinate number of things or letters in all possible orders one after the other.

Perone′al (Gr. *perone* the fibula), belonging to or lying near the small bone of the leg.

Perox′ide (Lat. *per* thoroughly, and Gr. *oxys* sharp), in chemistry, the oxide of a substance which contains most oxygen, but has not acid characters; the highest oxide of any metal.

Perox'idise, to oxidize to the highest degree.

Perphos'phate, in chemistry, a salt in which phosphoric acid is combined with an oxide at the maximum of oxidation.

Personnel' (Fr.), in military organization, the rank, appointment, and duties of the persons, men, or officers belonging to the army, as distinguished from the *matériel*, or provisions, arms, &c.

Perspec'tive (Fr. from Lat. *perspicio* to look through), relating to the science of vision; a glass through which things are viewed.—*Aërial perspective* is the act of giving due diminution to the strength of light, shade, and colours of objects, according to their distances, and of the gradation of their tints in proportion to the intervening air.—*Isometrical perspective*, the art of proportioning in size the relative objects seen in a painting, making them gradually less as they recede in the distance.—In the fine arts, *perspective* is the art of delineating, on a given transparent plane or superficies, objects as they appear to an eye placed at a given height and distance.

Perspec'tograph (Gr.), an instrument for taking the points and outlines of objects.

Persul'phate, in chemistry, a salt composed of sulphuric acid and a peroxide.

Persulta'tion (Lat. *persulto* to leap through), an eruption of the blood from an artery.

Pertus'sis (Lat. *per*, and *tussis* a cough), in pathology, the whooping-cough.

Peru'vian Bark, or **Cincho'na,** a bark from a Peruvian tree, much used in medicine.

Per'uvine, a substance distilled from balsam of Peru.

Pes'sary (Fr. from Gr. *pesso* to soften), in surgery, a small roll of lint, or other material, medicated for thrusting into the uterus on extraordinary occasions.

Petal (Gr. *petalon*), in botany, a flower-leaf; division of the corolla of a plant.

Pet'alite (Gr. *petalon*, and *lithos* a stone), a reddish mineral with a foliated texture. It is a silicate of alumina and lithia, and contains between 5 and 6 per cent. of the latter alkali.

Pétard (Fr.), in military science, a machine charged with powder, resem-

bling in shape a high-crowned hat, formerly much used for breaking gates, barricades, &c.

Pet'asus (Lat.), in architecture, a cupola in the form of a broad-brimmed hat.

Petau'rus, a marsupial animal which has the power of taking extensive leaps through the air.

Pete'chiæ (Ital.), in pathology, small red pestilential spots.

Petrifac'tion (Lat. from Gr. *petra* a stone, and *facio* to form), state of being petrified or turned to stone.

Pet'rilite (Gr.), a sort of felspar.

Petro'leum (Gr. *petros* rock, and Lat. *oleum* oil), a brown liquid bitumen, found in several parts of the world.—*Petroline*, a substance obtained by distilling petroleum.

Petrol'ogy (Gr.), a discourse concerning rocks.

Pet'rosal (Lat. *petra*), a name applied to the ossified portion in the fish.

Petrosi'lex (Lat.), hornstone, or compact felspar.

Petroste'arine (Gr. *petros*, and *stearos* solid), a term applied to the solid unctuous material of which the patent composite candles are made.

Petunse (Chinese), porcelain clay.

Petworth Marble, in geology, a variety of marble occurring in the Weald clay.

Peuced'anine (Gr.), in chemistry, a peculiar principle obtained from the sea-sulphurwort.

Phagede'na (Gr. *phago* to eat away), in surgery, a gangrenous ulcer which spreads and eats away the flesh.

Phalan'ges (Gr. *phalanx*), in anatomy, the small bones of the fingers and toes.

Phanæ'us (Gr. *phanos* bright), a family of coleopterous insects; fam. Scarabæidæ.

Phanerogam'ic, Phanerog'amous (Gr. *phaneros* visible, and *gamos* marriage), in botany, having the reproductive organs visible.

Phan'tascope, Phantas'mascope (Gr. *phantasma* a form, and *skopeo* to view), an optical instrument, by which fixed objects appear as if in motion.

Phantasmago'ria (Gr. *phantasma*), an optical apparatus, by means of which the images of objects can be magnified or diminished at pleasure.

Phantasmatog'raphy (Gr. *phantasma*, and *grapho* to describe), a description of celestial appearances, as the rainbow, &c.

Pharmaceu'tics (Gr. *pharmakon* medicine), the science of preparing medicines.

Pharmac'olite (Gr. *pharmakon*, and

lithos a stone), native arseniate of lime.

Pharmacol'ogy (Gr.), a treatise on pharmacy.

Pharma'con (Gr.), a poison; a medicine.

Pharmacopœ'ia (Gr.), a book published by the College of Physicians, containing directions for preparing medicines.

Phar'macy (Gr. *pharmakon* a drug), the art of preparing medicines; that branch of science which relates to the medical and chemical history of the different articles of the Materia Medica.

Pharyngeurys'ma (Gr. *pharynx*, and *euryno* to dilate), in pathology, a morbid dilatation of the pharynx.

Pharyngi'tis (Gr.), an inflammation of the membrane which forms the pharynx.

Pharyngol'ogy (Gr. *pharynx*, and *logos* a discourse), the part of anatomy which treats of the pharynx.

Pharyngople'gia (Gr. *pharynx*, and *plesso* to strike), paralysis of the muscles of the pharynx.

Pharyngot'omy (Gr.), the operation of cutting into the pharynx.

Pharynx (Gr.), the back part of the mouth, or the upper part of the gullet, below the larynx.

Phase (Gr. *phasis*, from *phaino* to shine), the appearance of any celestial body, as seen by an observer; the appearance or state of any phenomenon that undergoes a periodical change.—In astronomy, the term *phases* is applied to denote the different appearances of the moon or inferior planets, according as greater or smaller portions of the hemisphere illuminated by the sun are visible to the observer. The principal phases of the moon are the new moons, full moons, and quarter moons.

Phen'acite (Gr. *phoinikos* purple), a mineral resembling quartz.

Phengite (Gr.), a species of beautiful alabaster.

Phen'icine (Gr. *phoinikos*), in mineralogy, a purple powder which is precipitated when a sulphuric solution of indigo is diluted with water.

Phenoga'mian, Phenog'amous (Gr. *phaino* to show, and *gamos* marriage), in botany, having stamens and pistils distinctly visible.

Phenom'enon, *pl.* **Phenom'ena** (Gr. *phainomai* to appear), anything as it appears to the senses; commonly applied to those appearances of nature of which the cause is not immediately obvious, such as the phenomena of light, electricity, magnetism, &c., or to unusual natural appearances, as meteors, comets, &c.

Phil'lyrine, a non-azotized vegetable principle which occurs in the bark of *Phillyrea media* and *latifolia*.

Philadelpha'ceæ (Gr.), an order of exogenous plants, consisting of ornamental hardy shrubs, of which Philadelphus is the type.

Philan'thidæ, in entomology, a family of hymenopterous insects, of which Philanthus is the type.

Philip'site, in mineralogy, a species of haimotome, or cross-stone, consisting of silica, alumina, potash, lime, and water: sp. gr. 2·0—2·2; H = 4·5.

Philol'ogy (Gr. *phileo* to love, and *logos* a word), in literary science, the knowledge and study of languages, or the branches of learning connected with languages, as etymology, grammar, and literary criticism.

Philoprogen'itiveness (Gr. *philos* love, and Lat. *propigno* to bring forth), in phrenology, the love of offspring, situated in the region of the occipital bone.

Philos'opher's Stone, a stone which was fancied by the alchemists to convert base metals into gold.

Philos'ophy (Gr. *philos*, and *sophos* wisdom), the love of wisdom; knowledge, natural or moral, consisting of three departments, viz., *natural philosophy*, or physics; *intellectual* or *mental philosophy*, or metaphysics; and *moral philosophy*, or ethics.—*Philosopher* is a person well acquainted with the varied phenomena of nature, or the laws on which physical science is founded; one profoundly versed in any science.

Philotech'nic (Gr. *philos*, and *techne* art), fond of, or friendly to, the arts.

Philydra'ceæ (Gr.), in botany, a nat. order of dipetalous Exogens without a calyx, of which the Philydrum (lover of water) is the type.

Phimo'sis (Gr. *phimos* a muzzle), in pathology, an affection of the prepuce, in which it cannot be drawn back, so as to uncover the glans penis.

Phlebi'tis (Gr. *phleps* a vein), in pathology, an inflammation of the veins, distinguished by a hard, cord-like, tender line, pursuing the course of a vein or veins, from an incision or wound.

Phlebog'raphy (Gr. *phleps*, and *graphe* to describe), a description of the veins.

Phlebol'ogy (Gr.), the anatomy of the veins.

Phlebot'omy (Gr.), the opening of a vein for the purpose of taking away blood.

Phlegma (Gr.), in pathology, a tenacious matter secreted in the lungs.

Phleg'magogue (Gr. *phlegma*, and *ago* to drive away), medicine for carrying away phlegm.

Phlegma'tia (Gr. *phlegma*), extravasation of mucus or serum.

Phlegmatorrha'gia (Gr. *phlegma*, and *rhegnymi* to burst forth), an abundant discharge of mucus from the nostrils, unaccompanied by inflammation of the pituitary membrane.

Phlegmon (Gr. *phlego* to burn), in pathology, a burning tumour; an inflammatory swelling on the external surface.

Phlogis'ton (Gr. *phlogizo* to burn), the matter of fire fixed in combustible bodies; the old name for caloric.

Phlorid'zine (Gr. *phloios* bark, and *rhiza* a root), a peculiar vegetable matter existing in the bark of apple, pear, cherry, and plum trees.—*Phloridzeine* is a red powder precipitated by the addition of acids to a solution in ammonia of phloridzine previously moistened with that alkali, and exposed to the action of the atmosphere.

Phoca'ceans (Lat. *phoca* a seal), in zoology, a tribe of carnivorous amphibious Mammals, of which the Seal is the type.

Pho'cea, in astronomy, the name of one of the newly-discovered planets, first observed by Chacornac in 1853. Its mean distance from the sun is 228,940,000 miles, and its periodical revolution 3 years and 263 days.

Pho'cinine, a peculiar fatty matter contained in the oil of the porpoise.

Pho'cidæ (Lat.), a family of Cetaceans, of which Phoca, the Seal, is the type.

Pho'larite, a hydrated silicate of alumina.

Phona'tion (Gr.), the physiology of the voice.

Phonet'ic (Gr. *phone* voice, vocal sound), applied to that sort of writing in which sounds are represented by peculiar characters.

Phonet'ics (Gr.), the science which treats of the sounds of the human voice.

Phonics (Gr.), the doctrine of sounds; acoustics.

Pho'nograph (Gr. *phone*, and *grapho* to describe), a type or character for expressing sound; a character used in phonography.

Phonog'raphy (Gr.), the art of expressing sounds by characters or symbols; a brief system of shorthand writing, used instead of stenography.

Pho'nolite (Gr. *phone*, and *lithos* a stone), in mineralogy, a species of compact, sonorous basalt.

Phonol'ogy (Gr.), a treatise on the sounds of the human voice; phonics.

Pho'notype (Gr.), a type or character used in phonotypic printing.

Phonot'ypy (Gr.), the art of printing by sound, or by types or characters representing the human voice.

Phoronom'ics (Gr. *phero* to bear, and *nome* a law), the science of motion; mechanical philosophy.

Phosgene (Gr. *phos* light, and *gennao* to produce), applied to a gas compounded of chlorine and carbonic oxide formed in bright daylight.

Phosphate (Gr.), in chemistry, a salt formed of phosphoric acid and a base.—*Phosphate of lime* is a salt consisting of lime and phosphoric acid. It constitutes the base of the bones of animals.—*Mineral phosphate of lime* contains several species, as *apatite*, *asparagus stone*, &c.

Phosphite (Gr.), a salt formed of phosphorous acid and a base.

Phos'pholite (Gr. *phosphoros*, and *lithos* a stone), an earth united with phosphoric acid.

Phosphores'cence (Gr. *phos*), the emission of light by substances at common temperatures. — *Phosphorescence of the sea* is a luminous appearance of sea-water, arising from the presence of innumerable microscopic medusæ which people every region of the ocean, and being specifically lighter than the sea-water, float in incalculable numbers on its surface.

Phos'phorite, native phosphate of lime.

Phos'phorus (Gr. *phos*, and *phero* to bear), in chemistry, a substance which exists in minerals and animals, and is commonly obtained from bones and urine. When exposed to the air at a temperature of about 100°, it burns with intense brilliancy.—*Phosphoric acid* is an acid obtained by various methods from phosphorus. It is colourless, intensely sour, reddens litmus, and neutralizes alkalies. Its equivalent is 71·4; symb. P₂ + O₅.

Phos'phuret (Gr. *phos*), a compound formed of phosphorus combined with some other substances.—*Phosphuret of nitrogen* is a light, snow-white powder, insoluble in water, in dilute acids, or alkaline solutions; composed of 2 atoms of phosphorus and 1 atom of nitrogen. Its equivalent is 45·55; symb. N + 2 P. — *Phosphuretted hydrogen*, a combination of phosphorus and hydrogen, which was discovered in 1812 by Sir H. Davy. It is a transparent, colourless gas, of an exceedingly offensive smell and bitter taste.—*Metallic phosphurets* are combinations which may be made with most, if not all, of the metals, by bringing them, at a high temperature, into immediate contact with phosphorus.

Pho′tixite, a magnesian spar.

Photo- (Gr. *phos, photos* light), a prefix to numerous compound words connected with science, which denotes relation to or connection with light.

Photog′eny (Gr. *phos, photos,* and *gennao* to produce), the art or act of producing fac-similes, or representations of objects, by the chemical action of light on a prepared metallic tablet; called also *Daguerreotype,* from M. Daguerre, the inventor.

Pho′tograph (Gr. *phos,* and *grapho* to write), a fac-simile or likeness produced by photogeny, or daguerreotype.

Photog′raphy (Gr.), the art of delineating objects by means of light; photogeny.

Photohe′liograph (Gr. *phos,* and *helios* the sun), a drawing produced by the agency of the sun's light; a sun camera, or instrument for photographing the spots of the sun.

Photel′ogy (Gr. *phos, photos,* and *logos* a discourse), the science of, or a treatise on, light.

Photomag′netism (Gr. *phos,* and *magnetism*), that branch of science which describes the relation of the phenomena of magnetism to those of light.

Photom′etry (Gr.), the science or art of measuring light.—*Photometer,* an instrument for measuring the relative illuminating powers of different sources of light.

Photopho′bia (Gr. *phos, photos,* and *phobos* fear), in pathology, intolerance of light, a symptom of amaurosis.

Photop′sy (Gr. *phos, photos,* and *optomai* to see), in pathology, a morbid affection of the eyes, in which coruscations of light play before them; a symptom of amaurosis.

Pho′tosphere (Gr. *light of the sphere*), in astronomy, a term applied to the light which surrounds a star or planet.

Phrenet′ic (Gr. *phren* the mind), disordered with frenzy; affected in the brain.

Phrenic (Gr. *phrenes* the diaphragm), belonging to the diaphragm.

Phreni′tis (Gr. *phren*), inflammation of the brain; madness.

Phrenol′ogy (Gr. *phren,* and *logos* a discourse), the doctrine of the special faculties of the mind; the science of the brain, as connected with the intellectual, moral, and sensual dispositions and qualities of the individual, supposed to be developed on the external cranium.

Phrygan′idæ, a family of neuropterous insects, of which the genus Phryganea is the type.—*Phryganinæ,* or Mayflies, are a sub-family of this class.

Phthis′ic (Gr.), pulmonary consumption.

Phthisiol′ogy (Gr.), a treatise on consumption.

Phthisis (Gr. *phthio* to consume), in pathology, the disease commonly known as consumption.

Phyllid′iana, a family of gasteropodous Molluscs, including the genera Phyllidia, Chitonella, Chiton, Patella, Patelloidea, and Siphonaria.—*Phyllidina* are a sub-family of tectibranchiate Mollusca, consisting of Sea-slugs without shells.

Phyllite (Gr. *phyllon* a leaf, and *lithos* a stone), a mineral of a brownish-black colour; lustre semi-metallic. Its constituents are silica, alumina, peroxide of iron, magnesia, potash, and water: sp. gr. 2·89; H = 5·75.

Phyllo′dea (Gr. *phyllon*), in botany, a term applied to the petioles of certain leafless plants.

Phylloph′agans (Gr. *phyllon,* and *phago* to eat), in zoology, a tribe of Marsupials.—In entomology, a tribe of coleopterous insects which live on leaves.

Phys′alite (Gr. *physa* a bladder, and *lithos* a stone), a mineral that swells with heat; a species of topaz.

Physe′ter (Gr.), a filtering machine, consisting of a tub with an air-tight perforated stage.

Physian′thropy (Gr. *man's nature*), the philosophy of human life.

Physic (Gr. *physis* nature), the science of medicine, or the art of healing; medicine collectively.—*Physician* is one who professes or practises physic.

Phys′icist, Physiool′ogist (Gr.), one conversant with physics, or natural philosophy.

Physiool′ogy (Gr. *physikos* natural, from *physis* nature, and *logos* a discourse), a discourse on physics, or the general laws of nature; natural philosophy.

Phys′ico - mathemat′ics (Gr.), mixed mathematics.

Phys′ico-theol′ogy (Gr.), natural theology, or theology illustrated by natural philosophy.

Physics (Gr. *physis*), the science of nature; natural philosophy, or that department of science which has for its subject all things that exist independently of the mind's conception of them.

Physiognom′ics (Gr. *physis,* and *nomos* a law), certain indications on the countenance, by which the temperament or constitution of the body and mind may be determined.

Physiog'nomy (Gr. *physis*, and *gignosco* to know), the art of discovering the temper and character by the outward appearance, especially by the features of the face.

Physiog'notype (Gr.), a machine for taking casts and imprints of human faces or countenances, first practised in Paris.

Physiol'ogy (Gr. *physis*, and *logos* a discourse), the science of things generated or alive; the doctrine of vital phenomena; the science of natural organization, or of organized beings.—*Animal physiology*, the science of animals, or zoology.—*Vegetable physiology*, the science of vegetables, or botany.

Phytiph'agans (Gr. *phyton* a plant, and *phago* to eat), a tribe of Cetaceans, called also Herbivora.

Phyto- (Gr. *phyton*), a prefix to compound words, signifying *plant*.

Phyto-chem'istry (Gr. *phyton*), vegetable chemistry.

Phytogen'esis (Gr. *phyton*, and *gennao* to produce), the development of plants.

Phytog'raphy (Gr.), a description of plants; a branch of botany.

Phytol'ogy (Gr.), a discourse on botany; a book containing herbs and plants.

Phyton'omy (Gr.), the laws of the vegetable world.

Phytot'omy (Gr. *phyton*, and *tome* incision), the dissecting of plants.

Pia Mater (Lat.), in anatomy, a thin vascular membrane covering the convolutions of the brain and the spinal marrow.

Pianofor'te (Ital. *piano* soft, and *forte* loud), a musical stringed instrument played by keys.—*Piano monitor* is a bar of metal placed a little above and before the keys of a pianoforte, for enabling the young practitioner to rest on.

Piaz'za (Ital.), in architecture, a square open space surrounded by buildings; an open walk around a building usually enclosed by columns, and covered by a projecting story.

Pica (Lat.), in letter-press printing, the name of a type, so called because it was first used in printing the Pie, a Catholic service book.

Pic'idæ (Lat.), in ornithology, a family of birds, of which the Picus, or Woodpecker, is the type.

Picket (Fr.), in fortification, a stake used, in laying out grounds, to mark the bounds and angles. — In military science, a guard posted before an army to give notice of an enemy's approach.—*Outlying pickets* are de-

tachments of cavalry or infantry, sometimes with light guns, posted on the front and flanks of an army in the field in order to guard against surprise.

Pic'romel (Gr. *pikros* bitter, and *meli* honey), the chemical principle which exists in the bile and gall of animals.

Pic'rophyl (Gr.), in mineralogy, a species of serpentine.

Pic'rosmine, a siliceous mineral, the dihydrous bisilicate of magnesia, consisting of silica, magnesia, protoxide of iron, and water: sp. gr. 2·66; $H=2·5—3·6$.

Picrotox'ine (Gr. *pikros*, and *toxikon* poison), in chemistry, the bitter and poisonous principle of the *Cocculus Indicus*.

Pi'edroit (Fr.), in architecture, a pier or square pillar partly inserted in a wall, and being without capital or base.

Pieno (Ital. from Lat. *plenus*), in music, a term signifying that the composition where the word is appended is *full*, and that all the instruments are at that place performing.

Pier (Sax. *pere*), a column on which the arch of a bridge is raised; a mole projecting into the sea to break the force of the waves.

Pieri'næ, in entomology, a sub-family of lepidopterous insects, of which the Pieris, or White Garden Butterfly, is the type.

Pies'trum (Gr. *piezo* to compress), in surgery, an instrument to compress the head of a dead fœtus, to facilitate extraction, and save the parent.

Piezom'eter (Gr. *piezo*, and *metron* a measure), an instrument for ascertaining the compressibility of liquids.

Pig-iron, in metallurgy, a term applying to the mass of metal which sets in the main furrow leading immediately from the smelting furnace, called a *sow*, those in the smaller furrows leading from it being called *pigs*; and hence, in commerce, they are known as *pig* or *crude* iron.

Pigment (Lat.), in anatomy, the mucous secretion which covers the iris of the eye, and gives it its various colours; also the dark matter which covers the anterior surface of the choroid membrane, and the interior surface of the ciliary processes.

Pig'otite, a massive brownish mineral.

Pi'lary (Lat. *pilus* hair), in anatomy, pertaining to the assemblage of hairs which invest the exterior of many animals and plants.

Pilas'ter (Fr.), a square column or pillar set or inserted in a wall.

Pile (Sax. *pil*), in architecture and engineering, a stake, or strong piece of wood or timber, driven into the ground to make a firm foundation and support a superstructure.—In gunnery, a heap of shot piled up in horizontal courses in the form of a pyramid.—*Thermo-electric pile*, an instrument which shows that heat, under certain circumstances, produces a galvanic effect.—*Galvanic* or *voltaic pile*, a series of circles or elements acting in unison ; a galvanic battery.—*Pile-engine*, a machine for driving piles into the ground ; a pile-driver.

Piles (Lat. *pila* a ball), in pathology, a disease originating in a morbid dilatation of the veins in the rectum ; hæmorrhoids.

Pillar (Lat. *pila*), an irregular column, having the same diameter at the capital and base.

Pim'elite (Gr.), a green mineral, a variety of steatite coloured by chrome.

Pina'oeæ (Lat.), an important and extensive order of trees, the Conifers, of which the Pinus is the type and genus.

Pinchbeck, an alloy of copper and zinc ; a gold-coloured mixed metal.

Pine (Lat. *pinus*), a large evergreen tree of many varieties, of the order Pinaceæ, valued for timber.—*Pine-aster* is a variety of the Pine which throws out large spreading arms, but is naked in winter.

Pinguic'ola (Lat. *pinguis* fat), in pathology, a form of pterygium occurring in elderly persons, and consisting of little yellow granules towards the angles of the eye, under the conjunctiva.

Pinic Acid, an acid obtained from common resin and pure alcohol.

Pinion (Fr. *pignon*), in mechanical science, a small wheel which works in the teeth of a larger one ; sometimes only an arbor or spindle with notches or leaves, which are caught successively by the teeth of the wheel, and the motion by this means communicated.

Pinite, a crystallized mineral found in the mine Pini, in Saxony, composed of silex, alumina, and oxide of iron.

Pinites (Lat. *pinus* the fir tree), a generic term for fossil remains of plants allied to the coniferous order.

Pinna (Lat.), in anatomy, the *pinna auris* is the upper and broader part of the ear.

Pin'nacle (Fr.), in architecture, a small polygonal turret or elevation above the rest of the building.

Pinnat'iped (Lat. *pinna*, and *pedes* feet), in zoology, fin-footed ; a fin-footed bird.

Pint, a measure of capacity, the eighth part of a gallon, containing 34·659 cubic inches.

Pipera'oeæ (Lat.), a nat. order of incomplete Exogens, composed of creeping plants, of which Piper (Pepper) is the genus. The common pepper of commerce is the produce of *Piper nigrum*, a climbing East Indian plant.—*Piperine* is the peculiar principle of black pepper, consisting of carbon, hydrogen, oxygen, and nitrogen.

Pip'ridæ (Gr.), in ornithology, a family of birds of the order Dentirostres, of which Pipra, the Manakins, is the genus.

Piquet. (See *Picket*.)

Pisces (Lat. *piscis* a fish), in zoology, the fourth class in the systems of Linnæus and Cuvier.—In astronomy, the last of the winter signs of the zodiac, which the sun enters about the 19th of February.

Pisé (Fr.), in architecture, a species of wall constructed of stiff earth or clay, rammed down as the work is carried on.

Pi'siform (Lat. *pisum* a pea, and *forma*), in anatomy, *pisiforme os* is the first bone of the first row of the carpus. — *Pisiform iron ore* is a variety of argillaceous oxide of iron, occurring in small masses or grains, nearly or quite spherical, and often equal in size to a pea, or even larger. It occurs in secondary rocks, and is abundant in France, Switzerland, and Germany.

Pi'solite (Gr. *pison* a pea, and *lithos* a stone), a mineral resembling an agglutination of peas ; the pea-stone.

Pissas'phalt (Gr. *pissa* turpentine, and *asphaltos*), mineral pitch, an indurated bitumen.

Pissellæ'um In'dicum, a mineral fluid of the nature of the thicker bitumens ; Barbadoes tar.

Pistil (Lat.), in botany, the central organ of a flowering plant, consisting of the ovary, stylus, and stigma.

Piston (Fr.), a short cylinder of wood or metal, which fits exactly the cavity of a pump, or of other hydraulic machines, as an air-pump, &c. ; and, working up and down, causes suction.—*Piston-rod* is the rod attaching the piston to the adjoining machinery.

Pitch (Sax. *pic*), the residuum which remains after boiling tar in an open iron pot, much used in ship-building ; a resinous substance obtained by incision from the bark of the pine tree, *Abies picea*, commonly called *Burgundy pitch*.—In music, the degree of acuteness or graveness of a note.

Pitchblende, in mineralogy, a compound of the oxides of uranium and iron.

Pitchpipe, an instrument to regulate the voice, and to give the leading note of a tune.

Pitchstone, in mineralogy, a volcanic rock resembling indurated pitch. It occurs massive at Meissen in Saxony, at Newry in Ireland, in the Isle of Arran, &c.: sp. gr. 2·3—2·7; H — 5·0 —6·0.

Pitchy Iron Ore, a mineral with the aspect of resin, which occurs in several old mines in Saxony, Upper Silesia, Brittany, and Chili, consisting of oxide of iron, arsenic acid, sulphuric acid, protoxide of manganese, and water: sp. gr. 2·3—2·4; H — 2·5.

Pith (Sax. *pitha*), in botany, the cellular substance which forms the centre of the stems of exogenous plants, and round which the annual concentric vascular wood is arranged.—In zoology, the spinal cord of the animal economy.—*Pith-balls* are small balls made of the pith of the elder tree, extremely useful in numerous electrical experiments to show the effects of attraction and repulsion.

Pit'tacal (Gr. *pitta* pitch, and *kalos* beautiful), one of the curious principles found in wood-tar; a dark blue substance, somewhat like indigo.

Pit'tizite (Gr.), in mineralogy, a species of pitchy iron ore.

Pittospora'ceæ (Gr. *pitta*, and *sporos* a seed), in botany, a nat. order of exogenous plants, of which the Pittosporum is the type.

Pityri'asis (Gr. *pityron* bran), in pathology, a disease of the skin, characterized by bran-like scales.

Pit'uite (Fr.), in pathology, phlegm, mucus.

Piu (Ital.), in music, a little more; as, *piu presto*, a little quicker; *piu piano*, a little softer, &c.

Pivot, in military science, the officer or soldier stationed at the flank on which a company wheels.

Placebo (Lat. *I shall please*), in pathology, a medicine or prescription designed to please rather than benefit the patient.

Placen'ta (Lat.), the flat cellular substance which in parturition connects the mother with the child; the after-birth.—In botany, the part of the ovary to which the ovules are attached. —In geology, a name given to a section of the Catocysti, because the shells are flat.

Placenta'tion (Lat.), in botany, the disposition of the cotyledons in the germination of seed.

Places of Arms, in fortification, spaces contrived at the salient and re-entering angles of the covered way.

Placoid (Gr. *plax* flatness), in ichthyology, a term applied to an order of fishes covered with irregular plates of enamel.

Plagihe'dral (Gr. *plagios* oblique, and *hedra* a base), in mineralogy, having oblique sides.

Pla'gionite (Gr. *plagios*), a mineral, occurring in oblique four-sided prisms, and containing lead, antimony, and sulphur.

Plane (Lat. *planus* flat), in geometry, a completely flat or even surface or superficies.—In astronomy, an imaginary surface passing through any of the circles of the sphere, as the *plane* of the ecliptic, the *plane* of the earth's orbit, &c.—In optics, the *plane of reflection*, that which passes through the point of reflection; *plane of refraction*, a plane surface, drawn through the incident and refracted rays.—In dialling, the surface upon which any dial is drawn.—*Plane of gravitation*, a plane supposed to pass through the centre of gravity of any body.—*Horizontal plane*, a plane parallel to the horizon.—*Inclined plane*, a plane inclined to the horizon, and forming one of the mechanical powers.—In perspective, there are the *perspective plane*, or table on which the object is formed; the *geometrical* or *ground plane*, on which the former is supposed to stand at right angles; and the *vertical plane*. —In crystallography, the face of a crystal.—In mechanics, a tool used by joiners, &c., who work in wood.— *Plane problem*, in geometry, is a problem which can be solved by the intersection of straight lines and circles, without the aid of the conic sections, or any of the higher curves. —*Plane trigonometry*, the art of determining the sides and angles of plane triangles: it is used in almost every part of practical mathematics, navigation, and surveying, as very often by this science only can altitudes be ascertained.—*Plane sailing*, the operation of working a ship on a plane chart, constructed on the principle of the earth being an extended plane.—*Craig.*

Planet (Gr. *planao* to wander), a celestial body that revolves about another and larger body; a wandering star.—A *primary planet* is one which revolves round the sun.—A *secondary planet* is one which revolves round a primary planet; a satellite. Within the last few years no less than seventy-six new planets have been discovered, most of which are noticed under their respective names.

Planeta'rium (Lat. *planeta*), an orrery, or astronomical machine which exhibits the motions of the planets.

Planifo'lious (Lat.), in botany, consisting of plain leaves set together in circular rows.

Planim'etry (Lat. *planus* flat, and *metior* to measure), that part of geometry which treats of plane figures.

Planipen'nes (Lat. *planus*, and *penna* a wing), the name given by Cuvier to his second family of Neuroptera.

Pla'nisphere (Lat. *planus*, and *sphæra* a globe), a sphere projected on a plane; a map of one or both hemispheres.

Plano- (Lat. *planus*), a prefix to many scientific terms, signifying *plane* or *flat.—Plano-concave*, flat on one side and concave on the other ;—*Plano-conical*, flat on one side and conical on the other ; — *Plano-horizontal*, having a level horizontal surface or position;—*Plano-subulate*, smooth and awl-shaped.

Plantagina'ceæ, a nat. order of exogenous herbaceous plants, of which the Plantago is the genus.

Plantar (Lat. *planta* the sole of the foot), in anatomy, appertaining to the sole of the foot.—*Plantar aponeurosis* is the strong tendonous expansion which lies under the integuments in the sole of the foot.—*Plantaris* is a muscle of the foot connected with the leg.

Plan'tigrade (Lat. *planta*, and *gradus* a step), a class of animals that walk on the whole foot, as the Bear.

Plasma (Gr.), in mineralogy, a species of green gem.

Plaster (Fr.), in pharmacy, a composition for external application ; a kind of salve.

Plastic Clay (Gr. *plasso* to form), in geology, one of the beds of the eocene tertiary period.

Plastog'raphy (Gr.), the art of forming figures in plaster; counterfeit writing.

Platana'ceæ (Lat.), the Planes, an order of exogenous plants, of which Platanus is the genus.

Platen, the plate or flat part of a printing press, by which the impression is made.

Plat'ina, Plat'inum, the heaviest of metals, of a white colour, very hard, exceedingly ductile, malleable, and difficult of fusion: sp. gr. 17·33; H = 2·75.

Plat'inode, the cathode or negative pole of a galvanic battery.

Platoon (Fr.), a small square body of musketeers drawn out to strengthen

the angle of a larger square, or to do duty in ambuscade.

Platy- (Gr. *platys*), a prefix to compound words, signifying *flat* or *broad*,

Platyceph'alous (Gr. *platys*, and *kephale* a head), in fossilology, broad-headed.

Platycer'cinæ, the Loriets, a sub-family of birds, in which the tail is long and very broad ; fam. Psittacidæ.

Platycri'nite (Gr.), in geology, a broad, lily-shaped, fossil animal.

Platy'odon (Gr.), a broad-toothed animal.

Plat'ypod (Gr.), a broad footed animal.

Plat'ypus (Gr.), a flat-footed quadruped of New Holland, with a mouth like a duck's bill.

Platys'ma (Gr. *platyno* to widen), in anatomy, a broad, thin, muscular expansion at each side of the neck.

Plectogna'thes (Gr. *plektos* plaited, and *gnathos* a jaw), Cuvier's sixth order of fishes, formed of the two families Gymnodontes and Sclerodermes.

Plectrum (Lat.), the styloid process of the temporal bone.

Pledget, in surgery, a flat piece of lint laid over a wound.

Ple'iads, a northern constellation consisting of seven stars.

Plei'ocene (Gr. *pleion* more, and *kainos* new), in geology, a term applied to the upper tertiary group, containing more of recent than of extinct species.

Pleis'tocene (Gr. *most recent*), in geology, the newest division of the tertiary formation.

Plenist (Lat.), one who holds all space to be full of matter; opposed to *vacuist*.

Plenum (Lat. *full*), in natural philosophy, that state of things in which every portion of space is supposed to be occupied by material substance.

Pleodon'tes (Gr. *pleos* full, and *odontes* teeth), a sub-family of Lizards.

Ple'onaste (Gr. *abundant*), a black mineral allied to spinel. It occurs crystallized, and consists of alumina, silica, magnesia, lime, and oxide of iron : sp. gr. 3·64.

Plero'sis (Gr. *fulness*), in physiology, the filling up or restoration of the animal body when worn down by abstinence or disease.—*Plerotic*, in pharmacy, is an epithet applied to remedies which are calculated to effect the cicatrization of a wound or sore.

Plesiomor'phism (Gr. *plesios* near, and *morphe* form), a close resemblance of crystallized substances to each other.

Plesiosau'rus (Gr. *plesios*, and *saura*

a lizard), in geology, a genus of extinct marine Saurians, remarkable for a long neck.

Pleth'ora (Gr. *pletho* to fill), in pathology, a redundant fulness of the blood-vessels.—*Plethoric*, having a full habit of body, or the vessels overcharged with fluid.

Pleura (Gr.), in anatomy, a double membrane which covers the internal cavity of the thorax.—*Pleurisy*, or *Pleuritis*, is an inflammation of the pleura.

Pleurodyn'ia (Gr. *pleuron* the side, and *odyne* pain), in pathology, pain in the side resembling pleurisy.

Pleuronec'tidæ (Gr. *swimming on the side*), a family of fishes, of which the Pleuronectes is the type.

Pleurorrhœ'a (Gr. *pleuron*, and *rheo* to flow), in pathology, a collection of fluid in the sacs of the pleura.

Pleurorthopnœ'a (Gr. *pleuron*, and *orthopnoia* upright breathing), pain in the side which renders an erect posture necessary for respiration.

Pleu'rospasm (Gr.), in pathology, spasm in the side; the intercostal pain of hysterical females.

Pleurosthot'onos (Gr. *pleuron*, and *teino* to stretch), a spasmodic disease, in which the body is bent to one side.

Pleurotom'inæ (Gr.), in malacology, a sub-family of the Strombidæ, the shells of which are turreted and sub-fusiform, and of which the Pleurotoma, a genus of Gasteropods, is the type.

Plexus (Lat. *network*), in anatomy, a term applied to blood-vessel nerves, &c., when they are numerous, and exhibit a network formation.—*Plexus cardiacus* is a ganglion or network of nerves formed from the union of the eighth pair and the great sympathetic.—*Plexus reticularis*, a network of vessels under the brain.—*Plexus pulmonicus*, a ganglion formed by the union of the eighfh pair of nerves with the sympathetic.—*Plexus choroides*, a network of vessels situated in the lateral ventricles of the brain.—*Plexus pampiniformis*, the complication of vessels about the spermatic cord.

Plicipen'nes (Lat. *plico* to plait, and *penna* a wing), in entomology, the name given by Cuvier to his third family of the Neuroptera, the genera of which have the inferior wings usually wider than the others, and plaited longitudinally.

Plinth (Gr. *plinthos* a brick), in architecture, the square part under a pedestal, or the lower member of the base of a column, wall, &c.

Plinthite (Gr.), a brick-red mineral.

Pli'ocene (Gr. *plesion* nearer, and *kainos* recent), the most modern division of the tertiary period of geologists. The newer pliocene contains from 90 to 95 per cent. of recent species of shells, and the older from 35 to 50 per cent. The Mammalia and other organic remains of these deposits consist of both recent and extinct species.

Plombgomme, a mineral occurring in small reniform masses; hydrated alumina of lead.

Plonge (Fr.), in fortification, the superior slope given to the parapet.

Plumbagina'ceæ (Lat. *plumbum* lead), a nat. order of exogenous plants, of which the Plumbago, or Leadwort, is the type.

Plumba'gine, a vegetable principle existing in the root of the *Plumbago Europæa*.

Plumba'go, Graphite (Lat. *plumbum*), a mineral consisting of carbon and iron, commonly called *black-lead*.

Plumbane, a chloride of lead. It is the substance of which writing and other pencils are made. The finest kinds of it are found at Borrowdale, in Cumberland, from which a specimen was found to contain carbon, silica, alumina, oxide of iron and manganese, and water: sp. gr. 2·25; H = 1.

Plumb-line, a flexible line to which a heavy body, commonly a mass of lead, is attached, used to indicate the direction of terrestrial gravity in ascertaining the perpendicularity of buildings, &c.

Plumbo-calcite (Lat. *plumbum*, and *calx* lime), a mineral, in its form and cleavage similar to the primary rhomb of calcareous spar. It consists of carbonate of lime and carbonate of lead.

Plumbum (Lat. *lead*), a term much used in pharmacy, and applied in various pathological cases; as, *Plumbi acetas*, sugar of lead;—*Plumbi diacetatis liquor*, solution of diacetate of lead; —*Plumbi chloridum*, chloride of lead;—*Plumbi iodium*, iodide of lead;—*Plumbi oxydum hydratum*, hydrated oxide of lead;—*Plumbi carbonas*, subcarbonate of lead, commonly called *white-lead*;—*Plumbum corneum*, chloride of lead.

Plume Alum (Lat. *pluma* a feather), a kind of asbestos, so named from its feathery appearance.

Plumming, in mining, the operation of sounding the place where to sink an air-shaft, &c.

Plutoc'racy (Gr. *ploutos* wealth, and *kratos* power), the power of wealth, riches, or money.

Plu'tonist, one who advocates the theory that the formation of the earth was effected by igneous fusion, called the *Plutonic theory*.

Pluviam'eter (Lat. *pluvia* rain, and *metior* to measure), an instrument for measuring the quantity of water that falls during rain.

Plyers, in fortification, a kind of balance used in raising or letting down a drawbridge.

Plymouth Marble, a fine variety of bluish-white marble, streaked with red, found near Plymouth and other parts of Devonshire.

Pneumat'ics (Gr. *pneuma* air), the science which treats of the mechanical properties of elastic fluids, and particularly of atmospheric air.—*Pneumatic trough* is a tin or wooden box, sometimes only a tub or basin, indispensable to the chemist in collecting gases over water, mercury, &c.—*Pneumatic telegraph*, an invention for communicating signals to a great distance by means of the impulse given to a column of water at one end of the apparatus.—*Pneumatic* or *atmospheric railroad*, the name given to a system of locomotion on railways by means of the pressure of the atmosphere.—*Pneumatic filterer*, an instrument for filtering water and other liquids, operating by the pressure of the atmosphere on the surface of the liquid to be filtered, a vacuum being previously formed beneath the bottom of the containing vessel, which is full of holes like a sieve.

Pneumat'ocele (Gr. *pneuma*, and *hele* a tumour), in pathology, a hernia from wind in the scrotum.

Pneumatol'ogy (Gr. *pneuma*, and *logos* a discourse), the doctrine of the properties of elastic fluids.

Pneumato'sis (Gr. *flatulency*), a collection of air in the cellular membrane, generally arising from some wound which affects the lungs.

Pneumol'ogy (Gr.), the anatomy of the lungs.

Pneumo'nia (Gr.), in pathology, an inflammation of the lungs.

Pneumon'ica (Gr.), in pharmacy, medicines for diseases of the lungs.

Pneumonot'omy (Gr. *pneumon* a lung, and *tome* incision), anatomical dissection of the lungs.

Poco (Ital.), in music, signifies *little*; as, *poco largo*, a little slow.

Podag'ra (Gr. *podes* feet, and *agra* seizure), in pathology, gout in the feet.

Po'dium (Lat.), in architecture, the part of an amphitheatre projecting over the arena.

Pœ'cilite (Gr. *poikilos* barred), in geology, the new red sandstone.—*Pœcilitic*, applied to the new red sandstone formation.

Point (Fr. from Lat. *punctum* a point), a term used in physics.—*Point of sight* is that point which is exactly opposite the eye.—*Point of incidence*, the place where the motion is changed in direction.—*Point of view*, the place from which an object is seen.—*Point-blank*, in gunnery, denotes that when the piece is levelled, the shot goes directly forward to the mark.

Polar'iscope (Gr. *polos* a pole, and *skopeo* to view), an apparatus or instrument for exhibiting the polarization of light.

Polar'ity (Lat. *polus* the pole), in physics, that property of bodies in consequence of which they arrange themselves to certain determinate directions, and tend towards the poles of the earth.

Po'larize (Lat. *polus*), to render light incapable of reflection and transmission in certain directions, with an allusion to an imaginary conformity to the poles of a magnet.

Pole (Lat. *polus*, from Gr. *poleo* to turn), the extremity of any axis of rotation; one of the extremities of the imaginary axis of the earth.—In astronomy, the *altitude of the pole* is an arc of the meridian intercepted between the pole and the horizon of any place, and is equal to the latitude of that place.—The *poles* are the extremities of the earth's axis, or the points on the surface of the sphere through which the axis passes.—*Pole-star* is the north star; a star in Ursa Major, near the pole, by which navigators compute their northern latitude.—*Poles of the ecliptic* are points in the solstitial colure, 23° 30′ distant from the poles of the world.—*Poles of the horizon* are the two points of the meridian called the zenith and nadir, the one of which is exactly over our heads, and the other as exactly under under our feet.—*Poles of a magnet* are the two points of a magnet corresponding with the poles of the world, the one pointing to the north and the other to the south.—In mathematics, *pole* applies to any point 90° from the plane of any circle, and in the axis or line raised perpendicularly in its centre.

Pol'itics (Gr. *polis* a city), the science of government, or the art and practice of administering public affairs. —*Political economy* is the management of the resources of a country, and the science which develops the laws by which the civilization, wealth, and happiness of a nation may be best promoted.

Pollen (Lat. *fine flour*), the powder or pulverulent substance contained in the anther of a flower.—*Pollen-tube*, a membranous tube emitted by pollen after falling on the stigma.

Pol'lenine, in chemistry, a substance prepared from the pollen of tulips, which is extremely combustible; it burns with a bright flame, and with great rapidity.

Pollux, in astronomy, a fixed star; one of the twins forming the constellation Gemini.

Pol'verine (Ital. *polverino*, from Lat. *pulvis* dust), the calcined ashes of an alkaline plant, used in the manufacture of glass.

Poly-, a prefix to numerous words of Greek origin, signifying *many, much*, &c.—*Polyadelphia*, a class of plants having stamens combined into more than two parcels;—*Polyandria*, a class of plants with more than twenty hypogynous stamens;—*Polyautography*, the art of multiplying copies of autographs; a kind of lithography;—*Polybasite*, a mineral with numerous bases;—*Polychrest*, in chemistry and medicine, anything of multifarious virtues, or having various uses;—*Polychroite*, the colouring matter of saffron;—*Polychrome*, a colouring matter found in the horse chestnut and other plants;—*Polycotyledonous*, in botany, having more than two cotyledons;—*Polydipsia*, in pathology, excessive thirst;—*Polygalaceæ*, a nat. order of exogenous plants, of which Polygala is the type;—*Polygaline*, a bitter alkaline principle found in several species of Polygala;—*Polygamia*, the twenty-third class in the Linnæan system of botany;—*Polygamous*, having male, female, and hermaphrodite flowers on the same or different individuals;—*Polygastric*, having many stomachs, as the ox;—*Polygastrians*, one of the two great divisions of the Infusorial Animalculæ.

Pol'yglot (Gr. *polys*, and *glotta* a tongue), a book containing a work in several languages.

Pol'ygon (Gr. *polys*, and *gonia* an angle), a figure of many angles; a range of buildings with several corners or divisions.—In fortification, *exterior polygon*, the figure formed by lines connecting the points of the bastions of a fortress with one another quite round the work.

Pol'ygraph (Gr. *polys*, and *graphe* writing), an instrument for multiplying copies of a writing.

Polyg'raphy (Gr.), the art of writing in various ciphers, and of deciphering them.

Polyg'yn (Gr. *polys*, and *gyne* a female), in botany, a plant having many pistils.

Polyhal'lite (Gr. *polys*, and *als* salt), a mineral of a pale flesh-red colour.

Polyhe'dral, Polyhe'drous (Gr.), having many sides.

Polyhe'dron (Gr.), in geometry, a figure or a solid body of many sides.

Polyhy'drite (Gr.), in mineralogy, a silicate of the peroxide of iron.

Polyhym'nia, in astronomy, one of the newly-discovered planets, first observed by Chacornac in 1854. Its mean distance from the sun is 276,820,000 miles, and its periodical revolution 4 years and 326 days.

Pol'ylite (Gr. *polys*, and *lithos* stone), a mineral allied to pyroxene.

Polym'athy (Gr. *polys*, and *mathano* to learn), the knowledge of many arts and sciences; varied learning.

Polymig'nite (Gr. *polymiges*, much mixed), a black mineral occurring in prismatic crystals of metallic lustre. Its constituents are titanic acid, oxide of iron, oxide of cerium, oxide of manganese, zirconia, yttria, lime, potash, and silica: sp. gr. 4·806.

Polym'nite (Gr.), in mineralogy, a stone marked with dendrites and black lines.

Pol'ymorphy (Gr. *polys*, and *morphe* change), state of having many forms.

Polyne'sia (Gr. *polys*, and *nesos* an island), a space in the Pacific Ocean which includes many clusters of islands.

Polyon'omous (Gr.), having many names or terms.

Polyop'tron (Gr. *polys*, and *optomai* to see), a glass through which objects appear multiplied, but not diminished.

Polyora'ma (Gr. *polys*, and *orao* to see), an optical machine presenting many views.

Polypes (Gr. *polys*, and *podes* feet), the name of an extensive group of radiated animals, associated together by the common character of a fleshy body.

Polyphar'macy (Gr. *polys*, and *pharmakon* a drug), a prescription embracing many ingredients.

Polypia'ria (Gr. *polys*, and Lat. *pario* to bring forth), an extensive class of zoophytes, of which there are various sorts and classes; as, *Polypiaria solida*, the animals of which are contained in small calcareous cells with a terminal opening, accumulated into a solid fixed Polypiarium;—*Polypiaria membranacea*, animals very short;—*Polypiaria dubia*, animals provided with long tentacula;—*Poly-piaria nuda*, animals the body of which is gelatinous.

Pol'ypode (Gr. *polys*, and *podes* feet), in entomology, a millepede.

Polypodia'ceæ, *pl.* an order of the Ferns.

Polyprismat'ic (Gr.), in crystallography, having many planes.

Pol'ypus (Gr. *polys*, and *podes* feet), one of a group of radiated animals; a fleshy tumour, as in the nostrils or uterus.

Pol'yscope (Gr. *polys*, and *skopeo* to view), a lens consisting of several plane surfaces disposed under a convex form; a multiplying-glass.

Polys'pharite (Gr. *polys*, and *sphaira* sphere), a mineral occurring in roundish masses, having internally a radiated structure.

Polytech'nic (Gr. *polys*, and *techne* art), in mechanical science, a term comprising many arts.

Polythalma'ceæ (Gr.), an order of polythalmaceous Cephalopods, embracing many recent and extinct genera allied to Nautilus, Spirula, and Sepia. It embraces the families Nautilidæ, Ammonitidæ, Spirulidæ, and Belemnitidæ.

Polytro'phia (Gr. *polys*, and *trophe* nourishment), in pathology, excessive activity of the process of nutrition.

Polyzo'on (Gr. *polys*, and *zoon* an animal), in zoology, a species of compound animals.

Poma'ceæ (Lat. *pomum* an apple), a nat. order of exogenous plants, of which the Apple and Pear are familiar examples.

Pomade (Fr.), in pharmacy, a soft and unctuous compound for external applications, usually aromatized and coloured.

Pome (Lat. *pomum*), in botany, a fruit like that of the Apple, Pear, &c.

Pommelled, in heraldry, denoting the pommel of a sword or dagger.

Pomol'ogy (Lat. *pomum*, and *logos* a discourse), the art of cultivating fruit and fruit trees; a treatise on fruit.

Pomo'na, in astronomy, one of the recently-discovered planets, first observed by Goldschmidt in 1854. Its mean distance from the sun is 245,840,000 miles, and its periodical revolution 4 years and 51 days.

Pom'pholyx (Gr. a *water-bubble*), white oxide of zinc.—In pathology, an eruption of bubbles, or blebs, accompanied with fever, breaking and healing without scale or crust. The species of this disease are—*P. benignus*, mild water-blebs; *P. diritinus*, chronic water-blebs; and *P. solitarius*, solitary water-blebs.

Pompil'idæ, in entomology, a form of hymenopterous insects, of which Pompilus is the type.

Pompo'so (Ital.), in music, affectedly pompous.

Pomum Adami (Lat. *Adam's apple*), the protuberance in front of the neck formed by the thyroid gland, fancifully supposed to represent the forbidden apple eaten by Adam.

Pondera'tion (Lat. *the art of weighing*), in sculpture, painting, &c., the proper balancing or supporting of a figure or object, so that it shall not have the appearance of instability or tottering.

Pons Varo'lii (Lat. *Variolus's bridge*), in anatomy, the centrical part of the brain, situated between the cerebrum and the cerebellum, and united to both.

Pontoon (Fr.), in military science, a flat-bottomed boat; a floating bridge.

Poo'nahlite, a mineral allied to natrolite, brought from Poonah, in Hindostan; H = 5·0.

Poplit'eal, **Poplit'ic** (Gr. *poples* the ham), in anatomy, a term relating to the posterior part of the knee-joint or ham.

Pop'uline (Lat. *populus* the poplar tree), a crystallizable substance separated from the bark of the poplar.

Por'celain (Fr. from Ital. *porcellano*), the finest species of earthenware or pottery.

Por'celainite, in mineralogy, an opaque, brittle variety of jasper.

Pore (Gr. *poros* a passage), in anatomy, a passage for perspiration.

Porif'era (Lat. *porus* a pore, and *fero* to bear), a family of Polypi, including the genera Cellepora, Millepora, and Tubulipora; the term also designates, as a class, the fresh-water and marine Sponges.

Porism, a geometrical proposition; a general theorem drawn from another theorem already demonstrated.

Po'rocele (Gr. *poros*, and *kele* a tumour), in pathology, a hard tumour of the scrotum.

Porphyrox'ine (Gr.), in chemistry, a non-azotized principle found in Bengal opium, quite distinct from the other vegetable substances found in opium.

Por'phyry (Gr. *porphyros* purple), a hard stone of different colours, susceptible of a high polish.—In geology, an unstratified or igneous rock.

Por'rigo (Lat. *to stretch out*), in pathology, an eruption of straw-coloured pustules, of which there are various species.

Portcul'lis (Fr. *porte* a gate, and *écouler* to slide), a frame of bars placed over a gateway, to let down as a protection to the gate.

Portfire, in gunnery, a paper tube filled with powder, &c., used to fire guns instead of a match.

Por'tioo (Ital. from Lat. *porticus*), in architecture, a series of columns at the end of a building; a projection supported by columns.

Portland Stone, in mineralogy, a species of oolite; a whitish sandstone used for building.

Portulaca'ceæ (Lat. *porto* to carry, and *lac* milk), in botany, an order of exogenous plants, of which the Portulaca, or Purslane, is the type.

Portu'nidæ, a family of brachyurous Crustaceans, of which the Portunus is the genus.

Posi'tion (Lat.), in arithmetic, a rule of supposition, called also *Rule of False*. —In geometry, a line is said to be *given in position* when its direction is known; in magnitude, when its length is known.—In painting, the placing of the model in the manner best calculated for the end which the painter has in view.

Posol'ogy (Gr. *posos* so much, and *logos* a discourse), that part of medicine which teaches the right administration of doses.

Post-, a Lat. preposition used in the composition of many words, and signifying *after*.

Post-dilu'vial (Lat. *post*, and *diluvium* a deluge), posterior to or after the flood.

Post-merid'ian (Lat. *post*, and *meridies* noon-day), relating to or being in the afternoon.

Potalia'ceæ, in botany, a nat. order of exogenous plants, of which the Potalia, a beautiful flowering plant, is the genus.

Potash (Fr.), a saline matter, or alkaline salt, obtained from lixiviating the ashes of wood, of great use in the manufacture of soap, in bleaching, &c.—*Potash bisilicate of magnesia*, a mineral occurring in both a crystallized and an earthy state, friable, and easily reduced to soft powder; composition—silica, magnesia, potash, peroxide of iron, alumina, and lime: sp. gr. 2·87.

Potassa, in chemistry, an alkaline salt substance; a protoxide of potassium. The following are the preparations of potassa used in medicine:—*Acetas potassæ*, acetate of potassa; *arsenias potassæ*, arseniate of potassa; *bicarbonas potassæ*, bicarbonate of potassa; *bisulphas potassæ*, bisulphate of potassa; *bitartras potassæ*, bitartrate of potassa; *carbonas potassæ*, carbonate of potassa; *chloras potassæ*, chlorate of potassa; *chloridum potassæ*, chloride of potassa; *citras potassæ*, citrate of potassa; *hydras potassæ*, hydrate of potassa, called also *potassa fusa*, or the stronger caustic; *hydroides potassæ*, hydroide of potassa; *liquor potassæ*, solution of potassa; *potassa cum calce*, potassa with lime, or the milder caustic; *sulphas potassæ*, sulphate of potassa; *sulphuretum potassæ*, sulphuret of potassa; *tartras potassæ*, tartrate of potassa.

Potas'sium, the metallic base of potassa, discovered by Sir H. Davy in 1807. Its texture, when brittle, is crystalline; opaque; a good conductor of heat and electricity: sp. gr. at 60°, 0·865. It is the lightest known solid.

Potence (Fr.), in heraldry, a sort of cross which terminates like the head of a crutch.

Potin, a composition of copper, lead, tin, and silver, of which Roman coins were made.

Potstone, in mineralogy, a tough variety of steatite.

Potter's Clay, in mineralogy, a substance which differs from pipe-clay by containing a greater proportion of lime and oxide of iron.

Pounce (Fr. *pierre-ponce* pumice-stone), the powder of gum sandarac; a powder used to prevent ink from spreading after erasures, and other purposes.

Pound (Sax. *pund*, from Lat. *pondus*), a weight, being 12 ozs. troy, and 16 ozs. avoirdupois.—In money, the sum of 20*s*.

Pozzuola'na, volcanic ashes used as mortar for building; so called from Pozzuoli, a town of Naples.

Præ-, or **Pre-**, a Lat. preposition of frequent use in compound words, signifying *before*, or *in front of*.

Præcor'dia (Lat. *præ*, and *cors, cordis* the heart), in anatomy, the parts adjoining the heart; the diaphragm, the abdominal viscera, and the epigastrium.

Prase (Gr. *prason* a leek), a siliceous mineral, a variety of quartz, so called from its leek-green colour.

Pras'eolite, a green mineral, imperfectly crystallized.

Pras'ilite, a soft, green, fibrous mineral found in Scotland.

Pre. (See *Præ*.)

Pre-Ad'amite, one supposed to have lived before Adam.

Precen'tor (Lat.), in music, one who leads a choir; a chanter.

Preces'sion of the Equinoxes. (See *Equinox*.)

Prehnite, a greyish mineral, so called after M. Prehn, who brought it from the Cape of Good Hope. It occurs both crystallized and massive, and consists of silica, alumina, lime, oxide of iron, potash of soda, and water: sp. gr. 2·926.

Prepuce (Fr. from Lat. *præputium*), the skin which is removed by circumcision; that fold of integument which surrounds and envelops the glans penis.

Presbyo'pia (Gr. *presbys* old, and *ops* the eye), in pathology, a state of the eye observed in advanced age, arising from a flattening of the cornea, and partial loss of the refractive power of the eye.

Pressiros'ter (Lat. *pressus*, and *rostrum* a bill), in ornithology, a tribe of wading birds, including those which have a flattened or compressed beak.

Pretib'ial (Lat. *præ*, and *tibialis* belonging to the legs), in anatomy, situated anteriorly to the tibia.

Pricking-up, in architecture, the first coating of plaster in work of three coats.

Pri'mary (Lat. *primus* first), an epithet of frequent application in art and science.—In astronomy, *primary planets* are those which revolve round the sun as their centre, in distinction from *secondary planets* or satellites, which revolve round the *primaries.*—In painting, *primary colours* are those into which a ray of solar light may be decomposed. Newton supposed them to be seven: red, orange, yellow, green, blue, indigo, and violet.—In geology, *primary*, is a term sometimes applied to those old formations composed of gneiss, mica slate, chlorite slate, and clay slate or other rocks which have undergone great change.

Prime (Lat. *primus*), in dialling, *prime vertical* is a vertical circle which is perpendicular to the meridian.—In arithmetic, *prime numbers* are numbers which have no divisors.

Primit'iæ (Lat.), the first-fruits of any production of the earth, which were uniformly consecrated to the Deity by all the nations of antiquity.

Prim'itive (Lat.), a term frequently applied to scientific objects.—The *primitive form of a crystal* is one of the regular geometrical solids which a crystal presents on its being split as much as possible in its cleavage. —In painting, the *primitive colours* are red, yellow, and blue, from the mixtures of which all other colours are obtainable.

Primula'ceæ, in botany, a nat. order of herbaceous plants, of which Primula, or Primrose, is the type. The more common species are—the Primrose, *P. vulgaris;* the Cowslip, *P. veris;*

the Oxlip, *P. elatior;* and the Auricula, *P. auricula.*

Primum Mob'ile (Lat. *the first mover*), that which puts everything in motion; a term frequently used in ancient astronomy.

Prince's Metal, in metallurgy, an alloy of three parts of copper to one of zinc, forming one of the many varieties of brass; called also *Prince Rupert's metal.*

Prin'ciple (Lat. *principium* beginning), a term sometimes applied to an elementary substance; but sometimes those substances which are the peculiar results of the combination of organized with inorganic matter are called *proximate principles.*—In science generally, a truth admitted either without proof or as having been already proved.

Priodon'tes (Gr. *saw-teeth*), in zoology, a division of the Armadillos, consisting of *Dasypus gigas*, or Great Armadillo, distinguished by having twenty-two to twenty-four small teeth on each side of the jaws.

Prion'idæ (Gr.), a family of coleopterous insects.

Prism (Fr. from Gr. *prisma*), a geometrical figure or solid, whose two ends are parallel, equal, and straight, and whose sides are parallelograms. —In optics, an instrument or prism of glass whose ends are triangles.— *Prismatic,* relating to or formed as a prism.—*Prismatic colours,* the seven colours into which a ray of light is decomposed when refracted from a prism.

Pristi'na, in ichthyology, a sub-family of the Squalidæ, of which the Pristis, or Saw-fish, is the type.

Probe (Lat. *probo* to prove), a surgical instrument for examining wounds.— *Probe-scissors,* surgical scissors used to open wounds.

Probos'cis (Gr. *pro* before, and *bosko* to feed), a prehensile organ formed by the prolongation of the nose, as the trunk of an elephant.—*Proboscidians* are a family of pachydermatous Mammals, including those which have the nose prolonged into a prehensile trunk or proboscis, as the Elephant and Mastodon.

Problem (Gr. *proballo* to throw forward), in geometry, a proposition in which some operation or construction is required, as to divide a line, to raise a perpendicular, &c. It consists of three parts—the proposition, the resolution or solution, and the demonstration.

Procar'dium (Gr. *pro*, and *kardia* the orifice of the stomach), in anatomy, the pit of the stomach.

Procatarx'is (Gr. *pro*, and *archo* to begin), in pathology, the pre-existent cause of a disease.

Prochei'lon (Gr. *pro*, and *cheilon* a lip), in anatomy, the extreme projecting part or margin of the lips.

Pro'cidence (Lat. *procido* to fall down), in pathology, a falling down of any part; a prolapsus, as of the intestinum rectum.

Procœ'lian (Gr.), in anatomy and zoology, noting those vertebræ which have a cavity or cup at the fore part of the body, and a ball at the back part.

Procon'dyli (Lat. *pro*, and *condylus* a knuckle), in anatomy, the bones of the fingers next the back of the hand.

Proctag'ra, Proctal'gia, Procti'tis, and **Proctopeo'sis** (Gr. *proktos* the anus), in pathology, terms applied to painful affections of the anus.

Proc'tocele (Gr. *proktos*, and *kele* hernia), in pathology, inversion and prolapse of the mucous coat of the rectum, from relaxation of the sphincter.

Pre'cyon (Gr. *pro*, and *kyon* a dog), in astronomy, a star of the second magnitude in the constellation Canis Minor. It is uncertain whether this star, or Sirius, is properly the Dog-star of the ancients.

Product (Lat. *produco* to produce), in arithmetic and algebra, the result or quantity produced by multiplying one number by another; as, 24 is the *product* of 6 and 4, being produced by the multiplication of these numbers.—In geometry, the factum of two or more lines.

Proempto'sis (Gr. *happening before*), in chronology, the lunar equation or addition of a day, necessary to prevent the new moon from happening too soon according to the civil calculation.

Progno'sis (Gr. *pro*, and *ginosko* to know), in pathology, that part of medicine by which the progress and termination of diseases are judged.

Progres'sion (Lat.), in arithmetic and algebra, series of quantities or numbers advancing or proceeding in the same manner, or according to a certain law. It is either arithmetical, geometrical, or harmonical. An *arithmetical* progression is one of which the quantities proceed by some common difference, as 2, 4, 6, 8, &c., the common difference being 2. A *geometrical* progression is one in which the successive terms increase or decrease by a common ratio, as 2, 4, 8, 16, &c., the common ratio or multiplier being 2.—In music, a re-gular succession of chords or movement of parts in harmony.

Projec'tile (Lat. *projicio* to throw forward), a body projected or put in motion.—The science of *projectiles* is that branch of mechanical philosophy which treats of the motions of bodies impelled from the surface of the earth, and acted on by gravity and the resistance of the air.

Projec'tion (Lat.), a term applied to the projection of the sphere, of which there are three principal points—the *stereographic*, in which the eye is supposed to be placed on the surface of the sphere; the *orthographic*, in which the eye is conceived to be at an infinite distance; and the *gnomonic*, in which the eye is placed in the centre of the sphere.

Prolap'sus (Lat. *prolabor* to slide down), in pathology, the falling down or protrusion of a part through the orifice with which it is naturally connected, as of the uterus, rectum, &c.

Prolate (Lat. *prolatum* extended).—In geometry, a *prolate spheroid* is a solid produced by the revolution of an ellipse about its tranverse diameter; the figure produced by the revolution of an ellipse about its shorter axis is termed an *oblate spheroid*.

Prolegs, in entomology, the fleshy pediform organs which serve various larvæ instead of legs.

Prolep'sis (Gr. *pro*, and *lambano* to take), in chronological science, an anachronism when an event is dated before the usual time.—*Proleptical*, in pathology, is applied to a periodical disease, the paroxysm of which returns at an earlier hour at every repetition.

Promerop'idæ (Gr. *pro*, and *merops* the bee-eater), in ornithology, a family of tenuirostral birds, of the order Passeres, of which the Hoopoe is the genus.

Prome'thean, a small glass tube containing concentrated sulphuric acid, surrounded with an inflammable mixture.

Prom'ontory (Lat.), in geography, a high point of land projecting into the sea beyond the line of coast; a headland.

Promus'cis (Gr.), in entomology, a term applied to the sucking organ of hemipterous insects.

Prona'tion (Lat. *pronus* bending forward), in anatomy, that motion of the radius by which the palm of the hand is turned downward.

Prona'tor (Lat. *pronus*), in anatomy, a muscle used in turning the palm of the hand downwards.

Propædeu'tics (Gr. *pro*, and *paideuo* to

Pulse (Lat. *pulsus* struck), the pulsation or motion of an artery.—In botany, leguminous plants or their seeds, as Peas and Beans.

Pulsim'eter (Lat. *pulsus*, and Gr. *metron* a measure), in pathology, an instrument for measuring the quickness or force of the pulse.

Pulvil'lus (Lat.), in entomology, a membrane capable of being inflated, which covers the feet of insects, and by which they can create a vacuum, and thus suspend themselves or walk against gravity.

Pumice (Lat. *pumex*), a porous substance ejected from volcanoes.—*Pumice-stone*, a slag or cinder of some fossil.

Pump (Fr.), an engine or machine by which water is drawn up from wells. —The *forcing pump*, a pump which is capable of driving a stream of water above the pump-barrel by means of compressed air. — *Chain-pump*, a pump used in ships-of-war.

Pupip'ara (Lat. *pupa*, and *pario* to bring forth), in entomology, a family of dipterous insects distinguished by the larvæ issuing from the mother in the form of a soft white egg, the skin of which hardens and becomes a firm shell, from which, in time, the perfect insect emerges.

Purbeck, in geology, a fresh-water deposit, consisting of marl and limestone.—*Purbeck beds* constitute the lowest members of the Wealden group, lying below the Hastings sands, and immediately above the Portland beds. The *Purbeck limestone* abounds in organic remains.

Purlin, in architecture, a horizontal piece of timber lying on the main rafters.

Purple Wood, in botany, the wood of the *Copaifera pubiflora* of Guiana.

Purples, in pathology, spots of a livid red colour; a purple fever.

Pur'pura (Lat. *purple*), in heraldry, one of the tinctures used in blazonry, represented in engraving by diagonal lines from the sinister to the dexter side of the escutcheon.—In pathology, the scorbutus, or scurvy; an eruption of small, distinct, purple specks and patches, attended with languor, general debility, and pain in the limbs. The varieties are—*P. simplex*, petechial scurvy; *P. hæmorrhagica*, land scurvy; *P. urticans*, nettle-rash scurvy; *P. senilis*, scurvy of old age; *P. contagiosa*, contagious scurvy.

Pur'suivant (Fr.), in heraldry, a kind of probationer in the Heralds' College.

Pus (Lat.), in pathology, a peculiar fluid yielded from the blood in consequence of inflammation

Pustule (Lat.), in pathology, a cuticular elevation with an inflamed purulent base.

Puzzola'na (from *Puzzuoli*, whence it was brought), a substance formed of volcanic ashes more or less compacted together, and valuable for the foundation of lighthouses and other marine erections.

Pyæ'mia (Gr. *pyos* pus, and *haima* blood), in pathology, a dangerous disease, consisting of a peculiar alteration of the blood, and the formation of numerous abscesses in various parts of the body.

Pycnite (Gr. *pyknos* thick), a prismatic mineral, a variety of topaz, the constituents of which are alumina, silica, and fluoric acid: sp. gr. 3'57.

Pyc'nodonts (Gr. *thick-toothed*), in geology, an extinct family of fishes which prevailed extensively during the middle period of geological history.

Pycnogon'idæ (Gr. *pyknos*, and *gonon* race), a family of Entomostraca, consisting of spider-looking creatures, with eight very long unguiculated legs, of which the Pycnogonon is the type and genus.

Pyc'nostyle (Gr. *thick-columned*), in architecture, an arrangement of columns, in which the intercolumniations are equal to one diameter and a half.

Pycnoti'næ, in ornithology, a subfamily of dentirostral birds, of the order Passeres.

Pylo'rus (Gr.), in anatomy, the lower orifice of the stomach, through which the food passes into the intestines.

Pyophthal'mia (Gr. *pyon* pus, and *ophthalmia* inflammation of the eye), purulent ophthalmia.

Pyorrhœ'a (Gr. *pyon*, and *rheo* to flow), a continued purulent discharge, especially from the genital organs, lungs, and other parts.

Pyr-, or **Pyro-** (Gr.), a prefix to numerous scientific words, denoting *fire*, or the idea of *fever* or *heat*. Thus, in chemistry, the products which are obtained by subjecting certain organic acids to heat are termed *pyro-acids*, as pyro-citric, pyro-gallic, pyro-kinic, pyro-maric, pyro-meconic, and pyro-sorbic acids.

Pyral'lolite (Gr. *pyr*, *allos* another, and *lithos* a stone), a mineral which changes its colour by heat.

Pyr'amid (Gr.), a solid figure standing on a polygonal square or triangular base, and terminating in a point at the top.—In anatomy, an osseous eminence in the tympanum, enclosing the stapedius muscle.—In surgery, the pivot or centre-pin attached to the crown of the trephine.

Pyrar'gillite (Gr. *pyr*, and *argillos* clay), a mineral consisting of potash, soda, silica, alumina, oxide of iron, magnesia, and water: sp. gr. 2·50; H = 3·5.

Pyrene'ite, in mineralogy, a black variety of garnet, found in the Pyrenees, embedded in primitive limestone.

Pyret'ics (Gr.), medicine for fevers.

Pyretol'ogy (Gr.), a discourse on fevers.

Pyri'tes (Gr.), fire-stone; a sulphuret of iron or other metal. —*Pyretology*, a treatise on pyrites.

Pyro-acet'ic Spirit, in chemistry, a limpid, colourless, inflammable liquid, of an agreeable ethereal odour and pungent taste.

Pyro-acid, in chemistry, an acid made by subjecting another acid to heat.

Py'rochlore (Gr. *pyr*, and *chloros* greenish yellow), a reddish-brown or black mineral, consisting of titanic acid, lime, protoxide of uranium, peroxide of cerium, protoxide of manganese, peroxide of iron, peroxide of tin, and water: sp. gr. 4·20; H = 5.

Pyrocit'ric, in chemistry, noting an acid obtained by distilling citric acid.

Pyro-electric'ity, electricity developed by heat, as in certain crystals.

Pyrolig'neous, Pyrolig'nous (Gr. and Lat.), noting an acid obtained from wood.

Pyrolignite (Gr.), a salt formed by the union of pyroligneous acid with a base.

Pyrolith'ic (Gr.), noting an acid obtained from uric acid.

Pyrel'ogy (Gr.), a treatise on heat or fire.

Pyrolu'site (Gr. *pyr*, and *louo* to loosen), in mineralogy, common black manganese. It is the most important and most abundant of all the ores of manganese, and, according to Thomson, consists of binoxide of manganese, silica, and peroxide of iron: sp. gr. 4·97; H = 2—2·8.

Pyrema'lic Acid (Gr. *pyr*, and Lat. *malum* an apple), in chemistry, a volatile substance obtained by heating malic acid in close vessels.

Pyrem'etry (Gr. *pyr*, and *metron* a measure), the measurement of heat, or the expansion of bodies by heat.— *Pyrometer* is an instrument for the measurement of expansion caused by heat.

Pyromor'phite (Gr.), in mineralogy, native phosphate of lead.

Pyromu'cous (Gr. *pyr*, and *mucous*), in chemistry, noting an acid obtained from sugar, gum, and mucilage.— *Pyromucite*, a salt formed of pyromucous acid and a base.

Pyron'omy (Gr.), the laws of igneous action in chemical processes.

Pyrope (Gr.), in mineralogy, a fiery, brilliant red garnet, a gem highly prized.

Pyr'ophane (Gr. *appearance of fire*), a mineral said to change its colour by heat.

Pyroph'orus (Gr. *bearing fire*), a substance which spontaneously takes fire when exposed to air.

Pyrophos'phate (Gr.), in chemistry, a compound of pyrophosphoric acid with a base.

Pyrophosphor'ic (Gr.), in chemistry, an acid procured by exposing phosphoric acid to heat.

Pyrophyl'lite (Gr. *pyr*, *phyllon* a leaf, and *lithos* a stone), a foliated mineral of a light green colour.

Pyrophy'salite (Gr. *pyr*, and *physa* a bladder), in mineralogy, a variety of topaz.

Pyropneumat'ic (Gr.), noting a kind of lamp for producing instantaneous light by the action of inflammable air upon a metallic substance.

Pyr'oscope (Gr. *viewing the fire*), an instrument for measuring the intensity of heat radiating from a fire.

Pyrosid'erite (Gr. *fire-steel*), in mineralogy, a mineral composed of peroxide of iron and water.

Pyro'sis (Gr. *inflammation*), in pathology, a burning redness in the face.

Pyros'klerite (Gr. *pyr*, and *skleros* hard), an emerald-green mineral, consisting of silica, alumina, magnesia, protoxide of iron, oxide of chromium, and water.

Pyros'malite (Gr. *pyr*, *osme* smell, and *lithos* a stone), a native submuriate of iron.

Pyr'osome (Gr.), in entomology, a sort of compound Ascidian, which is remarkable for emitting phosphoric light.

Pyrotartar'ic, noting an acid obtained by distilling pure tartrate of potassa.

Pyrotar'trate, in chemistry, a salt formed by pyrotartaric acid and a base.

Pyr'otechny, or **Pyr'otechnics** (Gr. *pyr*, and *techne* art), the art or science of managing fire, particularly as applied to the art of war, and more especially the making of ornamental fireworks for amusement.

Pyrot'ic (Gr.), in pathology, a caustic medicine.

Pyrou'ric (Gr.), in chemistry, noting an acid obtained from uric acid.

Pyr'oxene (Gr.), in mineralogy, the augite; a crystallized mineral.

Pyrox'yle (Gr. *pyr*, and *xylon* wood), a term embracing all explosive substances obtained by immersing vegetable fibre in nitric or sulphuric acid. —*Pyroxylic*, in chemistry, applied to a spirit produced by the destructive distillation of wood.—*Pyroxyline*, a substance found in pyroxylic spirit.

Pyrr'hite (Gr. *pyrrhos* flame-coloured), a mineral of a deep orange yellow, and vitreous lustre.

Pyrrhooöraci'næ, or **Pyrrhuli'næ**, in ornithology, a sub-family of conirostral birds, of the order Passeres and family Corvidæ; Choughs.

Pyr'rhotine (Gr.), a mineral composed chiefly of sulphur and iron.

Pyul'con (Gr.), a surgical instrument for extracting pus from a cavity.

Pyu'ria (Gr. *pyon* pus, and *ouron* urine), in pathology, evacuation of pus along with the urine.

Pyx (Gr. *pyxis*), a box used for the trial of gold and silver coin.

Q.

In mathematical problems Q.E.D. stands for *quod erat demonstrandum*, which was to be demonstrated ; and, in chemistry, Q.S. stands for *quantum sufficit*.

Quadra (Lat. *quatuor* four), in architecture, a square moulding, border, or frame encompassing a bas-relief, &c.; a term applied to the plinth or lower member of the podium.—A prefix to compound words, signifying *four*.

Quad'rangle (Lat.), a plane figure with four angles.—In geometry, the fourth part of a circle ; an arc of 90°.

Quadrant (Lat. *the fourth part*), a mathematical instrument for taking altitudes ; an instrument used in gunnery for elevating and pointing cannon, &c.—*Quadrant of altitude* is an appendix to an artificial globe, consisting of a slip of brass graduated into 90°, of the same length as those on one of the great circles of the globe, and used as a scale for measuring the distance between places in degrees.

Quadrat (Lat. *quadratus* squared), a mathematical instrument for measuring altitudes, called also a geometrical square and line of shadow.—In printing, a square piece of metal to fill up a void space between words and letters.

Quad'ratrix (Lat.), in geometry, a mechanical line, by means of which right lines are found equal to the circumferences of circles.

Quad'rature (Lat. *quadratio* act of squaring), in mathematics, the determination of the area of a curve.—In astronomy, the position of the moon when she is 90° from the sun. —The *quadrature of the circle* is a problem of great celebrity in the history of mathematical science.—In anatomy, *quadratus lumborum*, a muscle arising from the crest of the ilium.—*Quadratus femoris*, a muscle arising from the tuber ischii.

Quad'ricorns (Lat. *quatuor*, and *cornua* horns), in entomology, a family of insects having four antennæ.—In zoology, a four-horned antelope.

Quadrifur'cate (Lat. *quatuor*, and *furca* a fork), doubly forked.

Quadrino'mial (Lat. *quatuor*, and *nomina* names), in algebra, having four terms.

Quadrip'artite (Lat.), divided into four parts.

Quadrisul'cate (Lat.), in zoology, an unguiculate quadruped, having the hoof divided into four parts.

Quadrox'alate, in chemistry, a salt composed of four equivalents of oxalic acid and one of base.

Quadru'mana (Lat. *four-handed*), in zoology, the second order of mammiferous animals in Cuvier's system, as the Apes, Monkeys, &c.

Quadrune, in mineralogy, a kind of grit-stone with a calcareous cement.

Quaquaver'sal (Lat. *quaquà* and *versus*, inclined on every side), in geology, noting the dip of beds to all points of the compass around a centre, as in the case of beds of lava around the crater of a volcano.

Quartan (Lat. *quartus* fourth), in pathology, applied to a form of ague ; occurring every fourth day.

Quarta'tion (Lat. *art of quartering*), in metallurgy, the separation of silver from gold by the agency of nitric acid.—In chemistry, a process by which the quantity of one thing is made equal to the fourth part of another.

Quartersil'icate, a mineral in which four atoms of silica are combined with one atom of some other substance.

Quartet (Ital.), in music, a piece arranged for four voices or four instruments.

Quartz (Germ.), a transparent mineral, composed of pure silex ; rock-crystal ; one of the ingredients of granite, found under every variety of form : sp. gr. 2·5—2·7 ; H = 7·0.

Quartzite (Germ.), in mineralogy, an aggregate of grains of quartz; quartz rock.

Quartz'sinter, in mineralogy, a substance found in the form of siliceous concretions.

Quaver (Welsh), in music, a note or

measure of time equal to half a crotchet, or the eighth of a semibreve.

Quer'citron (Fr.), the bark of an American oak, which furnishes an excellent yellow dye-stuff.—*Quercitrine* is the colouring principle of quercitron.

Queruli'næ (Lat.), in ornithology, a sub-family of dentirostral birds; order Passeres.

Queues d'Hironde [pron. **kew'deronde**], in fortification, lines composed of projecting tenailles, or works.

Quillai Bark, the bark of the *Quillaia saponaria*, used to make a lather instead of soap, when washing silks and woollens.

Quincite (Fr.), a mineral found in the limestone deposit in the neighbourhood of Quincey, in France. It consists of silica, magnesia, protoxide of iron, and water.

Quincunx (Lat. *quinque* five), an order or arrangement of five; a peculiar arrangement of anything in rows, as trees.

Quindec'agon (Lat. *quindecim* fifteen, and Gr. *gonia* an angle), in geometry, a plane figure of fifteen sides, and as many angles.

Quinine', or **Quin'ine**, an alkaline substance prepared from cinchona or yellow bark, much used in medicine as a tonic and febrifuge; Peruvian bark.

Quin'odine, a substance similar to quinine, extracted from the yellow bark.

Quinque- (Lat.), a prefix to many scientific words, denoting *five*; as, *Quinquangular*, having five angles;—*Quinquefid*, five-cleft;—*Quinquefoliated*, having five leaves;—*Quinquelobate*, having five lobes, applied in botany to parts which are divided into five distinct lobes;—*Quinquelocular*, having five cells;—*Quinquepartite*, divided into five parts;—*Quinquevalvular*, having five valves.

Quinsy (Gr. *kyon* a dog, and *ancho* to strangle), in pathology, an acute inflammation of the tonsils.

Quintet'to (Ital.), in music, a vocal or instrumental composition in five parts, in which each part is *obligato*, and performed by a single voice or instrument.

Quintile (Lat.), in astronomy, the aspect of planets when distant from each other the fifth of a circle.

Quiscali'næ, in ornithology, a sub-family of conirostral birds, of the order Passeres.

Quoin (Fr.), in architecture, a corner or angle of a building.—In gunnery, a loose wedge placed below the breech of a cannon to adjust its elevation.—In printing, a wedge used for fastening the type together.

R.

As an abbreviation, the letter R, with physicians, stands for *Recipe*.

Rabdol'ogy (Gr. *rabdos* a rod, and *logos* a discourse), in arithmetic, a contrivance to facilitate the performance of multiplication and division by means of rods; called also *Napier's bones*.

Ra'bies (Lat.), madness arising from the bite of a rabid animal.

Raceme (Lat. *racemus* a cluster of grapes), in botany, a form of inflorescence in which the flowers are arranged along an axis.—*Racemic*, in chemistry, is an epithet denoting an acid found in the tartar obtained from certain vineyards. —*Racemovinic acid* is an acid formed by the action of alcohol on racemic acid.

Rachis (Gr. *the spine*), in botany, the axis of inflorescence; the petiole of a leaf.—In zoology, the vertebral column of Mammals and birds.

Rachi'tis (Gr. *rachis*), in pathology, a disease affecting children; the rickets.

Rack (Sax.), in mechanics, a straight bar of metal with cogs or teeth cut along its edge, by which it is moved up and down.

Ra'diant (Lat. *shining*), in optics, the luminous point or object from which light emanates, that falls on a mirror or lens.

Radia'ta (Lat.), the fourth great division of the animal kingdom. The *radiated* animals are among the most frequent organic remains in the transition strata. These animals comprise all those which were formerly called zoophytes, or animal-plants, as the Corallines, &c.

Ra'diated (Lat. *issued in rays*), in mineralogy, having crystals diverging from a centre.—*Radiated pyrites* is a variety of sulphuret of iron, occurring most commonly in coal-beds.

Rad'ical (Lat. *radix* a root), in chemistry, an epithet equivalent to base, but applied only to acids; chlorine being the *simple radical* of muriatic acid, and cyanogen and iron the *compound radical* of ferrocyanic acid.—In algebra, a *radical quantity* is one affected by the radical sign.— The *radical sign*, $\sqrt{\ }$, is that by which the root of a quantity is expressed:

the particular root is indicated by a small figure placed to the left of this sign, which by itself denotes the square root;—$\sqrt[3]{}$, $\sqrt[4]{}$, $\sqrt[5]{}$, express the cubic root, the biquadrate, and the fifth roots, respectively.

Rad'icule (Fr.), in botany, that end of the embryo which is opposite to the cotyledons.

Ra'diolite (Lat. *radius* a little ray), in mineralogy, a variety of natrolite.

Radiom'eter (Lat. *radius*, and Gr. *metron* a measure), an instrument for taking altitudes.

Ra'dius, *pl.* **Ra'dii** (Lat.), in geometry, the semi-diameter of a circle.—In the higher geometry, *radius vector* is a right line drawn from the centre of force in any curve in which a body is supposed to move by centripetal force, to that point in which the body is imagined to be.—In anatomy, the *radius* is the small bone of the forearm.—In fortification, a term applied to a line drawn from the centre of the polygon to the extremity of the exterior side, there being the *exterior*, the *interior*, and the *right* radius.

Radix, *pl.* **Rad'ices** (Lat.), in arithmetic, any number which is arbitrarily made the fundamental number of a system.— In algebra, the root of a finite expression from which a series is raised.

Ragstone, in mineralogy, a dark grey siliceous sandstone, which has an uneven fracture.

Ra'idæ (Lat.), in ichthyology, a family of Flat-fishes; the Rays.

Railway, a way constructed of tracks of iron called *rails*, on which the wheels of the railway-carriages roll. —*Railway-chairs* are pieces of iron made to receive and support the rails, and which rest on the sleepers or blocks.—*Railway-sleepers* are the underlying timbers to which the chairs are fixed.

Rainbow, in meteorology, the brilliant-coloured arch which is seen when rain is falling in the region of the sky opposite to the sun.

Rain Gauge, an instrument for measuring the quantity of rain that falls; a pluviameter.

Rake, in military science, to fire in the direction of the length of anything, particularly of a ship; to enfilade.

Ral'lidæ, in ornithology, a family of birds, of the order Grallæ; the Rails.

Ralphite, in mineralogy, a sort of fibrous hornblende.

Ram, in astronomy, the sign of the zodiac Aries, which the sun enters on the 21st of March.—In the arts, the *ram's-horn* is a kind of scroll ornament.

Ramen'ta (Lat. *chips*), in botany, soft, chaff-like hairs growing upon the petioles of ferns.

Ramollisse'ment (Fr. from Lat. *mollis* soft), in pathology, a softening of the brain, or other parts of the body.

Rampant (Sax. *rempend*), a term of frequent use in heraldry, and applied to a lion or other beast when represented as standing on its hind legs. The *lion rampant,* as it betokens vigour and courage, is the most frequent of all bearings. When the lion stands upright on his hind legs, it is called *rampant gardant,* and *rampant regardant* when the beast looks behind.—In architecture, *rampant arch,* an arch the abutments of which spring from an inclined plane.

Rampart (Fr.), in fortification, an elevation or mound of earth round a place, capable of resisting the shot of an enemy, and formed into bastions, curtains, &c.

Ramphas'tidæ (Gr. *ramphos* a beak), in ornithology, a family of birds with enormous bills; the Toucans, of which the Ramphastos is the genus.

Ramps (Fr.), in fortification, the slopes or ways leading from the inward area or lower part of a work to the rampart.

Ramus (Lat. *a branch*), in anatomy, the branch of an artery.—*Ramus anastomaticus magnus* is a branch of the brachial artery.

Range, in nautology, a length of cable equal to the depth of water.—In gunnery, the horizontal distance to which a shot or other projectile is carried.

Ran'idæ (Lat. *rana* a frog), the family of batrachian reptiles, of which the Frog is the type.

Ranine (Lat. *rana*), in anatomy, applied to an artery of the tongue.

Ran'ula (Lat. *rana*), in pathology, an inflammatory tumour under the tongue, arising from an accumulation of saliva and mucus.

Ranuncula'ceæ (Lat.), in botany, a nat. order of Exogens, of which the Ranunculus, or Crow's-foot, is the type.

Rapha'nia (Gr. *raphanis* the radish), in pathology, a disease attended with spasms of the joints, trembling, &c.

Raphe (Gr. *a seam*), in botany, the vascular cord communicating between the nucleus of an ovule and the placenta.—In anatomy, a line having the appearance of a seam, as that of the corpus callosum, &c.

Raph'ides (Gr. *raphis* a needle), in botany, acicular and other crystals scattered in vegetable tissue.

Raph'ilite (Gr. *raphis*, and *lithos* a stone), a mineral occurring in diverging, acicular crystals; lustre glassy and silky; constituents—silica, lime, alumina, protoxide of iron, protoxide of manganese, magnesia, potash, and moisture: sp. gr. 2·85; H = 3·75.

Rapto'res (Lat. *robbers*, from *rapio* to snatch), in ornithology, an order of birds which live by rapine; birds of prey.

Rarefac'tion (Lat. *rarus* thin, and *facio* to make), state of being rarefied; applied specially to air and gales.

Raso'res (Lat. *rasor* a scraper, from *rado* to scratch), in ornithology, an order of birds, including the families Pavonidæ, Tetraonidæ, Strathonidæ, Columbidæ, and Megapodiidæ.

Ratafi'a (Fr. and Sp.), liquor compounded with alcohol, sugar, and the odoriferous or flavouring principles of vegetables.

Ratchet, in mechanical science, a piece of mechanism, one end of which abuts against a tooth of a wheel, called a ratchet-wheel.

Rath'ofite, in mineralogy, a species of garnet found in Sweden.

Ra'tio (Lat.), in mathematics, the mutual relation which two magnitudes or quantities of the same kind bear to each other: thus, the ratio of 6 to 3 is $\frac{6}{3}$ or 2; and the ratio of 3 to 6 is $\frac{3}{6}$ or $\frac{1}{2}$.—In arithmetic and algebra, a *rational quantity* is an expression in definite terms, or one in which no extraction of a root is left which cannot be extracted by known processes: thus, 2, $\sqrt{9}$, $\sqrt[3]{a6}$, are rational quantities, and $\sqrt{2}$, $\sqrt[3]{9}$, $\sqrt[4]{a6}$, are irrational or surd quantities.—In geography, *rational horizon* is the plane passing through the centre of the earth parallel to the *sensible horizon* of the place to which it is referred.

Ratlines, or **Ratlins**, in nautology, small horizontal lines extending over the shrouds, forming the steps of ladders.

Rauchwacke (Germ.), in geology, one of the calcareous members of the Zechstein formation.

Ravelin (Fr.), in fortification, a detached work, composed of two embankments. In this it differs from a half-moon, which is placed before an angle.

Ray'onnant (Fr.), in heraldry, darting forth rays.

Razee (Fr.), in nautology, a ship-of-war cut down to an inferior class.

Re-, or **Red-**, a Lat. preposition used in compound words, signifying *repetition*.

Reac'tion (Lat. *re*, and *ago* to act), in dynamics, the resistance made by a body to the action or impulse of another body.

Rea'gent (Lat.), in chemistry, a substance used to detect the presence ot other bodies.

Real'gar, a mineral occurring in splendid translucent crystals of a brilliant red colour, consisting of arsenic and sulphur; it is a protosulphuret of arsenic: sp. gr. 3·3—3·6. Realgar is also artificially prepared and used as a pigment.

Reaumuria'ceæ (in honour of *M. Réaumur*), in botany, a nat. order of exogenous plants, of which Reaumuria is the type.

Recip'rocal Ra'tio, in arithmetic and algebra, is that between the reciprocal of two quantities.—In geometry, *reciprocal figures* are two figures of the same kind, so related that two sides of the one form the *extremes* of an analogy, of which the *means* are the two corresponding sides of the other.

Recip'rocating Motion, in mechanical science, a form of action illustrated in the suspension of a rigid bar on an axis.

Reclina'tion (Lat. *re*, and *clino* to lean), in surgery, an operation for the cure of cataract.

Rec'tangle (Lat. *rectus* right, and *angulus* angle), any geometrical figure containing one or more right angles; a right-angled parallelogram.—*Rectangular*, having one or more angles of 90°.

Rectifica'tion (Lat.), in chemistry, the purification of any substance by repeated distillation.

Rectilin'ear (Lat.), in geometry, a figure whose boundaries are right lines.

Rectum (Lat. *rectus*), in anatomy, the last portion of the large intestines (the straight gut), terminating in the anus.

Rectus (Lat. *straight*), in anatomy, an epithet applied to several straight-formed muscles of the body.—*Rectus capitis* is the name of five muscles arising from the upper cervical vertebræ, and inserted into the occipital bone; these are the *R. capitis anticus major*; the *R. capitis anticus minor*; the *R. capitis lateralis*; the *R. capitis prosticus major*; and the *R. capitis prosticus minor*.—The muscles connected with the eye are, the *R. superior*, which raises the eye; the *R. inferior*, which depresses it; the *R. internus*, which draws it inwards; and the *R. externus*, which draws it outwards.—The *Rectus ab-*

and inflammability, solubility in alcohol, and insolubility in water.—*Highgate resin* is a mineral discovered during an attempt to pass a tunnel through Highgate Hill: sp. gr. 1·046; H = 2·5.—*Resinous electricity* is that kind of electricity which a tube of resin exhibits by friction on a rubber of wool, otherwise called *negative* electricity.

Res'inone, a product somewhat resembling alcohol, which differs from oil of turpentine in containing an additional atom of water.

Resolu'tion (Lat. *re*, and *solvo* to loosen), in chemistry, the process of separating the component parts of bodies.—In pathology, the subsidence of inflammation without abscess, ulceration, mortification, &c.—In algebra, *resolution of equations* is the finding of the values which the unknown quantity or quantities must have, so as to fulfil the conditions expressed in the proposed equation.—In geometry, the orderly enumeration of the things to be done to obtain what is required in a problem.—In mechanics, *the resolution of forces* is the act of finding the quantity of two or more forces or motions, which, taken together, shall produce a given resultant.

Resolve (Lat.), in algebra, to *resolve an equation* is to find the values which the unknown quantity or quantities must have, in order to fulfil the conditions of the problem.

Resol'vend (Lat.), in arithmetic, a number which arises from increasing the remainder after subtraction, in extracting the square or cube root.

Resol'vent (Lat.), that which causes solution.—In pathology, a substance employed to allay inflammation, and prevent suppuration.

Rest, in music, a pause or interval of time, during which there is an intermission of the voice or sound.—In physics, the continuance of a body in the same place when acted on by equal and opposing forces.

Restia'ceæ (Lat. *restis* a cord), a nat. order of plants, of which Restio is the type. They are used as cords at the Cape of Good Hope.

Resul'tant (Lat. *resulto* to leap back), in dynamics, the force which results from the composition of two or more forces acting upon a body.

Rete (Lat. *a net*), a term frequently applied in anatomy and natural history to cellular membranes, nerves, vessels, and other parts which have a *retiform* appearance.—In anatomy, *rete mirabile*, a network of blood-vessels at the base of the brain of quadrupeds;—*Rete mucosum*, the soft and apparently fibrous matter or layer situated between the cuticle and the cutis; it is the seat of the colour of the skin, which in the negro is black.

Reten'tion (Lat.), in pathology, the power of retaining, or that state of contraction of the elastic or muscular parts of the body by which they hold their proper contents, and prevent evacuation.

Retia'res (Lat. *rete*), in entomology, those spiders which spin a web or net to entrap their prey.

Reticula'ta (Lat. *reticulum* a little net), the name of a section of Lithophytes.—In architecture, *reticulated work* is a species of masonry formed of small square bricks or stones placed lozenge-wise.

Retic'ulum (Lat.), in comparative anatomy, the second cavity of the complex stomach of the ruminant quadrupeds, so called from the reticulate or honeycomb-like disposition of the sub-hexagonal cells which occupy its inner surface.

Ret'ina (Lat. from *rete* a net), the net-like expansion of the optic nerve; the seat of vision.

Retinac'ulum (Lat. *a band*), in botany, the viscid matter by which the pollen masses in Orchids adhere to a prolongation of the anther.

Retin'alite (Gr. *retine* resin, and *lithos* a stone), a translucent mineral of a brownish-yellow colour, consisting of silica, magnesia, soda, peroxide of iron, alumina, and water: sp. gr. 2·493; H = 3·75.

Retinas'phalt (Gr. *retine* and *asphaltos*), a mineral of a pale brownish-yellow colour; composition—resin, asphalt, and earthy substances: sp. gr. 1·1—1·2; H = 1·0—2·0.

Ret'inite (Gr. *retine*), a resinous substance found in some kinds of coal.

Retini'tis (Lat. *retina*), in pathology, inflammation of the retina of the eye.

Ret'irade (Fr. *retirer* to retire), in fortification, a kind of retrenchment in the body of the bastion or other work.

Retort (Lat. *re*, and *torqueo* to twist), in chemistry, a globular vessel with a long neck employed in distillation.

Retro- (Lat.), a preposition used in compound words, signifying *back* or *backward*.

Re'troflex (Lat. *retro*, and *flecto* to bend), in botany, bent backwards.

Re'trofract (Lat.), in botany, hanging back and down, as if broken.

Ret'rograde (Lat. *retro*, and *gradior* to step), in astronomy, apparently moving in the direction contrary to the order of the signs of the zodiac in which the sun appears to move.

Retrogres'sion (Lat.), in astronomy, the change of position undergone by the moon's nodes, in a direction contrary to the motion of the sun.

Retromin'gent (Lat. *retro*, and *mingo* to urinate), discharging the urine backwards; an animal staling backwards.

Return (Fr. *retourner*), in architecture, the continuation of a moulding, projection, &c., in the opposite direction.—In fortification, the *returns of a trench* are its several windings and lines.

Retuse (Lat. *re*, and *tundo* to bruise), in geometry, having a broad and slightly depressed apex.

Reus'site (from *M. Reuss*, the German mineralogist), in mineralogy, a substance containing sulphates of soda and magnesia.

Reveille (Fr. *awake*), in military affairs, the beat of drum about daybreak to arouse the soldiers.

Rever'beratory (Lat. *re*, and *verbero* to beat back), in chemistry and metallurgy, applied to a furnace in which a crucible or other object is heated by flame or hot air reverberated or beaten back from the roof.

Revet'ment (Fr.), in fortification, a strong wall built round the lower part of the rampart.

Reve'tus, in fortification, works constructed with stone or brick.

Revolu'tion (Lat. *revolvo* to turn about), in physics, the circular motion of a body on its axis; the motion of any body round a fixed point.—In geometry, the motion of any figure round a fixed line as an axis; thus a right-angled triangle, revolving round one of its legs as an axis, generates a cone.

Rhabdol'ogy. (See *Rabdology*.)

Rhamna'ceæ (Gr. *rhamnos* a branch), a nat. order of exogenous plants, of which the Rhamnus, or Buckthorn, is the type.

Rhamphas'tidæ. (See *Ramphastidæ*.)

Rhapon'ticine, in chemistry, a substance obtained from the *Rheum rhaponticum*.

Rhat'any, in pharmacy, the root of the *Krameria triandria*, imported from Peru, used as an astringent.

Rheine (Lat. *rheum* rhubarb), an inodorous, bitterish substance of a yellow colour, obtained by gently heating powdered rhubarb with 8 parts of nitric acid.

Rhenite, a translucent, vitreous mineral found at Rheinbreitbach, near Bonn, on the Rhine, consisting of

phosphoric acid, oxide of copper, and water: sp. gr. 4'2—4'3; H — 5'0.

Rheom'etry (Gr. *rheo* to flow, and *metron* a measure), in mathematics, the differential and integral calculus. —*Rheometer* is an instrument by which the force of an electric, magnetic, or galvanic current is measured.

Rhe'ostat (Gr. *rheos* a current, and *istemi* to stand), in galvanism, an apparatus for enabling a galvanic needle to be kept at the same point during an experiment.

Rhe'otome (Gr. *rheos*, and *temno* to cut), in electricity, an instrument for periodically interrupting an electric current.

Rhe'otrope (Gr. *rheo*, and *trepo* to turn), in electricity, an instrument for reversing the direction of a voltaic current.

Rheu'matism (Gr. *rheuma* a watery humour), in pathology, pain and inflammation about the joints and surrounding muscles;—*Articular rheumatism*, occurring in the joints and muscles of the extremities;—*Lumbago*, in the loins;—*Sciatica*, in the hip-joint;—*Spurious pleurisy* occurs in the muscles of the diaphragm.

Rheumic, in chemistry, an epithet denoting an acid obtained from rhubarb stalks.

Rhexis (Gr. *a bursting*), in pathology, the rupture of a vein, or the spontaneous bursting of a purulent collection.

Rhinantha'ceæ (Gr. *rhin* a snout, and *anthos* a flower), a nat. order of herbaceous plants, of which Rhinanthus, or Yellow-rattle, is the type.

Rhinocarcino'ma (Gr. *rhin*, and *karkinoma* cancer), in pathology, cancer of the nose.

Rhi'noplasty (Gr. *rhin*, and *plasso* to form), in pathology, the operation for forming a new nose.

Rhinopoti'næ, a sub-family of flat fishes; fam. Raidæ.

Rhipip'tera (Gr. *rhips* a fan, and *pteron* a wing), in entomology, an order of insects having only two wings folded like a fan.

Rhizanths (Gr. *rhiza* a root, and *anthos* a flower), in botany, a class of plants occupying a position between the flowering and the non-flowering species.

Rhizocar'pous (Gr. *rhiza*, and *karpos* fruit), an epithet applied to plants whose branches perish every year, but whose roots last many years.

Rhi'zopods (Gr. *rhiza*, and *podes* feet), in natural history, a class of simple organic beings, consisting of minute gelatinous masses, often provided with long, slender, contractile filaments, and generally covered by a shell.

Rho′dalite (Gr. *rhodon* a rose, and *lithos* a stone), a mineral discovered in Ireland of a flesh-red colour, consisting of silica, alumina, peroxide of iron, lime, magnesia, and water: sp. gr. 2·0; H = 2.

Rho′dium (Gr. *rhodon*), in mineralogy, a rose-coloured metal obtained from the ore of platinum.

Rhod′izite (Gr.), a rose-tinged mineral observed in small crystals.

Rhodizo′nate (Gr. *rhodon*), in chemistry, a salt composed of potassium and carbonic oxide, containing a peculiar acid, which has been named *rhodozinic acid*, and which is represented by the formula $C_7H_3O_{10}$.

Rhodocrini′tes (Gr. *rhodon*, and *krinon* a lily), a genus of Crinoideans.

Rho′donite (Gr. *rhodon*), a mineral of a pale rose colour, composed of oxide of manganese, silica, carbonic acid, alumina, oxide of iron, and water: sp. gr. 3·5.

Rhomb, Rhombus (Gr. *rhombo* to whirl round), in geometry, a quadrilateral figure whose sides are all equal, and its angles not right angles.

Rhombohe′dron (Gr. *rhombos* a rhomb, and *hedra* a side), in geometry, a solid figure of six sides.

Rhomboid (Gr. *like a rhomb*), in geometry, a quadrilateral figure, with the opposite sides equal, but not the adjacent sides.

Rhomboide′us (Lat. *rhombus*), in anatomy, the name given to a dorsal muscle.

Rhomb-star, in mineralogy, a crystalline magnesian carbonate of lime.

Rhonchus (Gr. *a snoring*), in pathology, a term applied to any unnatural sound produced by obstructions to the air tubes.

Rhubarb (Pers. *rhubar*, Gr. *rha*), a medicinal plant of the genus Rheum.

Rhumb (Gr. *rhombos*, from *rhombo* to turn round) in geography and navigation, a circle on the earth's surface making a given angle with the meridian of a place; a division on the compass card.—*Rhumb-line* is the track of a ship which cuts all the meridians at the same angle.

Rhynchopi′næ (Gr.), in ornithology, a sub-family of birds of the order Anseres.

Rhyn′colites (Gr. *a stone-beak*), in fossilology, the remains of the beaks of certain Cephalopods.

Rhynchoph′ora (Gr. *rhynchos* a snout, and *phoreo* to bear), the name of the first family of tetramerous Coleoptera, distinguished by the entire prolonga-

tion of the head, which forms a sort of snout or proboscis.

Rhythmom′eter (Gr. *rhythmos*, and *metron* a measure), an instrument for marking time to movements in music.

Rhytido′sis (Gr. *rhytidoo* to become wrinkled), in pathology, a state of the cornea in which it collapses so considerably, without its transparency being affected, that the sight is much impaired.

Rib (Sax.), one of the twelve bones on each side of the vertebræ of the human skeleton, proceeding from the vertebral column to the sternum, and serving to enclose and protect the heart and lungs.—In botany, a *rib* is the continuation of the petiole along the middle of a leaf, and from which the veins take their rise.

Ricin′ic, in chemistry, applied to an acid obtained from castor-oil.

Ric′ochet (Fr.), an epithet applied to the firing of a piece of ordnance, by which a shot or shell bounds along the opposite rampart.

Rideau (Fr.), in fortification, a small mound of earth to cover a camp from the approach of an enemy.

Rigel. (See *Regel*.)

Right (Sax. *riht*).—In geometry, *right* is used synonymously with straight, as a *right* line; but more generally in opposition to oblique, as a *right* angle, an angle of 90°.—In astronomy, *right ascension* is the angle at the pole of the equator formed by two great circles, one of which passes through the first point of Aries, and the other through a celestial body, and is consequently measured by the arc of the equator intercepted between those circles.—In the stereographic projection of the sphere, *a right circle* is one at right angles to the plane of projection.—*Right sphere*, that position of the sphere in which its poles are in the horizon.—*Right cone, cylinder, prism,* &c., figures whose axes are perpendicular to the plane of the base.—In navigation, *right sailing* is that in which a voyage is performed on some one of the four cardinal points, east, west, north, or south.

Rima (Lat. *a fissure*).—In anatomy, *rima glottidis* is the fissure of the glottis; the opening between the chordæ vocales.—*Rima* is, in conchology, the interstice between the valves when the hymen is removed.

Rinforzan′do (Ital. *strengthening*), in music, a direction to the performer that the sound is to be increased, marked thus, < ; when the sound is to be diminished, *diminuendo*, this mark > is used.

Ring Mountains, in astronomy, certain

roundish formations on the surface of the moon, of the same nature as bulwark plains.

Rings.—In gunnery, the *rings* of a gun are of five kinds: the *base ring*, *reinforce ring*, *trunnion ring*, *cornice ring*, and *muzzle ring*.

Ri'olite, in mineralogy, a substance containing selenium and zinc.

Ripie'no (Ital. *full*), in music, used in compositions of many parts, to distinguish those which fill up the harmony, and play only occasionally, from those which play throughout the piece.

Risus (Lat. *laughter*).—In pathology, *risus sardonicus* is a convulsive affection of the lips and cheek, which frequently precedes or accompanies tetanus;—*Risus caninus* is a spasmodic contraction of the muscles of one of the commissures of the lips, and of the corresponding cheek.

Ritornel'lo (Ital. *a return*), in music, a short repetition, such as that of an echo, or of the last words of a song.

Rivose (Lat. *rivus* a rivulet), in zoology, marked with furrows sinuate or not parallel.

Ro'borant (Lat. *strengthening*), in pharmacy, a medicine which strengthens the parts, and gives new vigour to the constitution.

Rocel'lic, in chemistry, applied to *rocellic acid*, a crystallized acid discovered in the *Rocella tinctoria*.

Rochelle Powders, a term applied to powders used for making an effervescing purgative drink when mixed in water or other liquid.

Rochelle Salt, a tartrate of soda and potassa.

Rock (Fr. *roc*, and Ital. *rocca*), a prefix of frequent occurrence in scientific words.—In mineralogy, *rock-butter* is a native alum which occurs in soft masses in the cavities or fissures of argillaceous slate, mingled with clay and oxide of iron.—*Rock-crystal* is a transparent crystallized quartz.—*Rock-milk* is an acidiferous earthy mineral, consisting of almost pure carbonate of lime.—*Rock-oil*, another name for petrol, or petroleum.—*Rock-ruby*, a name sometimes given to the garnet, when it is of a strong but not of a deep red.—*Rock-salt*, common salt found in solid masses or beds in different formations.—*Rock-soap*, a mineral composed chiefly of silica, alumina, and water.—*Rock-wood*, a variety of asbestos.—In conchology, *rock-shells* is the common name of certain univalves, characterized by the long straight canal which terminates the mouths of their shells.

Rocket (Ital.), an artificial firework, or

military projectile, consisting of saltpetre, sulphur, and charcoal, which is carried by its own conflagration to a considerable distance, and finally explodes.—*Congreve rockets*, which are employed as military projectiles, were first invented by Sir Wm. Congreve: they are of various sizes, from twenty-four to three pounders.

Roden'tia, or **Rodents** (Lat. *rodo* to gnaw), an order of quadrupeds with two incisor teeth in each jaw, adapted for gnawing, as Rats, Mice, Squirrels, Beavers, Hamsters, Jerboas, Marmots, Guinea-pigs, Cavias, &c.

Rolling, in mechanical science, an epithet applied to machinery, by which metals are compressed into sheets.—*Rolling-mill*, a mill for rolling or forming iron and other metals into plates or sheets.—*Rolling-press*, a cylinder rolling upon another cylinder, by which printing is performed on engraved plates.

Roman, an epithet frequently applied to terms connected with mechanical science; as, *Roman cement*, an excellent water cement, in general use for building purposes, usually obtained from a species of ferruginous limestone.—*Roman vitriol* is a name for sulphate of copper.—In pyrotechny, *Roman candle* is a particular kind of firework, characterized by the continued emission of a multitude of sparks, and the ejection, at regular intervals, of brilliant stars, which are thrown upwards as they become ignited.

Roman'zofite (from *Count Romanzoff*), a brown mineral from Finland.

Ro'meine (from *Rome de l'Isle*), a hyacinth-coloured mineral, which occurs in small square octahedrons, and consists of antimonious acid, lime, protoxide of manganese, protoxide of iron, and silica: hardness, scratches glass.—*Dana*.

Rondel (Fr. *a target*), in fortification, a small round tower erected in some particular cases at the foot of the bastion.

Root (Swed. *röt*), in botany, that part of a plant which grows downwards into the earth, while the stem ascends into the air; the smaller divisions of roots being called fibrils.—In arithmetic and algebra, the *root* of any quantity is an expression whose continued multiplication into itself a given number of times produces the quantity proposed.—The *root of an equation* is any quantity which fulfils the conditions proposed in such equation.

Rootstock, in botany, a prostrate stem which yearly produces young branches or plants, as is common in Iridaceæ.

Rosa'ceæ (Gr. and Lat. *rosa*, Celt. *ros*), a nat. order of exogenous plants, composed of herbaceous plants or shrubs, of which Rosa is the type and genus, distinguished by the beauty of the flowers. Don enumerates 205 species, some of which have many varieties.

Rose-cut, in jewellery, an epithet applied to such precious stones as are cut with a smooth rounded surface, to distinguish them from such as have numerous facets; as, *rose-diamond*, a diamond cut into twenty-four triangular planes.—In mineralogy, *rose-quartz* is a variety of quartz of a rose colour.

Ro'selite (from *Dr. Rose* of Berlin), a very rare mineral, which occurs in small, deep rose-coloured, twin crystals, and consists of oxide of cobalt, arsenic acid, lime, magnesia, and water: $H = 3·0$.

Rose'ola (Lat. *roseus* rosy), in pathology, rose-rash, a rose-coloured efflorescence, without wheals or papulæ, and not contagious.

Rosite (Lat. *rosa*), a rose-red mineral which occurs in small uncrystallized grains, and consists of silica, alumina, peroxide of iron, oxide of manganese, potash, lime, magnesia, soda, and water: sp. gr. 2.72; $H = 2·5$.

Rostrum (Lat. *the bill* or *beak of a bird*), in surgery, a crooked pair of scissors used for dilating wounds.—In chemistry, the pipe which conveys the distilling liquor into its receiver in the common alembic.

Rotheln (Germ.), in pathology, an eruptive febrile disease, partaking of the character of both scarlet fever and measles.

Rotif'era, or **Ro'tifers** (Lat. *rota* a wheel, and *fero* to carry), in entomology, an order of Infusoria, the Wheel Animalcules, which are distinguished by certain ciliated appendages at the anterior part of the body, which seem to move in a rapid rotatory manner.

Rouleaux (Fr.), in military science, a term applied to round bundles of fascines, which are tied together, and serve to cover men when the works are pushed close to a besieged town, or to mask the head of a work.

Roundel (Fr.), in fortification, a circular bastion; also a kind of target.

Roxburghia'ceæ, in botany, a nat. order of Dictyogens with bisexual flowers, of which Roxburghia (so called in honour of Dr. Roxburgh) is the genus. The stems have been known to attain a length of 600 feet.

Rubefa'cient (Lat. *making red*), in me-

dicine, a substance or external application which causes redness.

Ru'belite (Lat. *rubeus* red), red tourmaline, a mineral of a reddish colour, which consists of silica, alumina, soda, oxides of manganese and iron.

Rubeo'la (Lat. *redness*), in pathology, an eruption of crimson-coloured stigmata or dots, grouped in irregular circles or crescents, commonly called measles.

Rubi'go (Lat. *rubeus*), in botany, a genus of fungous parasitic plants, popularly known by the name of *mildew* or *blight*.

Ruby (Lat. *rubeus*), in mineralogy, a precious stone; a crystallized gem of various shades of red, very hard and valuable.—*Ruby-blend* is a red sulphuret of zinc.—*Ruby silver*, a sectile mineral, composed of sulphur, antimony, and silver.

Ru'denture (Fr.), in architecture, the figure of a rope or staff, with which the flutings of columns are sometimes filled up.

Rudol'phine, in astronomy, an epithet applied to a set of astronomical tables computed by Kepler, and founded on the observations of Tycho Brahé.

Rugæ (Lat. *folds* or *plaits*), in anatomy, the wrinkles or folds into which the mucous membrane of some organs is thrown in particular states.

Rule (Fr. *règle*, from Lat. *regula*), in arithmetic and algebra, a determinate mode prescribed for performing any operation.—*Rule of three*, that rule in arithmetic which directs, when three terms are given, how to find a fourth, which shall have the same ratio to the third term as the second has to the first.—*Sliding-rule* is a mathematical instrument serving to solve a number of questions from the change of the position of the slider by inspection, and therefore of much importance to the less educated artisan.

Rumen (Lat.), in anatomy, the paunch of a ruminant quadruped.

Ruminan'tia, or **Ru'minants** (Lat. *rumino*, from *rumen* the cud), in zoology, an order of herbivorous animals, provided with four stomachs—the first so situated as to receive a large quantity of vegetable matter, coarsely bruised by the first mastication, which passes into the second, where it is moistened and formed into little pellets, which the animal has the power of bringing again to the mouth to be re-chewed, after which it is swallowed into the third stomach, and thence passes to the fourth. It comprehends the Antelopes, Oxen, Stags, Musks, and Giraffes.—*Craig*.

Ru'pia (Gr. *rupis* filth), an eruption of

flat distinct vesicles, with a base slightly inflamed, containing a sanious fluid.

Ruta'ceæ (Sax. *ruta* or *rud*), a nat. order of exogenous plants, consisting of fetid herbs, as Garden Rue, of which Ruta, or Rue, is the genus.

Rutel'idæ (Lat. *rutilans*, shining), in entomology, a division of the family Scarabæidæ, or Sting Beetles.

Ruthe'nium, in chemistry, a very hard brittle metal, extracted from the ore of platinum.

Rutile (Lat. *rutile* to shine), in mineralogy, a reddish-brown mineral.

Ru'tilite, native oxide of titanium.

S.

As an abreviation S. stands for south; S.E. for south-east; S.W. for south-west; S.S.E. for south-south-east; S.S.W. for south-south-west; — F.R.S., Fellow of the Royal Society; F.G.S., Fellow of the Geological Society, &c.

Sabadil'la (Sp.), in botany, a species of Veratrum found in the West Indies and in Mexico, from which veratria, a considerable article of commerce, is obtained.—*Sabadilline* is a poisonous crystalline substance extracted from the root of the Sabadilla.

Sacchar'ic Acid, a product of the action of dilute nitric acid on cane or grape sugar.

Sac'charine (Lat. *saccharum* sugar), having the qualities of sugar.—*Saccharine fermentation*, a kind of spontaneous fermentation which takes place in various bodies, by which sugar is formed in them either at the expense of the gluten or of an acid.

Sac'charite, a mineral composed chiefly of silica, alumina, soda, and lime.

Saccharom'eter (Lat. *saccharum*, and Gr. *metron* a measure), an instrument for ascertaining the strength of brewers' and distillers' worts, and the richness of saccharine substances; also the degree to which the juice expressed from the sugar-cane is concentrated previously to undergoing the process of crystallization.

Saccha'rum (Lat. from Arab. *soukar* sugar), an important genus of plants from which sugar is obtained, the Sugar-cane; order Graminaceæ.—In chemistry and medicine, *saccharum saturni* is the acetate of lead—a salt which crystallizes in right rhombic prisms, or in needles, and is poisonous.

Saccholac'tic (Lat. *saccharum*, and *lac* milk), in chemistry, noting an acid obtained from the sugar of milk.—*Saccholactate* is a salt formed by saccholactic acid with a base.

Sacchul'mine, in chemistry, a crystalline substance of a colour nearly black, obtained by boiling cane sugar in dilute sulphuric acid.

Sacrum (Lat. *sacer* sacred), in anatomy, the bone which forms the basis of the vertebral column. — *Sacro-iliac*, pertaining to the articulation which exists between the sacral and iliac bones.—*Sacro-lumbalis*, a muscle arising from the sacrum.—*Sacro-lumbar*, pertaining to the sacro-lumbalis.—*Sacro-coccygeal*, belonging to the articulation which results from the union of the sacrum and coccyx. —*Sacro-sciatic*, pertaining to either of the two ligaments of the pelvis.— *Sacro-vertebral*, belonging to the articulation formed by the union of the sacrum with the last lumbar vertebra.—*Craig*.

Safety Lamp, a lamp covered with fine gauze to give light in mines, and so constructed as to burn without danger in an explosive atmosphere.

Safety Tube, a tube of various forms used in distillations.

Safety Valve, a valve on the boiler of a steam-engine, which opens outward from the boiler, facilitating the escape of steam.

Sagape'num (Arab.), in botany, a concrete gum resin imported from Alexandria, Smyrna, &c., in drops or masses of an olive or brownish-yellow colour, used only in medicine.

Sagger, a species of clay used in making the pots in which earthenware is baked.

Sagitta'lis (Lat. *sagitta* an arrow), in anatomy, the arrow-like suture of the cranium, which passes from the middle of the superior margin of the frontal to the angle of the occipital bone.

Sagitta'rius (Lat.), in astronomy, one of the signs of the zodiac, the figure of which is a centaur drawing a bow. The catalogue of the Astronomical Society gives 150 stars.

Sagit'tate (Lat.), in botany, shaped like the head of an arrow.

Sahlite (from *Sahla* in Sweden, where it is found), a variety of white augite, which consists of silica, lime, magnesia, oxide of iron, manganese, and alumina.

Saint Vitus's Dance, in pathology, a convulsive motion of the limbs.

Sal (Lat.), the scientific term for salt, as used in chemistry and pharmacy.—*Sal ammoniac* is a compound of 17 parts of ammonia and 37 of hydrochloric acid. — *Sal volatile*, carbonate of ammonia, a term frequently applied to a spirituous solution of the carbonate flavoured with aromatics.

Salalem'broth, in chemistry, a double salt, consisting of chloride of mercury and chloride of ammonium.

Salam Stone, in mineralogy, a species of sapphire.

Salica'ceæ (Lat. *Salix*, one of the genera), a nat. order of amentaceous Exogens; the Willows and Poplars.

Sal'icine (Lat. *salix*), a bitter crystallizable principle extracted from the willow.

Sa'lient (Lat. *salio* to leap), in geometry, applied to projecting angles.

Sal'ifiable (Lat. *sal*, and *fio* to become), in chemistry, capable of forming a salt by combining with an acid.

Saline (Lat. *sal*), in chemistry, containing the properties of salt.

Salinom'eter (Lat. *salinus* saline, and Gr. *metron* a measure), an apparatus for ascertaining the brine in steam-engine boilers.

Sali'no-terrene (Lat. *salinus*, and *terra* earth), in chemistry, partaking of salt and earth.

Sal'ivary (Lat. *saliva*), belonging to or conveying saliva.—*Salivary glands*, the glands which secrete the saliva, being the parotid, sublingual, and maxillary.

Saliva'tion (Lat.), in pathology, the process of producing an excessive flow of saliva.

Salmon'idæ, a family of malacopterygious fishes, of which the Salmo, or Salmon, is the type.

Salpin'go-pharyn'geus (Gr. *salpinx* a trumpet, and *pharynx* the pharynx), in anatomy, a muscle composed of a few fibres of the palato-pharyngeus, which it assists in dilating the mouth of the Eustachian tube.

Sal Prunel'la (Lat.), fused nitre, cast into cakes or balls.

Salseparine', in chemistry, a substance extracted by alcohol from sarsaparilla.

Salt (Germ. *salz*, Lat. *sal*), in popular language, the chloride of sodium, a substance which has been in common use as a seasoner and preserver of food from the earliest ages.—In chemistry, any substance resulting from the combination of two oxides or analogous bodies, of which one is highly basic and the other highly acid.

Saltato'ria (Lat. *salto* to skip), a family of orthopterous insects, comprising Grasshoppers, Crickets, &c.

Sal'tier (Fr.), in heraldry, one of the eight great ordinaries; a cross with two feet, as an X.

Sal'tigrades (Lat.), a family of Spiders which leap to seize their prey.

Saltpe'tre (Germ. *salpeter*), the nitrate of potash, a salt of very great importance, found in a natural state, but chiefly obtained by artificial processes.

Salt Rad'ical, in chemistry, an element which forms a salt by combination with a metal.

Salts, in chemistry, an important class of substances, composed of two or more dissimilar elements in such combination with each other as chemically to unite, forming a substance dissimilar to either, of which the following are a few of the more ordinary ones :—*Culinary, Rock*, or *Sea salt*, chloride of soda ;—*Purging* or *Epsom salt*, sulphate of magnesia ;—*Glauber salt*, sulphate of soda ;—*Salt of hartshorn*, carbonate of ammonia ;—*Sedative salt*, boracic acid; —*Rochelle salt*, tartrate of potash and soda :—*Salt of Silvius*, acetate of potash ;—*Salt of sorrel*, oxalate of potash ; — *Microcosmic salt*, triple phosphate of soda and ammonia ;— *Spirit of salt*, hydrochloric acid ;— *Salt of tartar*, carbonate of potash ; *Salt of lemons*, citric acid ;—*Salt of Saturn*, acetate of lead ;—*Salt of amber*, succinic acid ;—*Salt of vitriol*, or *White vitriol*, sulphate of zinc (*Craig*).—*Salts* is the popular name for salt taken as an opening medicine.

Salvatel'la (Germ. from Lat. *salus* safety), in anatomy, the name of a vein situated in the dorsal region, near the ulnar border of the human hand.

Sal Volat'ile (Lat. *volatile salt*), a sesquicarbonate of ammonia.

Samian Stone, a kind of polishing stone used by goldsmiths, brought from Samos.

Samyda'ceæ, a nat. order of exogenous plants, consisting of shrubs or little trees, of which the Samyda, or Birch, is the type.

Sand (Sax.), in mineralogy, flint or quartz broken fine by the action of water, but not reduced to powder.— In chemistry, a *sand-bath* is a vessel filled with sand and heated by a fire underneath ;—*Sand-heat*, the temperature produced by this apparatus. —In fortification, *sand-bag* is a bag containing usually about a cubic foot of sand, used in repairing breaches, erecting temporary bulwarks, &c.— *Sandstone* is an aggregate of siliceous grains, or any stone composed of grains of sand agglutinated together.

San'darach (Lat. *sandaraca,* from Arab. *sandros*), a resinous substance, or gum resin, which oozes from the common juniper, used in making varnish; a native fossil of a bright red colour. Sandarach is also a name for realgar, or sulphuret of arsenic.

Sanguina'ria (Lat. *sanguis* blood), in chemistry, a vegetable alkali obtained from the *Sanguinaria Canadensis.*

Sanguisorba'ceæ (Lat. *sanguis,* and *sorbeo* to absorb), an order of exogenous plants, consisting of herbs or under-shrubs, of which the Sanguisorba is the type and genus.

Sa'nies (Lat.), in physiology, a thin reddish discharge from sores or wounds.

San'tonine, a vegetable principle obtained from the *Artemisia santonica.*

Sap (Sax.), the vital juice of plants and trees, or the fluid which is absorbed by the roots.—In military science, a trench for undermining.—*Sap-green,* the inspissated juice of the berries of the Buckthorn, *Rhamnus catharticus.*—In botany, *sap-tubes* are those vessels by which the sap is conveyed.

Sapan-wood (Malabar), the wood of the tree *Cæsalpinia sapan,* used throughout Asia as a red dye-stuff.

Saphe'na (Gr. *saphes* distinct), in anatomy, the large vein of the leg, which ascends over the external ankle.

Sapinda'ceæ (Lat. *sapo* soap), a nat. order of exogenous plants, consisting of trees and shrubs, of which the Sapindus, or Soapwort, is the type.

Saponifica'tion (Lat. *sapo*), the change which fats undergo in contact with alkaline solutions at high temperatures; the formation of soap.

Sap'onine (Lat. *sapo*), a substance contained in the root of the *Saponaria officinalis,* producing lather.

Sap'onite, in mineralogy, a soft white mineral.

Sapota'ceæ (Lat. *sapo*), a nat. order of exogenous plants, consisting of exotic trees or shrubs, chiefly tropical and lactescent.

Sapph'irine, a mineral which occurs in translucent grains of a pale blue or green colour, and consists of alumina, silica, magnesia, lime, oxide of iron, oxide of manganese, and water: sp. gr. 3·42; H = 7·0—8·0.

Saproph'agans (Gr. *sapros* putrid, and *phago* to eat), a tribe of coleopterous insects, comprising those which feed on animal and vegetable substances in a state of decomposition.

Sar'cocarp (Gr. *sarx* flesh, and *karpos* fruit), in botany, the intermediate fleshy layer between the epicarp and endocarp.

Sar'cocele (Gr. *sarx,* and *kele* a tumour), in pathology, a tumefaction of the testicle.

Sarcocol'la (Gr. *sarx,* and *kolla* glue), the concrete juice of the *Penæa sarcocolla.*

Sar'coderm (Gr. *sarx,* and *derma* skin), in botany, the middle covering of a seed when it becomes succulent or juicy.

Sar'colite (Gr. *sarx,* and *lithos* a stone), in mineralogy, a variety of zeolite.

Sarcol'ogy (Gr. *sarx,* and *logos* a discourse), that part of anatomy which treats of the fleshy parts of the body.

Sarco'ma (Gr.), in pathology, a morbid tumour.

Sarcoram'phinæ (Gr. *sarx,* and *ramphos* a beak), in ornithology, a sub-family of birds, of the order Accipitres.

Sarco'sis (Gr. *sarx*), in pathology, the formation of flesh; a fleshy tumour.

Sarcot'ic (Gr.), a medicine which fills up ulcers with new flesh.

Sard (Gr. *sardion*), a mineral of a deep red colour; a variety of chalcedony.

Sar'dachate (Gr.), a sort of agate, containing sard.

Sar'donyx (Gr.), a precious stone; a chalcedony or cornelian.

Sarmen'tous (Lat. *sarmentum* a twig), in botany, applied to a stem which is long and almost destitute of buds or leaves.

Sarsaparil'la (Sp. *zarza* a bramble, and *parilla* a vine), a medicinal plant and its root; a species of Smilax.

Sarto'rius (Lat. *sartor* a tailor), in anatomy, the muscle which serves to throw one leg across the other, called the *tailor's muscle.*

Sas'soline, in chemistry, native boracic acid, which occurs in loose scaly particles. The pure varieties consist of borax and oxygen: sp. gr. 1·48. The name is derived from *Sasso,* at the hot springs of which it is deposited.

Sat'ellite (Lat. *satelles* an attendant), a secondary planet which revolves about a primary planet, as the moon round the earth.

Satin-spar, in mineralogy, fibrous limestone.—*Satin-wood,* a fine lemon-coloured wood, having a fragrant odour.

Satura'tion (Lat.), in chemistry, the union of one body with another by affinity, till the receiving body can contain no more.

Saturn, in astronomy, one of the primary planets of the solar system, which is attended by seven satellites.

Saturn's distance from the sun is above 890,000,000 miles; the mean diameter is 76,078 miles.

Satyr'idæ (Gr. and Lat.), the Argus Butterflies, some of which are among the largest butterflies in existence.

Saucisse, Saucis'son (Fr.), in fortification, a long pipe of pitched cloth or leather filled with powder, for the purpose of communicating fire to mines, caissons, &c.

Saur'ia, or **Sau'rians** (Gr. *sauros* a lizard), in zoology, the general term for the great family of Lizards. the second order of the class Reptilia of Cuvier. It consists of six families: the Crocodiles, Lizards, Iguanas, Geckos, Chamelions, and the Scincoidians.

Sauroid'ichnites (Gr.), in geology, a term applied to fossil footsteps of the saurian tribes.

Saus'surite, a mineral occuring in masses of a greenish white, and consisting of soda, silica, alumina, lime, magnesia, and oxide of iron: sp. gr. $3 \cdot 2—3 \cdot 4$; $H = 5 \cdot 5$. So called from M. Saussure, the discoverer.

Saxicav'idæ (Lat *saxum* a rock, and *cavea* a den), in malacology, a family of perforating bivalvular Molluscs, of which Saxicava is the type and genus.

Saxifraga'ceæ (Lat. *saxum,* and *frango* to break), a nat. order of exogenous plants, consisting of herbs or shrubs, of which Saxifraga, or Saxifrage, is the genus and type—a medicine which has the property of breaking the stone.

Sca'bies (Lat. *scabo* to scratch), in pathology, a contagious eruption, of which there are different species; as, *S. papuliformis,* Rank Itch; *S. lymphatica,* Watery Itch; *S. purulenta,* Pocky Itch; and *S. cachectica,* Scorbutic Itch.

Scaglio'la (Ital.), in architecture, a kind of ornamental plaster, or artificial stone, prepared from gypsum and Flanders glue, and made to imitate the colours of marble.

Scalene (Gr. *oblique*), in geometry, a triangle having the three sides unequal. —A *scalene cone* or *cylinder* is one of which the axis is inclined to the base.

Scales (Sax.), a mathematical instrument, consisting of various lines drawn on wood, ivory, brass, &c., and variously divided, according to the purpose they are intended to serve.— In arithmetic, the order of progression on which any system of notation is founded.

Scalezi'asis (Gr. *skaleuo* to root up, as pigs), in physiology, a disease peculiar to swine, which is purely parasitic, and depends for its origin on the introduction into the system of the mature and fecundated ova of *Tænia solium.* It is sometimes known as the measles; and the malady is most prevalent in those counties in Ireland where pigs are reared in small lots by poor people.—*Report of the Privy Council on Public Health and Diseases of Cattle.*

Scam'mony (Lat. *scammonia*), a species of Asiatic Convolvulus.—In pharmacy, a gum resin obtained from it, used as a drastic purge: sp. gr. $1 \cdot 23$.

Scanso'res (Lat. *climbers*), an order of birds, including those which have the toes arranged in pairs, two before and two behind.

Scapha (Gr. *skaphe* a skiff), in surgery, a double-headed roller for stopping hæmorrhage, &c.—In anatomy, the depression of the outer ear before the anti-helix.

Scaphidi'tes (Gr. *skaphe*), a family of clavicorn coleopterous insects, of which the Scaphidium is the type.

Scaphiduri'næ, a sub-family of the Sturnidæ or Starling family, of which the Scaphidura, or Boat-rails, is the type.

Scaphite (Gr. *skaphe*), in conchology, an elliptical-chambered shell of the family of the Ammonites.

Scap'olite (Gr. *skapos* a rod, and *lithos* a stone), in mineralogy, a siliceous mineral; pyramidal felspar, composed of silica, alumina, lime, and water: sp. gr. $2 \cdot 5$; $H = 5 \cdot 0$.

Scap'ula (Lat.), in anatomy, the shoulder-blade, which approaches nearly to a triangular figure.

Scarabæ'idæ (Lat.), a family of Lamellicorns, of which the Scarabæus, or Beetle, is the genus.

Scar'broite (from *Scarborough,* where it occurs), a mineral of a purely white colour, composed of alumina, silica, peroxide of iron, and water: sp. gr. $1 \cdot 48$.

Scarfing (Sax. *scearf*), in architecture, the act of covering with a scarf; the joining of two pieces of timber by notching or indenting, so as to appear but one.

Scarlati'na (Ital. *scarlattino*), that febrile exanthema called, in nosology, Rosalia; scarlet fever.

Scarp (Fr. *escarpe*), in fortification, the interior talus or slope of the ditch at the foot of the rampart.

Scelotyr'be (Gr. *skelos* the leg, and *tyrbe* commotion), in pathology, a contracted state of the limbs.

Scenog'raphy (Gr. *skene,* and *grapho* to write), the representation of solids in perspective; the art of perspective.

Schaal'stein (Germ.), in mineralogy, table-spar which occurs in laminated concretions.

Scheele's Green, an arseniate of copper;

a pigment obtained by mixing arseniate of potassa with sulphate of copper.

Scheel'ite (in honour of *Scheele*, who discovered it), a brittle mineral; a tungstate of lime.

Scheelium, in mineralogy, another name for tungsten.

Scher'erite (from *Scheerer*, who first discovered it), in mineralogy, an inflammable substance found in beds of lignite; resinous naphthaline.

Scherzan'do (Ital.), in music, noting a sportive style.

Schesis (Gr. *scheo* to hold), in medicine, habit or constitution of the body.

Schief'er-spar (Germ.), in mineralogy, slate spar; a foliated carbonate of lime.

Schil'ler-spar (Germ. *schillern* emitting rays of light), in mineralogy, a siliceous mineral, which occurs crystallized, composed of silica, magnesia, alumina, lime, oxide of iron, and water: sp. gr. 2·6; H = 3·5.

Schist (Gr. *schistos* cloven), in geology, a term adopted from the German, synonymous with slate.—*Schistose, Schistous*, relating to or containing schist; having a slaty texture.

Schizandra'ceæ, an order of exogenous plants, usually climbing shrubs, of which Schizandra is the type and genus.

Schneide'rian Membrane, in anatomy, the putuitary membrane, which secretes the mucus of the nose; so named from Schneider, the discoverer.

Schorl (Swed. *skor* brittle), a dark-coloured, opaque variety of tourmaline, composed of silica, potash, magnesia, and oxide of iron: sp. gr. 3·05—3·36. It is harder than hornblende.

Schorlite (Swed. *skor*, and Gr. *lithos* a stone), in mineralogy, a name sometimes given to topaz.

Schorly Granite, in geology, a kind of granite, consisting of schorl or tourmaline, quartz, felspar, and mica.

Schweinfurth Green, in chemistry, a double crystallizable salt of arsenite of copper and acetate of copper, used as a pigment,

Sciag'raphy (Gr. *skia* a shadow, and *graphe* description), the art of sketching or delineating shadows; art of dialling.—In architecture, the section or profile of a section of a building.—In astronomy, the art of finding the hour by the shadows of the sun or moon.

Sciat'ica (Gr. *ischion* the hip), in pathology, a rheumatic affection of the hip joint.—*Sciatic nerve*, the termination of the sacral or sciatic plexus, and the largest of all the nerves.

Science (Lat. *scientia*, from *scio* to know), the knowledge of things reducible to practice; a body of truths or principles; any species of knowledge or art; one of the seven liberal arts of the ancients—namely, grammar, rhetoric, logic, arithmetic, music, geometry, astronomy.—*Abstract science*, the knowledge of reasons and their conclusions.—*Natural science*, the knowledge of causes and effects, and of the laws of nature.—The *sciences* may be divided into three great classes: those which relate to number and quantity, those which relate to matter, and those which relate to mind. The first are called the mathematics; the second, natural philosophy; and the third, intellectual or moral philosophy. The terms *art* and *science* are frequently used without due discrimination and precision. In general, an *art* is that which depends on practice or performance, and *science* is that which depends on abstract or speculative principles. The theory of music is a *science*, the practice of it an *art*.

Scil'litine, in chemistry, the peculiar bitter principle obtained from the squill.

Scintilla'tion (Lat. *scintilla* a spark), in astronomy, the twinkling or tremulous motion of the light of the larger fixed stars.

Sciog'raphy. (See *Sciagraphy*.)

Sciol'to (Ital.), in music, a term denoting that the notes are to be performed in a distinct manner.

Sciop'tics (Gr. *skia* a shadow, and *optomai* to see), the science of exhibiting images of external objects, received through a double convex glass into a darkened room.

Sciop'tric (Gr.), a mechanical contrivance used in the camera obscura, for the purpose of giving motion to a lens in every direction.

Sciother'ic (Gr. *skia*), applied to an instrument for adjusting the time by means of the shadow.

Scir'rhus (Gr. *skirrhos* hard), in pathology, an induration of a gland, forming an indolent tumour not readily suppurating.

Scle'roderm (Gr. *skleros*, and *derma* skin), in ichthyology, a family of fishes having skins covered with hard scales.

Scle'rophthalmy (Gr. *skleros* hard, and *ophthalmos* the eye), in pathology, inflammation of the eye, with thickening of the orbicular muscle of the eyelids.

Sclero'sis (Gr.), a hard tumour.

Sclerot'ic (Gr.), in pathology, medicine which hardens and consolidates.

Sclerot'ica (Gr. *skleros*), in anatomy, one of the membranes of the eye.

Scleroti'tis (Gr. *skleros*), in pathology, sclerotic inflammation.

Scol'ecite (Gr. *skole* a worm), a crystallized mineral; the needle-stone; composed of silica, alumina, lime, soda, and water: sp. gr. 2·27.

Scom'bridæ (Lat. *scomber* a mackerel), in ichthyology, a family of marine acanthopterygious fishes, including the Mackerel, the Tunny, the Swordfish, &c.

Scorbu'tus (Sax. *scor*), in pathology, scurvy.

Score (Sax. *twenty*), in music, the original draft of the whole composition, in which the several parts are marked.

Sco'ria, *pl.* **Sco'riæ** (Lat.), ashes, dross, or slag from a smelting furnace; volcanic cinders.

Scor'odite (Gr. *skorodon* garlic, from the odour it emits under the blowpipe), a mineral of a pale leek-green, consisting of oxide of copper, arsenic acid, protoxide of iron, and water: sp. gr. 3·1; H = 3·5.

Scor'olite (Lat. *scoria* dross, and Gr. *lithos* a stone), a mineral of a reddish-brown colour, composed of silica, alumina, protoxide of iron, lime, and water: sp. gr. 1·71; H = 2.

Scorpæ'nidæ (Gr. *skorpios* a scorpion), in ichthyology, a family of fishes with smooth scales, of which the Scorpæna is the genus.

Scor'pion (Gr.), an insect or small reptile, having in its tail a venomous sting; a sea-fish; the eighth sign in the zodiac.—*Scorpion Grass, Scorpion Senna, Scorpion's Tail, Scorpion-wort*, names of plants or herbs.

Sco'tia (Gr. *darkness*), in architecture, a semicircular cavity or channel; a hollow moulding; a cavetto.

Scotodyn'ia (Gr. *dizziness*), in pathology, giddiness, with imperfect vision.

Scot'ograph (Gr. *skotos* dark, and *grapho* to write), an instrument with which a blind person may write.

Scot'omy (Gr. *skotoma*, from *skotoo* to darken), vertigo; dimness of vision.

Screw (Dutch *scroef*), one of the six mechanical powers, consisting of a spiral ridge winding round a cylinder. —The *double screw* consists in the combination of two screws of unequal fineness of thread, one of which works within the other.—The *micrometer screw* is a contrivance adapted to astronomical or optical instruments, for the purpose of measuring angles with great exactness.— *Screw propeller*, in nautology, an instrument for the propulsion of vessels, consisting of two or more twisted blades set on an axis running parallel with the keel, and revolving beneath the water at the stern.

Scrobic'ulus Cordis (Lat.), a name sometimes applied to the epigastric region; the pit of the stomach.

Scrof'ula (Lat.), in pathology, a disease characterized by indurated glandular tumours, especially about the neck.

Scroll, in architecture, a convolved or spiral ornament; also the volutes of the Ionic and Corinthian capitals.— In heraldry, the ornament placed under the escutcheon.

Scrophularia'ceæ (Lat. *scrofula*), in botany, an order of exogenous plants, consisting of herbs and sub-shrubs, of which Scrophularia, or Figwort, is the type.

Scrotal (Lat. *scrotum*), pertaining to or affecting the scrotum.—*Scrotal hernia*, protrusion of any of the contents of the abdomen into the scrotum.—*Scrotocele*, in pathology, a hernia descending into the scrotum.

Scrotum (Lat.), in anatomy, the cutaneous envelope of the testes.

Sculpture (Lat. *sculptura*), the act of imitating forms by chiselling and cutting away solid substances.

Scurvy (Lat. *scorbutus*), in pathology, a disease characterized by general debility, with hæmorrhage from various parts of the body.

Scutel'lum (Lat. *scutella* a saucer), in botany, the fructifying space upon the thallus of a lichen.

Scutibran'chiate (Lat. *scutis* a shell, and *branchiæ* gills), in ichthyology, having the gills covered by a shield-like shell.

Sea (Sax. *sæ*), a large body of salt water communicating with the ocean, as the Mediterranean Sea.—*Sea* is a word extensively used in composition, and its compounds may be formed almost at will.

Sea Anem'one, in botany, a plant; a highly-organized polype.

Seba'ceous (Low Lat. from *sebum* tallow), in anatomy, applied to glands which secrete an unctuous matter.

Secant (Lat. *secans*, from *seco* to cut), in geometry, a right line that cuts a curve or a circle.—In trigonometry, a straight line drawn from the centre of a circle to one extremity of an arc.

Secer'nent (Lat. *secerno* to separate), in pathology, medicine to promote secretion.—In anatomy, a secreting vessel of the body.

Second, in chronology, the sixtieth part of a degree of a circle, or of a minute.

Sec'ondary (Lat.), in geology, applied to a series of stratified rocks which lie above the primary and below the tertiary.—In pathology, a *secondary fever* is that which arises after a crisis, or the discharge of some morbid matter.

Secrete (Lat. *secerno*), in physiology, to separate some peculiar fluid or substance from the blood or nutritive fluid.—*Secretion* is the separation of this peculiar fluid.

Secre'tiveness, in phrenology, the organ which induces secrecy.

Sector (Lat. *a divider*), in geometry, a portion of the area of a circle, bounded by two radii and the intercepted arc; a mathematical instrument used in making diagrams, laying down plans, &c.; an astronomical instrument, constructed for determining the zenith distances of stars.

Sec'undine (Fr.), the fœtal membrane or membranes; the after-birth.

Secun'dum Artem (Lat. *according to art*), a term used in medical prescriptions, usually affixed when the making up of a recipe requires great care.

Sed'entaries (Lat. *sedentarius*, from *sedeo* to sit), a tribe of Spiders which rest motionless until their prey is entangled.

Sedum (Lat.), in medicine, an acrid substance which acts both as an emetic and a cathartic.

Segment (Lat. *a cutting*), in geometry, a part cut off from a figure by a line or plane; the part of a circle comprised between an arc and its chord.

Seidlitz Powders, in medicine, a term applied to powders used for making an effervescing aperient drink.—*Seidlitz water*, the mineral water of Seidlitz, in Bohemia, containing sulphate of magnesia, soda, and carbonic acid.

Seismom'eter (Gr. *seismos* an earthquake, and *metron* a measure), an instrument for measuring the shock of an earthquake and other concussions.

Sele'niate, in chemistry, a salt formed of selenic acid and a base.

Selen'ic (Gr. *selene* the moon), in chemistry, relating to selenium.—*Selenic acid* is a colourless liquid acid having a strong affinity for water, and capable of dissolving zinc, iron, copper, and gold. It consists of selenium and oxygen: sp. gr. 2·52.

Sele'niet, in mineralogy, a combination of selenium with zinc, lead, copper, silver, or palladium.—*Selenious acid* is an acid composed of selenium and oxygen.

Sele'nite (Gr.), in mineralogy, a crystallized sulphate of lime; sparry gypsum.

Sele'nium (Gr. *selene*), a sort of semi-metal, brittle, and not very hard.

Seleni'uret, a mineral composed chiefly of selenium, silver, and copper.

Selenog'raphy (Gr. *selene*, and *grapho* to describe), a description of the surface of the moon.

Sella Sphenoi'des, in anatomy, a part of the sphenoid bone, resembling a Turkish saddle.

Seltzer Water, a mineral water of Seltzer, in Germany, containing carbonic acid, &c.

Sematol'ogy (Gr. *semata* signs, and *logos* a treatise), the doctrine of lingual or verbal signs.

Semeiog'raphy, Semeiol'ogy (Gr. *semeion* a sign), in pathology, a description of symptoms or signs of disease.

Semen (Lat. *seed*), the fecundating fluid of animals; sperm.

Semi- (Lat.), a word of very frequent use as a prefix in composition, which signifies *half*, and sometimes *imperfect*; as, *semi-fluid*, *semi-transparent*, &c.

Sem'ibreve (Fr.), in music, a note of half the quantity of a breve, containing two minims, four crotchets, &c.

Sem'inal (Lat. *semen*), in botany, applied to the cotyledons or seed-leaves.

Semipal'mate (Lat. *semi* and *palma*), in zoology, having the toes connected together by a web.

Semiphyllid'ians (Lat. *semi*, and Gr. *phyllon* a leaf), a division of Gasteropods, consisting of those whose branchiæ are placed under the border of the mantle. It includes the genera Pleurobranchus and Umbrella, Ancyclus, Pleurobranchæa, Spericella, and Siphonaria.

Semi-pro'tolite (Lat. and Gr.), in geology, a semi-primigenous fossil.

Semiquaver, in music, a note whose duration is half that of a quaver.

Semit'ic (Gr. *sema* a sign or character), in philology, an epithet applied to the southern ramifications of the great stock of languages, consisting of the Arabic with the Ethiopic forms.

Sem'plice (Ital.), in music, implying that the movement is to be performed with simplicity and chasteness.

Sen'egine, in chemistry, the bitter acrid principle of senega.

Senna (Arab. *sana* or *sena*), a species of Cassia; the leaves of the tree used as a cathartic medicine.

Senso'rium (Lat.), in anatomy, the organ of sensation; the brain.

Sepal (Lat. *sepio* to enclose), in botany, a division or leaf of the calyx.

Se'pia (Lat. *the cuttle-fish*), a pigment prepared from a black juice secreted by the cuttle-fish.

Sepi'adæ (Lat.), a family of Cephalopods, including the various genera of the Cuttle-fishes, of which the Sepia is the type.

Sep'tangle, a figure having seven sides and seven angles.

Septa'ria (Lat. *septum* an enclosure), in geology and mineralogy, spheroidal masses of argillaceous limestone or ironstone, traversed interiorly by cracks in different directions.

Septen'trio (Lat.), that part of the heavens in which are the Seven Stars, or Charles's Wain ; the north.

Septici'dal (Lat. *septum*, and *cædo* to cut), in botany, an epithet applied to fruits or seed-vessels which open by dividing through the partitions of the ovary.

Sep'tuagint (Lat. *seventy*), the Greek version of the Old Testament, made at Alexandria about 284 B.C., so called because it was the work of seventy-two interpreters.

Septum, *pl.* **Septa** (Lat.), in anatomy, the partition of bone or muscle which separates two adjoining cavities ; as, *Septum cordis*, the fleshy substance which separates the right from the left ventricle of the heart ; *Septum lucidum*, the partition which divides the lateral ventricles of the brain.— In botany, any partition separating a body into two or more cells.

Seque'la (Lat. *sequor* to follow), in pathology, morbid affections which follow others, as anasarca after scarlatina, &c.

Seralbu'men (Lat.), albumen obtained from the serum of the blood.

Ser'aphine (Heb. *seraph*), a musical wind instrument of the organ species.

Sericul'ture (Lat.), the cultivation of silkworms.

Se'ries (Lat. *an order* or *succession*), in algebra, a number of quantities succeeding each other in regular increasing or diminishing order.

Serpenta'rius (Lat. *serpens* a serpent), in astronomy, a constellation in the northern hemisphere.—In ornithology, the Secretary Bird.

Ser'pentine (Lat. *serpens*), in mineralogy, a magnesian stone or rock, sometimes speckled like a serpent's back.

Serpi'go (Lat.), in pathology, a ringworm ; a tetter.

Serrate, Serra'ted (Lat. *serratus* notched like a saw).—In anatomy, *serratus magnus* is a muscle arising from eight or nine of the first ribs, and inserted into the base of the scapula ; —*Serratus posticus superior* is a muscle arising from the spinous processes of the last cervical, and the three upper dorsal vertebræ ;—*Serratus posticus inferior* is a muscle arising from the spinous processes of the dorsal and lumbar vertebræ.

Serum (Lat.), in physiology, the fluid which separates from blood during its coagulation.

Ses'amoid (Gr. *sesame* a seed, and *eidos* likeness), in anatomy, noting little bones at the articulations of the toes, resembling the seed of sesamum.

Ses'amum (Lat. *oily grain*), in botany, a genus of Oriental plants, from the seeds of which oil is obtained.

Sesqui-, a Latin prefix signifying *one and a half*, and used in chemistry to denote those compound substances in which there is one proportion and a half of oxygen, chlorine, or hydrogen, &c., to one of the base, as *sesquibromide*, a compound of 3 equivalents of bromine and 2 of a metal. —*Sesquitone*, in music, an interval of three semitones.

Sesquial'ter (Fr.), in geometry, having the ratio or proportion of 1½ to 1.

Sessile (Lat.), in botany, seated close upon anything without a stalk.

Seta, *pl.* **Setæ** (Lat. *a bristle*), in botany, the stalk that supports the theca, capsule, or sporangium of mosses.

Seton (Fr. from Lat. *seta*), in surgery, a kind of issue, usually made with a flat needle, threaded with a skein of silk.

Setose (Lat. *seta*), in botany and zoology, covered with bristles or stiff hairs.

Sev'erite, a siliciferous hydrate of alumina, so called from its being found near St. Sever, in France ; consisting of alumina, silica, and water : sp. gr. 2·06.

Sex- (Lat.), a prefix in compound words, signifying *six*.

Sex'angle (Lat. *sex*, and *angulus* an angle), in geometry, a figure having six sides and six angles.—*Sexangular*, having six angles.

Sextant (Lat. *a sixth part*), an astronomical instrument, formed of a sixth part of a circle, or 60°, for measuring the angular distances of objects by reflection. It is capable of very general application, but is chiefly used as a nautical instrument for measuring the altitudes of celestial objects.

Sextile (Lat.), in astrology, an aspect of two planets when distant from each other a sixth part of a circle, or 60°.

Sex'tuple (Lat. *sixfold*), in music, denoting a mixed sort of triple beaten in double time.

Sex'ual System, in botany, the classification founded by Linnæus on the number, position, &c., of the stamens and pistils.

Sforza'to (Ital.), in music, played forcibly.

Shaft, in architecture, the body of a column between the trunk and the capital.—In mechanics, a large and strong axle.

Shale (Germ. *schalen* to peel off), in geology, a term applied to all argillaceous or clayey strata which peel off in thin laminæ.

Shells, in the science of gunnery, hollow iron balls to throw out of mortars or howitzers;—*Message shells* are howitzer shells fired into a garrison or camp to communicate information;—*Shrapnel* shells are of a peculiar construction, invented by General Shrapnel.

Shingle, in geology, loose imperfectly-rounded stones and pebbles.

Shorlite, a mineral occurring at Altenburg, in Saxony.

Sial'ogogue (Gr. *sialon* saliva, and *agogos* drawing forth), a medicine that increases the flow of saliva and other fluids.

Sib'erite (from *Siberia*), in mineralogy, rubellite, or red tourmaline.

Sibthorpia'ceæ (from *Dr. Sibthorp* of Oxford), an order of exogenous plants, consisting of herbs with alternate undivided leaves.

Sidera'tion (Lat. *sidus* a star), in pathology, a name given to erysipelas of the face or scalp.

Side'real (Lat. *sideralis*, from *sidus*), pertaining to the stars.—The *sidereal day* is the time in which the earth makes a complete revolution on its axis according to the fixed stars, being nearly four minutes shorter than the solar day.—The *sidereal year* is the time in which the earth performs a complete revolution in its orbit, in reference to the fixed stars, which is equal to 365 days 6 hours 9 minutes 9·6 seconds.

Sid'erite (Gr. *sideros* iron), in mineralogy, the loadstone; a phosphate of iron.

Siderog'raphy (Gr. *sideros* steel, and *grapho* to write), the art or practice of engraving on steel.

Sider'olites (Gr. *sideros*, and *lithos* a stone), a name given to those nummulites which have a stellated appearance.

Sideroschis'tolite (Gr. *sideros*, *schistos* fissile, and *lithos* a stone), a black mineral which occurs in small six-sided prisms, composed of protoxide of iron, silica, alumina, and water: sp. gr. 3·0; H = 2·0—3·0.

Sid'eroscope (Gr. *sideros*, and *skopeo* to view), an instrument for detecting small particles of iron.

Si'enite (from *Siene* in Egypt), in mineralogy, a rock or stone compounded of quartz, felspar, and hornblende.

Sigilla'ria (Lat. *sigillum* a seal), in geology, a large genus of fluted tree stems, with seal-like punctures on the ridges.

Sigmoid (like the Greek letter *sigma*), in anatomy, a term applied to various structures in the body.

Sign (Lat. *signum*), in pathology, anything by which the presence of disease is known.—In astronomy, the twelfth part of the ecliptic.

Silex (Lat. *flint*), the siliceous material which constitutes the principal portion of most of the hard stones that compose the crust of the globe.

Silhouette' (Fr.), representation of an object, or a small portrait, filled in with a black colour; a profile likeness by shade.

Sil'ica, the scientific term for *silex*.

Silicalca'reous, consisting of silica and calcareous matter.

Silicate (Lat. *Silex*, which see), a compound of silicic acid and a salifiable base.—*Silicate of cerium* is a mineral which occurs in regular hexagonal prisms of a pale yellowish-brown colour.—The *silicates* constitute the greater number by far of the hard minerals which encrust the globe.

Silicical'ce (Lat. *silex*, and *calx* lime), a mineral substance which occurs in amorphous masses under strata of limestone in Provence.

Silicif'erous (Lat. *silex*, and *fero* to produce).—*Siliciferous hydrate of alumina*, a mineral which occurs in white and nearly opaque masses, perfectly sectile, and composed of alumina, silica, and water: sp. gr. 2·06—2·11. —*Siliciferous oxide of manganese*, a mineral which occurs massive, of a pale rose-red colour: sp. gr. 3·5; H = 5·0.

Silicifica'tion (Lat. *silex*), the conversion of a substance into stone by the infiltration of siliceous matter.

Silicimu'rite (Lat. *silex*, and *muria* brine), an earth composed of silica and magnesia.

Silic'eous, Silic'ious (Lat. *flinty*), containing silica. —*Siliceous oxide of zinc* is a mineral which occurs crystallized, stalactitic, mammillated, botryoidal, and massive; composed of oxide of zinc, silica, and water: sp. gr. 3·3—3·6; H = 5·0.

Sil'icite, a mineral composed of silica, alumina, lime, and soda.

Sili'cium, in chemistry, the metallic base of silica.

Sil'icon (Lat. *silex*), an elementary substance of a dark brown colour, incombustible in atmospheric air and oxygen gas, and infusible by the blowpipe.

Silic'ula, or **Sil'icule** (Lat.), in botany, a dry bivalve pericarp, divided interiorly by a membranous septum, which contains the seeds.

Sil'iqua (Lat.), in botany, the pod, husk, or shell of plants of the Pulse kind, as the Bean, Pea, &c.—In gold refinery, a carat, of which six make a scruple.

Sil'limanite, a mineral of a dark grey colour and vitreous lustre, so called from Professor Silliman, of Connecticut, composed of alumina, silica, oxide of iron, and water: sp. gr. 3·41; H = 6·0.

Sillon (Fr.), in fortification, a work raised in the middle of a ditch, in order to defend it when too wide.

Sil'phidæ (Gr. *silphe* a grub), a family of coleopterous insects, of which the Silpha is the type.

Silu'rian (from the ancient *Silures* of Wales), in geology, noting a series of rocks, or a group of fossiliferous strata, such as are found in Wales. The system is divided into the Ludlow rocks, Wenlock limestone, Caradoc sandstone, and Llandeilo rocks.

Silu'ridæ (Gr. *silouros*), a family of malacopterygious fishes, in which the body is mailed or naked, and without true scales: Silurus, or Cat-fish, is the type and genus.

Sil'vanite (Lat. *silva*), in mineralogy, a very sectile mineral of a metallic lustre, and composed of tellurium, gold, and silver.—*Dana*.

Silver (Ger. *silber*), in metallurgy, a white, malleable, ductile, and tenacious metal, of a brilliant lustre when polished. Silver is one of the fifty-five simple or elementary bodies, and included in the subdivision termed metals nearly white: sp. gr. when melted, 10·47; fusing point, 1873° Fahr.; symb. Ag; equiv. 108.—*German silver*, an alloy much used for the manufacture of domestic articles, such as forks, spoons, &c.; its ingredients being copper, nickel, and zinc.

Silvic, in chemistry, applied to an acid which, with pinic acid, constitutes the greater portion of common rosin.

Simaru'ba (Caribbean name), in medicine, the bark of the root *Quassia simaruba*, used as a tonic.

Simaruba'ceæ, a nat. order of exogenous plants, consisting of trees or shrubs, of which the Simaruba is the type.

Sim'ia (Lat. flat-nosed), in zoology, a genus of animals resembling man, as the Baboon, &c. The facial angle of the Orang-outang, a genus of Simia, or Ape-monkey, is 65°.

Sim'iadæ (Lat.), a family of the Quadrumana, distinguished by having eight cutting teeth, four canines, and twenty grinders.

Simoom (Ind.), a hot, suffocating wind which blows occasionally in Africa and Arabia.

Simple Equa'tion, in algebra, an equation in which the unknown quantity is only of one dimension, as $7\,ax = b$; $5x - ax = bc$.

Sina'pis (Lat. and Gr. *mustard*), a genus of cruciferous plants, from the seed of which is produced the well-known article mustard.—*Sinapine* is a peculiar principle extracted from mustard seed. It is supposed to contain sulphur, carbon, nitrogen, hydrogen, and oxygen.

Sina'pium (Lat. *sinapis*), in pharmacy, an infusion or decoction of mustard.

Sinap'oline (Lat. *sinapis*), a compound obtained by depriving oil of mustard of its sulphur by the action of baryta.

Sin'ciput (Lat.), in anatomy, the fore part of the head.

Sindon (Lat. *fine linen*), in surgery, a small rounded pledget of linen, with a thread attached thereto.

Sine (Lat. *sinus*), in geometry, a straight line drawn from one extremity of the arc of a circle, perpendicular to the radius, passing through the other extremity.—In trigonometry, a right line drawn from one end of an arc perpendicular upon the diameter.—The *cosine* of an arc is simply the *sine* of its complement.

Singul'tus (Lat. *a sob*), in pathology, a convulsive motion of the diaphragm; the hiccough.

Sin'ical Quadrant, an instrument formerly used for taking the altitude of the sun.

Sin'namine, a crystallized substance obtained from the oil of mustard.

Sinus (Lat. *an indentation*), in anatomy, a cavity in a bone widest at the bottom.—In surgery, an elongated cavity containing pus.

Sin'oper, **Sin'ople** (Gr.), in mineralogy, a red ferruginous quartz; a species of earth.

Siphon (Gr.), a bent tube used for drawing off liquids from casks.—*Siphon-gauge* is a glass siphon partly filled with mercury, used for indicating the degree of rarefaction which has been produced in the receiver of an air-pump.

Siphon'ifera, an order of testaceous Mollusca which have a siphon contained within a polythalamous shell.—*Brande*.

Siphonip'tera (Gr.), an order of dipterous insects which have a siphon-like mouth.

Siphonobran'chiate (Gr.), in zoology, an order of Gasteropods, including those in which the branchial cavity terminates in a tube or siphon.

Si'phuncle, a small siphon.

Sir'asis (Gr.), in pathology, a stroke of the sun; inflammation of the brain.

Sir'ius (Lat.), a star of the first magnitude in the constellation Canis Major, or the Great Dog; the brightest star in the heavens.

Siroc'co (Ital.), a periodical warm south wind, which generally blows in the south of Italy about Easter.

Sismon'dine, a mineral of a deep green colour, composed of silica, alumina, protoxide of iron, and water: sp. gr. 3·56.

Sitiol'ogy (Gr. *sition* food, and *logos*, a discourse), a treatise upon aliments.

Sitti'næ (Gr. *sitta* a woodpecker), a sub-family of the Certhiadæ, or Creepers, of which Sitta is the type.

Sivathe'rium (*Siva* a district in India, and Gr. *therion* a wild beast), in geology, an extinct genus of ruminant animals of great size.

Skeletol'ogy (Gr. *skeletos* dry), in anatomy, a treatise on the solid parts of the body.

Skel'eton (Gr. *skeletos*), the bones of an animal body separated from the flesh, and retained in their natural position.

Skew Bridge, in engineering and architecture, a kind of bridge introduced upon railroads, when the railway intersects obliquely any existing communication.

Skel'exite. (See *Scolecite*.)

Skor'odite. (See *Scorodite*.)

Skorzite, in mineralogy, a variety of epidote.

Slate (Fr. *éclater* to split; Irish *sglata* a tile), in geology, a dark-coloured stone of a structure termed schistose, which admits of being split into thin layers of considerable extent. It consists of silica, alumina, oxide of iron, manganese, potash, carbon, and water. The *Slate system* is divided into—*Plynlimmon rocks*, consisting of grauwacke and grauwacke slate; the *Bala limestone*, a dark limestone associated with slate, containing shells and corals; the *Snowdon rocks* consist of fine-grained slates, and of grauwacke and conglomerate.

Slubbing Machine, a machine used in the manufacture of woollen, for drawing out into slubs the rolls of wool.

Slugs, in gunnery, pieces of metal discharged from a gun.

Smalt (Germ. *schmalz*), a beautiful blue substance made by fusing glass with oxide of cobalt, by which a blue glass is formed, which, after being pulverized, is employed for relieving the yellow tint of writing paper and linen, staining glass, porcelain, and earthenware.

Smaragd, **Smarag'dus** (Gr.), in mineralogy, a name for the emerald.—*Smaragdine*, made of or resembling emerald.

Smarag'dite (Gr.), in mineralogy, a green diallage of a brilliant or emerald green colour.

Smelt (Germ. *schmelter* to melt), in metallurgy, to melt, as ore, for the purpose of separating the metal from extraneous substances.

Smila'ceæ, in botany, an order of dictyogenous herbaceous plants, so called from Smilax, the Greek name given to several plants, more especially to the Yew-tree.

Smyr'neæ, a family of umbelliferous plants, of which Smyrnium, or Myrrh, is the genus.

Snifting Valve, a valve in the steam-engine, so called because it makes a noise like a man *snifting* with a cold.

Snow (Sax. *snaw*), in meteorology, congealed watery vapour which falls from the bosom of the atmosphere in white flakes.—*Snow-line* is the elevation at which mountains are covered with perpetual snow.

Soap (Lat. *sapo*, Gr. *sapon*), a chemical compound of oily substances boiled with potash or alkaline solutions, and prepared for the purposes of washing, shaving, &c.—*Soap-stone*, in mineralogy, a magnesian stone, apparently unctuous to the touch. It is composed of silica, alumina, magnesia, potash, oxide of iron, and water: sp. gr. 2·4.

Socle (Ital. *zoccolo* a shoe), in architecture, a square member of less height than its horizontal dimension, serving to support vases or other ornaments.

Soda (Ital. and Sp.), in chemistry, a mineral or fixed alkali; an oxide of sodium; natron.—In commerce, it generally occurs as a *carbonate*, either pure, or in the impure forms of *barilla* and *kelp*.—The *carbonate of soda* is an article of the greatest importance in the soap, glass, and other manufactures.—*Soda-water*, a refreshing drink formed by dissolving carbonate of soda in water, and saturating the solution with carbonic acid.

Soda Alum, in mineralogy, a crystalline mineral, soluble in water, and composed of sulphate of soda, alumina, and water.

Soda Ash, in chemistry, an impure carbonate of soda.

So'dalite (*soda*, and Gr. *lithos* a stone), a mineral composed chiefly of silica, alumina, and soda.

So'dium, in mineralogy, the base of the alkali soda, and one of the fifty-five elementary substances: it is a metal possessing a strong lustre, and a colour very analogous to that of silver;

it fuses at 200°, and rises into vapour at a red heat: sp. gr. 0·97.

Solana'ceæ (Lat. *solanum* nightshade), a nat. order of exogenous plants, consisting of herbs or shrubs, of which Solanum is the genus.

Sola'nia, in chemistry, the active principle of *Solanum dulcamara*, or Woody Nightshade.

Sol'anine (Lat. *solanum*), a vegetable principle which occurs in several species of Solanum.

Sola'num (Lat.), in botany, a genus of plants of which there are different species; as, *S. tuberosum*, the plant of which the Potato is the root; *S. nigrum*, the Common Nightshade; *S. lycopersicum*, Love-apple or Tomato.

Solar (Lat. *sol* the sun), an epithet of frequent use in astronomy and chronology, as *solar* month, *solar* year.—The *solar system* is that part of the universe which comprises the sun and the various heavenly bodies that revolve around him.—*Solar cycle* is a period of twenty-eight years, which being elapsed, the Dominical or Sunday letters return to their former place, and proceed in the same order as before.—*Solar month* is the time which the sun takes to run through one entire sign of the ecliptic, the mean quantity of which is 30 days, 10 hours, 29 min., 5 sec.—In anatomy, *solar plexus* is an assemblage of ganglia, which are distributed to all the divisions of the aorta.

Solen (Gr. *a channel*), a surgical machine in which a broken leg is placed.

Solfata'ra (Ital.), in geology, a volcanic vent, from which sulphureous gases are emitted.

Solid (Lat. *solidus*), in geometry, a body which has length, breadth, and thickness.—A *solid angle* is an angle formed by three or more plane angles meeting in a point, and of which the sum of all the plane angles is less than 360°.—A *regular solid* is one which is terminated by equal and similar planes, so that the apex of their solid angles may be inscribed in a sphere.—In military science, *solid square* is a square body of troops; a body in which the ranks and files are equal.—In anatomy and medical science, the *solids* are the bones, flesh, &c., of animals, distinct from the fluids.

Solidun'gulates (Lat. *solidus*, and *ungula* a hoof), a tribe of Mammalia, which includes those with only a single hoof on each foot, as the Horse.

Sol'ipeds (Lat. *solidus*, and *pedes* feet), a class of animals with a single hoof on each foot, as the Horse, the Ass, and the Zebra.

Solmiza'tion, in music, a repetition of the notes of the gamut.

Solpu'gidæ, a family of tracheal Arachnides.

Solstice (Lat. *solstitium*, from *sol* the sun, and *sto* to stand), the time at which the sun is at the greatest distance from the equator; midsummer and mid-winter.—*Solstitial*, belonging to or happening at the solstice.—*Solstitial points*, the two points in the ecliptic at which the sun arrives at the time of the solstice.

Solu'tion (Lat. *solutio*, from *solvo* to loosen), the act of separating the parts by means of a fluid; thus, in dissolving salt in water we obtain a solution of the salt.—In pathology, the termination of a disease.—In surgery, *solution of continuity* is a dissolving the unity and continuity of parts, as in wounds, fractures, &c.—In mathematics, *solution* is the geometrical construction of a problem, or the algebraical expression of its conditions by an equation which gives the value of the unknown quantity.

Solvent (Lat. *solvo* to dissolve), in chemistry, any fluid or substance which renders other bodies liquid.

Somatol'ogy (Gr. *soma* the body, and *logos* a discourse), the doctrine of material substances; a treatise on the human body.

Som'ervillite, a crystallized mineral which occurs among the ancient scoriæ of Vesuvius.—*Dana*.

Sommite, a mineral, so called from Monte Somma, a part of Vesuvius, where it occurs.

Somnop'athy (Lat. *somnus* sleep, and Gr. *pathos* a passive state), a kind of mesmeric sleep; somnambulism.

Sona'ta (Ital. *sonare* to sound), a tune or composition to be performed wholly by instruments.—*Sonatina*, a short and simple sonata.

Sonom'eter (Lat. *sonus* sound, and Gr. *metron* a measure), an instrument for measuring sounds, or the intervals of sounds.

Sopra'no (Ital.), in music, the highest vocal part.

Sorbic Acid, an acid found in many fruits, particularly the apple, but most commonly obtained from the *Sorbus aucuparia*.

Sorbine, a crystalline, saccharine substance obtained from berries of the mountain-ash.

Sordaw'alite, a mineral occurring in opaque, greyish, or bluish-black coloured masses, so called from Sordawala, in Finland. Composition—silica, alumina, peroxide of iron, magnesia, phosphoric acid, and water : sp. gr. 2·53 ; H = 2·5—3·0.

Sordes (Lat.), in pathology, the viscid matter discharged from ulcers, &c.

Soric'idæ, in zoology, a family of Mammals, comprehending the Shrews, Moles, and Hedgehogs, of which Sorex, the Shrew, is the type.

Soro'sis (Gr.), in botany, a sort of fleshy fruit formed of compound receptacles.

Soru'binæ (Lat.), in ichthyology, a subfamily of the Cobitidæ, consisting of fishes with large lengthened heads, of which the Sorubium is the type.

Sorus (Gr. *soros* a heap), in botany, one of the small clusters of capsules or fruit dots on the back of the fronds of ferns.

Sospi'ro (Ital.), in music, a breathing rest.

Soteriol'ogy (Gr. *soterios* salubrious, and *logos* a discourse), a treatise on health, or the science of preserving health.

Sotto-voce (Ital.), in music, with a softened or under voice.

South (Sax.), one of the cardinal points of the compass ; the direction in which the sun always appears at noon to the inhabitants of the northern hemisphere.

Spadix (Lat.), in botany, a form of inflorescence in which the flowers are arranged round a fleshy rachis.

Spandrel, in architecture, the triangular space included between the curve of an arch and the square drip-stone over it.

Spar'gelstein (Germ.), in mineralogy, a variety of apatite of a wine-yellow colour ; asparagus-stone.

Sparia'næ (Lat.), in ichthyology, a subfamily of the Chætodonidæ.

Spar'idæ, a family of acanthopterygious fishes, resembling the Perches.

Spar'talite (Gr. *spartos* scattered, and *lithos* a stone), in mineralogy, red oxide of zinc, translucent and brittle : sp. gr. 5·4 ; H = 4·0.

Spasm (Gr. *spao* to draw), in anatomy, an abnormal involuntary contraction of muscular fibres.

Spasmol'ogy (Gr. *spasma* spasm, and *logos* a discourse), a treatise on convulsions.

Spathe (Gr. *spathe* a broad blade), in botany, a large coloured bract which encloses a spadix.

Spathic (Germ. *spath* spar), in mineralogy, foliated or lamellar.

Spathose Iron (Germ. *spath*), a mineral of a lamellar or prismatic structure, and a pearly lustre, composed of protoxide of iron, carbonic acid, oxide of manganese, and lime : sp. gr. 3·6 ; H = 3·5.

Spat'ulate (Lat. *spatula* a broad leaf),

in botany, applied to leaves narrow at the base, and widening towards a broad-crowned top.

Spavin (Fr.), in farriery, a disease of horses which generally causes lameness.

Species (Lat.), in botany and zoology, a class comprehended under a genus. A male and female of the same genus may procreate, and the offspring is called a mule or hybrid. Hybrids in the vegetable kingdom produce endless varieties, but not new species.— In mineralogy, *species* is determined by the form of the primitive crystal, or the ingredients of which a mineral is composed.

Specific (Fr.), in pathology, an efficacious medicine appropriated to the cure of some particular disease.

Specific Gravity, in chemistry and physicology, a term of very general application, as denoting the relative proportion of the weight of bodies of the same bulk as compared with rain water. Specific gravities are usually stated in whole numbers and decimal parts, that of water being stated as 1, except as relates to the gases, when the weight of atmospheric air is the unit. The following is a list of the specific gravities of the most common substances :—

Acid, acetic	1·062
—— arsenious	3·728
—— muriatic	1·200
—— nitric	1·271
—— sulphuric	1·850
Alcohol (pure)	·797
Alum	1·714
Barytes, sulphate of	4·865
Basalt	3·000
Blood, human	1·053
Butter	·942
Chalk	2·675
Cider	1·018
Coal, from	1·020 to 1·300
Diamond	3·521
Ether, sulphuric	·632
Fat of beef	·923
Felspar	2·700
Flint (black)	2·582
Gases : Atmospheric air	1·000
Carbonic acid	1·527
Carburetted Hydrogen	·972
Chlorine	2·500
Hydrogen	·069
Nitrogen	·972
Oxygen	1·111
Prussic acid	·937
Glass (flint)	3·000
Granite, from	2·613 to 2·956
Gunpowder, solid	1·745
——————— loose	·836
Gypsum	2·288
Honey	1·450

Ironstone (Carron)	3·281
Lead-glance	7·786
Limestone, compact	3·000
Marble, Carrara	2·716
Parian	2·560
Metals: Antimony	6·702
Arsenic	5·763
Bismuth	9·880
Brass	8·306
Cobalt	8·600
Copper	8·900
Gold, cast	19·25
—— hammered	19·35
Iridium, hammered	23·00
Iron, cast	7·248
—— bar, hardened	7·788
Lead	11·35
Manganese	8·000
Mercury (solid)	15·61
—— at 32° Fahr.	13·61
Platinum	21·47
Potassium	·865
Silver	10·49
—— hammered	10·51
Sodium	·972
Steel, hardened	9·840
Tin	7·291
Zinc, from	6·900 to 7·191
Mica	2·934
Milk	1·032
Naphtha, from	·700 to ·847
Nitre	1·900
Oil, essential, of Amber	·868
—————— Caraway	·904
—————— Cinnamon	1·043
—————— Cloves	1·036
—————— Lavender	·894
—————— Turpentine	·870
— expressed, of Linseed	·940
—————— Olives	·915
Opium	1·336
Pearl (Oriental)	2·750
Phosphorus	1·770
Plumbago	2·400
Porcelain (China)	3·384
Porphyry	2·972
Quartz, from	2·624 to 3·750
Spar, fluor	3·791
Spermaceti	·943
Steam of water	·481
Stone, paving	2·708
—— Portland	2·496
Sugar	1·606
Sulphur (native)	2·033
Talc	3·000
Vinegar, from	1·013 to 1·080
Water, distilled	1·000
—— of the sea	1·028
Wax (bees')	·964
Wine, Port	·997
—— Champagne	·997
Wood: Ash	·845
Box (Dutch)	1·398
Lignum Vitæ	1·333
Mahogany	1·063
Oak, heart of, sixty years old	1·170

Specifica'tion (Fr.), in architecture and building, a description at length of the materials and workmanship to be used in the erection of a building.

Spectrum, *pl.* **Spectra** (Lat.), in optics, the image of something seen after closing the eyes ; an optical image of the sun, or other luminous body, formed on a wall or screen by a beam of light.

Spec'ular Iron, a mineral which occurs lamellar and crystallized in many forms : sp. gr. 5·0 ; H = 5·5.

Spec'ulum, *pl.* **Spec'ula** (Lat.), a reflector formed of polished metal.—*Speculum metal* is an alloy of 2 parts of copper and 1 of tin, of which the reflectors of telescopes are usually made.

Speiss (Germ.), a brittle, reddish alloy, composed chiefly of nickel and arsenic.

Spelter, in mineralogy, native impure zinc, containing lead, copper, iron, arsenic, manganese, and plumbago.

Spermace'ti (Gr. *sperma* seed, and *ketos* a whale), a substance obtained from the oil found in the head of whales, employed for making ointments.

Sper'maphore (Gr. *sperma*, and *phero* to bear), in botany, that part of the ovary from which the ovule rises.

Spermat'ocele (Gr. *sperma*, and *kele* a tumour), in pathology, a hernia or swelling of the testicles.

Spermatozo'a (Gr. *sperma*, and *zoon* an animal), in zoology, minute bodies, considered by physiologists to be essential to impregnation.

Spermatozo'id (Gr.), in physiology, one of the reputed animalcules seen in sperm.—In botany, one of the vegetable filaments produced in the organs called antheridia, and which exist in the plants of many cryptogamous families.

Sperm-cell (Gr. *sperma*), in anatomy, one of the cells contained in the semen, in which the spermatozoa are formed.

Sphac'elus (Gr.), in pathology, a deep-seated gangrene of a limb or organ ; the death of a bone.

Sphæren'chyma (Gr. *sphaira* a sphere, and *enchyma* a tissue), in botany, vegetable tissue composed of spherical cells.

Sphæ'ronites (Gr. *sphaira*), in geology, a group of fossil Echinodermata found in the Silurian and Devonian strata.

Sphærula'cea (Gr.), in zoology, a family of Foraminifera, comprising the genera Miliola, Melenia, Saracenaria, and Textularia.

Sphæ'rulite (Gr. *sphaira*, and *lithos* a stone), a mineral which occurs in small botryoidal and spheroidal masses, composed of silica, alumina, potash and soda, magnesia, oxide of iron, and water: sp. gr. 2·4; H = 7—7·5.

Spheo'idæ, a family of hymenopterous insects, of which Sphex is the genus.

Sphene (Gr. *sphen* a wedge), a mineral of a foliated texture and vitreous lustre; an oxide of titanium.

Spheno- (Gr.), in anatomy, a prefix to compound words, implying connection with or relation to the sphenoid bone; as, *Spheno-maxillary,* belonging to the sphenoid and jaw bones;—*Spheno-parietal,* belonging to the sphenoid and parietal bones;—*Spheno-temporal,* belonging to the sphenoid and temporal bones.

Sphenoid (Gr. *sphen,* and *eidos* likeness), in anatomy, a bone at the base of the cranium.

Sphere (Gr. *sphaira*), in geometry, a solid body bounded by a surface of which every point is equally distant from the centre within a globe.—In astronomy, the concave expanse of the heavens.—In geology, the representation of the earth on the surface of a globe.—*Spherical trigonometry* is the science of spherical triangles.—*Armillary sphere,* an artificial representation of the circles of the sphere by means of brass rings.

Spherics, the doctrine and properties of the sphere; spherical trigonometry. —*Spherical angle* is an angle formed on the surface of a sphere by the intersection of two great circles, or circles whose planes pass through the centre.

Spheroid (Gr. *sphaira,* and *eidos* a likeness), in geometry, a solid approaching the figure of a sphere, produced by the revolution of a semi-ellipsis about its axis.

Spherom'eter (Gr. *sphaira,* and *metron* a measure), an instrument for measuring the thickness of small bodies, the dimensions of a sphere, the curvature of optical glasses, &c.

Spherostil'bite, a mineral that occurs in globular masses, which present a radiated structure and a brilliant fracture.

Spher'ulite (Gr. *sphaira,* and *lithos* a stone), in mineralogy, obsidian or pearl-stone.

Sphincter (Gr. *sphincho* to close), in anatomy, a general name for those muscles which close or contract the orifices they surround.

Sphragis'tics (Gr. *sphragis* a seal), the science of seals; the knowledge or study of seals and autographs.

Sphygmom'eter (Gr.), an instrument for counting arterial pulsations and measuring their strength.

Spica (Lat. *an ear of corn*), in surgery, a bandage, so called from its turns being thought to resemble the rows of an ear of corn.—In astronomy, *Spica Virginis* is the name of a bright fixed star of the first magnitude.—*Spicular,* resembling a dart; having sharp points.

Spicca'to (Ital.), in music, a term directing a division of the notes distinctly from each other.

Spic'ulum (Lat. *a dart*), in surgery, a small pointed piece of bone or other hard matter.

Spigelia'ceæ, a nat. order of exogenous plants, consisting of shrubs or sub-shrubs, of which Spigelia is the type,

Spikelet (Lat. *spica*), in botany, a small cluster of flowers, as in grasses.

Spikenard (Lat. *spica nardi*), a perennial plant or shrub; the oil or balsam produced from the plant.

Spilus (Gr. *spilos* a spot), in pathology, a partial thickening of the rete mucosum.

Spina Bif'da (Lat. *spina* a thorn, *bis* twice, and *findo* to cleave), in pathology, a disease attended with an incomplete state of some of the vertebræ, and a fluid swelling.

Spinal Cord, in anatomy, that part of the nervous system contained in the canal of the vertebral column.— *Spinal system of nerves,* in anatomy, the nerves which convey impressions to and from the spinal cord.

Spindle (Sax.), in geometry, a solid generated by the evolution of a curve line about its base.—In mechanics, the axis of a wheel or roller.

Spine (Lat. *spina*), in anatomy, the vertebral column or backbone.

Spinel'lane, in mineralogy, a dodecahedral variety of zoolite, composed of soda, silica, alumina, lime, oxide of iron, sulphuric acid, and water: sp. gr. 2·28.—*Dana.*

Spinelle (Fr.), in mineralogy, a crystallized ruby; a mineral exhibiting various shades of red, violet, or yellow; composition—alumina, magnesia, silica, lime, and protoxide of iron: sp. gr. 3·5; H = 8·0.

Spinthere (Fr.), a mineral of a greenish-grey colour, found in the department of the Isère, in France.

Spi'racle (Lat. *spiro* to breathe), a term applied to the external openings of the air-tubes of insects.

Spiral (Lat. *spira* a spire), in geometry, the name given to a class of curves distinguished by the general property of continually receding from a centre or pole, while they continue to revolve about it.

Spirit Level, in surveying and levelling, an instrument for determining a plane parallel to the horizon, consisting of a tube of glass nearly filled with spirit of wine, and hermetically sealed, so that when placed in an exactly horizontal position the bubble of air in the liquid stands exactly in the centre of the tube.

Spirito'so, or **Con Spir'ito** (Ital.), in music, a term denoting a movement to be spiritedly performed.

Spirom'eter (Lat. *spiro* to breathe, and Gr. *metron* a measure), in pathology, an instrument for measuring the quantity of air employed in respiration, and the capacity of the lungs.

Spiru'lidæ, a family of polythalamous, decapodous, dibranchiate Cephalopods, of which Spirula is the only genus.

Spis'situde (Lat. *spissus* thick), in chemistry and medicine, a term applied to substances which are neither perfectly solid nor perfectly liquid.

Splanchnog'raphy, Splanchnol'ogy (Gr. *splanchna* the bowels), that part of anatomy which treats of the viscera.

Splanchnot'omy (Gr.), dissection or anatomy of the viscera.

Spleen (Gr.), a spongy viscus of an oval form.

Splenal'gia (Gr. *splen* the spleen, and *algos* pain), in pathology, a painful affection of the spleen.

Splene'tis (Gr. *splen*), in pathology, inflammation of the spleen.—*Splenic apoplexy* is one of the disorders peculiar to horned cattle and sheep, which generally results from high feeding, when there is a transudation of blood in the substance of the spleen, accompanied by discharges of fæces and urine tinged with blood, when the animal bellows, moans, and soon dies.—*Report of the Privy Council on Public Health and Diseases of Cattle.*

Sple'nius (Gr. *splen*), in anatomy, a cervical muscle which brings the head and neck backwards laterally.

Spleniza'tion (Gr. *splen*), in pathology, a change induced in the lungs by inflammation, causing them to resemble the spleen.

Splen'ocele (Gr. *splen*, and *kele* a tumour), in pathology, hernia of the spleen.

Splenol'ogy (Gr.), a treatise on the spleen.

Splenot'omy (Gr. *splen*, and *tome* incision), dissection of the spleen.

Spod'umene (Gr. *spodoo* to reduce to ashes), a mineral found in laminated masses, and composed of silica, alumina, lithia, and oxide of iron: sp. gr. 3·0; H = 6·5.

Spondia'ceæ, a nat. order of exogenous plants, consisting of tall trees, of which Spondias, or the Hog-plum, is the genus.

Spongia'ria (Gr. *spongos* a sponge), in natural history, a class of beings including Sponges.

Spongio'sa Ossa (Lat. *spongia* a sponge), in anatomy, applied to bones situated in the lower part of the side of the nose.

Sporad'ic (Gr. *scattered*), in pathology, applied to diseases which attack few at a time.

Sporan'gium (Gr. *spora* a seed), in botany, the case in which the reproductive matter of many cryptogamic plants is enclosed.

Spore (Gr.), a seed.

Sporules (Gr. *spora*), in botany, the minute organs in flowerless plants which are the analogues of seeds in flowering plants.

Spring (Sax.), a word from which many useful compounds are formed in mechanical science; as, *Spring-balance*, a machine in which the elasticity of a spring of tempered steel is employed to measure weight or force; —*Spring-box*, the cylindrical box which contains the spring of a watch; —*Spring-tides*, the tides at the new and full moon, when the sun and moon are in a straight line with the earth, and by their joint effect the waters of the ocean are raised.

Spur (Sax.), in architecture, a brace which props the two pillars supporting a wooden bridge.—In fortification, a wall that crosses a part of the rampart, and joins the town wall.— In machinery, *spur-gear* are wheels whose axles are parallel to each other, or wheels whose teeth are perpendicular to their axles.

Sputum (Lat. *spuo* to spit), in pathology, that which is discharged from the mouth in disorders of the breathing organs.

Squal'idæ (Lat. *squalis* a shark), in ichthyology, the Shark family.

Squali'næ, a sub-family of the Squalidæ.

Squama (Lat. *a scale*), in botany, an epithet applied to the scale-like plates with which various parts or organs of plants are invested.—In zoology, the term is employed to denote the hard and horny covering of many animals, as in reptiles, fishes, &c.—*Squamous suture*, in anatomy, is the suture between the temporal and parietal bones, the one overlapping the other like a scale.

Squamose (Lat. *squama*), in anatomy, an epithet applied to a suture of the cranium, from the edges covering it like the scales of a fish.—In botany and zoology, applied to surfaces covered with scales.—In conchology, consisting of scales spreading every way, or standing upright.

Squamipen'nes (Lat. *squama*, and *penna* a fin), in ichthyology, a family of acanthopterygious fishes.

Square (Lat. *quadratus*), in geometry, a right-angled figure, having four equal sides, and as many right angles.—In algebra and arithmetic, the *square root* of any quantity is the quantity which, being multiplied into itself, produces the given one.—*Square number*, a number whose root can be exactly found, or the product of a number multiplied by itself. — *To square the circle* is to attempt to produce a rectilineal figure equal to a given figure. — In architecture, *square staff*, a piece of wood used for fortifying the angles of plaster-work intended to be papered over.—In military affairs, a form into which troops are disposed on particular occasions, as in resisting a charge of cavalry.

Stacca'to (Ital.), in music, a character (') denoting that the notes over which it is placed should be performed in a separate manner.

Stackhous'eæ, Stackhousia'ceæ, a nat. order of exogenous plants, consisting of herbs, occasionally somewhat shrubby.

Stacte (Gr.), the gum that distils from the myrrh tree.

Staff, *pl.* **Staves** (Sax. *stæf*), in music, the five lines, and the spaces between them, on which music is written.—In military science, the officers who are attached to a commander of an army, comprising a quartermaster-general, adjutant-general, &c.

Stagma (Gr.), in chemistry, any distilled liquor.

Stalac'tite, *pl.* **Stalac'tites** (Gr. *stalaktos*, from *stalasso* to drop), in mineralogy, a concretion of carbonate of lime, found pendent, like icicles, from the roofs and sides of arches and caves in calcareous regions.

Stalag'mite (Gr. *stalagmos* a drop), in mineralogy, a stalactitical deposit of carbonate of lime, found upon the floors of calcareous caverns.

Stamen, *pl.* **Stamens** (Lat.), in botany, the male apparatus or fertilizing organ of a flower, consisting of filament, anther, and pollen.

Stan'nary (Lat. *stannum* tin), the tin mines of a district; the royal rights with respect to tin mines.

Stapes (Lat. a *stirrup*), in anatomy, one of the bones of the internal ear, so called from its shape.

Staph'yline (Gr. *staphyle* a bunch of grapes), having the form of a bunch of grapes.—In anatomy, pertaining to the uvula.

Staphylin'idæ, in entomology, a family of coleopterous insects which fly with great velocity, and of which the Staphylinus, or Rover Beetle, is the type.

Staphylo'ma, or **Staphylo'sis** (Gr. *staphyle* a grape), in pathology, an increase in the size of the cornea of the eye, almost invariably accompanied by more or less opacity.

Staphylon'ous (Gr. *staphyle*, and *onkos* a swelling), in pathology, tumefaction of the uvula.

Staphylor'aphy (Gr. *staphyle*, and *raphe* a suture), in surgery, an operation for uniting a cleft palate.

Starch, a vegetable product which occurs abundantly in the seeds of the Cerealia, and in many roots, as the potato and arrowroot.

Statics (Gr. *statike*), in physics, that branch of mechanics which treats of the equilibrium, weight, or pressure of bodies while at rest.

Statis'tics (Lat.), the science which treats of the condition of a country in relation to its extent, population, and resources.

Stat'uary (Lat. *statuarius*), a statue or a group of statues; art of carving or of casting statues.

Stau'rolite (Gr. *stauros* a cross, and *lithos* a stone), in mineralogy, a silicate of baryta and alumina.

Stau'rotide (Gr. *stauros*), in mineralogy, the prismatic garnet or grenatite.

Steam (Sax.), in physics, the elastic fluid into which water is converted by continued application of heat.—*Steam-engine*, an engine acted upon by the expansive force of steam, and employed to impel boats, cars, and other machinery.—*Steam-gauge*, a contrivance to show the exact amount of pressure of steam.—*Steam-gun*, an instrument by which balls and other projectiles may be projected by steam.—*Steam-whistle*, a pipe attached to the boiler of a steam-engine, from which steam escapes with a bold, hissing noise.

Ste'arate (Gr. *stear* suet), in chemistry, a salt consisting of stearic acid and a base.

Ste'arine (Gr.), one of the proximate elements of animal fat, as lard, tallow, &c.—*Stearic acid* is an acid obtained from stearine, an impure variety of which is largely used as a substitute for wax in candle-making.

Stearop'tene, a crystalline substance obtained from many of the essential oils.

Ste'atite (Gr. *stear*), in mineralogy, a magnesian mineral of fatty lustre and greasy feel; a kind of soapstone; composition—silica, magnesia, oxide of iron, and water: sp. gr. 2·65.

Steat'ocele (Gr. *stear*, and *kele* a tumour), in pathology, a hernia or tumour in the scrotum containing fat.

Steato'ma (Gr.), an encysted tumour; a species of wen.

Steel (Sax. *styl*), in metallurgy, iron combined with a portion of carbon; hardened and refined iron.

Steganog'raphy (Gr. *steganos* covered, and *graphe* writing), the art of writing in secret characters or ciphers.

Steg'anopods (Gr. *steganos*, and *podes* feet), a family of Swimming birds.

Stegno'sis (Gr.), in pathology, constipation.

Stegnot'ic (Gr.), a binding or costive medicine.

Stein'erite, in mineralogy, a variety of iolite, of a blue colour.

Stein'mannite, a mineral with a fine granular composition and metallic lustre: sp. gr. 6·83; H = 2·5.

Stella (Lat. *a star*), in surgery, a bandage or roller so as to keep back the shoulders.

Stella'tion (Lat. *stella*), radiation of light, as from a star.

Steller'idæ (Lat.), in ichthyology, a family of Radiata, including the Starfishes.

Stellite (Lat. *stella*), a snow-white translucent mineral observed in the neighbourhood of Kilsyth, near Glasgow.

Sten'idæ (Gr. *stenos* narrow), in entomology, a family of coleopterous insects, of which Stenus is the type.

Stenocar'dia (Gr. *stenos*, and *kardia* the heart), in pathology, constriction of the heart.

Stenog'raphy (Gr. *stenos*, and *graphe* writing), the art of writing in shorthand.

Steppe (Rus.), in physical geography, a plain of vast extent, uncultivated, but sometimes covered with luxuriant vegetation.—In pathology, *steppe disease* is a dangerous and often fatal disease peculiar to the ox tribe. It proves the most fatal of all cattle plagues when it crosses the Russian frontier into Central Europe.—*Report of the Privy Council on Public Health and Diseases of Cattle.*

Sterculia'ceæ (Lat. *sterculium* a dunghill), an order of exogenous plants, composed of large, umbrageous, tropical trees, of which the Sterculia is genus.

Sterelmin'tha (Gr. *stereos* solid, and *helmins* a worm), parasitic worms.

Stereog'raphy (Gr. *stereos*, and *graphe* description), the representation of solids on a plane. That branch of solid geometry which demonstrates the properties, and shows the construction, of all regularly-defined solids.

Stereom'etry (Gr. *stereos*, and *metron* measure), the art of measuring solid bodies.—*Stereometer* is an instrument for determining the specific gravities of bodies.

Ster'eoscope (Gr. *stereos*, and *skopeo* to view), in optics, a binocular instrument for viewing small pictures, consisting of a double tube, through which two objects, taken from different points of view, appear as if concentrated into one, while the relief, or perspective, is so wonderfully brought out as to make the two pictures look like one solid reality, agreeably to the laws of monocular and binocular vision.—*National Cyc. Suppt.*

Stereot'omy (Gr.), the art of cutting solid bodies for certain purposes, as walls, arches, &c.

Ster'eotype (Gr. *stereos*, and *typos* type), the art of casting, from movable types, solid metallic plates, to be used in printing. — *Stereotypography* is stereotype printing.

Sternach'idæ (Lat.), a family of apodal fishes.

Stern'bergite, in mineralogy, a foliated ore of silver; composition—silver, iron, and sulphur: sp. gr. 4·2; H = 1·0.

Sternum (Lat.), in anatomy, the breastbone; the simple or compound bone which completes the thoracic cage anteriorly.—*Sternalgia* is pain about the sternum.

Sternu'tatory (Lat. *sternuo* to sneeze), in pharmacy, medicine that provokes sneezing.

Stethom'eter (Gr. *stethos* the breast, and *metron* a measure), an instrument for measuring the comparative mobility of the chest in cases of diseases of the lungs.

Steth'oscope (Gr. *stethos*, and *skopeo* to view), in pathology, an instrument for exploring the chest, or ascertaining its diseases by sounds.

Sthenic (Gr. *sthenos* strength), an epithet applied to diseases which are the result of inflammatory or increased action.

Stib'ium (Lat.), antimony.

Stigma, *pl.* **Stig'mata** (Gr. *a brand*), in botany, the upper extremity of the pistil, or that part which receives the pollen.

Stilagina'ceæ (Lat.), a nat. order of exogenous plants, consisting of trees or shrubs, of which the Stilago is the type.

Stilbite (Gr. *stilbo* to glitter), a white mineral of a vitreous lustre, consisting of silica, alumina, lime, and water: sp. gr. 2·0; H = 3·5.

Stil'latory (Lat. *stillo* to distil), a vessel in which distillation is performed; a laboratory.

Stilpnom'elan (Gr. *stilpnos* glittering, and *melan* ink), a dark greenish mineral which occurs in crystalline, lamellar, and fibrous masses.

Stilpnosid'erite (Gr. *stilpnos*, and *sideros* iron), a dark-coloured mineral, which occurs in botryoidal groups, massive and dendritic; composition —oxide of iron, silica, and water: sp. gr. 3·6; H = 4·5.

Stim'ulant, Stim'ulus (Lat.), in medicine, that which produces a rapid and transient increase of vital energy.

Stipe (Lat. *stipes* a stake), in botany, the stem or base of a frond.

Stip'ula (Lat.), in botany, a scale which protects the nascent leaves of plants.

Stockade (Ital. *stocco*), in fortification, a sharpened post or stake; a line or enclosure formed with pointed stakes.

Stoichiom'etry (Gr. *stoichizo* to arrange, and *metron* a measure), in chemistry, that branch which treats of the proportions that substances must have when they neutralize each other.

Stomach Pump, a small pump or syringe for drawing liquids out of the stomach.

Stomach'ic (Gr. *stoma* the stomach), a medicine that strengthens the stomach, and excites its action.

Stoman'thrax (Gr. *stoma*, and *anthrax* inflammation), an inflammatory disease of the stomach in cattle and sheep.

Stom'apods (Gr. *stoma*, and *podes* feet), in zoology, an order of Crustaceans.

Stom'ata (Gr.), in botany and zoology, oval orifices in the covering of some plants, and the cuticle of some animals.

Stomatog'raphy (Gr. *stoma*, and *graphe* description), an anatomical description of the mouth.

Stomatorrha'gia (Gr. *stoma*, and *rhegnymi* to burst forth), in pathology, hæmorrhage from the stomach.

Stone (Sax. *stan*), a mineral not ductile or malleable; an indurated mass of earthy matter; a concretion of some species of earth, as lime, silex, clay, and the like; a measure of weight in different parts of Europe, the standard British stone being 14 lbs. avoirdupois.

Storax (Gr. *gum resin*), a fragrant balsam, the produce of the plant *Styrax officinalis*.

Strabis'mus (Lat.), an unnatural obliquity in the axis of the eye; a squinting.—*Strabotomy*, in surgery, is removal of strabismus by dividing the muscle or muscles which distort the eyeball.

Strahlstein (Germ. *strahl* a beam, and *stein* a stone), in mineralogy, a variety of hornblende

Stram'eny (Gr.), a narcotic plant used in medicine; the Thorn Apple.

Stran'gury (Gr. *strangx* a drop, and *ouron* urine), in pathology, a difficulty in voiding urine, attended with pain.

Strasci'no (Ital.), in music, a grace note used only in slow passages.

Strass, in mineralogy, a compound substance used in making artificial gems.

Stratarith'metry (Gr. *stratos* an army, *arithmos* number, and *metron* measure), the act of drawing up an army or body of men in a geometrical figure.

Strateget'ics (Gr. *stratos*), that branch of military science which relates to the disposition and arrangement of an army for battle; military tactics.

Strat'egy (Gr. *stratos*), the art or science of arraying and conducting an army.

Stratog'raphy (Gr. *stratos*, and *grapho* to describe), a description of armies, or whatever relates to them.

Stratum, *pl.* **Strata** (Lat.), in mineralogy and geology, a layer or bed of anything.

Stratus (Lat. *spread abroad*), in meteorology, a cloud that rests on the earth's surfaces.

Strepito'so (Ital. *noisy*), in music, denoting the passage to be executed in an impetuous style.

Strepsip'tera (Gr. *strepho* to turn, and *pteron* a wing), in ornithology, an order of insects in which the first pair of wings are represented by twisted rudiments.

Stretto (Ital. *narrow*), in music, the opposite of *largo*, to indicate that it is to be performed short and concisely.

Striæ (Lat.), in conchology, the small channels in the shells of cockles and scallops.—In architecture, fillets or rays that separate the furrows of fluted columns.

Stridor Den'tium (Lat.), in pathology, grinding of the teeth, a common symptom during sleep in children affected with intestinal irritation.

Striges (Lat.), in architecture, the channels of a fluted column.

Strig'idæ, a family of rapacious birds, generally of nocturnal habits, of which Strix, the Owl, is the genus.

Strigose (Lat.), covered with rough strong hairs, pressed together.

Strob'ilites (Gr.), fossil remains of cone-like fruit.

Strom'bidæ, a family of Gasteropods with winged shells, of which Strombus is the genus.

Stron'gylus (Gr. *cylindrical*), in entomology, a parasitic insect which abounds in the respiratory organs of calves and pigs. These parasites are very fatal to cattle. Camper noticed a perfect ball of these worm-like parasites in the air passages of a calf, which effectually obstructed the windpipe.—*Report of the Privy Council on Public Health and Diseases of Cattle.*

Stron'tia, a white earth contained in a mineral found at Strontian, in Scotland.—*Strontianite* is the native carbonate of strontia.—*Strontium* is a peculiar metal which forms the metallic base of strontia.

Stroph'ulus (Lat.), an eruption of pimples on the skin, peculiar to infants.

Struma (Lat.), in pathology, an enlarged gland; scrofula.—In botany, a cellular swelling where the leaf joins the midrib.

Struthion'idæ, in ornithology, a family of gigantic birds, generally with wings too short to support flight, of which Struthio, the Ostrich, is the genus.

Strychna'ceæ, an order of exogenous plants, of which Strychnos is the genus.

Strych'nia, a poisonous alkaline substance extracted from the *Strychnos nux vomica;* strychnine.—In botany, a kind of nightshade.

Strychnine, an alkaline principle, excessively poisonous.

Stucco (Ital.), a kind of plaster, mortar, or calcareous cement, used for laying on the surface of buildings, &c.

Stufa (Ital.), a jet of steam issuing from a fissure in the earth; not uncommon in volcanic countries.

Sturion'idæ (Lat.), in ichthyology, a family of cartilaginous fishes, the Sturgeons, the bodies of which are covered with large osseous plates or tubercles.

Stur'nidæ (Lat. *sturnus* the starling), a family of birds smaller and less robust than the Corvidæ, or Crows.—*Sturninæ,* a sub-family of the Sturnidæ.

Stycos'tega, a family of microscopic Foraminifera.

Stylagalma'ic (Gr. *stylos* a column, and *alma* an ornament), in architecture, applied to figures which serve as columns.

Style (Gr. *stylos*), in botany, the stalk or elongation of the ovarium which supports the stigma.

Stylida'ceæ (Gr. *stylos*), in botany, a nat. order of plants, consisting of caulescent herbs or shrubs, of which Stylidium is the genus.

Sty'lobate (Gr. *stylos,* and *basis* a base), in architecture, an uninterrupted base below a range of columns or pillars.

Styloid (Gr. *stylos*), a term of frequent application in anatomy, and generally applied to a process of the temporal bone.—*Stylo-hyoideus,* a muscle arising from the styloid process, and inserted into the os hy-

oides, which it raises.—*Stylo-glossus,* a muscle arising from the styloid process and the stylo-maxillary ligament, and inserted into the root of the tongue.—*Stylo-pharyngeus,* a muscle arising from the styloid process, and inserted into the pharynx and back part of the thyroid cartilage.—*Stylo-mastoid,* applied to a foramen situated between the styloid and mastoid processes, through which the portio dura of the seventh pair of nerves passes.—*Stylo-maxillary,* a ligament which extends from the styloid to the angle of the jaw.—*Craig.*

Stylom'eter (Gr. *stylos,* and *metron* a measure), in architecture, an instrument for measuring columns.

Stylop'idæ (Gr. *stylos,* and *ops* the countenance), in entomology, a family of parasitical insects found on several genera of bees and wasps, of which Stylops is the genus.

Styptic (Gr. *styptikos,* from *stypho* to restrain), a remedy to check the flow of blood or hæmorrhage; an astringent medicine.

Styra'ceæ (Gr. *styrax* a reed), a nat. order of exogenous plants, consisting of elegant trees, of which Styrax is the type.—*Styracine* is a substance extracted from Styrax.

Sub-, a Latin preposition of frequent use in scientific terms, signifying *under* or *below;* and in composition it signifies a less or subordinate degree.

Sub-Ap'ennine, in geology, a term applied to strata of the older pliocene period, resting upon the inclined beds of the Apennine range, all consisting of tertiary deposits.

Subcar'bonate, in chemistry, a salt or carbonate having an excess of the base.

Subcar'buretted, carburetted in a subordinate degree.

Subcla'vian (Lat. *sub,* and *clavis* a key), in anatomy, applied to vessels, nerves, &c.; as, the *subclavian* arteries.

Subdiaphragmat'ic (Lat. *beneath the diaphragm*), in anatomy, applied to a plexus distributed to the diaphragm.

Subdu'plicate (Lat.), in arithmetic and algebra, the *subduplicate* ratio of two qualities is that of their square roots.

Suber'ic Acid (Lat. *suber* the cork tree), an artificial substance produced by treating rasped cork with diluted nitric acid.

Subhydrosul'phuret, a compound of sulphuretted hydrogen with a base.

Sub'limate (Lat.) is the product of sublimation, as of quicksilver raised in the retort.

Sublima'tion (Lat.), in chemistry, a process by which solids are converted into vapour, which is again condensed, and often reduced to a crystalline form.

Subli'tion (Lat.), in painting, the laying of the ground colour under the perfect colour.

Submas'toid, in anatomy, an epithet applied to a branch given off by the seventh pair of nerves.

Submax'illary, situated under the jaw.

Submul'tiple, a number or quantity which has a geometrical ratio to another number or quantity, by being contained in it a certain number of times exactly; thus 3 is a submultiple of 21.

Subnor'mal (Lat.), in geometry, that part of the axis of a curved line which is intercepted between the ordinate and the normal.—In all curves it is the third proportional to the subtangent and the ordinate.

Sub-ovate (Lat. *sub*, and *ovum* an egg), nearly in the shape of an egg.

Sub-oxide, a compound consisting of 2 equivalents of the positive elements and 1 of oxygen.

Subperitone'al (Lat. *sub*, and *peritoneum*), in anatomy, lying beneath the peritoneal membrane.

Subplinth, in architecture, a lower plinth placed under the principal one in columns and pedestals.

Subquad'rate (Lat.), nearly square.

Subquin'tuple (Lat.), having the ratio of 1 to 5.

Sub-resin, a name applied to that portion of a resin which is soluble only in boiling alcohol, and is thrown down again as the alcohol cools.

Subsalt, in chemistry, a salt having an excess of the base.

Sub-scap'ular, in anatomy, being beneath the scapula.

Subsoil, in agriculture and geology, the soil under the superficial soil.

Substra'tum, *pl.* **Substra'ta** (Lat. *spread under*), a stratum lying under another stratum; a subsoil.

Substyle, in dialling, the straight line formed by the intersection of the face of the dial with the perpendicular plane which passes through the gnomon.

Subsul'phate, in chemistry, a sulphate with excess of the base.

Subsul'tus (Lat. *sub*, and *sultus* a leaping), in pathology, sudden and irregular snatches of the tendons.

Subtan'gent, in geometry, the part of the axis of a curve intercepted between the tangent and the ordinate.

Subtend (Lat. *sub*, and *tendo* to stretch), to extend under or opposite to.

Subter-, a Latin preposition, signifying *under*; equivalent to *sub*, as a prefix.

Sub'trahend (Lat. *subtraho* to subtract), in arithmetic, a number which is to be subtracted from a larger number, called the *minuend*.

Subtrip'licate, in arithmetic and algebra,

subtriplicate ratio is the ratio of the cube roots.

Subu'licorns (Lat. *subula* an awl, and *cornu* a horn), a family of neuropterous insects, distinguished by their awl-shaped antennæ.

Succen'tor (Lat.), a bass singer in a concert.

Succin'amide, in chemistry, a substance obtained from succinic acid and ammonia.

Suc'cinate, in chemistry, a salt formed of succinic acid and a base.

Succin'ic (Lat. *succinum* amber), pertaining to amber.—*Succinic acid* is an acid which exists ready formed in amber, and in the resins of certain Coniferæ.

Suc'cinite (Lat. *succinum*), in mineralogy, an amorphous variety of topazolite, not hard enough to scratch glass, but easily pulverized.—*Succinone* is an oily liquid obtained from the distillation of succinic acid with lime.

Suc'cula, in mechanics, a bare axis or cylinder with staves on it to move it round.

Suffru'ticose (Lat. *sub*, and *frutex* fruit), in botany, permanent or woody at the base, but decaying yearly above.

Sulcate (Lat. *sulcus* a furrow), deeply marked with longitudinal lines.

Sulphameth'ylene, a crystalline substance, obtained from the action of dry ammonia on neutral sulphate of methyl.

Sulphar'sine, an ethereal liquid substance obtained from mustard seed.

Sulphate, in chemistry, a salt formed of sulphuric acid and an oxidized base.—In mineralogy, the following are the principal sulphates:—*Sulphate of alumina*, found native in crystalline masses: sp. gr. 1·66;—*Sulphate of ammonia*, a mineral of a greyish colour;—*Sulphate of baryta*, a mineral called also *heavy-spar*;—*Sulphate of cobalt*, a mineral investing other minerals in small friable pieces;—*Sulphate of copper*, a mineral which occurs massive, stalactitic, and pulverulent: sp. gr. 2·21; H = 2·5;—*Sulphate of iron*, a mineral which occurs massive, pulverulent, and in stalactites: sp. gr. 1·84; H = 2·0;—*Sulphate of lead*, a mineral of a white, grey, or yellowish colour; structure lamellar: sp. gr. 6·23; H = 3·0;—*Sulphate of lime*, gypsum, plaster of Paris;—*Sulphate of magnesia*, a mineral of a white or grey colour: sp. gr. 1·66—1·75;—*Sulphate of potash*, a mineral which occurs massive: sp. gr. 1·731; H = 2·5—3·0;—*Sulphate of soda*, a mineral which occurs in efflorescences of a yellow or greyish-white colour: sp. gr. 1·47;—*Sulphate of zinc*, a mineral of a greenish white: sp. gr. 2·0;—*Sulphato-carbonate of lead*, a mineral of a greenish white, pale yellow, or grey colour: sp. gr. 6·8; H = 2·5;—*Sulphato-tricarbonate of lead*, a mineral of a white, pale yellow, green, or grey colour: sp. gr. 6·2; H = 2·5.—*Sulphite* is a salt compounded of sulphurous acid and an oxidized base.

Sulphobenzo'ic Acid, in chemistry, an acid obtained by treating an acid solution of hyposulphobenzoate of baryta with sulphuric acid.

Sulphocyan'ic Acid, in chemistry, a compound of sulphur, carbon, hydrogen, and nitrogen.

Sulphocyan'ogen, in chemistry, a yellow powder, insoluble in water, alcohol, and ether.

Sulphonaphthal'ic Acid, a compound of sulphuric acid and naphthaline.

Sulphosacchar'ic Acid (Lat. *sulphur*, and *saccharum* sugar), in chemistry, an acid obtained by the action of sulphuric acid on sugar of starch.

Sulpho-salt, in chemistry, a salt formed by the combination of a salt with sulphuretted hydrogen.

Sulphosinap'isine (Lat. *sulphur*, and *sinapi* mustard), in chemistry, a crystallizable substance obtained from mustard seed.

Sulphovin'ic Acid (Lat. *sulphur*, and *vinum* wine), an acid formed by the action of sulphuric acid upon alcohol.

Sulphur (Lat. *brimstone*), a yellow, brittle, mineral product, most abundant in volcanic regions.—*Sulphur-base* is a base in which oxygen is represented by sulphur.

Sul'phuret, in chemistry, a combination of sulphur with an alkali, earth, or metal, having no sensible properties of acid. The most usual of sulphurets noticed by mineralogists are the *sulphurets of antimony*, of *arsenic*, of *bismuth*, of *cobalt*, of *copper*, of *lead*, of *manganese*, of *mercury*, of *nickel*, of *silver*, of *tin*, and of *zinc*.

Sulphu'ric, pertaining to sulphur.—*Sulphuric acid* is frequently called oil of vitriol. When pure it boils at 620° Fahr., and has a specific gravity, in its most concentrated form, of from 1·84 to 1·85.—*Sulphuric ether* is ether obtained by distilling a mixture of sulphuric acid in alcohol.

Su'mach (Fr.), a large shrub of the genus Rhus, used in medicine, dyeing, and tanning.

Sump, in metallurgy, a round pit of stone, lined with clay, for receiving the metal on its first fusion.

Sun-stone, in mineralogy, a species of felspar, the Adularia, an ornamental stone.

Super-, a Latin preposition, signifying *above, over*; used in composition as a prefix, denoting *above, over*, or *excess*.—In chemistry, when prefixed to the name of salt, it denotes an excess of acid.

Supercil'ium (Lat.), in physiology, the ridge of hair above the eyelids.

Superfeta'tion (Lat. *super*, and *fœtus*), a conception after a prior one, and before the birth of the first.

Superox'ide, an oxide containing more equivalents of oxygen than of the base with which it is combined.

Su'persalt, a salt in which there is an excess of acid, commonly distinguished by the prefixes *bi* and *di*; as, *bitartrate* of potash.

Supersul'phate, a sulphate with an excess of acid.

Supersul'phuretted, combined with an excess of sulphur.

Supina'tor (Lat. *supinus* upward), in anatomy, a muscle which turns the hand upwards.

Supra-, a Latin preposition, signifying *above, over*, or *beyond*, used in composition.

Supracreta'ceous (Lat. *supra*, and *creta* chalk), in geology, applied to rocks superimposed on the cretaceous or chalk formation.

Supraor'bital (Lat. *supra*, and *orbis* round), in anatomy, applied to an artery sent off by the ophthalmic along the superior wall of the orbit of the eye.

Suprare'nal (Lat. *supra*, and *ren* a kidney), in anatomy, above the kidneys.

Sural (Lat.), in anatomy, belonging to the calf of the leg.

Surbase, in architecture, a cornice or series of mouldings on the top of the base of a pedestal, &c.

Surd (Lat. *surdus* deaf), in arithmetic and algebra, a term applied to magnitudes which cannot be expressed by rational quantities, as the $\sqrt{2}$.

Sur'gery, that department of medicine in which diseases or injuries of the body are cured by the hand alone, or by instruments.

Surox'ide, in chemistry, that which contains an addition of oxide.

Sursol'id, in arithmetic, the fifth power of a number, as 32 is the fifth power of 2.—*Sursolid problem*, that which cannot be resolved but by curves of a higher nature than a conic section.

Suture (Lat. *sutura*, from *suo* to sew), in anatomy, the junction of bones by their serrated or toothed margins. These sutures have been distinguished into the *coronal*, which passes transversely over the skull;—the *sagittal*, which passes from the middle of the superior margin of the frontal to the angle of the occipital bone;—the *lamboidal*, which begins at the termination of the sagittal suture;—the *squamous*, which joins the superior portions of the temporal bones to the parietals.—In surgery, the uniting of the edges of wounds by sewing.—In botany, the part of a capsule which forms a kind of furrow on the external surface, in which the valves are placed.—In conchology, the line of junction in the whorls of spiral shells.—In entomology, the line at which the elytra meet.—In mammalogy, the line formed by the incumbent series of converging hairs of the integument.

Suzan'nite, a mineral which occurs in the form of a right rhomboid prism.

Sychnocar'pous (Gr.), in botany, an epithet applied to a plant which produces fruit many times without perishing.

Syco'sis (Gr. *sykos* a fig), in pathology, a tubercular eruption upon the scalp or bearded part of the face.

Syd'erolite, a kind of Bohemian ware resembling Wedgwood ware.

Sy'enite, a granitic rock from Syene, in Egypt.

Syl'vanite, in mineralogy, a species of tellurium of a steel-grey colour, approaching to tin-white, composed of tellurium, gold, and silver: sp. gr. 5·7; H = 1·5—2·0.

Syl'viadæ (Lat. *sylva* a wood), a family of small birds, the Warblers, including the Stonechats, Nightingales, True Warblers, Titmice, and Wagtails; order Inessores.—*Sylvianæ* is a sub-family of Perching birds, very small in size, and weak in structure.

Sylvic Acid (Lat. *sylva*), an acid extracted from ligneous resin by weak alcohol, and purified by stronger alcohol.

Sympathet'ic Ink (Fr. *sympathique*), a sort of ink which changes its colour when acted upon by heat.

Sympet'sis, in pathology, a concoction or ripening of inflammatory humours.

Symphyseot'omy (Gr. *symphysis*, and *tome* a cutting), in surgery, the operation of dividing the symphysis; the Sigauitian operation.

Sym'physis (Gr. *a growing together*), in anatomy, a junction of certain bones or joints not admitting motion, as the *symphysis pubis*.—In pathology, the first intention of cure in a wound.

Sympiesom'eter (Gr. *sympiezo* to compress, and *metron* a measure), an instrument for measuring the weight of the atmosphere by the compression of a column of gas.

Symptomatol'ogy (Gr.), that branch of pathology which treats of the symptoms of diseases.

Syn-, a Greek preposition, signifying *with* or *together*, which forms a prefix to numerous scientific words.

Synanchi'næ, a sub-family of the Scorpænidæ (the Hog-fishes), characterized by the body being without scales.

Synarthro'sis (Gr. *syn*, and *arthron* a joint), in anatomy, a close conjunction of two bones.

Synbran'chidæ (Gr. *syn*, and *branchia* gills), a family of apodal fishes, which have the body eel-shaped.

Synchondro'sis (Gr. *syn*, and *chondros* a cartilage), in anatomy, an articulation by cartilage.

Syn'chysis (Gr. *synchyo* to confound or dissolve), in pathology, confusion of the humours of the eye from blows.

Syn'clinal (Gr.).—In geology, *synclinal lines*, lines bounding the surfaces of parallel superincumbent strata.

Syn'copal (Gr. *syncope*), in pathology, an epithet applied to a variety of intermittent fever, every paroxysm of which is characterized by fainting.

Syncopa'tion (Gr. *syn*, and *kopto* to cut off), in music, an interruption of the regular measure.

Syn'cope (Gr.), in pathology, fainting; sudden and complete loss of feeling and voluntary motion.

Syndesmog'raphy, or **Syndesmol'ogy** (Gr. *syndesmos* a ligament), in anatomy, a description of the ligaments.

Syndesmo'sis (Gr. *syndesmos*, from *syn*, and *deo* to bind), the union of one bone with another by means of ligament.

Syn'drome (Gr. *a running together*), in pathology, the assemblage of symptoms which characterize morbidity.

Synech'ia (Gr. *syn*, and *echo* to hold), in pathology, adhesion of the uvea to the crystalline capsule, or of the iris to the cornea.

Syn'ergy (Gr.), in pathology, the cooperation of different organs in health or disease.

Syngene'sia (Gr. *syn*, and *genesis* production), in botany, a class of plants that have the stamens united in a cylindrical form by the anthers; the nineteenth class of the Linnæan system.

Syngnath'idæ (Gr. *syn*, and *gnathos* the jaw), in ichthyology, a family of cheliform fishes; the Pipe-fishes.

Synize'sis (Gr. *synizo* to coalesce), in pathology, an obliteration of the pupil of the eye.

Synneuro'sis (Gr. *syn*, and *neuron* a nerve), in anatomy, union of one bone with another by means of a membrane.

Syn'ocha (Gr.), in pathology, an inflammatory fever.—*Synochus* is a continued fever, compounded of synocha and typhus.

Synod'ic (Gr. *syn*, and *odos* way), in astronomy, an epithet applied to the common lunar month, or the period of time which the moon takes in returning to any given phase; also to the motion of a planet.

Synosteol'ogy (Gr. *osteon* a bone, and *logos* a discourse), in anatomy, a treatise on the joints.

Synosteot'omy (Gr. *osteon*, and *temo* to cut), dissection of the joints.

Syno'via (Gr. *syn*, and Lat. *ovum* an egg), an unctuous fluid secreted from certain glands in the joints.—*Synovitis* is inflammation of a synovial membrane.

Syntex'is (Gr.), in pathology, a wasting of the body; consumption.

Syn thesis (Gr. *a putting together*), in chemistry, the uniting of elements into a compound, as in combining oxygen and hydrogen to form water. —In surgery, the operation by which the divided parts are reunited.

Syn'tonin (Gr. *stretched*), in anatomy, fibrine of muscle or flesh.

Syph'ilis (Gr. *siphlos* crippled), in pathology, the venereal disease.

Syringot'omy (Gr. *syrinx* a pipe, and *tome* an incision), in surgery, the art or practice of cutting fistulas or hollow sores.

Syr'phidæ, a tribe of dipterous insects, of which Syrphus is the genus.

Syssarco'sis (Gr. *syn*, and *sarx* flesh), in anatomy, a junction of bones by intervening muscles.

Systal'tic (Gr. *syn*, and *staltikos* drawing together), having alternate contraction and dilatation.

System'ic, in pathology, belonging to the general system, as *systemic* circulation.

Sys'tole (Gr.), in anatomy, the contraction of the heart and arteries.

Systyle (Fr.), in architecture, the arrangement of columns which are two diameters apart.

Syz'ygy (Gr. *syn*, and *zygoo* to join), in astronomy, the place of the moon, or of a planet, when in conjunction with, or opposition to, the sun.

T.

T, as an abbreviation, sometimes stands for theology, as in S.T.D., Doctor of Sacred Theology.

Taban'idæ, in entomology, a family of dipterous insects, of which Tabanus is the genus.

Tabes (Lat.), in pathology, a wasting of the flesh; emaciation; consumption.

Tab'lature (Lat. *tabula* a table), in anatomy, a division or parting of the skull into two tables.—In painting, a pictorial decoration on walls or ceilings.

Table-land, an extensive elevated plain, with steep acclivities on all sides; a plateau.—*Table-spar*, in mineralogy, a silicate of lime of a greyish white; called also *tabular spar*.

Tablette (Fr.), in fortification, a flat coping-stone placed at the top of the revetment of the escarp.

Tab'lorins (Fr.), in artillery, the thick boards that constitute the platform on which a cannon is mounted.

Tacca'ceæ (Malay *tacca*), in botany, an order of exogenous plants, consisting of large perennial herbs, with tuberous roots, of which Tacca is the genus.

Tachom'eter (Gr. *tachys* quick, and *metron* a measure), an instrument which indicates minute variations in the velocity of machines.

Tachyg'raphy (Gr. *tachys*, and *graphe* writing), a term applied to short-hand writing.

Tach'ylite (Gr. *tachys*, and *lithos* a stone), in mineralogy, a mineral which occurs laminated and massive, and resembles obsidian.

Tachyn'idæ (Gr. *tachys*), a family of coleopterous insects, remarkable for swiftness of flight.

Tac'tics (Gr. *taktikos*), the science and art of disposing military and naval armaments for battle; evolutions and manœuvres.

Tæ'nia (Gr. *teino* to stretch), in pathology, an intestinal worm; the Tapeworm.—In surgery, a ligature.—In anatomy, the *tænia seminicularis* is a white line running between the convex surface of the optic thalami and the corpora striata.

Tænioï'dea, Cuvier's third family of intestinal worms, of which Tænia, or Tape-worm, is the type.

Tagl'ia (Ital.), in mechanical science, the name given to a particular combination of pulleys, consisting of a system of fixed pulleys in one common block, to which the weight is attached.

Tagliaco'tian, in surgery, an epithet applied to the operation of artificially restoring the nose, an invention due to Tagliacotius, a surgeon of Venice.

Talc (Germ. *talk* isinglass), in mineralogy, a foliated magnesian mineral of unctuous feel; sometimes used for tracing lines on wood, cloth, &c., instead of chalk.

Talcite, in mineralogy, a synonym of *nacrite*.

Tal'ipes (Lat. *talus* an ankle, and *pes* a foot), a deformity known as club-foot.

Talmud (Heb.), the book containing the traditionary or unwritten laws of the Jews.

Talpa (Lat. *the mole*), in pathology, a tumour under the skin, compared to a mole under the ground.

Tal'pidæ (Lat.), in zoology, a family of the Moles.

Talus (Lat. *the ankle*), in anatomy, a bone in the ankle.—In fortification, a surface inclined to the horizon.—In geology, an accumulation of fragments broken off from the face of a steep rock by the action of water.

Tamariscin'eæ, a nat. order of exogenous plants, consisting of shrubs or herbs, of which Tamarix is the genus.

Tambour (Fr. and Sp.), a frame resembling a drum, on which a kind of embroidery, with threads of gold, silver, coloured silk, &c., is worked. —In architecture, a member of the Corinthian and Composite capital, somewhat resembling a drum.—In fortification, a work formed of palisades or long pieces of wood planted close together, and driven two or three feet into the ground.—*Tambours* are also solid pieces of earth made in that part of the covert-way which is joined to the parapet, and serve to prevent the covert-way being enfiladed.

Tamping, in mining, the filling up of holes bored in a rock for blasting.

Tangent (Lat. *tangens* touching), in geometry, a straight line which meets or touches a circle or other curve without intersecting it.—In trigonometry, the straight line which touches a circular arc at one of its extremities. —*Cotangent*, the tangent of the complement of the arc or angle, or of what it wants of 90°.—*Subtangent*, a line lying beneath the tangent.— *Artificial* or *logarithmic tangents* are the logarithms of the tangents of arcs.—*Tangential force* is a force which gives a tendency to any body to fly off from the centre.

Tannate, in chemistry, a substance formed of tan, or tannic acid, and a base.

Tannin, or **Tannic Acid**, in chemistry, the astringent principle of vegetables, which has the power of converting skins into leather. Tannic acid combines with the skin of animals, forming an insoluble compound which does not putrefy. Formula, $C_{18}H_5 O_9 + 3\,HO$.—*Tanno-gelatine* is a white precipitate formed when tannic

acid is added to a solution of gelatine.

Tantal'idæ, a family of large birds (the Ibises), of which Tantalus is the type.

Tan'talite, in mineralogy, the ferruginous oxide of columbium; composition—oxide of tantalum, oxide of iron, oxide of manganese, and oxide of tin: sp. gr. 6·3; $H = 6·0$.

Tan'talus Cup, a philosophical toy, which amusingly exhibits the principle of the siphon.

Tape'tum (Lat. *a carpet*), in anatomy, the coloured layer of the choroid coat of the eye.

Tapio'ca, a farinaceous and glutinous substance used for food.

Taran'tula (Ital.), a sort of large spider, so called from Tarento, in Italy, whose bite is fabled to be cured by music.

Tar'digrades (Lat. *slow-paced*), in zoology, a family of quadrupeds of the order of Edentata, which have obtained their name from the slowness of their motions. The only existing genus is the Bradypus, or Sloth.

Tarse, or **Tarsus** (Gr. *tarsos* the sole of the foot), in zoology and anatomy, a collection of small bones between the tibia and metatarsus, or those which constitute the first part of the foot; the instep.—*Tarsal* is an epithet pertaining to the tarsus; as, the *tarsal articulations* and *tarsal artery*.

Tarso-metatar'sal (Gr.), in anatomy, pertaining to the tarsus and to the metatarsus.

Tartar, an acid substance that concretes on the inside of wine casks; an incrustation on the teeth.—*Tartaric acid* is an acid contained in grape juice, and in tamarinds and several other fruits.—*Tartaric ether* is an ether formed by distilling together 5 parts of tartaric acid, 7 of alcohol, and 2 of sulphuric ether.

Tartar Emet'ic, in chemistry, a double salt, consisting of tartaric acid combined with potassa and protoxide of antimony.

Tar'tarin, in chemistry, a fixed vegetable alkali or potassa.

Tar'tarized, impregnated with tartar; as, *tartarized iron*, a salt used in medicine: it is a compound of tartrate of potash and sesquioxide of iron.

Tar'tarum, a preparation of tartar, called *petrified tartar*.

Tartrate, in chemistry, a salt composed of tartaric acid and a base.

Tartrometh'ylate, a compound of tartrate of oxide of methyl with a base.

Tasco, in mineralogy, a sort of clay for making melting-pots.—*Crabb*.

Tasto (Ital. *to touch*), in music, a term used in conjunction with *solo* to signify that the instruments are only to play single sounds till the direction is contradicted by the word *accordo*.

Tastu'ra (Ital.), in music, the whole range or set of keys in an organ, harpsichord, pianoforte, or other similar keyed instrument.

Taurine (Lat. *taurus*), a peculiar crystallizable substance contained in the bile.

Tau'rocol (Gr.), a gluey substance made from a bull's hide.

Taurus (Lat. *a bull*), in astronomy, the second in order of the twelve zodiacal constellations. There are several remarkable stars in this constellation: particularly *Aldebaran*, of the first magnitude.

Tau'tochrone (Gr. *tautos* the same, and *chronos* time), in mechanical science, a curve line whose property is that a heavy body descending along it by the action of gravity will always arrive at the lowest point in the same time.

Tau'tolite, a velvet-black mineral which occurs crystallized: sp. gr. 3·86; H = 6·5.

Taxa'ceæ (Gr. *taxos* an arrow), in botany, a nat. order of Gymnogens, of which Taxus, the Yew tree, is the type.

Tax'icorns (Lat. *taxus* the yew, and *cornu* a horn), in entomology, a family of coleopterous insects.

Tax'idermy (Gr. *taxis* arrangement, and *derma* a skin), the art of arranging and preserving specimens of natural history, as the skins of quadrupeds, birds, &c.

Taxon'omy (Gr. *taxis*, and *nomos* a law), in botany, the arrangement of plants and animals according to certain principles in divisions and groups.

Taylor's Theorem, in mathematics, a remarkable formula of most extensive application in analysis. Demonstrations of this important theorem are given in every treatise on the differential calculus.

Technics (Gr. *techne* art), the doctrine of arts in general, or such branches of learning as pertain to the arts.—*Technology*, a discourse or treatise on the arts.

Techtibran'chiates (Lat. *tego* to cover, and *branchiæ* the gills), an order of Gasteropods, characterized by having the gills covered by a process of the mantle, containing a shell.

Teg'ument (Lat. *tego* to cover), in entomology, the covering of the wings of the order Orthoptera.

Tei'noscope (Gr. *teino* to extend, and *skopeo* to view), the name of an instrument called a prism telescope, formed by combining prisms in a par-

ticular manner, so that the chromatic aberration of the light is corrected, and the linear dimensions of objects seen through them increased or diminished.

Telangiec'tasis (Gr. *a stretching out*), in pathology, distension of the vessels.

Telamo'nes (Gr. *telaio* to bear up), in architecture, figures of men used for supporting entablatures.

Tel'egram (Gr.), a message or despatch by telegraph.

Tel'egraph (Gr. *tele* far off, and *grapho* to write), any instrument by which intelligence can be communicated rapidly to a considerable distance. —*Electro-magnetic telegraph*, an instrument or apparatus for communicating words or language to a distance by means of electricity. There are also the *indicator telegraph*, which conveys its signals by the movements of pointers; the *type-printing telegraph*; the *symbol-printing telegraph*; and the *chemical-printing telegraph*.

Teleg'raphy (Gr.), the art or practice of communicating intelligence by a telegraph.

Telen'giscope (Gr. *tele*, *enggys* near, and *skopeo* to view), in optics, an instrument which combines the power of the telescope and the microscope.

Tel'ephone (Gr. *tele*, and *phone* sound), an instrument for conveying sound to a great distance.

Tel'escope (Gr. *tele*, and *skopeo* to view), an optical instrument employed in viewing distant objects, as the heavenly bodies. The essential parts of a telescope are the object-glass and speculum, and the eye-glass.—The *Newtonian telescope* is a reflecting telescope of the form invented by Sir I. Newton, in which the image is reflected by a plane mirror to the eye through one side of the tube, where it is viewed by the eye-glass.

Tellin'idæ, a family of solid and close bivalve Mollusca, of which Tellina, a species of Mussel, is the type.—*Tel-lininæ* is a sub-family of the Tel-linidæ, of which the animal is marine, and the siphons excessively long.

Tel'lurate (Lat. *tellus* the earth), in chemistry, a compound of telluric acid and a base.—*Telluric acid* is a compound of tellurium and oxygen in its anhydrous state.

Tellu'rion (Lat. *tellus*), an instrument for showing the earth's motions and the obliquity of her axis.

Tel'lurite (Lat. *tellus*), a compound of tellurous acid and a base.

Tellu'rium (Lat. *tellus*), a metal of a colour between silver and tin.

Tellu'rous, in chemistry, noting an acid composed of tellurium and oxygen.

Temple (Lat. *templum*), in anatomy, the upper part of the side of the head, where the pulse is felt.

Templet, in architecture, a piece of timber or stone laid under a girder or beam; also a moulding used by bricklayers and plasterers.

Tempo (Ital.), in music, a word constantly used to express *time*.

Tem'poral (Lat. *temporalis*, from *tempus* time), in anatomy, pertaining to the temples of the head: as, the *temporal artery*, a branch of the carotid, which gives off the frontal artery; the *temporal* bones, the bones constituting part of the lateral parietes of the cranial vault.

Tenac'ulum (Lat. *teneo* to hold), a surgical instrument for drawing out the mouths of bleeding arteries, in order to secure them.

Tenaille, Tenail'lon (Fr.), in fortification, a kind of outwork made on each side of a small ravelin.

Tendon (Lat. from *tendo* to stretch), a ligature attaching a muscle to a bone, by which a joint is moved.—*Tendo Achillis*, the large tendon which passes from the muscles of the calf of the leg to the heel.

Tenebrion'idæ (Lat. *tenebræ* darkness), a tribe of coleopterous insects, of which the Tenebrio is the type; fam. Scarabæidæ.

Tenes'mus (Gr. *teino* to strain), in pathology, a straining or ineffectual attempt to void the contents of the bowels.

Ten'nantite, in mineralogy, an arsenical sulphuret of copper and iron.

Tenon (Fr.), in architecture, the end of a timber cut to be fitted into a mortise in another timber.

Tenontag'ra (Gr. *tenon* a sinew, and *agra* seizure), in pathology, gouty or rheumatic pains in the tendons.

Tenor (Lat.), in music, the mean or middle part of a composition.—*Counter-tenor* is only a higher kind of tenor.

Tenot'omy (Gr. *tenon*, and *temno* to cut), in surgery, the operation of dividing a tendon.

Tension (Lat. *tensio* distension).—*Tension-bridge* is a sort of suspension-bridge, the roadway of which is suspended from iron rods, and these from an iron arch.

Tensor (Lat. from *tendo* to stretch), in anatomy, a muscle used in stretching some part.

Tentac'ulum, or **Ten'tacle** (Lat. *tento* to feel or try), in zoology, a thread-like organ situated about the mouth or other part of the body of many invertebrate animals.

Tento'rium (Lat. *tendo*), in anatomy, a membranous partition which separates the cerebrum from the cerebellum.

Tenuiros'ters (Lat. *tenuis* slender, and *rostrum* a beak), a tribe of suctorial birds, including those Insessores with long and slender bills.

Tenu'te (Ital.), in music, a term signifying that the notes are to be sustained.

Tephroïte (Gr.), a mineral of an ash-grey colour.

Teratol'ogy (Gr. *teras* a prodigy, and *logos* a discourse), that branch of physiology which treats of the malformations and monstrosities of the organic kingdoms of nature, or of departures from the normal forms of beings.

Terebintha'ceæ (Gr. *terebinthos* the turpentine tree), a nat. order of plants, consisting of trees or shrubs full of resinous, gummy, or caustic juices, of which Terebinth is the type.

Terebran'tia (Lat. *terebro* to bore), a section of hymenopterous insects (the Borers), characterized by the possession of an anal instrument organized for the perforation of animal or vegetable bodies for the deposition of their eggs.

Termit'idæ (Lat. *termes* an ant), a family of neuropterous insects (the White Ants), which, in their larva state, commit the most extraordinary ravages.

Tern (Lat. *sterna*), a common name of birds of the genus Sterna; the species being the Sea-Swallow, or Great Tern, and the Lesser Tern.

Ternstrœmia'ceæ, an important order of exogenous plants, of which the Ternstrœmia is the genus; the Tea trees and Camellias constituting a family of this order.

Terra-cotta (Ital. *baked clay*), in the arts, a name given to statues, figures, vases, architectural decorations, &c. modelled in potter's clay.

Terre-plein (Fr.), in fortification, a platform or horizontal surface of a rampart, on which cannon are placed.

Terre'-verte (Fr.), green earth used by painters.—In mineralogy, a species of chlorite of a green or olive colour, found in Germany, France, Italy, and North America.

Tersul'phuret, a sulphuret containing three equivalents of sulphur.

Tertian, in medicine, an intermitting fever or ague, the paroxysms of which return every other day.

Ter'tiary (Lat. *tertius* third), in geology, a term applied to the *tertiary strata*, which comprise a series of sedimentary rocks that lie above the primary and secondary strata, and are distinguished from them by their organic remains. The term is applied to all geological deposits which are newer than the chalk system, and older than the creation of the human race, and are divided into the newer pliocene, older pliocene, miocene, and eocene periods.

Terzet'to (Ital.), in music, a composition in three parts.

Tessella'tion (Lat. *tessella* a square tile), mosaic work, or the operation of making it.

Tes'sera (Lat.), a die in the form of a square, or a square piece of stone, porcelain, &c., for pavements.

Testa'cea (Lat. *testa* a shell), in conchology, molluscous animals having a shelly covering. The Testacea differ from the Crustacea; the calcareous part of the shells of the former being carbonate of lime, and of the latter phosphate of lime.

Testudin'idæ (Lat. *testudo* a tortoise), a family of chelonian reptiles, the Land Tortoises, of which the genus Testudo is the type.

Testu'do (Lat.), a genus of Land Tortoises, characterized by the sternum being immovable in all its parts, and consisting of eleven or twelve divisions.—In pathology, a broad soft tumour between the skull and the skin.

Tet'anus (Gr. *tetanao* to stretch), in pathology, a spasmodic affection of the muscles, the varieties of which are:—*Trismus*, or locked-jaw, in which all the body becomes rigid;—*Emprosthotanus*, in which the body is bent forward;—*Ophisthotanus*, in which the muscles of the back are chiefly affected;—*Pleurosthotanus*, in which the body is drawn to one side.

Tête-de-pont (Fr.), in fortification, a work for defending the entrance of a bridge.

Tetra- (Gr.), a prefix to numerous compound words, signifying *four*.

Tetrabranchia'ta (Gr. *tetra*, and *branchia* gills), in zoology, an order of Cephalopods, having four gills, and protected by an external shell. It includes the families of Nautilidæ and Ammonitidæ.

Tetracau'lodon, in geology, a fossil extinct animal, allied to the Mastodon.

Tet'rachord (Gr. *tetra*, and *chorde* a chord), in music, a concord consisting of three degrees or intervals, and four terms.

Tetradac'tyl (Gr. *tetra*, and *dactylos* a toe), in zoology, an animal having four toes.

Tetradyna'mia (Gr. *tetra*, and *dynamis* power), in botany, a class of plants having four stamens stronger than the others, and forming the fifteenth class of the sexual system of Linnæus, composed chiefly of cruciferous plants.

Tet'ragon (Gr. *tetra*, and *gonia* an angle), in geometry, a figure of four angles, the faces being convex.

Tetragonia'ceæ (Gr. *tetra*, and *gonia* an angle), a nat. order of plants, of which Tetragonia is the genus.

Tetragram'maton (Gr. *tetra*, and *grammata* letters), the mystic number *four*, which was anciently symbolized to represent the Deity, whose name was expressed in several languages by four letters.

Tetrahe'dral (Gr. *tetra*, and *hedra* a side), having four sides.—*Tetrahedral angle* is an angle bounded by four plane angles.

Tetragyn'ia (Gr. *tetra*, and *gyne* a female), in botany, an order comprising plants which have four pistils, or female organs.

Tetrahe'dron (Gr. *tetra*, and *hedra* a side), in geometry, a solid figure comprehended under four equilateral and equal triangles.

Tetrahexahe'dral (Gr. *tetra*, *hex* six, and *hedra* a side), exhibiting four ranges of faces, each range containing six faces.

Tetran'dria (Gr. *four males*), the fourth class of the sexual system of Linnæus, comprehending such plants as have four stamens.

Tetraon'idæ, a family of birds, comprehending the various species of Grouse, Quails, &c.—*Tetraoninæ* is a subfamily of the Tetraonidæ, comprehending different genera.

Tetraphar'macon (Gr. *tetra*, and *pharmaxis* medical treatment), in medicine, an ointment composed of four ingredients, viz., wax, resin, lard, and pitch.

Tet'rastyle (Gr. *tetra*, and *stylos* a column), in architecture, a building with four columns or pillars in front.

Tetter (Sax. *tetr*, *teter*), in medicine, an eruptive disease of the skin; herpes, or ringworm.

Tettigon'idæ, a family of hemipterous insects, the Grasshoppers, of which Tettigonia is the type.

Teu'thidæ (Gr.), a family of dibranchiate Cephalopods, of which the Calamary (*Loligo vulgaris*) is the type. It comprehends various genera.

Thalamiflo'ræ (Gr. *thalamos* a bridal chamber, and *flos* a flower), a subclass of Exogens, consisting of those dichlamydeous plants which contain all the polyandrous plants of Linnæus.

Thal'amus (Gr. *a bed*), in anatomy, the portion of the brain from which the optic nerves have part of their origin.—In botany, the part on which the ovary is seated.

Thalassamen'idæ (Gr. *thalassios* marine), a family of Annelids, allied to the Earth-worms, comprehending the genera Thalassema and Sternopsis.

Thalassin'ians, a tribe of Crustaceans of the Lobster kind, composed of various genera.

Thali'a, in astronomy, one of the newly-discovered planets, first observed by Hind in 1852. Its mean distance from the sun is 250,420,000 miles, and its periodical revolution 4 years, 93 days.

Thallite (Gr. *thallos* a green shoot), in mineralogy, a substance variously denominated by different authors.

Thallus (Lat.), in botany, a term given to the organs of vegetation of liverworts, lichens, and seaweeds.

Thamnophili'næ, a sub-family of birds of the Laniadæ, or Shrikes, of which the Thamnophilus is the genus.

Thau'matrope (Gr. *thauma* a wonder, and *trepo* to turn), an optical toy representing figures in a succession of different positions in performing some action.

Thebaine, a substance derived from opium by the action of lime, which forms colourless crystals.

Theca (Lat.), in anatomy, a fibrous sheath, in which certain soft parts of the body are enclosed.—In botany, the case which contains the sporules of flowerless plants.

Thecosom'ata (Gr. *theke* a case, and *soma* a body), in entomology, a family of Aporobranchiata, including the families Cleodoridæ, Limacinidæ, Cuvieridæ, and Cymbuliadæ.

The'codonts (Gr. *theke*, and *odous* a tooth), in palæontology, a tribe of extinct lacertian reptiles, distinguished by having their teeth planted in distinct sockets.

Thelphu'sians (Gr. *thele* a nipple, and *physao* to breathe), a tribe of brachyurous Crustaceans, of which Thelphusa, a genus of Crabs, is the type.

Themis, in astronomy, one of the newly-discovered planets, first observed by De Gasparis in 1849. Its mean distance from the sun is 299,870,000 miles, and its periodical revolution 5 years, 210 days.

Theod'olite (Gr. *theo* to run, and *dolichos* long), an instrument used by surveyors for computing the heights and distances of remote objects.

The'orem (Gr.), in geometry, a truth or position proposed to be proved; a position laid down as an acknowledged truth.

Theoret'ics (Gr.), the speculative parts of a science.

The'ory (Gr. *theoreo* to see), in physical science, an explanation of natural phenomena, founded on facts known to be true from evidence independent of those phenomena.

Therapeu'tics (Gr. *therapeuo* to cure), a branch of pathology relating to the application of remedies and the cure of diseases.

Thereol'ogy (Gr.), the study of diseases, and the practice of medicine.

Thermal (Gr. *therme* heat), in natural science, a term applied to springs, of which the temperature is above 60° Fahr.

Thermo-elec'trics (Gr. *therme*), metallic bodies, the union of which shows the effects attributed to thermo-electricity.

Thermo-lamp, an instrument for furnishing light by means of inflammable gas.

Thermom'eter (Gr. *therme*, and *metron* a measure), an instrument for measuring the variations of heat or temperature, founded on the property which heat possesses of expanding all bodies. The thermometers usually employed are Fahrenheit's, the Centigrade, and Réaumur's. In Fahrenheit's thermometer, the freezing-point is marked at 32°, and the boiling at 212°.

Ther'moscope (Gr. *therme*, and *skopeo* to view), the name given to that modification of the air called a differential thermometer.

Ther'mostat (Gr. *therme*, and *statos* standing), an apparatus for regulating temperature in vaporization, ventilization, &c.

Thermot'ics (Gr.), the principles and science of heat.

Thetis, in astronomy, the name of one of the newly-discovered planets, first observed by Luther in 1852. Its mean distance from the sun is 235,880,000 miles, and its periodical revolution 3 years, 325 days.

Thionu'ric, in chemistry, an epithet denoting an acid obtained by the action of nitric acid on uric acid.—*Miller*.

Thol'obate, in architecture, the part of a building on which a cupola is placed.

Thom'sonite, in mineralogy, a variety of zeolite.

Thora'cic (Gr. *thorax* the chest), in ichthyology, a fish with ventral fins placed beneath the pectorals.—*Thoracic duct* is the great trunk which conveys the contents of the lacteals and absorbents into the blood.

Thorax (Gr.), in anatomy, that part of the body between the neck and the abdomen, which contains the heart and lungs, the œsophagus, the thoracic duct, &c.

Thorite, a mineral found in Norway, being a hydrated silicate of thorina. —*Thoria*, a primitive earth extracted from thorite.—*Thorium* is the metallic base of thorina, procured by the action of potassium on chloride of thorium.

Thraulite (Gr. *thraulos* easily frangible), in mineralogy, a hydrated silicate of iron.

Threpsol'ogy (Gr. *threpsis* nutrition, and *logos* a discourse), in pathology, a treatise on the nutrition of organized bodies.

Throm'bolite, in mineralogy, an amorphous green phosphate of copper.

Thrombus (Gr. *thrombos* a lump), in pathology, a small tumour caused by blood-letting.

Throttle Valve, in steam-engines, a valve contrived to regulate the supply of steam to the cylinder, being brought into operation by the action of the governor.

Thulite, a rare mineral from Norway, which occurs in crystalline masses, of a red-rose colour; composition—silica, alumina, lime, and magnesia; H = 6·0.

Thu'merstone, a crystallized mineral.

Thun'derbolt, in meteorology, a term applied to a stream of the electric fluid, particularly if acting in a direction towards the earth.—*Thunderstone*, crystallized iron pyrites of a cylindrical form, found in chalk beds.

Thus (Lat. from Gr. *thyo* to sacrifice), the resin of the spruce fir; the term *frankincense* being also applied to it.

Thyite, a species of indurated clay, of a smooth, regular texture, and of a pale green colour.

Thylacothe'rium (Gr. *thylakos* a pouch, and *therion* a wild beast), the name given to a small marsupial animal; the first and only mammiferous animal whose remains occur in strata older than the tertiary formation.

Thymela'ceæ, a nat. order of exogenous plants, mostly shrubs.

Thymus (Gr. *thyme*), a genus of odoriferous plants. — In anatomy, a glandular body divided into lobes situated behind the sternum, in the duplicature of the mediastinum.

Thy'reocele (Gr. *thyreos* a shield, and *kele* a swelling), in pathology, a swelling of the thyroid gland.

Thyroid (Gr. *thyreos*, and *eidos* like), in anatomy, applied to a cartilage placed perpendicularly to the cricoid cartilage of the larynx, commonly called *Adam's apple*.

Thyrsus (Lat. from Gr. *thyrsos*), in botany, a kind of inflorescence resembling a bunch of grapes.

Thysanou'rans (Gr. *thysanouros* having a long busby tail), in entomology, an order of apterous insects with fringed tails.

Tib'ia (Lat. *a flute*), in anatomy, the larger of the two bones which form the second segment of the leg.

Tic (Fr.), in pathology, a local and habitual convulsive motion of certain muscles.—*Tic douloureux*, an acute twitching pain in the face.

Tide (Sax. *tid*), the alternate ebb and flow, or rise and fall, of the ocean or sea.—*Spring-tides* are the high tides, and *neap-tides* the low ones, which are both influenced by the position of the sun and moon.—*Tide-gate*, a gate through which water passes into a basin when the tide flows, and which is shut to retain the water from flowing back at the ebb.

Tie, in architecture, a piece of timber or metal for binding two bodies together.—*Tie-beam*, that beam in a roof which extends from one wall to the opposite.

Tile (Sax. *tegel*, from Lat. *tego* to cover), a thin piece or plate of baked clay or other material, used for the external covering of a roof, and also in making drains. — *Tile-earth*, a kind of strong, clayey earth.—In architecture, *tile-creasing*, two rows of plain tiles placed horizontally under the coping of a wall, to throw off the rain-water.—In mineralogy, *tile-ore*, a variety of red oxide of copper.—In botany, *tile-root*, a plant of the genus Geissorhiza, natives of the Cape of Good Hope.

Tilgate Beds, in geology, the great series of strata in the weald of Kent and Sussex.

Tilia'ceæ, in botany, an order of exogenous plants, consisting of herbs, shrubs, and trees, of which Tilia, the Lime tree, is the type.

Tilmus (Gr. *tillo* to pluck), in pathology, the picking of the bedclothes, a symptom of fatal termination in some disorders.

Timali'næ, in ornithology, a sub-family of dentirostral birds, the Babblers, of which Timalia is the genus.

Timbre (Fr.), an acoustic property by which sounds of the same note and loudness are distinguished from each other.

Time (Sax. *timme* an hour), the measurement of duration, marked by periods, whether past, present, or future.—*Apparent time* is time deduced from the motions of the sun.—*Mean time* is that shown by a well-regulated clock, and would be the same as apparent time if the sun were always in the equator.—*Sidereal time* is the portion of a sidereal day which has elapsed since the transit of the first point of Aries.—*Civil time* is mean time adapted to the purposes of civil life.—*Astronomical time of day* is the time past mean noon of that day, and is reckoned on to twenty-four hours in mean time.—In music, *time*, that affection of sound by which shortness or length is denominated as regards its continuity on the same degree of tune; thus, *common time*, of four crotchets in a bar, is represented by a character placed at the beginning of the tune; any other time is represented by a fraction similarly placed. — *Time-table*, in music, is a tabular representation of the several notes, and their relative lengths and durations.

Timeist, in music, a performer who preserves a just and steady time.

Timoro'so (Ital.), in music, a style expressive of awe or fear.

Tin (Sax.), a metal of a brilliant white colour, very malleable, ductile, and tenacious: sp. gr. about 7·29; equiv. 57·9; symb. Sn.—*Tin-white cobalt*, a mineral of a tin-white colour, inclining, when massive, to steel-grey; composition—cobalt, arsenic, iron, copper, and sulphur: sp. gr. 6·4; H = 5·5.

Tincture (Lat. *tingo* to tinge), the volatile parts of a substance separated by a menstruum.—In pharmacy, a preparation generally consisting of an active remedy dissolved in rectified or proof spirit.—In heraldry, *tinctures* are of three descriptions, metals, colours, and furs; the first are *or* and *argent*; the second, *gules, azure, sable, vert, sanguine*, and *tenny*.

Tinei'dæ (Lat. *tinea* a moth), in entomology, a family of lepidopterous insects, of which Tinea is the type.

Tinni'tus Au'rium (Lat.), in pathology, ringing in the ears.—*Pliny*.

Tinstone, in mineralogy, an oxide of tin: sp. gr. 6·4; H = 6·0—7·0.

Tissue (Fr. *woven*), in botany and anatomy, a thin membranous organization of parts. According to anatomists, there are thirteen simple tissues: the cellular, the adipose, the vascular, the nervous, the osseous, the fibrous, the cartilaginous, the muscular, the erectile, the mucous, the serous and synovial, the corneous, and the glandular.

Tita'nia, in astronomy, one of the newly-discovered planets, first observed by Ferguson in 1860.

Tita'nium, in chemistry and mineralogy, a rare and extremely hard metal, found in Cornwall, of a copper colour, and brittle.—*Titanite* is a native oxide of titanium.—*Titanic acid* is the peroxide of titanium, which occurs as a mineral, most commonly crystallized, and of a brownish-red colour.

Tithor'tic (Gr.), in physiology, an epithet pertaining to those rays of light which produce chemical effects.

Tituba'tion (Lat. *titubo* to stumble), in pathology, general restlessness, the fidgets, accompanied with a perpetual desire to change the position.

Tityri'næ, a sub-family of dentirostral birds, the Becards.

Toadstone, in mineralogy, a species of igneous or basaltic stone.

Tocol'ogy (Gr. *tokos* parturition, and *logos* a discourse), the science of obstetrics, or midwifery.

Tolu (from *Tolu*, the place whence it was first brought), a brownish-red balsam extracted from the stem of a South American tree.

Tolu'idine, in chemistry, a volatile, oily, organic base, containing no oxygen.

Tomen'tum (Lat. *down*), in botany, a species of pubescence, very soft to the touch, and giving a downy appearance to the surface on which it exists.—In anatomy, the small vessels on the surface of the brain.—*Tomentose*, covered with a down-like wool.

Tom'pions (Fr.), in gunnery, wooden cylinders put into the mouths of cannon to keep the inside dry and clean.

Ton (Sax.), a measure of weight = 20 cwts., or 2,240 lbs. avoirdupois. In the measurement of a ship it is reckoned at 40 cubic feet.

Tone (Fr.), in painting, the prevailing hue or degree of harmony in the colouring of a picture.—In music, a property of sound which brings it under the relation of grave or acute.

Tonic (Gr. *tonos* that which tightens), in pharmacy, medicine that strengthens the tone or muscular action of the system.—In music, the principal note of the key; the chief sound upon which all regular melodies depend.

Tonic'ity (Gr. *tonos*), in physiology, the faculty that determines the general tone of the solids; the property of muscles by which they remain in a state of contraction.

Tonquin Bean, the fruit of the *Dipteryx odorata*, a shrubby plant of Guiana, which affords a crystalline volatile oil of a peculiarly agreeable odour.

Tonsil (Fr.), in anatomy, a gland shaped like an almond, situated on each side of the fauces.—*Tonsillitis*, inflammation of the tonsils.

Topaz (Fr. from Gr. *topazion*), a crystallized mineral or precious stone of a yellowish colour, composed of alumina, silica, and fluoric acid: sp. gr. 3·49—3·56; H = 8·o.

Topaz'olite (Gr. *topazion*, and *lithos* a stone), a variety of garnet of a pale yellow colour, composed of silica, alumina, lime, glucina, iron, and manganese.

Tophus (Lat. *sandstone*), in mineralogy, a porous deposit of calcareous matter from water.—In pathology, a chalky deposit on the joints from gout.

Topic (Lat. from Gr. *topos* place), in medicine, anything applied externally to a particular part, as a blister or poultice.

Topina'ria, in pathology, a tumour of the scalp.

Topog'raphy (Gr. *topos*, and *graphe* description), the art or science of describing cities, towns, places, or particular localities.

Topol'ogy (Gr.), the art of assisting the memory by associating the object to be remembered with some place or building, the parts of which are well known.

Toreumatog'raphy, Toreumatol'ogy (Gr. *tcreutos* worked in relief), the science or art of sculpture, or a description of ancient and modern sculpture and bas-relief.

Toreu'tic (Gr.), in sculpture, an epithet applied to such objects as are executed with high finish.

Tormen'til (Lat.), a medicinal plant and root, used as an astringent; Septfoil.

Tor'mina (Lat. *torqueo* to twist), in pathology, griping pains.

Torna'do (Sp. *tornar* to turn), a whirlwind hurricane prevalent in the tropical regions.

Torpedi'næ, a sub-family of fishes, the Torpedo Rays, of which Torpedo is the type; fam. Raidæ.

Torpe'do, the name of a machine, invented for destroying ships by explosion.

Tor'relite (so called from *Dr. Torrey*, of the United States), a mineral of a dull vermilion colour, composed of peroxide of cerium, silica, protoxide of iron, alumina, lime, and water.

Torricel'lian Vac'uum (from *Torricelli*, the inventor of the mercurial barometer), a term applied to the upper part of the mercurial tube of the barometer.

Torsion Balance (Lat. *torqueo* to twist), an instrument for determining the amount of torsion which may take place in a thread of any substance by loading its extremity with different weights. — *Torsion electro-*

meter and *torsion galvanometer* are instruments by which the force of an electric or galvanic current is measured by the amount of torsion produced in a filament of glass or other non-conducting material by the action of these agents.—*Craig.*

Torso (Ital.), in sculpture, the trunk of a statue deprived of the head and limbs.

Torsten, an iron ore of a bluish-black colour.

Tortoise, in zoology, a common name applied to reptiles of the families Chelonidæ, Emydæ, Testudinidæ, and Trionycidæ.

Torus (Lat. *a rope*), in architecture, a large round moulding used in the base of columns.

Tourbil'lion (Fr.), in pyrotechnics, an ornamental firework, peculiar for turning round when in the air.

Tour'maline, in mineralogy, a mineral of various colours; a superior kind of schorl, composed of soda, silica, alumina, oxide of iron, oxide of manganese, boracic acid, magnesia, and lime: sp. gr. 3·o; H = 7·o.

Tour'niquet (Fr.), a bandage used in amputations to prevent hæmorrhage, being tightened by a screw.

Tourquois, a mineral of a bluish-green colour, composed of alumina, phosphoric acid, oxide of copper, protoxide of iron, and water: sp. gr. 2·65—3·25.

Tower Bastion, in fortification, a small tower in the form of a bastion, with rooms or cells underneath for men and guns.

Toxæ'mia (Gr. *toxicon* poison, and *haima* blood), a poisoned state of the blood.

Toxicol'ogy (Gr. *toxicon*, and *logos* a discourse), a treatise or discourse on poison.

Tox'odon (Gr. *toxon* a bow, and *odontes* teeth), a name given to a gigantic mammiferous animal referable to the order Pachydermata, the remains of which were found on the east coast of America.

Trabs (Lat.), in architecture, a horizontal piece of timber lying on a wall, for the reception of the ends of timbers.

Trache'æ (Gr. *trachea* the windpipe), the spiral vessels of leaves and insects.

Trachea'ria (Gr. *trachea*), in zoology, an order of the class Arachnides.

Trachei'tis (Gr.), inflammation of the trachea; croup.

Trachel'ides (Gr. *trachys* rough), a name applied to Lamarck's fourth family of heteronomous Coleoptera.

Trachel'ipods (Gr. *trachelos* the neck, and *podes* feet), an order of Mollusca which comprehends such genera as have the body spirally convolved.

Trache′lo - mastoi′deus (Gr. *trachelos* the neck), in anatomy, a muscle arising from the transverse processes of the last four cervical, and sometimes of the first dorsal vertebræ.—*Trachelo-scapular* is a term applied to certain veins, which arise near the neck and shoulder, and contribute to form the external jugular vein.

Tra′cheocele (Gr. *tracheia*, and *kele* a tumour), in pathology, an enlargement of the thyroid gland.

Tracheot′omy (Gr. *tracheia*, and *temno* to cut), the operation of making an opening into the trachea, or windpipe.

Trachini′næ (Gr.), in ichthyology, a sub-family of the Scorpænidæ.

Trachi′tis (Gr.), inflammation of the windpipe.

Tracho′ma (Gr. *trachys* rough), in pathology, an asperity in the internal superficies of the eyelid; a violent ophthalmia.

Trachypteri′næ (Gr.), in ichthyology, a sub-family of the Gymnetres, or Ribbon-fishes.

Trachyte (Gr. from *trachys* rough), a kind of lava, containing hornblende and augite, which passes into the varieties of trap.

Tractor (Lat.), an instrument of tractive power, consisting of two small bars of metal, imagined to possess magnetic powers.

Trac′tory (Lat. *traho* to draw), in geometry, a curve whose tangent is always equal to a given line.

Trade Winds, certain winds favourable to navigation and trade, which occur in the open seas, about 30° north and south of the equator.

Tradot′to (Ital.), in music, a term denoting that a composition has been transposed or rearranged to suit the convenience of some particular instrument.

Trag′acanth (Lat.), an African plant, and a yellowish gum obtained from the plant, familiarly called *gum dragon.*—*Tragacanthine* is the principle of tragacanth.

Tragus (Gr. *tragos* a goat), in anatomy, the small cartilaginous eminence at the entrance of the external ear, upon which hair often grows like the beard of a goat.—*Craig.*

Trajec′tory (Lat.), in geometry, the curve which a body describes in space, as a stone thrown obliquely upwards in the air.

Transcenden′tal (Lat. *transcendo* to climb), in mathematics, an epithet applied to any equation, curve, or quantity which cannot be represented or defined by an algebraical equation of terms.

Transept (Lat. *trans* beyond, and *septum* a division), in ecclesiastical architecture, the transverse portion of a cruciform church or cathedral.

Transfer′rer (Lat. *trans*, and *fero* to carry), in experimental philosophy, an instrument used with the air-pump for purposes of experiment.

Transforma′tion (Lat. *transformo*), in pathology, those adventitious or accidental tissues which usurp the place of the natural structure of organs.

Transfu′sion (Lat.), the operation of transferring the blood of one animal into the veins of another.

Transit (Lat. *trans*, and *eo* to pass over), in astronomy, the culmination or passage of a celestial object across the meridian of a place.—*Transit circle* is an apparatus for making astronomical observations.—*Transit instrument* is a telescope formed at right angles to a horizontal axis, which axis is so supported that the line of collimation may move in the plane of the meridian.

Transi′tion Rocks, in geology, a term applied by some geologists to those rocks which were considered as newer than those denominated primary, and older than those called secondary.

Transmuta′tion (Lat.), in physics, the change of anything into another substance, or into something of a different nature, as the *transmutation* of water into oxygen and hydrogen. —In geometry, the change of one figure or body into another of equal area or solidity.

Transom (Lat. *trans*), in architecture, a horizontal piece or bar running across a double window, dividing it into two stories.

Transpira′tion (Lat. *emission in vapour*).—*Pulmonary transpiration* is the exhalation of watery vapour constantly going on from the blood circulating through the lungs.

Transposi′tion (Lat.), changing, or putting a thing in the place before occupied by another.—In algebra, the act of transposing a term of an equation from one side to the other.

Transver′sal (Lat.), in geometry, a line drawn across several others so as to cut them all.—In anatomy, applied to organs, or parts of organs, situated in a transverse direction, as the *transversalis abdominis*, a muscle arising from the cartilages of the seven lower ribs, &c.

Transverse (Lat. *being across*), in conic sections, *transverse axis* is the diameter which passes through both foci. In the ellipse, the transverse is the longest of all the diameters; in the hyperbola it is the shortest.—In anatomy, *transversus perinæi* is a muscle which keeps the perinæum in its proper place.

Trap (Sax. *a hair*), in mineralogy, a name applied to basalt rock, which is divided into two families, *Common Trap* and *Figurate Trap*. The term is also applied to various igneous rocks, merely in reference to their form.

Trape'zium (Lat. and Gr.), in geometry, a four-sided figure, of which neither two of the opposite sides are equal or parallel.—In anatomy, a bone in the wrist.

Trape'zius (Lat.), in anatomy, a muscle situated immediately below the integuments of the posterior part of the neck and back.—*Craig.*

Trap'ezoid (Gr. *trapezion*, and *eidos* likeness), in anatomy, a bone resembling a trapezium.—In geometry, a plane figure like a trapezium, differing from it in having two of its sides parallel.

Trass, a deposit of volcanic ashes and scoria thrown out of the Eifel volcanoes, and accumulated in old lakes.

Traumat'ic (Gr. *trauma* a wound), in surgery, relating to or arising from wounds.

Traverse (Fr.), in architecture, a gallery of communication in a church or other large building.—In fortification, a trench with a little parapet for protecting the men on flank.—*Traverse sailing*, in nautical science, is a method of working or calculating traverses, so as to bring them all into one.

Travers'ing, in fencing, the change of ground made by moving to the right or left round the circle of defence.—In gunnery, the turning a piece of ordnance as on a centre, to make it point to any particular object.

Trav'ertine (Ital.), in mineralogy, a species of limestone deposited from the water of springs which hold lime in solution.

Treble (Lat. *three-fold*), in music, the highest or acutest part in music. —*Half-treble*, a high counter-tenor.

Trefoil (Lat. *trifolium* three-leaved), in botany, the common name of different kinds of three-leaved plants, as the *Trifolium repens, Trifolium minus*, &c.—In architecture, an ornament of three cusps in a circle, resembling three-leaved clover.

Tremandra'ceæ (Gr. *tremo* to tremble, and *anera* male), a nat. order of exo-genous plants, consisting of slender-like shrubs, of which Tremandra is the genus.

Trem'olo (Ital.), in music, a term intimating that the notes are to be drawn out with a tremulous motion.

Trench (Fr. *trancher* to cut), in fortification, a deep ditch cut for defence, or to interrupt the approach of an enemy; hence the phrases, to mount the *trenches*, to clear the *trenches*, &c.

Trepan, or **Trephine** (Fr.), in surgery, a circular saw for perforating the skull.

Tri- (Lat. and Gr. *three*), a common prefix to compound words, signifying *three*.

Triacontahe'dral, in geometry, having thirty sides.

Triad (Lat. *the union of three*), in music, the common chord or harmony, consisting of the third, fifth, and eighth.

Triadel'phous (Gr. *treis*, and *adelphos* a brother), in botany, having stamens united by their filaments so as to form three sets or bundles.

Trian'dria (Gr. *treis*, and *andres* males), the name of a class in Linnæus's sexual system, consisting of plants having three stamens, or male organs.

Tri'angle (Lat. *tres*, and *angulus* an angle), in geometry, a figure of three angles and three sides.—In music, a small triangular instrument of percussion open at one of its angles.

Triangula'tion (Lat.), in surveying, act of triangulating; the network of triangles with which the face of a country is covered in a triangular survey.

Trias, Trias'sic (Gr.), in geology, the new red sandstone series or group, so called from its consisting of three divisions.

Tribas'ic (Gr. *treis*, and *basis* a base), in chemistry, applied to a class of salts with three atoms of base to one of acid.

Tribe (Lat. *tribus*), in natural history, a number of things having certain characters or resemblances in common; as, a *tribe* of plants.

Tribom'eter (Gr. *tribo* to rub, and *metron* a measure), in mechanical science, a sort of apparatus for measuring the force of friction.

Tricap'sular (Lat. *tres*, and *capsula* a little chest), having three capsules.

Triceps (Lat. *tres*, and *capita* heads), in anatomy, the three-headed muscle which occupies all the exterior part of the os humeri.

Trichi'asis (Gr.), in pathology, a disease of the eyelids, in which the eyelashes grow inwards.

Trichiuri'næ (Gr. *trichios* hairy, and

oura a tail), in ichthyology, a sub-family of the Coryphænidæ, which have the ventral fins wanting.

Trichoderma'ceæ (Gr. *thrix* hair, and *derma* the skin), in botany, a division of the Gasteromycetes, of the nat. order Fungi.

Trichom'atose (Gr.), in pathology, applied to the hair when affected by a disease called *plica*.

Tri'chroism (Gr. *treis*, and *chroa* colour), an appearance which some bodies present of having three different colours, according to the way in which the rays of light traverse them.

Tric'linate (Gr. *treis*, and *klino* to lean), in mineralogy, a term applied to crystals, in which the three axes are all obliquely inclined to one another.

Tricus'pid (Lat.), in anatomy and botany, having three points.

Tridac'tylous (Gr.), in zoology, having three fingers or toes.

Trifa'cial (Lat. *tres*, and *facia* a face), in anatomy, a term applied to one of the cranial nerves, from its division into three large branches.

Trifid (Lat. *tres*, and *findo* to cleave), in botany, divided half-way into three parts; whence we have *trifoliate*, having three leaves; *trifurcate*, having three forks, &c.

Trig'lidæ (Gr.), in ichthyology, a family of malacopterygious fishes, which have the head covered with bony plates.

Triglyph (Gr. *treis*, and *glyphe* a channel), in architecture, an ornament of the Doric frieze, placed directly over each column, and at equal distances.

Trigonom'etry (Gr. *trigonos* a triangle, and *metreo* to measure), the art of measuring the sides and angles of triangles, and of ascertaining the relations between them.

Trigyn'ia (Gr. *treis*, and *gyne* a female), in botany, an order of plants having three pistils.

Trihe'dral (Gr. *treis*, and *hedra* a base), having three equal sides.

Trillan'do (Ital.), in music, with shakes or quavers.

Tril'obite (Gr. *treis*, and *lobos* a lobe), in geology, an extinct genus of articulated animals found in the transition rocks.

Trino'mial (Lat. *tres*, and *nomen* a name), in algebra, a name for an expression which consists of three terms, as $a + b + c$.

Trice'cia (Gr. *treis*, and *oikos* a dwelling), an order of plants having male, female, and bisexual flowers on the separate plants.

Tri'ones, in astronomy, the seven principal stars in the constellation of Ursa Major.

Trieny'cidæ (Gr. *treis*, and *onyx* a claw), a family of reptiles (the Soft Tortoises), consisting of the genera Trionyx and Emyda.

Tripartite (Lat.), divided into three parts.

Tripet'alous (Gr.), having three petals.

Triphane (Gr.), a mineral nearly allied to felspar.

Triph'yline (Gr. *treis*, and *phyle* union), a mineral substance containing phosphoric acid and iron.

Triplite, an imperfectly-crystallized mineral.

Tripoli, a mineral of an earthy fracture brought from Tripoli, used as a grinding and polishing substance.

Triptych (Gr. *treis*, and *ptyx* a fold), in the fine arts, a term applied to a picture with two hanging doors or leaves.

Trismus (Gr. *trizo* to gnash), tetanus affecting the jaw.

Trisoctahe'dron (Gr.), a solid bounded by twenty-four equal faces.

Trit'icum (Lat. *wheat*), a genus of plants, the most useful of the Grasses, its flour making the best bread; order Graminaceæ.

Tritox'ide, in chemistry, an oxide containing one atom of base united to three atoms of oxygen.

Tritu'rium, a chemical vessel for separating liquors of different densities.

Trochan'ter (Gr. *trochazo* to run along), in anatomy, one of the two processes at the upper end of the thigh-bone.

Troche (Gr. *a wheel*), a form of medicine in a circular lozenge for dissolving in the mouth.

Troche'ter (Gr. *trochao* to turn), in anatomy, a name given to the great tuberosity of the scapular extremity of the os brachii.

Troch'idæ (Gr. *trochos* a top), a family of testaceous Mollusca, the shells of which are usually trochiform, and of which Trochus is the genus.—*Trochinæ*, a sub-family of the Trochidæ.

Trochil'idæ (Gr.), a family of birds (the Humming-birds) remarkable for the extreme richness of their plumage; they comprehend the following genera:—Lampornis, Trochilus, Cynanthus, Phæthornis, and Campylopterus.

Trochite (Gr.), in mineralogy, a kind of figured fossil stone.

Troch'lea (Lat.), in anatomy, the cartilage through which the tendon of the trochleary muscle passes.

Troch'lear (Gr. *a pulley*), in anatomy, a term applied to the superior oblique muscle of the human eye, from the reflection of its tendon over a cartilaginous pulley.

Trochoi'dal (Gr. *trochos* a pulley).—In mathematics, the *trochoidal curve* consists of a large number of lines which are produced by the composition of two circular motions, including the straight line, the circle, and the ellipse.

Trochoi'des (Gr. *trochos*), in anatomy, a species of movable connection of bones, in which one bone rotates upon another.

Trochom'eter (Gr. *trochos*, and *metron* a measure), a machine for computing the revolutions of a carriage-wheel.

Trogi'næ, in entomology, a sub-family of the Scarabæidæ, or Beetles, distinguished by the head being sunk in the thorax.

Trog'lodytes (Gr.), in zoology, a subgenus of Quadrumana (the Chimpanzee), which, with the Orangoutang (*Simia satyrus*), makes the nearest approach of any other animal to the human form.

Trogon'idæ, in ornithology, a family of fissirostral birds, of which the Trogon is the genus.

Trombone (Ital.), a deep-toned trumpet, composed of sliding tubes, by means of which every sound is obtained in perfect tone.

Tropæola'ceæ (Gr. *tropaion* a trophy), in botany, a nat. order of exogenous plants, consisting of smooth trailing herbs, of which the Tropæolum, or Indian Cress, is the type and genus.

Tropics (Gr.), in astronomy, two circles parallel to the equator, between which the sun's annual path is traversed.—In geography, two parallels of latitude, one 23° 28' north, the other 23° 28' south, of the equator. That on the north is called the Tropic of Cancer, and that on the south the Tropic of Capricorn.

Trou-de-rat (Fr.), in military science, a disadvantageous position into which troops have been imprudently driven.

Troy Weight, a scale of weights used by goldsmiths for weighing gold, silver, diamonds, &c.

Truss (Fr.).—In the language of botanists, a *truss*, or *bunch*, is a tuft of flowers formed at the top of the main stalk of certain plants.—In architecture, *truss* is a combination of timber framing, so arranged that, if suspended at two given points, and charged with one or more weights in certain others, no timber would press transversely on another. — *Trussed roof* is a roof so constructed as to support the principal rafters and tie-beam to certain points where bending of the timber is likely to occur.

Tube (Fr. from Lat. *tuba*), in chemistry, an instrument commonly constructed of glass, and employed in divers processes.—In botany, the inferior portion of a monopetalous corolla or monophyllous calyx.—In gunnery, an instrument made of tin or quill for firing guns and mortars.

Tuber (Lat. *a bunch*), in anatomy, a rounded projection of a bone.—In botany, a thick underground stem, as the potato.

Tu'bercle (Lat. *a little swelling*), in pathology, a peculiar diseased deposit in the lungs and other parts, frequently attended by symptoms of consumption.

Tuber'cula Quadrigem'ina (Lat.), a term applied to four rounded projections at the base of the brain.

Tuberculo'sis (Lat. *tuberculum* a little knob), in pathology, a term applied to the condition under which tubercle is deposited in the organs of the body.

Tubic'ola (Lat. *tuba* a tube, and *colo* to inhabit), in zoology, a term applied to an order of animals which live in calcareous tubes.

Tubicor'nea (Lat. *tuba*, and *cornu* a horn), in zoology, a family of Ruminants which have the horns composed of an axis enveloped in a sheath.

Tubipor'idæ (Lat. *tuba*, and *porus* a pore), a group of Actinozoaria, forming the first family of the Zoophytaria.

Tubula'rii (Lat.), a family of Polypiaria, the polypi of which inhabit tubes, of which the common gelatinous body traverses the axis.

Tubulibranchia'ta (Lat. *tuba*, and *branchiæ* gills), in malacology, a tribe of bivalve shells, in which the branchiæ appear in the form of a spiral tube.

Tubuliflo'ræ (Lat. *tuba*, and *flora* a flower), in botany, a sub-order of composite plants.

Tufa, or **Tuff**, in mineralogy, a term applied to the scoria and ashes about a volcanic crater, which are re-aggregated so as to make a coherent mass.

Tu'lipa (Fr.), a genus of plants remarkable for the beauty and rich colouring of their cup-shaped flowers; order Liliaceæ.

Tumbrel (Fr.), in military science, a cart used for implements of pioneers or artillery stores.

Tungsten (Swed.), a mineral which is a tungstate of lime; a metal obtained from the mineral: sp. gr. 17·14.— *Tungstic acid* is an acid which consists of oxygen and tungsten, and occurs pulverulent in small friable masses: sp. gr. 6·0.

Tu'nicated (Lat. *tunica* a covering), in geology, applied to a class of Mollusca enveloped in an elastic tunic, not covered by a shell.—In botany, applied to a bulb covered by thin scales, as the onion.

Tur'bidæ (Lat. *turbo* a top), a family of univalve Mollusca, the shells of which are solid, but not perlaceous.—*Turbinæ*, a sub-family of the Turbidæ, the Winkles.

Turbinel'lidæ (Lat. *turbo*), a family of testaceous, univalve, marine Mollusca.—*Turbellinæ* are a sub-family of the Turbinellidæ.

Tu'rio (Lat. *a tendril*), in botany, a young shoot covered with scales, springing from an underground stem, as the Asparagus.

Turnera'ceæ (so named from *Dr. Turner*, author of the "New Herbal"), a nat. order of calyciflorous Exogens, consisting of shrubs and herbaceous plants.

Tur'nerite, a mineral which occurs in attached crystals, and consists principally of lime and magnesia.

Tur'pentine, a resinous juice extracted from several trees belonging to the Pine family.

Turquoise (Fr.), a greenish-blue mineral, which occurs in botryoidal mammillated masses, composed of phosphoric acid, alumina, oxide of copper, oxide of iron, and water: sp. gr. $2\cdot8$—3; $H = 5$—6.

Tu'tenag, a metallic compound brought from China, composed of copper, zinc, and iron.

Tutti (Ital.), in music, a direction for all the parts to play in full concert.

Tympani'tis (Gr. *tympanon* a drum), in pathology, excessive distension of the abdomen, arising from the accumulation of gas in the intestinal canal.

Tym'panum (Lat. *a drum*), in anatomy, the barrel or drum of the ear.—In architecture, the naked face of a pediment; the die of a pedestal.

Type (Gr. and Lat.), the mark of anything; a symbol; a stamp.—In natural history, the most strongly-characterized genus or species of an order, tribe, or family.—In architecture, the canopy over a pulpit.—In pathology, the character assumed by diseases.

Typhoon (Gr. *typhon* a whirlwind), a violent hurricane in the Chinese seas; a tropical storm; a hot, suffocating wind.

Typhus, in pathology, a fever characterized by weak and unequal pulse, with great prostration of strength.—*Typhoid* is applied to an asthenic or low form of fever.

Typ'ocosmy (Gr. *typos* a type, and *kosmos* the world), a representation of the world.

Typog'raphy (Gr. *typos*, and *graphe* description), emblematic or figurative representation; the art of printing.

Typ'olite (Gr. *typos*, and *lithos* a stone), in mineralogy, a stone or fossil having various figures impressed on it.

Tyranni'næ, a sub-family of the Laniadæ, or Shrike family.

U.

Udom'eter (Gr. *hydos* rain, and *metron* a measure), an instrument for measuring the quantity of rain which falls in a given period of time.

Ulcer (Lat. *ulcus*), in pathology, a sore on any soft part of the body, attended with a secretion of purulent matter.

Ulcus'cule (Lat. *a little ulcer*), in botany, the name of a tree, the milky juice of which yields the elastic gum called *ulc* in Mexico.

Ullage (Lat. *uligo* oosiness), in gauging, the quantity of fluid which a cask wants of being full, in consequence of the oozing of the liquor.

Ulma'ceæ (Lat. *ulmus* an elm), a nat. order of exogenous plants, most of which are valuable for their timber.

Ulmic Acid (Lat. *ulmus*), a vegetable acid exuding from the elm, chestnut, oak, &c.

Ulmine (Lat.), in chemistry, a dark brown substance which exudes from the bark of trees, particularly of the elm.

Ulna (Gr. *olnene* the cubit), in anatomy, the larger of the two bones of the forearm.

Ultra-, a Latin adverb signifying *beyond*, which is often used in composition.

Ultramarine' (Lat.), the blue colouring matter of the lapis lazuli.—*Ultramarine ashes* are a pigment which is the residuum of lapis lazuli after the ultramarine has been extracted.

Umbel (Lat. *umbella* a screen), in botany, a fan-like form of inflorescence.

Umbellif'eræ (Lat.), a nat. order of plants, bearing the inflorescence called 'an umbel, comprising the Parsnip, Celery, &c.

Umber (from *Ombre*, in Italy, where first found), an ore of iron used as a brown pigment, consisting of oxide of iron, oxide of manganese, silica, alumina, and water: sp. gr. 2 20.—In ornithology, a name of the *Scopus umbretta*, a bird of the Heron family.

Umbil'ical Cord, in anatomy, the navel-string.—In botany, the elongation of the placenta in the form of a little cord.

Umbo (Lat. *a protuberance*), in conchology, the point of a bivalve shell immediately above the hinge.

Umbra (Lat. *a shadow*), in astronomy, the dark cone projected from a planet or satellite on the side opposite to the sun.

Um'rakee, a vernacular name for the Myrobalan of the *Emblica officinalis*, used for tanning leather, and as a remedy in diarrhœa.—*Simmonds*.

Un-, a Saxon prefix of a negative character, equivalent to the privative *a* of the Greeks and *in* of the Latins.

Un'cia (Lat.), in pharmacy, an ounce troy; or, in liquids, the twentieth part of a pint.

Un'ciæ (Lat.), in algebra, the name given by old authors to the coefficients of the letters in the expansion of any power of a binomial.

Un'cial (Lat. *uncialis* roundish), an epithet denoting letters of large size, used in ancient manuscripts.

Un'ciform (Lat. *hook-shaped*), in anatomy, a bone of the carpus, and certain eminences of the brain.

Undec'agon (Lat. *undecim* eleven, and Gr. *gonia* an angle), in geometry, a plane figure of eleven equal sides or angles.

Undula'tion (Lat. *unda* a wave), in physics, the vibration of a substance in the manner of waves.—In optics, the *undulating theory* supposes light to be produced by the undulation of a subtle fluid, as sound is produced by the undulations of the air.

Unguic'ulate (Lat. *unguis* a claw), in zoology, a Mammal which has the digits armed with claws, with the under surface free for touch.

Unguis (Lat.), in anatomy, a small bone situated in the anterior and internal part of each orbit, which contributes to the formation of the lachrymal groove and nasal duct.—In botany, the lower part of a petal.

Un'gula (Lat. *a hoof*), a solid formed by cutting off a part from a cylinder, cone, or other solid, by a plane passing obliquely through the base; a sort of hooked surgical instrument.

Ungula'ta (Lat. *ungula* a claw), in zoology, a class of quadrupeds which have the digits enclosed in hoofs, as in the Pachydermata, Anotheres, Edentata, Ruminata, and the Solipedes.

Uni- (Lat. *unus*), a prefix to compound words, signifying *one*.

Uniax'al (Lat. *unus*, and *axis* an axle), in mineralogy, having but one axal.

Unicap'sular (Lat.), having one capsule.

U'nicorn (Lat. *unus*, and *cornu* a horn), a beast or quadruped that has only one horn.—In heraldry, the representation of a horse with a single horn.

Unilat'eral (Lat. *unus*, and *latus* side), in botany, growing on one side only of the common peduncle in flowers.

Uniloc'ular (Lat. *one partition*), in conchology, not divided into chambers, as shells.—In botany, not separated into cells.

Union'idæ, a family of Mollusca, consisting of what are called the River-mussels, or Unios.—*Unioninæ*, a sub-family of the Unionidæ.

Unipelta'ta (Lat.), a family of marine Crustaceans of the order Stomapoda, the shell of which consists of a single shield.

Unisex'ual (Lat. *unus*, and *sexus* six), in botany, a term applied to plants having separate male and female flowers.

Unis'oni (Ital. *one sound*), in music, a term implying that the parts in a score over which it is written are in unison with each other.

U'nivalve (Lat. *unus*, and *valva* a valve), a shell having only one valve.

U'niverse (Lat.), the whole creation; the general system of things.

Univer'sity (Lat.), a seminary or place of learning where the arts and sciences are taught and studied.

Unstrat'ified (Sax. *un* not, Lat. *stratum* a layer, and *facio* to make), in geology, a term applied to rocks which do not occur in strata or layers, but in shapeless masses, as the rocks of primary formation.

Upu'pidæ (Lat. *upupa* a lapwing), in ornithology, a family of Perching birds, placed between the Bee-eaters (*Merops*) and Creepers (*Certhia*).—*Upupina*, a sub-family of tenuirostral birds; the Hoopoes.

U'rachus (Gr. *ouron* urine), in anatomy, the ligamentous cord which arises from the base of the urinary bladder.—*Urucrasia*, in pathology, is involuntary excretion or incontinence of urine.

U'ramil, in chemistry, a substance containing carbon, oxygen, azote, and hydrogen, from the decomposition of which uramilic acid is formed.

Ura'nia, in astronomy, one of the newly-discovered planets, first observed by Hind in 1854. Its mean distance from the sun is 228,020,000 miles, and its periodical revolution 3 years, 254 days.

U'ranite, a mineral which consists of oxide of uranium, phosphoric acid, lime, magnesia and oxide of manganese, silica and oxide of iron, barytes, and water : sp. gr. 3·12.

Ura'nium, in mineralogy, a rare metal of an iron-grey colour.

Urano'chere, an ore of titanium, containing the metal in an oxidized state.

Uranog'raphy (Gr. *ouranos* heaven, and *grapho* to describe), a description of the heavenly bodies.

Uranol'ogy (Gr. *ouranos*, and *logos* a treatise), a discourse on the heavens.

Ura'nus (Gr. *heaven*), in astronomy, the name of the planet discovered in 1781 by Dr. Herschel, and called by him the Georgium Sidus. It is about 1,800 millions of miles distant from the sun.

Ura'o (Sp.), in chemistry, the native name of a sesquicarbonate of soda found in Mexico.

Urate, in chemistry, a salt composed of uric acid and a base.

Ur'ceolate (Lat. *pitcher-shaped*), in conchology, applied to shells which swell in the middle.—In botany, applied to the corolla or calyx swelling out like a pitcher.

U'rea, a principle proper to the animal urine; an organic compound found in the animal body.

Ure'ter (Gr.), in anatomy, the membranous tube which conveys the urine from the kidneys to the urinary bladder.

U'rethane, in chemistry, a white, fusible, volatile substance.

Ure'thra (Gr.), in anatomy, the membranous tube or canal by which the urine is voided.—*Urethritis*, inflammation of the urethra.

Urethrot'omy (Gr.), in surgery, incision of the urethra.

Uret'ic (Gr. *ouretikos*), in pathology, a medicine which increases the secretory action of the kidneys.

Uri'asis (Lat. *urina* urine), in pathology, the formation of urinary calculi in the animal body.

Uric (Lat. *urina*), in chemistry, noting an acid obtained from urinary calculi.

Urine (Lat. *urina*), the water or fluid secreted by the kidneys, and collected by the bladder.—*Urination* is the act of secreting the urine from the kidneys.—*Urinometer* is an instrument for ascertaining the weight ·of urine.

Urocele' (Gr. *ouron* urine, and *kele* a swelling), in pathology, infiltration of urine into the tissue of the scrotum.

Uroche'zia (Gr. *ouron*, and *chezo* to evacuate), in pathology, evacuation of urine per anum.

Urodyn'ia (Gr. *ouron*, and *odyne* pain), in pathology, a sense of pain in the passing of urine.

Uropla'nia (Gr. *ouron*, and *plane* error), in pathology, deviation of the urine from its usual channel.

Uros'copy (Gr. *ouron*, and *skopeo* to view), inspection of the urine for distinguishing diseases.

Ursa (Lat.), in astronomy, the name of two constellations, *Ursa Major*, the Great Bear, and *Ursa Minor*, the Lesser Bear.

Ur'sidae, in zoology, a family of plantigrade animals.

Urtica'ceæ (Lat.), a nat. order of exogenous plants, of which Urtica, the Nettle, is the genus.

Urtica'ria (Lat. *urtica*), in pathology, a genus of cutaneous diseases.

Ustula'tion (Lat. *act of burning*), in metallurgy, the operation of expelling one substance from another by heat.

U'terine, pertaining to the structure of the uterus or womb.

Uterogesta'tion, gestation in the uterus from conception to birth.

U'tricle (Lat. *utriculus* a little bottle), in botany, a kind of capsule resembling a small bladder.

U'vea (Lat.), in anatomy, the posterior surface of the iris in the eye.

U'vula (Lat.), in anatomy, a small fleshy protuberance attached to the soft palate, and hanging over the tongue.

V.

Vac'cina, Vacci'ola (Lat. *vacca* a cow), in pathology, the disease resulting from vaccination ; cow-pox.—*Vaccination* is the art or practice of inoculating with the virus of the cow-pox, which protects the individual from the malignant virus of the small-pox.

Vaco'a, in commerce, the scientific name for a species of Screw Pine the *Pandanus utilis*, which abounds in the Mauritius and Bourbon, where, from the tough fibres of the leaves, sacks for colonial produce are manufactured.— *Simmonds*.

Vac'uum (Lat.), in physics, a portion of space void of matter. — *Vacuum-pump* is a pump attached to a marine steam-engine.

Vagi'na (Lat.), in botany, a sheath formed by the convolution of a flat petiole round a stem.—In anatomy, the canal which leads from the external orifice of females to the uterus.

Vaginopen'nous (Lat.), in entomology, having the wings covered with sheaths.

Vair (Fr.), in heraldry, a kind of fur employed in blazonry.

Valeriana'ceæ (Lat. *valere* to make well), a nat. order of monopetalous Exogens, consisting of annual or perennial herbs or under-shrubs, of which Valeriana is the type.

Vallec'ula (Lat. *vallis* a valley), in botany, the interval between the ribs in the front of umbelliferous plants.

Valves (Lat. *valvæ* folding doors), in anatomy, membranous folds which exist at the orifices or in the course of certain cavities of the animal body, and are destined to prevent regurgitation.—In conchology, a term applied to the pieces or divisions of a shell when it consists of more than one piece.—In botany, a *valve* is the outer coat, shell, or covering of a capsule or other pericarp.—*Valvate*, opening by valves.

Val'vula (Lat. *a little valve*), in anatomy, a term applied to the *valvula Eustachii*, a membranous semilunar valve which separates the right auricle from the inferior vena cava.

Vana'dium, in mineralogy, a rare metal remarkable for its ductility. It is soluble in nitric and nitromuriatic acids, with which it yields solutions of a fine dark blue colour.

Vanfoss, in fortification, a ditch outside of the counterscarp, usually full of water.

Vanilla'ceæ, a nat. order of plants, of which the Vanilla, an aromatic used in confectionery, is the genus.

Van'ishing-point, in painting and perspective, the point at which an imaginary line cuts the horizon.

Vapour (Lat.), an invisible elastic fluid rendered aëriform by heat, and capable of being condensed or brought back to the liquid or solid state by cold.—*Vaporization* is the rapid conversion of a fluid into a vapour by heat.

Vara'nidæ (Lat. *vara* a pimple), a family of Lizards, the Broad-backed Saurians.

Variamen'to (Ital.), in music, a free and varied manner.

Varia'tion (Lat.), in astronomy, inequality of motion.—In nautical science, the *variation of the compass* is the deviation of the magnetic needle from an exact parallel with the meridian. —In arithmetic and algebra, a term applied to the different arrangements that can be made of any number of things.

Varicel'la (Lat. *varix* a distended vein), in pathology, a disease characterized by eruptions on the body; the chicken-pox.

Var'icocele (Lat. and Gr.), a swelling of the veins of the spermatic cord.

Varicom'phalus (Lat. *varix*, and Gr. *omphalos* the navel), in pathology, a varicose tumour of the navel.

Var'icose (Lat.), swelled, as a vein; diseased with dilatation.

Vari'ety (Lat. *varius* differing), in natural history, a plant or animal differing from the rest of its species in some accidental circumstances, which are not constant or permanent.

Vari'ola (Lat. *small-pox*), in pathology, a cutaneous disease introduced from the East into Europe about the twelfth century.

Va'riolite (Lat. and Gr.), in mineralogy, a porphyritic rock, consisting of an imperfectly crystallized aggregate of felspar and quartz.

Vari'oloid, in pathology, small-pox modified by previous inoculation.

Var'iscite, in mineralogy, a reniform, green mineral.

Varix (Lat.), in pathology, a dilatation or swelling of a vein.

Varnish (Low Lat. *varnix*), a fluid which, when spread thin upon a solid substance, becomes dry, and forms a glossy coating impervious to air and moisture.

Var'vicite, in mineralogy, an ore of manganese found in Warwickshire.

Vas (Lat.), in anatomy, a term applied to arteries, ducts, veins, &c.

Vas'cular (Lat. *vasculum* a vessel), having vessels that contain air or fluids.—*Vascular system* is that part of the animal economy which relates to the blood-vessels.

Vascula'res (Lat. *vasculum*), in botany, a term applied to the two principal classes of plants, Exogens and Endogens, on account of their highly vascular tissues.

Vaunt'mure (Fr.), a work raised before the main wall of a fort.

Vauque'linite (so called from *Vauquelin*, the French chemist), a dark green or blackish mineral.

Vector (Lat.), in astronomy, a line conceived to be drawn from the centre of a planet to the centre of the sun; called also *radius vector*.

Veg'etable (Lat. *vigeo* to grow), a plant or organized body destitute of sense and voluntary motion, and fed by means of external roots.—The *vegetable kingdom* is composed of the following grand divisions:—Exogens, Gymnosperms, Endogens, Rhizanths, and Acrogens.—*Vegetable ivory* is a name given to the seed of certain South American trees.—*Vegetable-marrow*, the name given to the Gourd, *Cucurbita ovifera*, of which there are several varieties. — In horticulture, *vegetable earth* is called mould; and in agriculture, the term is applied to the surface soil of hollows which contain alluvial soil beneath.

Vegeta'tion (Lat.), the process of growth, as plants, by means of nourishment imbibed from water and air, and received through roots and leaves.

Vein (Lat. *vena*), in animal physiology, a vessel or canal which receives the blood from the extreme capillary arteries, and conveys it to the heart. —In botany, an assemblage of tubes, by which the sap is transmitted through the leaves.—In geology, a fissure or rent filled with mineral or metallic matter, differing from the rock in which it occurs.

Vellica'tion (Lat. *vellico* to pull), in pathology, a twitching or convulsion of a muscular fibre.

Velocim'eter (Lat. *velox* swift, and Gr. *metron* a measure), a machine for measuring the speed of machinery.

Velo'cipede (Lat. *velox*, and *pedes* feet), a sort of machine with two wheels, placed one before the other, and connected by a beam, on which a person sits astride; and the vehicle is propelled by the muscular power of the rider acting upon treadles and levers, which communicate with a cranked-wheel axle.

Vena (Lat. *a vein.* See *Vein*).—*Vena portæ* (vein of the gate), the large vein which conveys the blood from the intestines into the liver.—The *vena cava* are the large hollow veins which pour the blood collected from the body into the heart.—*Venation*, in botany, is the arrangement of the veins in leaves.—*Venous system* is the collective name for the veins.

Veneri'næ, a sub-family of close bivalve-shelled Mollusca, of the family Tellinidæ.

Venesec'tion (Lat. *vena*, and *sectio* a cutting), the act or operation of opening a vein; phlebotomy.

Vene'tian Chalk, a white compact talc or steatite, used for marking on cloth, &c.

Vene'tian Red, a bright red ore, usually prepared from sulphate of iron.

Venice Tur'pentine, an oleo-resinous material obtained from the *Larix Europæa*.

Venter (Lat.), any cavity of the body; the abdomen.

Ven'tricle (Lat. *ventriculus*, from *venter* the belly), a small cavity in an animal body.—In anatomy, the term is applied to two cavities of the heart which propel the blood into the arteries and also to cavities in different parts of the brain.

Ven'tricose (Lat. *venter*), in botany and zoology, big-bellied.—In conchology, inflated or swelled in the middle of the shell.

Ventril'oquism (Lat. *venter*, and *loquor* to speak), the art of speaking inwardly, so that the sound appears to issue from some distant spot.

Ven'turine, a powder made of fine gold wire, which is strewed upon the first layer of varnishing laid in japanning.

Venus (Lat.), in astronomy, a brilliant planet, the second in order of distance from the sun, and the most brilliant of all the planetary bodies. Her distance from the sun is about 68,000,000 miles.

Vera'trine, a vegetable alkali discovered in white hellebore and some other plants.

Verbe'na, the name of a fine and costly perfume, obtained by distillation from the citron-scented leaves of the *Aloysia citriodora*.

Verbena'ceæ, in botany, a nat. order of Exogens, consisting of trees, or herbaceous plants, of which Verbena, or Vervain, is the type.

Verd-antique (Fr.), the green incrustation found on the surface of ancient copper and brass coins.—In mineralogy, a beautiful mottled-green marble.

Verdate (Lat. *viridis* green), a salt consisting of verdic acid with a salifiable base.

Verdic Acid (Lat. *viridis*), an acid so named from its becoming green when exposed to the atmosphere.

Ver'digris (Fr.), the blue-green rust of copper or brass.

Ver'diter (Fr.), a blue pigment.—In chemistry, a hydrated percarbonate of copper.

Vermeol'ogy (Lat. *vermis* a worm, and Gr. *logos* a discourse), a treatise on worms; helminthology.

Vermes (Lat. *worms*), in zoology, a class of invertebrated animals that have no antennæ, legs, voice, or true blood.

Vermic'ulite (Lat. *vermiculus* a little worm), a mineral which consists of micaceous-looking plates, composed of silica, magnesia, peroxide of iron, alumina, and water: sp. gr. 2; H = 1.

Ver'mifuge (Lat. *worm-expelling*), in pathology, a medicine for destroying intestinal worms.

Vermil'ion (Fr. *vermeil*), red sulphuret of mercury ; cinnabar.

Verna'tion (from Lat. *ver* the spring), the manner in which the young leaves are arranged in their leaf-bud foliation.

Ver'nier (Fr.), a contrivance for measuring intervals between the divisions of graduated scales or circular instruments, so named from the inventor.

Ver'ruca (Lat.), a wart.—*Verrucose*, full of warts, or having elevations resembling warts.

Ver'tebra (Lat.), a joint in the back or spine; pl. *Vertebræ*, the bones of the spine.

Vertebra'ta (Lat. *vertebra*), one of the great divisions of the animal kingdom, including those animals which are furnished with a back-bone, as the Mammalia, birds, reptiles, and fishes.

Vertex (Lat. from *verto* to turn), the point of a cone, pyramid, angle, or figure.—In astronomy, the zenith or point of the heavens perpendicularly over the head.

Ver'tical (Lat. *vertex*), being perpendicular to the horizon. — *Vertical angles* are opposite angles formed by two straight lines which intersect each other.—In astronomy, *vertical circle* is a great circle of the sphere passing through the zenith and nadir. —*Vertical line* is a line perpendicular to the horizon.—In conic sections, it is a right line drawn on the vertical plane, and passing through the vertex of the cone.—*Vertical plane* is a plane passing through the vertex, and parallel to the plane of the section.—*Prime vertical*, a great circle of the sphere, perpendicular to the horizon, and passing through the zenith, and the east and west points.

Ver'ticil (Lat.), in botany, a little whorl. —*Verticillate* is an epithet applied to flowers or leaves which grow in whorls.

Ver'tigo, or **Verti'go**, *pl.* **Vertig'ines** (Lat. *verto*), a sense of giddiness or swimming of the head.

Vesa'niæ (Lat. *vesanus* insane), in pathology, a class of diseases which includes the various forms of insanity.

Vesculo'sa (Lat. *vesica* a bladder), a tribe of dipterous insects (the Tanystoma) which have the abdomen in the form of a bladder.

Ves'icant (Lat. *vesica*), in medicine, a substance that raises blisters on the skin.

Ves'icle (Lat. *vesicula* a little bladder), any small membranous cavity in animals or vegetables, as those of the lungs, or of sea-weed.

Vespertilion'idæ (Lat. *vespertilio* a bat), in ornithology, the Bat family, which comprehends the sub-families Phyllostominæ, Noctilioninæ, Rhinolophinæ, Vespertilioninæ, and Pteropinæ.

Ves'pidæ, in entomology, a family of hymenopterous insects, of which the Vespa, or Wasp, is the type.

Vessel (Lat. *vas, vasis*), any utensil for holding liquors and other things.—In anatomy and botany, a tube ; a canal or duct which contains a fluid or other substance.—In vegetable physiology, a tube of very small diameter, in which the vegetable sap is conveyed.

Vesta, in astronomy, one of the four small planets which circulate between the orbits of Mars and Jupiter; an asteroid.—*Vesta* is also the name of one of the newly-discovered planets, first observed by Olbers in 1807. Its mean distance from the sun is 225,290,000 miles, and its periodical revolution 3 years, 230 days.

Vesu'vian (from *Mount Vesuvius*), in mineralogy, volcanic garnet ; a subspecies of pyramidal garnet ; a brownish mineral substance crystallized ; a name of the mineral idocrase.

Vexil'lum (Lat. *a standard*), in botany, the upper petal of a papilionaceous flower.

Via (Lat.).—In astronomy, *Via Lactea* is a term applied to the galaxy, or milky way, the white circle which encompasses the whole firmament, composed of an infinite number of stars.

Vi'aduct (Lat. *via* a way, and *duco* to lead), an extensive bridge or series of arches for conducting a road above the level ground in crossing a valley or other declivity.

Viam'eter (Lat. *via*, and Gr. *metron* a measure), an instrument to measure the distance passed over ; an odometer.

Via'rian (Lat. *via*), pertaining to roads, or travelling by public ways; as, the *viarian* communications of a country, by railway or otherwise.

Viatec'ture (Lat. *via*, and *tectum* a covering), the art of constructing roads, bridges, railroads, canals, and water-works ; civil engineering.

Vibra'tion (Lat. *vibro* to move to and fro), in physics, alternate and reciprocal motion, as the *vibrations* of the nervous fluid.—In music, the undulation of any body by which sound is produced.

Vi'brio (Lat. *vibro*), in entomology, a term applied to certain minute thread-like animalcules sometimes existing in fluids.

Victo'ria, in astronomy, one of the recently-discovered planets, first observed by Hind in 1850. Its mean distance from the sun is 223,770,000 miles, and its periodical revolution 3 years, 207 days.—In botany, a genus of magnificent stove aquatics, with immense spreading white flowers, so named in honour of her Majesty Queen Victoria; order Nymphæaceæ.—*Lindley*.

Vil'larsite, a crystallized yellowish mineral, composed of silica, magnesia, protoxide of iron, protoxide of manganese, lime, potash, and water; $H = 3 \cdot 0 - 3 \cdot 5$.

Villi (Lat. *villus* wool or hair), in botany, long, straight, soft hairs on the surface of a plant.—In anatomy, minute projections from the surface of a mucous membrane, presenting the appearance of the nap of cloth. —*Villous*, having a covering resembling hair or wool.—*Villosity*, the condition of being covered with villi.

Vin'culum (Lat. *a band* or *tie*), in algebra, a connecting mark or line drawn over a quantity, by which various terms are compounded into one, as in $\overline{a+b+cx}$, $(a+b+c)\,x$ $[a+b+c]\,x$, &c., which are, by the vinculum, prevented from being confounded with $a + b + cx$.

Viol (Ital. *viola*), an ancient musical instrument, the parent of all the modern instruments of the violin kind. —*Tenor viol* is a larger kind of violin, to which the part between the second violin and bass is assigned.

Viola'ceæ (Lat. *viola* the violet), a nat. order of plants, consisting of herbs and shrubs.

Violoncel'lo (Ital.), a bass viol, with four strings, an octave lower than the violin.

Violo'ne (Ital.), a large bass violin with three strings; a double bass.

Vireoni'næ, a sub-family of the Ampelidæ, or Fruit-eaters.

Virgin'ia, one of the lately-discovered planets, first observed by Ferguson in 1857.

Virgo (Lat.), in astronomy, the Virgin, one of the twelve zodiacal signs, which the sun enters about the 22nd of August.

Vir'tual (Lat. *virtus* force or power), in mechanical science, an epithet applied to the velocity which a body in equilibrium would acquire in the first instant of its motion, if the equilibrium were disturbed.—In optics, a term applied to the focus from which rays which have appeared divergent seem to issue.

Virtuo'so (Ital.), one skilled in antique or natural curiosities, or who has a taste for the fine arts, as painting, statuary, and architecture.

Virus (Lat. *poison*), the agent for transmitting infectious diseases.—*Virulent*, very poisonous.

Vis (Lat. *force*), in physics, any natural force or power.—In anatomy, that property by which a muscle contracts after the death of an animal.—*Vis inertiæ*, the resistance of matter to change as respects motion.—*Vis insita* (Lat. *inherent force*), in anatomy, the property by which a muscle, when irritated, contracts independently of the will of the animal, and without sensation.—*Vis nervosa*, the property of nerves by which they convey stimuli to muscles.

Vis'cera (Lat. *pl.* of *viscus*), in anatomy, the intestines or inward parts.

Viscus (Lat.), an internal organ of the body; an entrail.

Vis'ual (Lat. *pertaining to sight*).—In optics, *visual angle* is the angle under which an object is seen.—*Visual rays* are lines of light conceived to come from the object to the eye.—*Visual point*, in perspective, is a point in the horizontal line in which all the rays meet.

Vita'ceæ (Lat. *vitis* the vine), a nat. order of plants, consisting of scrambling, climbing shrubs, of which Vitis, the grape-producing Vine, is the genus. This order has been named Vitis, Viniferæ, Sarmentaceæ, and Ampelideæ.

Vital'ity (Lat.), the principle of life; the living principle.

Vitel'lary (Lat. *vitellus* a yolk), belonging to the yolk of an egg.

Vit'reous (Lat. *vitrum* glass), belonging to or resembling glass.—*Vitreous body* is a large, globular, transparent structure, occupying the centre of the eyeball, being the largest of the transparent media of the eye.—*Vitreous electricity*, a term sometimes applied to positive electricity, because developed by rubbing glass.—*Vitrifaction*, the process of converting a substance into glass by the action of heat.—*Vitrescence*, glassiness, or capability of being formed into glass.

Vit'riol (Ital. *vitriolo*, from Lat. *vitrum* glass), a name given to certain combinations of sulphur and oxygen, or of these with the metals; as, *oil of vitriol*, sulphuric acid; *blue vitriol*, sulphate of copper; *green vitriol*, sulphate of iron; *white vitriol*, the sulphate of zinc.

Vittæ (Lat. *vitta* a fillet), the receptacles of oil found in the fruits of umbelliferous plants.

Viverri'næ, a sub-family of the Gennets, or Musk Weasels, of which Viverra is the type.

Viv'ianite, in mineralogy, a phosphate of iron, which occurs crystallized in the form of a right oblique-angled prism. Its constituents are protoxide of iron, phosphoric acid, and water.

Vivip'arous (Lat. *bringing forth alive*), in botany, applied to stems that produce leaf-buds or buds in place of fruit.

Voohya'ceæ, a nat. order of exogenous plants, consisting of trees and shrubs with opposite leaves, so called from Vochy, the name of a species in Guiana.

Volatil'ity (Lat.), capability of rising in an aëriform state.

Vol'atilize, to cause to pass off in vapour, or in an aëriform state.

Volca'no (Ital. from *Vulcan*), an opening in the surface of the earth or other planet, from which smoke, flames, and lava, ashes or stones, are ejected. There are about 200 active volcanoes on the earth at present, and numbers which have become extinct.—*Volcanic rocks* are rocks which have been produced from the discharges of volcanic matter.

Volkon'skoite, a Siberian mineral containing oxide of chromium.

Voltag'raphy, the art of copying in metals any form or pattern which is made the negative surface of a voltaic circuit.

Volta'ic Electric'ity, the form of electrical action discovered by Galvani, but first described by Volta, in which any two conductors of electricity being brought into contact, an electric action is produced.

Vol'taism, galvanism or electricity, as improved or modified by Volta, to whom we owe the first knowledge of the powers of voltaic or galvanic currents.—*Voltaic battery* is any arrangement of galvanic circles made so as to produce an effect greater than a simple circle could occasion.

Vol'taite, in mineralogy, a species of iron alum.

Voltam'eter, an instrument for measuring voltaic electricity.

Vol'taplast, a kind of galvanic battery adapted for electrotyping.

Vol'tatype, a metallic plate containing a copy of a device upon a medal or coin; called also *electrotype*.

Voltzite, in mineralogy, a sulphuret of zinc, the constituents of which are sulphuret of zinc, oxide of zinc, oxide of iron, and organic matter: sp. gr. 3·60; H = 4·5.

Volume (Lat. *volumen*), in music, the compass of a voice from grave to acute.—In philosophy, the apparent space which a body occupies.

Volun'tary Muscles are those muscles which are thrown into action in obedience to the will; those which act independently of the will are called *involuntary muscles*.

Volu'ta (Lat. *volvo* to roll), in malacology, a genus of Mollusca, the shells of which are large and ventricose.

Volute (Fr. from Lat. *volvo*), in architecture, the spiral scroll appended on each side to the capital of the Ionic order. The Corinthian and Composite orders are also decorated with volutes, but they are smaller, and always diagonally placed.

Volu'tidæ, a family of Gasteropods, characterized by the shells being destitute of a channel.—*Volutinæ*, a sub-family of the Volutidæ, constituting the true Volutes.

Vomer (Lat. *ploughshare*), in anatomy, a thin bone which constitutes the inferior posterior part of the septum of the nasal fossæ.

Vom'ica (Lat.), in pathology, a collection of pus within the cavity of the thorax, which is expectorated by a kind of vomiting.

Vorant (Lat. *voro* to devour), in heraldry, an epithet applied to a fish, bird, beast, or reptile represented as swallowing any other creature.

Vorticel'la (Lat. *vortex*), a genus of Polypiaria; order Gelatinosi. Also, a genus of pedicellate Infusoria.

Voussoir (Fr.), in architecture, a stone in the shape of a truncated wedge, which forms the arch in a bridge; a keystone to an arch.

Vulcaniza'tion, a process of preparing india-rubber by impregnating it with sulphur.

Vulca'nian, relating to the Vulcanists, or their theory of the earth.—According to the *Vulcanian theory*, the present form of the earth has been produced by the action of fire.

Vul'nerary (Lat. *vulnerarius*), useful in healing wounds.

Vul'pinite, in mineralogy, an anhydrous sulphate of lime found at Vulpino, in Italy.

Vulsel'lum (Lat.), in surgery, an instrument for drawing parts into a convenient position for performing an operation.

Vultu'ridæ (Lat. *vultur*), a family of large rapacious birds, of which the Vulture is the type; head and neck, in general, more or less naked.

Vulva (Lat.), in anatomy, the orifice situated between the labia majora, which leads into the vulvo-uterine canal.—*Vulva cerebri*, an orifice which exists anteriorly to the optic thalami.

W.

Wacke (Germ.), in mineralogy, a rock nearly allied to basalt, of which it is a soft and earthy variety, and chiefly composed of silica.

Wag'nerite, a rare mineral resembling the Brazilian topaz. It consists of phosphoric and fluoric acids, magnesia, the oxide of iron, and manganese.

Wal'lerite, a variety of orthoclase, found in small compact masses, yellowish and translucent.

Wall-plate, in architecture, a piece of timber lying on a wall, on which girders, joists, &c., rest. — *Wall-spring*, a spring issuing from stratified rocks.

War'wickite, a mineral containing titanium.

Watch (Swed.), in mechanical science, a small portable time-piece, the machinery of which is moved by a spring. Those watches intended for astronomical or nautical observations are called chronometers, sometimes made with such precision as to vary but a few seconds in the course of a year. At Goldsmiths' Hall, from 14,000 to 15,000 gold watches, and from 80,000 to 90,000 silver ones, are annually assayed.—In *watch-making* there are various trades or professions called into action, as the watch-dial silverer, the watch-glass maker, the watch-tool maker, watch balance-wheel maker, watch-barrel maker, watch-cap maker, watch-case maker, &c.

Water (Sax.), a colourless, inodorous, transparent fluid, composed of oxygen and hydrogen, in the relative proportions, by weight, of 8 to 1. Water presents itself in three distinct forms: first, in a state of vapour or steam; secondly, in its liquid state; and, lastly, in its frozen or solidified state. When fluid, it is not in its most simple state, for its fluidity depends on a certain quantity of caloric, which enters into combination with it, and insinuating itself between the particles of the water, renders them capable of moving in all directions. —In the arts and mechanical science there are various combinations of this word as a prefix; as, *Water-gauge*, an instrument for measuring the depth and quantity of water;—*Water-line*, in nautical science, the line which distinguishes that part of a ship which is under water from that part which is above;—*Water-ram*, a machine by which water is raised much above its level by the momentum of a larger stream than the one raised;—*Water-spout*, a remarkable meteorological phenomenon, which appears as a conical pillar descending from a dense cloud;—*Water-thermometer*, an instrument for ascertaining the degree of cold at which water ceases to be condensed;—*Water-wheel*, a wheel of a mill moved by water; an engine for raising water out of a deep well;—*Water-works*, hydraulic engines or structures; artificial spouts of water.

Wa'vellite (in honour of *Dr. Wavel*, the discoverer), a mineral consisting of small slender crystals radiating from a centre, composed of phosphoric acid, alumina, water, fluoric acid, lime, oxides of iron and manganese: sp. gr. 3·33; $H = 3·5—4·0$.

Weald, or **Wealden** (Dutch), in geology, a term signifying a peculiar formation or strata of rocks, so named from the wealds of Kent or Sussex. The great *wealden formation* is a series of fresh-water deposits, covering an area 200 miles in length from east to west, and 220 miles from north-west to south-east, the total thickness averaging about 2,000 feet. The organic remains consist of leaves, stems, and branches of plants of a tropical character; bones of enormous reptiles of extinct genera, of crocodiles, turtles, flying reptiles, birds, and fishes. The wealden is supposed to have formed the estuary of an immense river.—*Wealden clay* is the blue clay which forms part of the wealden group.

Weasand (Sax.), in anatomy, the windpipe or trachea, the canal through which air passes to and from the lungs.

Wedgwood Ware, in the arts, a superior kind of earthenware, so called from its inventor, Mr. Wedgwood.—*Wedgwood's pyrometer* is an instrument used for ascertaining very high degrees of heat.

Wehrlite, in mineralogy, a mineral containing iron.

Weighing Machine, in mechanical science, a machine for weighing heavy bodies, and particularly wheel-carriages at turnpike gates.

Weight (Sax.), in statics, the pressure which a body exerts vertically downwards, in consequence of the action of gravity; anything to be raised, sustained, or moved by a machine. —In natural philosophy, the weight of a body is synonymous with its specific gravity multiplied by its bulk.

Weissite (in honour of *Professor Weiss*, of Berlin), a translucent mineral found at Falun in Sweden. Its constituents are potash, soda, silica, alumina, magnesia, protoxide of iron, protoxide of manganese, oxide of zinc, and water: sp. gr. 2·80.

Weld (Germ. *wellen* to join), according to the laws of mechanical affinity, to unite two or more pieces, generally of iron, by hammering them together when softened by heat.

Werne'rian The'ory, in geology, the doctrine propounded by Werner, the celebrated German mineralogist, which ascribed the origin of all rocks to aqueous deposition, as opposed to the Huttonian theory.

Wer'nerite (in honour of *Professor Werner*), in mineralogy, a silicate of alumina, lime, and oxide of iron. It is found massive and crystallized in octahedral prisms.

Whale (Sax. and Swed.), the general name for an order of Mammalia inhabiting the ocean, arranged under the name Cetacea.—The Greenland whale is the largest animal of this or former ages of the earth.

Wheel (Dutch and Swed.), in mechanical science, a simple machine, consisting of a round piece of wood, metal, or other material, which revolves on an axis. It is one of the principal powers which science has applied to mechanism.—*Wheel-axle* is a machine consisting usually of a cylinder, to which a wheel is firmly united, so that the mathematical axes of both are coincident.

Wheel An'imals, in natural history, the popular name of the Rotifera, a genus of Infusoria which have their tentacula arranged in a wheel-like form.

Whelk (Sax. *weoloc*, *hwylca*), in zoology, the common name given to the marine shell *Buccinum undatum*, or Trumpet-shell.—In pathology, an unsuppurative tubercular tumour, generally occurring on the face.

Whinstone (Scotch *quhyn* resounding), in mineralogy, a provincial term applied to greenstone, clinkstone, porphyretic, and other trap rocks.

Whirling Machine, in mechanical science, an apparatus for determining the resistance of air.—*Whirling-table*, a machine contrived to exhibit the principal laws of gravitation, or the phenomena in philosophy and nature relative to the power of the centrifugal force.

Whirlwind, in physics or pneumatics, a body of air moving in a circular or spiral form, as if round an axis, and at the same time having a progressive motion.

White (Sax.), a negative colour, which is the most significant of light, and reflects all its rays, as pure snow.—*White* is a prefix to numerous terms connected with mineralogical science and the arts.—*White antimony* is a mineral of a snow-white or grey colour, consisting of antimony and oxygen: sp. gr. 5·5; H = 3·5.—*White copper*, a term applied to Chinese copper, which is alloyed with zinc, and forms a very hard white metal, but little disposed to tarnish.—*White enamel*, or *calcine*, an enamel made by calcining about 30 parts of tin and 60 parts of lead.—*White-lead*, the white oxide of lead, used for numerous purposes of painting, &c.—*White-lead ore* is the carbonate of lead, which occurs in tabular crystals in six-sided prisms, variously terminated, and consists of carbonic acid and protoxide of lead: sp. gr. 6·3; H = 3·0.—*White manganese* is an ore of manganese; carbonated oxidized manganese.—*White metal*, a kind of queen's metal, made by fusing together 10 ounces of lead, 6 ounces of bismuth, and 4 drachms of regulus of antimony.—*White precipitate* is a compound of ammonia and corrosive sublimate, or of metallic mercury, hydrogen, and oxygen. —*Spanish-white*, a substance used in painting, prepared from chalk by separating it from its siliceous impurities.—*White vitriol* is the sulphate of zinc, a mineral found principally in the deserted galleries of old mines. Its constituents are oxide of zinc, sulphuric acid, oxide of manganese, oxide of iron, and water: sp. gr. 2·0; H = 2.—In botany, *white balsam* is pubescent myrrh-seed, the South American tree, *Myrospermum pubescens*, from which the perfume of quinquina is obtained.—In pathology, *white gum* is the *Strophulus albinus*, a species of gum-rash, in which the pimples are minute, hard, and whitish, surrounded by a reddish halo.

Whooping-cough, in pathology, a violent convulsive cough, returning by fits at longer or shorter intervals.

Whorl, in conchology, a wreath, convolution, or turn of the spire of a univalve shell: the axis of revolution is termed the *columella*, and the turns of the spiral are denominated *whorls*.—In botany, a species of inflorescence, in which the flowers surround the stem in the form of a ring.

Wide Gauge, in railway science, a term

applied to the widest gauge used on railways, as distinguished from the narrow gauge; the rails of the former being seven feet apart.

Wil'lemite, a mineral of resinous lustre and yellowish colour.

Wind (Sax.), in meteorology, a current in the atmosphere, conveying the air, with greater or less velocity, from one part to another.—In pathology, *wind-dropsy* is a tumour filled with air.—*Wind-gauge* is an instrument for ascertaining the velocity and force of wind.—*Wind-gall*, in farriery, a soft flatulent tumour which grows on each side of the fetlock joints, and makes a horse halt when on hard ground.—*Wind-sail*, a wide tube or funnel of canvas used to convey a stream of air into the lower apartments of a ship.

Windage, in gunnery, the difference between the diameter of the bore of a gun or other piece, and that of the ball or shell.

Windlass, in mechanical science, a machine for raising weights, in which a rope or chain is wound about a cylindrical body moved by levers.

Winter Solstice, in cosmography, the entrance of the sun into the sign Capricorn, on the 21st of December.

With'amite, a siliceous crystallized mineral, found encrusting the surface of trap rock by Mr. Witham. Its constituents are silica, alumina, peroxide of iron, lime, and water: sp. gr. 2·85; H = 6·0.

Woad (Sax.), the common name of plants of the genus Isatis: also the name of the plant *Reseda luteola,* known otherwise as Dyer's-woad.—

Woad-blue is of a deep hue, and is the base of many other shades of colour.

Wolfe's Appara'tus, in chemistry, a term applied to a bottle with two or more openings, used for generating gases.

Wolfram, in mineralogy, a native tungstate of iron and manganese.

Wol'lastonite, in mineralogy, a species of prismatic augite; a silicate of lime.

Works, in military science, a term generally applied to the fortifications about the body of a place. The word is also used to signify the approaches of the besiegers, and the several lines, trenches, &c., made for security.

Worm (Sax.), in natural history, the class Vermes of Linnæus, including Intestinal Worms; the Mollusca, or Snails; the Testacea, or Shell-fish; and Zoophytes, or compound animals, including Corals, Polypes, and Sponges.—In distillation and chemistry, *worm* is a spiral leaden pipe placed in a tub of water, in which it is cooled and condensed.

Wor'mian Bones, in anatomy, the small triangular pieces of bone sometimes found lying between the other bones of the skull.—*Dr. Henry*.

Wort (Sax.), in brewing and distillation, the fermentable infusion of malt grain, consisting of saccharine matter, starch, gluten, and tannin.

Worthite, a white and translucent mineral discovered by Von Worth, of St. Petersburg, consisting of silica, alumina, magnesia, and water.

Wyvern, in heraldry, an imaginary bird with a serpent's tail.

X.

X begins no word truly English, but is chiefly used in words of Greek origin, and hence it is frequently applied to terms of a scientific character.—In arithmetical science, as a numeral, it stands for 10; when laid horizontally, ⋈, for 1,000; and, on account of its corresponding with the Greek digraph Ch, it is used as a contraction for Christ.

Xan'thian, an epithet pertaining to Xanthus, the ancient capital of Lydia, as the *Xanthian marbles* in the British Museum.

Xanthic (Gr. *yellow*), in chemistry, an epithet denoting an acid composed of sulphur, carbon, and oxygen.

Xanthid'ium (Gr. *xanthizo* to render yellow), a name given to minute organic bodies found in chalk and flint, supposed to be fossil Infusoria.

Xanthine (Gr.), in chemistry, the yellow dyeing matter contained in madder.

Xanthite (Gr.), a mineral of a light grey or yellow colour. Its constituents are silica, alumina, lime, peroxide of iron, peroxide of manganese, and water: sp. gr. 3·20.

Xan'thogen (Gr. *xanthos* yellow, and *gennao* to generate), in chemistry, the base of an acid, procured by the action and reaction of carburet of sulphur and potash.—*Xanthide* is a compound of xanthogen and a metal.

Xan'thophylle (Gr. *xanthos*, and *phyllon* a leaf), the yellow colouring matter or sappy exudation in plants.

Xanthopic'rine (Gr. *xanthos*, and *pik-*

ros bitter), a bitter principle obtained from the bark of the Xanthoxylum.

Xanthoram'nine (Gr.), in chemistry, an organic compound existing in the ripe berries of certain species of Rhamnus.

Xan'thortite (Gr.), in mineralogy, a yellowish variety of allanite.—*Dana*.

Xanthous (Gr.), in ethnology, a term applied to varieties of mankind with yellow, red, or brown hair.

Xanthoxyla'cese (Gr. *xanthos*, and *xylon* wood), in botany, a nat. order of exogenous plants, consisting of trees or shrubs, of which Xanthoxylum, or Prickly Ash, is the type and genus.

Xen'otime (Gr.), an opaque crystal mineral; a phosphate of yttria.

Xera'sia (Gr. *dryness*), in pathology, a disease of the hair.

Xero'des (Gr. *dryness*), in pathology, something of a drying nature; a dry tumour.

Xiph'ias (Gr. *xiphos* a sword), in ichthyology, the Sword-fish.—In astronomy, a comet like a sword.

Xiphoid (Gr. *sword-like*), in anatomy, denoting a ligament or cartilage connected with the sternum, resembling a sword.

Xiphosu'ra (Gr. *xiphos*, and *oura* a tail), in malacology, a family of Crustaceans with sword-shaped tails.

Xy'lidine (Gr.), in chemistry, an artificial organic base or alkaloid, consisting of hydrogen, nitrogen, and carbon.

Xylo- (Gr. *xylon* wood), a prefix to numerous words connected with mechanical science and the arts, of which wood is the chief material.

Xylobal'samum (Gr. *xylon*, and Lat. *balsamum*), the wood of the Balsam tree; a balsam obtained by decoction of the leaves of the *Amyris Gileadensis*.

Xylog'raphy (Gr. *xylon*, and *graphe* writing), the art of engraving on wood; wood-engraving.

Xy'lochlore (Gr. *xylon*, and *chloros* green), an olive-green crystalline mineral, closely resembling apophyllite.—*Dana*.

Xylo'idine, in chemical science, a term applied to paper after it has been immersed in strong nitric acid, and washed in distilled water; the paper then assumes the toughness of parchment, and is so combustible as to serve for tinder.

Xy'lole, in chemistry, a hydrocarbon found among the oils separated from crude wood-spirit by the addition of water.—*Miller*.

Xy'lotile, in mineralogy, an opaque green mineral, consisting of silver, iron, and magnesia.

Xylor'etine, in chemistry, a crystallizable compound found on the remains of pine trees.

Xylopyrog'raphy (Gr. *xylon*, *pyroo* to burn, and *graphe* engraving), the art or practice of engraving on charred wood.

Xyphirrhyn'chus (Gr. *xiphos* a sword, and *rhynchos* a beak), a family of fishes, of which the Sword-fish is the type.

Xyster (Gr. *xystron* a scraper), in surgery, an instrument for scraping and shaving bones.

Y.

Yapon, in botany, the name of a South Sea Tea, the Cassine, the produce of the *Ilex cassine*, which is applied medicinally, and used as a tea. It is the produce of the southern states of South America.

Yarrawa'ra, in botany, a tree of New South Wales, one of the largest of the Eucalipti, which produces excellent timber.

Year (Sax.), in chronology and natural philosophy, an important division of time, embracing the four seasons, and determined by the revolution of the earth in its orbit.—The *civil year* is the year of the calendar, *i.e.* 12 months, or 365 days in common years, and 366 in leap years, beginning with the 1st of January.—The *sidereal year* is the space of time the sun takes in passing from any fixed star till his return to it again; the length of this is 365 d. 6 h. 9' 11".—A *lunar year* is the space of twelve lunar months.—The *Julian year* consists of 365¼ days. Julius Cæsar ordered that the civil year should consist of 365 days for three successive years, and the fourth of 366 days.

Yeast (Sax.), a substance generated during the vinous fermentation of vegetable juices and decoctions, rising to the surface in the form of froth.

Yellow (Sax.), the lightest and warmest of the prismatic colours, situated in the solar spectrum between red and blue.

Yel'lowing, in the arts, a term for cleaning pins by boiling them in sour beer or solution of tartar.

Yenite, an opaque mineral of a black colour, with a shade of brown or green, consisting of silica, lime, protoxide of iron, protoxide of manganese, alumina, and water: sp. gr. 3·99.

Y-level, in surveying, an instrument for measuring altitude and distance.

Yt'trium, a peculiar metal, discovered in the state of an oxide in Sweden; when heated to redness in the air, it takes fire, burns with splendour, and is converted into yttria.

Yttroco'rite, a mineral which occurs crystallized and massive, and whose constituents are fluoric acid, yttria, oxide of cerium, and lime: sp. gr. 3·44.

Yttrocolum'bite, the name of a mineral, of which there are three species—the yellow, brown, and black.

Yttrotan'talite, a mineral containing yttria and oxide of columbium.

Yu, in mineralogy, nephrite or jade.

Z.

Zaffre, in chemistry, the residuum or impure oxide of cobalt, after sulphur, arsenic, and other volatile matters have been expelled by calcination.

Zamite, in geology, a fossil Zamia, which is a kind of Palm.

Zamtite (Sp.), a hydrous carbonate of nickel of an emerald-green colour.

Zaph'ara, in the arts, a mineral used by potters to make a sky colour.

Zar'athan, in pathology, a hard tumour of the breast, resembling a cancer.

Zarnich, a genus of fossils that burns with a whitish flame.

Zea (Gr. *zoo* to live), a genus of important Grasses, Indian Corn or Maize, extensively cultivated in warm countries as an article of food.

Zebra Wood, a beautiful cabinet wood obtained from Demerara.

Zechstein (Germ.), in mineralogy, a magnesian limestone lying under the red sandstone.

Zenith (Ital. *zenit*), in natural philosophy and ouranology, that point in the visible celestial hemisphere which is vertical to the spectator; the point directly overhead, and opposite to the nadir.—*Zenith distance* is the distance of a star or planet from the zenith, measured on the vertical circle passing through the zenith.—*Zenith sector* is an astronomical instrument for measuring, with great accuracy, the distances from the zenith of stars which pass near that point.

Zeolite (Gr. *zeo* to foam, and *lithos* a stone), in mineralogy, a family of minerals, consisting of silica, alumina, lime, and water; natrolite.

Zero (Ital.), in meteorology, the point at which the graduation of the thermometer commences.—The *zero* of Réaumur's and of the Centigrade thermometers is the freezing-point of water; that of Fahrenheit's thermometer, 32° below the freezing-point.

Zetet'ics (Gr. *zeteo* to inquire), a part of algebra which consists in the direct search after unknown quantities.

Zeuxite (Gr.), a greenish-brown mineral, consisting of silica, alumina, protoxide of iron, lime, and water: sp. gr. 3·0; H = 4·25.

Zigzag (Fr.), an ornament in Gothic architecture; another name for the chevron.

Zigzags, in fortification, trenches or paths with several indented windings, so cut that the besieger cannot be enfiladed in his approaches.

Zi'mome (Gr. *zyme* ferment), in chemistry, that part of the gluten of wheat which is insoluble in alcohol.

Zinc (Germ.), a metal of a bluish-white colour, brittle when cold, but malleable when heated; much used in the manufacture of brass and other alloys. It is found in solid masses, sometimes in six-sided prisms, having the ends terminated in pentagons.—*Sulphate of zinc* is found efflorescent in the form of stalactites, or in rhombs.—*Sulphuret of zinc* is the most abundant of the zinc ores.—*Flowers of zinc,* the oxide of zinc which flies up on the exposure of the metal to a temperature in the air very little above the melting-point, in the form of white flowers.—*Zinc-amyl,* a colourless transparent liquid, composed of amyl and zinc. *Zinc-bloom,* an opaque mineral of a greyish dull lustre, composed of carbonic acid, oxide of zinc, and water.—*Zinc-ethyl,* a colourless, transparent, and poisonous liquid, consisting of ethyl and zinc.—*Zinco-methyl,* a volatile liquid of a very fetid smell, and consisting of carbon, hydrogen, and zinc.—*Zinc-white,* the oxide of zinc, used as a pigment for the same purposes as white-lead.

Zincog'raphy (Germ. *zink,* and Gr. *grapho* to write), the art of drawing upon, and printing from, plates of zinc.

Zingibera'ceæ, a nat. order of aromatic endogenous plants, of which Zingiber is the type.

Zin'kenite, a crystallized mineral containing antimony, sulphur, lead, and copper: sp. gr. 5·30; H = 3—3·5.

Zircon, a mineral composed chiefly of zirconia and silica, found in Ceylon.

Ziroo'nia, in mineralogy, a rare earth extracted from zircon and hyacinth. —*Zirconium* is the metallic base of zirconia.

Zoantho'ria (Gr. *zoon* an animal, and *anthos* a flower), in botany and zoology, a class of Zoophytes; animal-flowers.

Zoan'thropy (Gr. *zoon*, and *anthropos* a man), in pathology, a species of monomania, in which the patient believes himself transformed into one of the lower animals.

Zoar'chidæ (Gr. *zoarchos* a guiding animal), a family of the acanthopterygious fishes, of which Zoarchus is the type and genus.

Zo'diac (Gr. *zodiakos*, from *zoon* an animal), in astronomy, an imaginary zone or belt in the heavens, extending about 8° or 9° on each side of the ecliptic. It is divided into twelve equal parts, called *signs*. —*Zodiacal light* is a faint nebulous brightness which accompanies the sun immediately before sunrise or after sunset.

Zoia'tria (Gr. *zoon*, and *iatria* medical treatment), in pathology, the treatment of the diseases of the lower animals.

Zo'isite (so called from *Baron von Zois*), a grey crystalline mineral, consisting of silica, alumina, lime, and protoxide of iron: sp. gr. 3·32; H = 6·25.

Zone (Lat. and Gr. *zona*), in geology, a division of the earth's surface by means of parallel lines. The zones are five in number, viz., the *torrid zone*, two *temperate zones*, and two *frigid zones*.

Zoo- (Gr. *zoon*), in natural history, a prefix to compound words relating to animals or animal life.

Zoochem'ical (Gr.), pertaining to the chemistry of animal organization.

Zooch'omy (Gr.), that science which pertains to animal chemistry.

Zoog'eny (Gr.), the doctrine of animal formation.

Zoog'raphy (Gr.), in natural history, a description of animals.

Zooid (Gr. *zoon*), resembling an animal.

Zo'olite (Gr. *zoon*, and *lithos* a stone), in geology, the fossil remains of a petrified animal.

Zoolithol'ogy (Gr.), a treatise on fossil animal remains.

Zool'ogy (Gr. *zoon*, and *logos* discourse), in natural history, the science of animals, teaching their nature, properties, classification, &c.

Zoon'omy (Gr. *zoon*, and *nomos* a law), in natural history, a treatise on the laws of animal life; the structure and functions of animals.

Zoopathol'ogy (Gr. *zoon*, *pathos* disease, and *logos* a discourse), a treatise on the diseases of animals.

Zooph'agous (Gr. *zoon*, and *phago* to eat), eating animals; carnivorous.

Zo'ophyte (Gr. *zoon*, and *phyton* a plant), a name applied to an order of Vermes, comprehending those beings supposed to partake of the nature both of vegetables and animals.

Zo'ospore (Gr.), in zoology, a moving spore, provided with cilia or vibratile organs.

Zoot'omy (Gr. *zoon*, and *tome* an incision), that branch of anatomy which relates to the structure of the lower animals; dissection of the bodies of animals.

Zoster (Gr. *a girdle*), in pathology, a cutaneous disease, commonly known as the Shingles.

Zurlite, the name of a recently-discovered Vesuvian mineral.

Zygo'ma (Gr.), in anatomy, a bone of the upper jaw; the process of the cheek bone.

Zygophylla'ceæ (Gr. *zygon* a yoke, and *phyllon* a leaf), in botany, a nat. order of Exogens, consisting of herbaceous plants, shrubs, or trees, of which Zygophyllum is the type.

Zymic (Gr. *zyme* fermentation), in chemistry, an epithet denoting an acid procured from a fermented substance, as leaven.

Zymol'ogy (Gr.), the doctrine of fermentation.

Zymom'eter, Zymosim'eter (Gr. *zyme*, and *metron* a measure), an instrument for measuring the degree of fermentation.

Zymo'sis (Gr. *zymoo* to ferment), in pathology, an epidemic or contagious affection, including fever, small-pox, cholera, &c.—*Zymotic* is an epithet pertaining to zymosis, or to an epidemic or contagious fever.

THE END.

PRINTED BY VIRTUE AND CO., CITY ROAD, LONDON.

Z